THE GREEN LANTERN

SEASON TWO

VOL. 1

THE GREEN LANTERN SEASON ONE

GRANT MORRISON writer
LIAM SHARP XERMANICO artists
STEVE OLIFF colorist
TOM ORZECHOWSKI STEVE WANDS letterers
LIAM SHARP collection cover artist

SUPERBOY created by **JERRY SIEGEL**
SUPERMAN created by **JERRY SIEGEL** and **JOE SHUSTER**
By special arrangement with the JERRY SIEGEL family

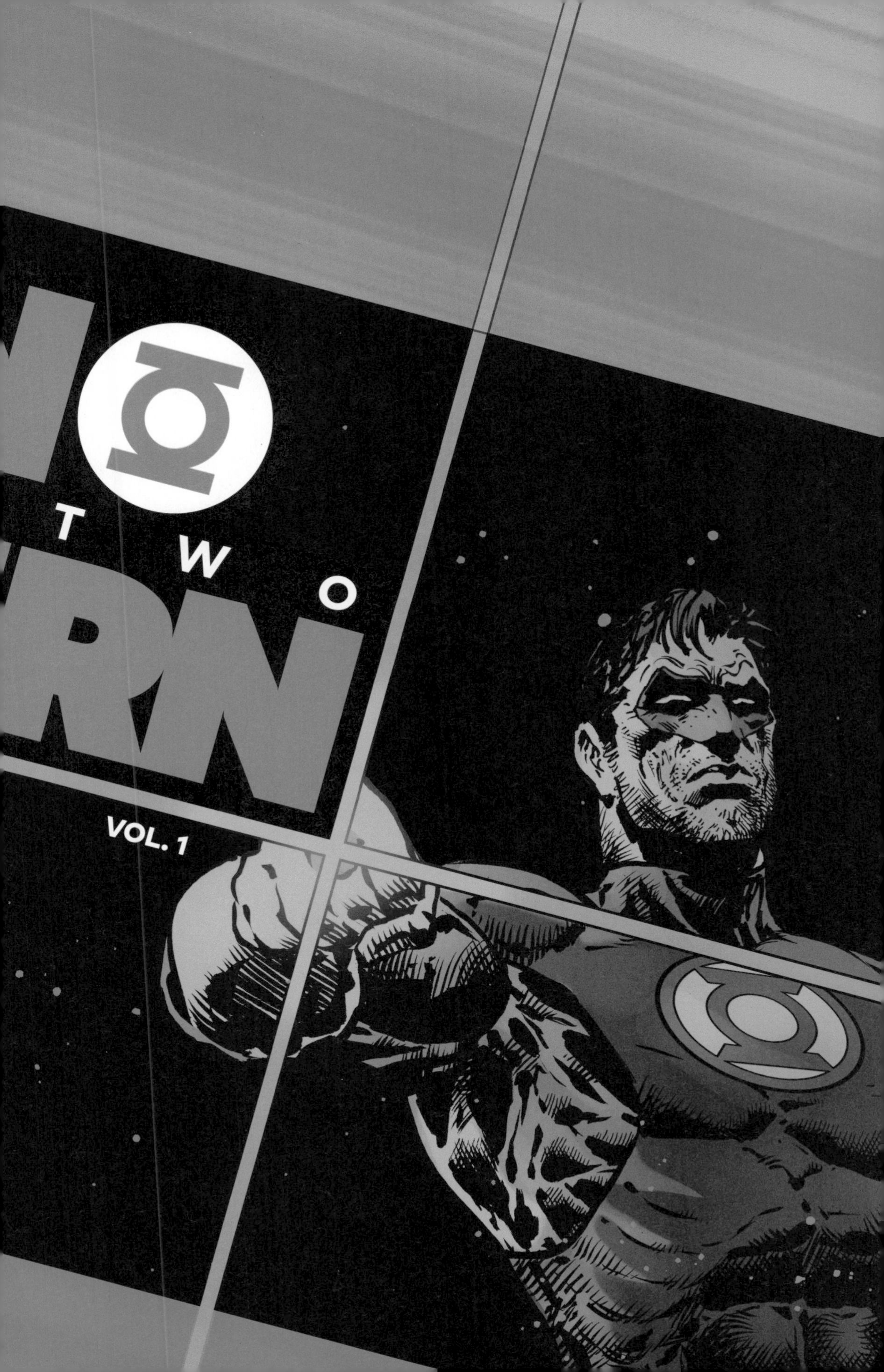
T W O
VOL. 1

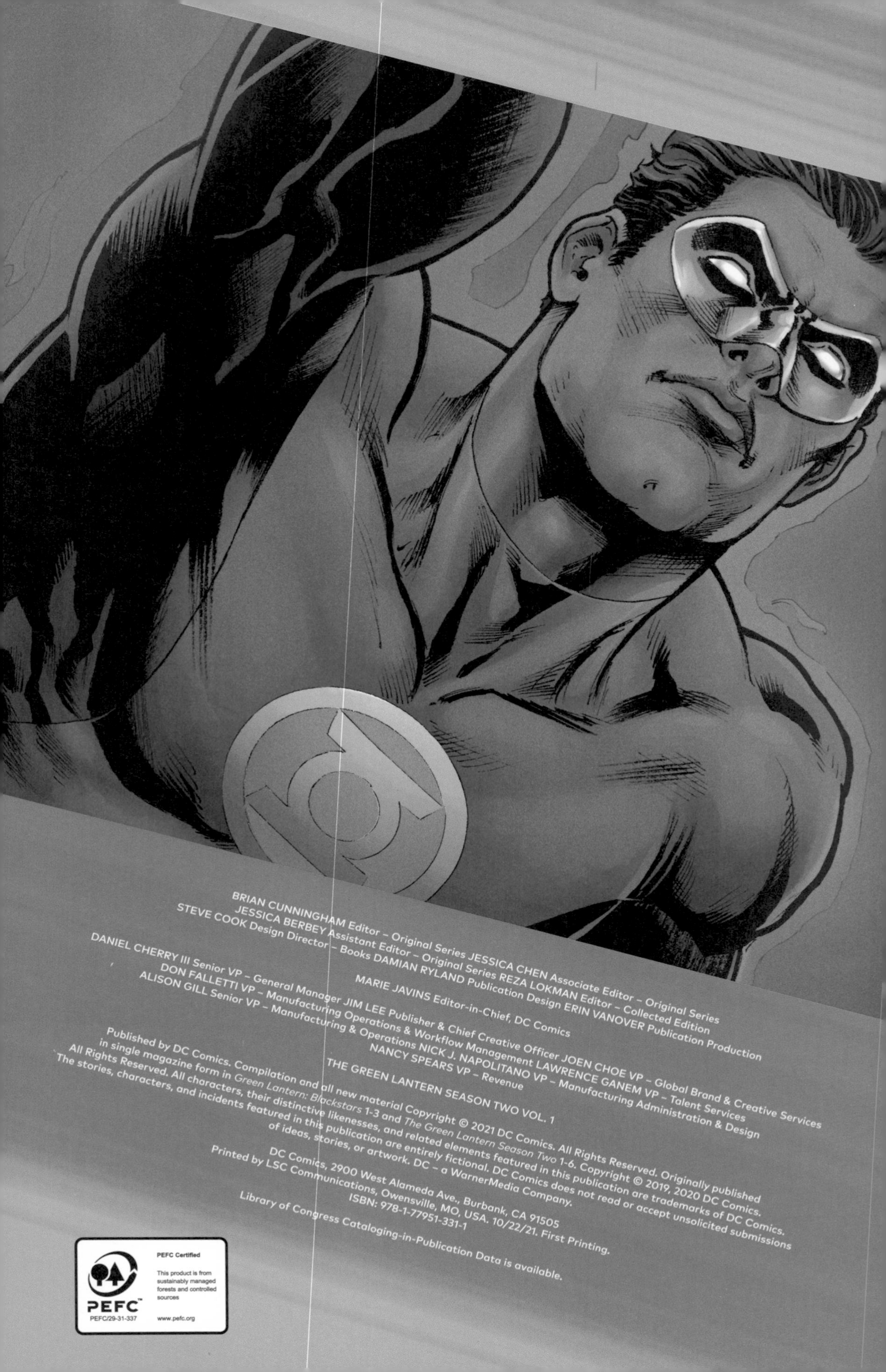

BRIAN CUNNINGHAM Editor – Original Series JESSICA CHEN Associate Editor – Original Series
JESSICA BERBEY Assistant Editor – Original Series REZA LOKMAN Editor – Collected Edition
STEVE COOK Design Director – Books DAMIAN RYLAND Publication Design ERIN VANOVER Publication Production

MARIE JAVINS Editor-in-Chief, DC Comics

DANIEL CHERRY III Senior VP – General Manager JIM LEE Publisher & Chief Creative Officer JOEN CHOE VP – Global Brand & Creative Services
DON FALLETTI VP – Manufacturing Operations & Workflow Management LAWRENCE GANEM VP – Talent Services
ALISON GILL Senior VP – Manufacturing & Operations NICK J. NAPOLITANO VP – Manufacturing Administration & Design
NANCY SPEARS VP – Revenue

THE GREEN LANTERN SEASON TWO VOL. 1

Published by DC Comics. Compilation and all new material Copyright © 2021 DC Comics. All Rights Reserved. Originally published in single magazine form in *Green Lantern: Blackstars* 1-3 and *The Green Lantern Season Two* 1-6. Copyright © 2019, 2020 DC Comics. All Rights Reserved. All characters, their distinctive likenesses, and related elements featured in this publication are trademarks of DC Comics. The stories, characters, and incidents featured in this publication are entirely fictional. DC Comics does not read or accept unsolicited submissions of ideas, stories, or artwork. DC – a WarnerMedia Company.

DC Comics, 2900 West Alameda Ave., Burbank, CA 91505
Printed by LSC Communications, Owensville, MO, USA. 10/22/21. First Printing.
ISBN: 978-1-77951-331-1

Library of Congress Cataloging-in-Publication Data is available.

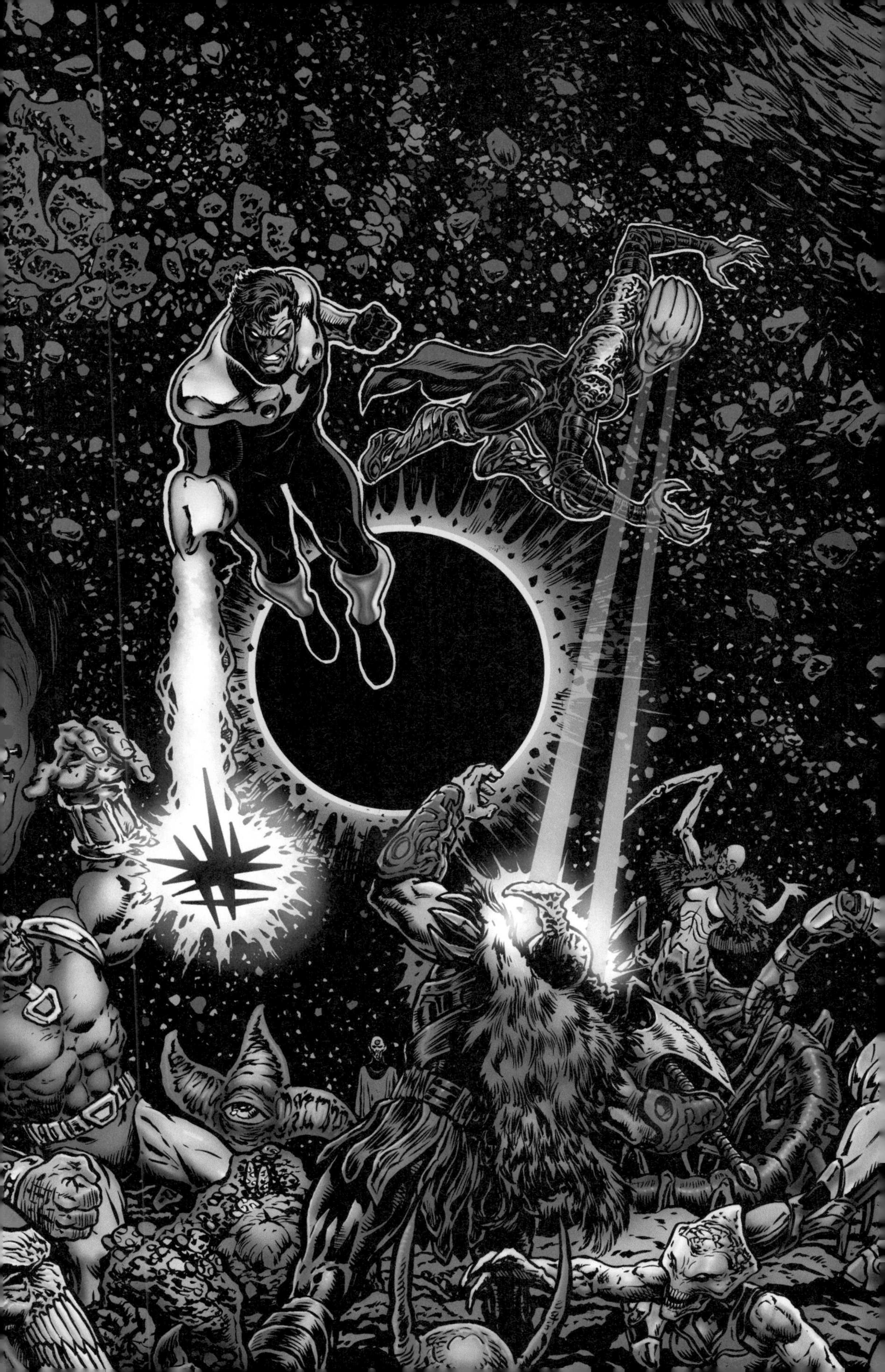

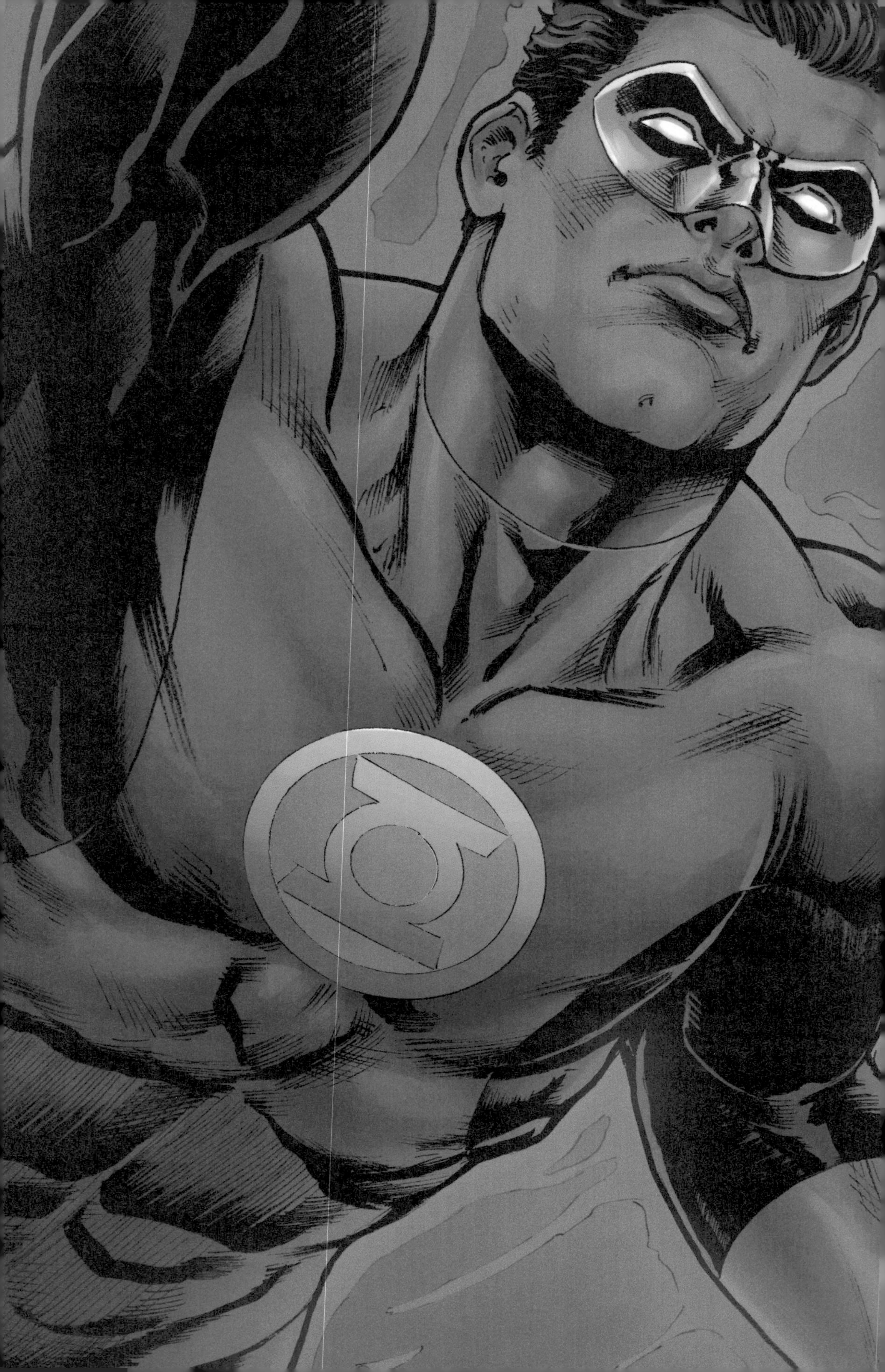

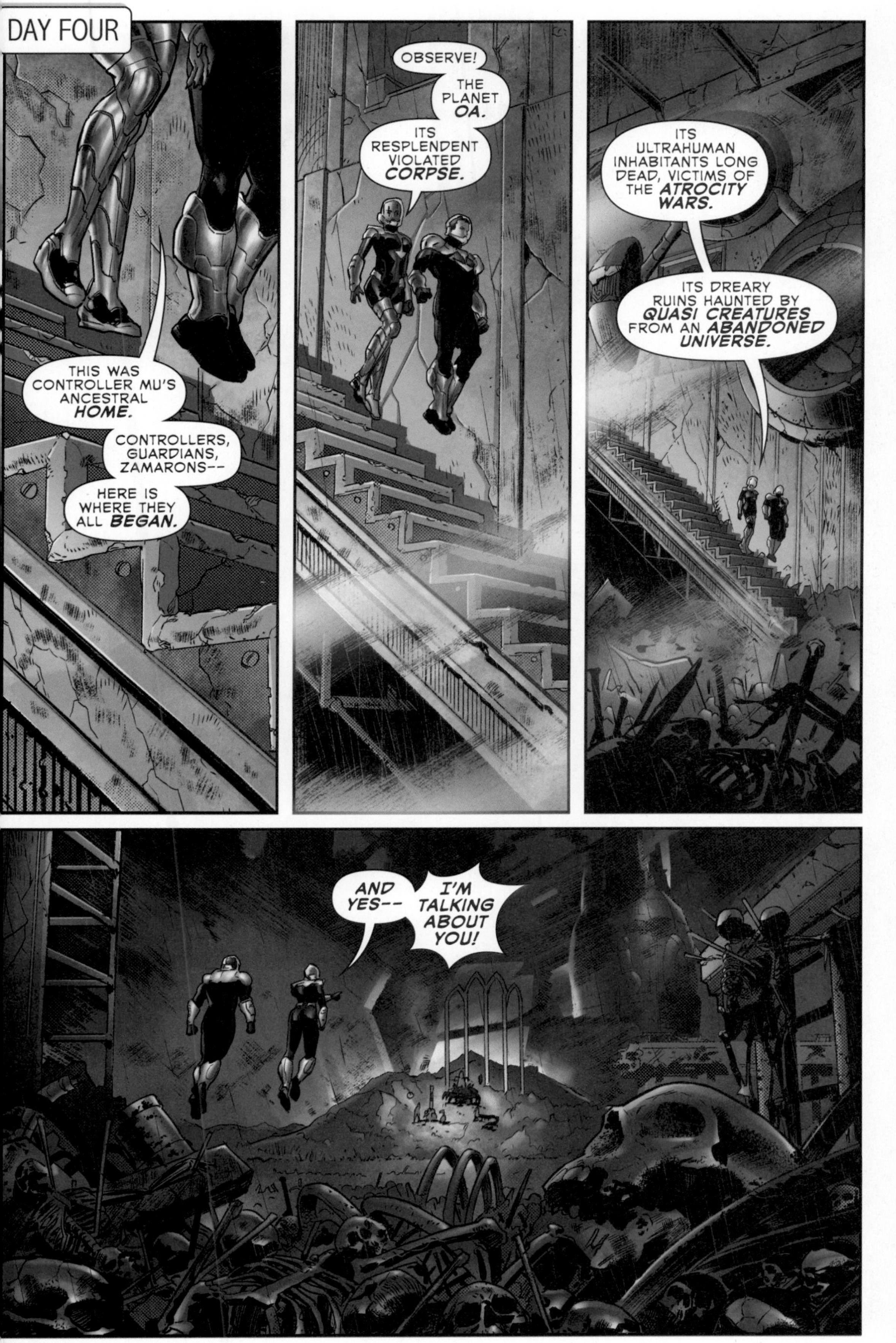
DAY FOUR
THIS WAS CONTROLLER MU'S ANCESTRAL HOME.
CONTROLLERS, GUARDIANS, ZAMARONS--
HERE IS WHERE THEY ALL BEGAN.
OBSERVE!
THE PLANET OA.
ITS RESPLENDENT VIOLATED CORPSE.
ITS ULTRAHUMAN INHABITANTS LONG DEAD, VICTIMS OF THE ATROCITY WARS.
ITS DREARY RUINS HAUNTED BY QUASI CREATURES FROM AN ABANDONED UNIVERSE.
AND YES--
I'M TALKING ABOUT YOU!

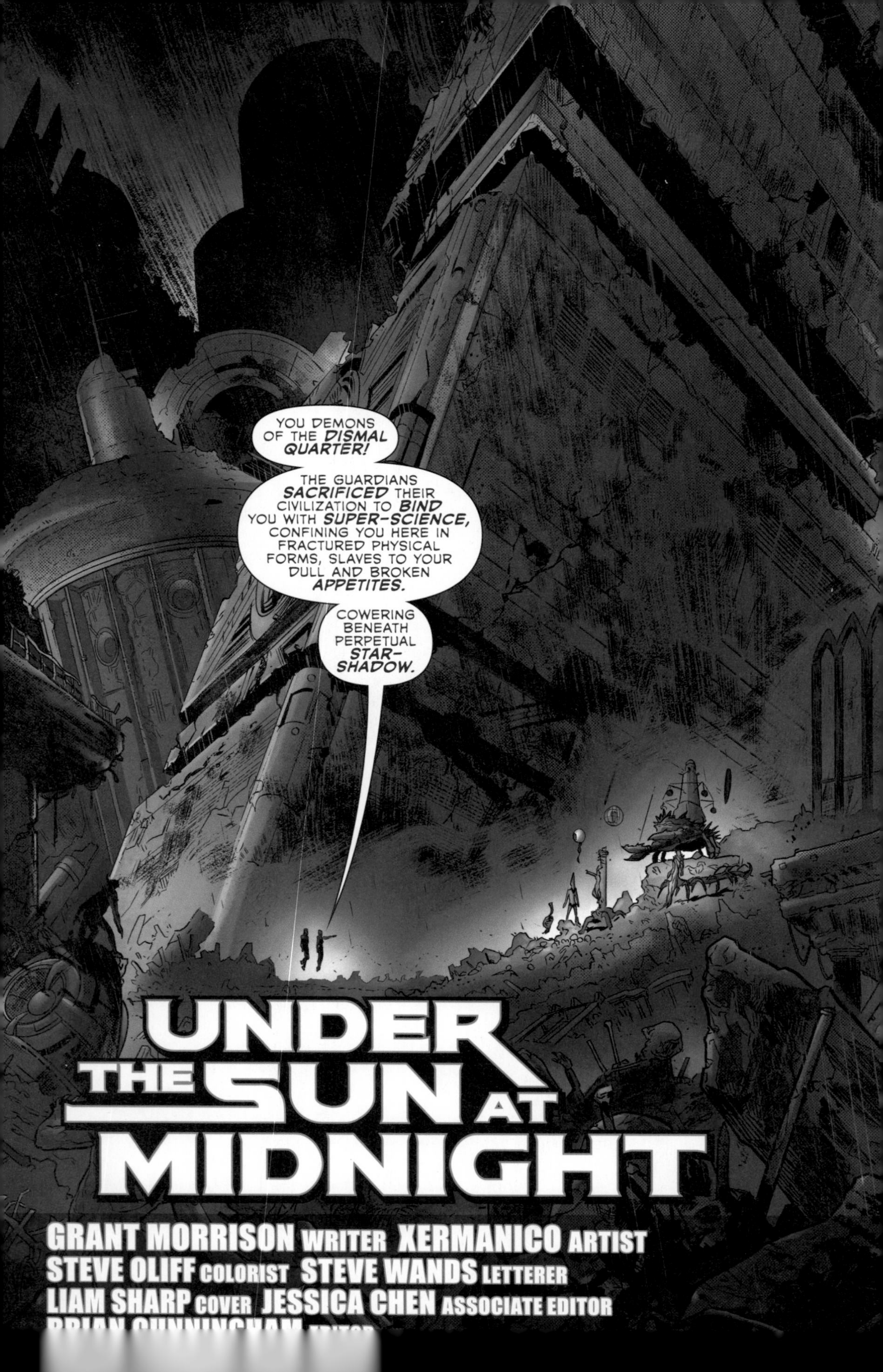
YOU DEMONS OF THE DISMAL QUARTER!
THE GUARDIANS SACRIFICED THEIR CIVILIZATION TO BIND YOU WITH SUPER-SCIENCE, CONFINING YOU HERE IN FRACTURED PHYSICAL FORMS, SLAVES TO YOUR DULL AND BROKEN APPETITES.
COWERING BENEATH PERPETUAL STAR-SHADOW.
UNDER THE SUN AT MIDNIGHT
GRANT MORRISON WRITER XERMANICO ARTIST
STEVE OLIFF COLORIST STEVE WANDS LETTERER
LIAM SHARP COVER JESSICA CHEN ASSOCIATE EDITOR

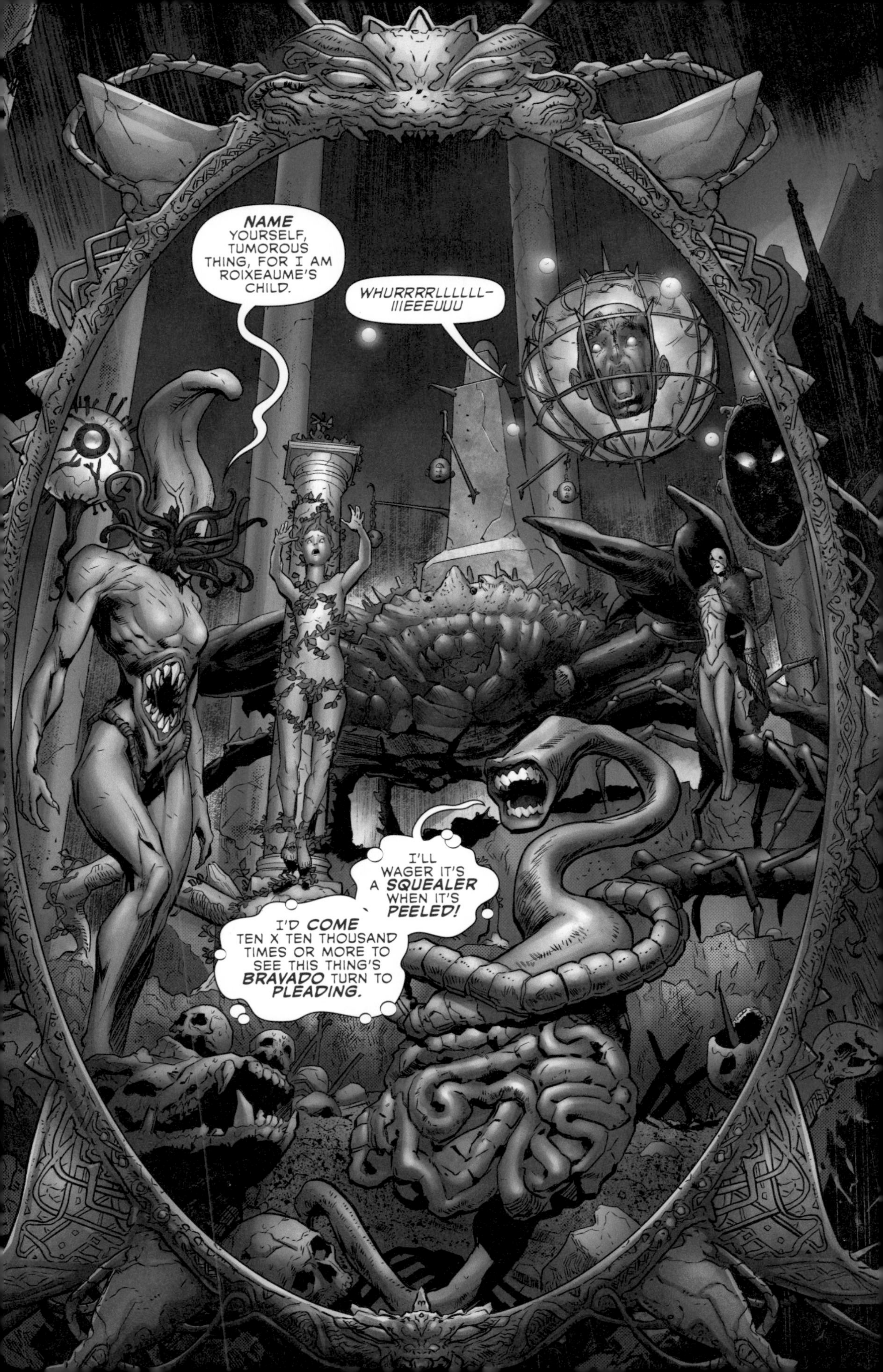
NAME YOURSELF, TUMOROUS THING, FOR I AM ROIXEAUME'S CHILD.
WHURRRRLLLLLL-IIIEEEUUU
I'LL WAGER IT'S A SQUEALER WHEN IT'S PEELED!
I'D COME TEN X TEN THOUSAND TIMES OR MORE TO SEE THIS THING'S BRAVADO TURN TO PLEADING.

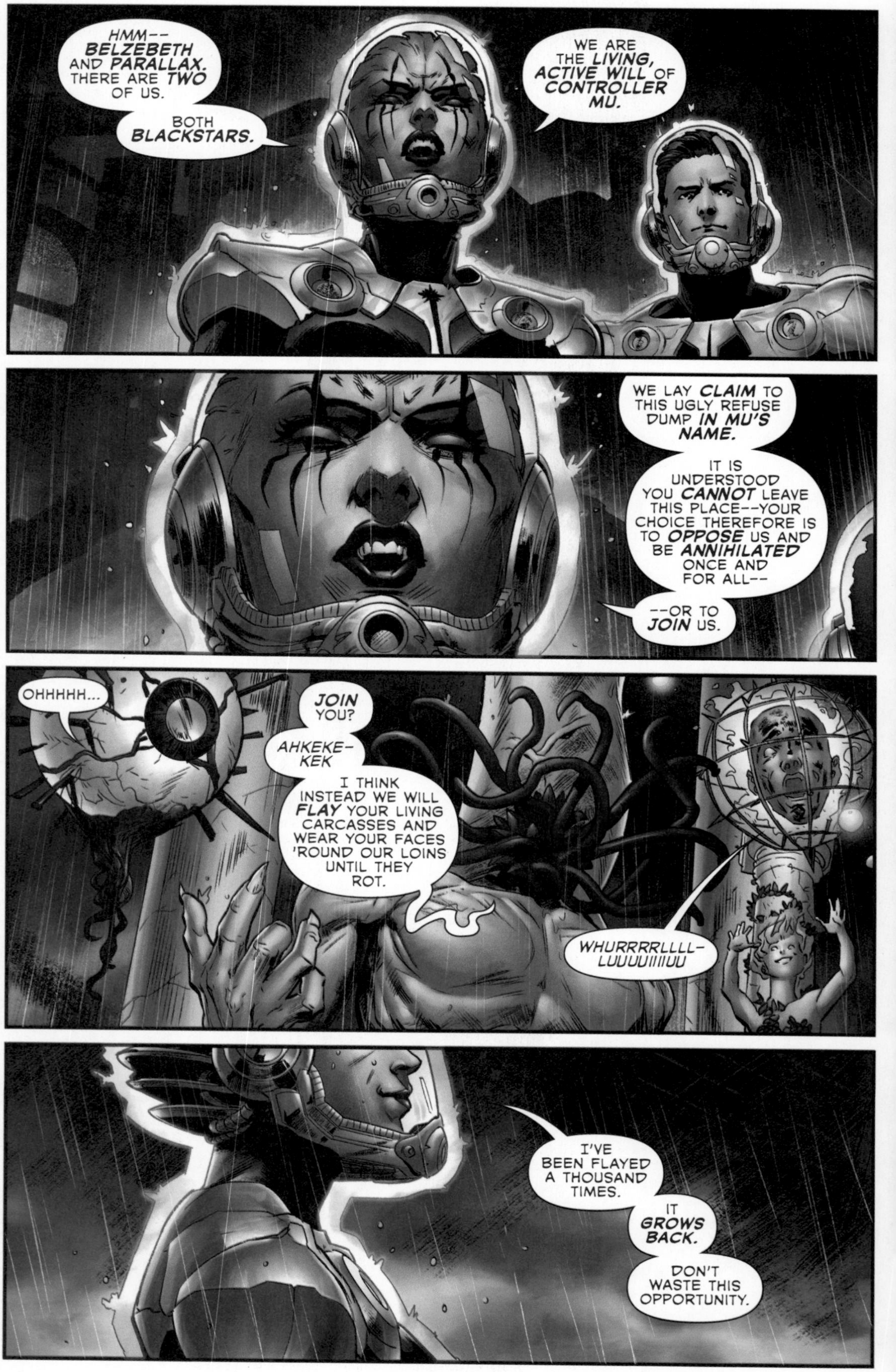
HMM-- BELZEBETH AND PARALLAX. THERE ARE TWO OF US.
BOTH BLACKSTARS.
WE ARE THE LIVING, ACTIVE WILL OF CONTROLLER MU.
WE LAY CLAIM TO THIS UGLY REFUSE DUMP IN MU'S NAME.
IT IS UNDERSTOOD YOU CANNOT LEAVE THIS PLACE--YOUR CHOICE THEREFORE IS TO OPPOSE US AND BE ANNIHILATED ONCE AND FOR ALL--
--OR TO JOIN US.
OHHHHH...
JOIN YOU?
AHKEKE-KEK
I THINK INSTEAD WE WILL FLAY YOUR LIVING CARCASSES AND WEAR YOUR FACES 'ROUND OUR LOINS UNTIL THEY ROT.
WHURRRRLLLL-LUUUUIIIIUU
I'VE BEEN FLAYED A THOUSAND TIMES.
IT GROWS BACK.
DON'T WASTE THIS OPPORTUNITY.

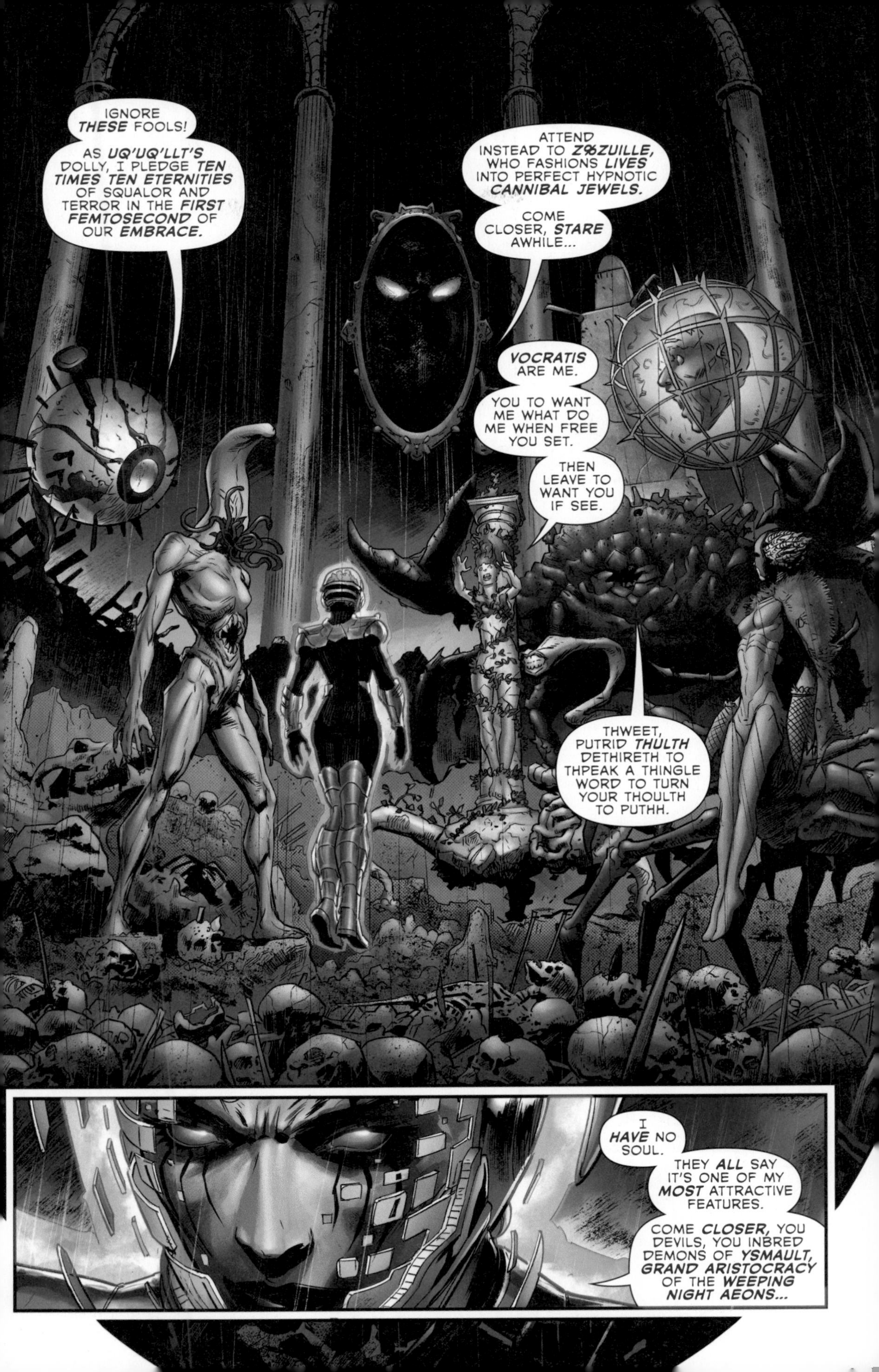
IGNORE THESE FOOLS!
AS UQ'UQ'LLT'S DOLLY, I PLEDGE TEN TIMES TEN ETERNITIES OF SQUALOR AND TERROR IN THE FIRST FEMTOSECOND OF OUR EMBRACE.
ATTEND INSTEAD TO Z%ZUILLE, WHO FASHIONS LIVES INTO PERFECT HYPNOTIC CANNIBAL JEWELS.
COME CLOSER, STARE AWHILE...
VOCRATIS ARE ME.
YOU TO WANT ME WHAT DO ME WHEN FREE YOU SET.
THEN LEAVE TO WANT YOU IF SEE.
THWEET, PUTRID THULTH DETHIRETH TO THPEAK A THINGLE WORD TO TURN YOUR THOULTH TO PUTHH.
I HAVE NO SOUL.
THEY ALL SAY IT'S ONE OF MY MOST ATTRACTIVE FEATURES.
COME CLOSER, YOU DEVILS, YOU INBRED DEMONS OF YSMAULT, GRAND ARISTOCRACY OF THE WEEPING NIGHT AEONS...

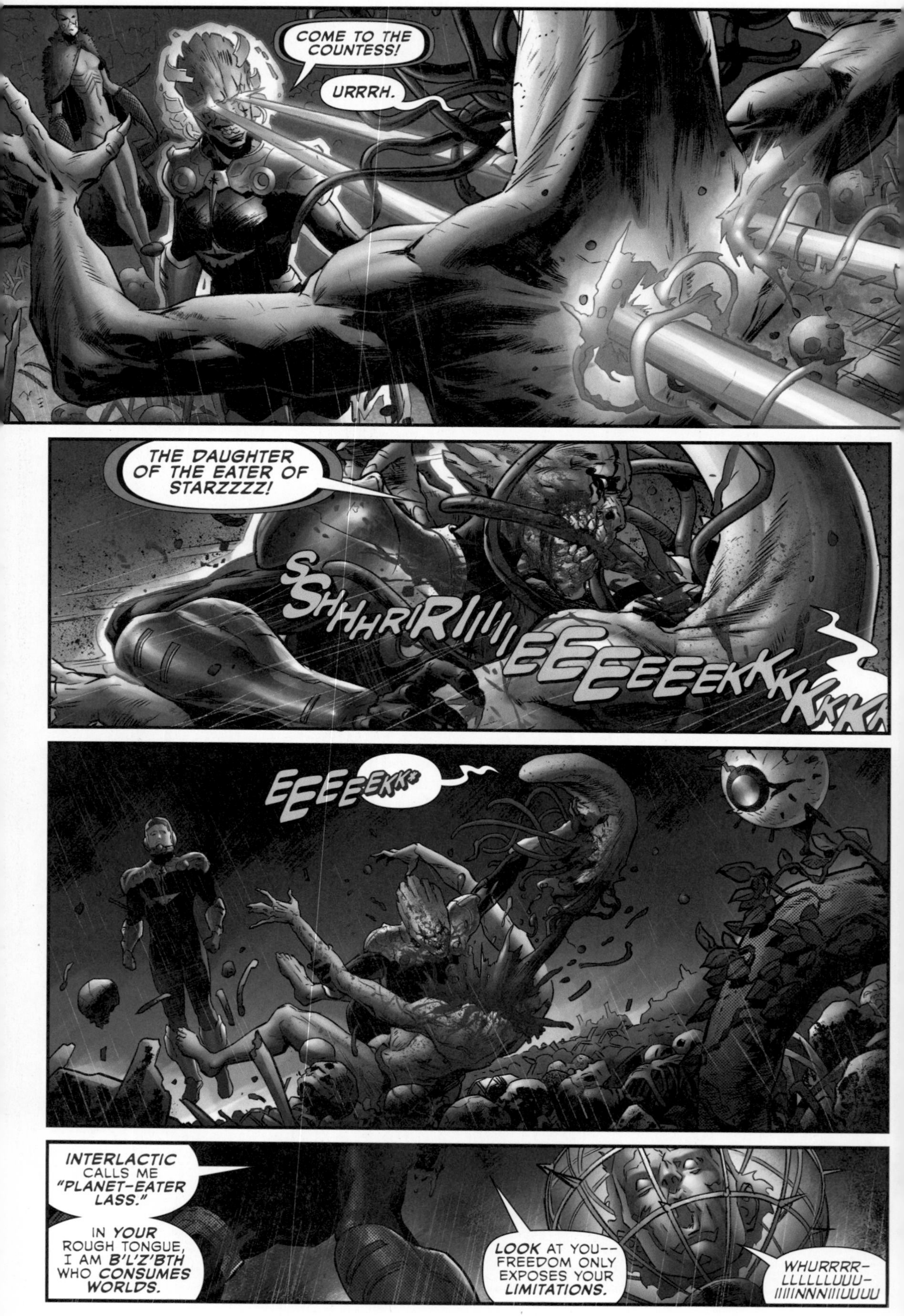
COME TO THE COUNTESS!
URRRH.
THE DAUGHTER OF THE EATER OF STARZZZZZ!
SSHHHRIRIIIIIEEEEEEEKKKKKK
EEEEEKK*
INTERLACTIC CALLS ME "PLANET-EATER LASS."
IN YOUR ROUGH TONGUE, I AM B'L'Z'BTH WHO CONSUMES WORLDS.
LOOK AT YOU-- FREEDOM ONLY EXPOSES YOUR LIMITATIONS.
WHURRRR-LLLLLLUUU-IIIIINNNIIIUUUU

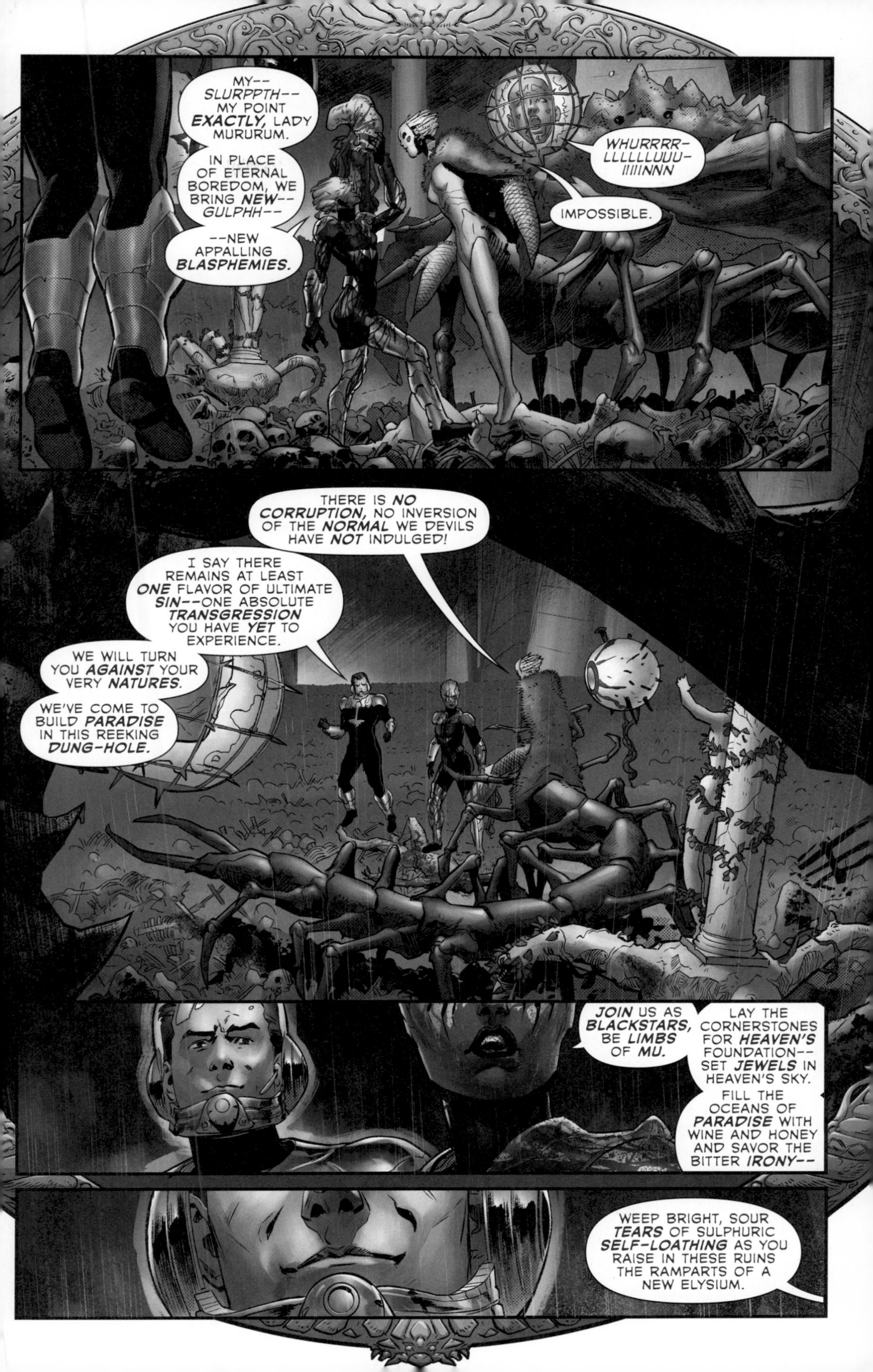
MY-- SLURPPTH-- MY POINT EXACTLY, LADY MURURUM.
IN PLACE OF ETERNAL BOREDOM, WE BRING NEW-- GULPHH--
--NEW APPALLING BLASPHEMIES.
WHURRRR-LLLLLLUUU-IIIIINNN
IMPOSSIBLE.
THERE IS NO CORRUPTION, NO INVERSION OF THE NORMAL WE DEVILS HAVE NOT INDULGED!
I SAY THERE REMAINS AT LEAST ONE FLAVOR OF ULTIMATE SIN--ONE ABSOLUTE TRANSGRESSION YOU HAVE YET TO EXPERIENCE.
WE WILL TURN YOU AGAINST YOUR VERY NATURES.
WE'VE COME TO BUILD PARADISE IN THIS REEKING DUNG-HOLE.
JOIN US AS BLACKSTARS, BE LIMBS OF MU.
LAY THE CORNERSTONES FOR HEAVEN'S FOUNDATION-- SET JEWELS IN HEAVEN'S SKY.
FILL THE OCEANS OF PARADISE WITH WINE AND HONEY AND SAVOR THE BITTER IRONY--
WEEP BRIGHT, SOUR TEARS OF SULPHURIC SELF-LOATHING AS YOU RAISE IN THESE RUINS THE RAMPARTS OF A NEW ELYSIUM.

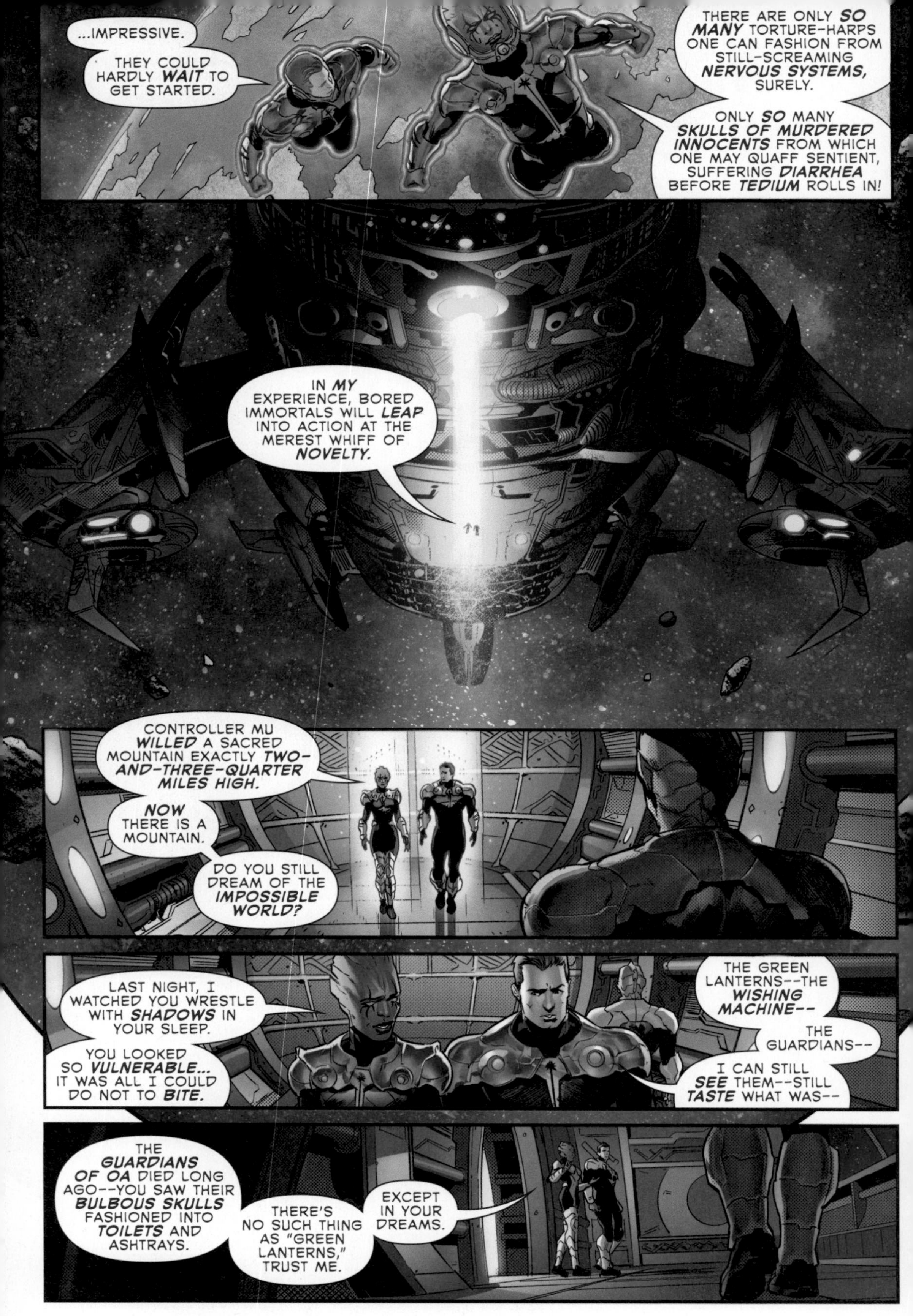
...IMPRESSIVE.
THEY COULD HARDLY WAIT TO GET STARTED.
THERE ARE ONLY SO MANY TORTURE-HARPS ONE CAN FASHION FROM STILL-SCREAMING NERVOUS SYSTEMS, SURELY.
ONLY SO MANY SKULLS OF MURDERED INNOCENTS FROM WHICH ONE MAY QUAFF SENTIENT, SUFFERING DIARRHEA BEFORE TEDIUM ROLLS IN!
IN MY EXPERIENCE, BORED IMMORTALS WILL LEAP INTO ACTION AT THE MEREST WHIFF OF NOVELTY.
CONTROLLER MU WILLED A SACRED MOUNTAIN EXACTLY TWO-AND-THREE-QUARTER MILES HIGH.
NOW THERE IS A MOUNTAIN.
DO YOU STILL DREAM OF THE IMPOSSIBLE WORLD?
LAST NIGHT, I WATCHED YOU WRESTLE WITH SHADOWS IN YOUR SLEEP.
YOU LOOKED SO VULNERABLE... IT WAS ALL I COULD DO NOT TO BITE.
THE GREEN LANTERNS--THE WISHING MACHINE--
THE GUARDIANS--
I CAN STILL SEE THEM--STILL TASTE WHAT WAS--
THE GUARDIANS OF OA DIED LONG AGO--YOU SAW THEIR BULBOUS SKULLS FASHIONED INTO TOILETS AND ASHTRAYS.
THERE'S NO SUCH THING AS "GREEN LANTERNS," TRUST ME.
EXCEPT IN YOUR DREAMS.

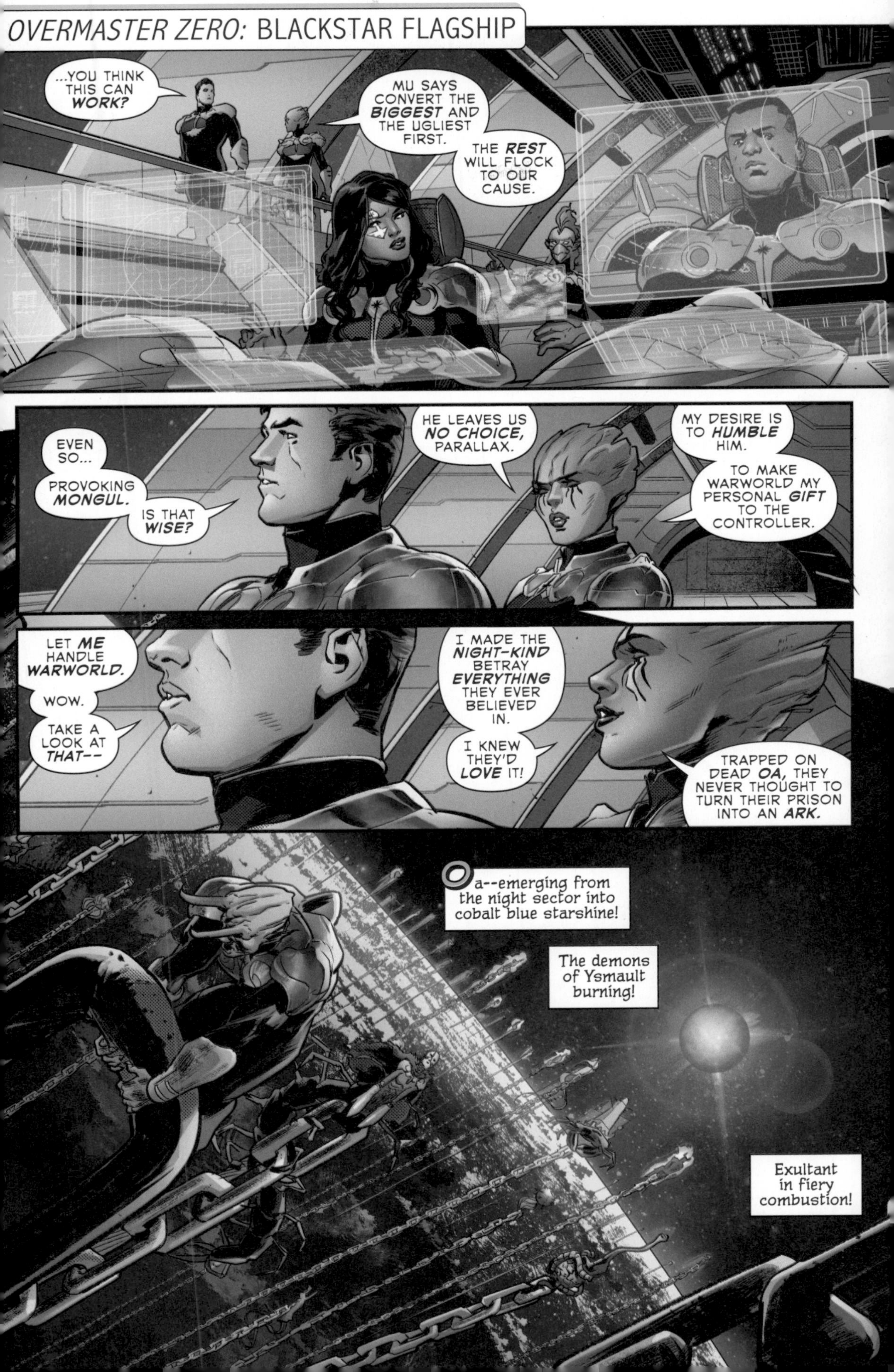
OVERMASTER ZERO: BLACKSTAR FLAGSHIP
...YOU THINK THIS CAN WORK?
MU SAYS CONVERT THE BIGGEST AND THE UGLIEST FIRST.
THE REST WILL FLOCK TO OUR CAUSE.
EVEN SO...
PROVOKING MONGUL.
IS THAT WISE?
HE LEAVES US NO CHOICE, PARALLAX.
MY DESIRE IS TO HUMBLE HIM.
TO MAKE WARWORLD MY PERSONAL GIFT TO THE CONTROLLER.
LET ME HANDLE WARWORLD.
WOW.
TAKE A LOOK AT THAT--
I MADE THE NIGHT-KIND BETRAY EVERYTHING THEY EVER BELIEVED IN.
I KNEW THEY'D LOVE IT!
TRAPPED ON DEAD OA, THEY NEVER THOUGHT TO TURN THEIR PRISON INTO AN ARK.
Oa--emerging from the night sector into cobalt blue starshine!
The demons of Ysmault burning!
Exultant in fiery combustion!

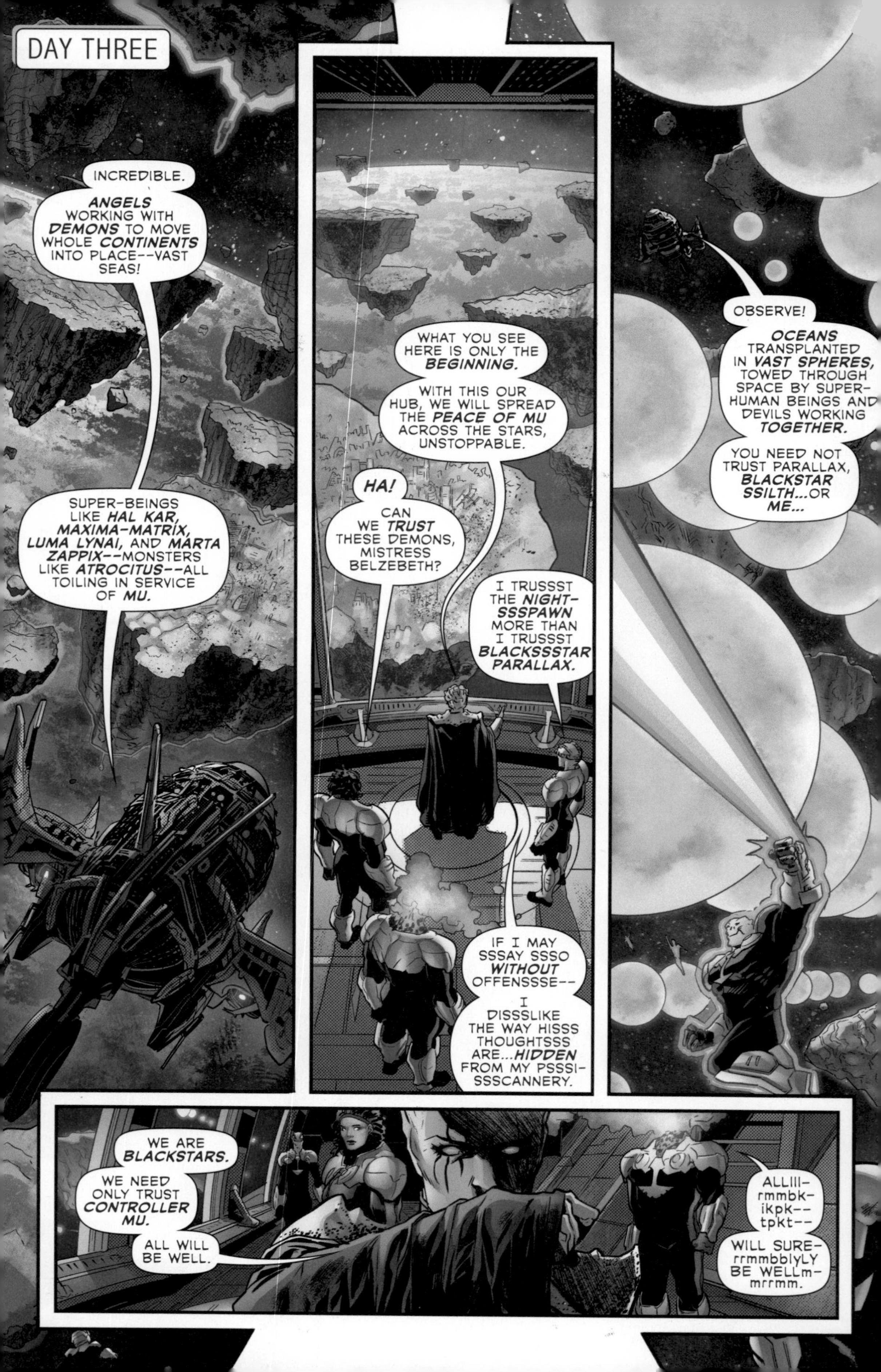
DAY THREE
INCREDIBLE.
ANGELS WORKING WITH DEMONS TO MOVE WHOLE CONTINENTS INTO PLACE--VAST SEAS!
SUPER-BEINGS LIKE HAL KAR, MAXIMA-MATRIX, LUMA LYNAI, AND MARTA ZAPPIX--MONSTERS LIKE ATROCITUS--ALL TOILING IN SERVICE OF MU.
WHAT YOU SEE HERE IS ONLY THE BEGINNING.
WITH THIS OUR HUB, WE WILL SPREAD THE PEACE OF MU ACROSS THE STARS, UNSTOPPABLE.
HA!
CAN WE TRUST THESE DEMONS, MISTRESS BELZEBETH?
I TRUSSST THE NIGHT-SSSPAWN MORE THAN I TRUSSST BLACKSSSTAR PARALLAX.
IF I MAY SSSAY SSSO WITHOUT OFFENSSSE--
I DISSSLIKE THE WAY HISSS THOUGHTSSS ARE...HIDDEN FROM MY PSSSI-SSSCANNERY.
OBSERVE!
OCEANS TRANSPLANTED IN VAST SPHERES, TOWED THROUGH SPACE BY SUPER-HUMAN BEINGS AND DEVILS WORKING TOGETHER.
YOU NEED NOT TRUST PARALLAX, BLACKSTAR SSILTH...OR ME...
WE ARE BLACKSTARS.
WE NEED ONLY TRUST CONTROLLER MU.
ALL WILL BE WELL.
ALLIII-rrmmbk-ikpk--tpkt--
WILL SURE-rrmmbblyLY BE WELLm-mrrmm.

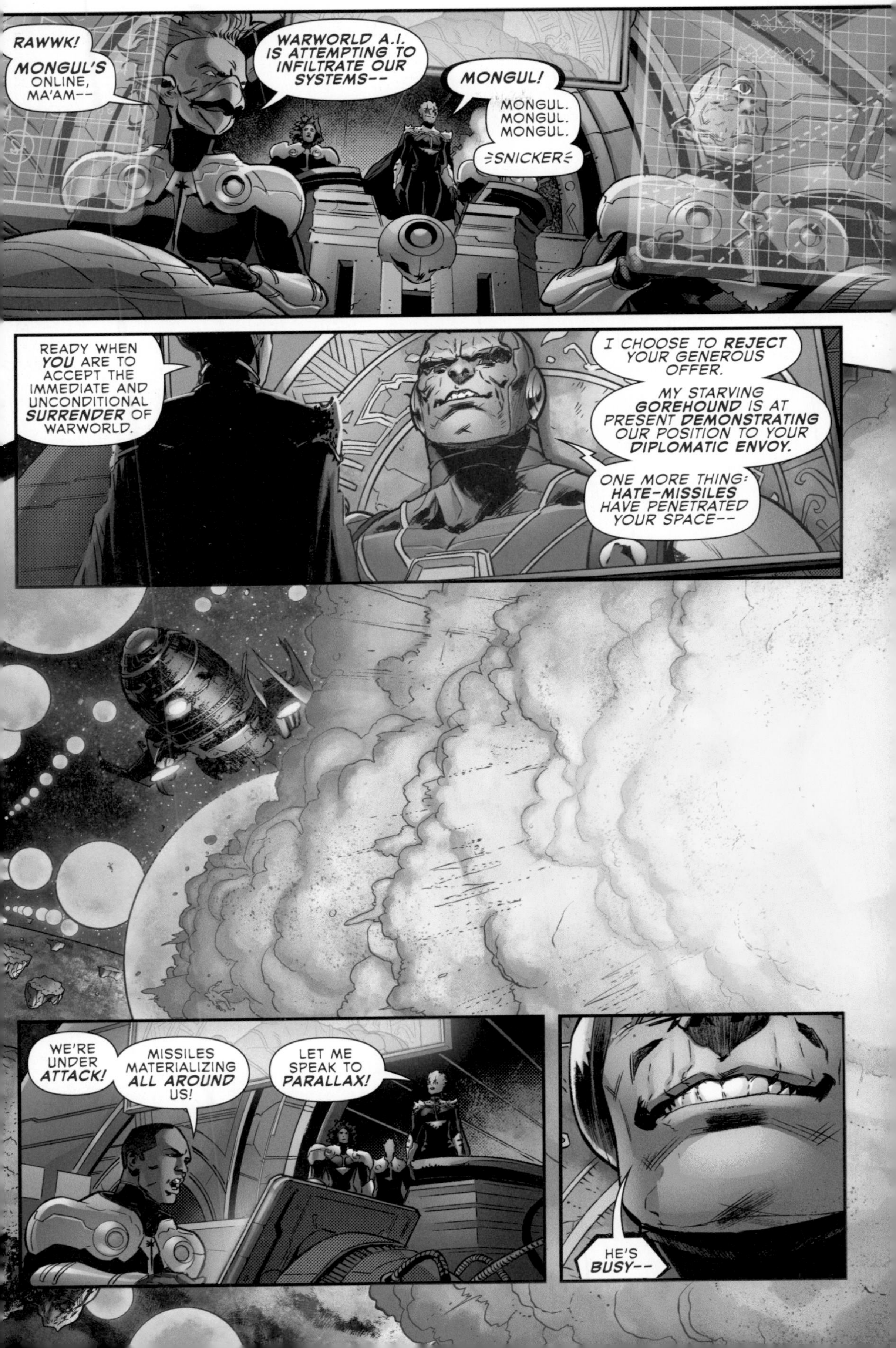
RAWWK! MONGUL'S ONLINE, MA'AM--
WARWORLD A.I. IS ATTEMPTING TO INFILTRATE OUR SYSTEMS--
MONGUL!
MONGUL. MONGUL. MONGUL.
SNICKER
READY WHEN YOU ARE TO ACCEPT THE IMMEDIATE AND UNCONDITIONAL SURRENDER OF WARWORLD.
I CHOOSE TO REJECT YOUR GENEROUS OFFER.
MY STARVING GOREHOUND IS AT PRESENT DEMONSTRATING OUR POSITION TO YOUR DIPLOMATIC ENVOY.
ONE MORE THING: HATE-MISSILES HAVE PENETRATED YOUR SPACE--
WE'RE UNDER ATTACK!
MISSILES MATERIALIZING ALL AROUND US!
LET ME SPEAK TO PARALLAX!
HE'S BUSY--

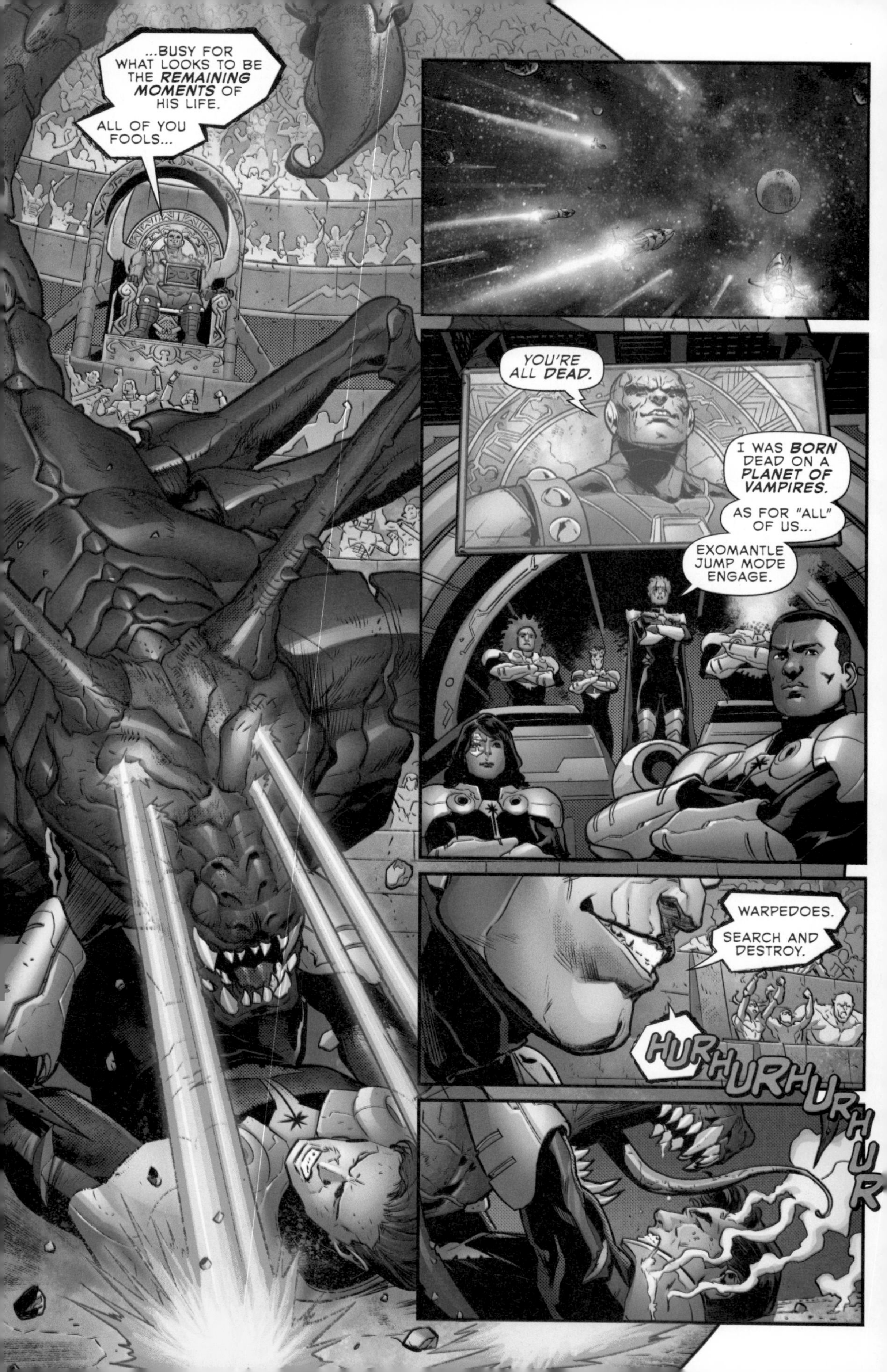
...BUSY FOR WHAT LOOKS TO BE THE **REMAINING MOMENTS** OF HIS LIFE.
ALL OF YOU FOOLS...
YOU'RE ALL **DEAD.**
I WAS **BORN** DEAD ON A **PLANET OF VAMPIRES.**
AS FOR "ALL" OF US...
EXOMANTLE JUMP MODE ENGAGE.
WARPEDOES.
SEARCH AND DESTROY.
HURHURHURHURHUR

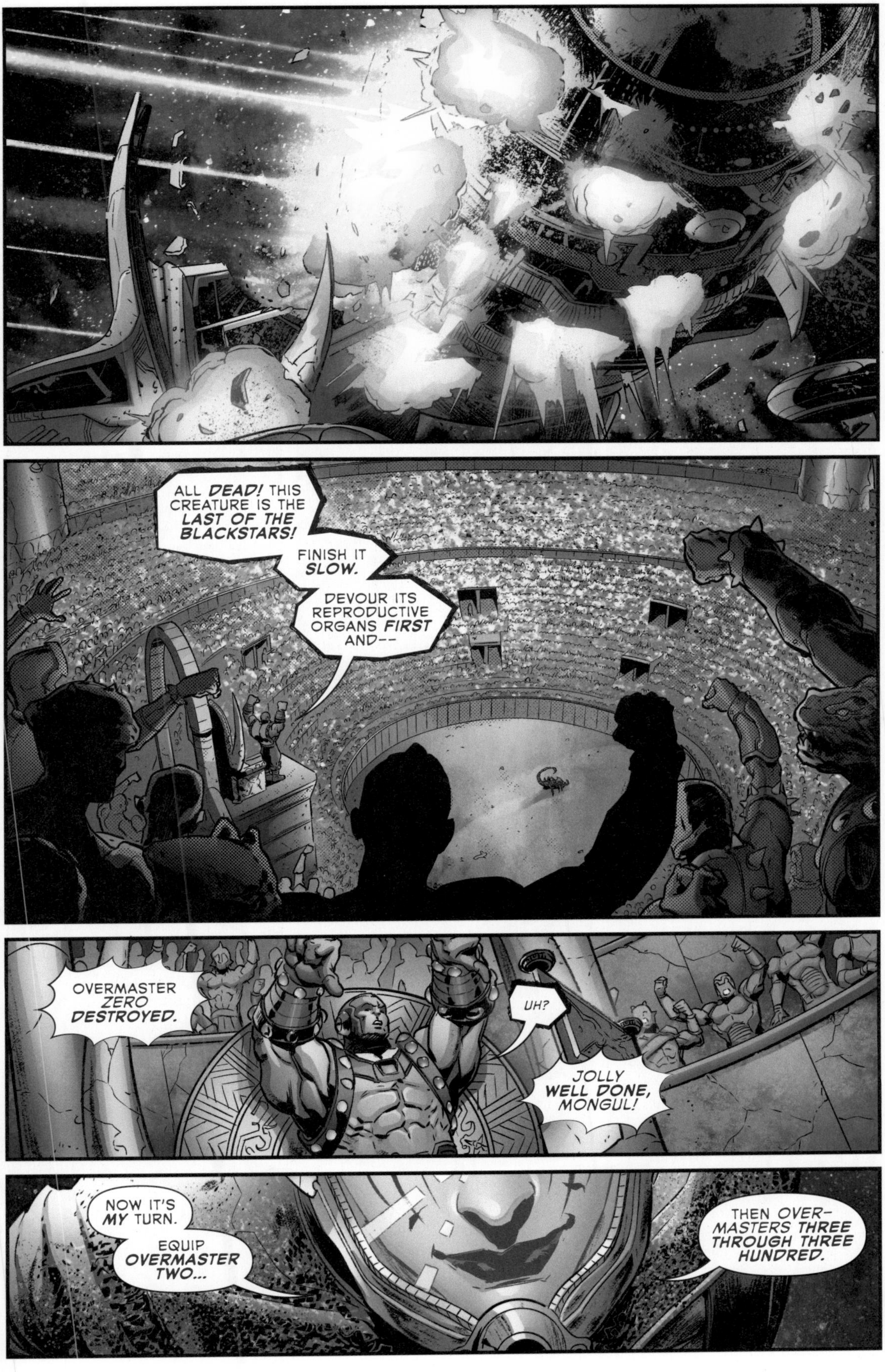
ALL DEAD! THIS CREATURE IS THE LAST OF THE BLACKSTARS!
FINISH IT SLOW.
DEVOUR ITS REPRODUCTIVE ORGANS FIRST AND--
OVERMASTER ZERO DESTROYED.
UH?
JOLLY WELL DONE, MONGUL!
NOW IT'S MY TURN.
EQUIP OVERMASTER TWO...
THEN OVER-MASTERS THREE THROUGH THREE HUNDRED.

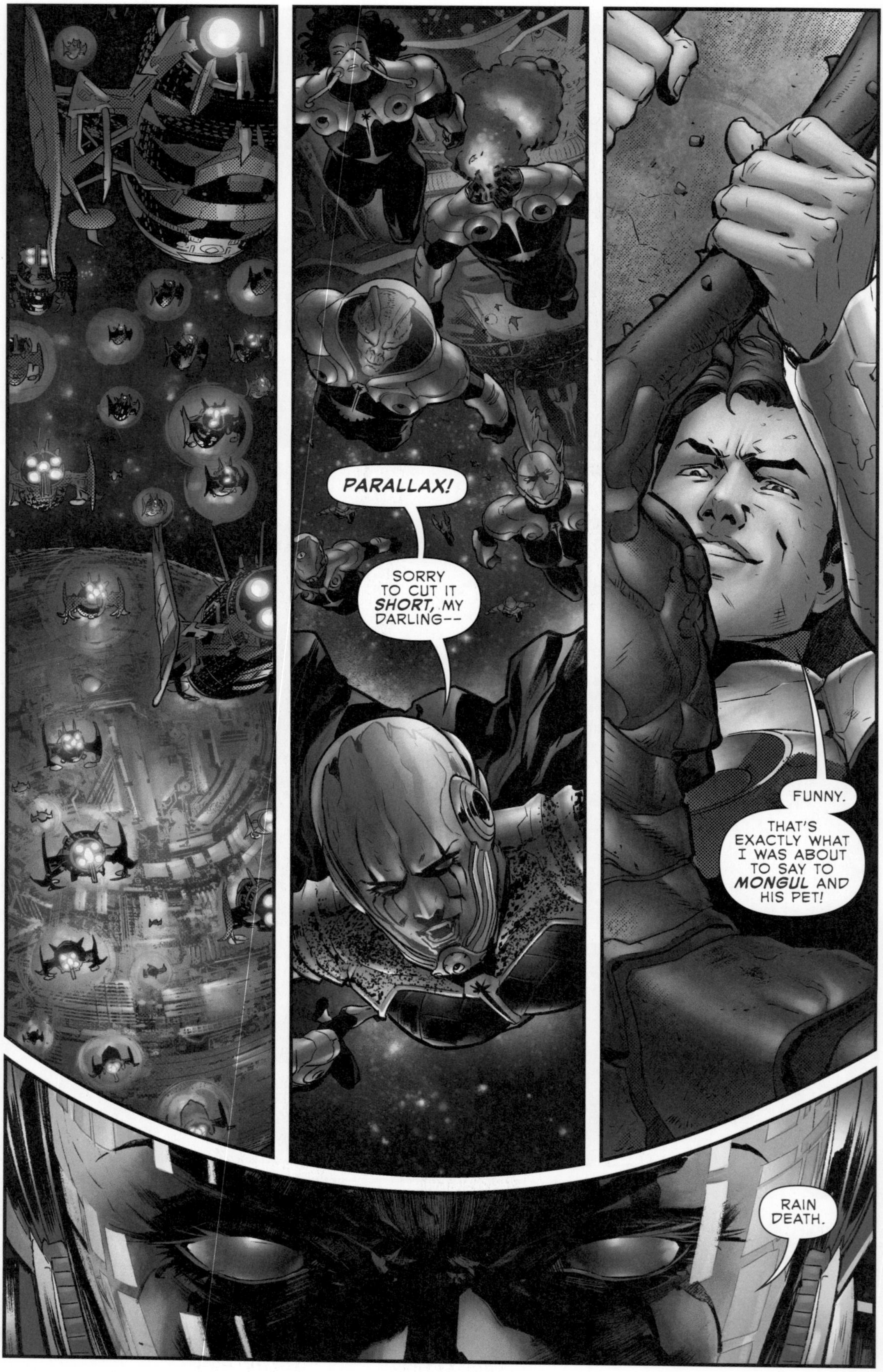
PARALLAX!
SORRY TO CUT IT SHORT, MY DARLING--
FUNNY.
THAT'S EXACTLY WHAT I WAS ABOUT TO SAY TO MONGUL AND HIS PET!
RAIN DEATH.

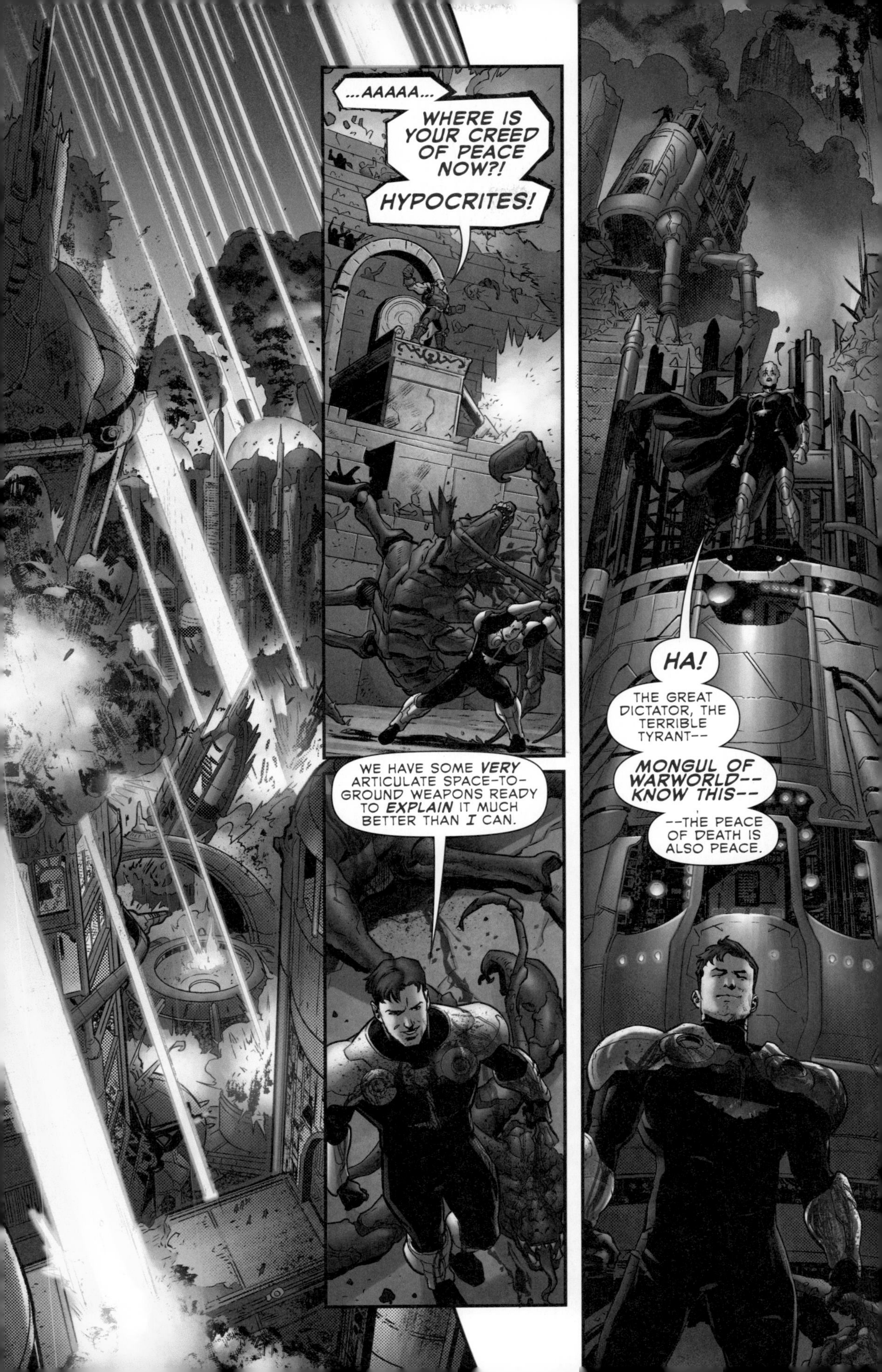
...AAAAA...
WHERE IS YOUR CREED OF PEACE NOW?!
HYPOCRITES!
WE HAVE SOME VERY ARTICULATE SPACE-TO-GROUND WEAPONS READY TO EXPLAIN IT MUCH BETTER THAN I CAN.
HA!
THE GREAT DICTATOR, THE TERRIBLE TYRANT--
MONGUL OF WARWORLD-- KNOW THIS--
--THE PEACE OF DEATH IS ALSO PEACE.

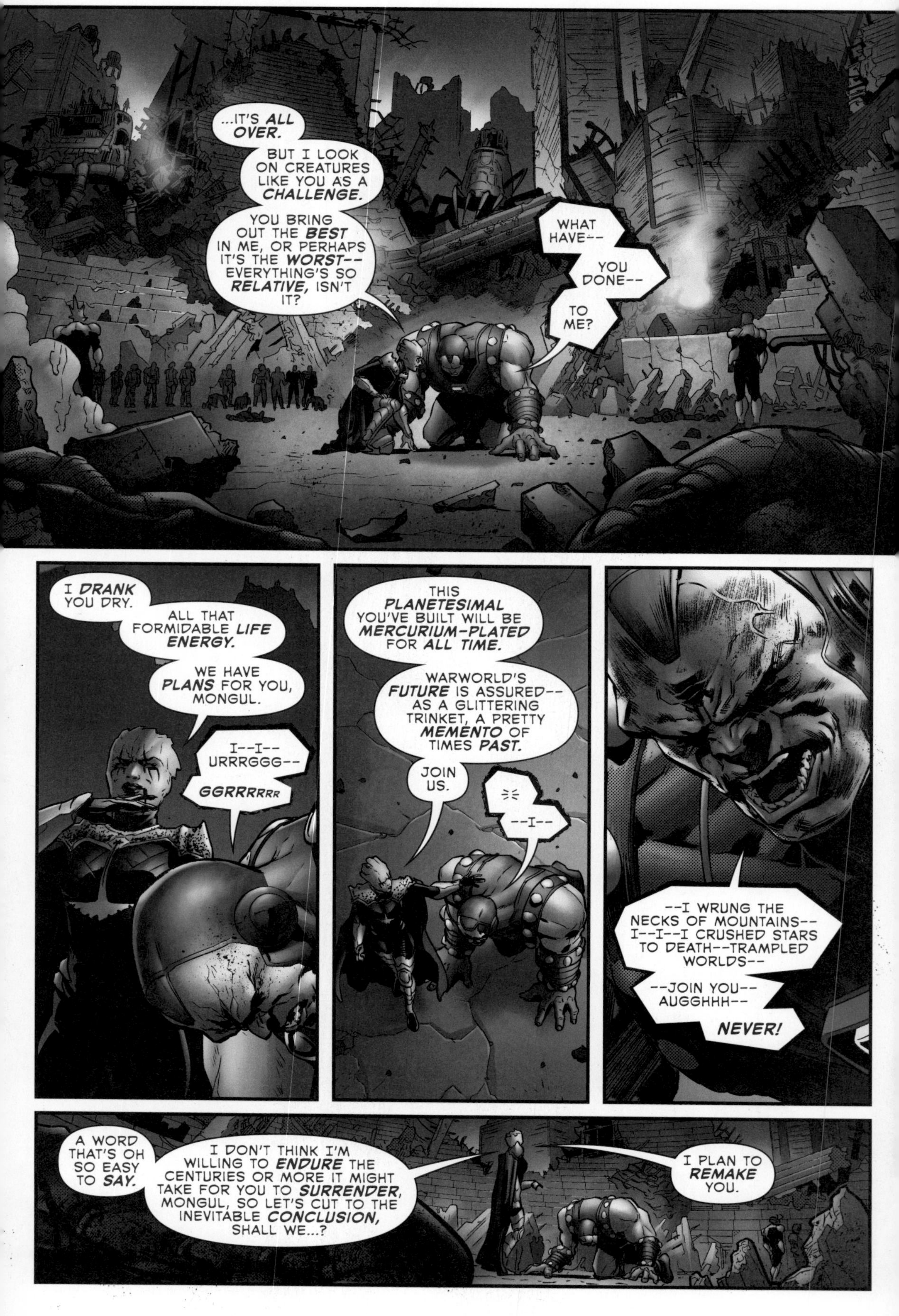
...IT'S ALL OVER.
BUT I LOOK ON CREATURES LIKE YOU AS A CHALLENGE.
YOU BRING OUT THE BEST IN ME, OR PERHAPS IT'S THE WORST--EVERYTHING'S SO RELATIVE, ISN'T IT?
WHAT HAVE--
YOU DONE--
TO ME?
I DRANK YOU DRY.
ALL THAT FORMIDABLE LIFE ENERGY.
WE HAVE PLANS FOR YOU, MONGUL.
I--I--URRRGGG--
GGRRRRRRR
THIS PLANETESIMAL YOU'VE BUILT WILL BE MERCURIUM-PLATED FOR ALL TIME.
WARWORLD'S FUTURE IS ASSURED--AS A GLITTERING TRINKET, A PRETTY MEMENTO OF TIMES PAST.
JOIN US.
--I--
--I WRUNG THE NECKS OF MOUNTAINS--I--I--I CRUSHED STARS TO DEATH--TRAMPLED WORLDS--
--JOIN YOU--AUGGHHH--
NEVER!
A WORD THAT'S OH SO EASY TO SAY.
I DON'T THINK I'M WILLING TO ENDURE THE CENTURIES OR MORE IT MIGHT TAKE FOR YOU TO SURRENDER, MONGUL, SO LET'S CUT TO THE INEVITABLE CONCLUSION, SHALL WE...?
I PLAN TO REMAKE YOU.

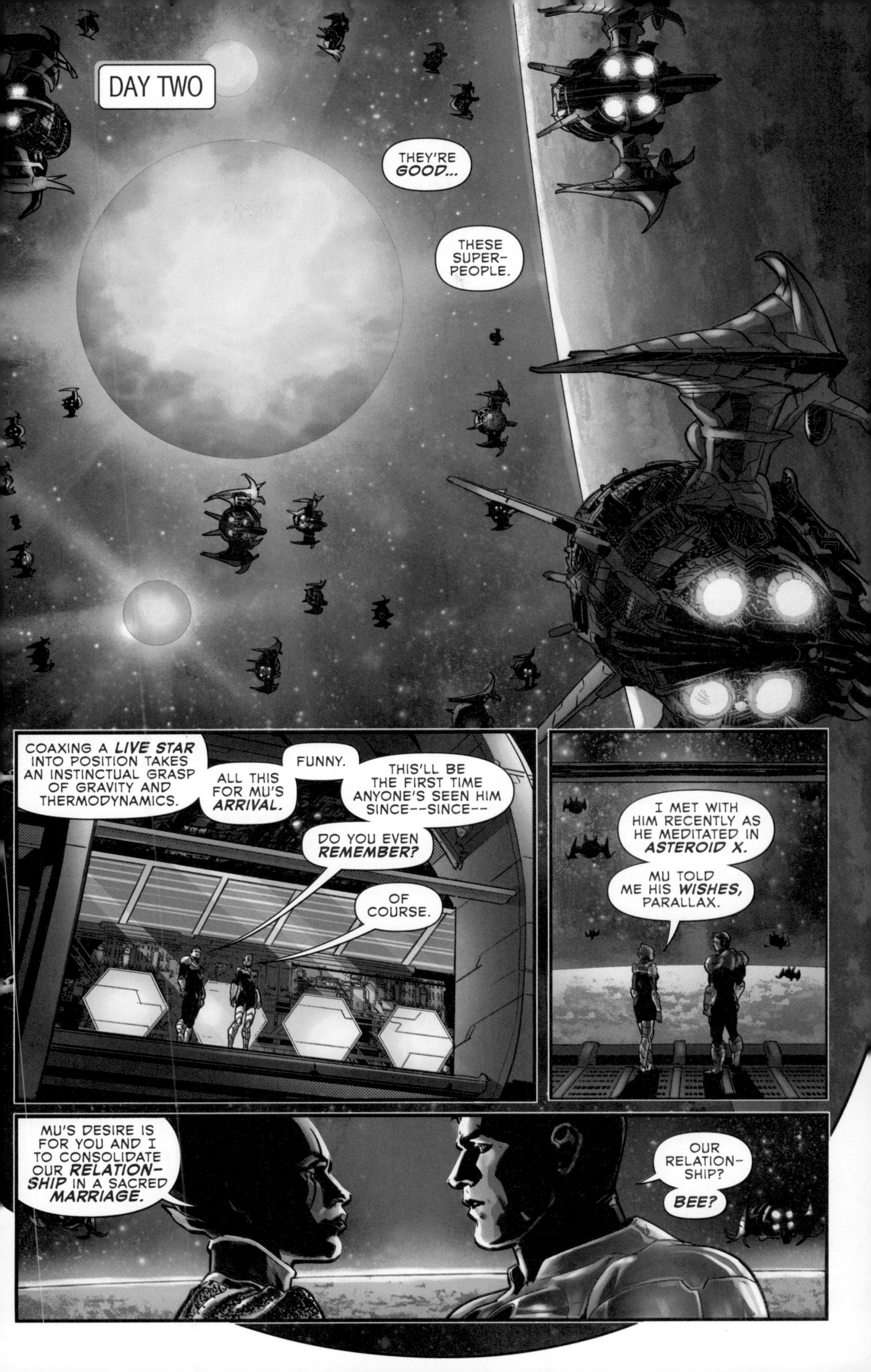
DAY TWO
THEY'RE GOOD...
THESE SUPER-PEOPLE.
COAXING A LIVE STAR INTO POSITION TAKES AN INSTINCTUAL GRASP OF GRAVITY AND THERMODYNAMICS.
ALL THIS FOR MU'S ARRIVAL.
FUNNY.
THIS'LL BE THE FIRST TIME ANYONE'S SEEN HIM SINCE--SINCE--
DO YOU EVEN REMEMBER?
OF COURSE.
I MET WITH HIM RECENTLY AS HE MEDITATED IN ASTEROID X.
MU TOLD ME HIS WISHES, PARALLAX.
MU'S DESIRE IS FOR YOU AND I TO CONSOLIDATE OUR RELATION-SHIP IN A SACRED MARRIAGE.
OUR RELATION-SHIP?
BEE?

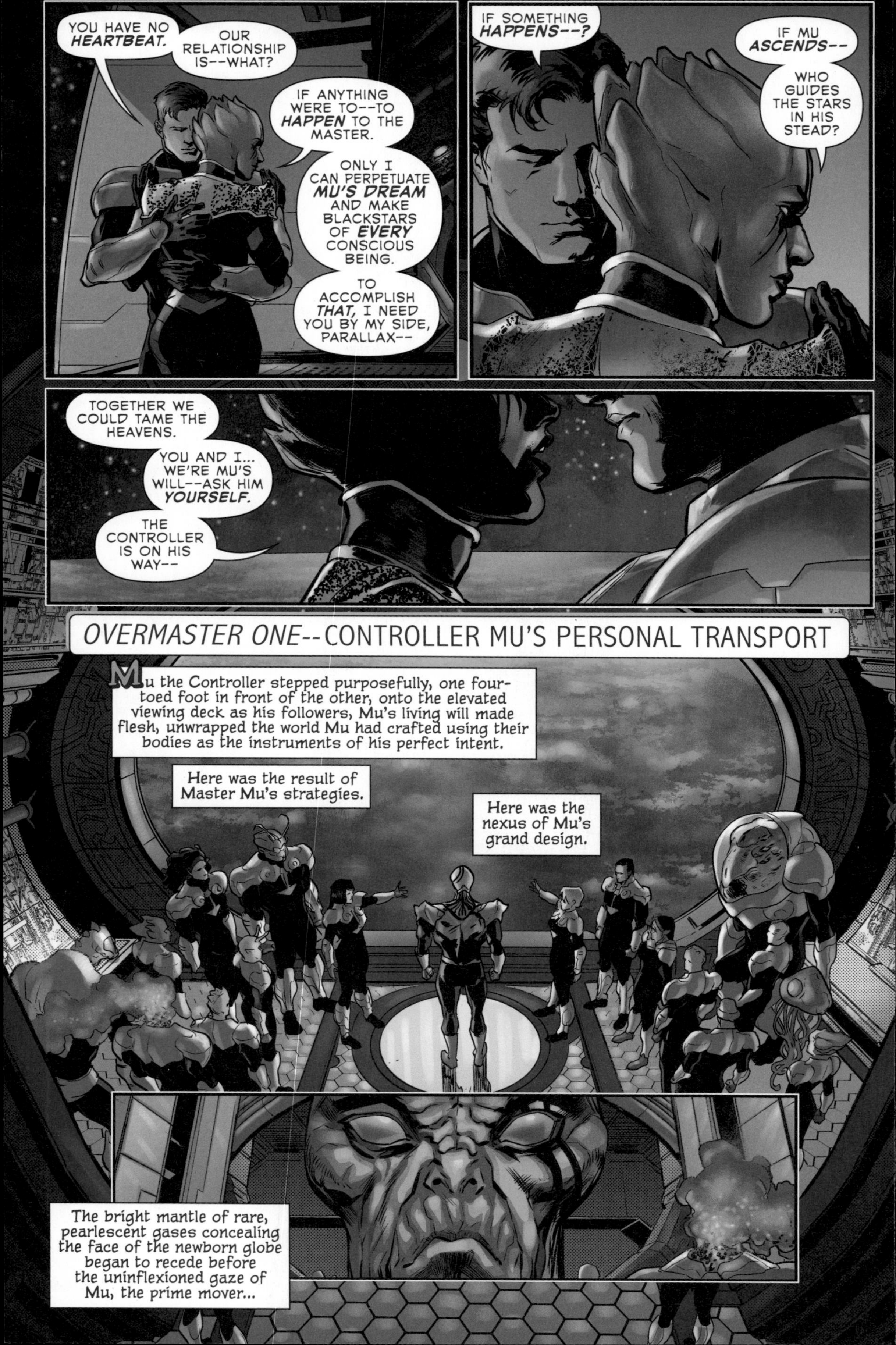

YOU HAVE NO *HEARTBEAT.*
OUR RELATIONSHIP IS--WHAT?
IF ANYTHING WERE TO--TO *HAPPEN* TO THE MASTER.
ONLY I CAN PERPETUATE *MU'S DREAM* AND MAKE BLACKSTARS OF *EVERY* CONSCIOUS BEING.
TO ACCOMPLISH *THAT,* I NEED YOU BY MY SIDE, PARALLAX--
IF SOMETHING *HAPPENS--?*
IF MU *ASCENDS--*
WHO GUIDES THE STARS IN HIS STEAD?
TOGETHER WE COULD TAME THE HEAVENS.
YOU AND I... WE'RE MU'S WILL--ASK HIM *YOURSELF.*
THE CONTROLLER IS ON HIS WAY--
OVERMASTER ONE--CONTROLLER MU'S PERSONAL TRANSPORT
Mu the Controller stepped purposefully, one four-toed foot in front of the other, onto the elevated viewing deck as his followers, Mu's living will made flesh, unwrapped the world Mu had crafted using their bodies as the instruments of his perfect intent.
Here was the result of Master Mu's strategies.
Here was the nexus of Mu's grand design.
The bright mantle of rare, pearlescent gases concealing the face of the newborn globe began to recede before the uninflexioned gaze of Mu, the prime mover...

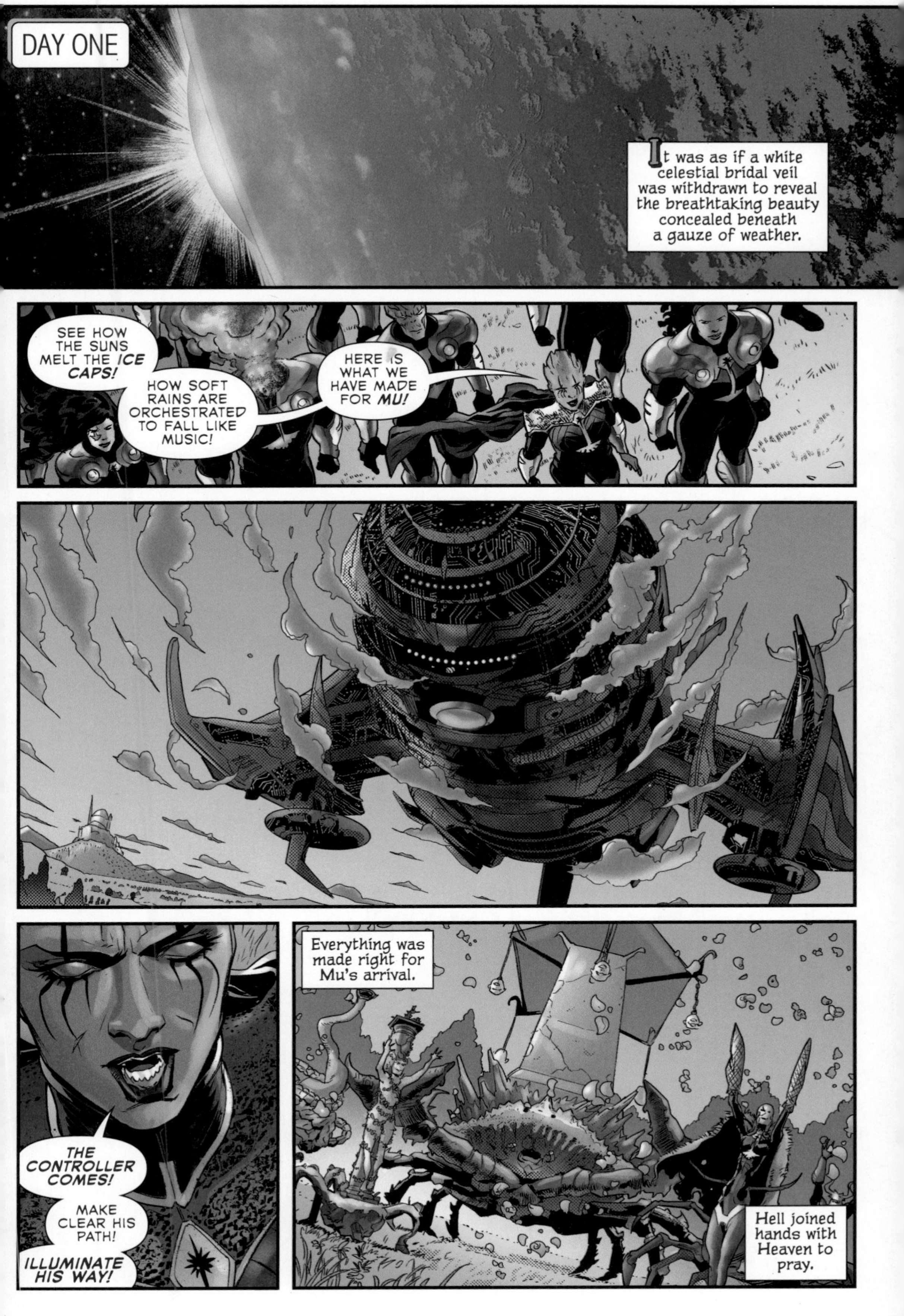
DAY ONE
It was as if a white celestial bridal veil was withdrawn to reveal the breathtaking beauty concealed beneath a gauze of weather.
SEE HOW THE SUNS MELT THE ICE CAPS!
HOW SOFT RAINS ARE ORCHESTRATED TO FALL LIKE MUSIC!
HERE IS WHAT WE HAVE MADE FOR MU!
THE CONTROLLER COMES!
MAKE CLEAR HIS PATH!
ILLUMINATE HIS WAY!
Everything was made right for Mu's arrival.
Hell joined hands with Heaven to pray.

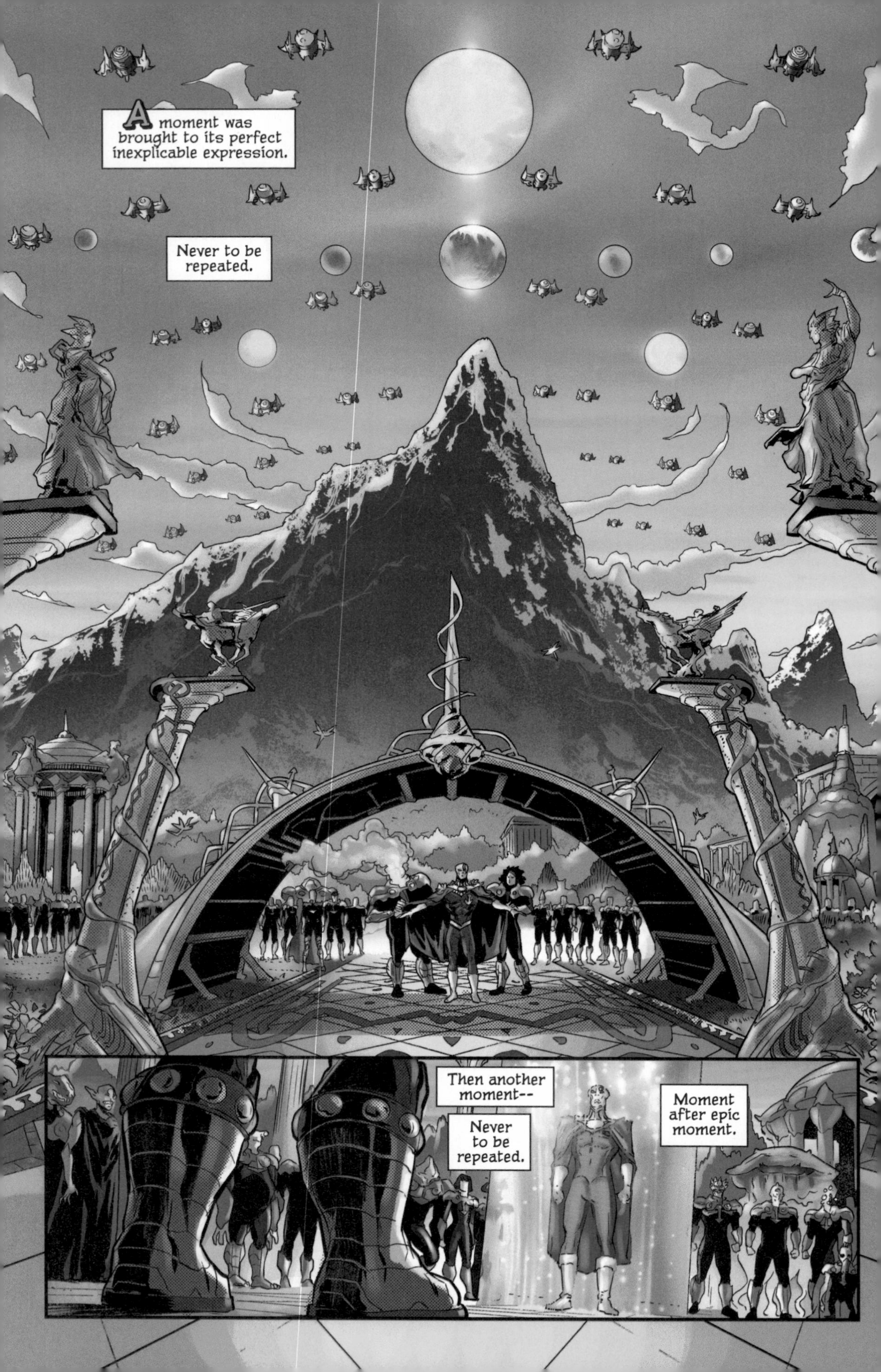
A moment was brought to its perfect inexplicable expression.
Never to be repeated.
Then another moment--
Never to be repeated.
Moment after epic moment.

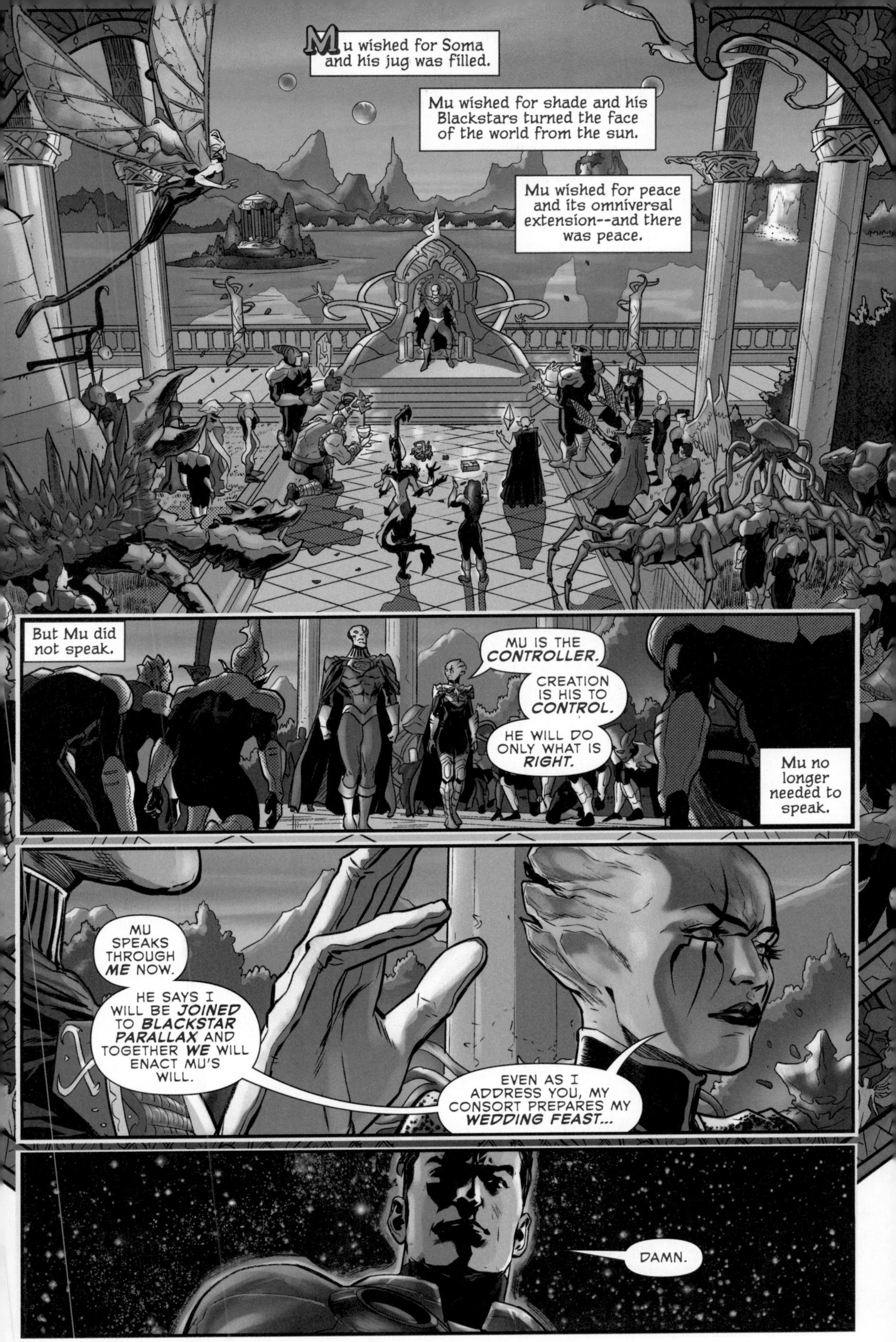
Mu wished for Soma and his jug was filled.
Mu wished for shade and his Blackstars turned the face of the world from the sun.
Mu wished for peace and its omniversal extension--and there was peace.
But Mu did not speak.
MU IS THE CONTROLLER.
CREATION IS HIS TO CONTROL.
HE WILL DO ONLY WHAT IS RIGHT.
Mu no longer needed to speak.
MU SPEAKS THROUGH ME NOW.
HE SAYS I WILL BE JOINED TO BLACKSTAR PARALLAX AND TOGETHER WE WILL ENACT MU'S WILL.
EVEN AS I ADDRESS YOU, MY CONSORT PREPARES MY WEDDING FEAST...
DAMN.

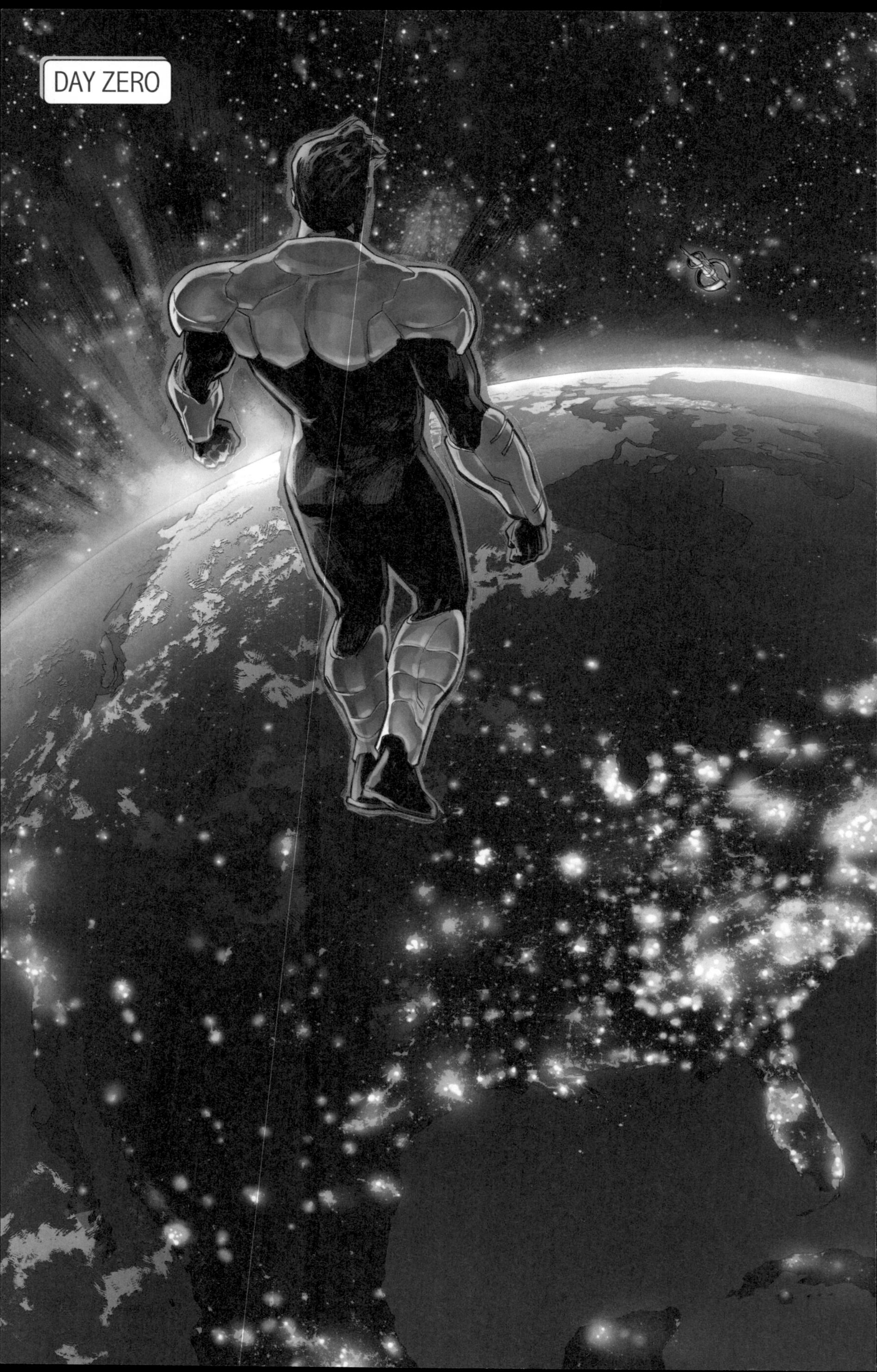
DAY ZERO

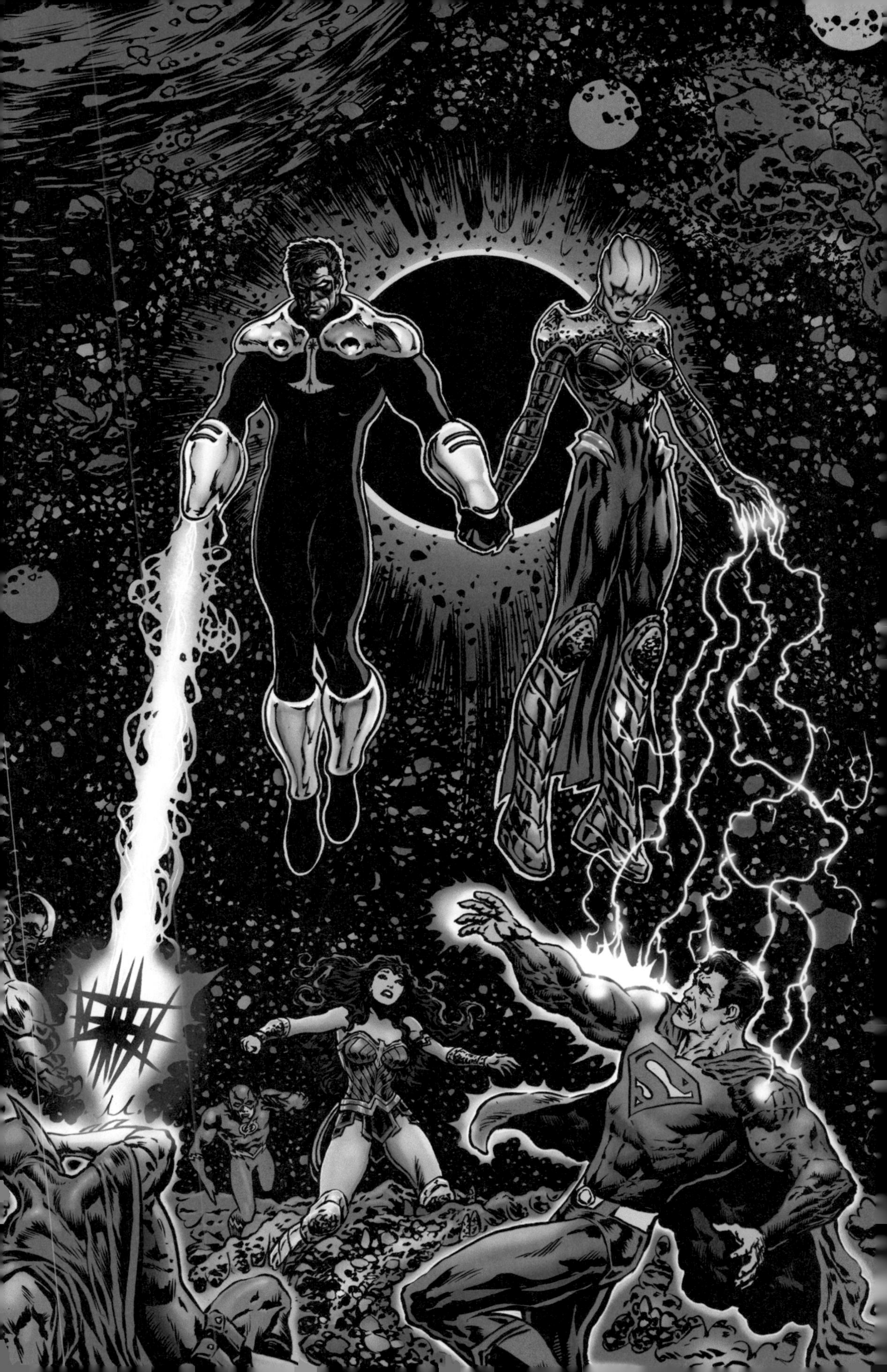

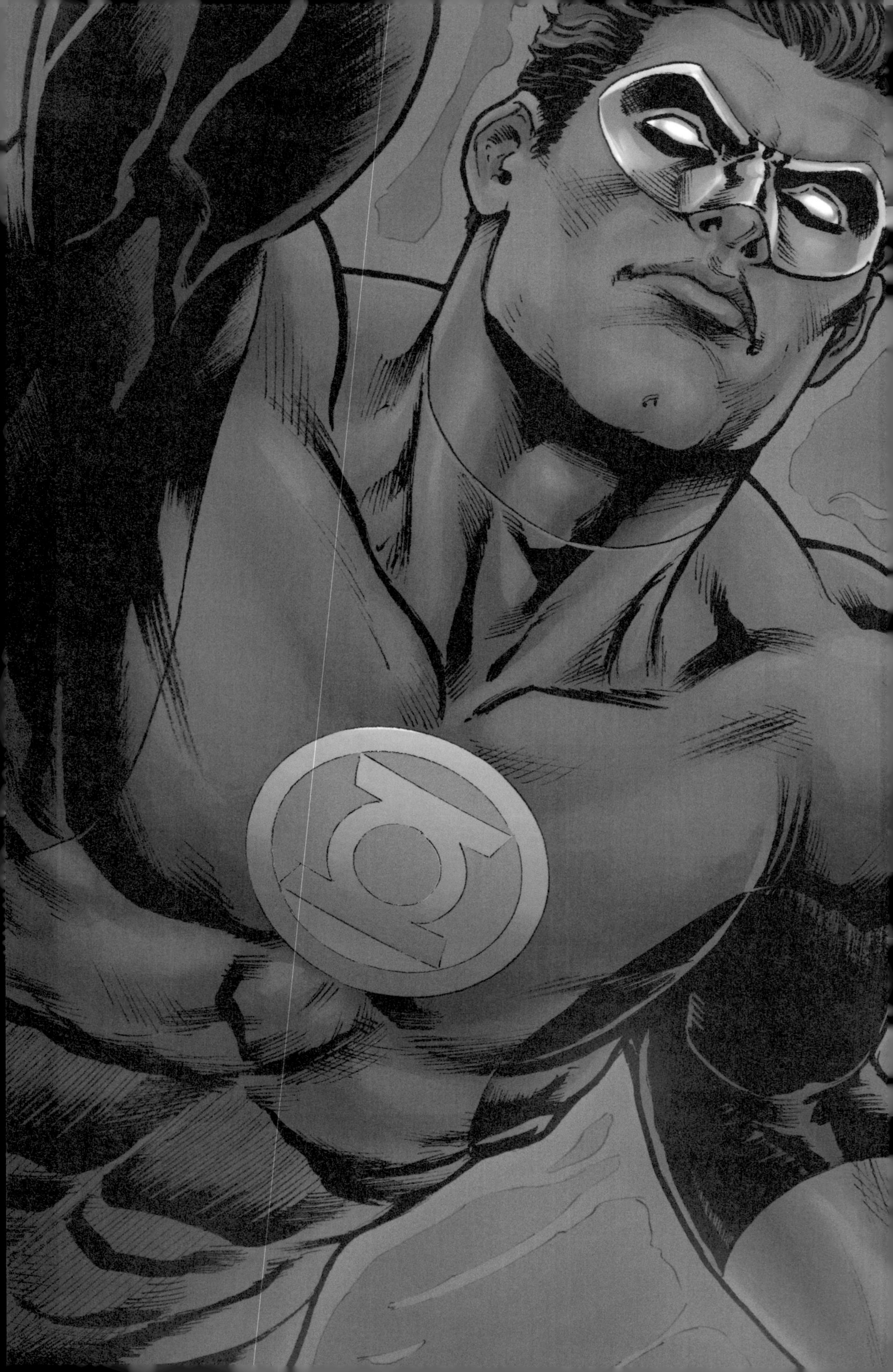

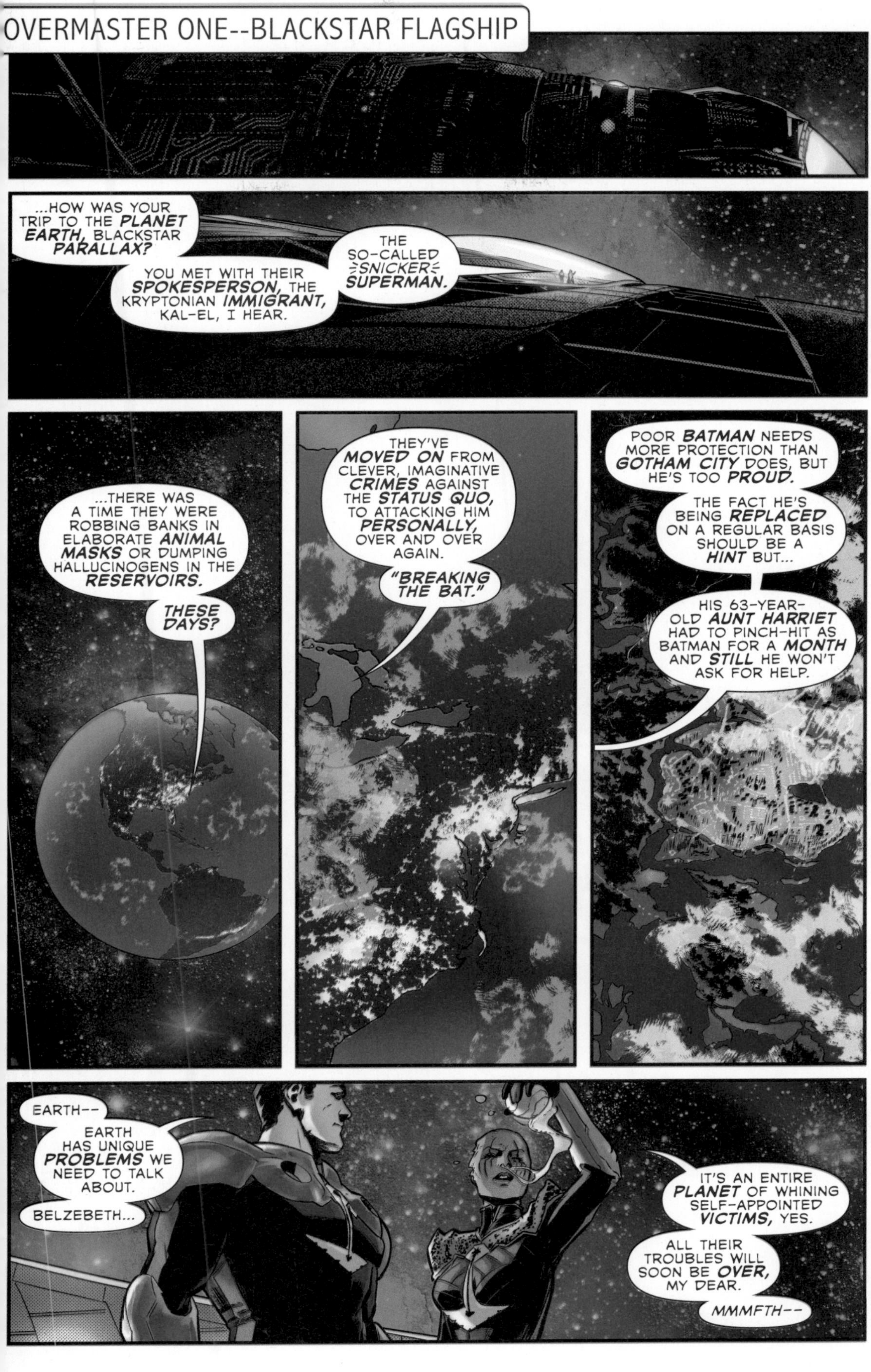
OVERMASTER ONE--BLACKSTAR FLAGSHIP
...HOW WAS YOUR TRIP TO THE PLANET EARTH, BLACKSTAR PARALLAX?
YOU MET WITH THEIR SPOKESPERSON, THE KRYPTONIAN IMMIGRANT, KAL-EL, I HEAR.
THE SO-CALLED SNICKER SUPERMAN.
...THERE WAS A TIME THEY WERE ROBBING BANKS IN ELABORATE ANIMAL MASKS OR DUMPING HALLUCINOGENS IN THE RESERVOIRS.
THESE DAYS?
THEY'VE MOVED ON FROM CLEVER, IMAGINATIVE CRIMES AGAINST THE STATUS QUO, TO ATTACKING HIM PERSONALLY, OVER AND OVER AGAIN.
"BREAKING THE BAT."
POOR BATMAN NEEDS MORE PROTECTION THAN GOTHAM CITY DOES, BUT HE'S TOO PROUD.
THE FACT HE'S BEING REPLACED ON A REGULAR BASIS SHOULD BE A HINT BUT...
HIS 63-YEAR-OLD AUNT HARRIET HAD TO PINCH-HIT AS BATMAN FOR A MONTH AND STILL HE WON'T ASK FOR HELP.
EARTH--
EARTH HAS UNIQUE PROBLEMS WE NEED TO TALK ABOUT.
BELZEBETH...
IT'S AN ENTIRE PLANET OF WHINING SELF-APPOINTED VICTIMS, YES.
ALL THEIR TROUBLES WILL SOON BE OVER, MY DEAR.
MMMFTH--

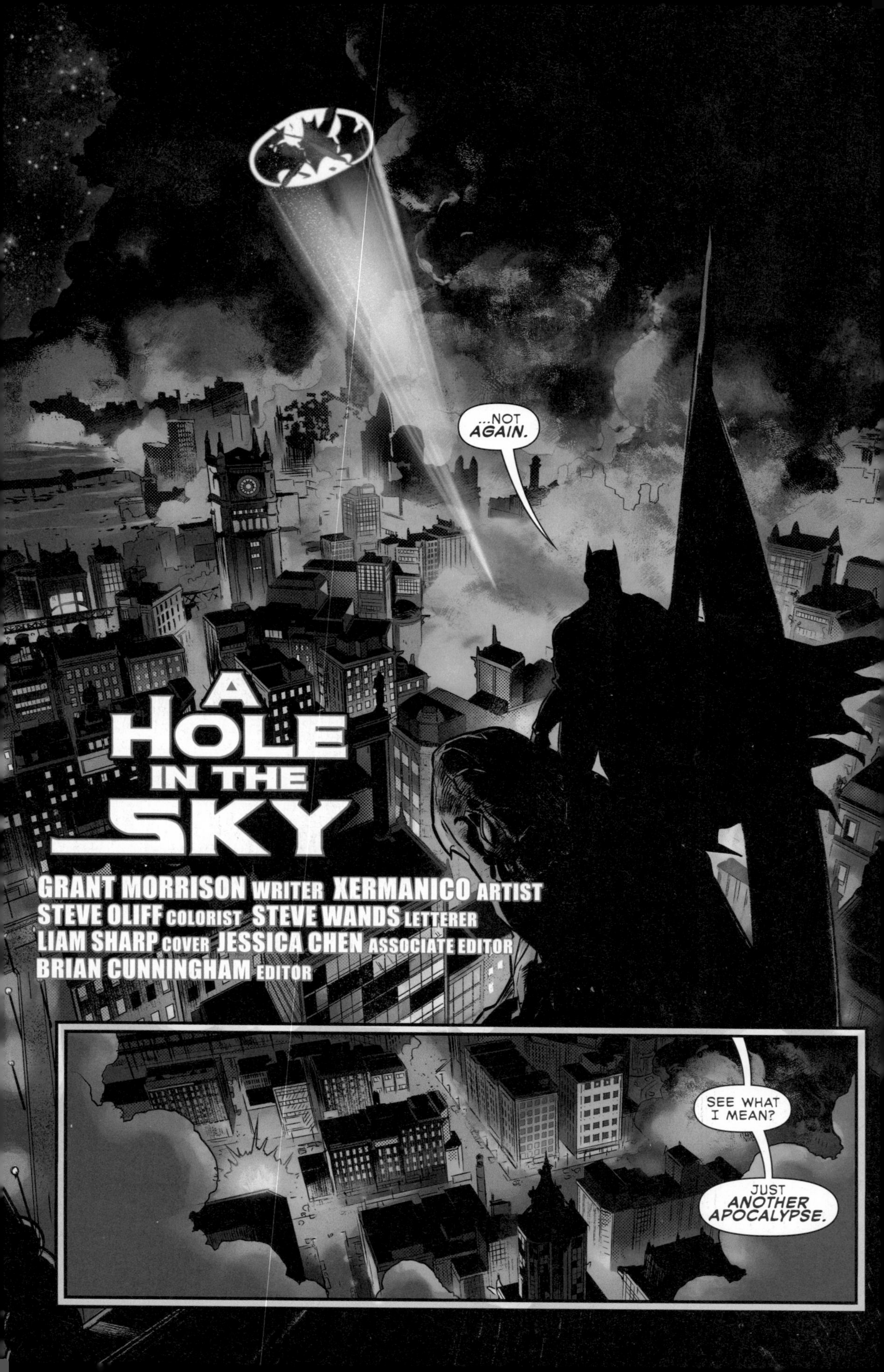
...NOT AGAIN.
A HOLE IN THE SKY
GRANT MORRISON WRITER XERMANICO ARTIST
STEVE OLIFF COLORIST STEVE WANDS LETTERER
LIAM SHARP COVER JESSICA CHEN ASSOCIATE EDITOR
BRIAN CUNNINGHAM EDITOR
SEE WHAT I MEAN?
JUST ANOTHER APOCALYPSE.

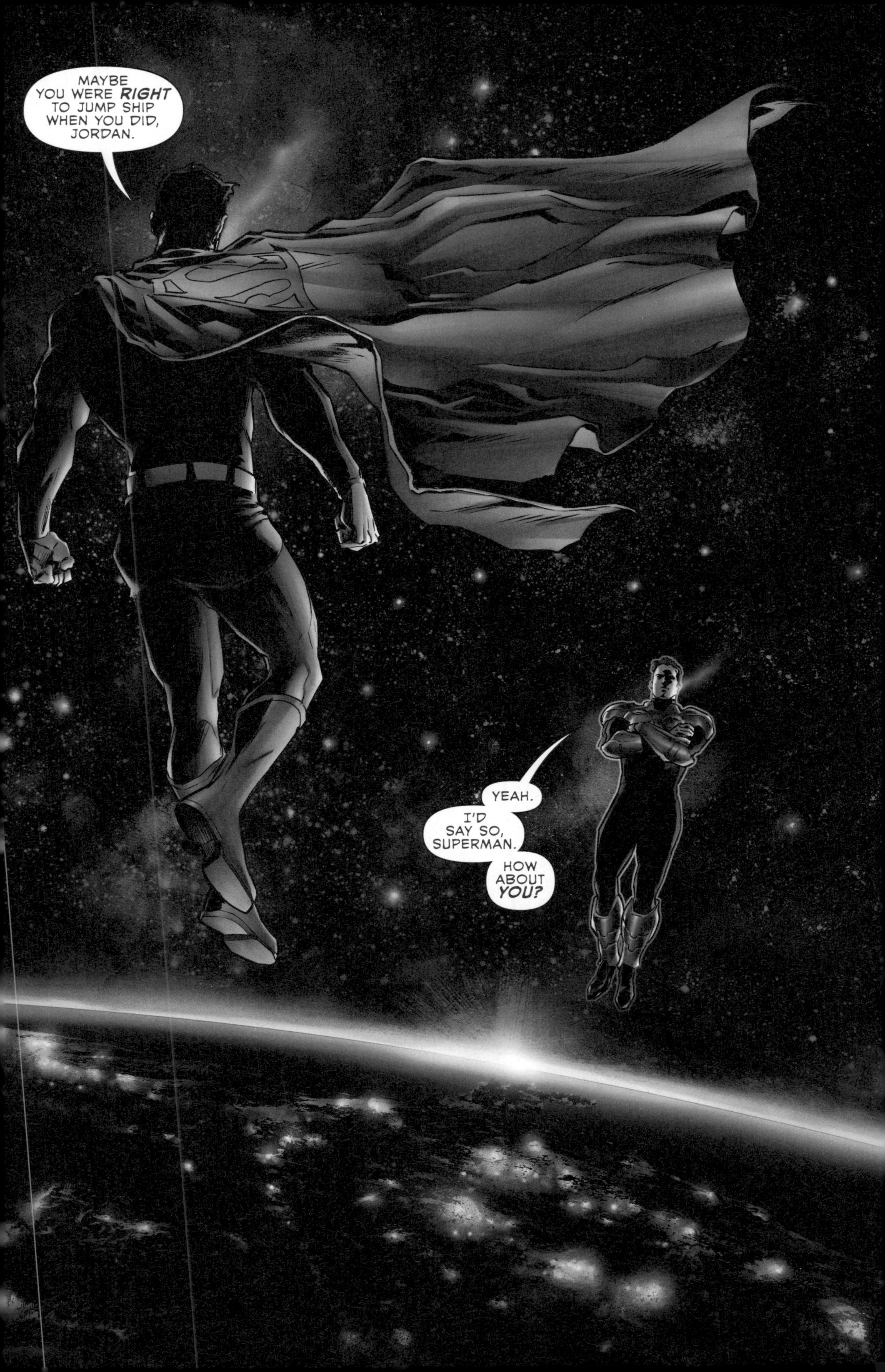
MAYBE YOU WERE **RIGHT** TO JUMP SHIP WHEN YOU DID, JORDAN.
YEAH.
I'D SAY SO, SUPERMAN.
HOW ABOUT **YOU?**

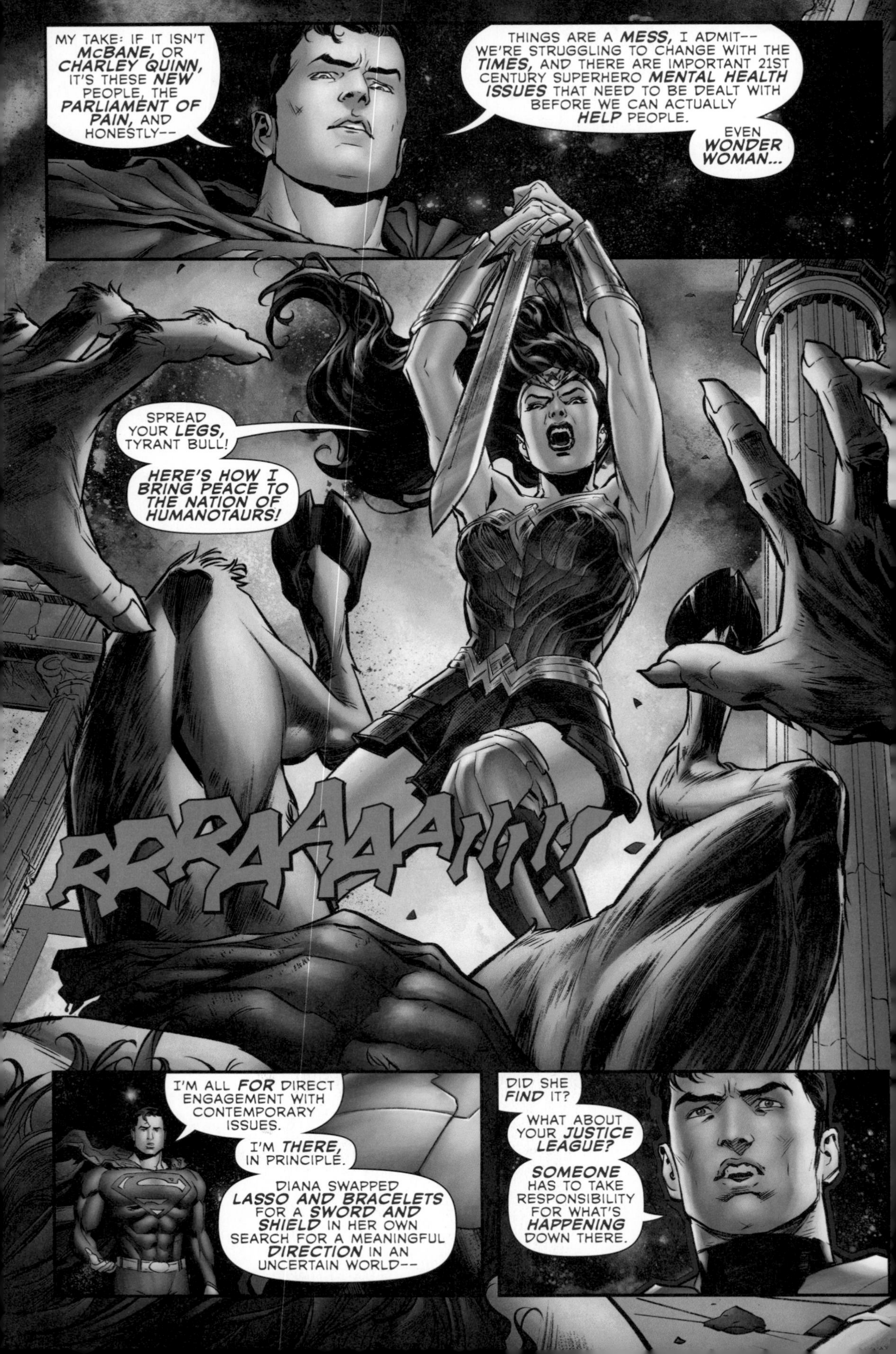
MY TAKE: IF IT ISN'T McBANE, OR CHARLEY QUINN, IT'S THESE NEW PEOPLE, THE PARLIAMENT OF PAIN, AND HONESTLY--
THINGS ARE A MESS, I ADMIT-- WE'RE STRUGGLING TO CHANGE WITH THE TIMES, AND THERE ARE IMPORTANT 21ST CENTURY SUPERHERO MENTAL HEALTH ISSUES THAT NEED TO BE DEALT WITH BEFORE WE CAN ACTUALLY HELP PEOPLE.
EVEN WONDER WOMAN...
SPREAD YOUR LEGS, TYRANT BULL!
HERE'S HOW I BRING PEACE TO THE NATION OF HUMANOTAURS!
RRRAAAAIII!!
I'M ALL FOR DIRECT ENGAGEMENT WITH CONTEMPORARY ISSUES.
I'M THERE, IN PRINCIPLE.
DIANA SWAPPED LASSO AND BRACELETS FOR A SWORD AND SHIELD IN HER OWN SEARCH FOR A MEANINGFUL DIRECTION IN AN UNCERTAIN WORLD--
DID SHE FIND IT?
WHAT ABOUT YOUR JUSTICE LEAGUE?
SOMEONE HAS TO TAKE RESPONSIBILITY FOR WHAT'S HAPPENING DOWN THERE.

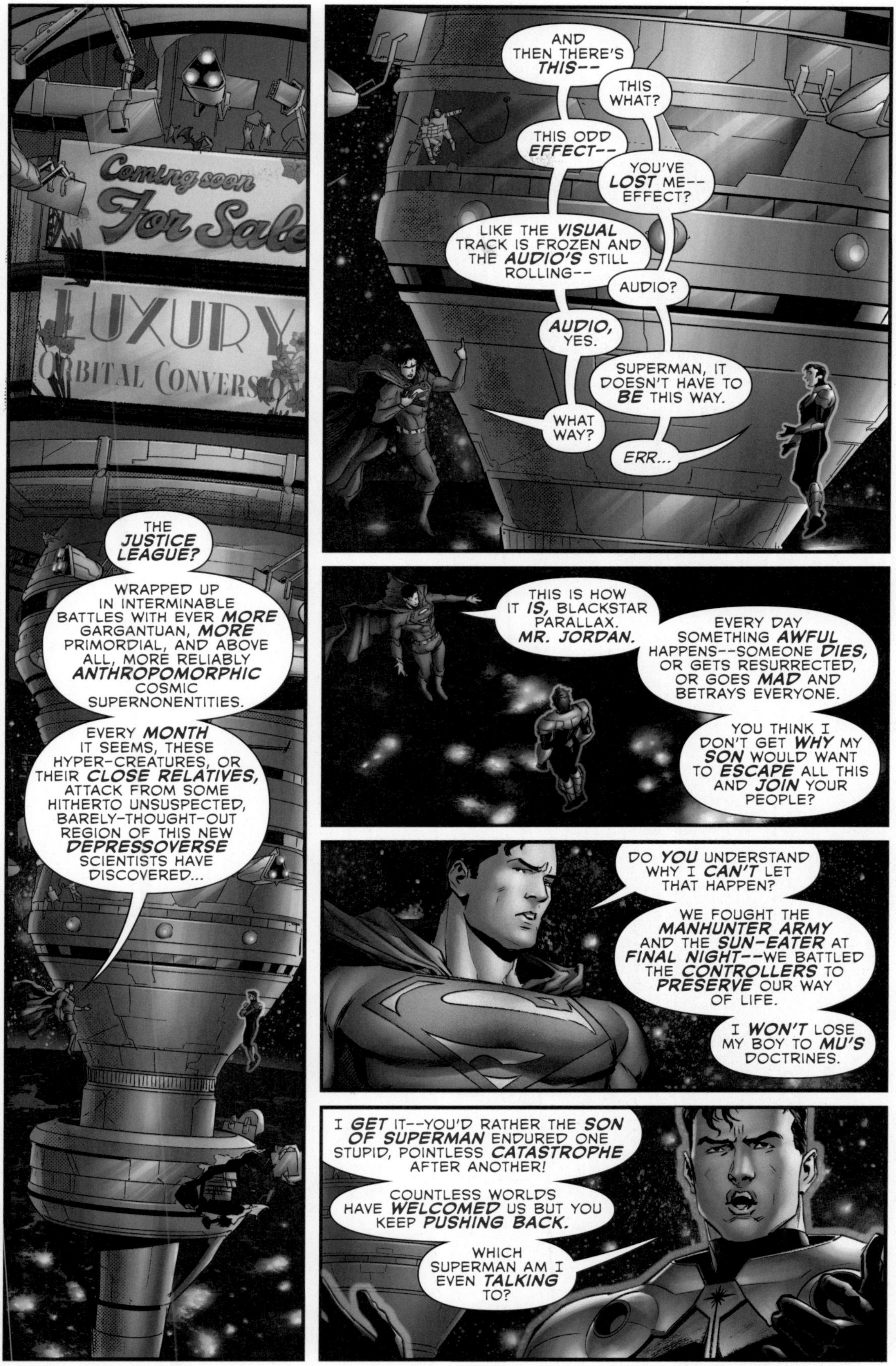
Coming soon For Sale
LUXURY ORBITAL CONVERSION
THE JUSTICE LEAGUE?
WRAPPED UP IN INTERMINABLE BATTLES WITH EVER MORE GARGANTUAN, MORE PRIMORDIAL, AND ABOVE ALL, MORE RELIABLY ANTHROPOMORPHIC COSMIC SUPERNONENTITIES.
EVERY MONTH IT SEEMS, THESE HYPER-CREATURES, OR THEIR CLOSE RELATIVES, ATTACK FROM SOME HITHERTO UNSUSPECTED, BARELY-THOUGHT-OUT REGION OF THIS NEW DEPRESSOVERSE SCIENTISTS HAVE DISCOVERED...
AND THEN THERE'S THIS--
THIS WHAT?
THIS ODD EFFECT--
YOU'VE LOST ME--EFFECT?
LIKE THE VISUAL TRACK IS FROZEN AND THE AUDIO'S STILL ROLLING--
AUDIO?
AUDIO, YES.
SUPERMAN, IT DOESN'T HAVE TO BE THIS WAY.
WHAT WAY?
ERR...
THIS IS HOW IT IS, BLACKSTAR PARALLAX. MR. JORDAN.
EVERY DAY SOMETHING AWFUL HAPPENS--SOMEONE DIES, OR GETS RESURRECTED, OR GOES MAD AND BETRAYS EVERYONE.
YOU THINK I DON'T GET WHY MY SON WOULD WANT TO ESCAPE ALL THIS AND JOIN YOUR PEOPLE?
DO YOU UNDERSTAND WHY I CAN'T LET THAT HAPPEN?
WE FOUGHT THE MANHUNTER ARMY AND THE SUN-EATER AT FINAL NIGHT--WE BATTLED THE CONTROLLERS TO PRESERVE OUR WAY OF LIFE.
I WON'T LOSE MY BOY TO MU'S DOCTRINES.
I GET IT--YOU'D RATHER THE SON OF SUPERMAN ENDURED ONE STUPID, POINTLESS CATASTROPHE AFTER ANOTHER!
COUNTLESS WORLDS HAVE WELCOMED US BUT YOU KEEP PUSHING BACK.
WHICH SUPERMAN AM I EVEN TALKING TO?

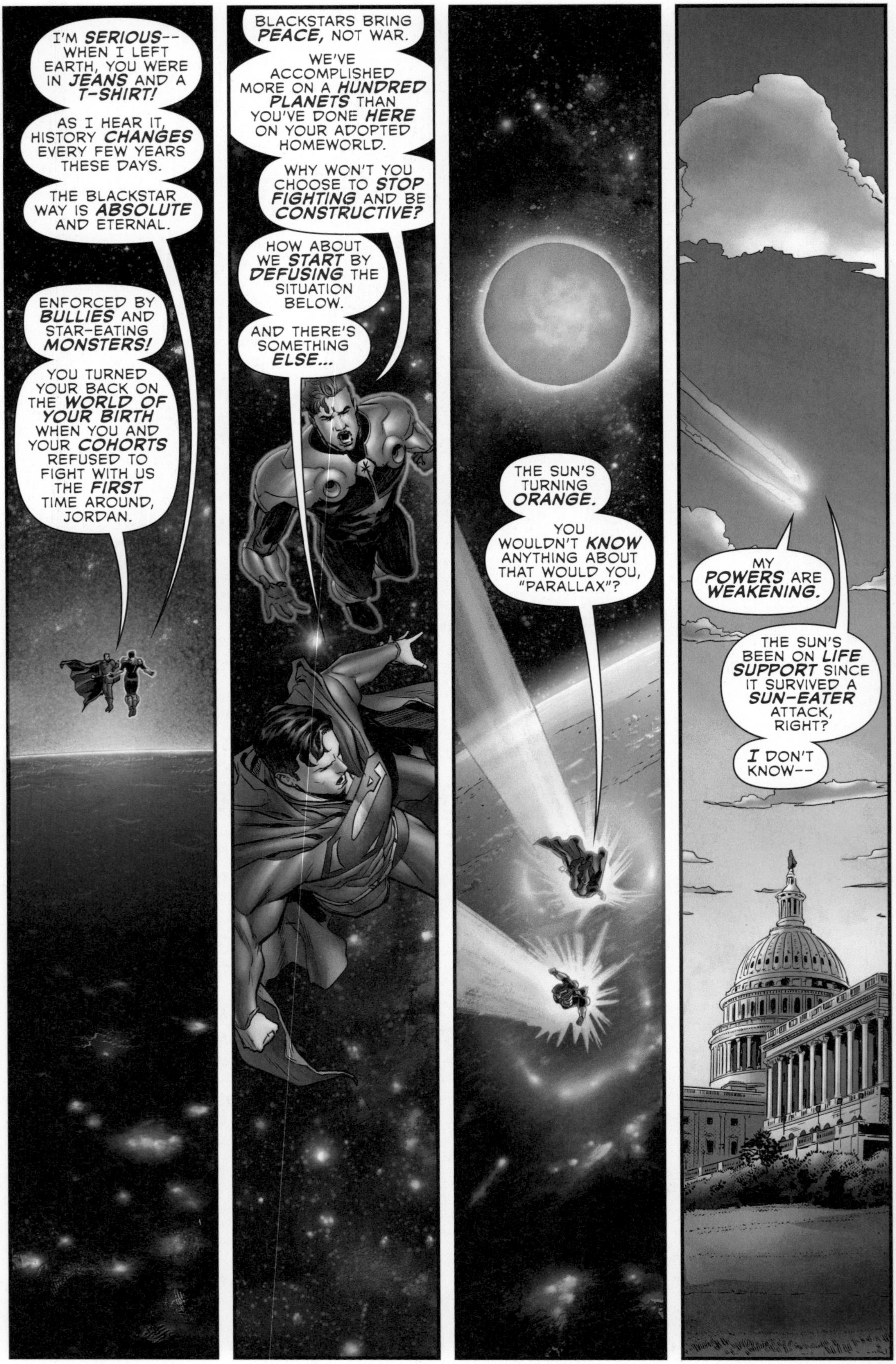
I'M SERIOUS-- WHEN I LEFT EARTH, YOU WERE IN JEANS AND A T-SHIRT!
AS I HEAR IT, HISTORY CHANGES EVERY FEW YEARS THESE DAYS.
THE BLACKSTAR WAY IS ABSOLUTE AND ETERNAL.
ENFORCED BY BULLIES AND STAR-EATING MONSTERS!
YOU TURNED YOUR BACK ON THE WORLD OF YOUR BIRTH WHEN YOU AND YOUR COHORTS REFUSED TO FIGHT WITH US THE FIRST TIME AROUND, JORDAN.
BLACKSTARS BRING PEACE, NOT WAR.
WE'VE ACCOMPLISHED MORE ON A HUNDRED PLANETS THAN YOU'VE DONE HERE ON YOUR ADOPTED HOMEWORLD.
WHY WON'T YOU CHOOSE TO STOP FIGHTING AND BE CONSTRUCTIVE?
HOW ABOUT WE START BY DEFUSING THE SITUATION BELOW.
AND THERE'S SOMETHING ELSE...
THE SUN'S TURNING ORANGE.
YOU WOULDN'T KNOW ANYTHING ABOUT THAT WOULD YOU, "PARALLAX"?
MY POWERS ARE WEAKENING.
THE SUN'S BEEN ON LIFE SUPPORT SINCE IT SURVIVED A SUN-EATER ATTACK, RIGHT?
I DON'T KNOW--

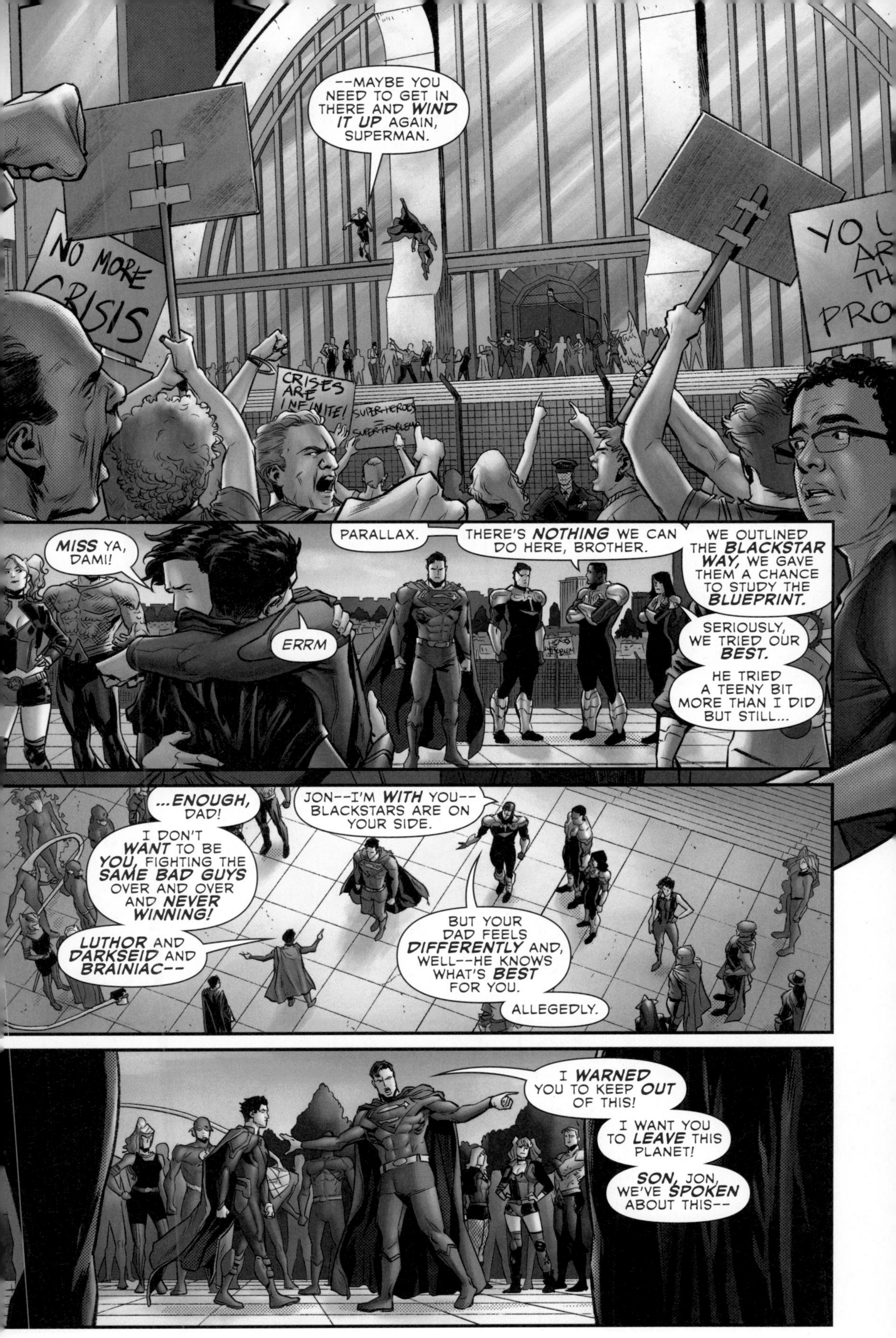
--MAYBE YOU NEED TO GET IN THERE AND WIND IT UP AGAIN, SUPERMAN.
NO MORE CRISIS
CRISES ARE INFINITE!
SUPER-HEROES = SUPER-PROBLEMS
MISS YA, DAMI!
ERRM
PARALLAX.
THERE'S NOTHING WE CAN DO HERE, BROTHER.
WE OUTLINED THE BLACKSTAR WAY, WE GAVE THEM A CHANCE TO STUDY THE BLUEPRINT.
SERIOUSLY, WE TRIED OUR BEST.
HE TRIED A TEENY BIT MORE THAN I DID BUT STILL...
...ENOUGH, DAD!
I DON'T WANT TO BE YOU, FIGHTING THE SAME BAD GUYS OVER AND OVER AND NEVER WINNING!
LUTHOR AND DARKSEID AND BRAINIAC--
JON--I'M WITH YOU--BLACKSTARS ARE ON YOUR SIDE.
BUT YOUR DAD FEELS DIFFERENTLY AND, WELL--HE KNOWS WHAT'S BEST FOR YOU.
ALLEGEDLY.
I WARNED YOU TO KEEP OUT OF THIS!
I WANT YOU TO LEAVE THIS PLANET!
SON, JON, WE'VE SPOKEN ABOUT THIS--

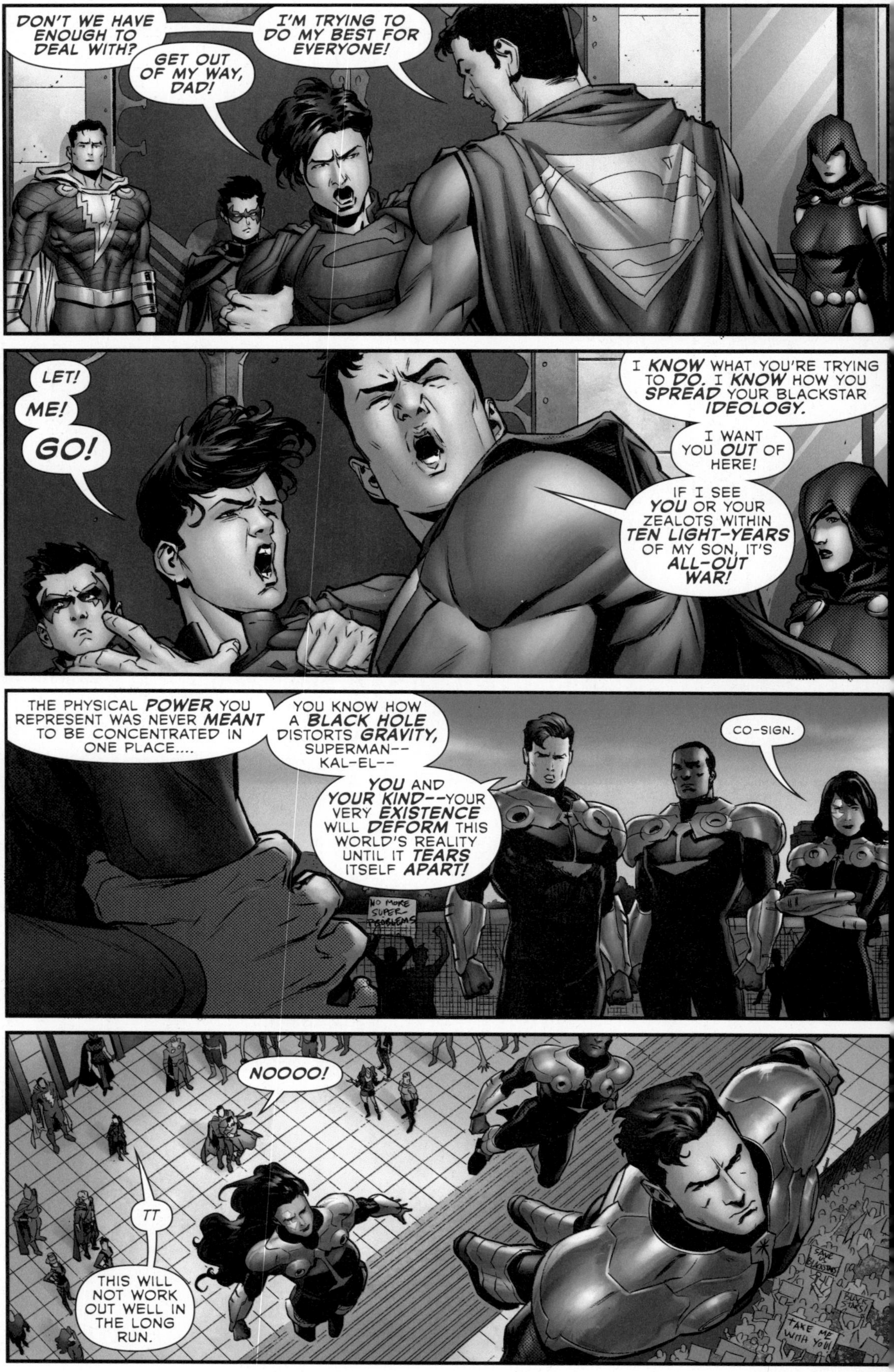
DON'T WE HAVE ENOUGH TO DEAL WITH?
I'M TRYING TO DO MY BEST FOR EVERYONE!
GET OUT OF MY WAY, DAD!
LET!
ME!
GO!
I KNOW WHAT YOU'RE TRYING TO DO. I KNOW HOW YOU SPREAD YOUR BLACKSTAR IDEOLOGY.
I WANT YOU OUT OF HERE!
IF I SEE YOU OR YOUR ZEALOTS WITHIN TEN LIGHT-YEARS OF MY SON, IT'S ALL-OUT WAR!
THE PHYSICAL POWER YOU REPRESENT WAS NEVER MEANT TO BE CONCENTRATED IN ONE PLACE....
YOU KNOW HOW A BLACK HOLE DISTORTS GRAVITY, SUPERMAN-- KAL-EL--
YOU AND YOUR KIND--YOUR VERY EXISTENCE WILL DEFORM THIS WORLD'S REALITY UNTIL IT TEARS ITSELF APART!
CO-SIGN.
NO MORE SUPER-PROBLEMS
NOOOO!
TT
THIS WILL NOT WORK OUT WELL IN THE LONG RUN.
TAKE ME WITH YOU!

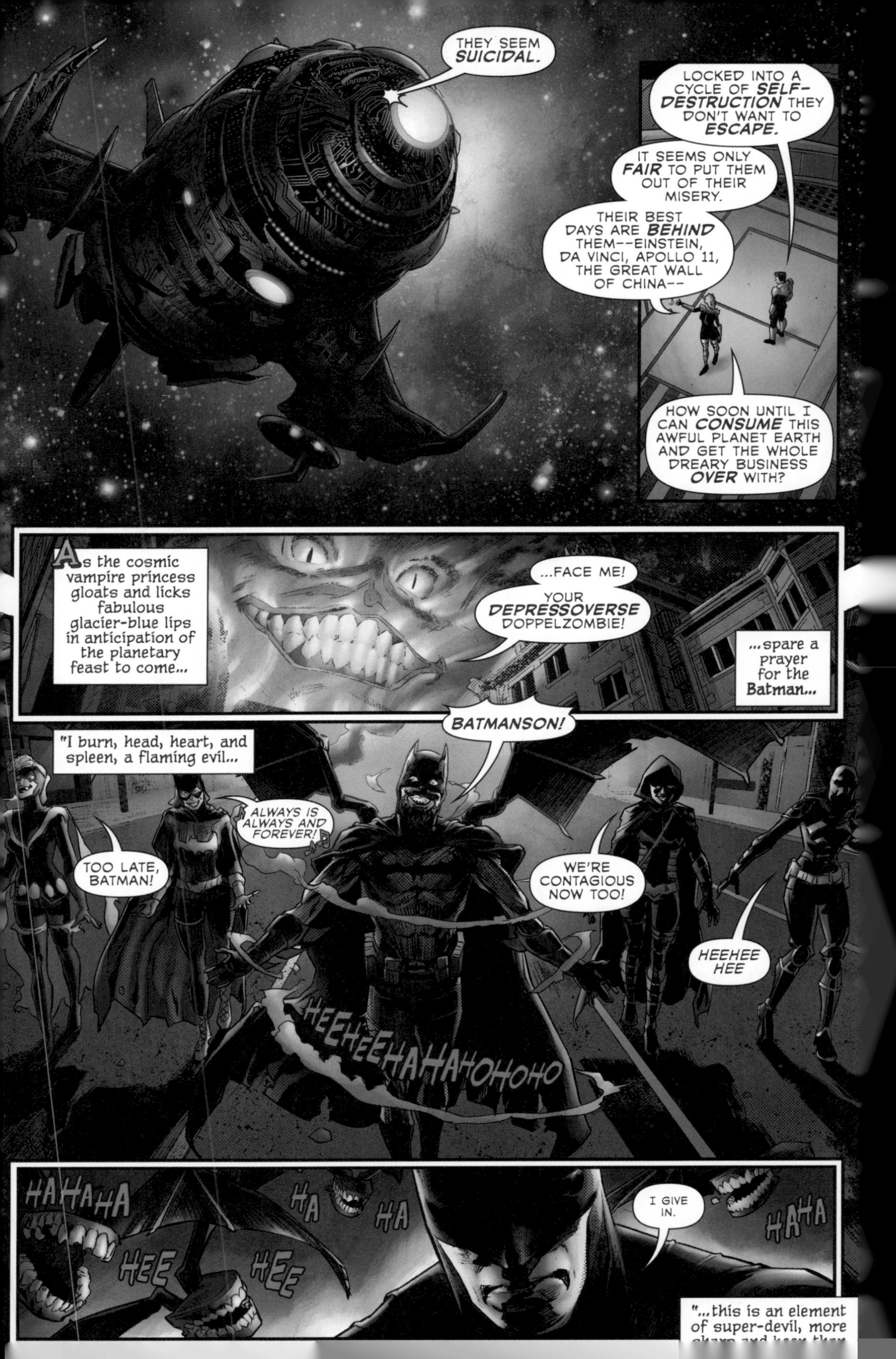

THEY SEEM SUICIDAL.
LOCKED INTO A CYCLE OF SELF-DESTRUCTION THEY DON'T WANT TO ESCAPE.
IT SEEMS ONLY FAIR TO PUT THEM OUT OF THEIR MISERY.
THEIR BEST DAYS ARE BEHIND THEM--EINSTEIN, DA VINCI, APOLLO 11, THE GREAT WALL OF CHINA--
HOW SOON UNTIL I CAN CONSUME THIS AWFUL PLANET EARTH AND GET THE WHOLE DREARY BUSINESS OVER WITH?
As the cosmic vampire princess gloats and licks fabulous glacier-blue lips in anticipation of the planetary feast to come...
...FACE ME!
YOUR DEPRESSOVERSE DOPPELZOMBIE!
...spare a prayer for the Batman...
BATMANSON!
"I burn, head, heart, and spleen, a flaming evil...
TOO LATE, BATMAN!
ALWAYS IS ALWAYS AND FOREVER!
WE'RE CONTAGIOUS NOW TOO!
HEEHEE HEE
HEEHEEHAHAHAHOHOHO
HAHAHA
HA
HA
HEE
HEE
I GIVE IN.
HAHA
"...this is an element of super-devil, more

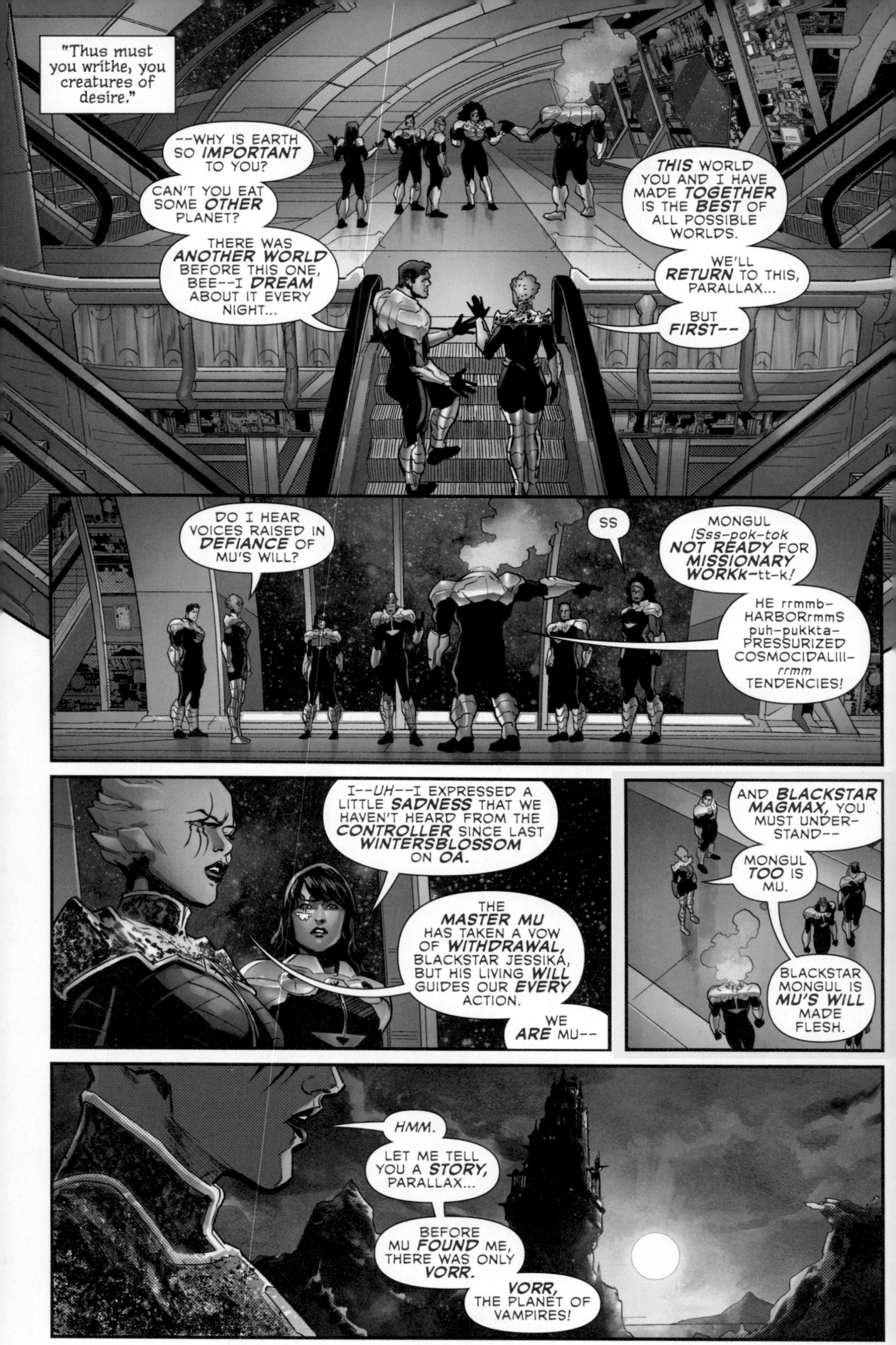
"Thus must you writhe, you creatures of desire."
--WHY IS EARTH SO IMPORTANT TO YOU?
CAN'T YOU EAT SOME OTHER PLANET?
THERE WAS ANOTHER WORLD BEFORE THIS ONE, BEE--I DREAM ABOUT IT EVERY NIGHT...
THIS WORLD YOU AND I HAVE MADE TOGETHER IS THE BEST OF ALL POSSIBLE WORLDS.
WE'LL RETURN TO THIS, PARALLAX...
BUT FIRST--
DO I HEAR VOICES RAISED IN DEFIANCE OF MU'S WILL?
SS
MONGUL ISss-pok-tok NOT READY FOR MISSIONARY WORKk-tt-k!
HE rrmmb-HARBORrmmS puh-pukkta-PRESSURIZED COSMOCIDALlll-rrmm TENDENCIES!
I--UH--I EXPRESSED A LITTLE SADNESS THAT WE HAVEN'T HEARD FROM THE CONTROLLER SINCE LAST WINTERSBLOSSOM ON OA.
THE MASTER MU HAS TAKEN A VOW OF WITHDRAWAL, BLACKSTAR JESSIKÁ, BUT HIS LIVING WILL GUIDES OUR EVERY ACTION.
WE ARE MU--
AND BLACKSTAR MAGMAX, YOU MUST UNDER-STAND--
MONGUL TOO IS MU.
BLACKSTAR MONGUL IS MU'S WILL MADE FLESH.
HMM.
LET ME TELL YOU A STORY, PARALLAX...
BEFORE MU FOUND ME, THERE WAS ONLY VORR.
VORR, THE PLANET OF VAMPIRES!

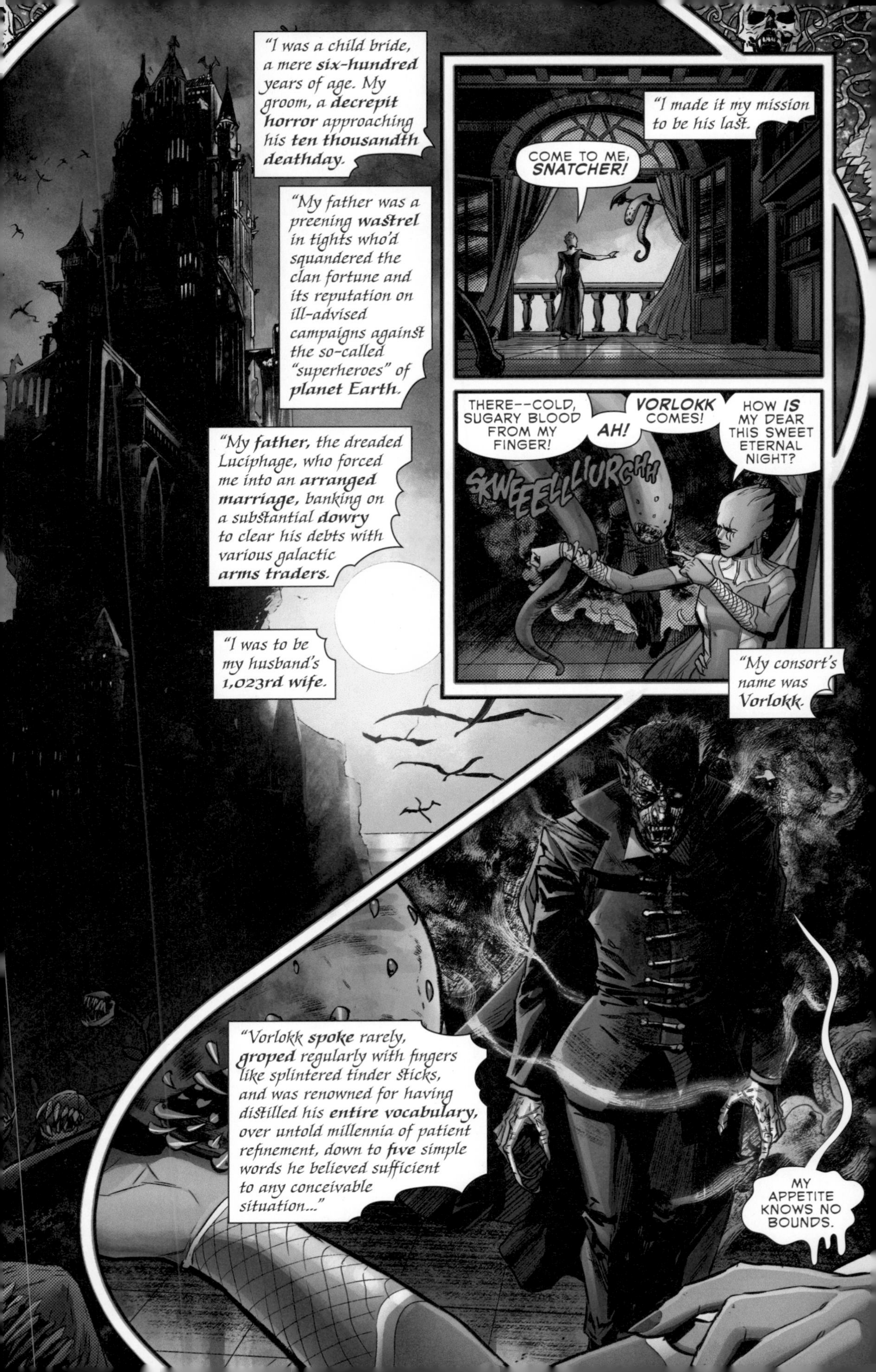
"I was a child bride, a mere six-hundred years of age. My groom, a decrepit horror approaching his ten thousandth deathday.
"My father was a preening wastrel in tights who'd squandered the clan fortune and its reputation on ill-advised campaigns against the so-called "superheroes" of planet Earth.
"My father, the dreaded Luciphage, who forced me into an arranged marriage, banking on a substantial dowry to clear his debts with various galactic arms traders.
"I was to be my husband's 1,023rd wife.
"I made it my mission to be his last.
COME TO ME, SNATCHER!
THERE--COLD, SUGARY BLOOD FROM MY FINGER!
AH!
VORLOKK COMES!
HOW IS MY DEAR THIS SWEET ETERNAL NIGHT?
SKWEEEELLLIURCHH
"My consort's name was Vorlokk.
"Vorlokk spoke rarely, groped regularly with fingers like splintered tinder sticks, and was renowned for having distilled his entire vocabulary, over untold millennia of patient refinement, down to five simple words he believed sufficient to any conceivable situation..."
MY APPETITE KNOWS NO BOUNDS.

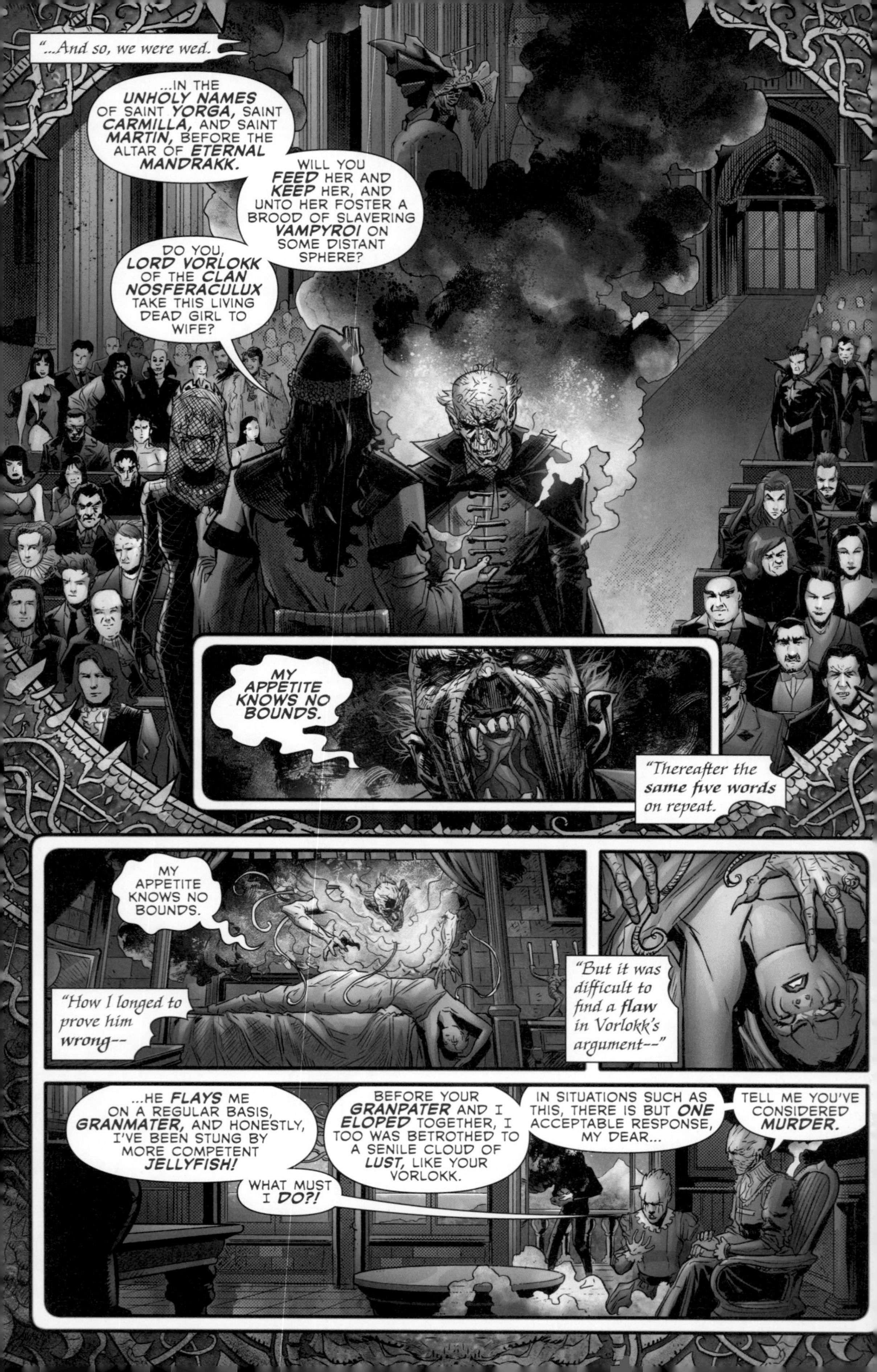
"...And so, we were wed.
...IN THE UNHOLY NAMES OF SAINT YORGA, SAINT CARMILLA, AND SAINT MARTIN, BEFORE THE ALTAR OF ETERNAL MANDRAKK.
WILL YOU FEED HER AND KEEP HER, AND UNTO HER FOSTER A BROOD OF SLAVERING VAMPYROI ON SOME DISTANT SPHERE?
DO YOU, LORD VORLOKK OF THE CLAN NOSFERACULUX TAKE THIS LIVING DEAD GIRL TO WIFE?
MY APPETITE KNOWS NO BOUNDS.
"Thereafter the same five words on repeat.
MY APPETITE KNOWS NO BOUNDS.
"How I longed to prove him wrong--
"But it was difficult to find a flaw in Vorlokk's argument--"
...HE FLAYS ME ON A REGULAR BASIS, GRANMATER, AND HONESTLY, I'VE BEEN STUNG BY MORE COMPETENT JELLYFISH!
WHAT MUST I DO?!
BEFORE YOUR GRANPATER AND I ELOPED TOGETHER, I TOO WAS BETROTHED TO A SENILE CLOUD OF LUST, LIKE YOUR VORLOKK.
IN SITUATIONS SUCH AS THIS, THERE IS BUT ONE ACCEPTABLE RESPONSE, MY DEAR...
TELL ME YOU'VE CONSIDERED MURDER.

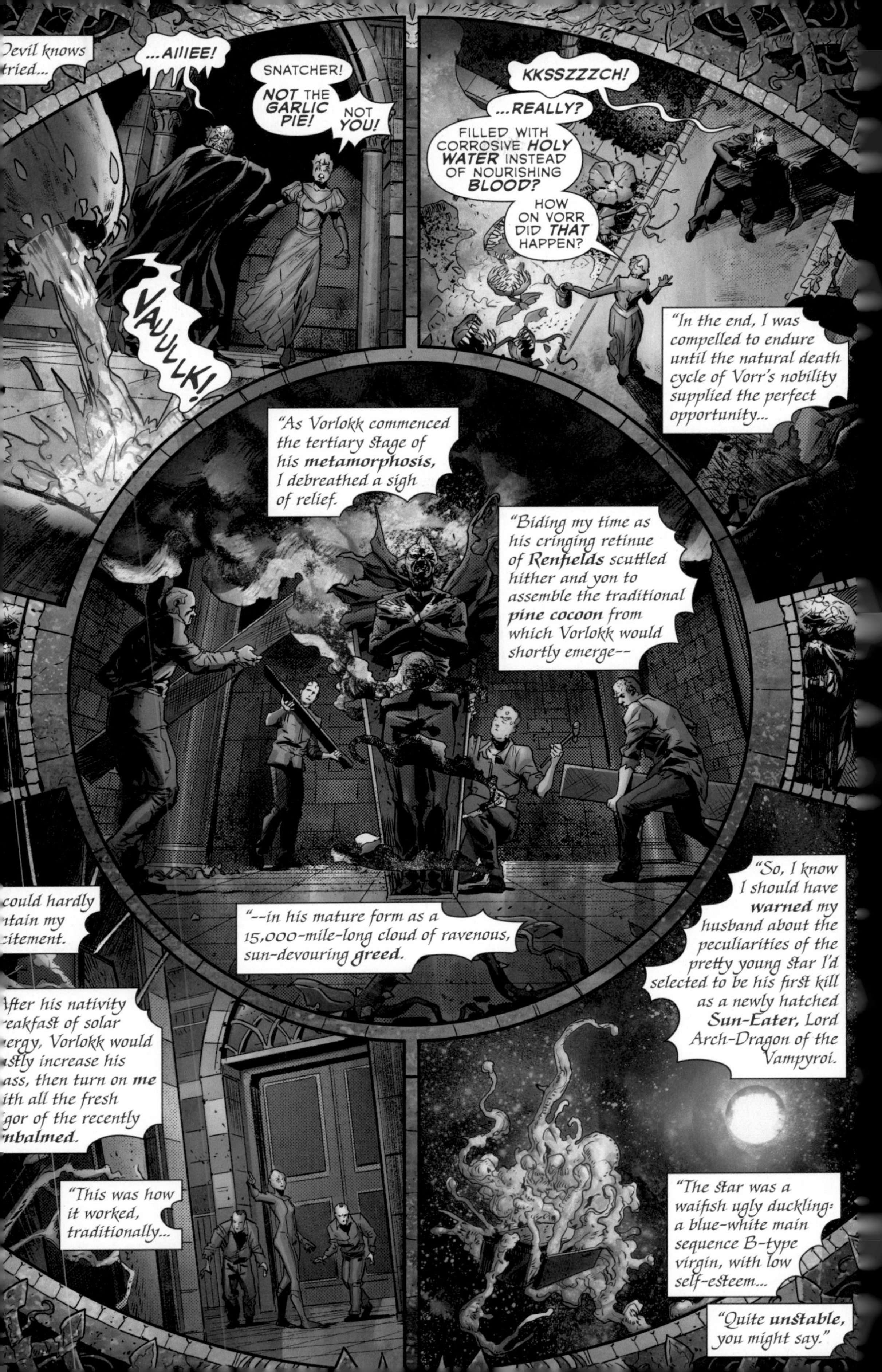

Devil knows
tried...
...AIIIEE!
SNATCHER!
NOT THE GARLIC PIE!
NOT YOU!
VAULLK!
KKSSZZZCH!
...REALLY?
FILLED WITH CORROSIVE HOLY WATER INSTEAD OF NOURISHING BLOOD?
HOW ON VORR DID THAT HAPPEN?
"In the end, I was compelled to endure until the natural death cycle of Vorr's nobility supplied the perfect opportunity...
"As Vorlokk commenced the tertiary stage of his metamorphosis, I debreathed a sigh of relief.
"Biding my time as his cringing retinue of Renfields scuttled hither and yon to assemble the traditional pine cocoon from which Vorlokk would shortly emerge--
"--in his mature form as a 15,000-mile-long cloud of ravenous, sun-devouring greed.
could hardly
ntain my
citement.
After his nativity
reakfast of solar
ergy, Vorlokk would
stly increase his
ass, then turn on me
ith all the fresh
gor of the recently
nbalmed.
"This was how it worked, traditionally...
"So, I know I should have warned my husband about the peculiarities of the pretty young star I'd selected to be his first kill as a newly hatched Sun-Eater, Lord Arch-Dragon of the Vampyroi.
"The star was a waifish ugly duckling: a blue-white main sequence B-type virgin, with low self-esteem...
"Quite unstable, you might say."

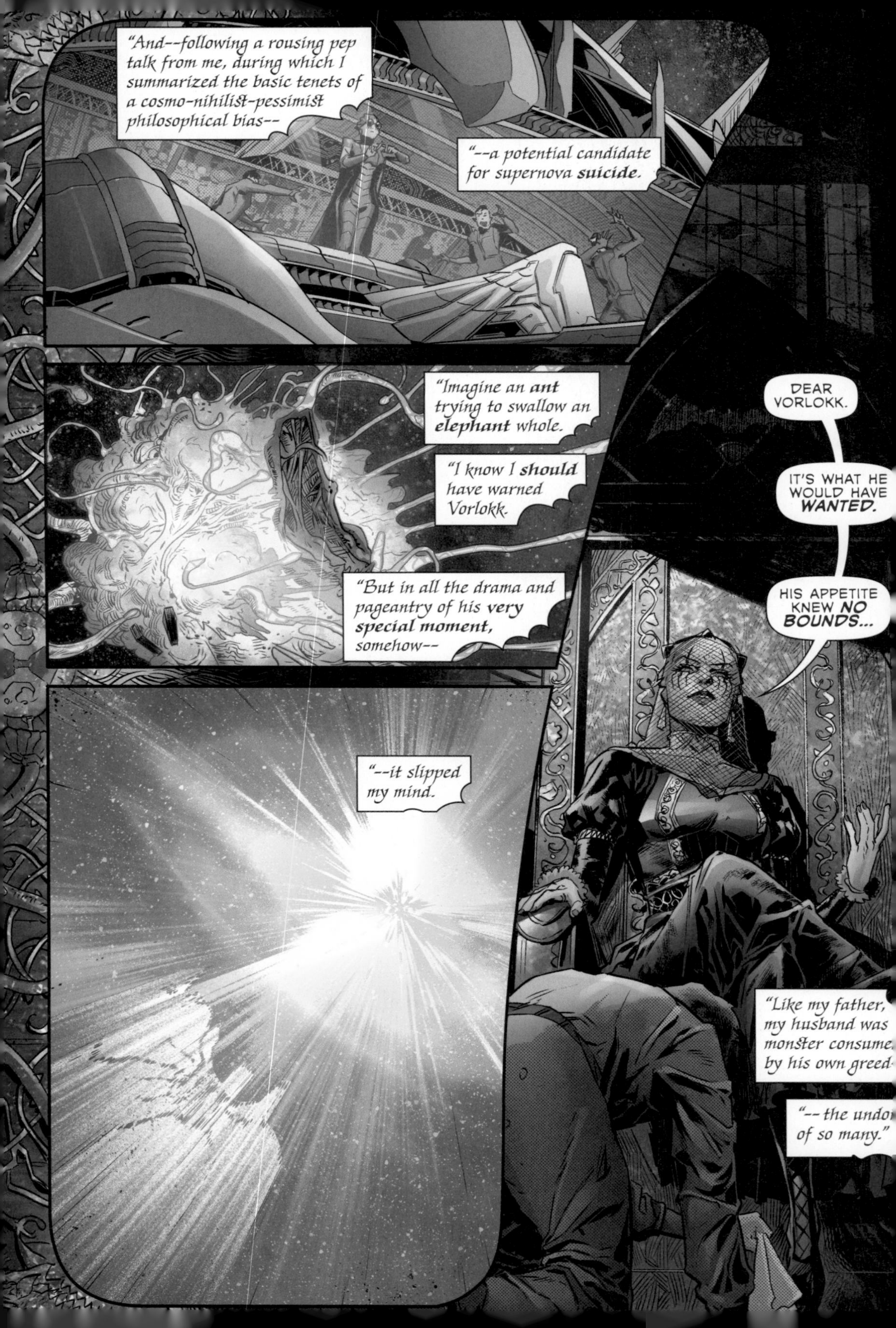
"And--following a rousing pep talk from me, during which I summarized the basic tenets of a cosmo-nihilist-pessimist philosophical bias--
"--a potential candidate for supernova suicide.
"Imagine an ant trying to swallow an elephant whole.
"I know I should have warned Vorlokk.
"But in all the drama and pageantry of his very special moment, somehow--
"--it slipped my mind.
DEAR VORLOKK.
IT'S WHAT HE WOULD HAVE WANTED.
HIS APPETITE KNEW NO BOUNDS...
"Like my father, my husband was monster consume by his own greed
"-- the undo of so many."

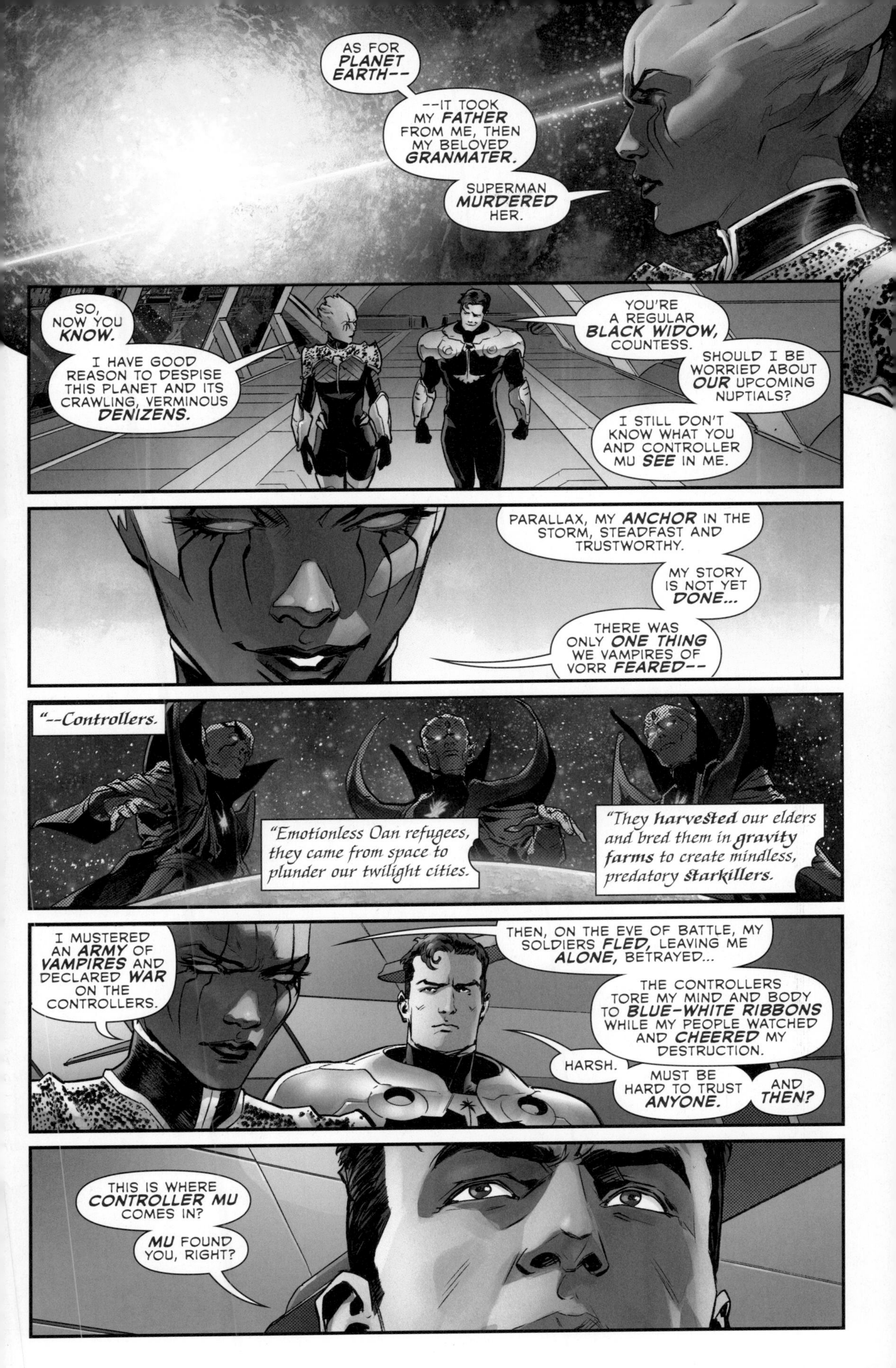
AS FOR PLANET EARTH--
--IT TOOK MY FATHER FROM ME, THEN MY BELOVED GRANMATER.
SUPERMAN MURDERED HER.
SO, NOW YOU KNOW.
I HAVE GOOD REASON TO DESPISE THIS PLANET AND ITS CRAWLING, VERMINOUS DENIZENS.
YOU'RE A REGULAR BLACK WIDOW, COUNTESS.
SHOULD I BE WORRIED ABOUT OUR UPCOMING NUPTIALS?
I STILL DON'T KNOW WHAT YOU AND CONTROLLER MU SEE IN ME.
PARALLAX, MY ANCHOR IN THE STORM, STEADFAST AND TRUSTWORTHY.
MY STORY IS NOT YET DONE...
THERE WAS ONLY ONE THING WE VAMPIRES OF VORR FEARED--
"--Controllers.
"Emotionless Oan refugees, they came from space to plunder our twilight cities.
"They harvested our elders and bred them in gravity farms to create mindless, predatory starkillers.
I MUSTERED AN ARMY OF VAMPIRES AND DECLARED WAR ON THE CONTROLLERS.
THEN, ON THE EVE OF BATTLE, MY SOLDIERS FLED, LEAVING ME ALONE, BETRAYED...
THE CONTROLLERS TORE MY MIND AND BODY TO BLUE-WHITE RIBBONS WHILE MY PEOPLE WATCHED AND CHEERED MY DESTRUCTION.
HARSH.
MUST BE HARD TO TRUST ANYONE.
AND THEN?
THIS IS WHERE CONTROLLER MU COMES IN?
MU FOUND YOU, RIGHT?

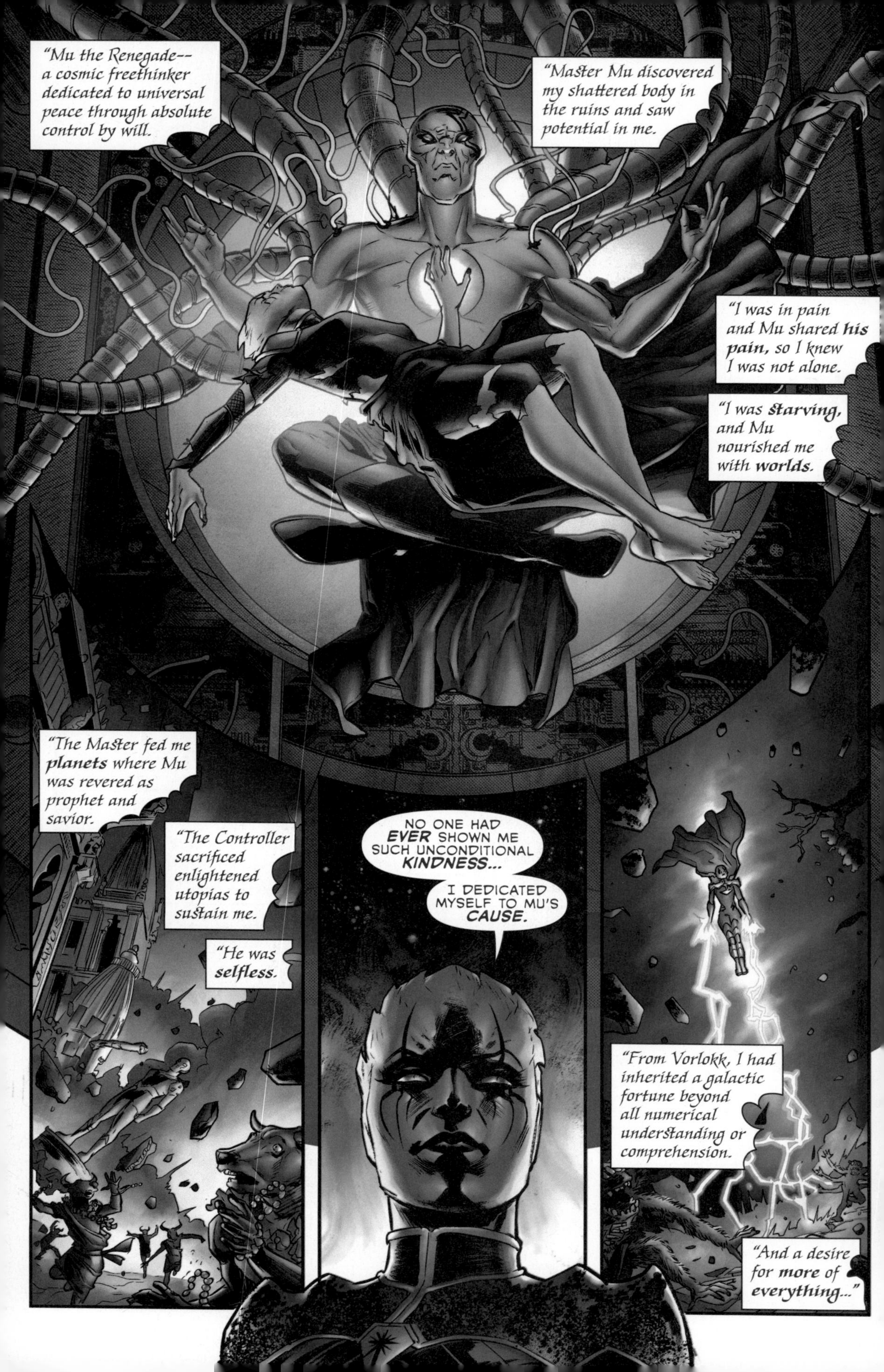
"Mu the Renegade-- a cosmic freethinker dedicated to universal peace through absolute control by will.
"Master Mu discovered my shattered body in the ruins and saw potential in me.
"I was in pain and Mu shared his pain, so I knew I was not alone.
"I was starving, and Mu nourished me with worlds.
"The Master fed me planets where Mu was revered as prophet and savior.
"The Controller sacrificed enlightened utopias to sustain me.
"He was selfless.
NO ONE HAD EVER SHOWN ME SUCH UNCONDITIONAL KINDNESS...
I DEDICATED MYSELF TO MU'S CAUSE.
"From Vorlokk, I had inherited a galactic fortune beyond all numerical understanding or comprehension.
"And a desire for more of everything..."

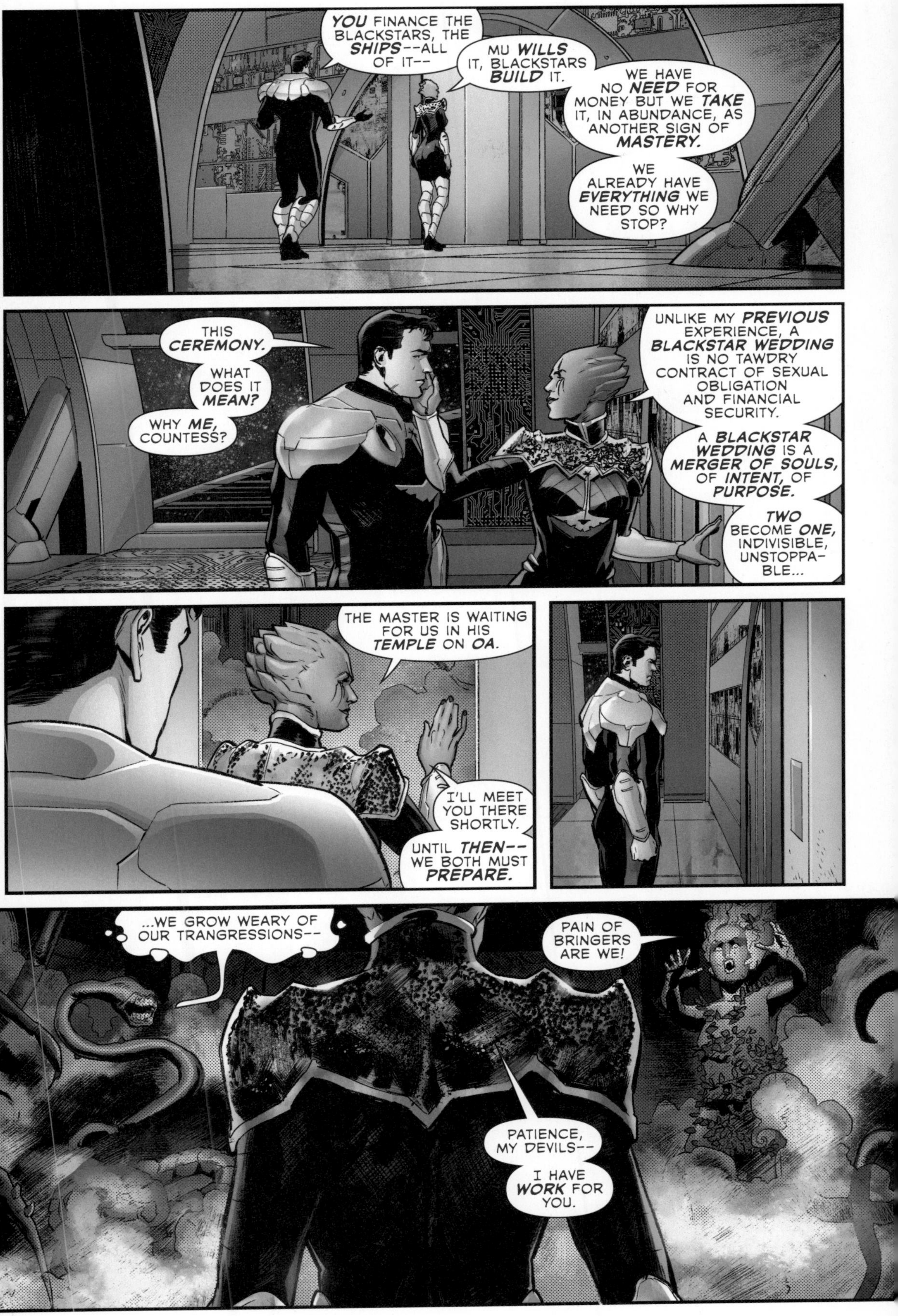
YOU FINANCE THE BLACKSTARS, THE SHIPS--ALL OF IT--
MU WILLS IT, BLACKSTARS BUILD IT.
WE HAVE NO NEED FOR MONEY BUT WE TAKE IT, IN ABUNDANCE, AS ANOTHER SIGN OF MASTERY.
WE ALREADY HAVE EVERYTHING WE NEED SO WHY STOP?
THIS CEREMONY.
WHAT DOES IT MEAN?
WHY ME, COUNTESS?
UNLIKE MY PREVIOUS EXPERIENCE, A BLACKSTAR WEDDING IS NO TAWDRY CONTRACT OF SEXUAL OBLIGATION AND FINANCIAL SECURITY.
A BLACKSTAR WEDDING IS A MERGER OF SOULS, OF INTENT, OF PURPOSE.
TWO BECOME ONE, INDIVISIBLE, UNSTOPPA-BLE...
THE MASTER IS WAITING FOR US IN HIS TEMPLE ON OA.
I'LL MEET YOU THERE SHORTLY.
UNTIL THEN--WE BOTH MUST PREPARE.
...WE GROW WEARY OF OUR TRANGRESSIONS--
PAIN OF BRINGERS ARE WE!
PATIENCE, MY DEVILS--
I HAVE WORK FOR YOU.

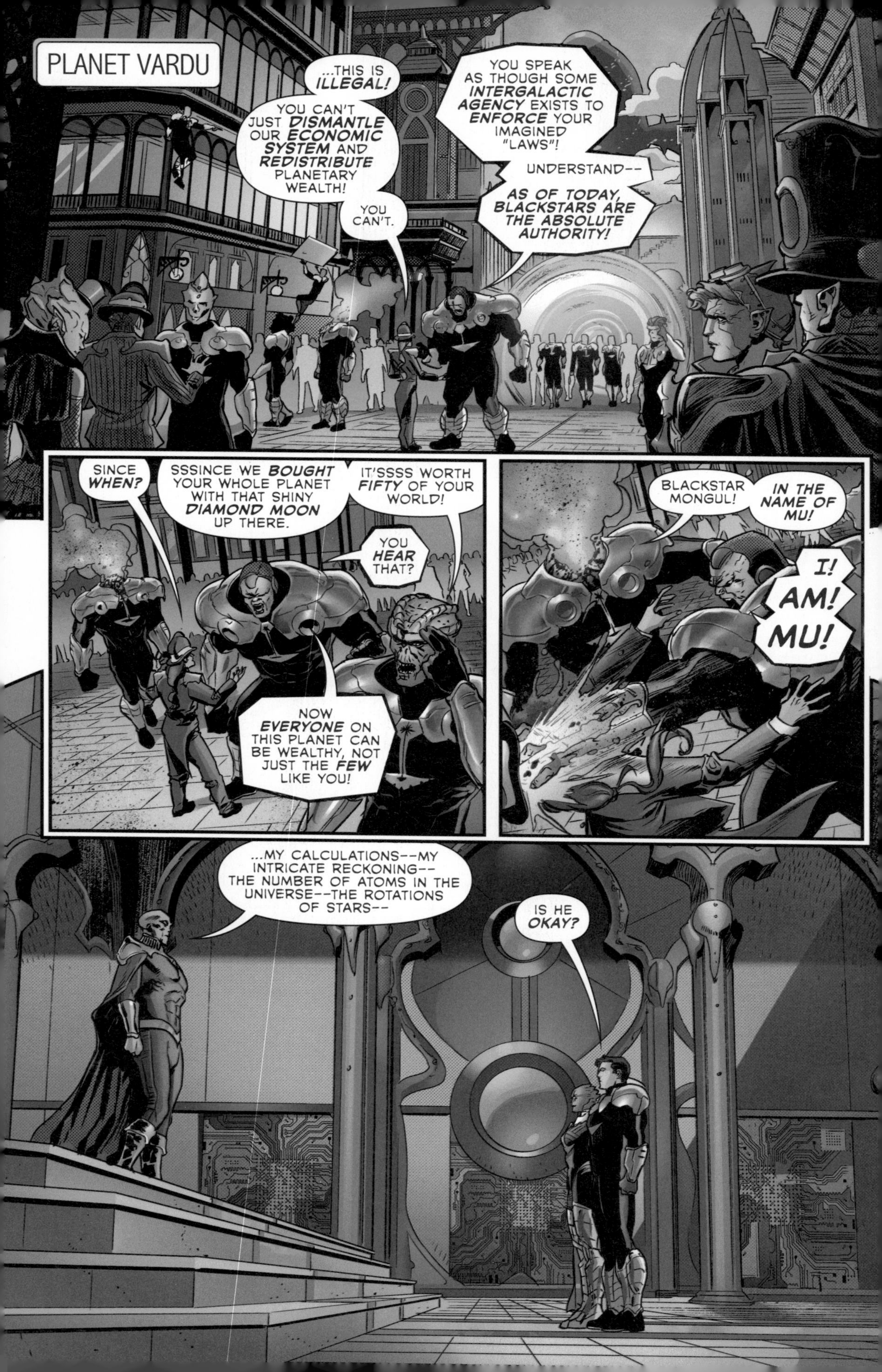
PLANET VARDU
...THIS IS ILLEGAL!
YOU CAN'T JUST DISMANTLE OUR ECONOMIC SYSTEM AND REDISTRIBUTE PLANETARY WEALTH!
YOU CAN'T.
YOU SPEAK AS THOUGH SOME INTERGALACTIC AGENCY EXISTS TO ENFORCE YOUR IMAGINED "LAWS"!
UNDERSTAND--
AS OF TODAY, BLACKSTARS ARE THE ABSOLUTE AUTHORITY!
SINCE WHEN?
SSSINCE WE BOUGHT YOUR WHOLE PLANET WITH THAT SHINY DIAMOND MOON UP THERE.
IT'SSSS WORTH FIFTY OF YOUR WORLD!
YOU HEAR THAT?
NOW EVERYONE ON THIS PLANET CAN BE WEALTHY, NOT JUST THE FEW LIKE YOU!
BLACKSTAR MONGUL!
IN THE NAME OF MU!
I! AM! MU!
...MY CALCULATIONS--MY INTRICATE RECKONING--THE NUMBER OF ATOMS IN THE UNIVERSE--THE ROTATIONS OF STARS--
IS HE OKAY?

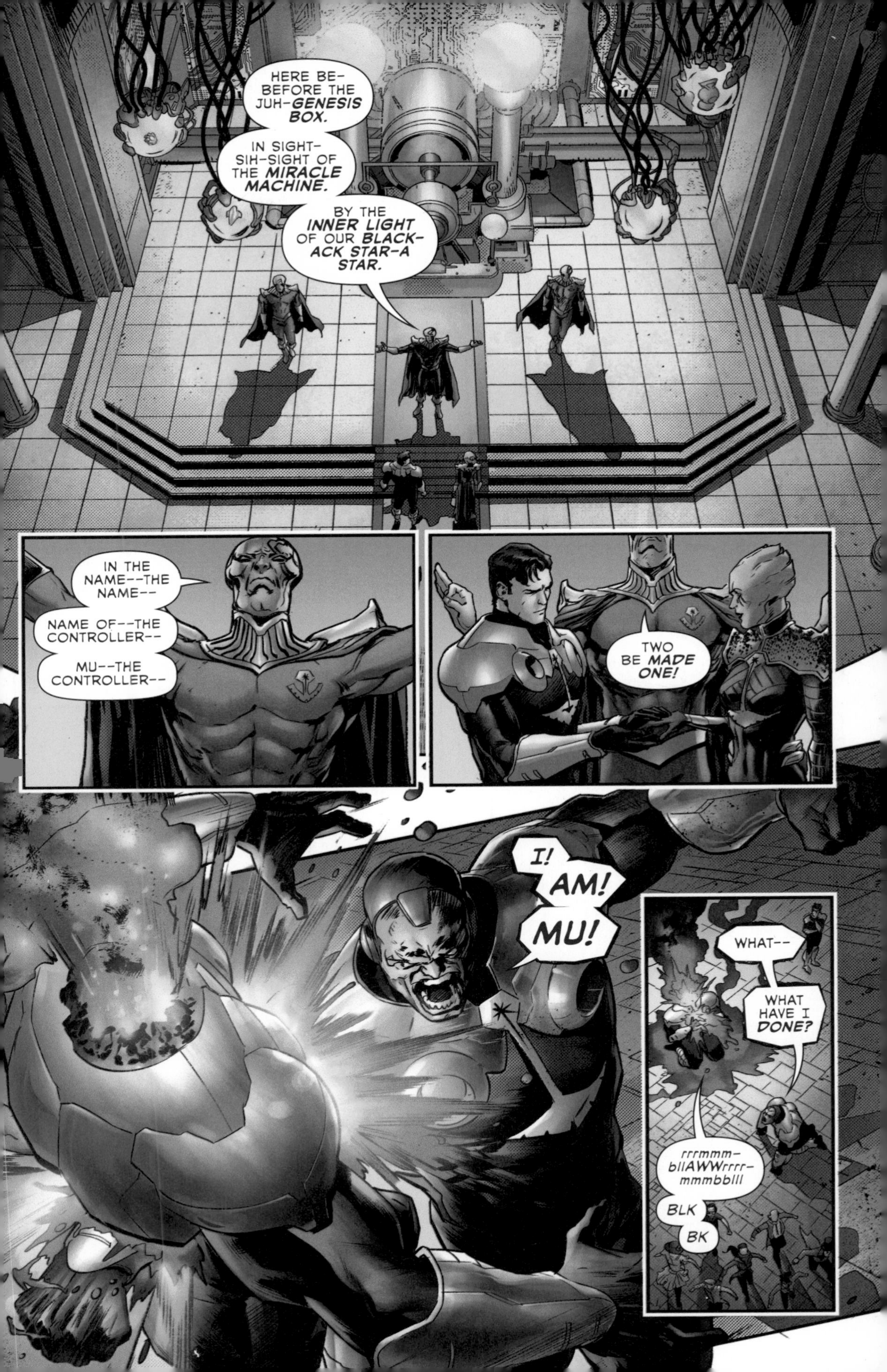
HERE BE-
BEFORE THE
JUH-GENESIS
BOX.
IN SIGHT-
SIH-SIGHT OF
THE MIRACLE
MACHINE.
BY THE
INNER LIGHT
OF OUR BLACK-
ACK STAR-A
STAR.
IN THE
NAME--THE
NAME--
NAME OF--THE
CONTROLLER--
MU--THE
CONTROLLER--
TWO
BE MADE
ONE!
I!
AM!
MU!
WHAT--
WHAT
HAVE I
DONE?
rrrmmm-
bllAWWrrrr-
mmmbblll
BLK
BK

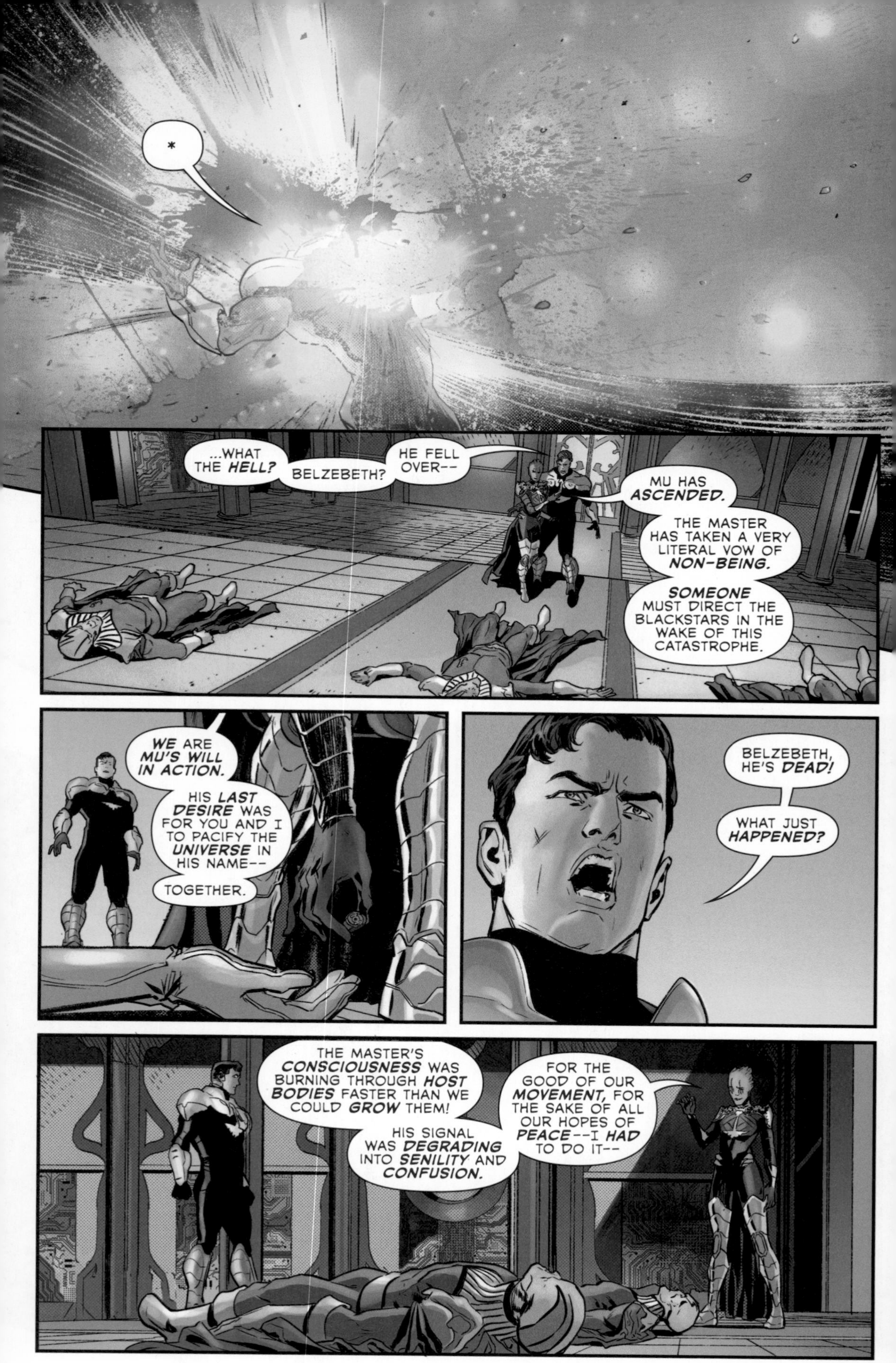

*
...WHAT THE HELL?
BELZEBETH?
HE FELL OVER--
MU HAS ASCENDED.
THE MASTER HAS TAKEN A VERY LITERAL VOW OF NON-BEING.
SOMEONE MUST DIRECT THE BLACKSTARS IN THE WAKE OF THIS CATASTROPHE.
WE ARE MU'S WILL IN ACTION.
HIS LAST DESIRE WAS FOR YOU AND I TO PACIFY THE UNIVERSE IN HIS NAME--
TOGETHER.
BELZEBETH, HE'S DEAD!
WHAT JUST HAPPENED?
THE MASTER'S CONSCIOUSNESS WAS BURNING THROUGH HOST BODIES FASTER THAN WE COULD GROW THEM!
HIS SIGNAL WAS DEGRADING INTO SENILITY AND CONFUSION.
FOR THE GOOD OF OUR MOVEMENT, FOR THE SAKE OF ALL OUR HOPES OF PEACE--I HAD TO DO IT--

NO ONE MUST KNOW.

THEY MUST CONTINUE TO BELIEVE *MU* IS IN *CONTROL*, OR WE ARE *LOST*.

WE MUST CONTINUE *HIS GREAT WORK.*

THAT *RING*--

THE LAST FRAGMENT OF THE *OTHER* WORLD--THE GREEN LANTERN.

THERE WAS ANOTHER WORLD BEFORE THIS!

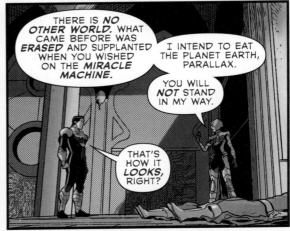

THERE IS *NO OTHER WORLD.* WHAT CAME BEFORE WAS *ERASED* AND SUPPLANTED WHEN YOU WISHED ON THE *MIRACLE MACHINE.*

I INTEND TO EAT THE PLANET EARTH, PARALLAX.

YOU WILL *NOT* STAND IN MY WAY.

THAT'S HOW IT *LOOKS*, RIGHT?

THIS IS *SUPERMAN!*

WHAT?

WE HAVE YOU SURROUNDED!

WHAT HAVE YOU *DONE?*

I COULDN'T LET YOU EAT *MY HOME PLANET,* BEE, I'M SORRY.

I HAD TO THINK OF *SOMETHING*--SO--GUESS *WHAT?*

WHAT?

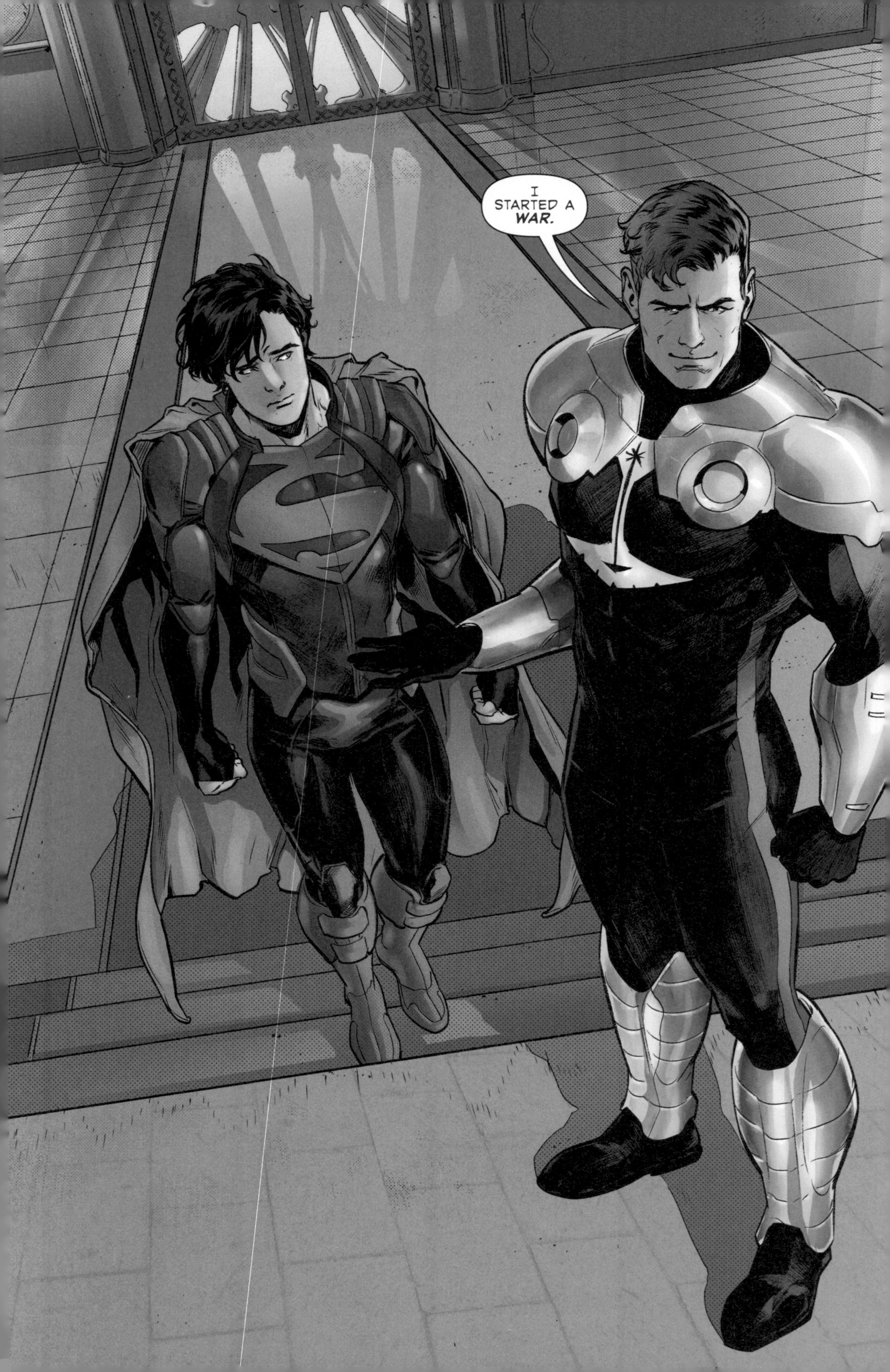
I STARTED A WAR.

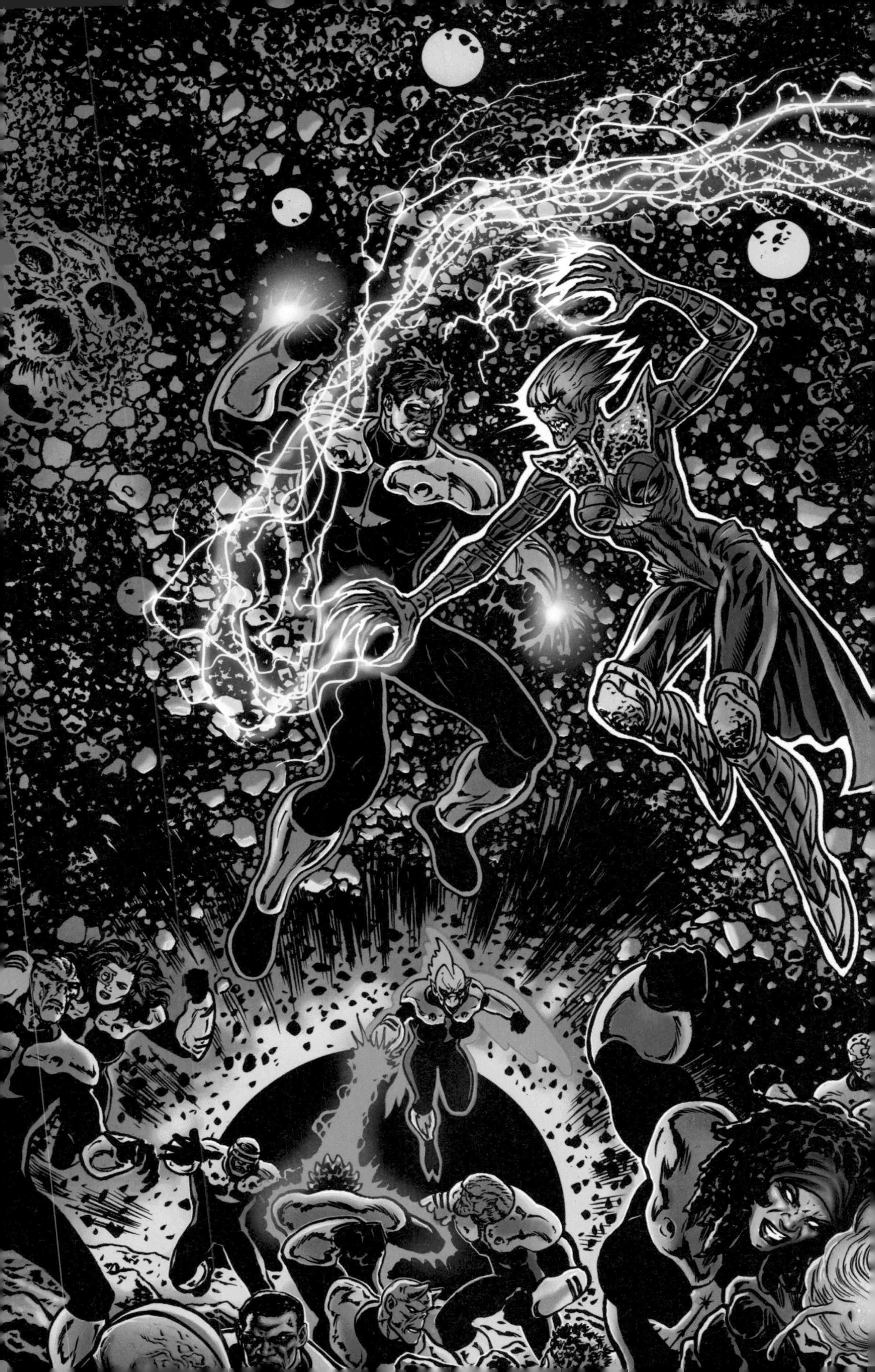

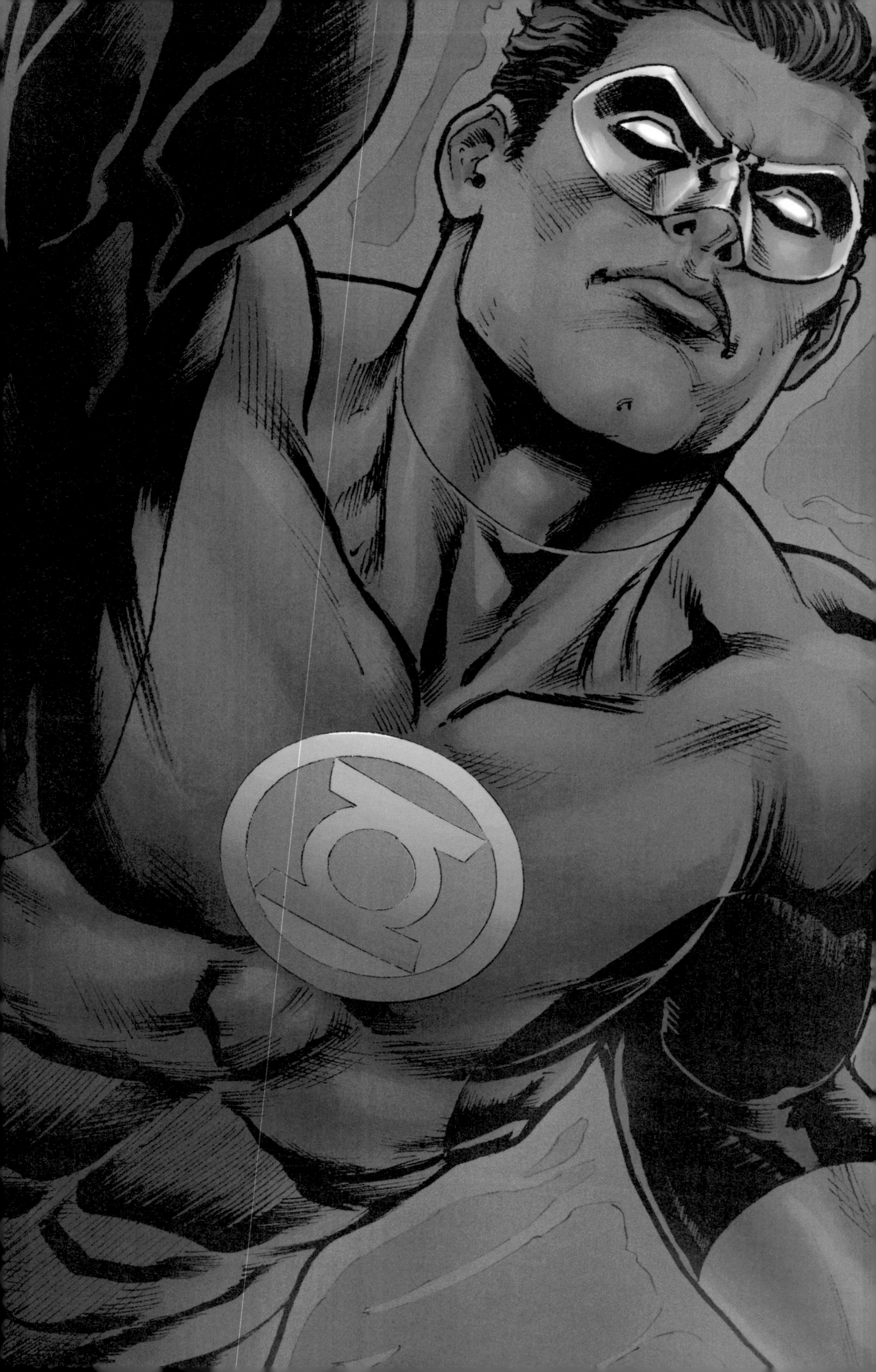

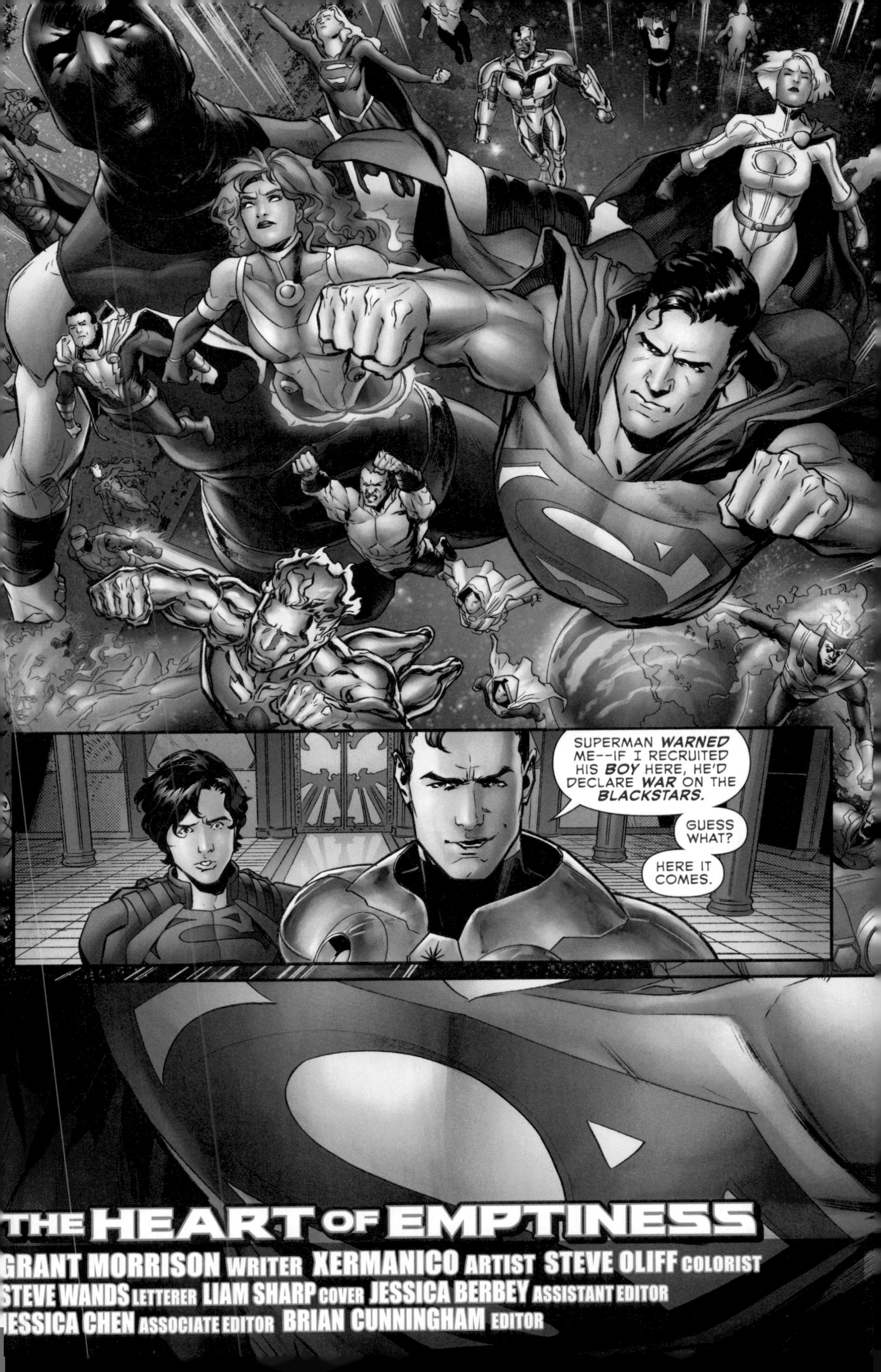
SUPERMAN WARNED ME--IF I RECRUITED HIS BOY HERE, HE'D DECLARE WAR ON THE BLACKSTARS.
GUESS WHAT?
HERE IT COMES.
THE HEART OF EMPTINESS
GRANT MORRISON WRITER XERMANICO ARTIST STEVE OLIFF COLORIST
STEVE WANDS LETTERER LIAM SHARP COVER JESSICA BERBEY ASSISTANT EDITOR
JESSICA CHEN ASSOCIATE EDITOR BRIAN CUNNINGHAM EDITOR

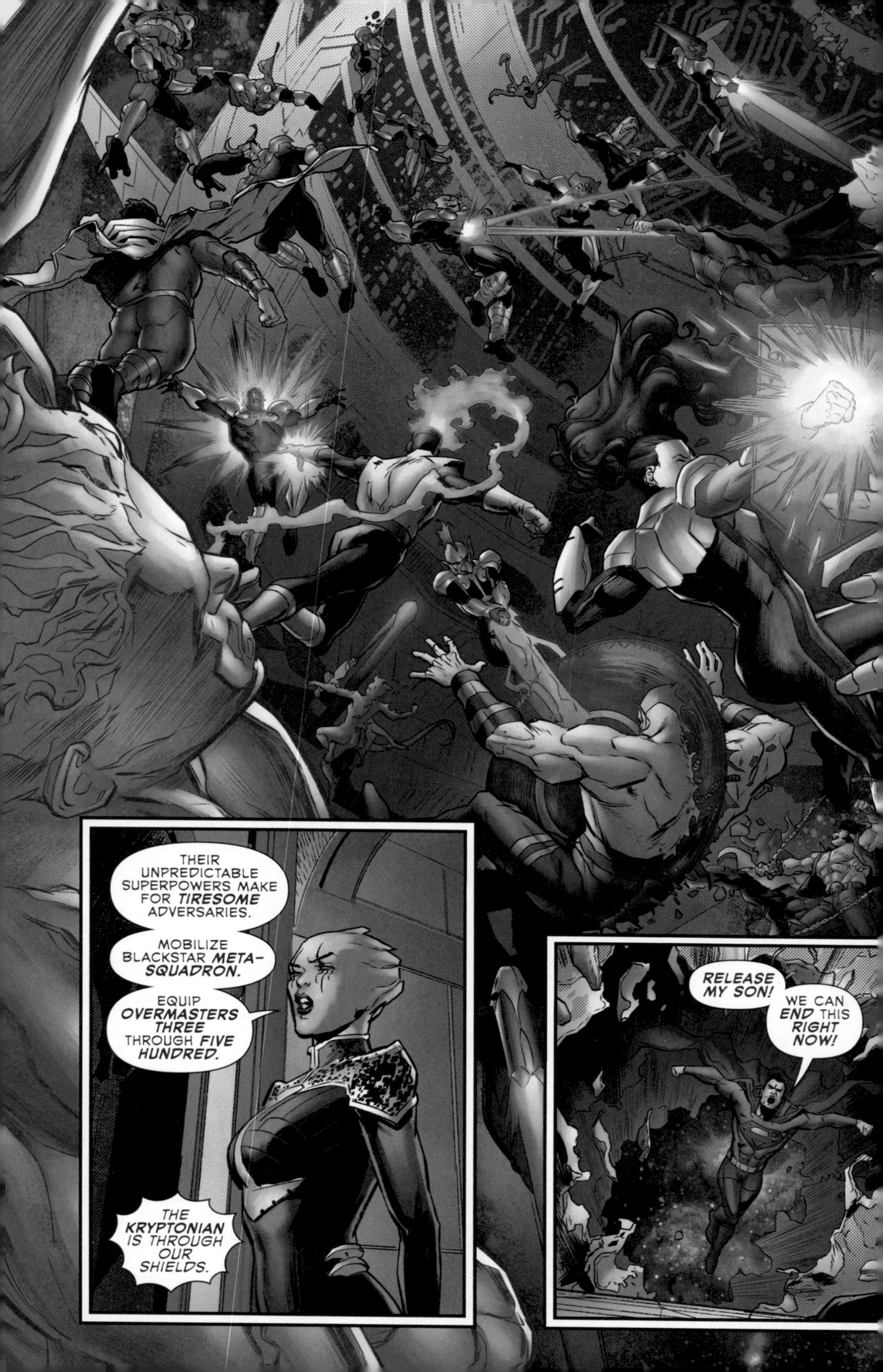
THEIR UNPREDICTABLE SUPERPOWERS MAKE FOR TIRESOME ADVERSARIES.
MOBILIZE BLACKSTAR META-SQUADRON.
EQUIP OVERMASTERS THREE THROUGH FIVE HUNDRED.
THE KRYPTONIAN IS THROUGH OUR SHIELDS.
RELEASE MY SON!
WE CAN END THIS RIGHT NOW!

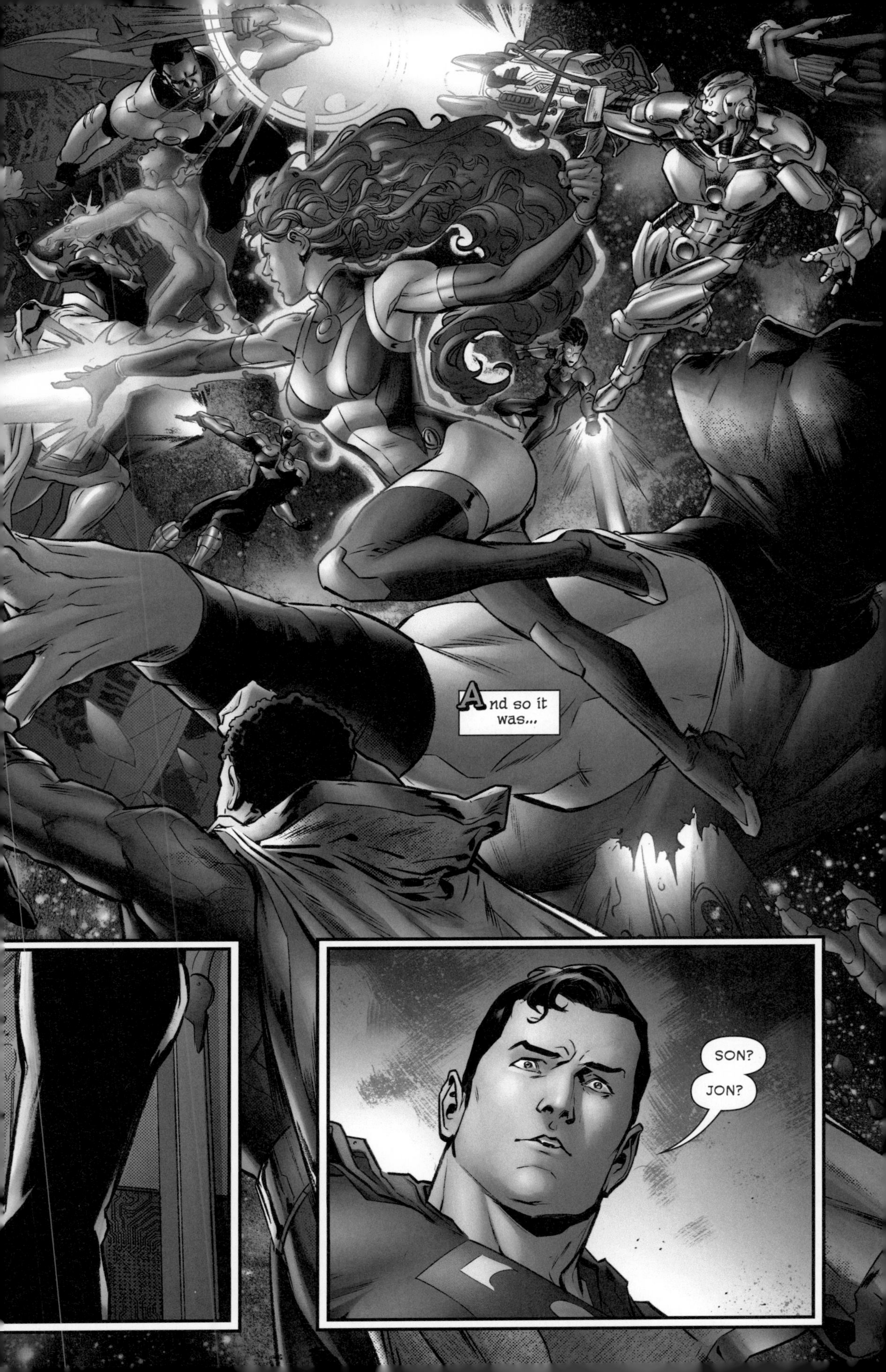
And so it was...
SON?
JON?

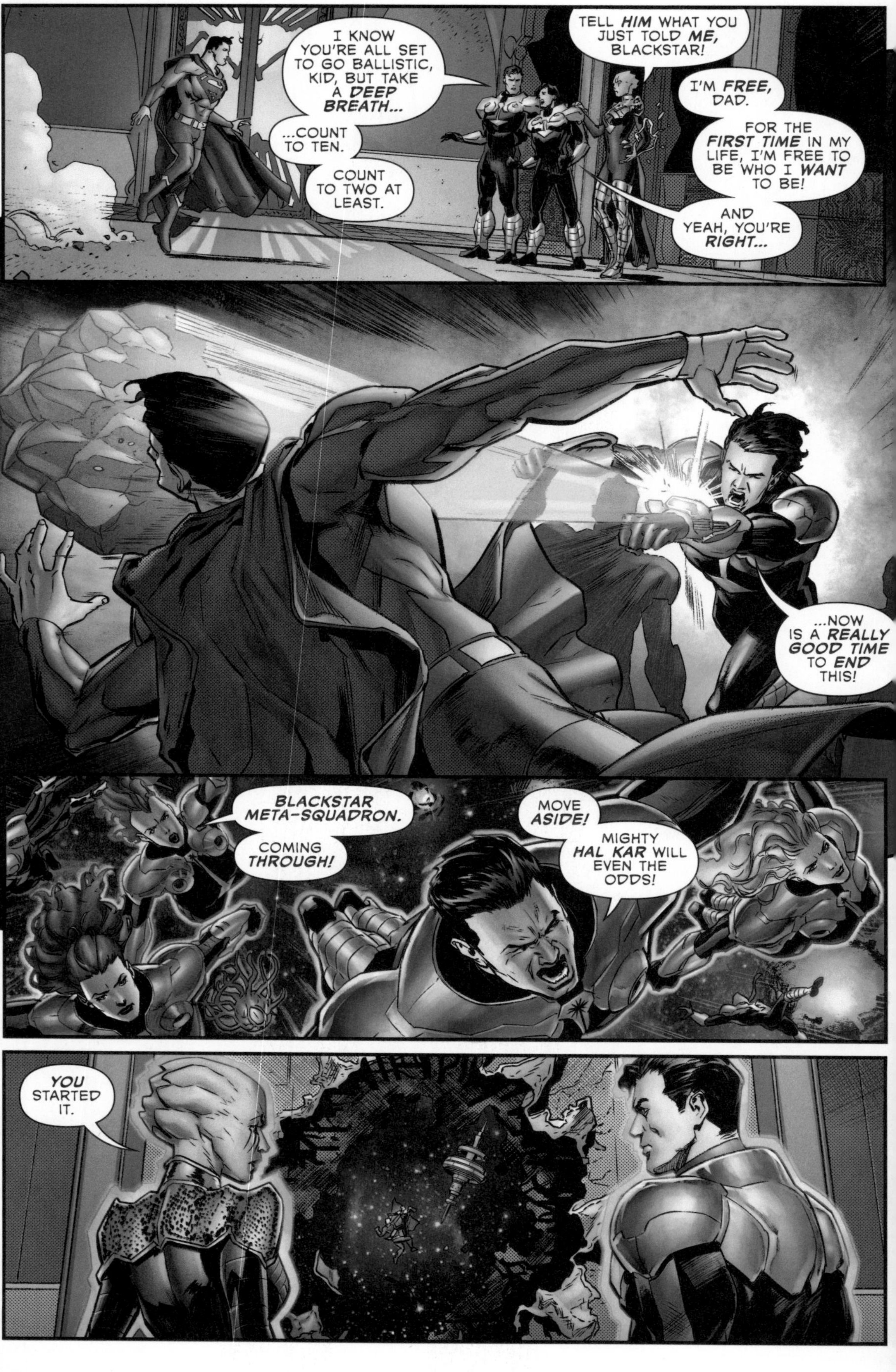
I KNOW YOU'RE ALL SET TO GO BALLISTIC, KID, BUT TAKE A DEEP BREATH...
...COUNT TO TEN.
COUNT TO TWO AT LEAST.
TELL HIM WHAT YOU JUST TOLD ME, BLACKSTAR!
I'M FREE, DAD.
FOR THE FIRST TIME IN MY LIFE, I'M FREE TO BE WHO I WANT TO BE!
AND YEAH, YOU'RE RIGHT...
...NOW IS A REALLY GOOD TIME TO END THIS!
BLACKSTAR META-SQUADRON.
COMING THROUGH!
MOVE ASIDE!
MIGHTY HAL KAR WILL EVEN THE ODDS!
YOU STARTED IT.

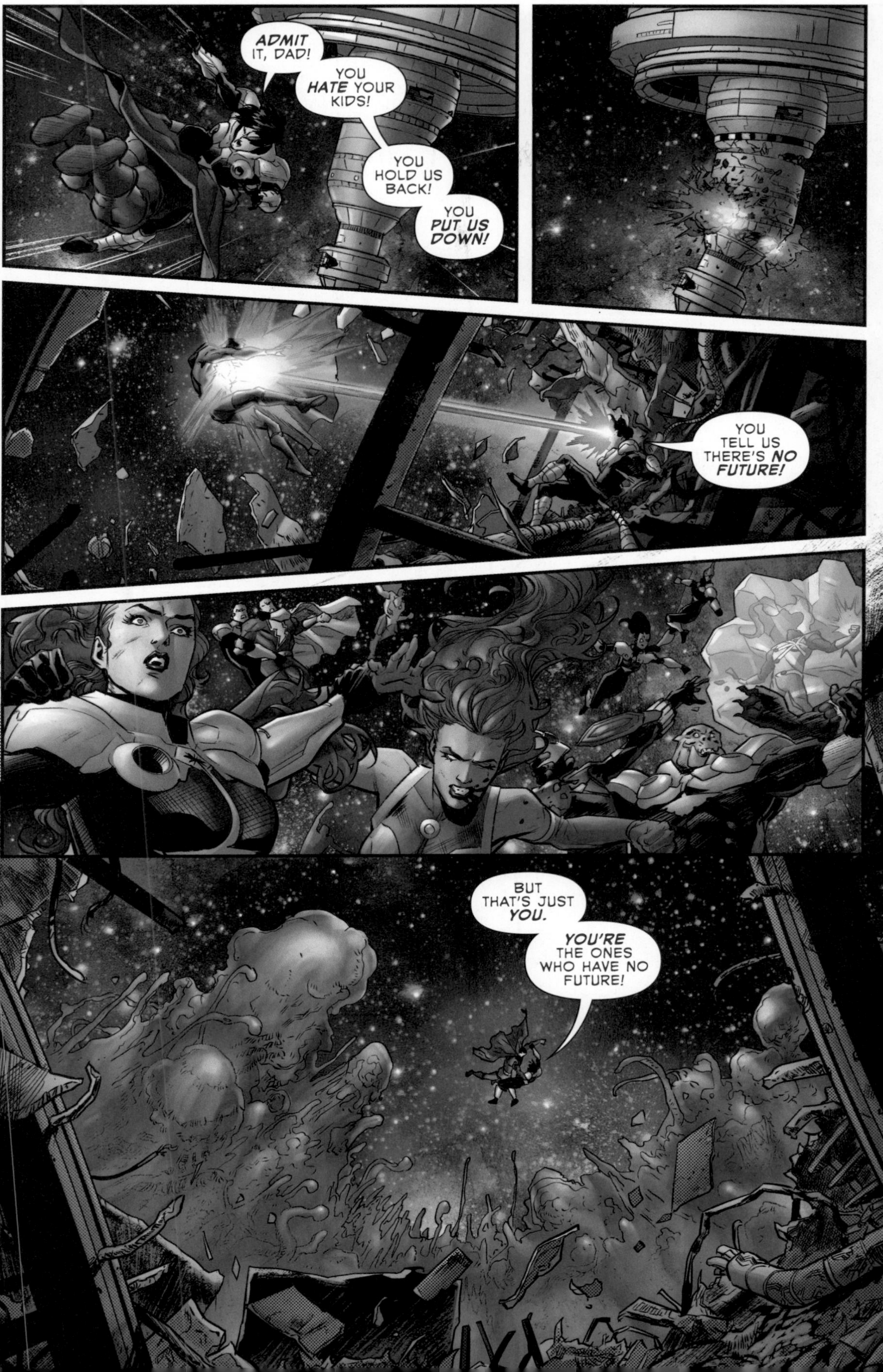
ADMIT IT, DAD!
YOU HATE YOUR KIDS!
YOU HOLD US BACK!
YOU PUT US DOWN!
YOU TELL US THERE'S NO FUTURE!
BUT THAT'S JUST YOU.
YOU'RE THE ONES WHO HAVE NO FUTURE!

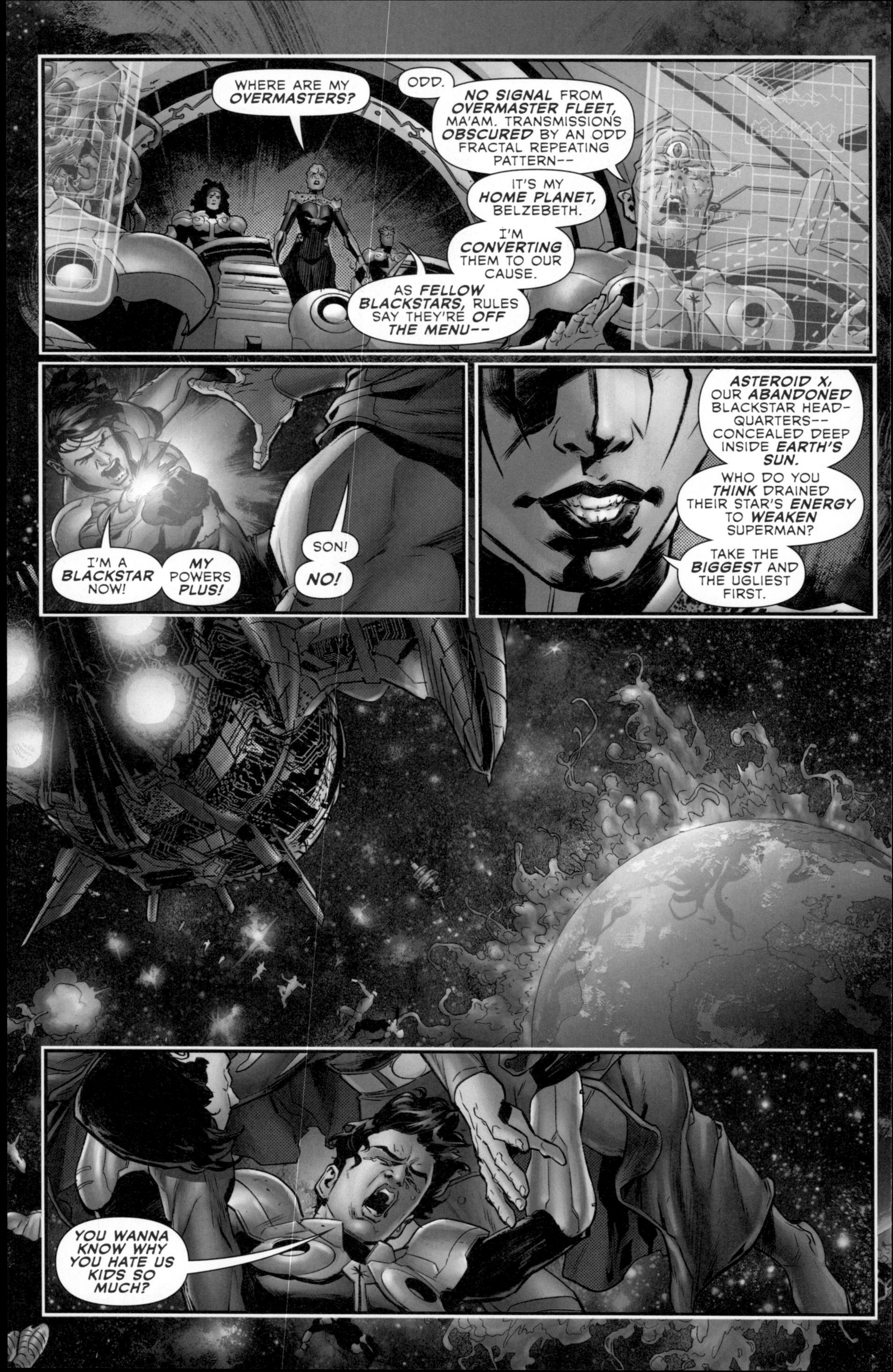
WHERE ARE MY OVERMASTERS?
ODD.
NO SIGNAL FROM OVERMASTER FLEET, MA'AM. TRANSMISSIONS OBSCURED BY AN ODD FRACTAL REPEATING PATTERN--
IT'S MY HOME PLANET, BELZEBETH.
I'M CONVERTING THEM TO OUR CAUSE.
AS FELLOW BLACKSTARS, RULES SAY THEY'RE OFF THE MENU--
I'M A BLACKSTAR NOW!
MY POWERS PLUS!
SON!
NO!
ASTEROID X, OUR ABANDONED BLACKSTAR HEAD-QUARTERS--CONCEALED DEEP INSIDE EARTH'S SUN.
WHO DO YOU THINK DRAINED THEIR STAR'S ENERGY TO WEAKEN SUPERMAN?
TAKE THE BIGGEST AND THE UGLIEST FIRST.
YOU WANNA KNOW WHY YOU HATE US KIDS SO MUCH?

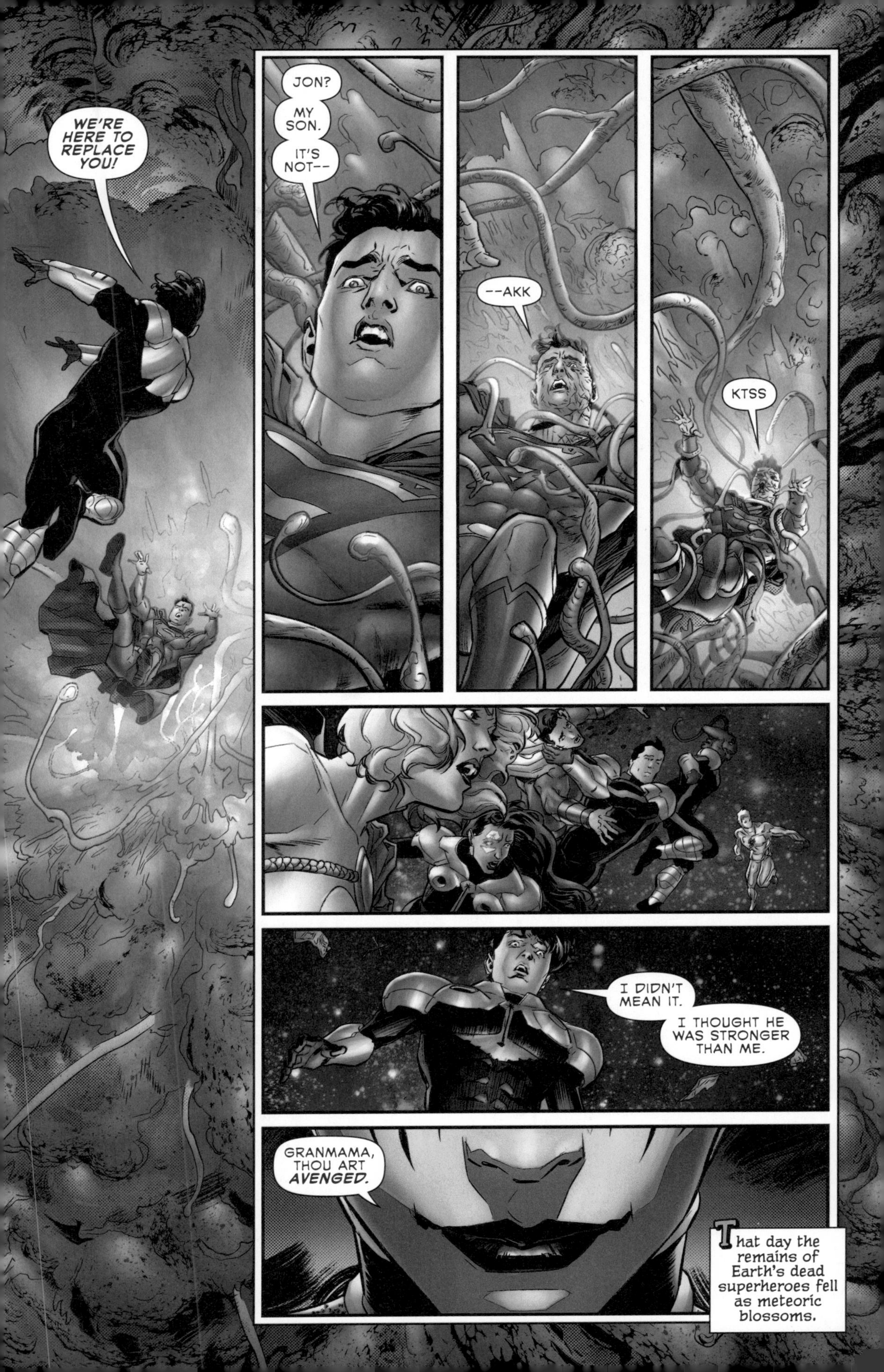
WE'RE HERE TO REPLACE YOU!
JON?
MY SON.
IT'S NOT--
--AKK
KTSS
I DIDN'T MEAN IT.
I THOUGHT HE WAS STRONGER THAN ME.
GRANMAMA, THOU ART AVENGED.
That day the remains of Earth's dead superheroes fell as meteoric blossoms.

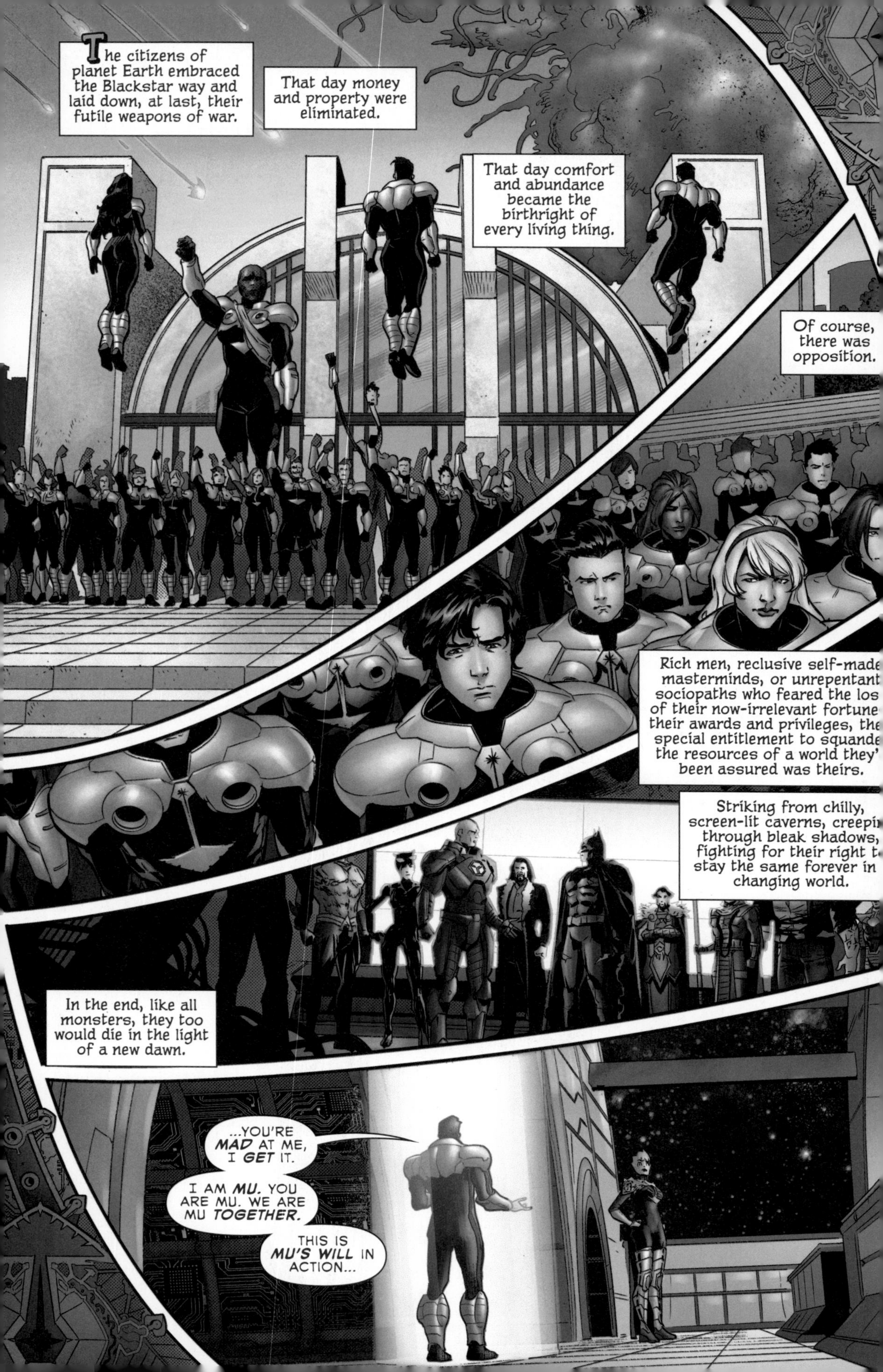
The citizens of planet Earth embraced the Blackstar way and laid down, at last, their futile weapons of war.
That day money and property were eliminated.
That day comfort and abundance became the birthright of every living thing.
Of course, there was opposition.
Rich men, reclusive self-made masterminds, or unrepentant sociopaths who feared the los of their now-irrelevant fortune their awards and privileges, the special entitlement to squande the resources of a world they' been assured was theirs.
Striking from chilly, screen-lit caverns, creepi through bleak shadows, fighting for their right t stay the same forever in changing world.
In the end, like all monsters, they too would die in the light of a new dawn.
...YOU'RE MAD AT ME, I GET IT.
I AM MU. YOU ARE MU. WE ARE MU TOGETHER.
THIS IS MU'S WILL IN ACTION...

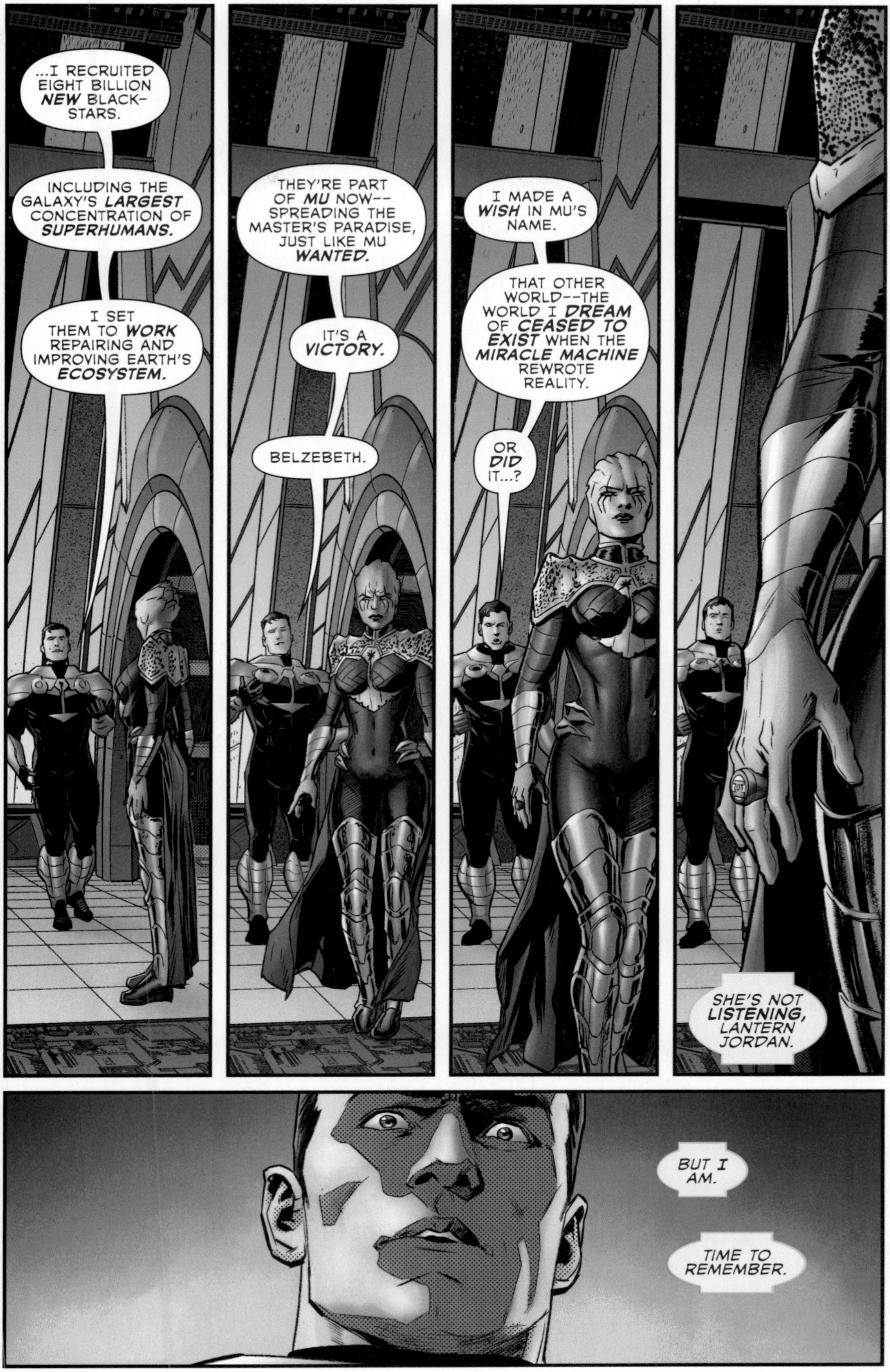

...I RECRUITED EIGHT BILLION NEW BLACK-STARS.
INCLUDING THE GALAXY'S LARGEST CONCENTRATION OF SUPERHUMANS.
I SET THEM TO WORK REPAIRING AND IMPROVING EARTH'S ECOSYSTEM.
THEY'RE PART OF MU NOW--SPREADING THE MASTER'S PARADISE, JUST LIKE MU WANTED.
IT'S A VICTORY.
BELZEBETH.
I MADE A WISH IN MU'S NAME.
THAT OTHER WORLD--THE WORLD I DREAM OF CEASED TO EXIST WHEN THE MIRACLE MACHINE REWROTE REALITY.
OR DID IT...?
SHE'S NOT LISTENING, LANTERN JORDAN.
BUT I AM.
TIME TO REMEMBER.

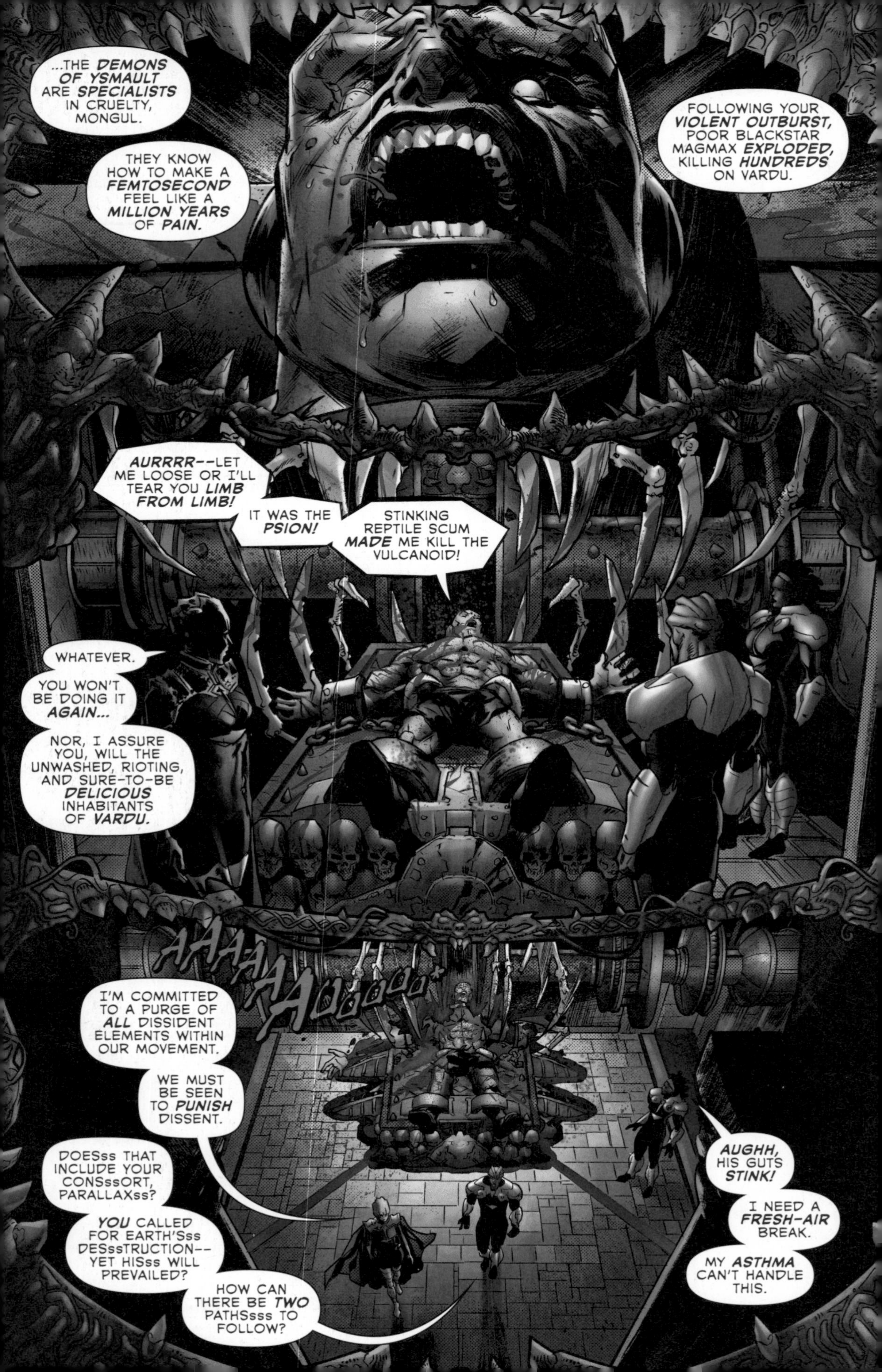
...THE DEMONS OF YSMAULT ARE SPECIALISTS IN CRUELTY, MONGUL.
THEY KNOW HOW TO MAKE A FEMTOSECOND FEEL LIKE A MILLION YEARS OF PAIN.
FOLLOWING YOUR VIOLENT OUTBURST, POOR BLACKSTAR MAGMAX EXPLODED, KILLING HUNDREDS ON VARDU.
AURRRR--LET ME LOOSE OR I'LL TEAR YOU LIMB FROM LIMB!
IT WAS THE PSION!
STINKING REPTILE SCUM MADE ME KILL THE VULCANOID!
WHATEVER.
YOU WON'T BE DOING IT AGAIN...
NOR, I ASSURE YOU, WILL THE UNWASHED, RIOTING, AND SURE-TO-BE DELICIOUS INHABITANTS OF VARDU.
AAAAAAAAaaaaa*
I'M COMMITTED TO A PURGE OF ALL DISSIDENT ELEMENTS WITHIN OUR MOVEMENT.
WE MUST BE SEEN TO PUNISH DISSENT.
DOESss THAT INCLUDE YOUR CONSssORT, PARALLAXss?
YOU CALLED FOR EARTH'Sss DESssTRUCTION-- YET HISss WILL PREVAILED?
HOW CAN THERE BE TWO PATHSsss TO FOLLOW?
AUGHH, HIS GUTS STINK!
I NEED A FRESH-AIR BREAK.
MY ASTHMA CAN'T HANDLE THIS.

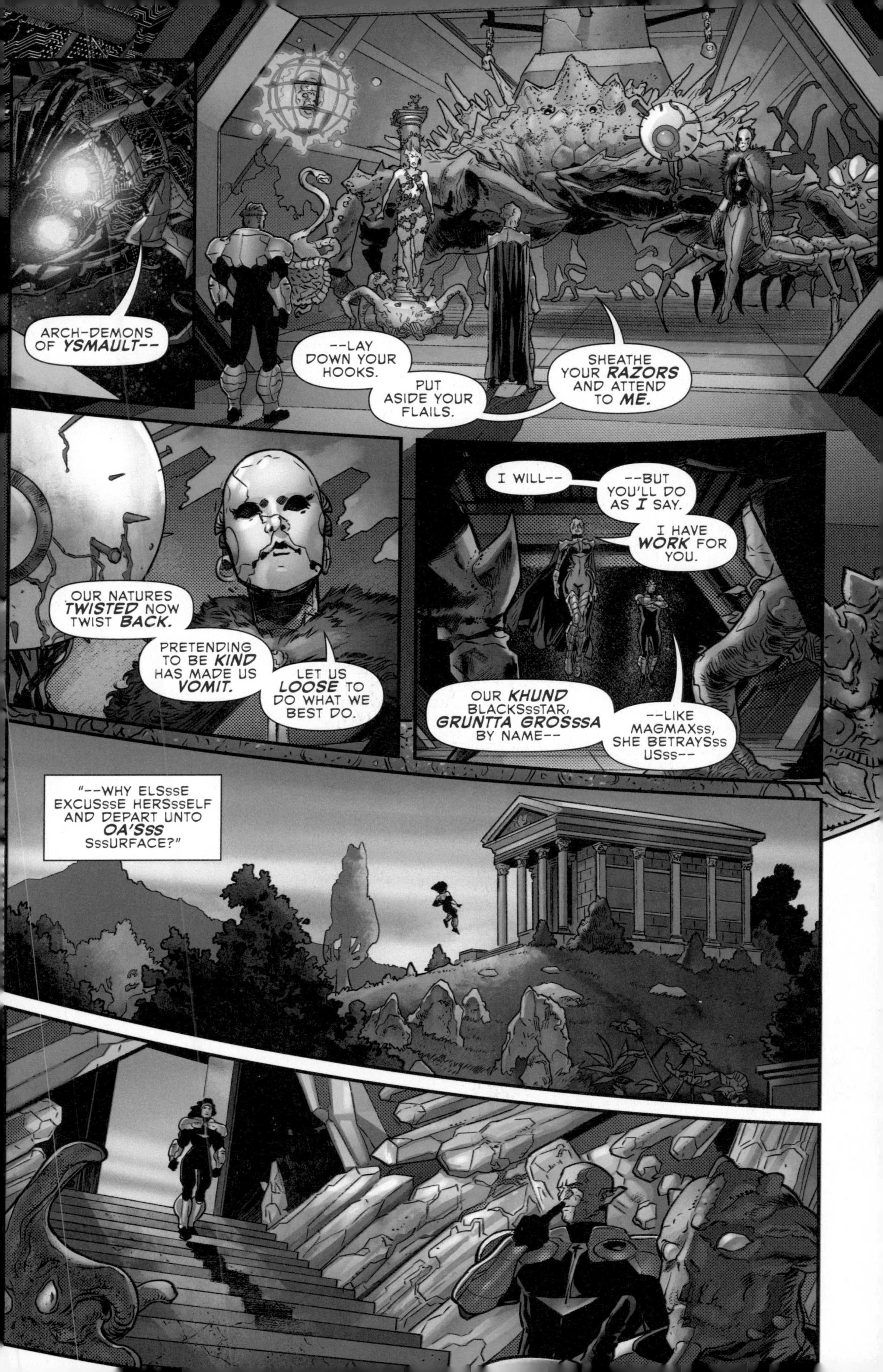

ARCH-DEMONS OF YSMAULT--
--LAY DOWN YOUR HOOKS.
PUT ASIDE YOUR FLAILS.
SHEATHE YOUR RAZORS AND ATTEND TO ME.
OUR NATURES TWISTED NOW TWIST BACK.
PRETENDING TO BE KIND HAS MADE US VOMIT.
LET US LOOSE TO DO WHAT WE BEST DO.
I WILL--
--BUT YOU'LL DO AS I SAY.
I HAVE WORK FOR YOU.
OUR KHUND BLACKSssTAR, GRUNTTA GROSSSA BY NAME--
--LIKE MAGMAXSS, SHE BETRAYSSS USss--
"--WHY ELSssE EXCUSssE HERSssELF AND DEPART UNTO OA'SSS SssURFACE?"

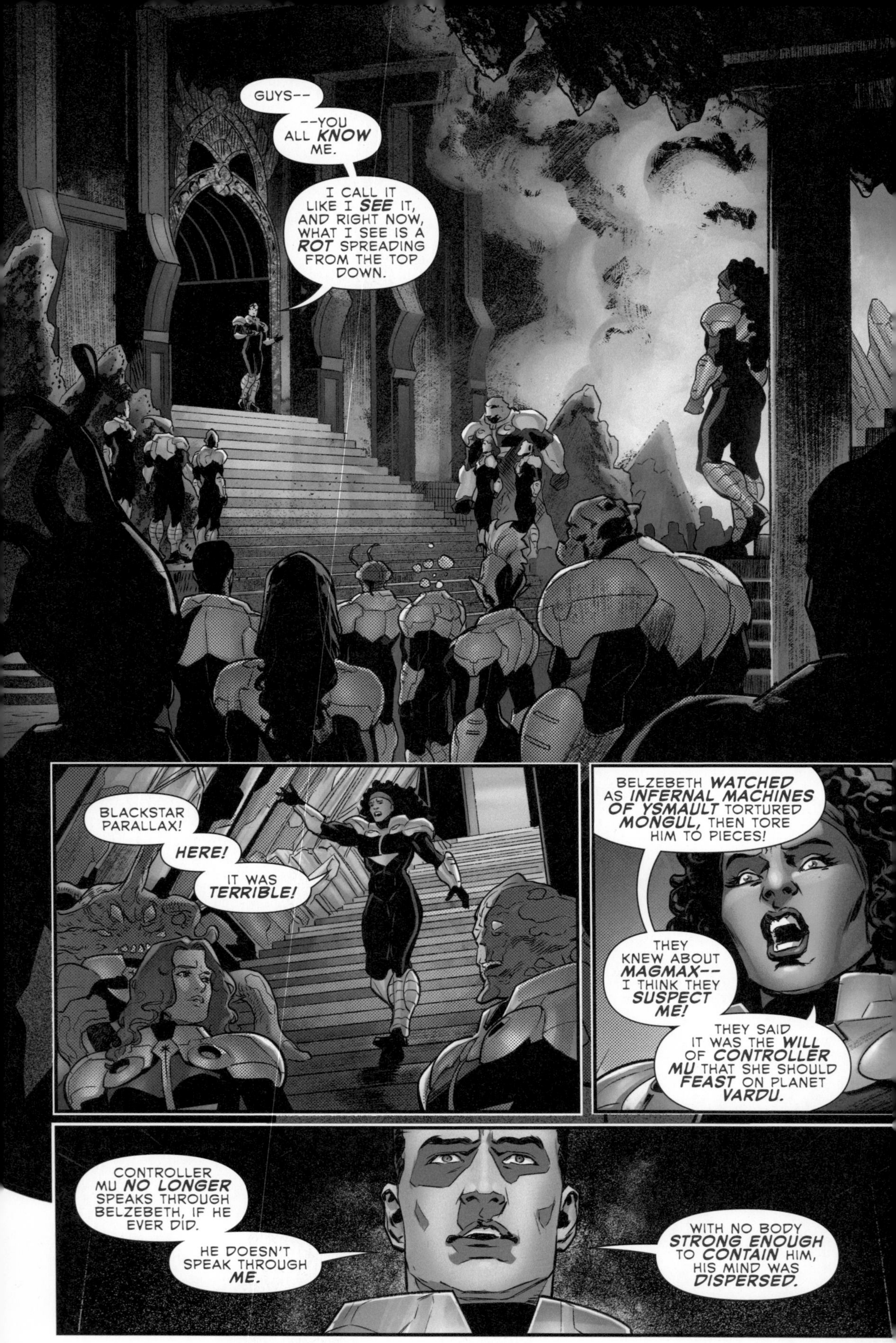
GUYS--
--YOU ALL KNOW ME.
I CALL IT LIKE I SEE IT, AND RIGHT NOW, WHAT I SEE IS A ROT SPREADING FROM THE TOP DOWN.
BLACKSTAR PARALLAX!
HERE!
IT WAS TERRIBLE!
BELZEBETH WATCHED AS INFERNAL MACHINES OF YSMAULT TORTURED MONGUL, THEN TORE HIM TO PIECES!
THEY KNEW ABOUT MAGMAX-- I THINK THEY SUSPECT ME!
THEY SAID IT WAS THE WILL OF CONTROLLER MU THAT SHE SHOULD FEAST ON PLANET VARDU.
CONTROLLER MU NO LONGER SPEAKS THROUGH BELZEBETH, IF HE EVER DID.
HE DOESN'T SPEAK THROUGH ME.
WITH NO BODY STRONG ENOUGH TO CONTAIN HIM, HIS MIND WAS DISPERSED.

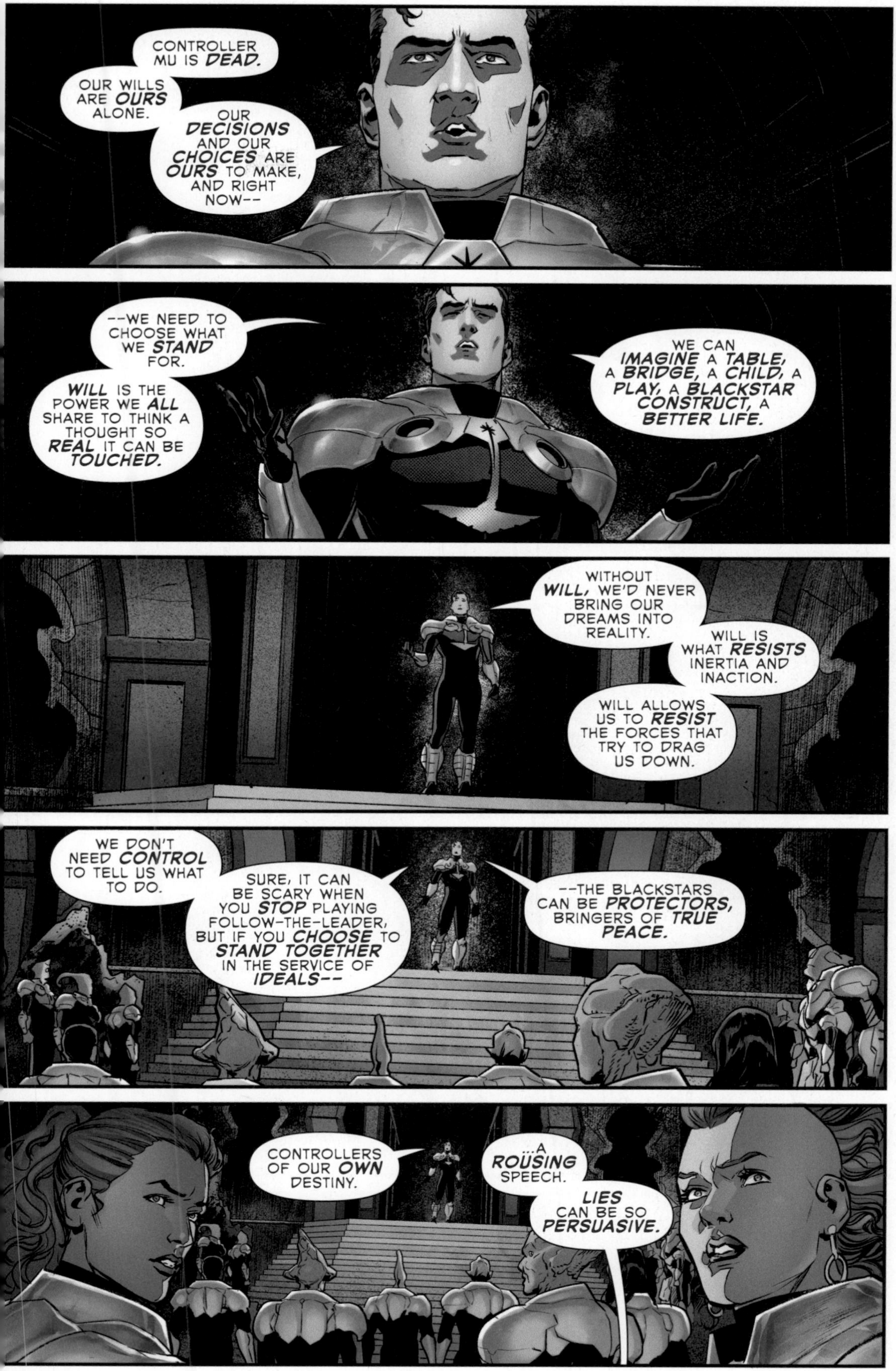
CONTROLLER MU IS DEAD.
OUR WILLS ARE OURS ALONE.
OUR DECISIONS AND OUR CHOICES ARE OURS TO MAKE, AND RIGHT NOW--
--WE NEED TO CHOOSE WHAT WE STAND FOR.
WILL IS THE POWER WE ALL SHARE TO THINK A THOUGHT SO REAL IT CAN BE TOUCHED.
WE CAN IMAGINE A TABLE, A BRIDGE, A CHILD, A PLAY, A BLACKSTAR CONSTRUCT, A BETTER LIFE.
WITHOUT WILL, WE'D NEVER BRING OUR DREAMS INTO REALITY.
WILL IS WHAT RESISTS INERTIA AND INACTION.
WILL ALLOWS US TO RESIST THE FORCES THAT TRY TO DRAG US DOWN.
WE DON'T NEED CONTROL TO TELL US WHAT TO DO.
SURE, IT CAN BE SCARY WHEN YOU STOP PLAYING FOLLOW-THE-LEADER, BUT IF YOU CHOOSE TO STAND TOGETHER IN THE SERVICE OF IDEALS--
--THE BLACKSTARS CAN BE PROTECTORS, BRINGERS OF TRUE PEACE.
CONTROLLERS OF OUR OWN DESTINY.
...A ROUSING SPEECH.
LIES CAN BE SO PERSUASIVE.

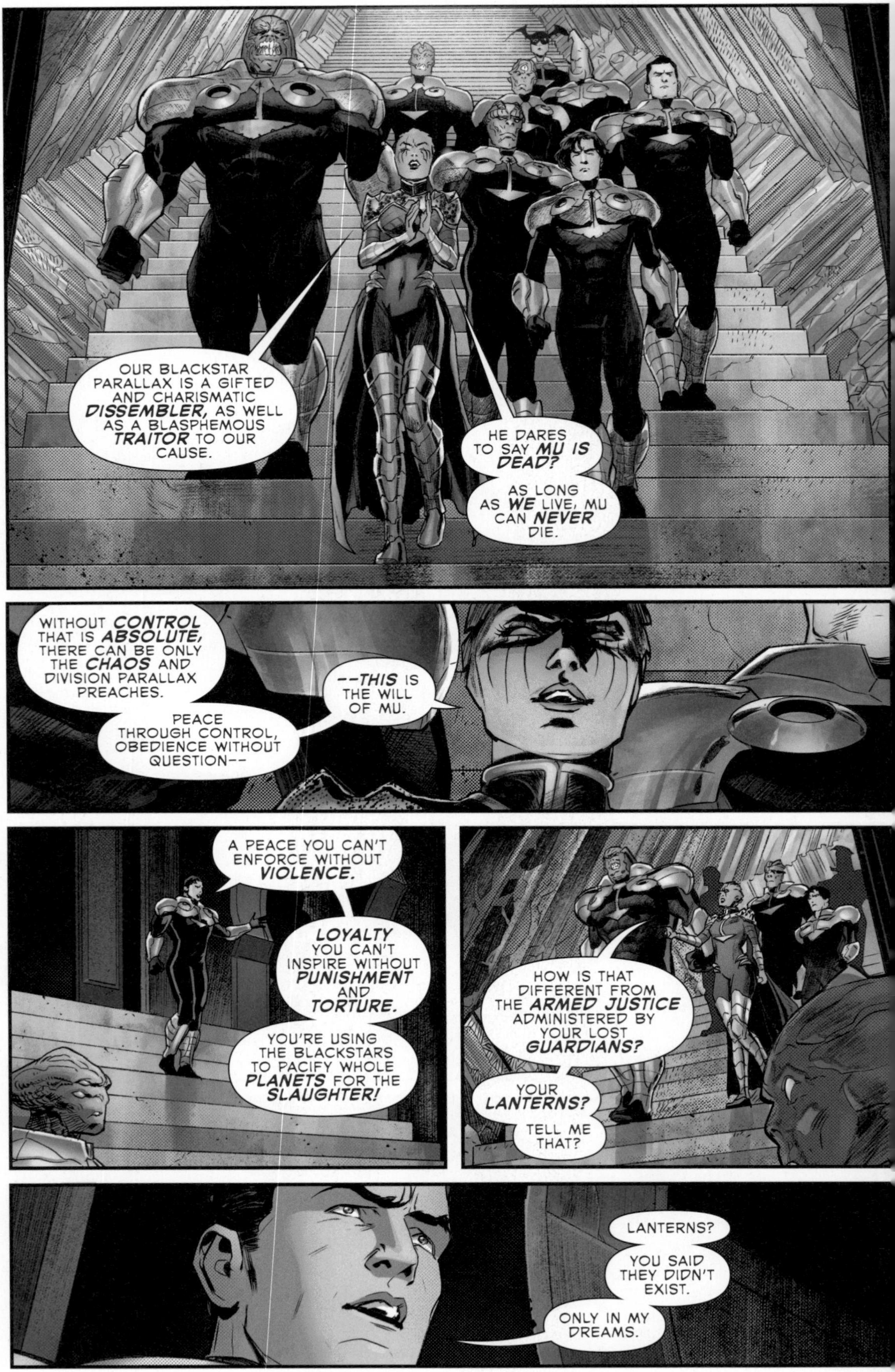
OUR BLACKSTAR PARALLAX IS A GIFTED AND CHARISMATIC DISSEMBLER, AS WELL AS A BLASPHEMOUS TRAITOR TO OUR CAUSE.
HE DARES TO SAY MU IS DEAD?
AS LONG AS WE LIVE, MU CAN NEVER DIE.
WITHOUT CONTROL THAT IS ABSOLUTE, THERE CAN BE ONLY THE CHAOS AND DIVISION PARALLAX PREACHES.
PEACE THROUGH CONTROL, OBEDIENCE WITHOUT QUESTION--
--THIS IS THE WILL OF MU.
A PEACE YOU CAN'T ENFORCE WITHOUT VIOLENCE.
LOYALTY YOU CAN'T INSPIRE WITHOUT PUNISHMENT AND TORTURE.
YOU'RE USING THE BLACKSTARS TO PACIFY WHOLE PLANETS FOR THE SLAUGHTER!
HOW IS THAT DIFFERENT FROM THE ARMED JUSTICE ADMINISTERED BY YOUR LOST GUARDIANS?
YOUR LANTERNS?
TELL ME THAT?
LANTERNS?
YOU SAID THEY DIDN'T EXIST.
ONLY IN MY DREAMS.

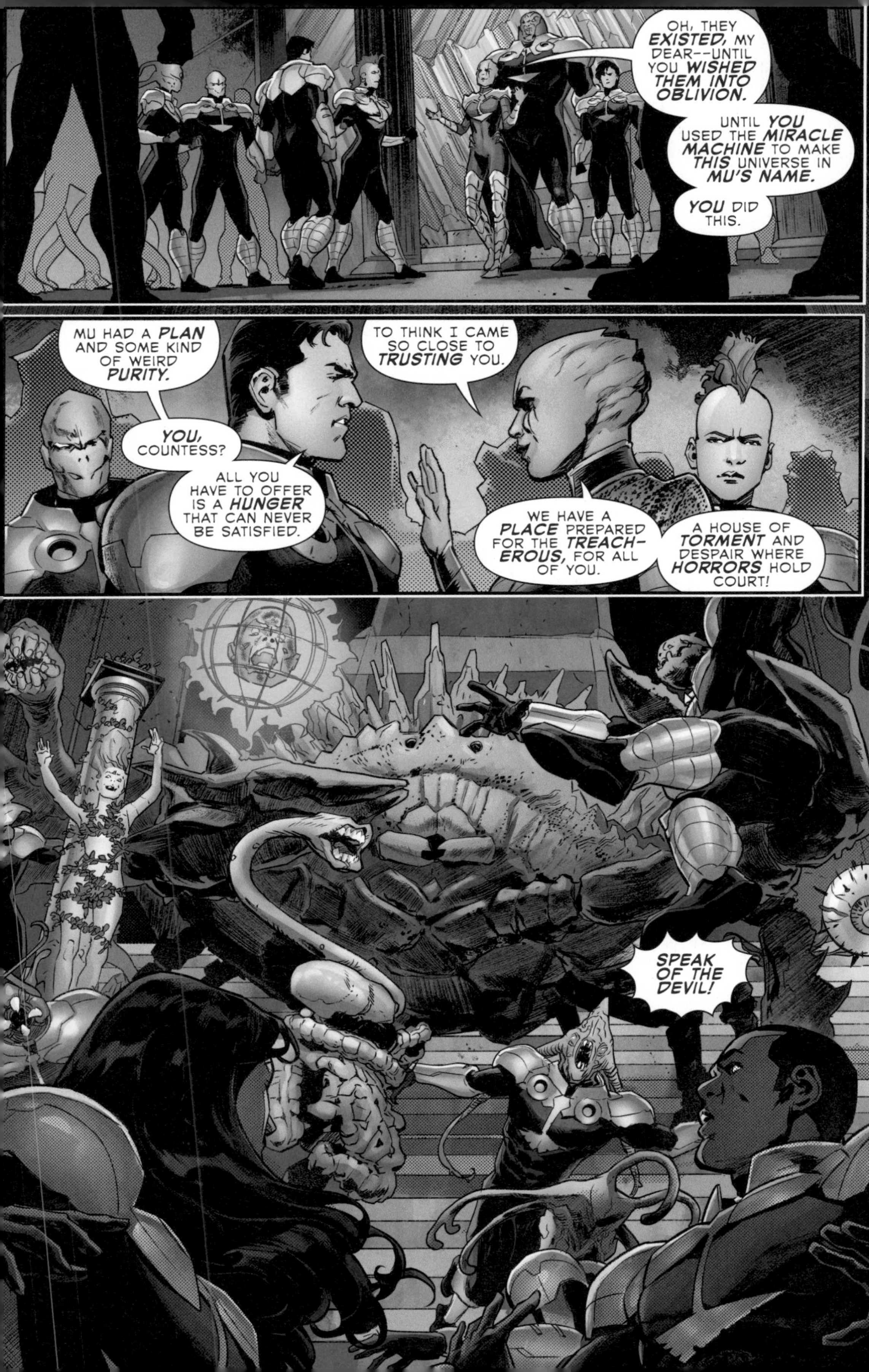
OH, THEY EXISTED, MY DEAR--UNTIL YOU WISHED THEM INTO OBLIVION.
UNTIL YOU USED THE MIRACLE MACHINE TO MAKE THIS UNIVERSE IN MU'S NAME.
YOU DID THIS.
MU HAD A PLAN AND SOME KIND OF WEIRD PURITY.
YOU, COUNTESS?
ALL YOU HAVE TO OFFER IS A HUNGER THAT CAN NEVER BE SATISFIED.
TO THINK I CAME SO CLOSE TO TRUSTING YOU.
WE HAVE A PLACE PREPARED FOR THE TREACHEROUS, FOR ALL OF YOU.
A HOUSE OF TORMENT AND DESPAIR WHERE HORRORS HOLD COURT!
SPEAK OF THE DEVIL!

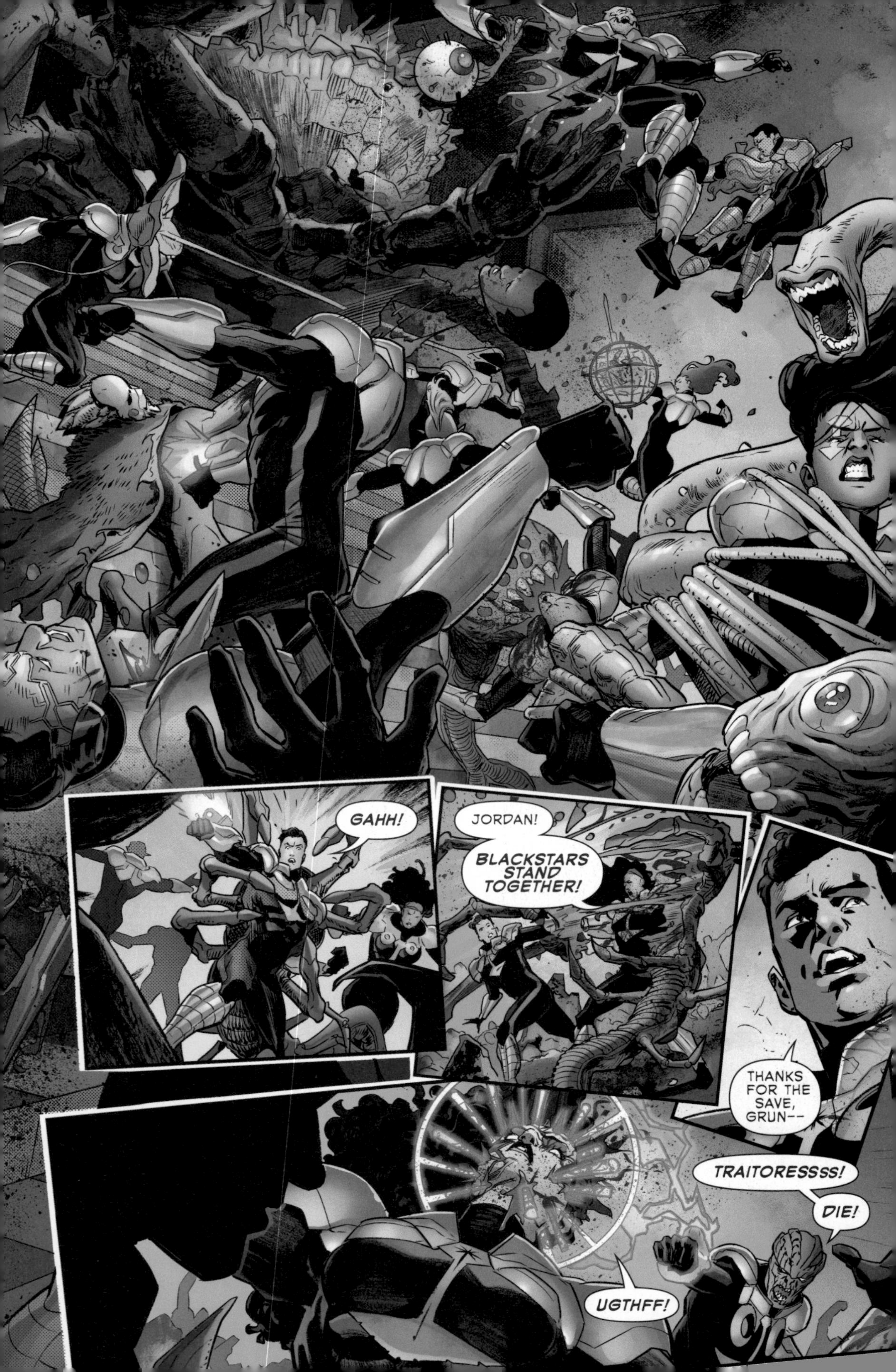
GAHH!
JORDAN!
BLACKSTARS STAND TOGETHER!
THANKS FOR THE SAVE, GRUN--
TRAITORESSSS!
DIE!
UGTHFF!

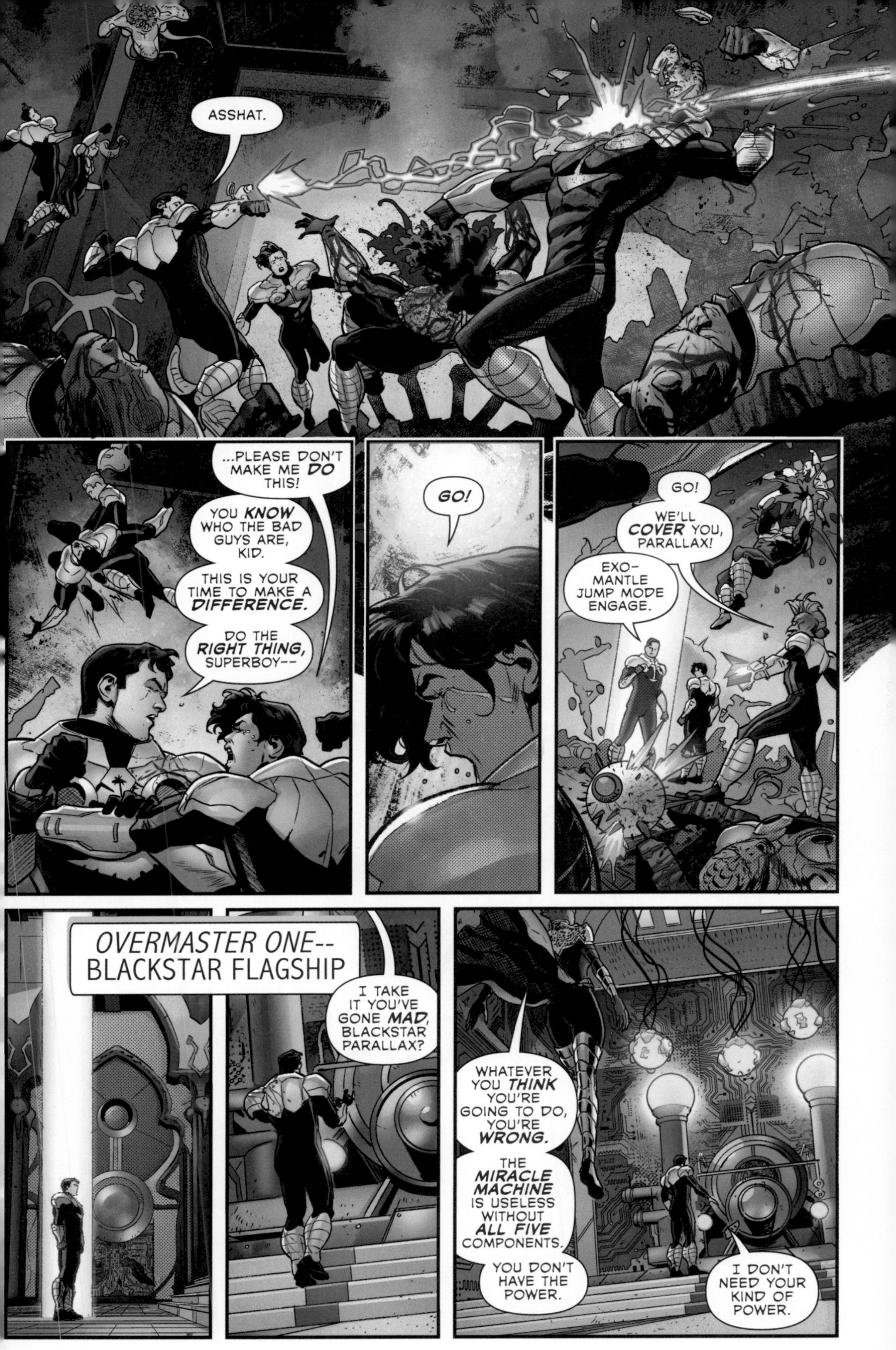
ASSHAT.
...PLEASE DON'T MAKE ME DO THIS!
YOU KNOW WHO THE BAD GUYS ARE, KID.
THIS IS YOUR TIME TO MAKE A DIFFERENCE.
DO THE RIGHT THING, SUPERBOY--
GO!
GO!
WE'LL COVER YOU, PARALLAX!
EXO-MANTLE JUMP MODE ENGAGE.
OVERMASTER ONE-- BLACKSTAR FLAGSHIP
I TAKE IT YOU'VE GONE MAD, BLACKSTAR PARALLAX?
WHATEVER YOU THINK YOU'RE GOING TO DO, YOU'RE WRONG.
THE MIRACLE MACHINE IS USELESS WITHOUT ALL FIVE COMPONENTS.
YOU DON'T HAVE THE POWER.
I DON'T NEED YOUR KIND OF POWER.

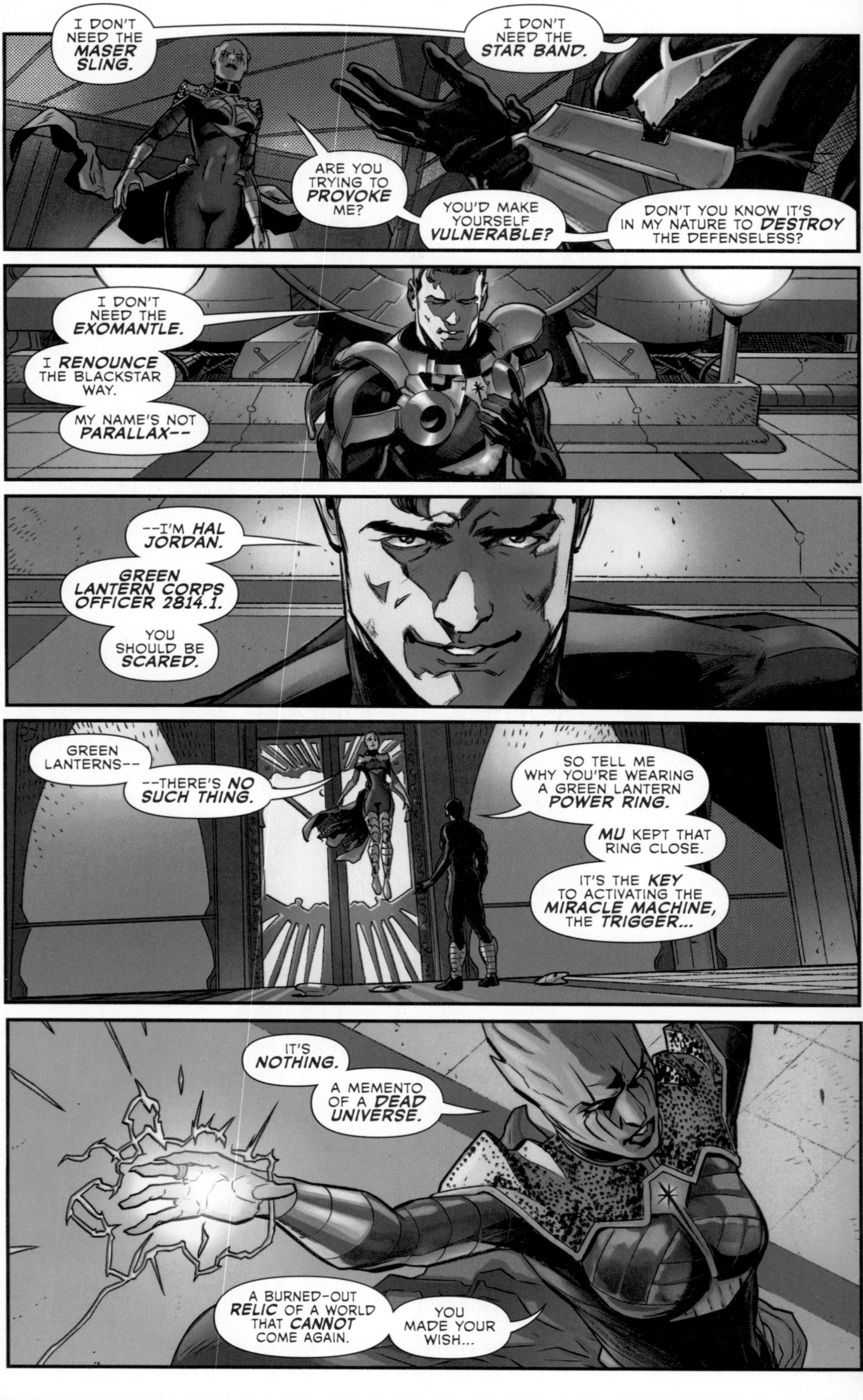
I DON'T NEED THE MASER SLING.
I DON'T NEED THE STAR BAND.
ARE YOU TRYING TO PROVOKE ME?
YOU'D MAKE YOURSELF VULNERABLE?
DON'T YOU KNOW IT'S IN MY NATURE TO DESTROY THE DEFENSELESS?
I DON'T NEED THE EXOMANTLE.
I RENOUNCE THE BLACKSTAR WAY.
MY NAME'S NOT PARALLAX--
--I'M HAL JORDAN.
GREEN LANTERN CORPS OFFICER 2814.1.
YOU SHOULD BE SCARED.
GREEN LANTERNS--
--THERE'S NO SUCH THING.
SO TELL ME WHY YOU'RE WEARING A GREEN LANTERN POWER RING.
MU KEPT THAT RING CLOSE.
IT'S THE KEY TO ACTIVATING THE MIRACLE MACHINE, THE TRIGGER...
IT'S NOTHING.
A MEMENTO OF A DEAD UNIVERSE.
A BURNED-OUT RELIC OF A WORLD THAT CANNOT COME AGAIN.
YOU MADE YOUR WISH...

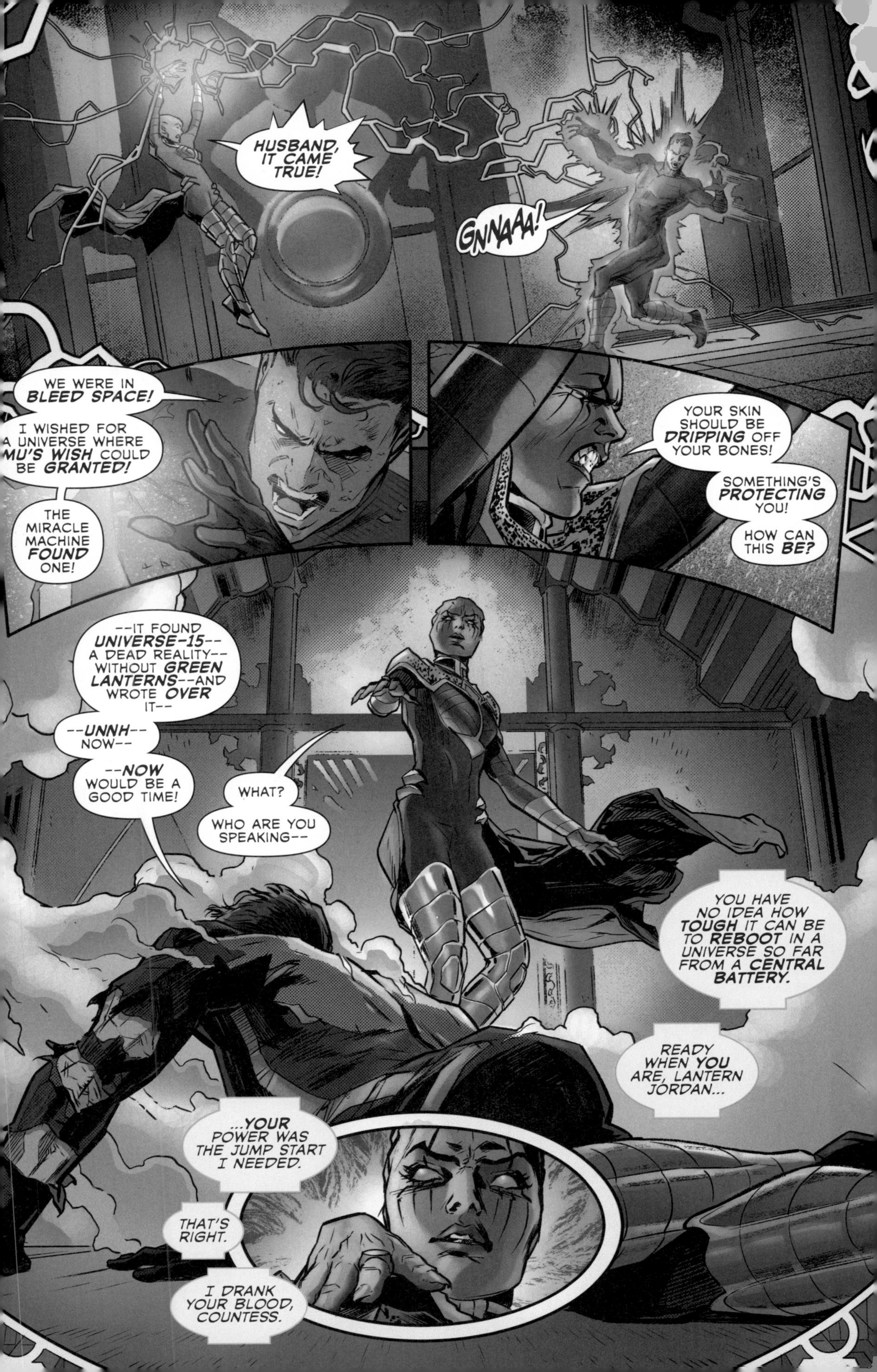
HUSBAND, IT CAME TRUE!
GNNAAA!
WE WERE IN BLEED SPACE!
I WISHED FOR A UNIVERSE WHERE MU'S WISH COULD BE GRANTED!
THE MIRACLE MACHINE FOUND ONE!
YOUR SKIN SHOULD BE DRIPPING OFF YOUR BONES!
SOMETHING'S PROTECTING YOU!
HOW CAN THIS BE?
--IT FOUND UNIVERSE-15-- A DEAD REALITY-- WITHOUT GREEN LANTERNS--AND WROTE OVER IT--
--UNNH-- NOW--
--NOW WOULD BE A GOOD TIME!
WHAT?
WHO ARE YOU SPEAKING--
YOU HAVE NO IDEA HOW TOUGH IT CAN BE TO REBOOT IN A UNIVERSE SO FAR FROM A CENTRAL BATTERY.
READY WHEN YOU ARE, LANTERN JORDAN...
...YOUR POWER WAS THE JUMP START I NEEDED.
THAT'S RIGHT.
I DRANK YOUR BLOOD, COUNTESS.

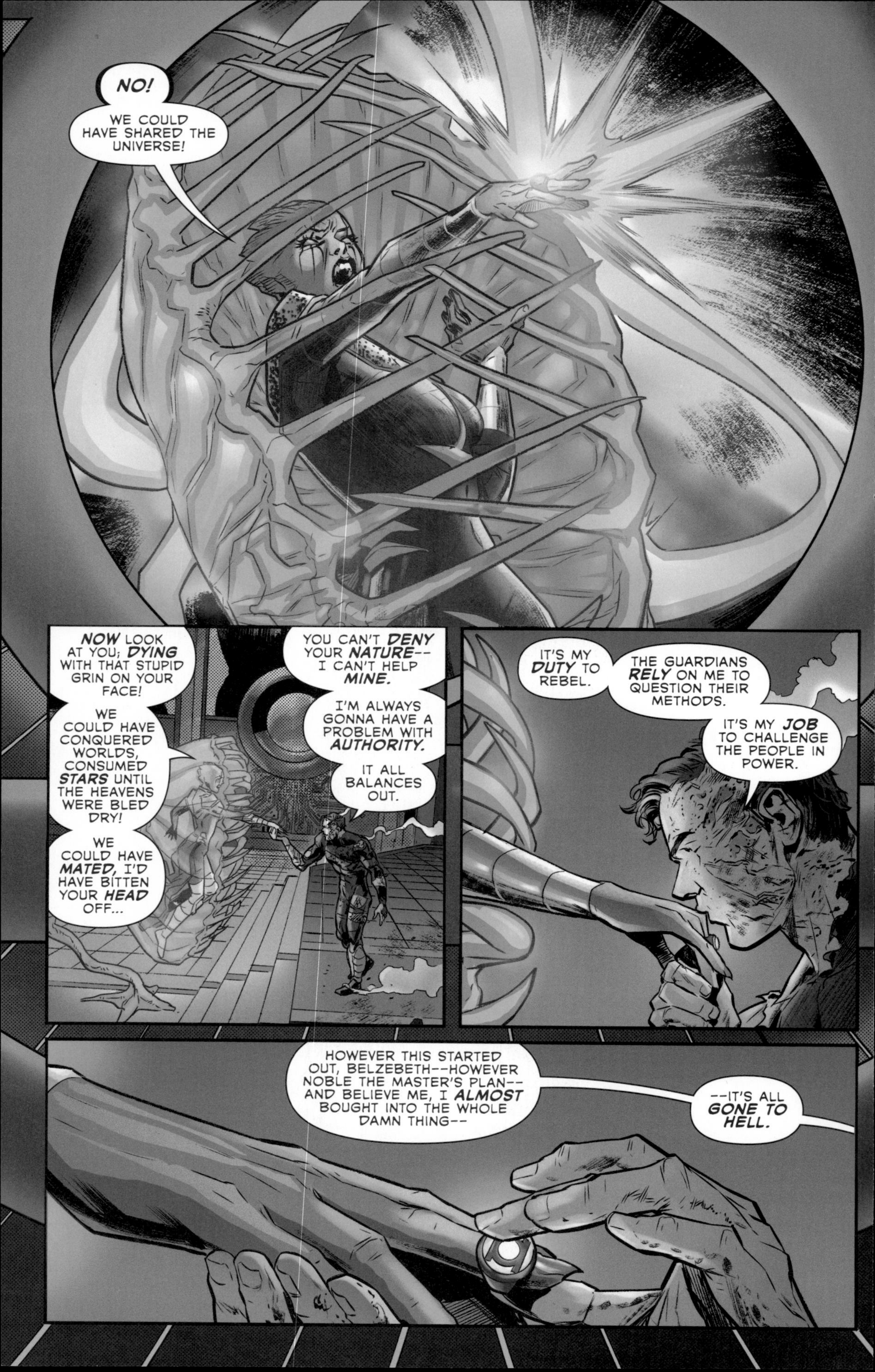
NO!
WE COULD HAVE SHARED THE UNIVERSE!
NOW LOOK AT YOU; DYING WITH THAT STUPID GRIN ON YOUR FACE!
WE COULD HAVE CONQUERED WORLDS, CONSUMED STARS UNTIL THE HEAVENS WERE BLED DRY!
WE COULD HAVE MATED, I'D HAVE BITTEN YOUR HEAD OFF...
YOU CAN'T DENY YOUR NATURE-- I CAN'T HELP MINE.
I'M ALWAYS GONNA HAVE A PROBLEM WITH AUTHORITY.
IT ALL BALANCES OUT.
IT'S MY DUTY TO REBEL.
THE GUARDIANS RELY ON ME TO QUESTION THEIR METHODS.
IT'S MY JOB TO CHALLENGE THE PEOPLE IN POWER.
HOWEVER THIS STARTED OUT, BELZEBETH--HOWEVER NOBLE THE MASTER'S PLAN-- AND BELIEVE ME, I ALMOST BOUGHT INTO THE WHOLE DAMN THING--
--IT'S ALL GONE TO HELL.

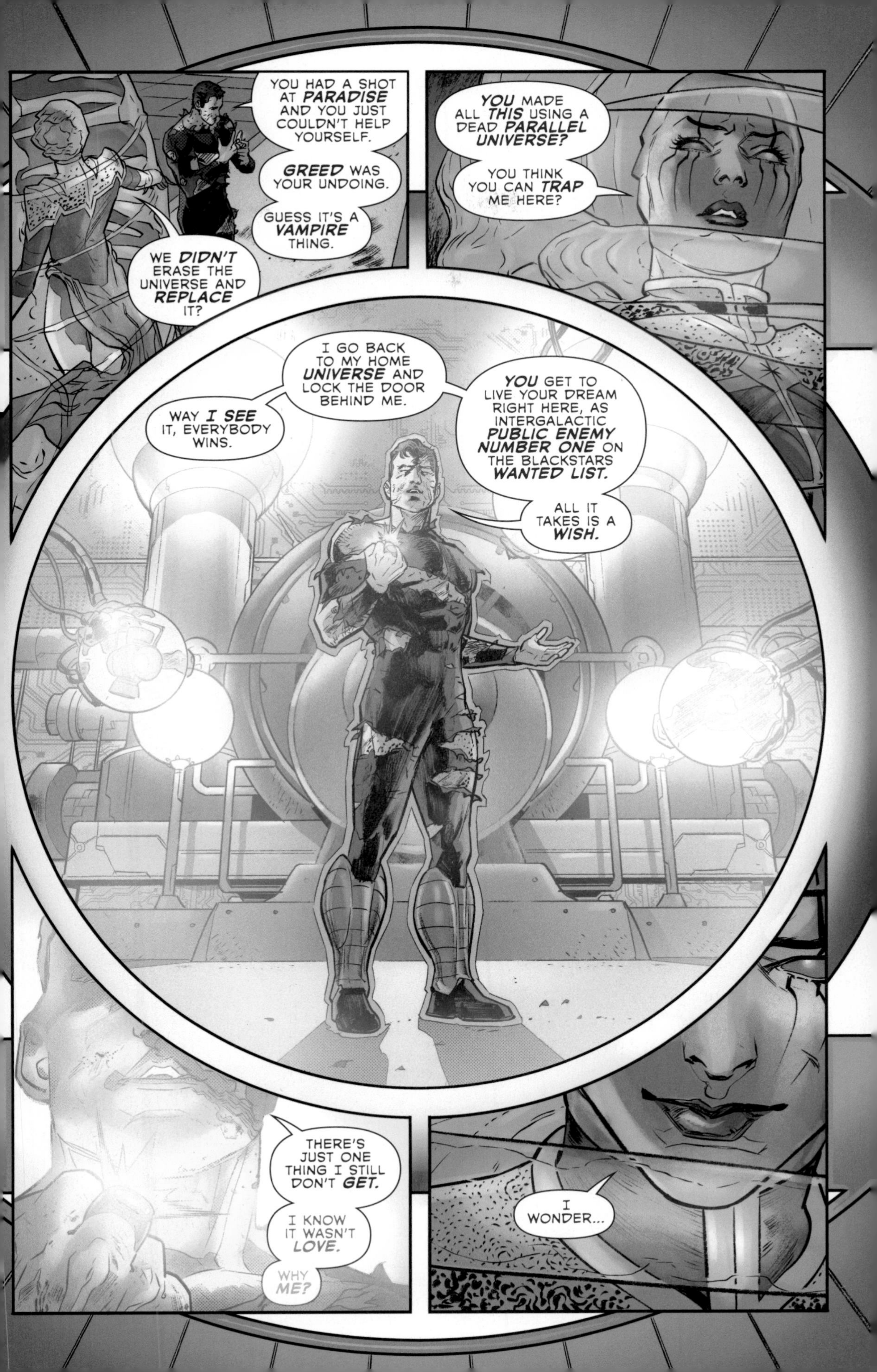
YOU HAD A SHOT AT PARADISE AND YOU JUST COULDN'T HELP YOURSELF.
GREED WAS YOUR UNDOING.
GUESS IT'S A VAMPIRE THING.
WE DIDN'T ERASE THE UNIVERSE AND REPLACE IT?
YOU MADE ALL THIS USING A DEAD PARALLEL UNIVERSE?
YOU THINK YOU CAN TRAP ME HERE?
WAY I SEE IT, EVERYBODY WINS.
I GO BACK TO MY HOME UNIVERSE AND LOCK THE DOOR BEHIND ME.
YOU GET TO LIVE YOUR DREAM RIGHT HERE, AS INTERGALACTIC PUBLIC ENEMY NUMBER ONE ON THE BLACKSTARS WANTED LIST.
ALL IT TAKES IS A WISH.
THERE'S JUST ONE THING I STILL DON'T GET.
I KNOW IT WASN'T LOVE.
WHY ME?
I WONDER...

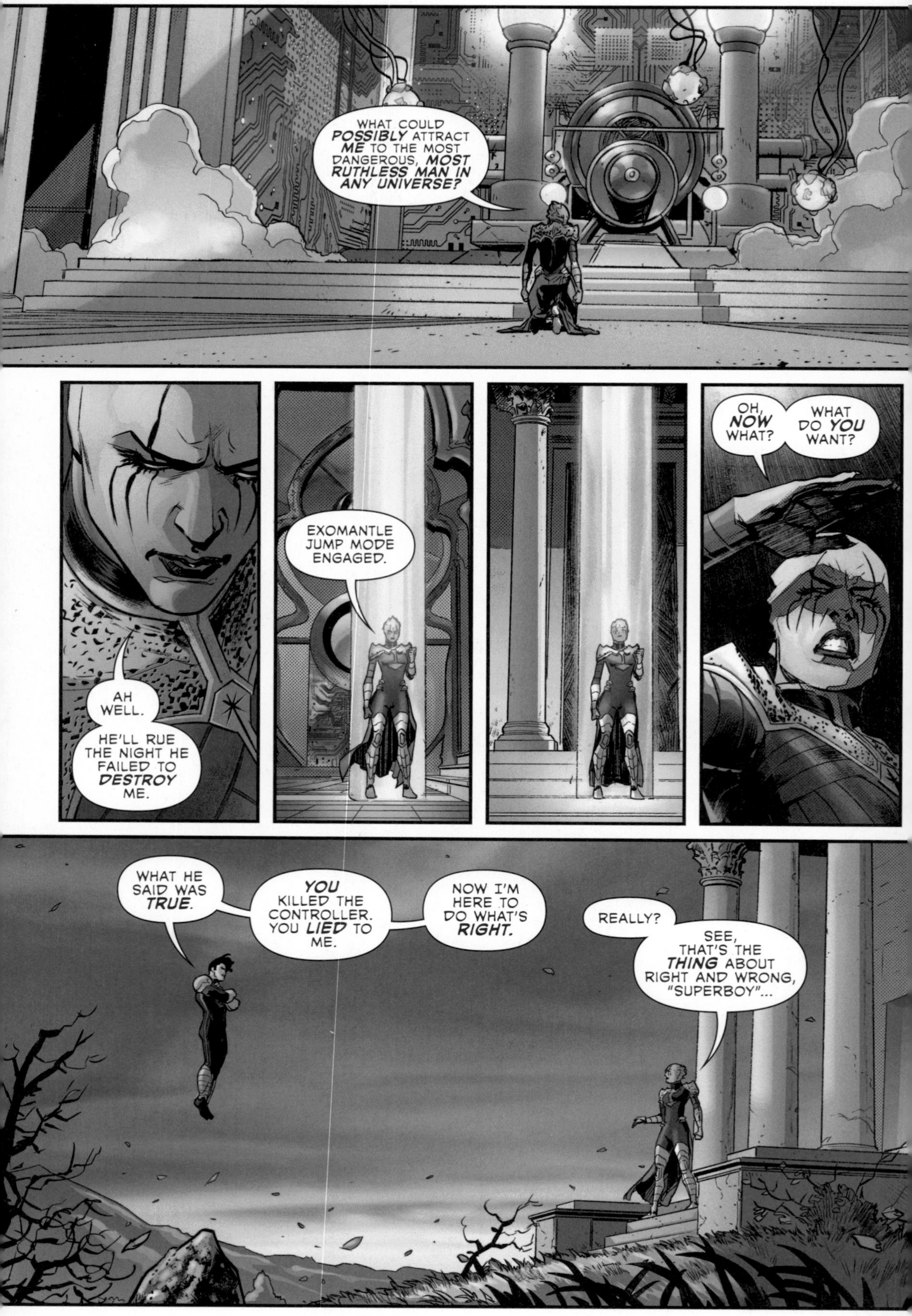
WHAT COULD ***POSSIBLY*** ATTRACT ***ME*** TO THE MOST DANGEROUS, ***MOST RUTHLESS MAN IN ANY UNIVERSE?***
AH WELL.
HE'LL RUE THE NIGHT HE FAILED TO ***DESTROY*** ME.
EXOMANTLE JUMP MODE ENGAGED.
OH, ***NOW*** WHAT?
WHAT DO ***YOU*** WANT?
WHAT HE SAID WAS ***TRUE.***
YOU KILLED THE CONTROLLER. YOU ***LIED*** TO ME.
NOW I'M HERE TO DO WHAT'S ***RIGHT.***
REALLY?
SEE, THAT'S THE ***THING*** ABOUT RIGHT AND WRONG, "SUPERBOY"...

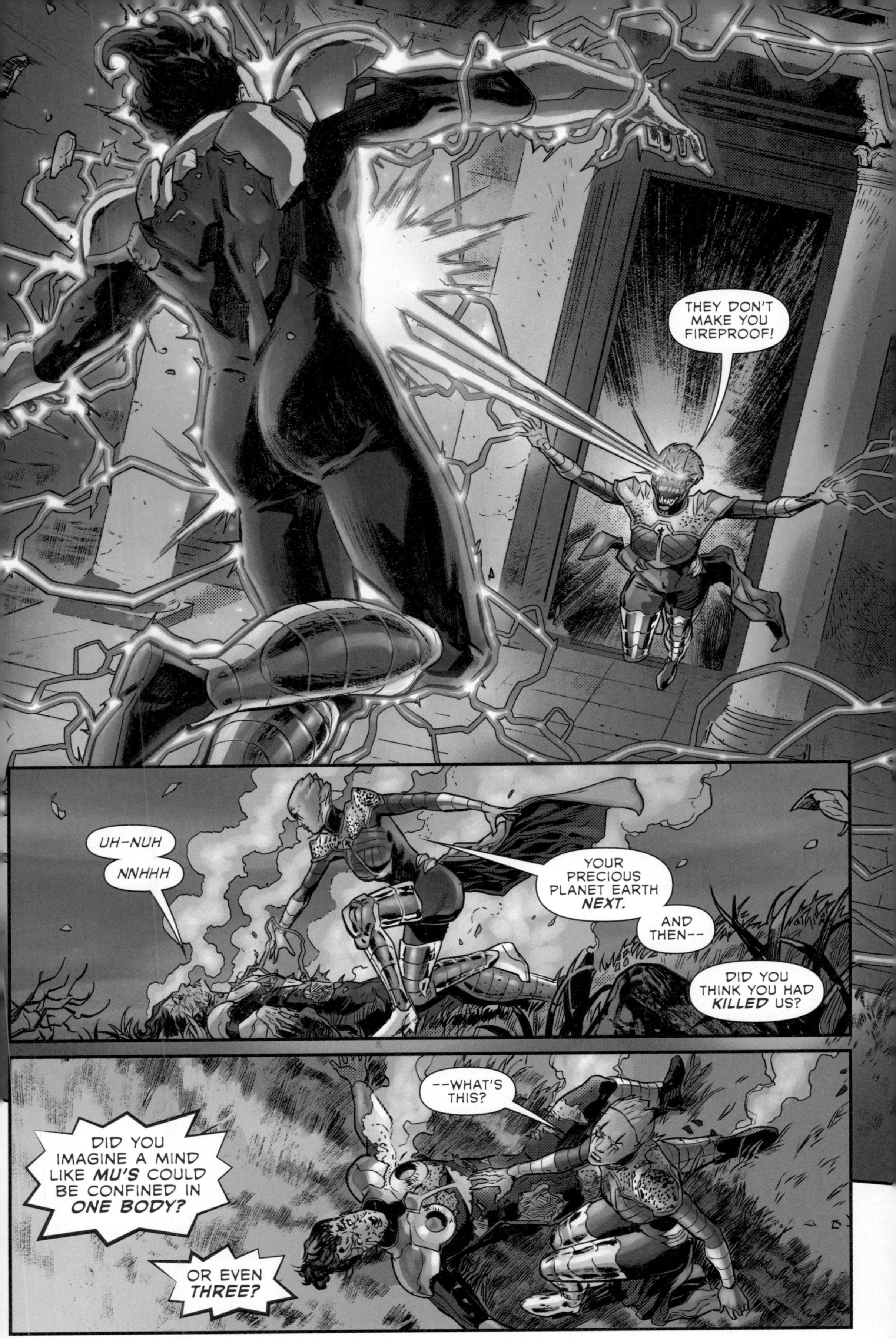
THEY DON'T MAKE YOU FIREPROOF!
UH-NUH
NNHHH
YOUR PRECIOUS PLANET EARTH **NEXT.**
AND THEN--
DID YOU THINK YOU HAD **KILLED** US?
--WHAT'S THIS?
DID YOU IMAGINE A MIND LIKE **MU'S** COULD BE CONFINED IN **ONE BODY?**
OR EVEN **THREE?**

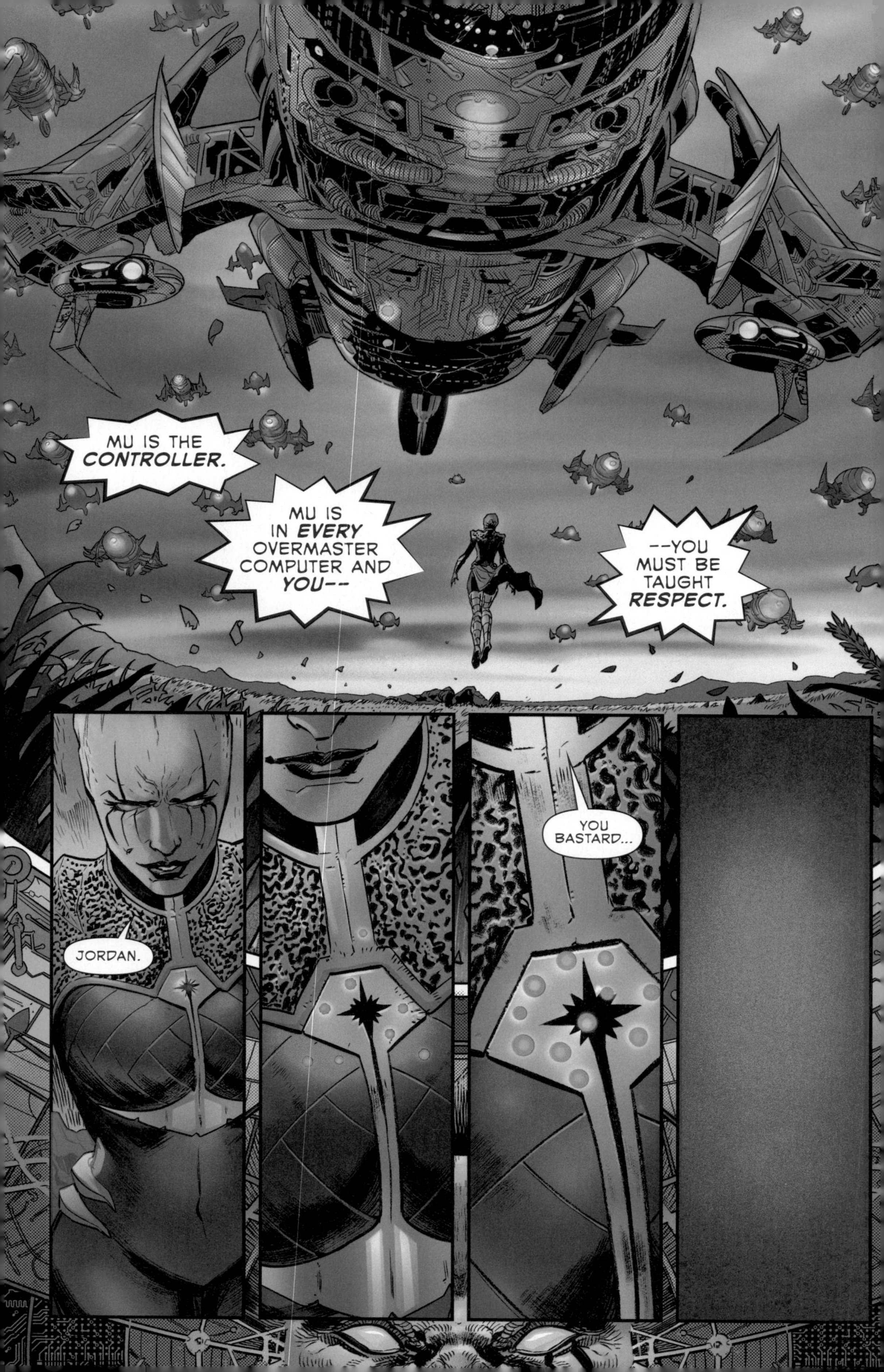
MU IS THE *CONTROLLER.*
MU IS IN *EVERY* OVERMASTER COMPUTER AND *YOU*--
--YOU MUST BE TAUGHT *RESPECT.*
JORDAN.
YOU BASTARD...

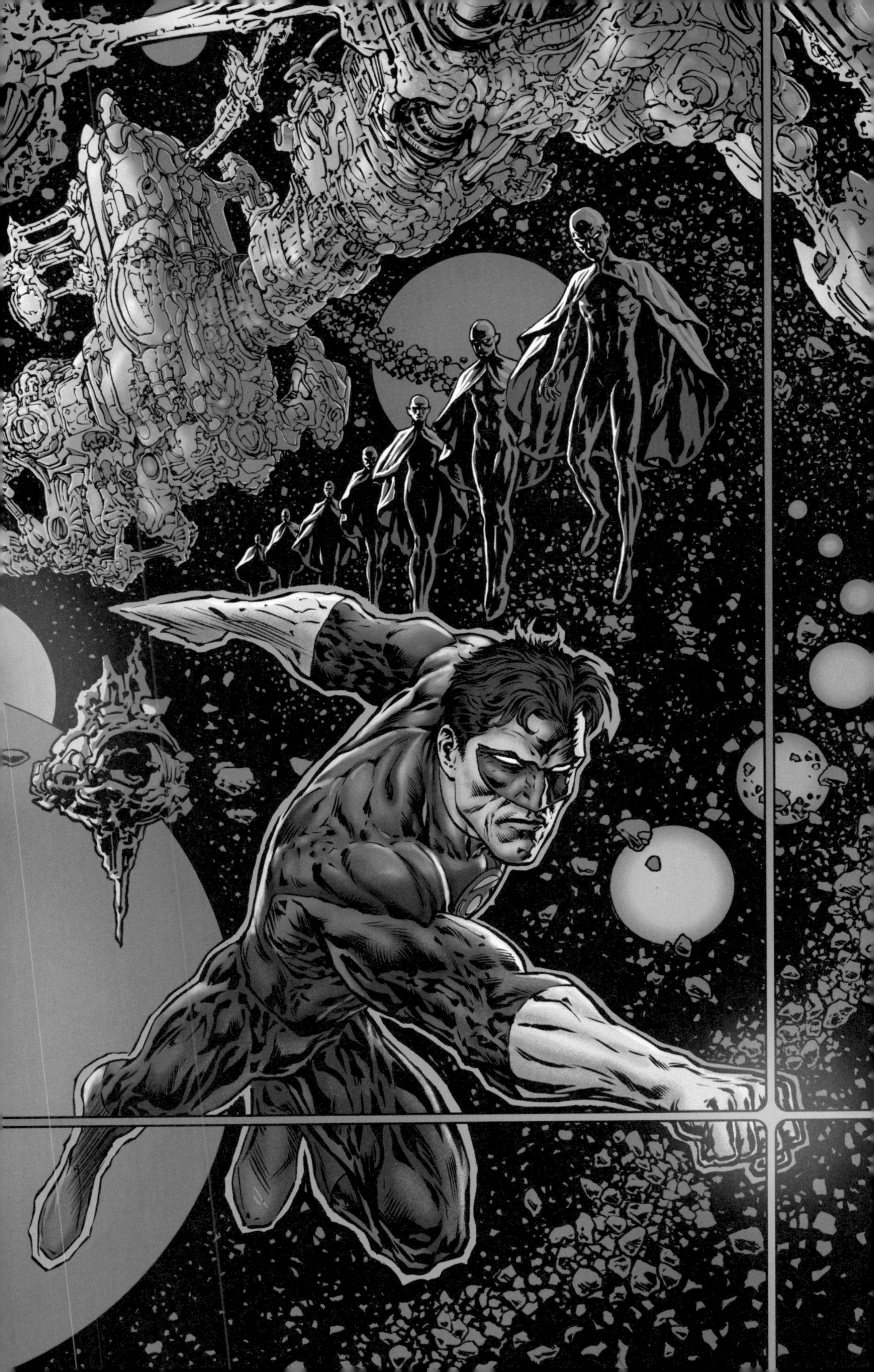

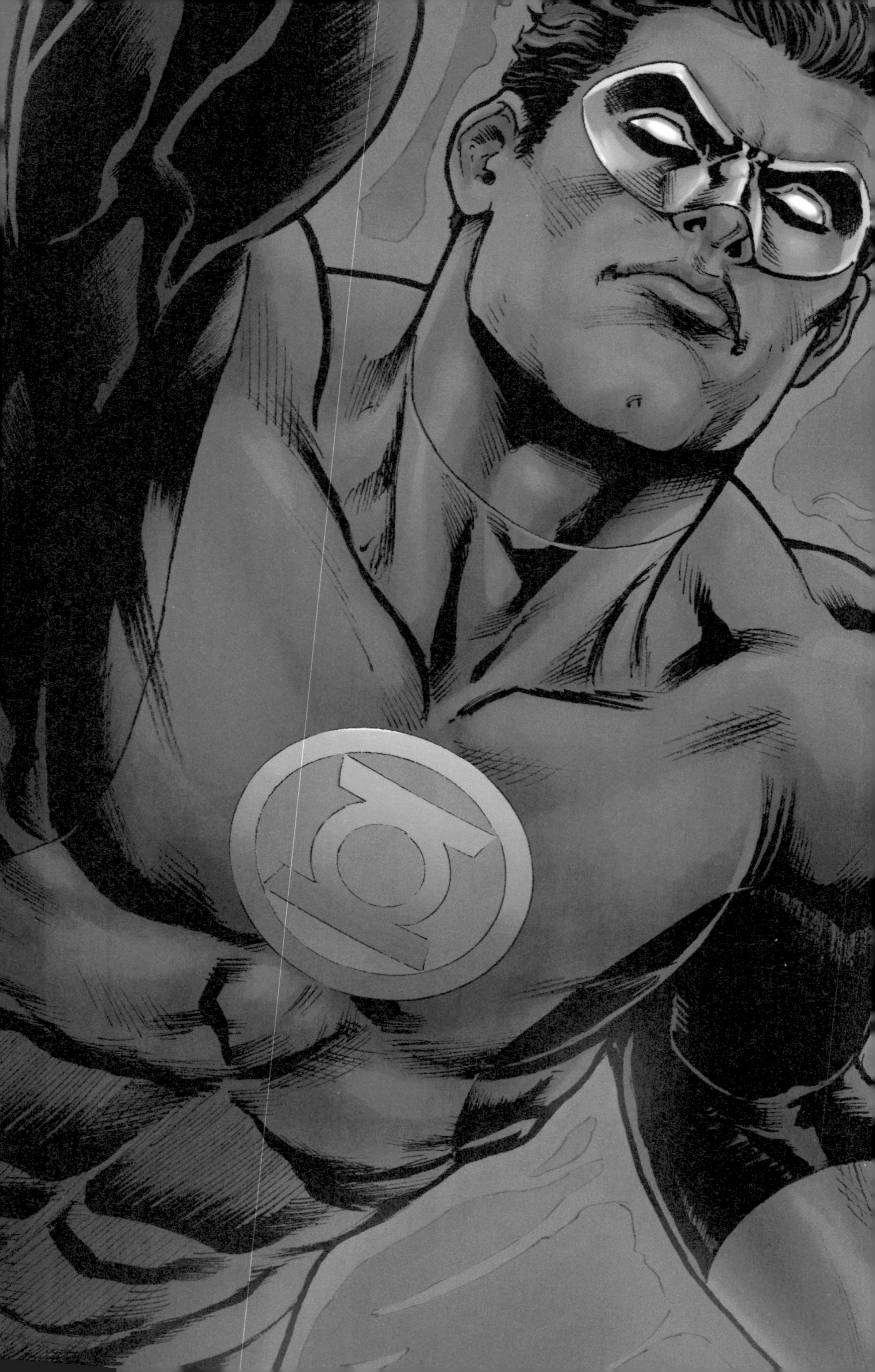

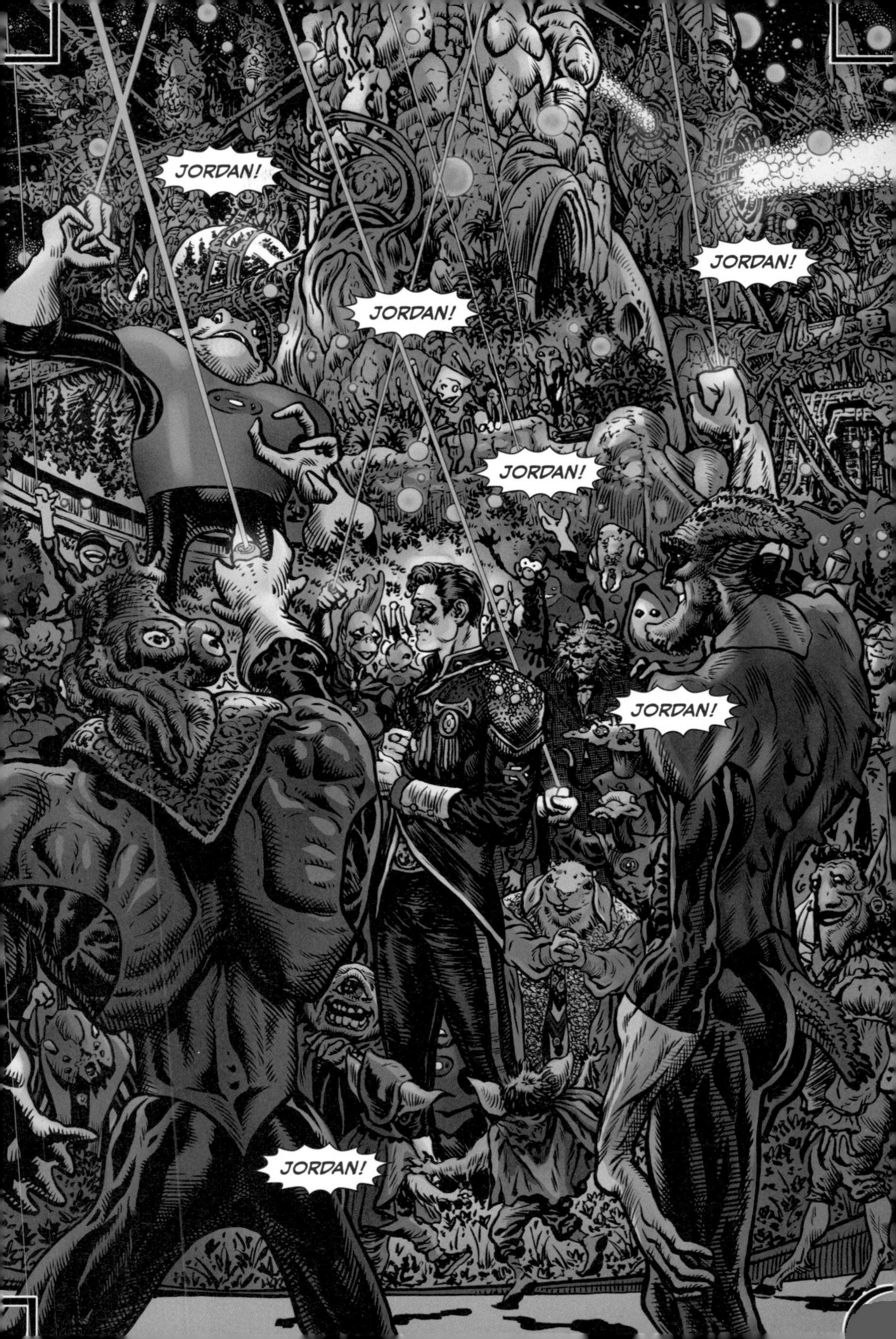
JORDAN!
JORDAN!
JORDAN!
JORDAN!
JORDAN!
JORDAN!

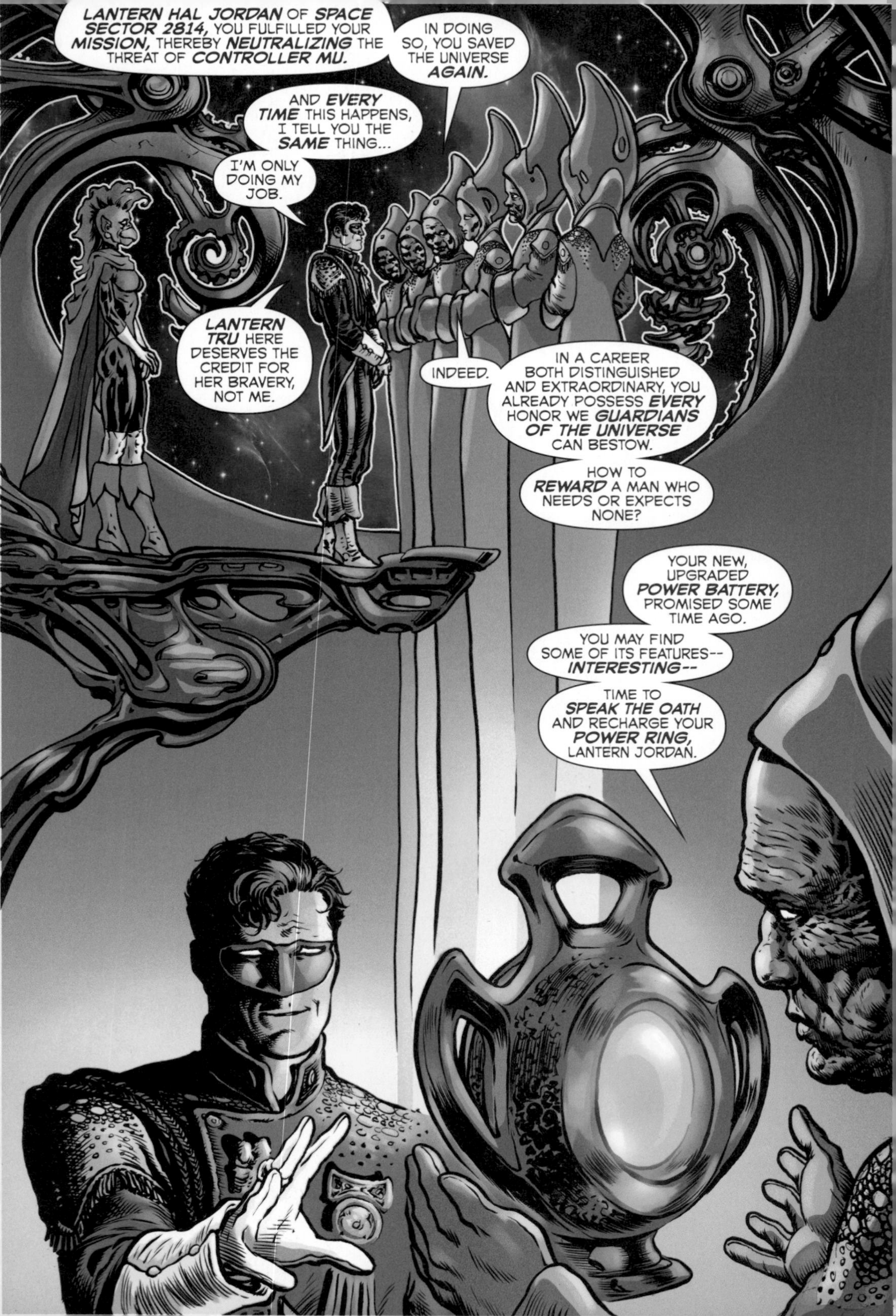
LANTERN HAL JORDAN OF SPACE SECTOR 2814, YOU FULFILLED YOUR MISSION, THEREBY NEUTRALIZING THE THREAT OF CONTROLLER MU.
IN DOING SO, YOU SAVED THE UNIVERSE AGAIN.
AND EVERY TIME THIS HAPPENS, I TELL YOU THE SAME THING...
I'M ONLY DOING MY JOB.
LANTERN TRU HERE DESERVES THE CREDIT FOR HER BRAVERY, NOT ME.
INDEED.
IN A CAREER BOTH DISTINGUISHED AND EXTRAORDINARY, YOU ALREADY POSSESS EVERY HONOR WE GUARDIANS OF THE UNIVERSE CAN BESTOW.
HOW TO REWARD A MAN WHO NEEDS OR EXPECTS NONE?
YOUR NEW, UPGRADED POWER BATTERY, PROMISED SOME TIME AGO.
YOU MAY FIND SOME OF ITS FEATURES-- INTERESTING--
TIME TO SPEAK THE OATH AND RECHARGE YOUR POWER RING, LANTERN JORDAN.

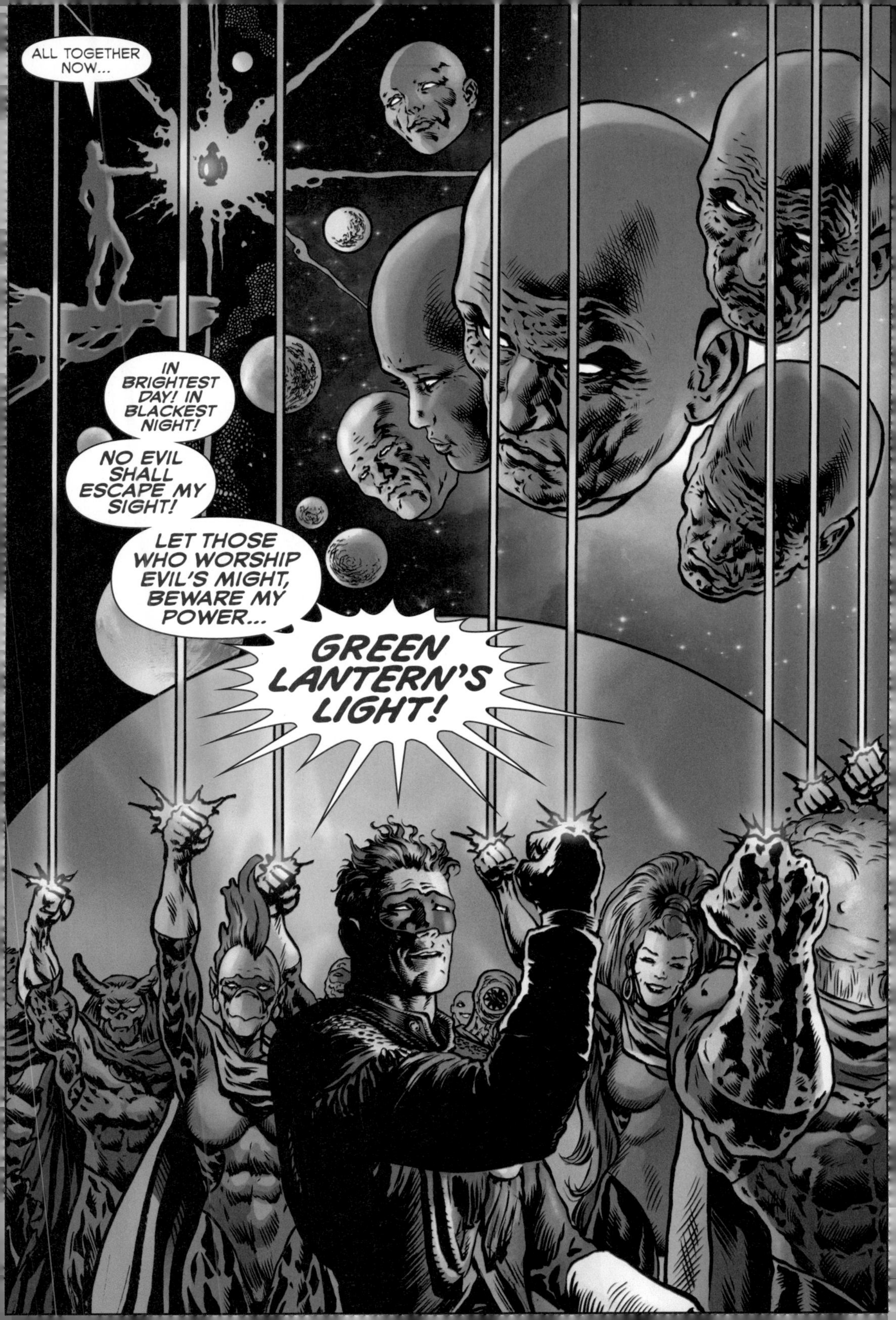
ALL TOGETHER NOW...
IN BRIGHTEST DAY! IN BLACKEST NIGHT!
NO EVIL SHALL ESCAPE MY SIGHT!
LET THOSE WHO WORSHIP EVIL'S MIGHT, BEWARE MY POWER...
GREEN LANTERN'S LIGHT!

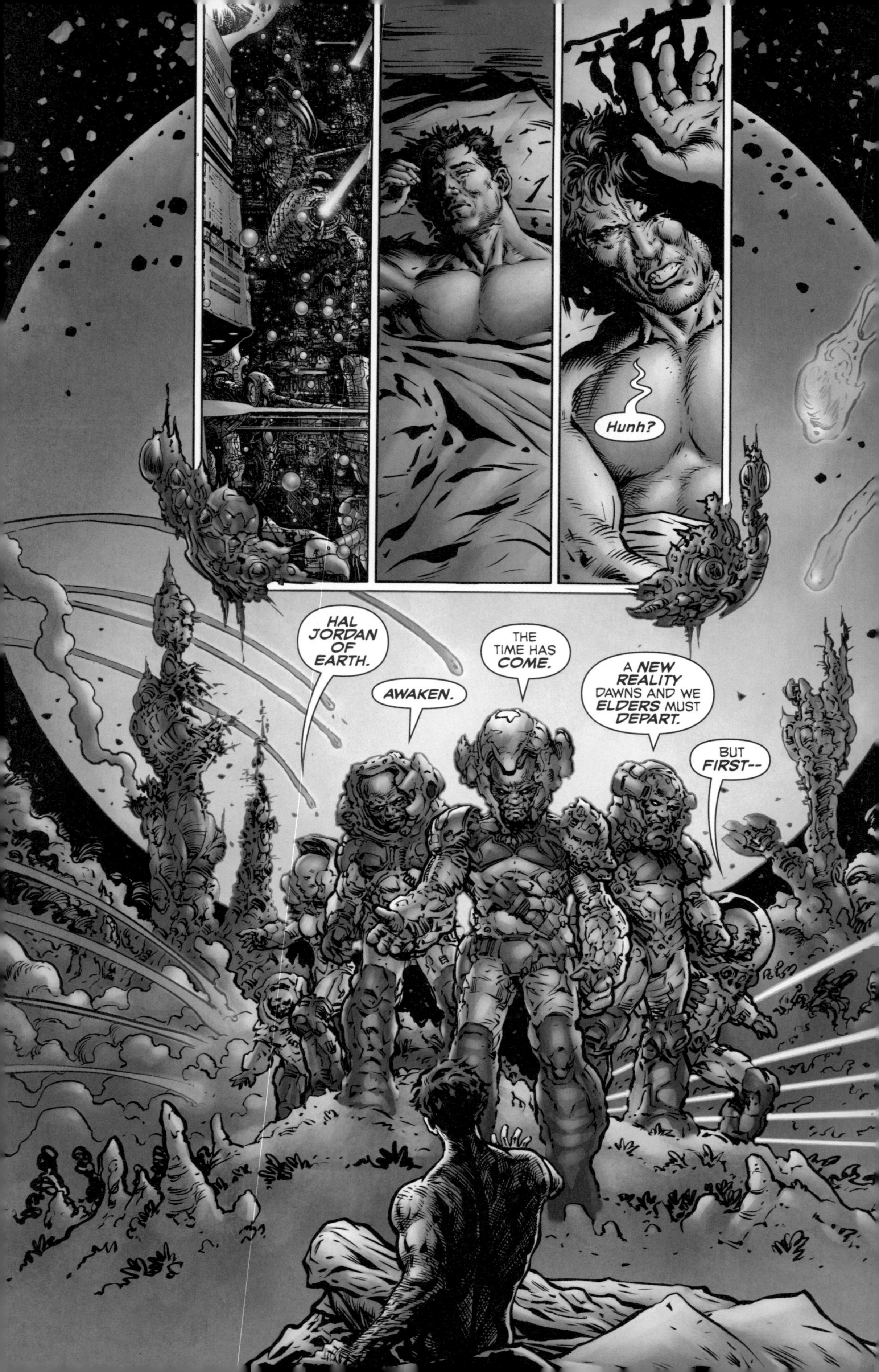
Hunh?
HAL JORDAN OF EARTH.
AWAKEN.
THE TIME HAS COME.
A NEW REALITY DAWNS AND WE ELDERS MUST DEPART.
BUT FIRST--

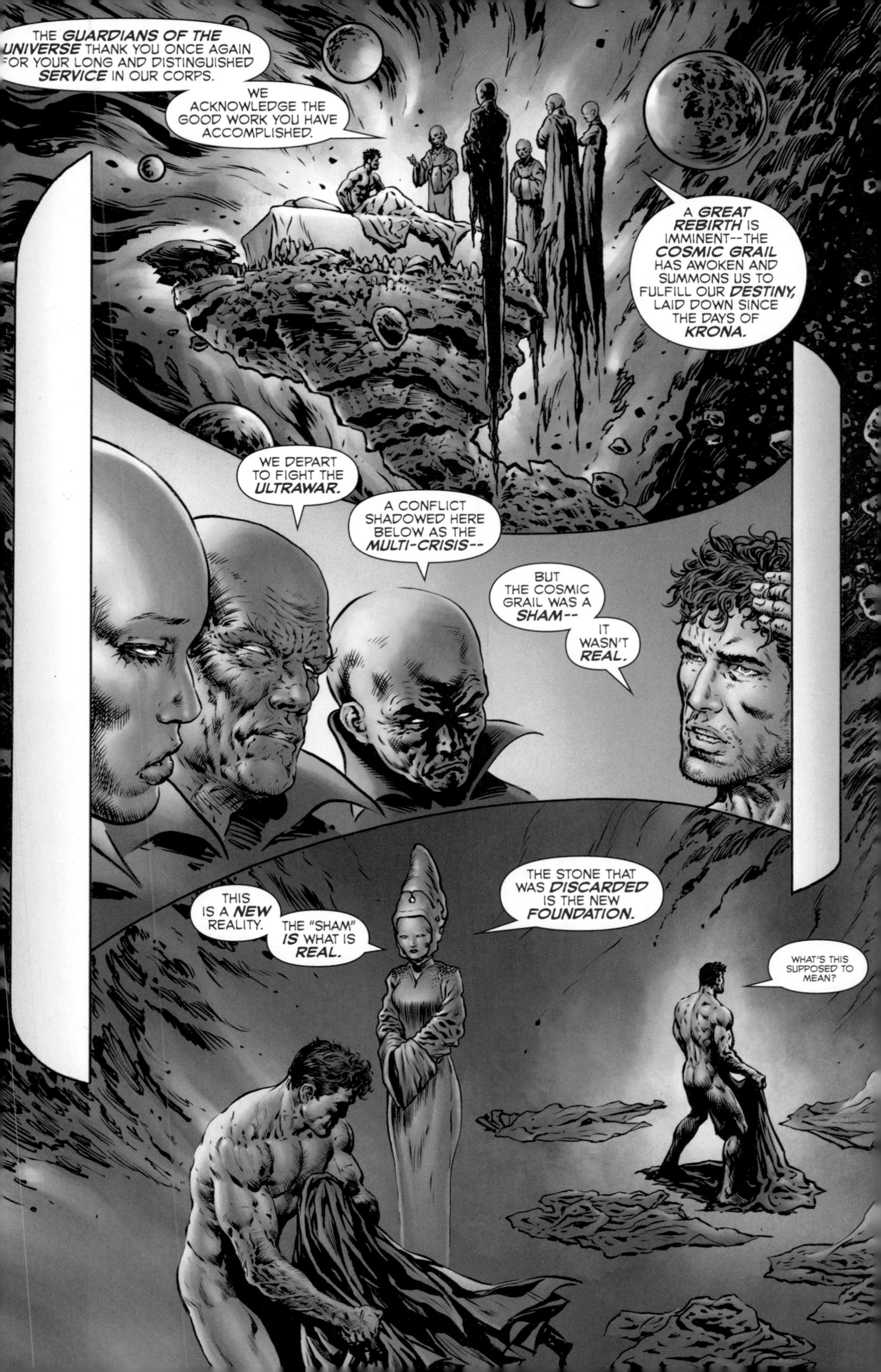
THE GUARDIANS OF THE UNIVERSE THANK YOU ONCE AGAIN FOR YOUR LONG AND DISTINGUISHED SERVICE IN OUR CORPS.
WE ACKNOWLEDGE THE GOOD WORK YOU HAVE ACCOMPLISHED.
A GREAT REBIRTH IS IMMINENT--THE COSMIC GRAIL HAS AWOKEN AND SUMMONS US TO FULFILL OUR DESTINY, LAID DOWN SINCE THE DAYS OF KRONA.
WE DEPART TO FIGHT THE ULTRAWAR.
A CONFLICT SHADOWED HERE BELOW AS THE MULTI-CRISIS--
BUT THE COSMIC GRAIL WAS A SHAM--
IT WASN'T REAL.
THIS IS A NEW REALITY.
THE "SHAM" IS WHAT IS REAL.
THE STONE THAT WAS DISCARDED IS THE NEW FOUNDATION.
WHAT'S THIS SUPPOSED TO MEAN?

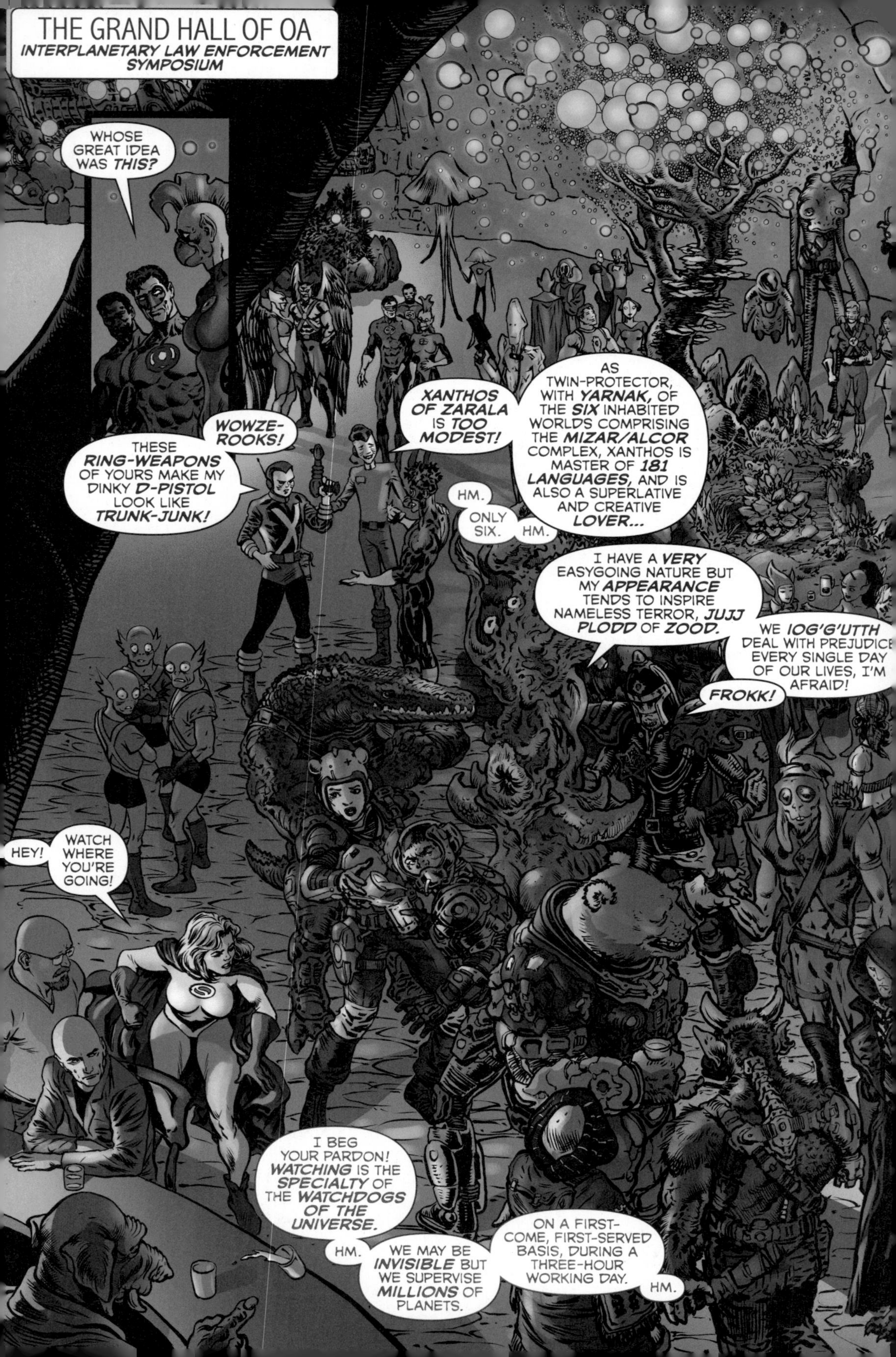
THE GRAND HALL OF OA
INTERPLANETARY LAW ENFORCEMENT SYMPOSIUM
WHOSE GREAT IDEA WAS THIS?
WOWZE-ROOKS!
THESE RING-WEAPONS OF YOURS MAKE MY DINKY D-PISTOL LOOK LIKE TRUNK-JUNK!
XANTHOS OF ZARALA IS TOO MODEST!
AS TWIN-PROTECTOR, WITH YARNAK, OF THE SIX INHABITED WORLDS COMPRISING THE MIZAR/ALCOR COMPLEX, XANTHOS IS MASTER OF 181 LANGUAGES, AND IS ALSO A SUPERLATIVE AND CREATIVE LOVER...
HM.
ONLY SIX.
HM.
I HAVE A VERY EASYGOING NATURE BUT MY APPEARANCE TENDS TO INSPIRE NAMELESS TERROR, JUJJ PLODD OF ZOOD.
WE IOG'G'UTTH DEAL WITH PREJUDICE EVERY SINGLE DAY OF OUR LIVES, I'M AFRAID!
FROKK!
HEY!
WATCH WHERE YOU'RE GOING!
I BEG YOUR PARDON! WATCHING IS THE SPECIALTY OF THE WATCHDOGS OF THE UNIVERSE.
HM.
WE MAY BE INVISIBLE BUT WE SUPERVISE MILLIONS OF PLANETS.
ON A FIRST-COME, FIRST-SERVED BASIS, DURING A THREE-HOUR WORKING DAY.
HM.

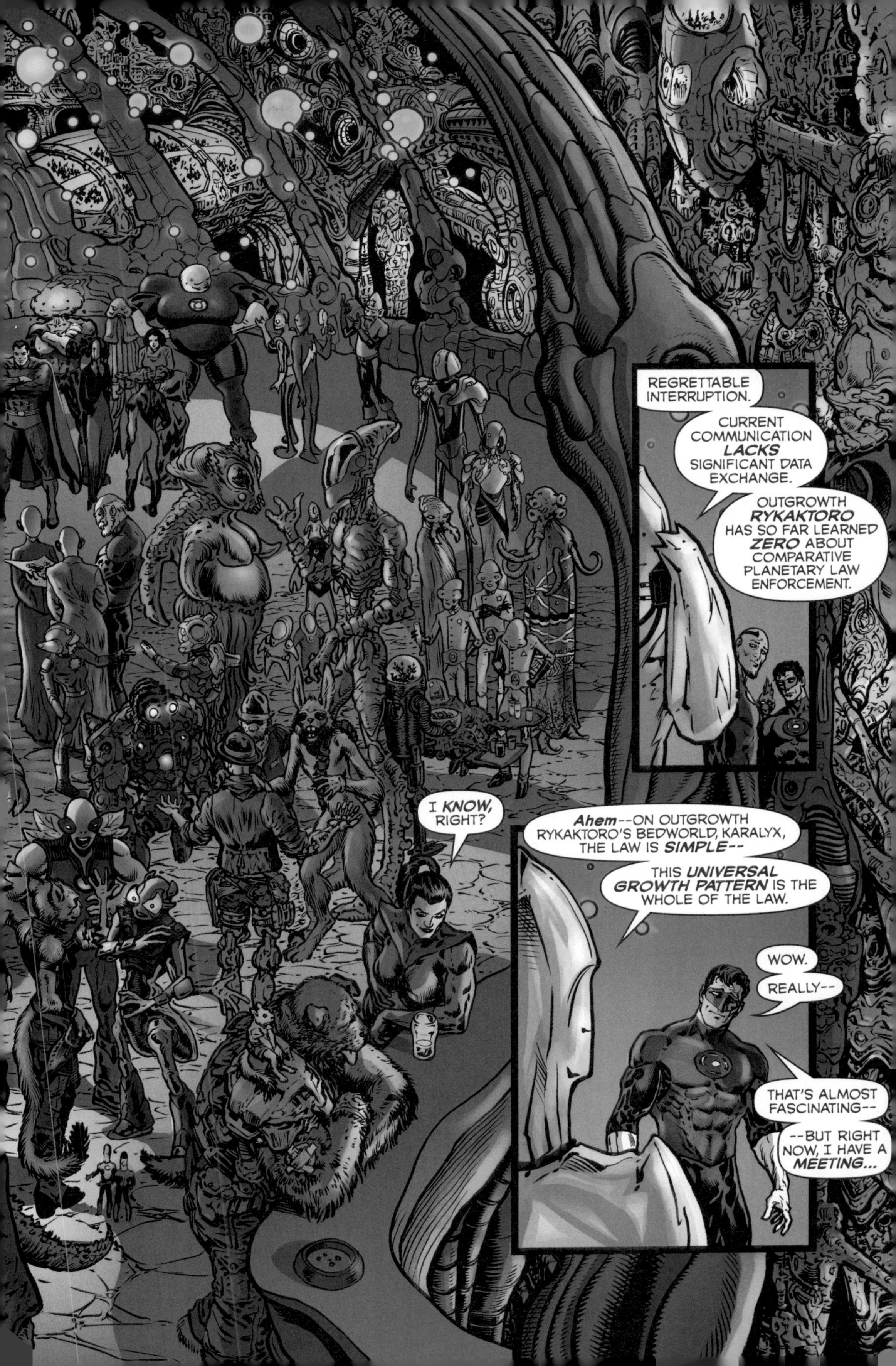
REGRETTABLE INTERRUPTION.
CURRENT COMMUNICATION **LACKS** SIGNIFICANT DATA EXCHANGE.
OUTGROWTH **RYKAKTORO** HAS SO FAR LEARNED **ZERO** ABOUT COMPARATIVE PLANETARY LAW ENFORCEMENT.
I **KNOW,** RIGHT?
Ahem--ON OUTGROWTH RYKAKTORO'S BEDWORLD, KARALYX, THE LAW IS ***SIMPLE***--
THIS ***UNIVERSAL GROWTH PATTERN*** IS THE WHOLE OF THE LAW.
WOW.
REALLY--
THAT'S ALMOST FASCINATING--
--BUT RIGHT NOW, I HAVE A ***MEETING...***

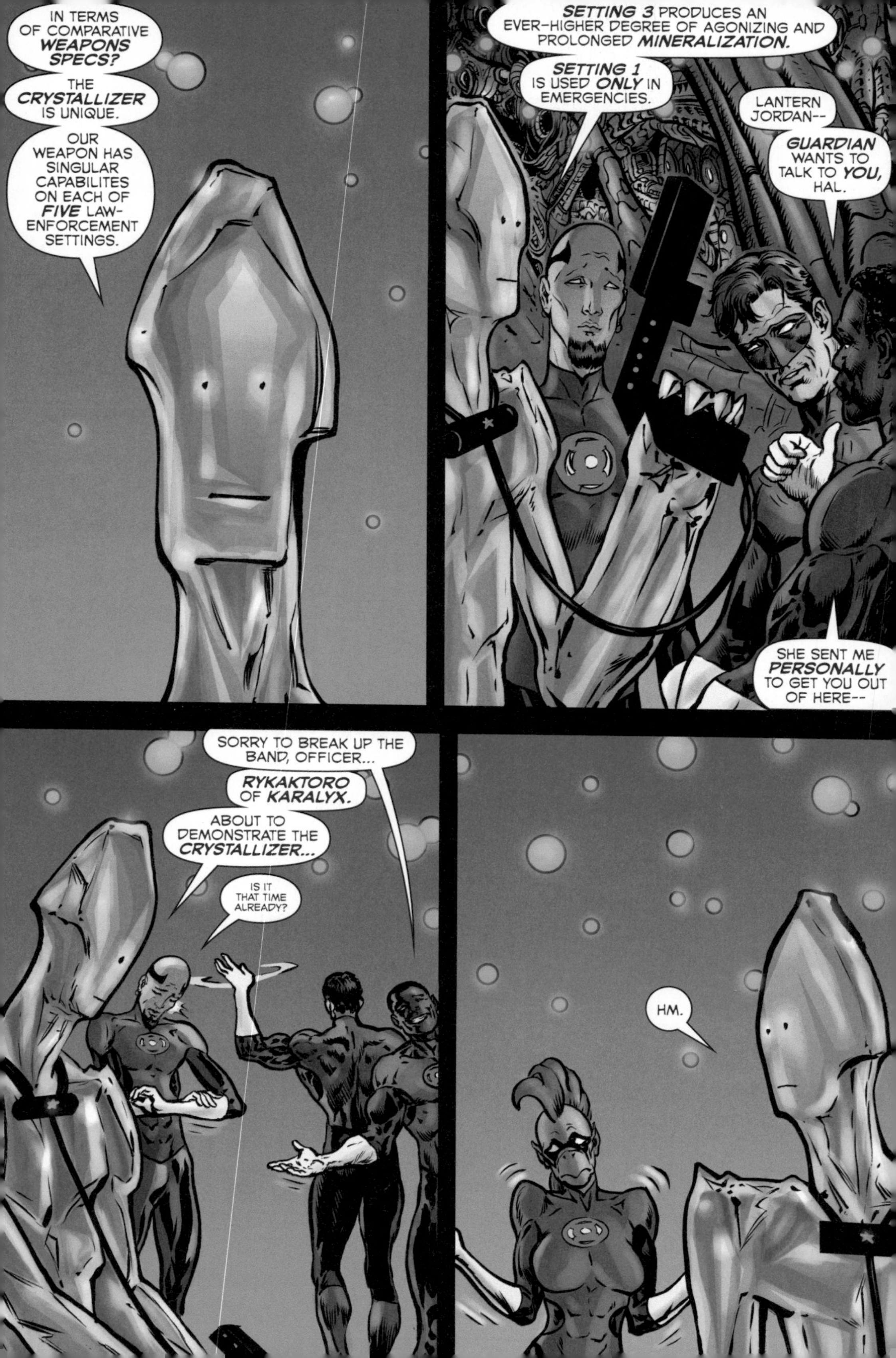
IN TERMS OF COMPARATIVE WEAPONS SPECS?
THE CRYSTALLIZER IS UNIQUE.
OUR WEAPON HAS SINGULAR CAPABILITES ON EACH OF FIVE LAW-ENFORCEMENT SETTINGS.
SETTING 3 PRODUCES AN EVER-HIGHER DEGREE OF AGONIZING AND PROLONGED MINERALIZATION.
SETTING 1 IS USED ONLY IN EMERGENCIES.
LANTERN JORDAN--
GUARDIAN WANTS TO TALK TO YOU, HAL.
SHE SENT ME PERSONALLY TO GET YOU OUT OF HERE--
SORRY TO BREAK UP THE BAND, OFFICER...
RYKAKTORO OF KARALYX.
ABOUT TO DEMONSTRATE THE CRYSTALLIZER...
IS IT THAT TIME ALREADY?
HM.

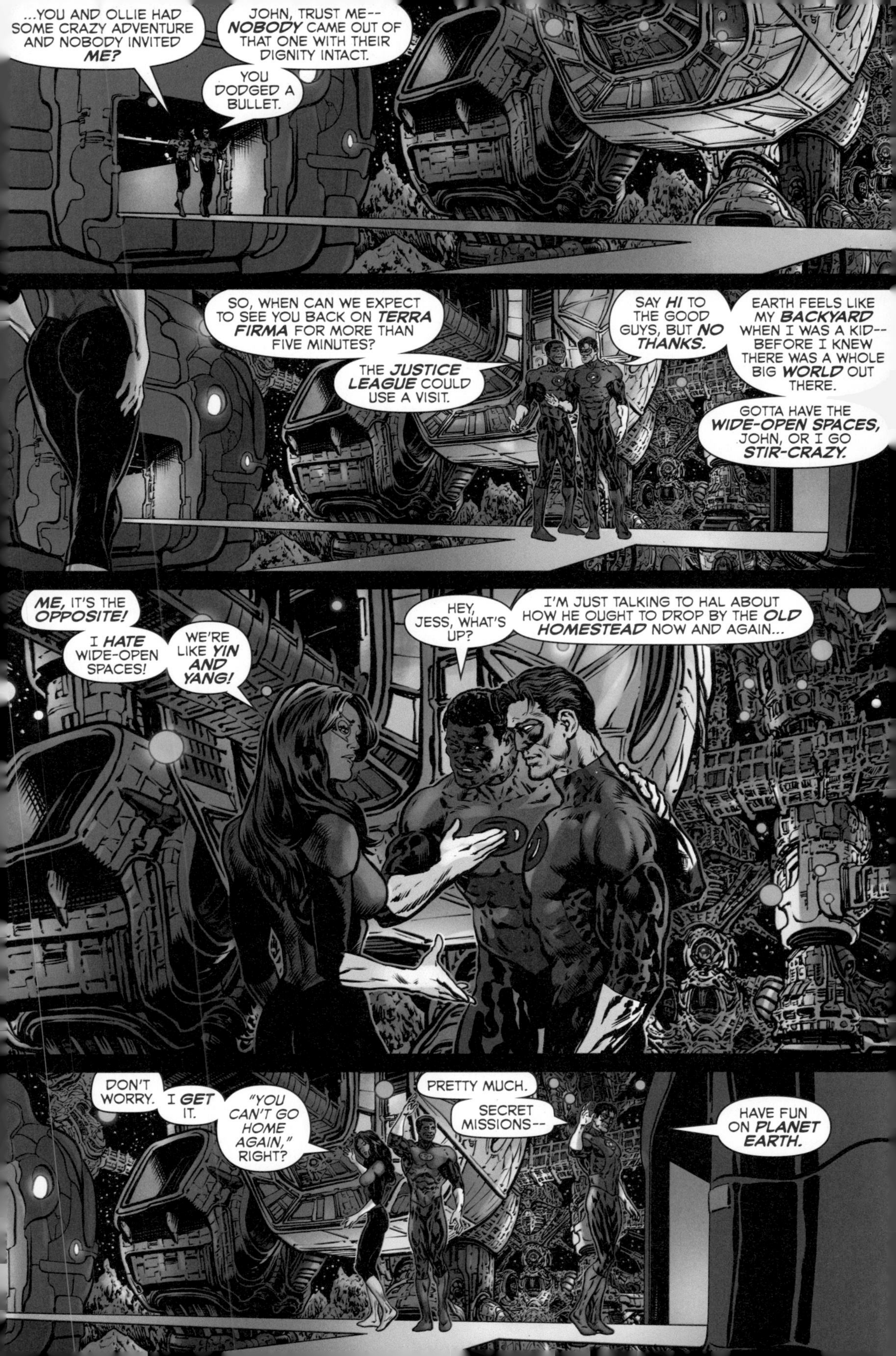
...YOU AND OLLIE HAD SOME CRAZY ADVENTURE AND NOBODY INVITED ME?
JOHN, TRUST ME-- NOBODY CAME OUT OF THAT ONE WITH THEIR DIGNITY INTACT.
YOU DODGED A BULLET.
SO, WHEN CAN WE EXPECT TO SEE YOU BACK ON TERRA FIRMA FOR MORE THAN FIVE MINUTES?
THE JUSTICE LEAGUE COULD USE A VISIT.
SAY HI TO THE GOOD GUYS, BUT NO THANKS.
EARTH FEELS LIKE MY BACKYARD WHEN I WAS A KID-- BEFORE I KNEW THERE WAS A WHOLE BIG WORLD OUT THERE.
GOTTA HAVE THE WIDE-OPEN SPACES, JOHN, OR I GO STIR-CRAZY.
ME, IT'S THE OPPOSITE!
I HATE WIDE-OPEN SPACES!
WE'RE LIKE YIN AND YANG!
HEY, JESS, WHAT'S UP?
I'M JUST TALKING TO HAL ABOUT HOW HE OUGHT TO DROP BY THE OLD HOMESTEAD NOW AND AGAIN...
DON'T WORRY.
I GET IT.
"YOU CAN'T GO HOME AGAIN," RIGHT?
PRETTY MUCH.
SECRET MISSIONS--
HAVE FUN ON PLANET EARTH.

THAT SEEMED POINTLESS.

HOW MUCH CAN WE *LEARN* FROM SOME SMALL-TIME INTERPLANETARY COPS?

OUR PLAN IS TO INDUCT A NUMBER OF *NEW* LANTERNS TO THE CORPS, JORDAN.

SOME OF THESE *LOCAL* SPACE AGENCIES WERE RECOMMENDED AS FERTILE GROUNDS FOR *RECRUITMENT,* WHICH BRINGS ME TO THE MATTER AT HAND--

--THE TIME HAS COME TO SEEK OUT *REPLACEMENTS* FOR OUR *DEPARTED* GUARDIANS.

REPLACEMENTS? HOW EASY IS *THAT?*

ANCIENT, WISE IMMORTALS DON'T EXACTLY GROW ON TREES.

TRUE-- THEY DO NOT.

THEY GROW IN THE *BODY-ORCHARDS OF MOTHER JUNA* ON THE PLANET *MALTUS.*

YOUR TRIP HAS BEEN ARRANGED

YOUNG GUARDIANS

GRANT MORRISON, writer
LIAM SHARP, artist & cover
STEVE OLIFF, colorist
TOM ORZECHOWSKI, letterer
JESSICA BERBEY, assistant editor
JESSICA CHEN, associate editor
BRIAN CUNNINGHAM, editor

YOUR *PARTNER* ASSIGNED.

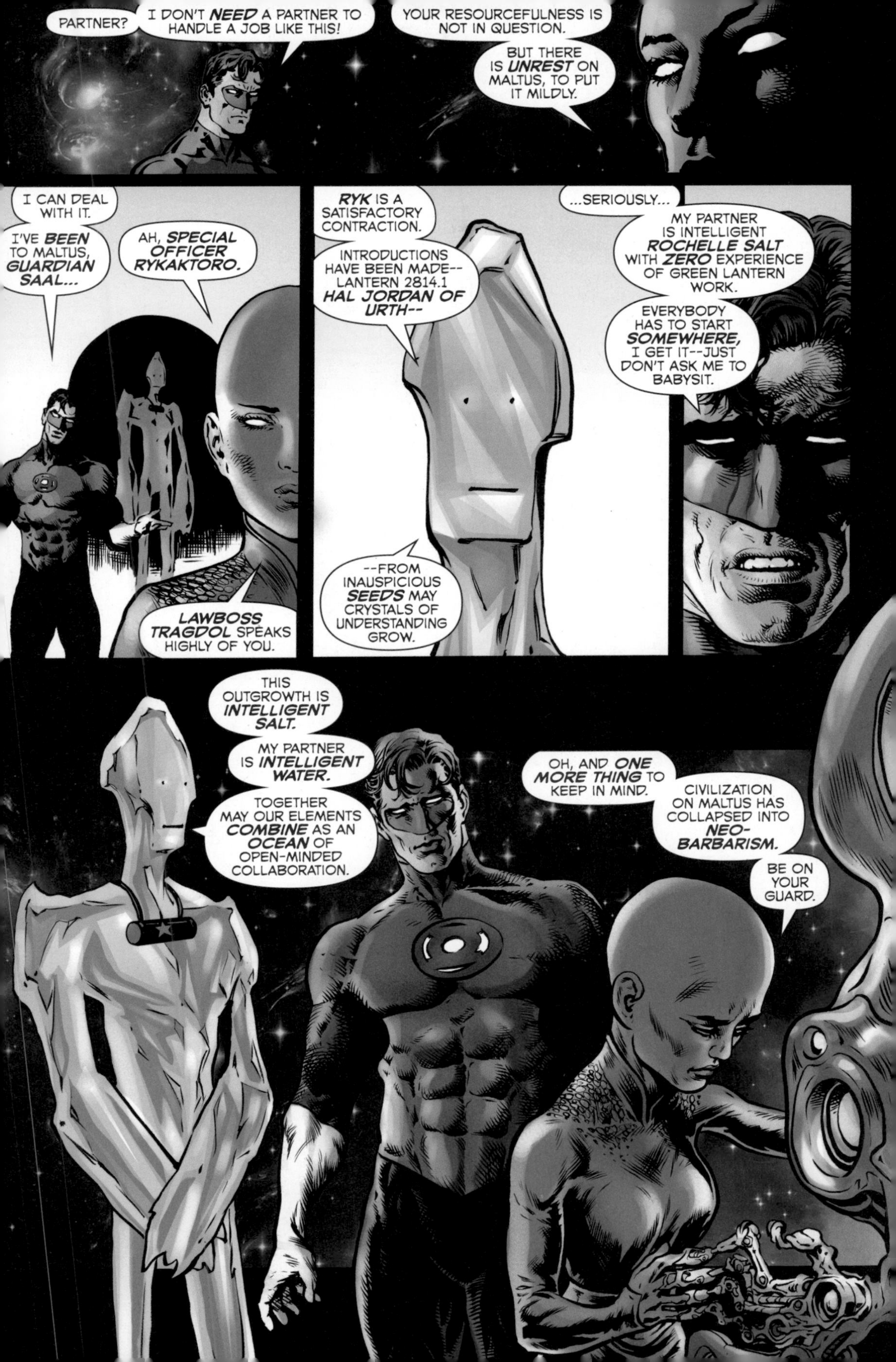
PARTNER?
I DON'T NEED A PARTNER TO HANDLE A JOB LIKE THIS!
YOUR RESOURCEFULNESS IS NOT IN QUESTION.
BUT THERE IS UNREST ON MALTUS, TO PUT IT MILDLY.
I CAN DEAL WITH IT.
I'VE BEEN TO MALTUS, GUARDIAN SAAL...
AH, SPECIAL OFFICER RYKAKTORO.
LAWBOSS TRAGDOL SPEAKS HIGHLY OF YOU.
RYK IS A SATISFACTORY CONTRACTION.
INTRODUCTIONS HAVE BEEN MADE-- LANTERN 2814.1 HAL JORDAN OF URTH--
--FROM INAUSPICIOUS SEEDS MAY CRYSTALS OF UNDERSTANDING GROW.
...SERIOUSLY...
MY PARTNER IS INTELLIGENT ROCHELLE SALT WITH ZERO EXPERIENCE OF GREEN LANTERN WORK.
EVERYBODY HAS TO START SOMEWHERE, I GET IT--JUST DON'T ASK ME TO BABYSIT.
THIS OUTGROWTH IS INTELLIGENT SALT.
MY PARTNER IS INTELLIGENT WATER.
TOGETHER MAY OUR ELEMENTS COMBINE AS AN OCEAN OF OPEN-MINDED COLLABORATION.
OH, AND ONE MORE THING TO KEEP IN MIND.
CIVILIZATION ON MALTUS HAS COLLAPSED INTO NEO-BARBARISM.
BE ON YOUR GUARD.

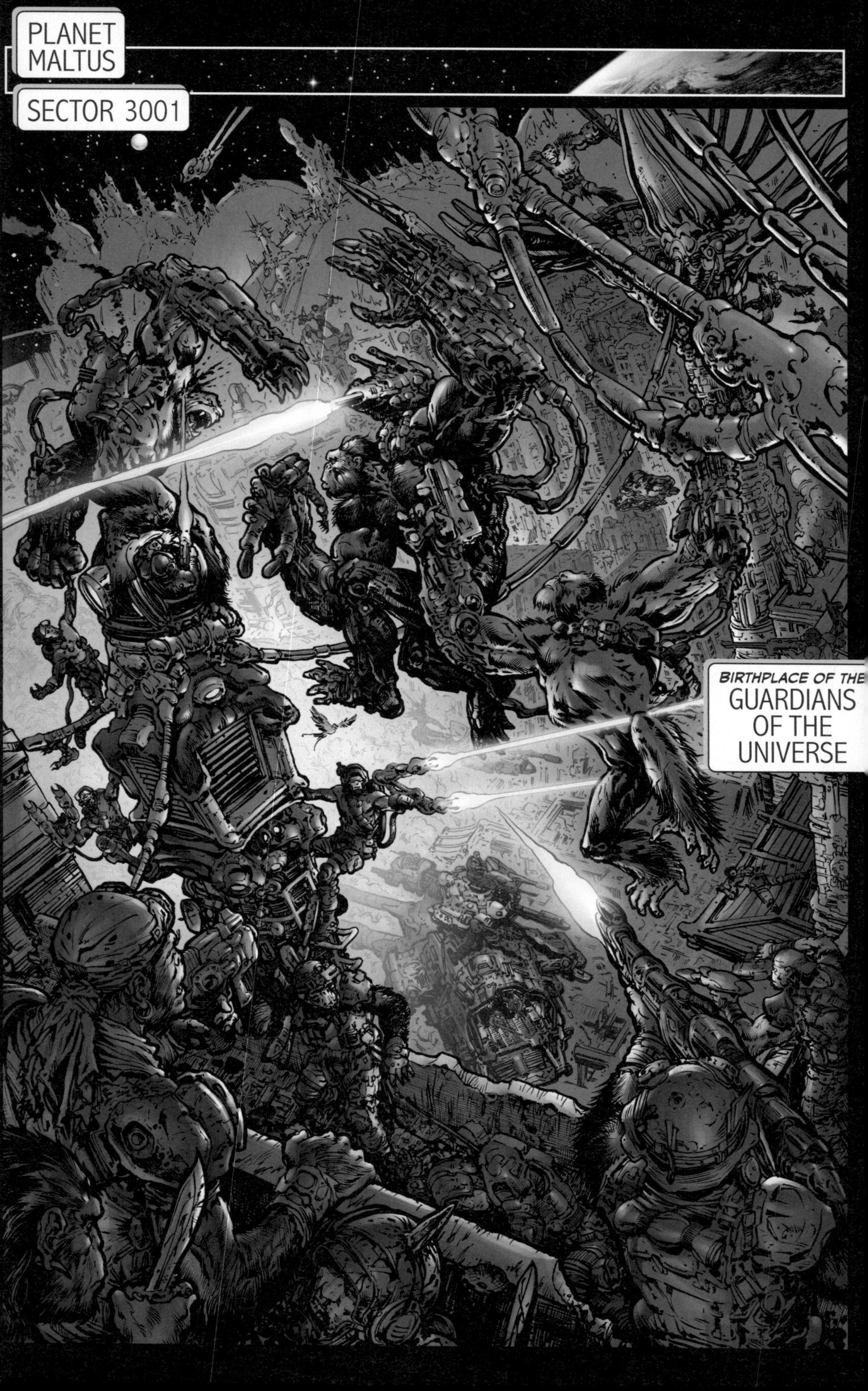
PLANET MALTUS
SECTOR 3001
BIRTHPLACE OF THE GUARDIANS OF THE UNIVERSE

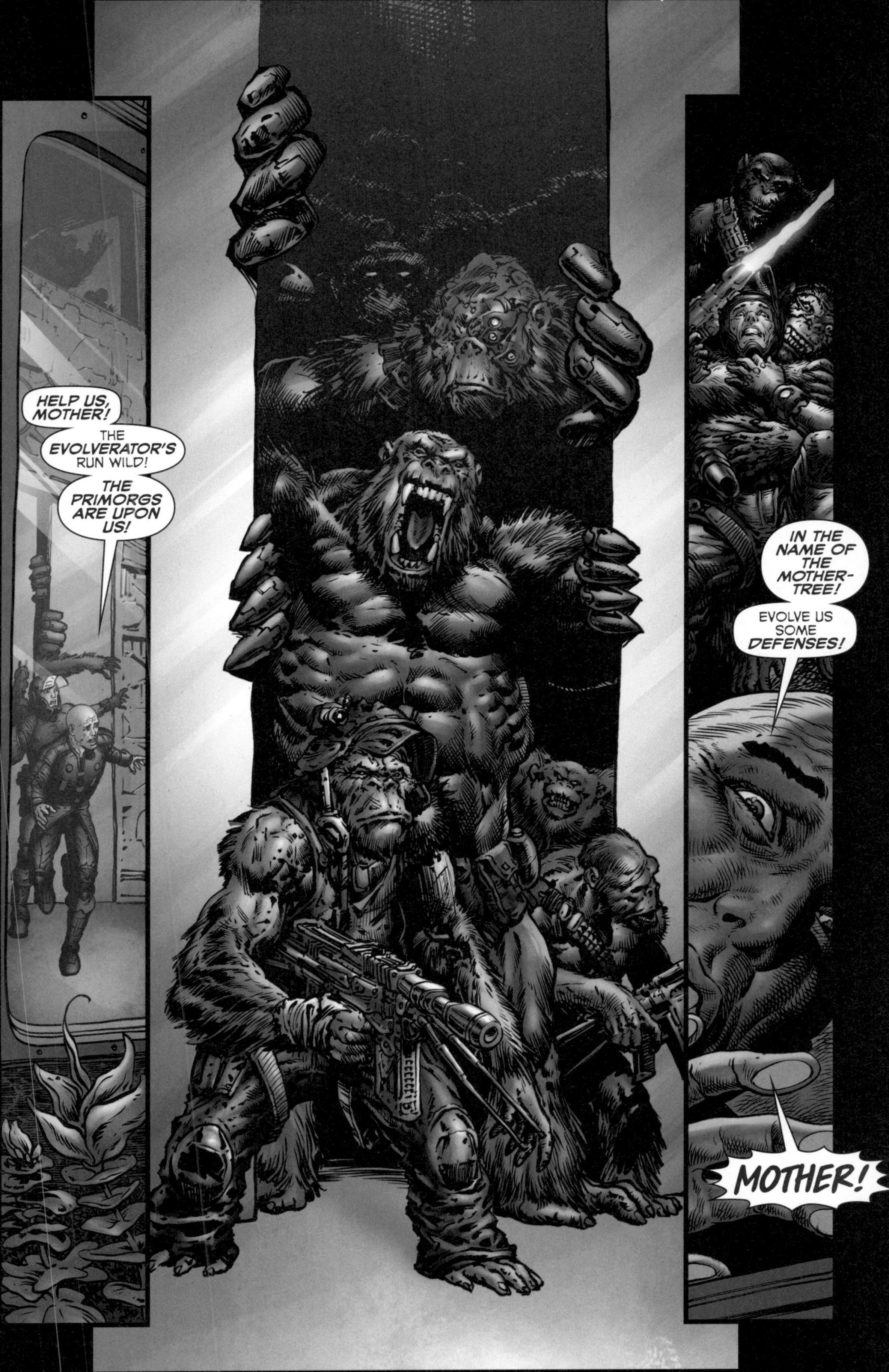
HELP US, MOTHER!
THE EVOLVERATOR'S RUN WILD!
THE PRIMORGS ARE UPON US!
IN THE NAME OF THE MOTHER-TREE!
EVOLVE US SOME DEFENSES!
MOTHER!

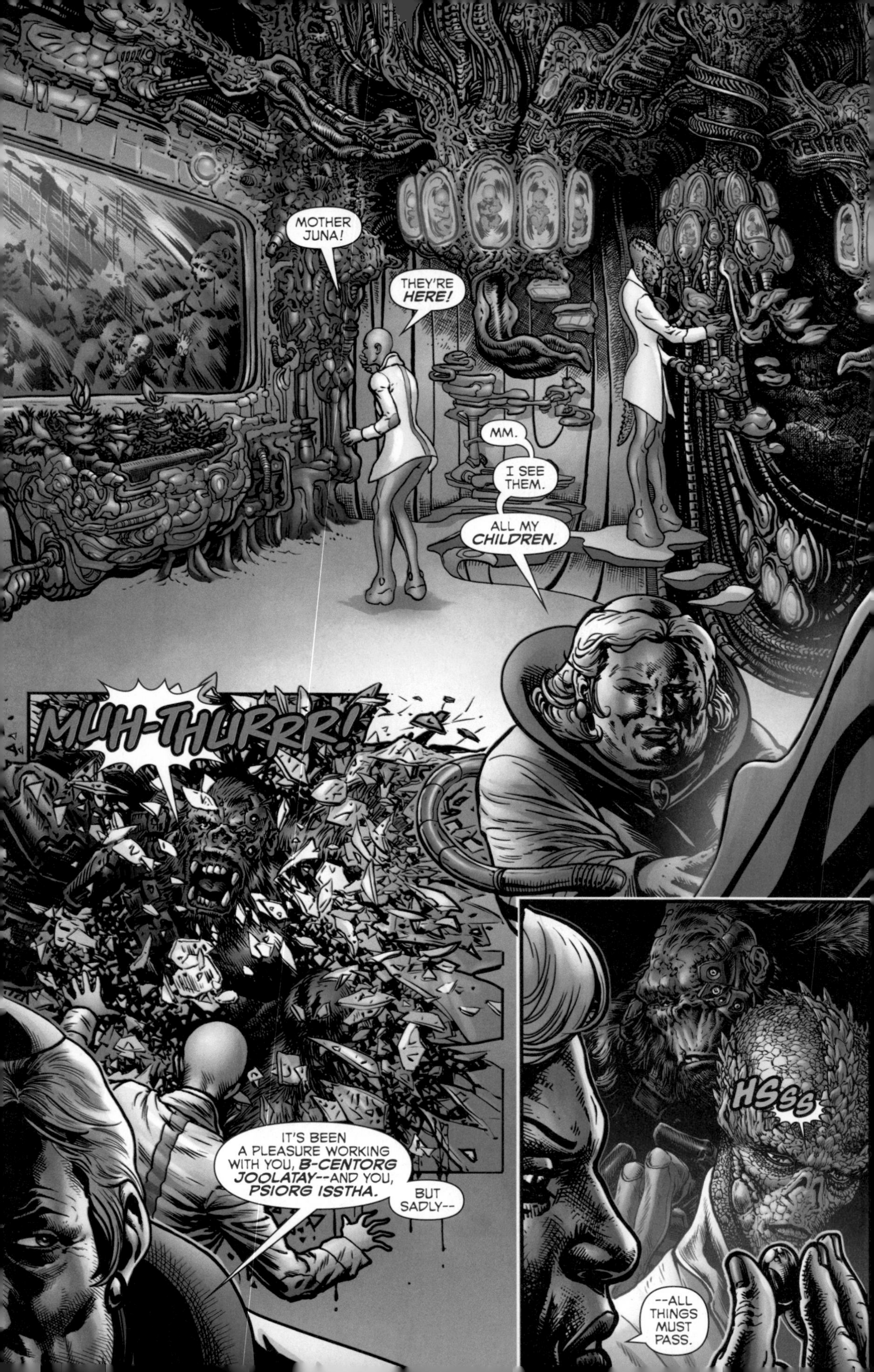
MOTHER JUNA!
THEY'RE HERE!
MM.
I SEE THEM.
ALL MY CHILDREN.
MUH-THURRR!
IT'S BEEN A PLEASURE WORKING WITH YOU, B-CENTORG JOOLATAY--AND YOU, PSIORG ISSTHA.
BUT SADLY--
HSSS
--ALL THINGS MUST PASS.

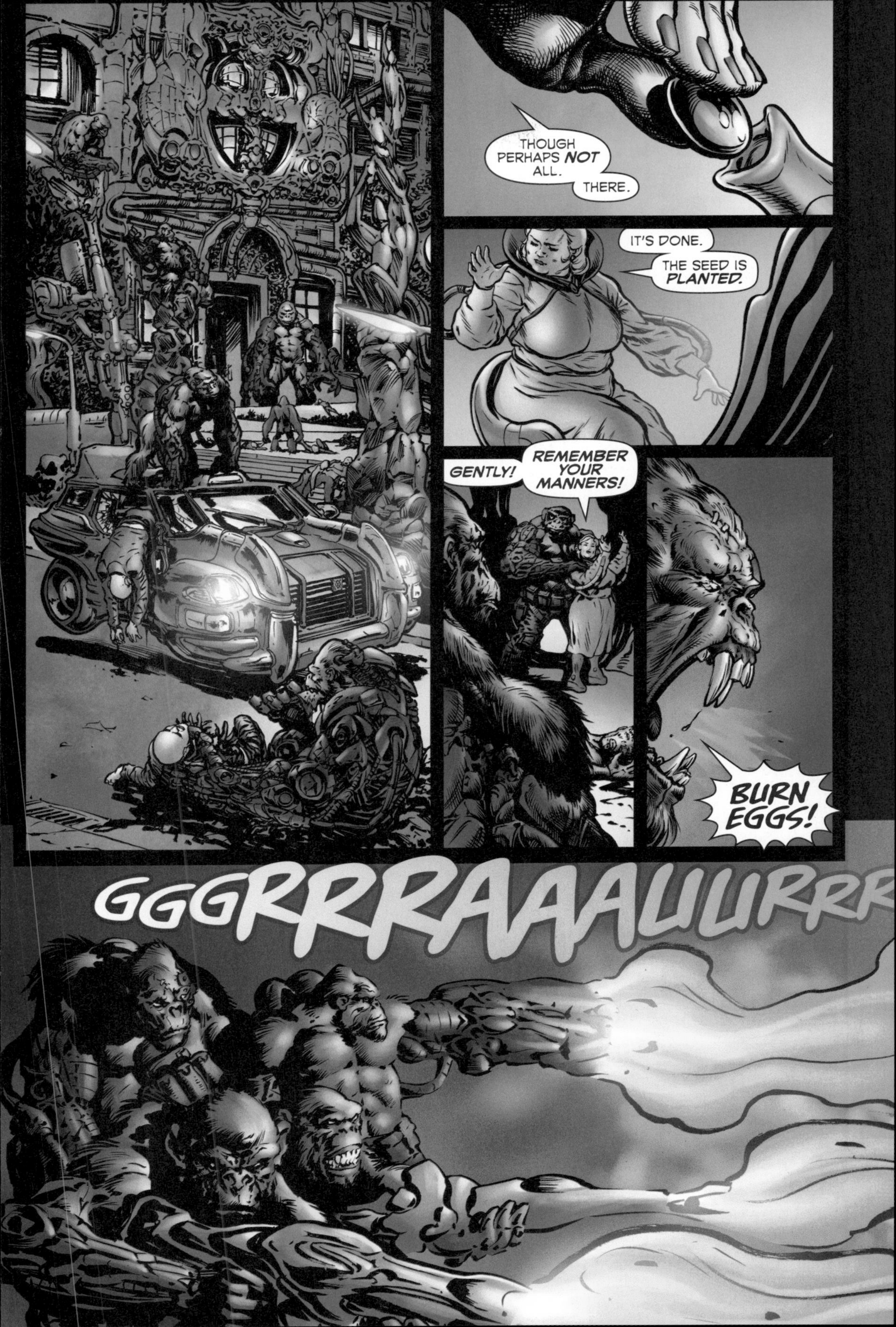
THOUGH PERHAPS NOT ALL.
THERE.
IT'S DONE.
THE SEED IS PLANTED.
GENTLY!
REMEMBER YOUR MANNERS!
BURN EGGS!
GGGRRRAAAAULRRR

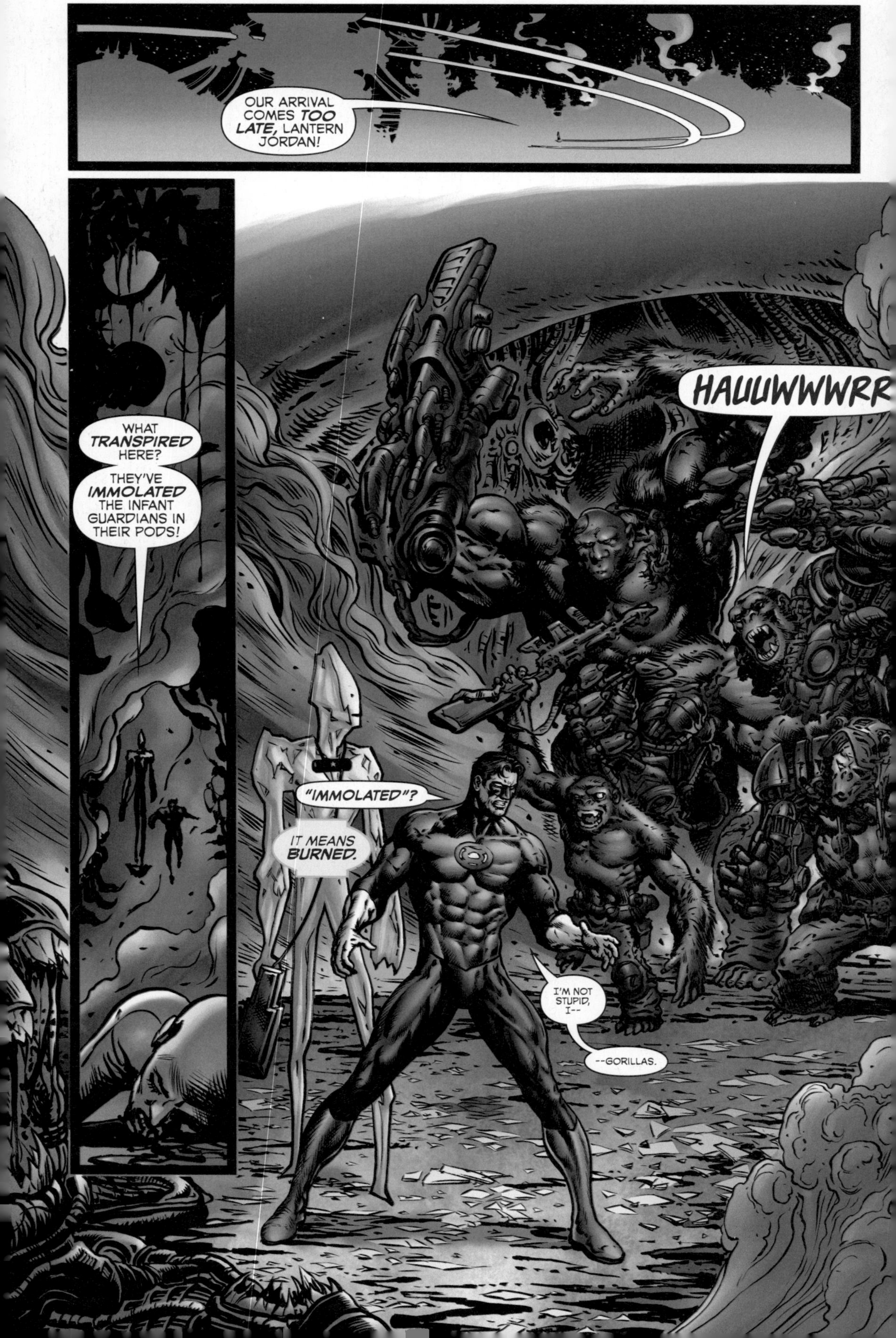
OUR ARRIVAL COMES TOO LATE, LANTERN JORDAN!
WHAT TRANSPIRED HERE?
THEY'VE IMMOLATED THE INFANT GUARDIANS IN THEIR PODS!
"IMMOLATED"?
IT MEANS BURNED.
I'M NOT STUPID, I--
--GORILLAS.
HAUUWWWRR

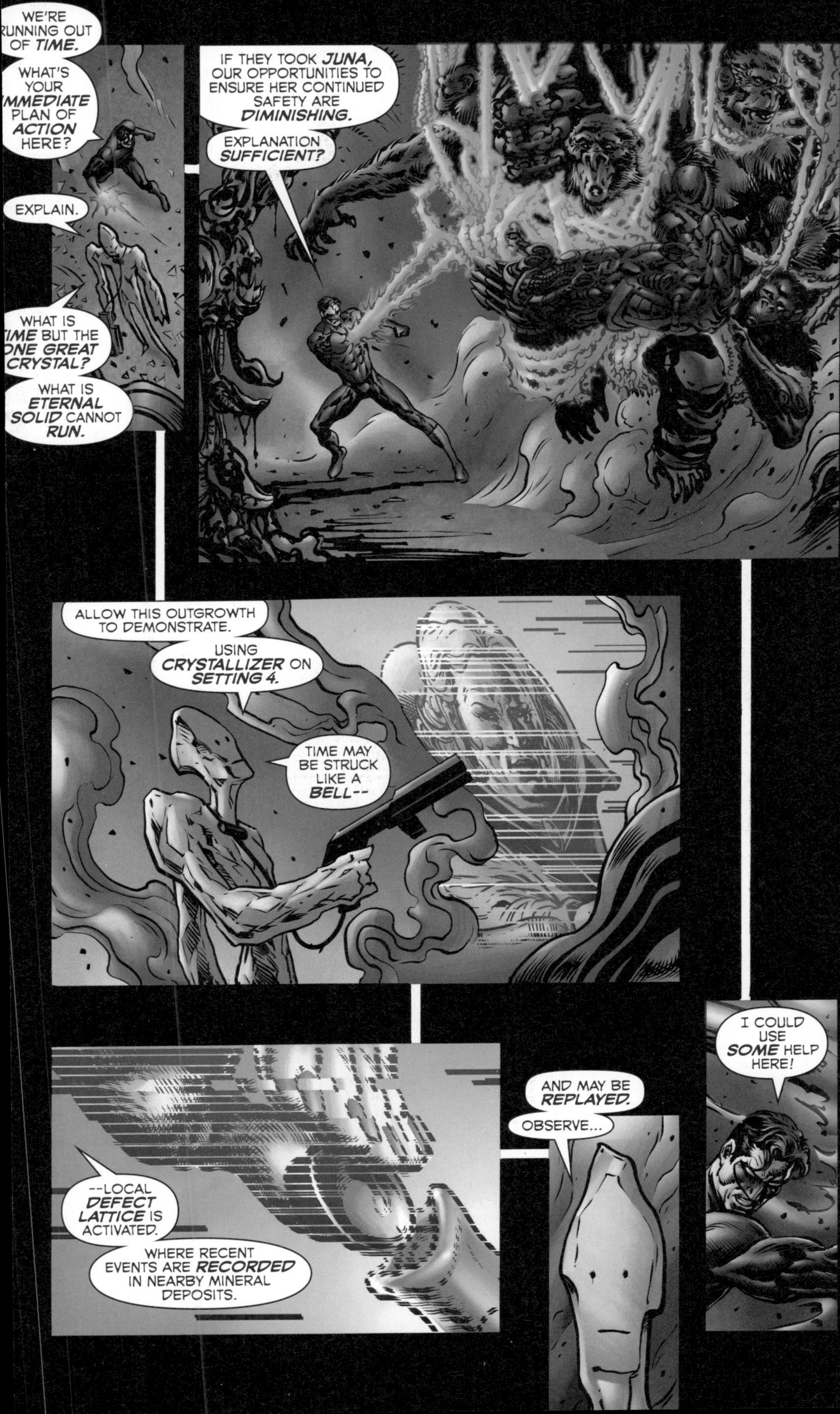
WE'RE RUNNING OUT OF TIME.
WHAT'S YOUR IMMEDIATE PLAN OF ACTION HERE?
EXPLAIN.
IF THEY TOOK JUNA, OUR OPPORTUNITIES TO ENSURE HER CONTINUED SAFETY ARE DIMINISHING.
EXPLANATION SUFFICIENT?
WHAT IS TIME BUT THE ONE GREAT CRYSTAL?
WHAT IS ETERNAL SOLID CANNOT RUN.
ALLOW THIS OUTGROWTH TO DEMONSTRATE.
USING CRYSTALLIZER ON SETTING 4.
TIME MAY BE STRUCK LIKE A BELL--
--LOCAL DEFECT LATTICE IS ACTIVATED.
WHERE RECENT EVENTS ARE RECORDED IN NEARBY MINERAL DEPOSITS.
AND MAY BE REPLAYED.
OBSERVE...
I COULD USE SOME HELP HERE!

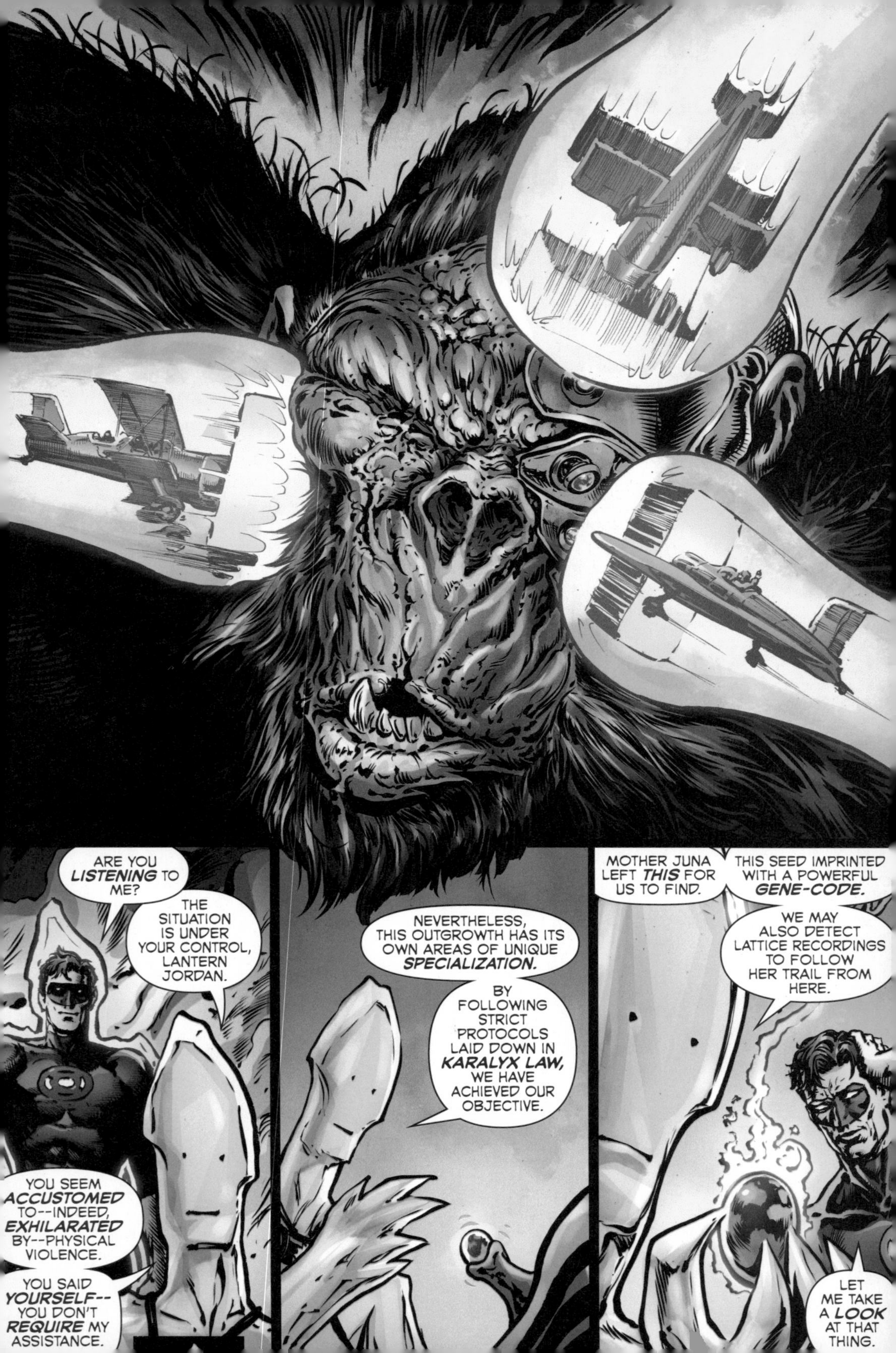

ARE YOU *LISTENING* TO ME?
THE SITUATION IS UNDER YOUR CONTROL, LANTERN JORDAN.
YOU SEEM *ACCUSTOMED* TO--INDEED, *EXHILARATED* BY--PHYSICAL VIOLENCE.
YOU SAID *YOURSELF--* YOU DON'T *REQUIRE* MY ASSISTANCE.
NEVERTHELESS, THIS OUTGROWTH HAS ITS OWN AREAS OF UNIQUE *SPECIALIZATION.*
BY FOLLOWING STRICT PROTOCOLS LAID DOWN IN *KARALYX LAW,* WE HAVE ACHIEVED OUR OBJECTIVE.
MOTHER JUNA LEFT *THIS* FOR US TO FIND.
THIS SEED IMPRINTED WITH A POWERFUL *GENE-CODE.*
WE MAY ALSO DETECT LATTICE RECORDINGS TO FOLLOW HER TRAIL FROM HERE.
LET ME TAKE A *LOOK* AT THAT THING.

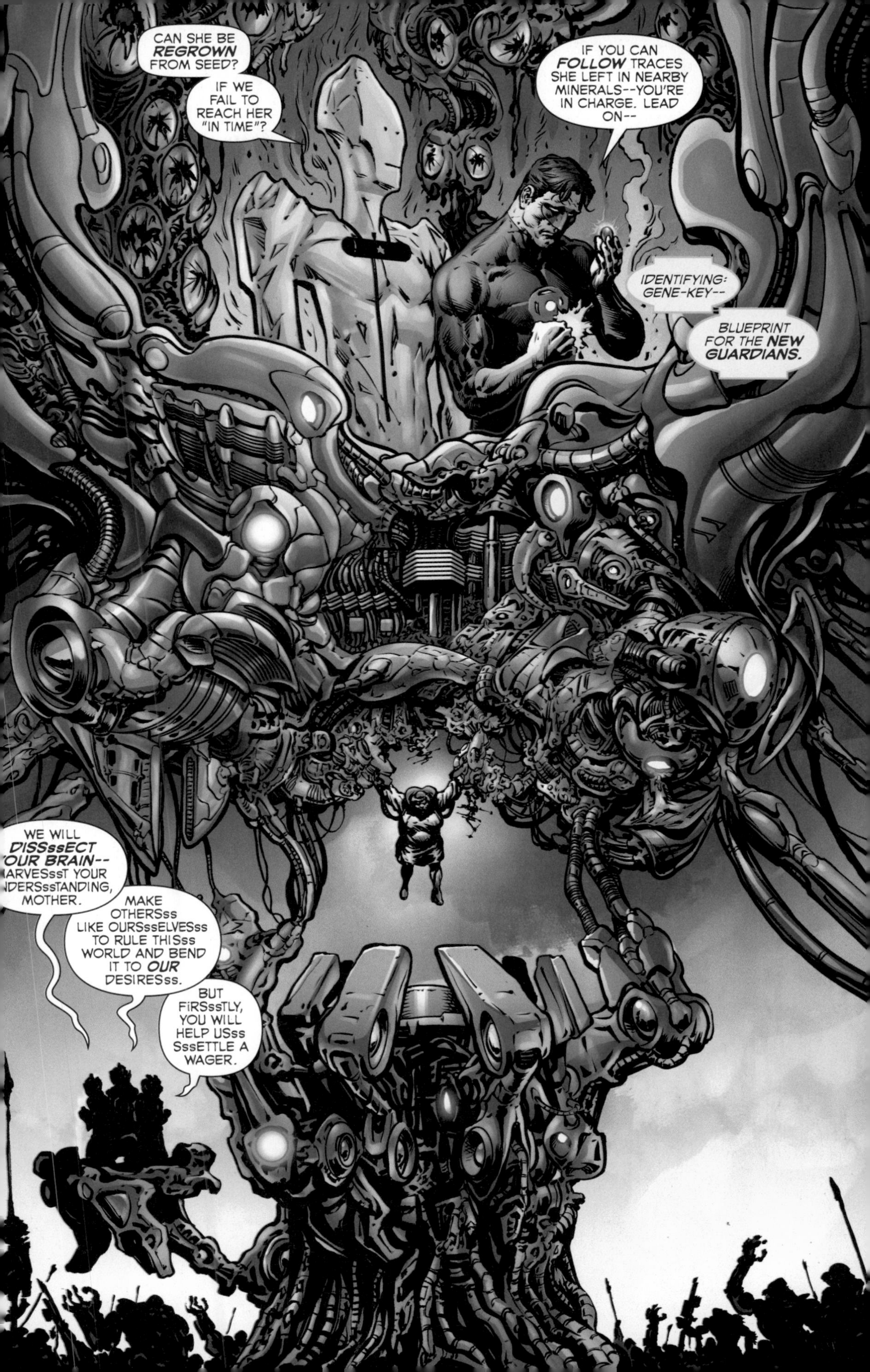
CAN SHE BE **REGROWN** FROM SEED?
IF WE FAIL TO REACH HER "IN TIME"?
IF YOU CAN **FOLLOW** TRACES SHE LEFT IN NEARBY MINERALS--YOU'RE IN CHARGE. LEAD ON--
IDENTIFYING: GENE-KEY--
*BLUEPRINT FOR THE **NEW GUARDIANS.***
WE WILL ***DISSssECT*** ***OUR BRAIN--*** ARVESSsT YOUR NDERSSsTANDING, MOTHER.
MAKE OTHERSss LIKE OURSssELVESss TO RULE THISss WORLD AND BEND IT TO ***OUR*** DESIRESss.
BUT FiRSssTLY, YOU WILL HELP USss SssETTLE A WAGER.

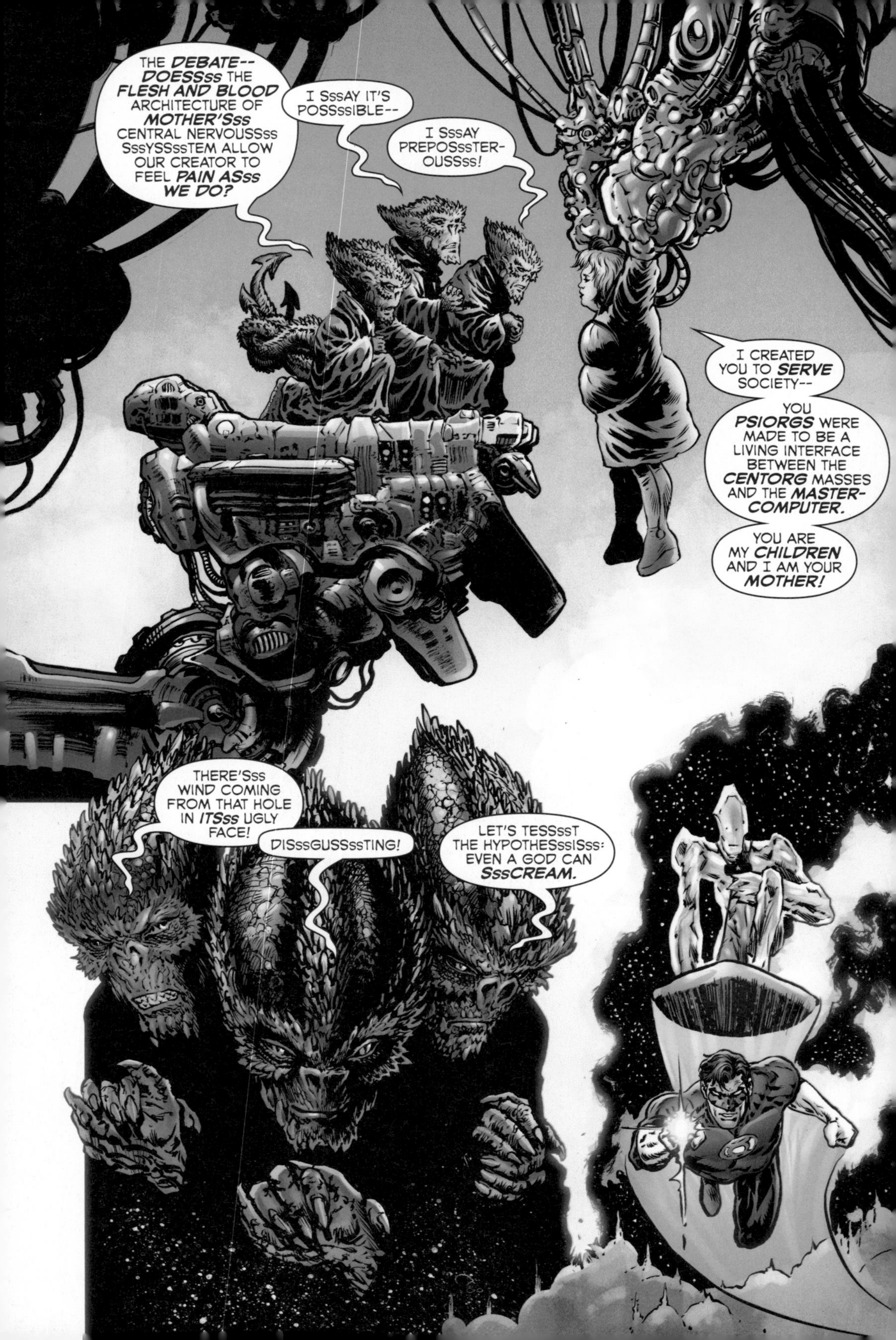
THE DEBATE-- DOESSss THE FLESH AND BLOOD ARCHITECTURE OF MOTHER'Sss CENTRAL NERVOUSSss SssYSSssTEM ALLOW OUR CREATOR TO FEEL PAIN ASss WE DO?
I SssAY IT'S POSSssIBLE--
I SssAY PREPOSssTER-OUSSss!
I CREATED YOU TO SERVE SOCIETY--
YOU PSIORGS WERE MADE TO BE A LIVING INTERFACE BETWEEN THE CENTORG MASSES AND THE MASTER-COMPUTER.
YOU ARE MY CHILDREN AND I AM YOUR MOTHER!
THERE'Sss WIND COMING FROM THAT HOLE IN ITSss UGLY FACE!
DISssGUSSssTING!
LET'S TESSssT THE HYPOTHESssISss: EVEN A GOD CAN SssCREAM.

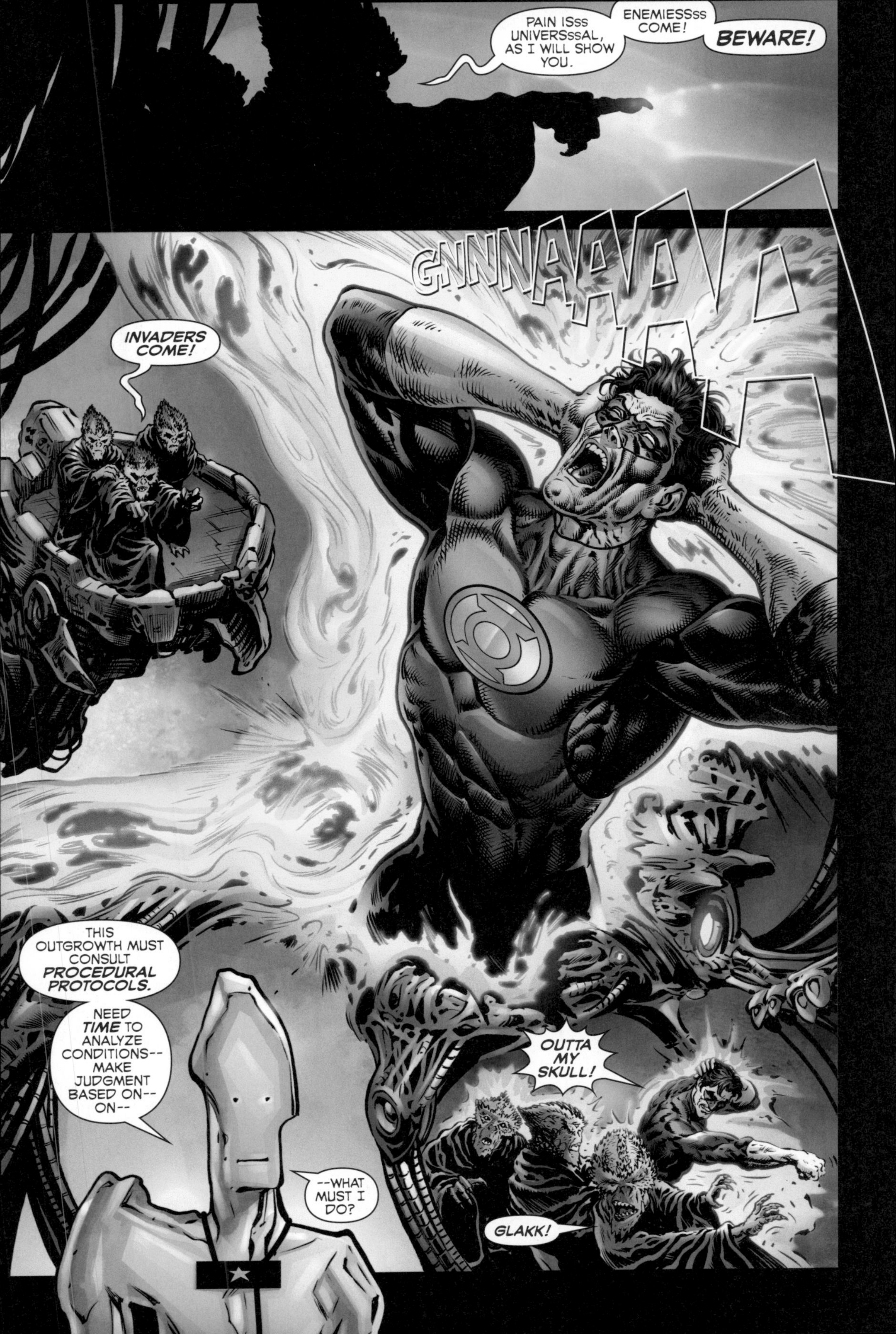

PAIN ISss UNIVERSssAL, AS I WILL SHOW YOU.
ENEMIESSSss COME!
BEWARE!
GNNNAAAAAAAA
INVADERS COME!
THIS OUTGROWTH MUST CONSULT PROCEDURAL PROTOCOLS.
NEED TIME TO ANALYZE CONDITIONS-- MAKE JUDGMENT BASED ON-- ON--
--WHAT MUST I DO?
OUTTA MY SKULL!
GLAKK!

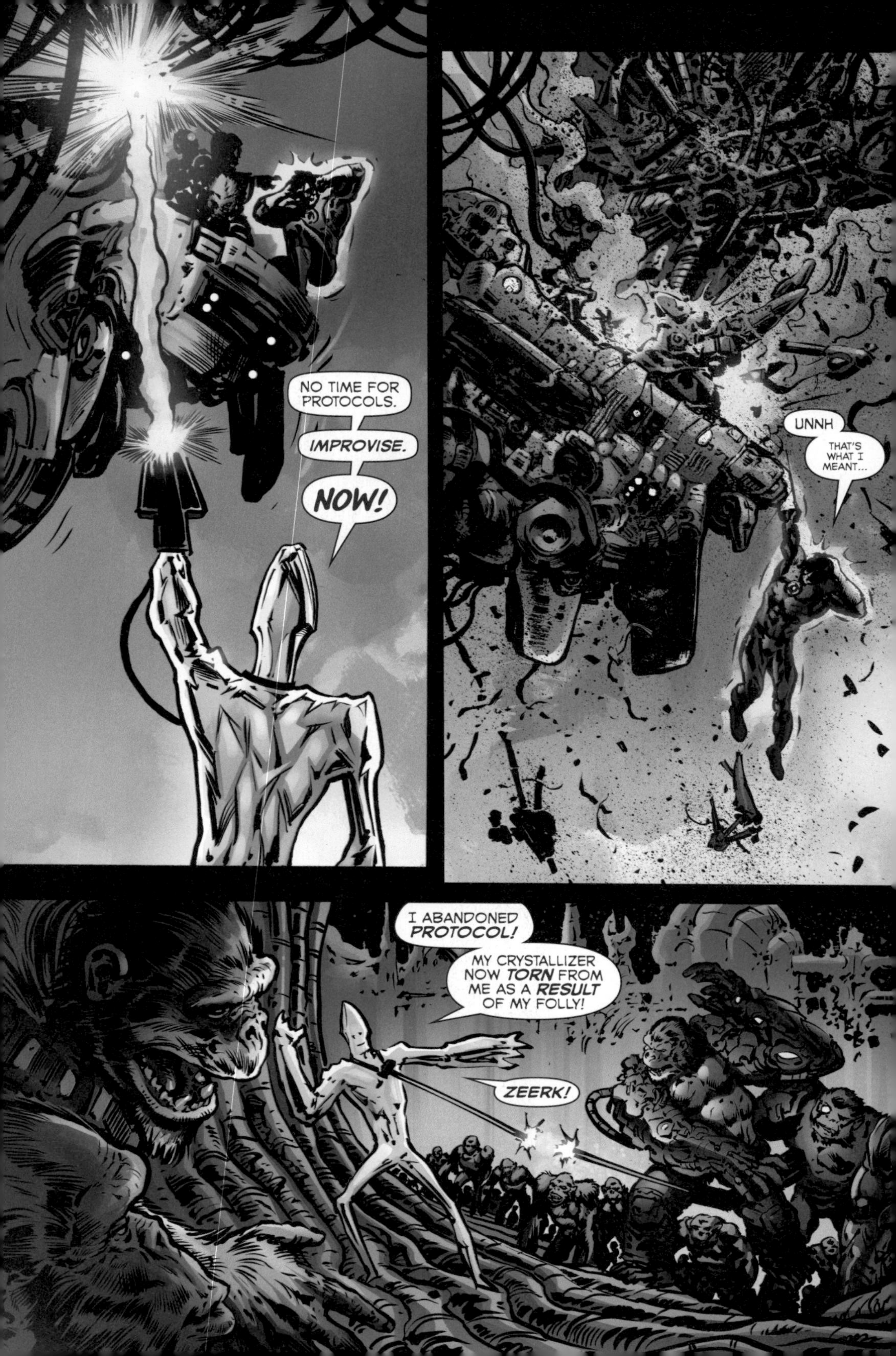
NO TIME FOR PROTOCOLS.
IMPROVISE.
NOW!
UNNH
THAT'S WHAT I MEANT...
I ABANDONED PROTOCOL!
MY CRYSTALLIZER NOW TORN FROM ME AS A RESULT OF MY FOLLY!
ZEERK!

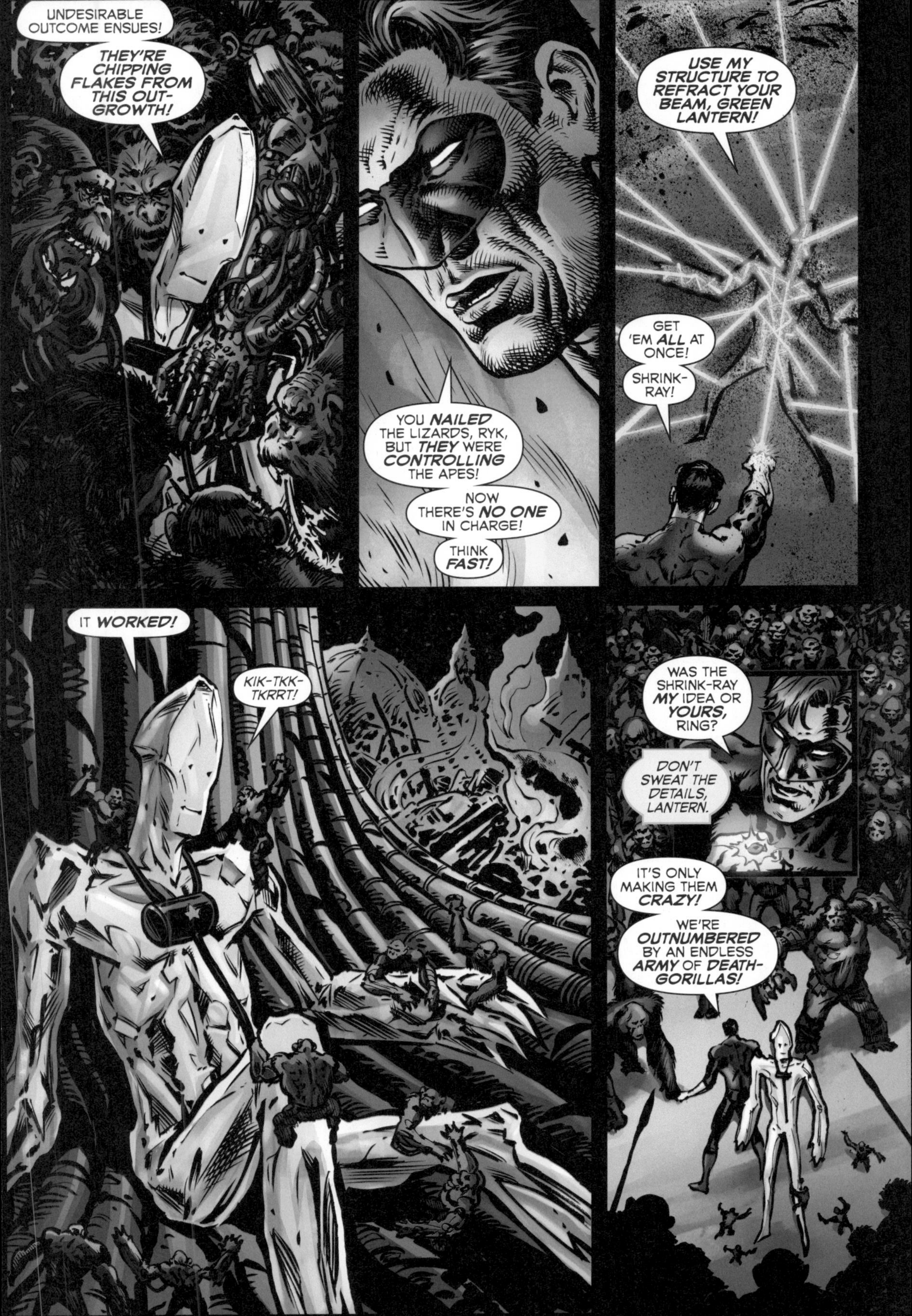
UNDESIRABLE OUTCOME ENSUES!
THEY'RE CHIPPING FLAKES FROM THIS OUT-GROWTH!
YOU NAILED THE LIZARDS, RYK, BUT THEY WERE CONTROLLING THE APES!
NOW THERE'S NO ONE IN CHARGE!
THINK FAST!
USE MY STRUCTURE TO REFRACT YOUR BEAM, GREEN LANTERN!
GET 'EM ALL AT ONCE!
SHRINK-RAY!
IT WORKED!
KIK-TKK-TKRRT!
WAS THE SHRINK-RAY MY IDEA OR YOURS, RING?
DON'T SWEAT THE DETAILS, LANTERN.
IT'S ONLY MAKING THEM CRAZY!
WE'RE OUTNUMBERED BY AN ENDLESS ARMY OF DEATH-GORILLAS!

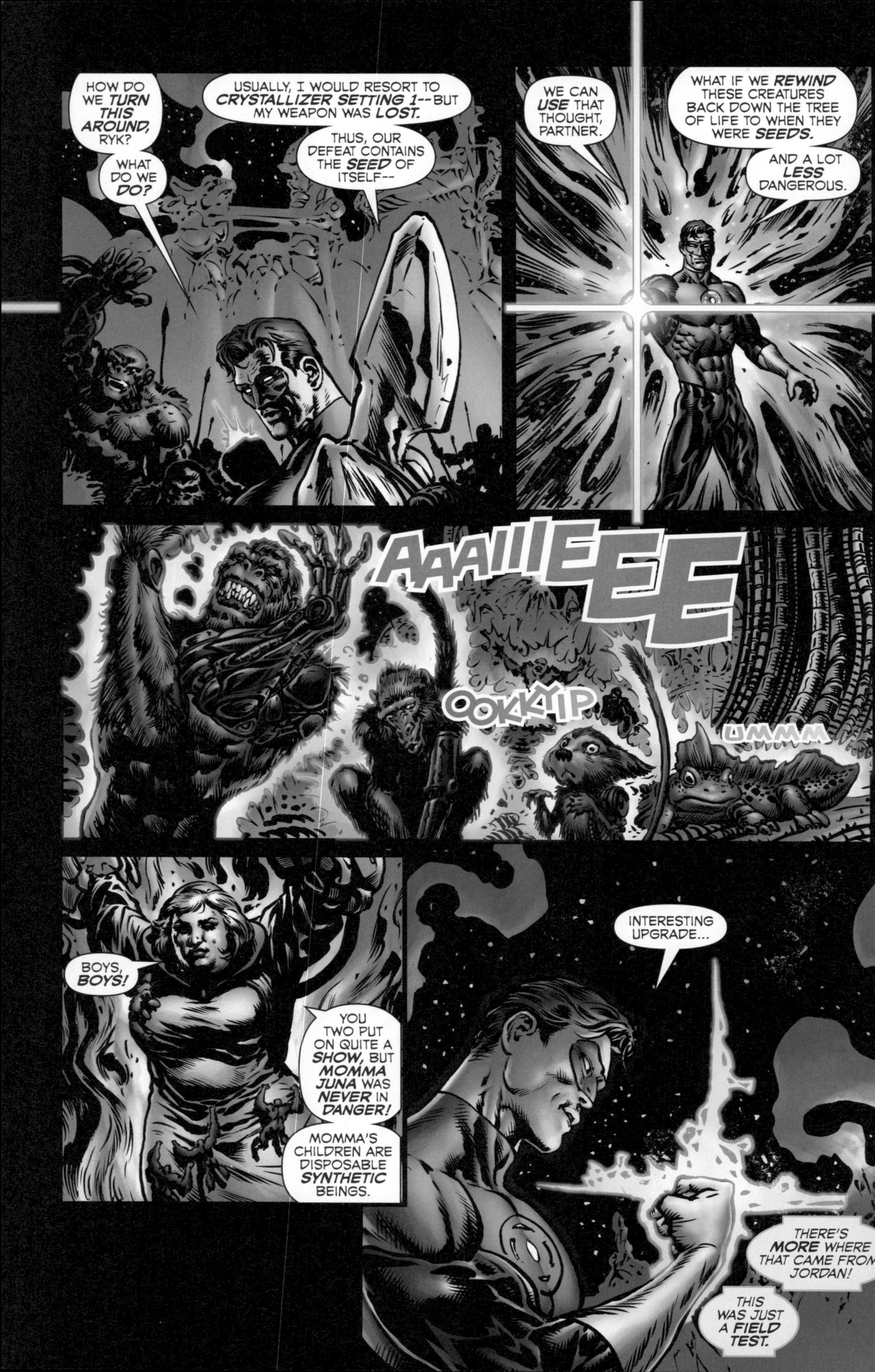
HOW DO WE TURN THIS AROUND, RYK?
WHAT DO WE DO?
USUALLY, I WOULD RESORT TO CRYSTALLIZER SETTING 1-- BUT MY WEAPON WAS LOST.
THUS, OUR DEFEAT CONTAINS THE SEED OF ITSELF--
WE CAN USE THAT THOUGHT, PARTNER.
WHAT IF WE REWIND THESE CREATURES BACK DOWN THE TREE OF LIFE TO WHEN THEY WERE SEEDS.
AND A LOT LESS DANGEROUS.
AAAIIIEEE
OOKKYIP
UMMM
BOYS, BOYS!
YOU TWO PUT ON QUITE A SHOW, BUT MOMMA JUNA WAS NEVER IN DANGER!
MOMMA'S CHILDREN ARE DISPOSABLE SYNTHETIC BEINGS.
INTERESTING UPGRADE...
THERE'S MORE WHERE THAT CAME FROM JORDAN!
THIS WAS JUST A FIELD TEST.

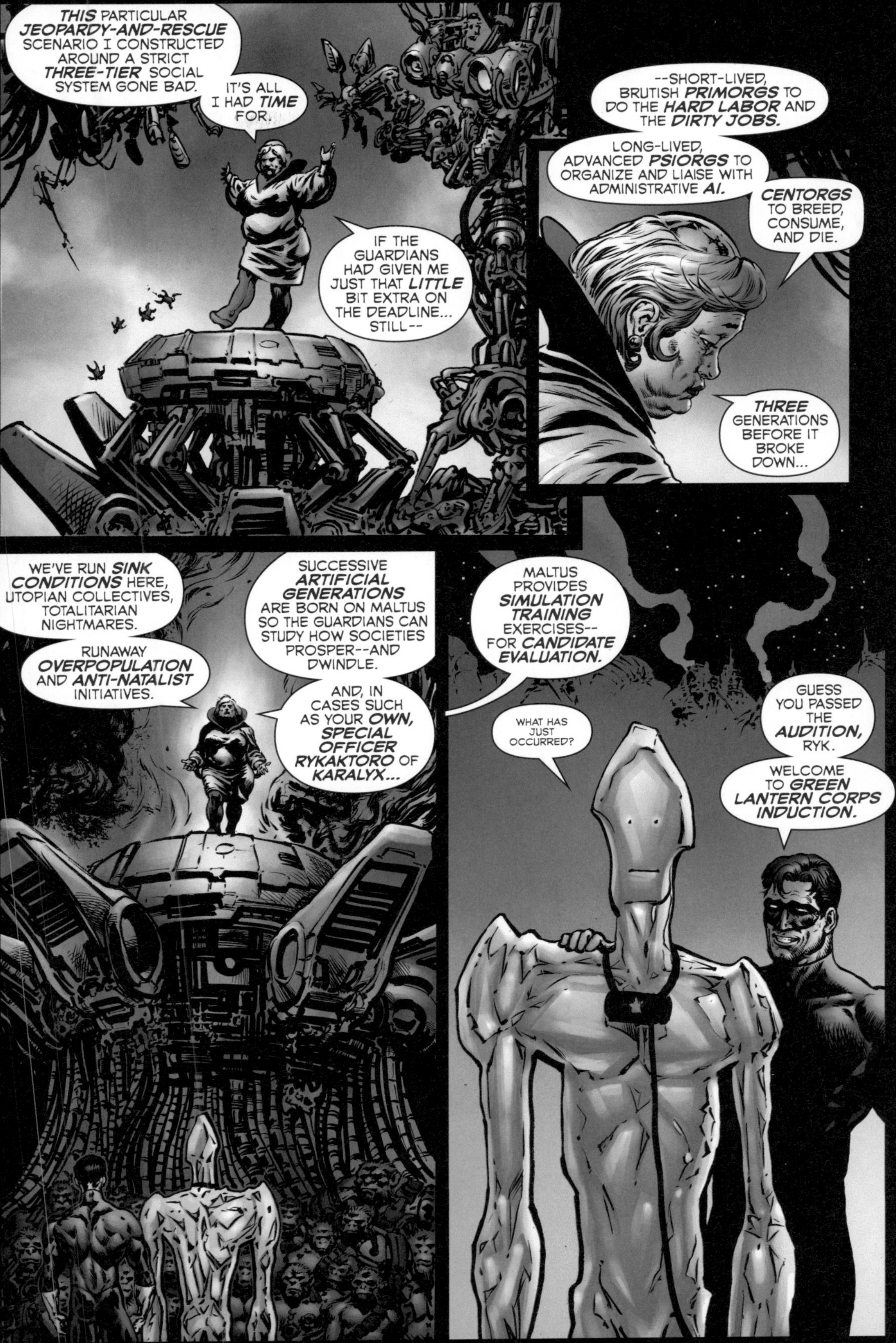
THIS PARTICULAR JEOPARDY-AND-RESCUE SCENARIO I CONSTRUCTED AROUND A STRICT THREE-TIER SOCIAL SYSTEM GONE BAD.
IT'S ALL I HAD TIME FOR.
IF THE GUARDIANS HAD GIVEN ME JUST THAT LITTLE BIT EXTRA ON THE DEADLINE... STILL--
--SHORT-LIVED, BRUTISH PRIMORGS TO DO THE HARD LABOR AND THE DIRTY JOBS.
LONG-LIVED, ADVANCED PSIORGS TO ORGANIZE AND LIAISE WITH ADMINISTRATIVE AI.
CENTORGS TO BREED, CONSUME, AND DIE.
THREE GENERATIONS BEFORE IT BROKE DOWN...
WE'VE RUN SINK CONDITIONS HERE, UTOPIAN COLLECTIVES, TOTALITARIAN NIGHTMARES.
RUNAWAY OVERPOPULATION AND ANTI-NATALIST INITIATIVES.
SUCCESSIVE ARTIFICIAL GENERATIONS ARE BORN ON MALTUS SO THE GUARDIANS CAN STUDY HOW SOCIETIES PROSPER--AND DWINDLE.
AND, IN CASES SUCH AS YOUR OWN, SPECIAL OFFICER RYKAKTORO OF KARALYX...
MALTUS PROVIDES SIMULATION TRAINING EXERCISES--FOR CANDIDATE EVALUATION.
WHAT HAS JUST OCCURRED?
GUESS YOU PASSED THE AUDITION, RYK.
WELCOME TO GREEN LANTERN CORPS INDUCTION.

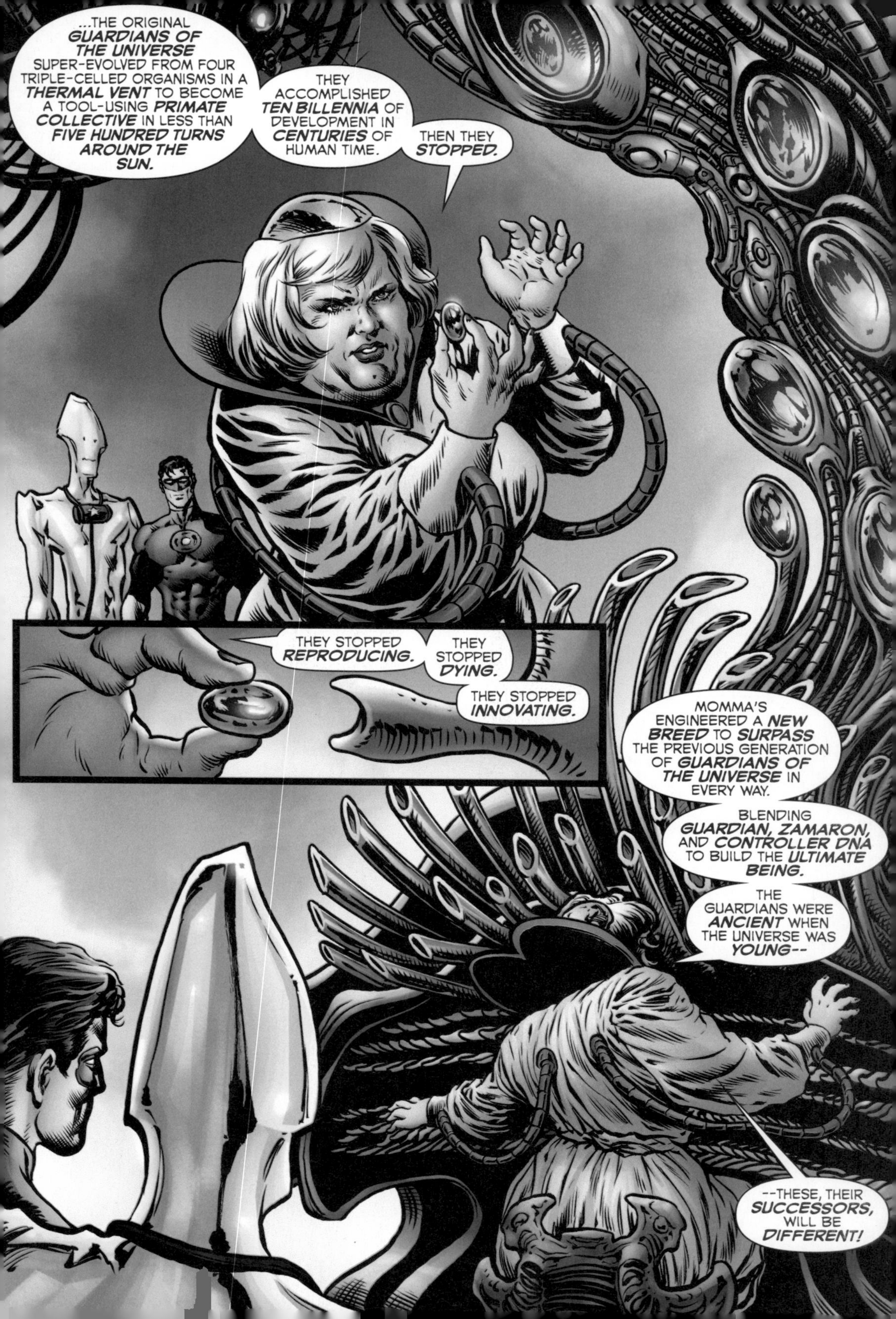
...THE ORIGINAL GUARDIANS OF THE UNIVERSE SUPER-EVOLVED FROM FOUR TRIPLE-CELLED ORGANISMS IN A THERMAL VENT TO BECOME A TOOL-USING PRIMATE COLLECTIVE IN LESS THAN FIVE HUNDRED TURNS AROUND THE SUN.
THEY ACCOMPLISHED TEN BILLENNIA OF DEVELOPMENT IN CENTURIES OF HUMAN TIME.
THEN THEY STOPPED.
THEY STOPPED REPRODUCING.
THEY STOPPED DYING.
THEY STOPPED INNOVATING.
MOMMA'S ENGINEERED A NEW BREED TO SURPASS THE PREVIOUS GENERATION OF GUARDIANS OF THE UNIVERSE IN EVERY WAY.
BLENDING GUARDIAN, ZAMARON, AND CONTROLLER DNA TO BUILD THE ULTIMATE BEING.
THE GUARDIANS WERE ANCIENT WHEN THE UNIVERSE WAS YOUNG--
--THESE, THEIR SUCCESSORS, WILL BE DIFFERENT!

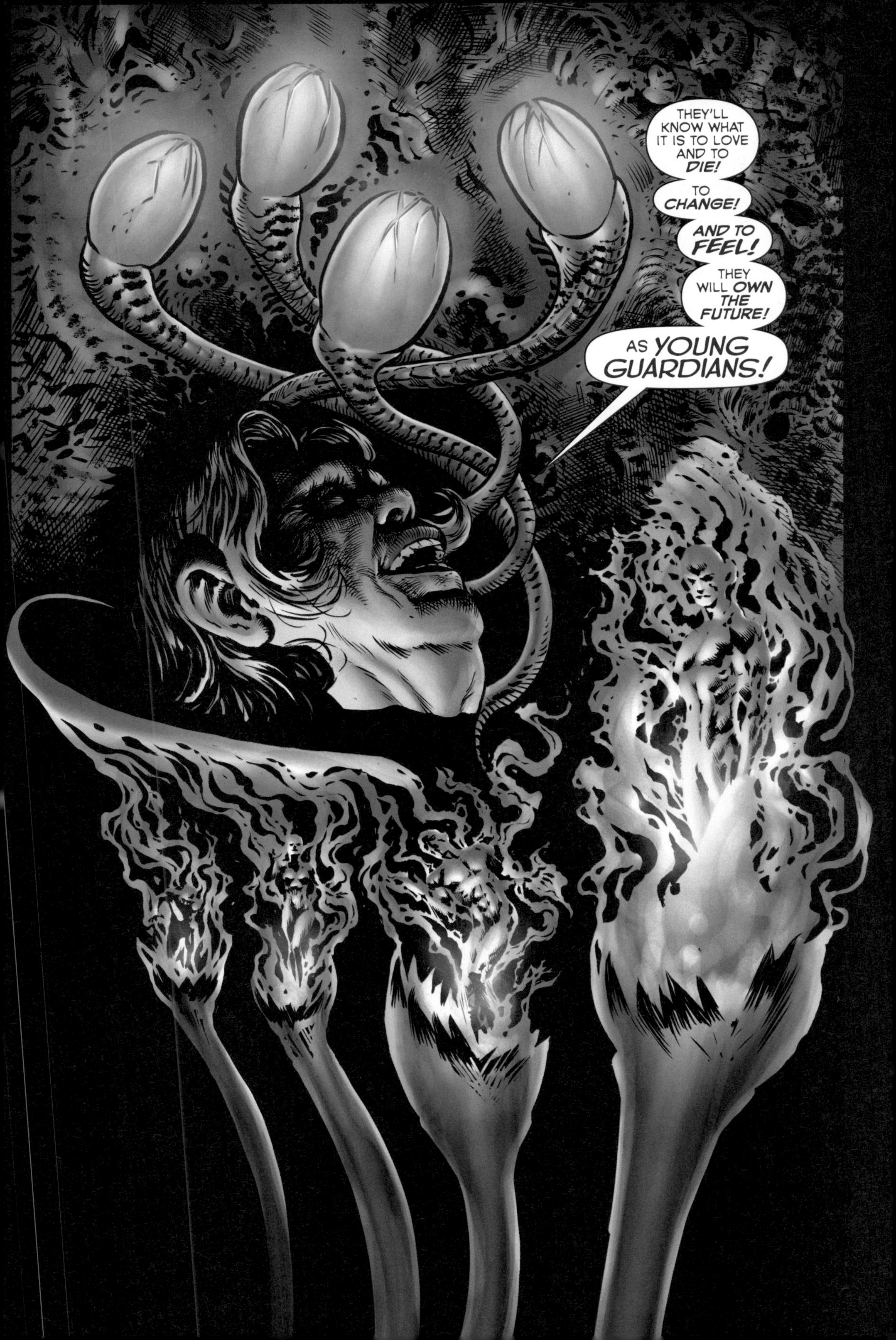

THEY'LL KNOW WHAT IT IS TO LOVE AND TO DIE!
TO CHANGE!
AND TO FEEL!
THEY WILL OWN THE FUTURE!
AS YOUNG GUARDIANS!

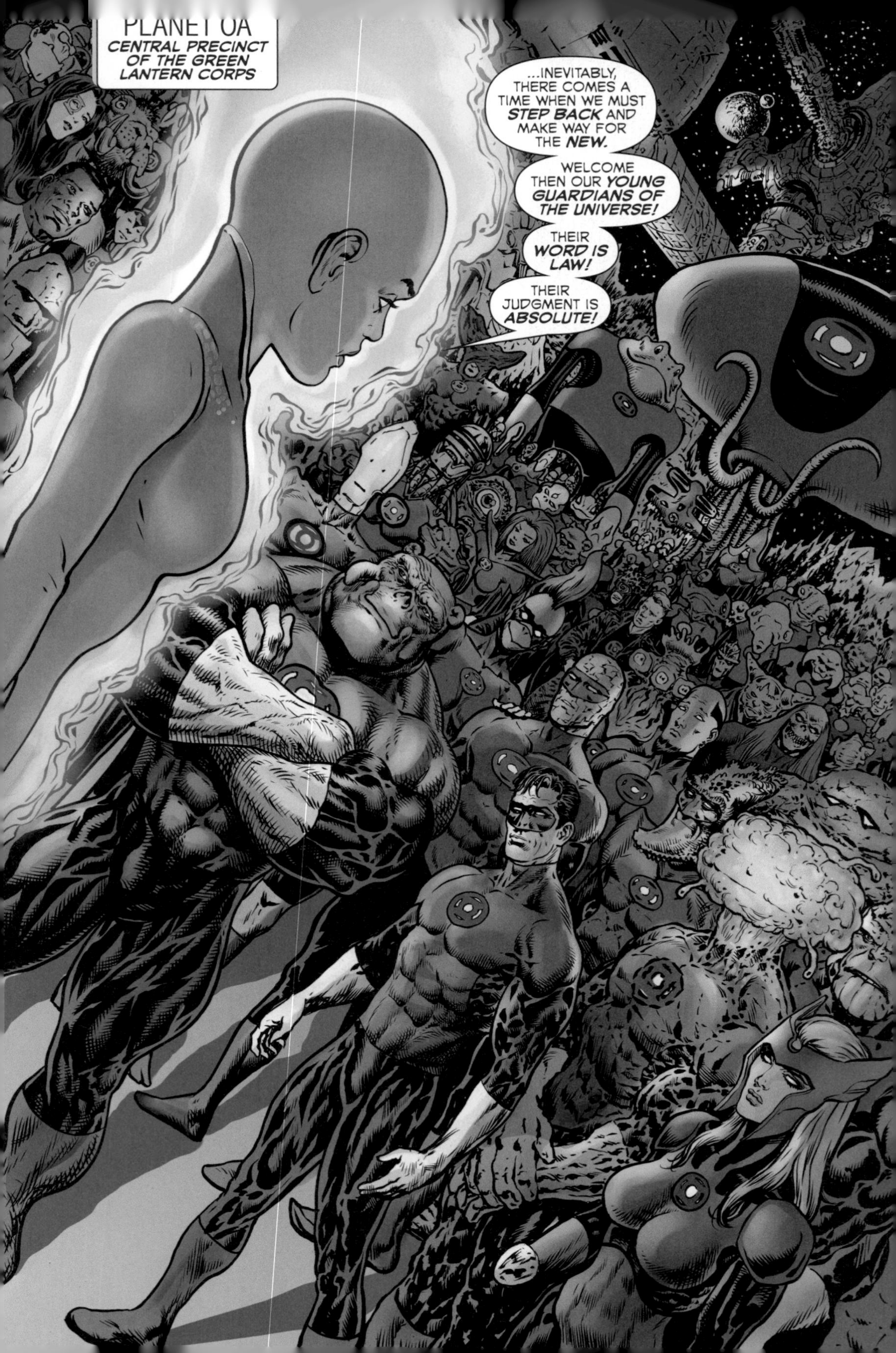
PLANET OA
CENTRAL PRECINCT OF THE GREEN LANTERN CORPS
...INEVITABLY, THERE COMES A TIME WHEN WE MUST STEP BACK AND MAKE WAY FOR THE NEW.
WELCOME THEN OUR YOUNG GUARDIANS OF THE UNIVERSE!
THEIR WORD IS LAW!
THEIR JUDGMENT IS ABSOLUTE!

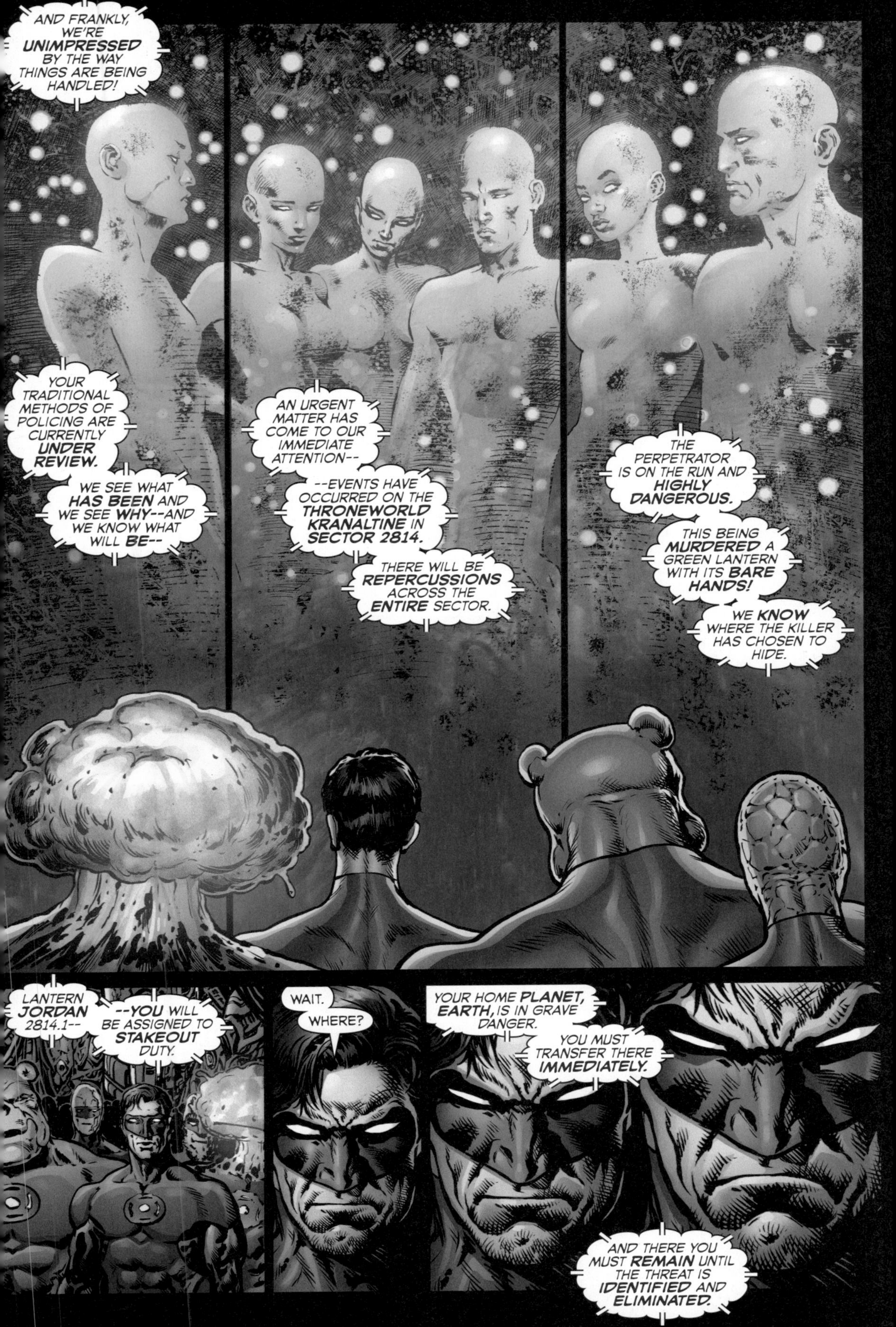

AND FRANKLY, WE'RE UNIMPRESSED BY THE WAY THINGS ARE BEING HANDLED!
YOUR TRADITIONAL METHODS OF POLICING ARE CURRENTLY UNDER REVIEW.
WE SEE WHAT HAS BEEN AND WE SEE WHY--AND WE KNOW WHAT WILL BE--
AN URGENT MATTER HAS COME TO OUR IMMEDIATE ATTENTION--
--EVENTS HAVE OCCURRED ON THE THRONEWORLD KRANALTINE IN SECTOR 2814.
THERE WILL BE REPERCUSSIONS ACROSS THE ENTIRE SECTOR.
THE PERPETRATOR IS ON THE RUN AND HIGHLY DANGEROUS.
THIS BEING MURDERED A GREEN LANTERN WITH ITS BARE HANDS!
WE KNOW WHERE THE KILLER HAS CHOSEN TO HIDE.
LANTERN JORDAN 2814.1--
--YOU WILL BE ASSIGNED TO STAKEOUT DUTY.
WAIT.
WHERE?
YOUR HOME PLANET, EARTH, IS IN GRAVE DANGER.
YOU MUST TRANSFER THERE IMMEDIATELY.
AND THERE YOU MUST REMAIN UNTIL THE THREAT IS IDENTIFIED AND ELIMINATED.

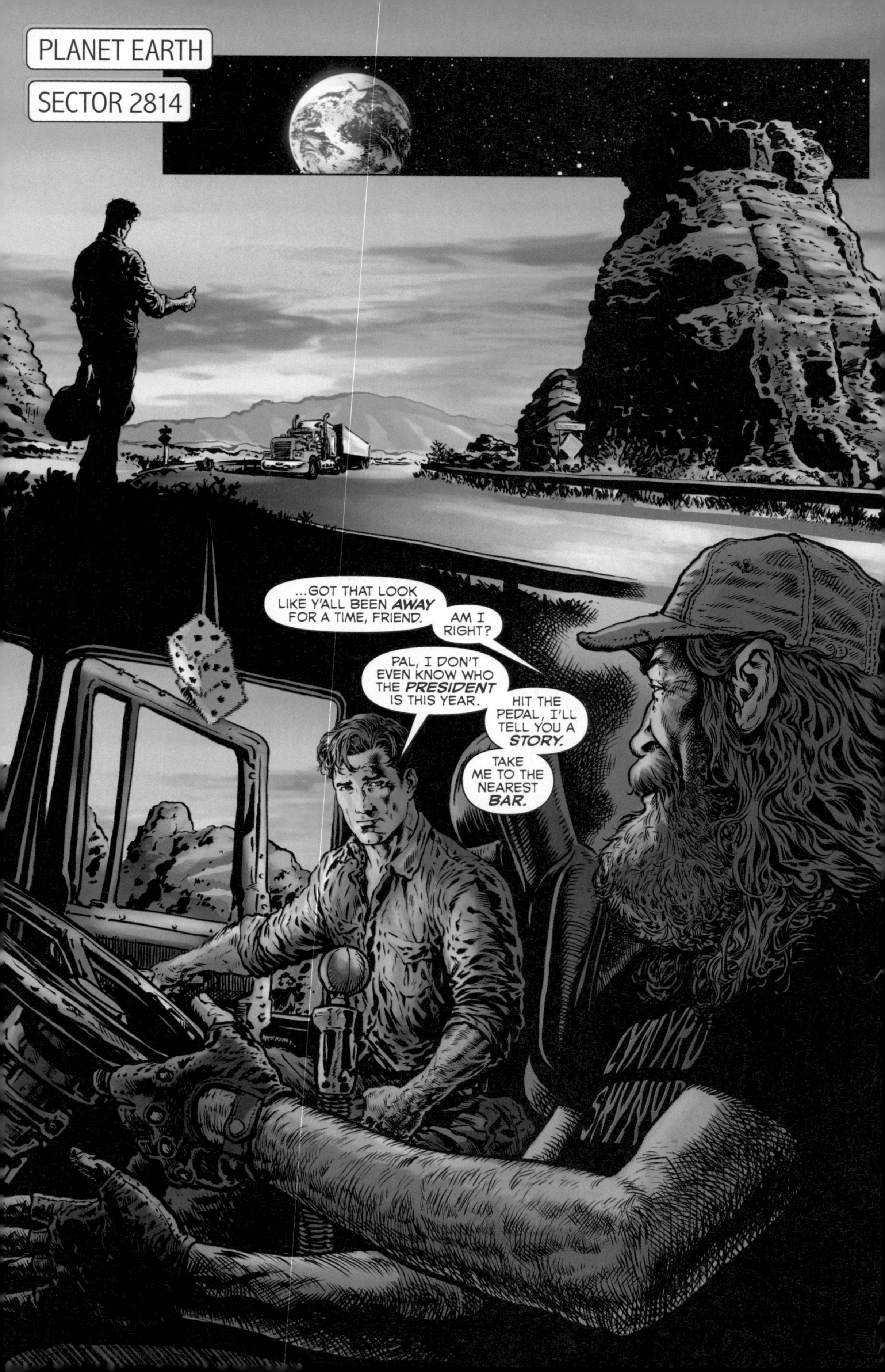
PLANET EARTH
SECTOR 2814
...GOT THAT LOOK LIKE Y'ALL BEEN AWAY FOR A TIME, FRIEND.
AM I RIGHT?
PAL, I DON'T EVEN KNOW WHO THE PRESIDENT IS THIS YEAR.
HIT THE PEDAL, I'LL TELL YOU A STORY.
TAKE ME TO THE NEAREST BAR.

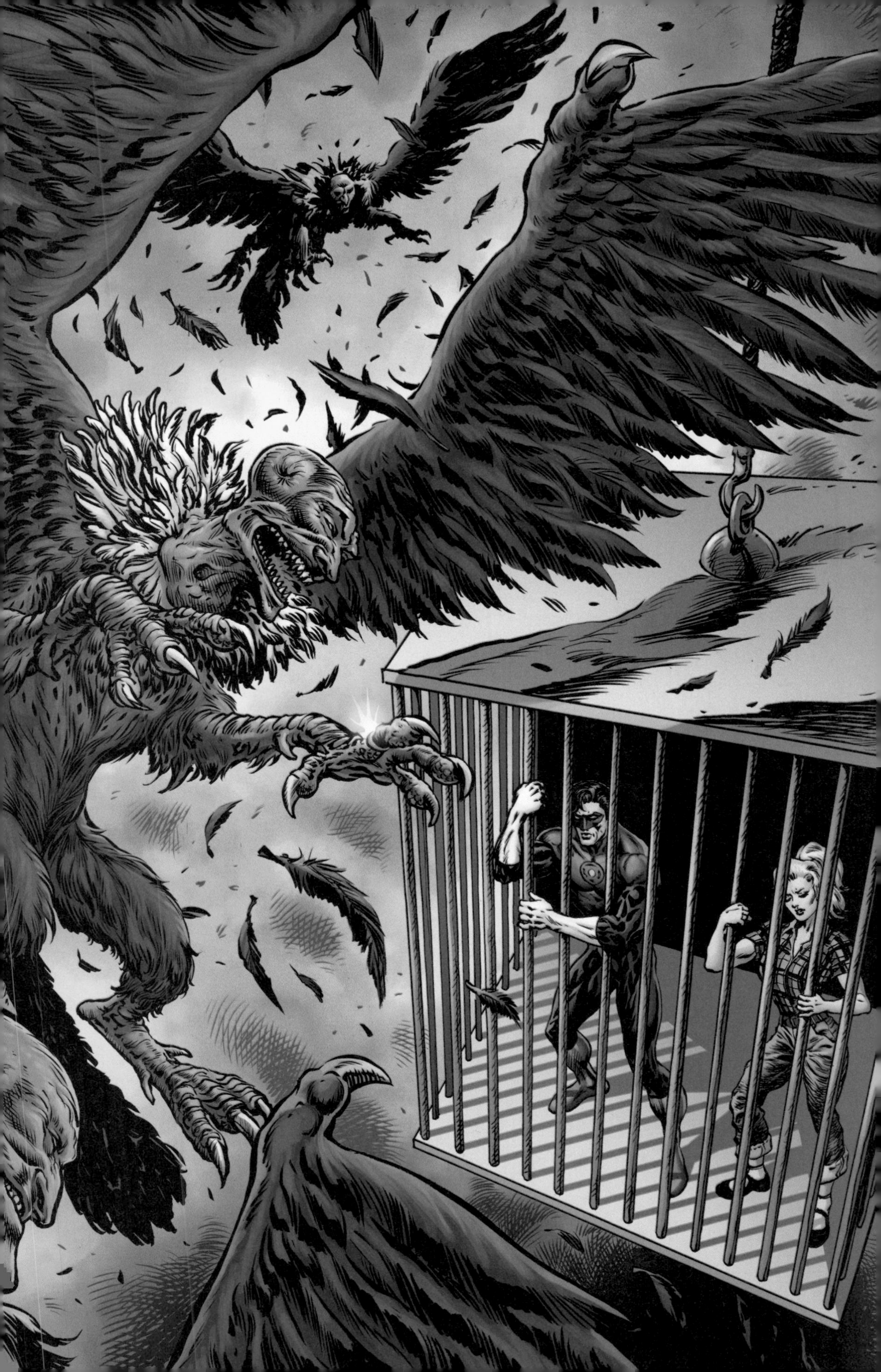

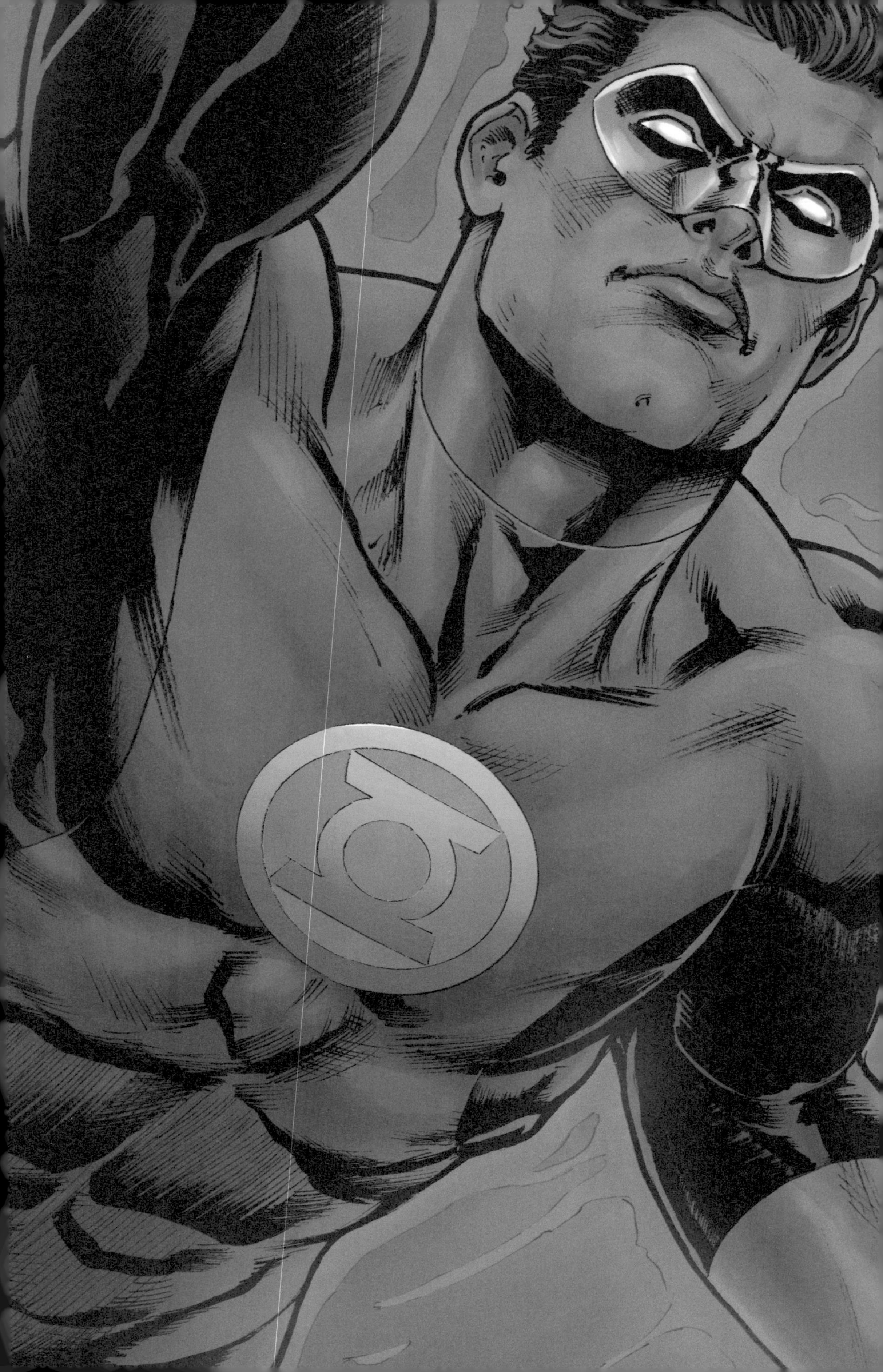

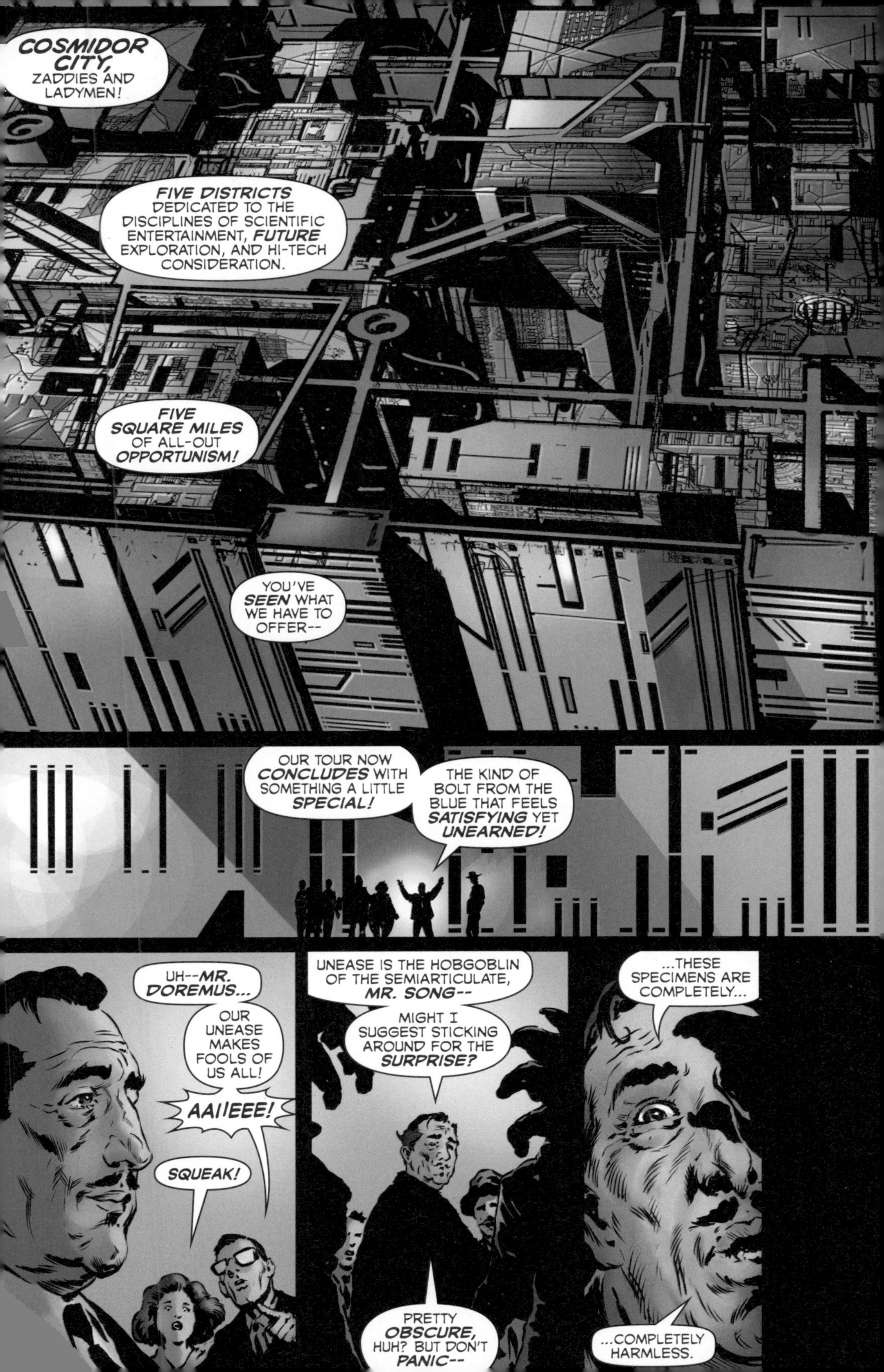
COSMIDOR CITY, ZADDIES AND LADYMEN!
FIVE DISTRICTS DEDICATED TO THE DISCIPLINES OF SCIENTIFIC ENTERTAINMENT, FUTURE EXPLORATION, AND HI-TECH CONSIDERATION.
FIVE SQUARE MILES OF ALL-OUT OPPORTUNISM!
YOU'VE SEEN WHAT WE HAVE TO OFFER--
OUR TOUR NOW CONCLUDES WITH SOMETHING A LITTLE SPECIAL!
THE KIND OF BOLT FROM THE BLUE THAT FEELS SATISFYING YET UNEARNED!
UH--MR. DOREMUS...
OUR UNEASE MAKES FOOLS OF US ALL!
AAIIEEE!
SQUEAK!
UNEASE IS THE HOBGOBLIN OF THE SEMIARTICULATE, MR. SONG--
MIGHT I SUGGEST STICKING AROUND FOR THE SURPRISE?
PRETTY OBSCURE, HUH? BUT DON'T PANIC--
...THESE SPECIMENS ARE COMPLETELY...
...COMPLETELY HARMLESS.

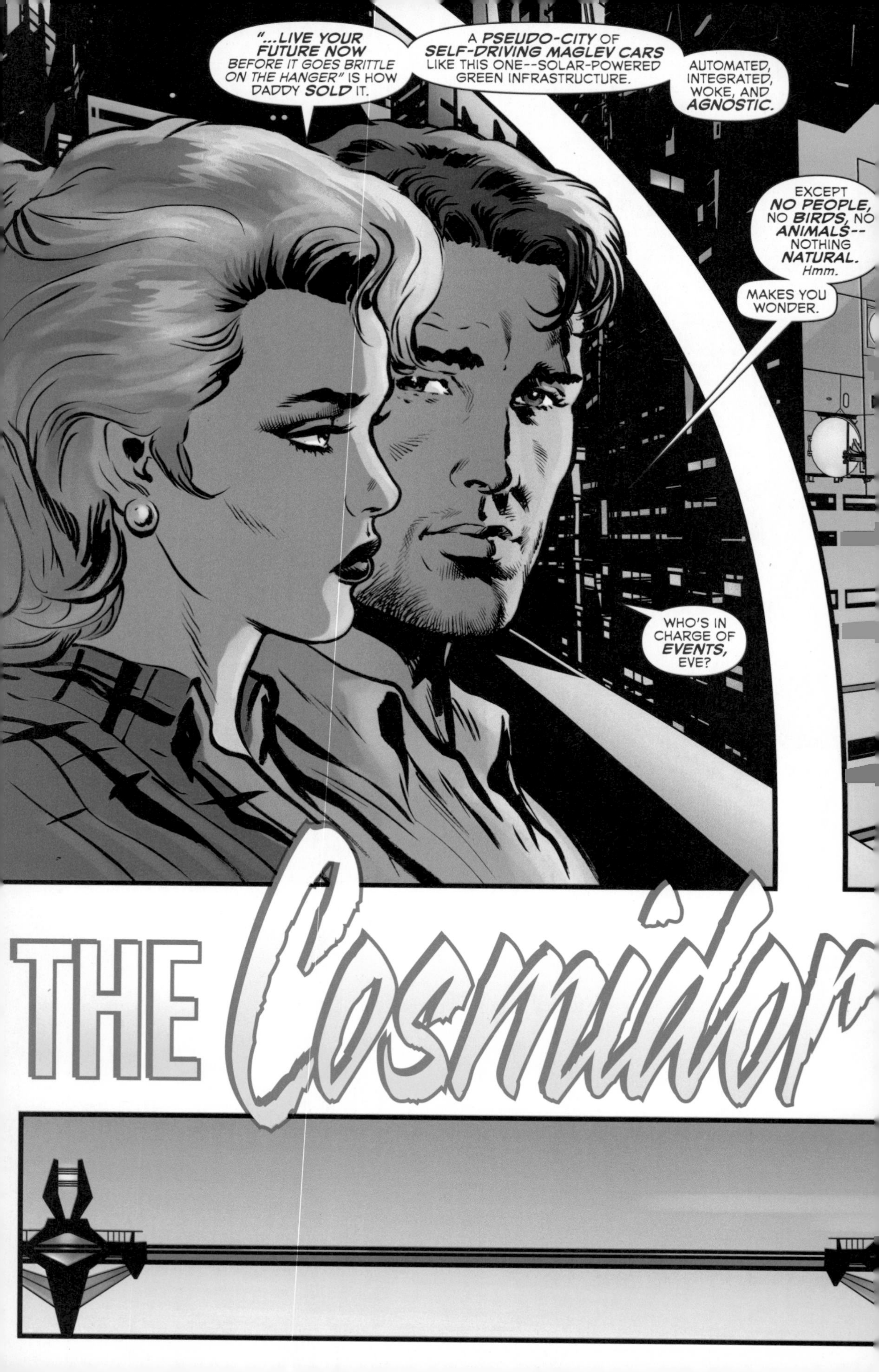
"...LIVE YOUR FUTURE NOW BEFORE IT GOES BRITTLE ON THE HANGER" IS HOW DADDY SOLD IT.
A PSEUDO-CITY OF SELF-DRIVING MAGLEV CARS LIKE THIS ONE--SOLAR-POWERED GREEN INFRASTRUCTURE.
AUTOMATED, INTEGRATED, WOKE, AND AGNOSTIC.
EXCEPT NO PEOPLE, NO BIRDS, NO ANIMALS--NOTHING NATURAL. Hmm.
MAKES YOU WONDER.
WHO'S IN CHARGE OF EVENTS, EVE?
THE Cosmidor

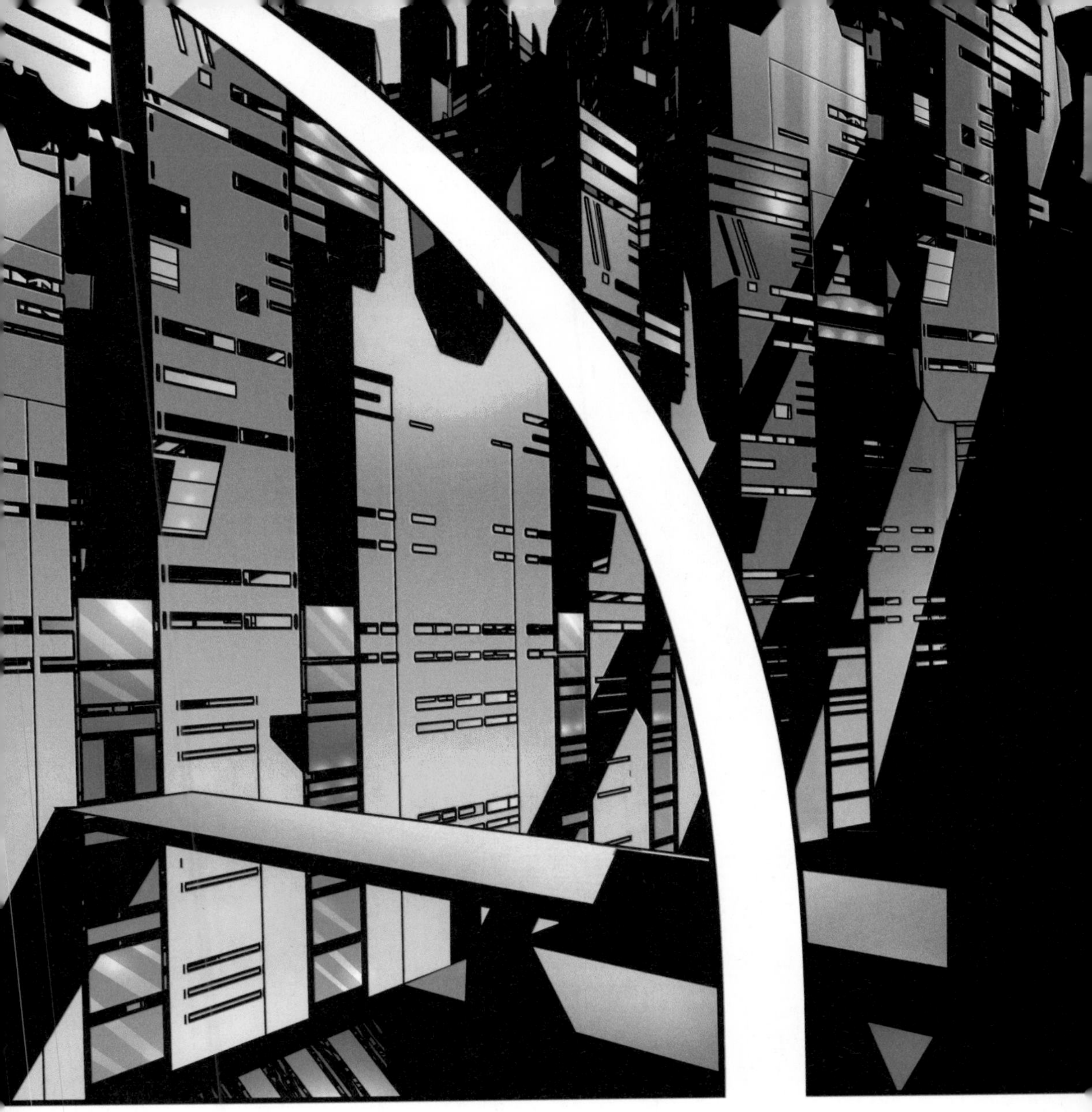

CONSPIRACY

GRANT MORRISON, writer
LIAM SHARP, artist & cover
STEVE OLIFF, colorist
TOM ORZECHOWSKI, letterer
BRIAN CUNNINGHAM, editor

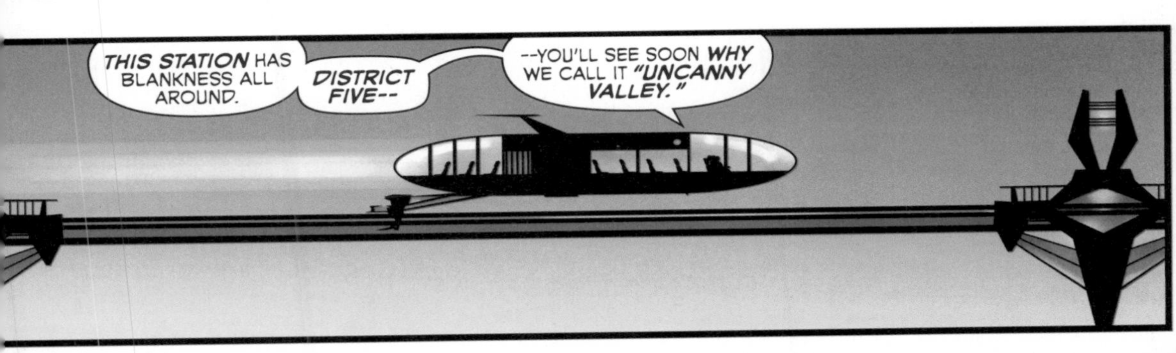

THIS STATION HAS BLANKNESS ALL AROUND.
DISTRICT FIVE--
--YOU'LL SEE SOON WHY WE CALL IT "UNCANNY VALLEY."

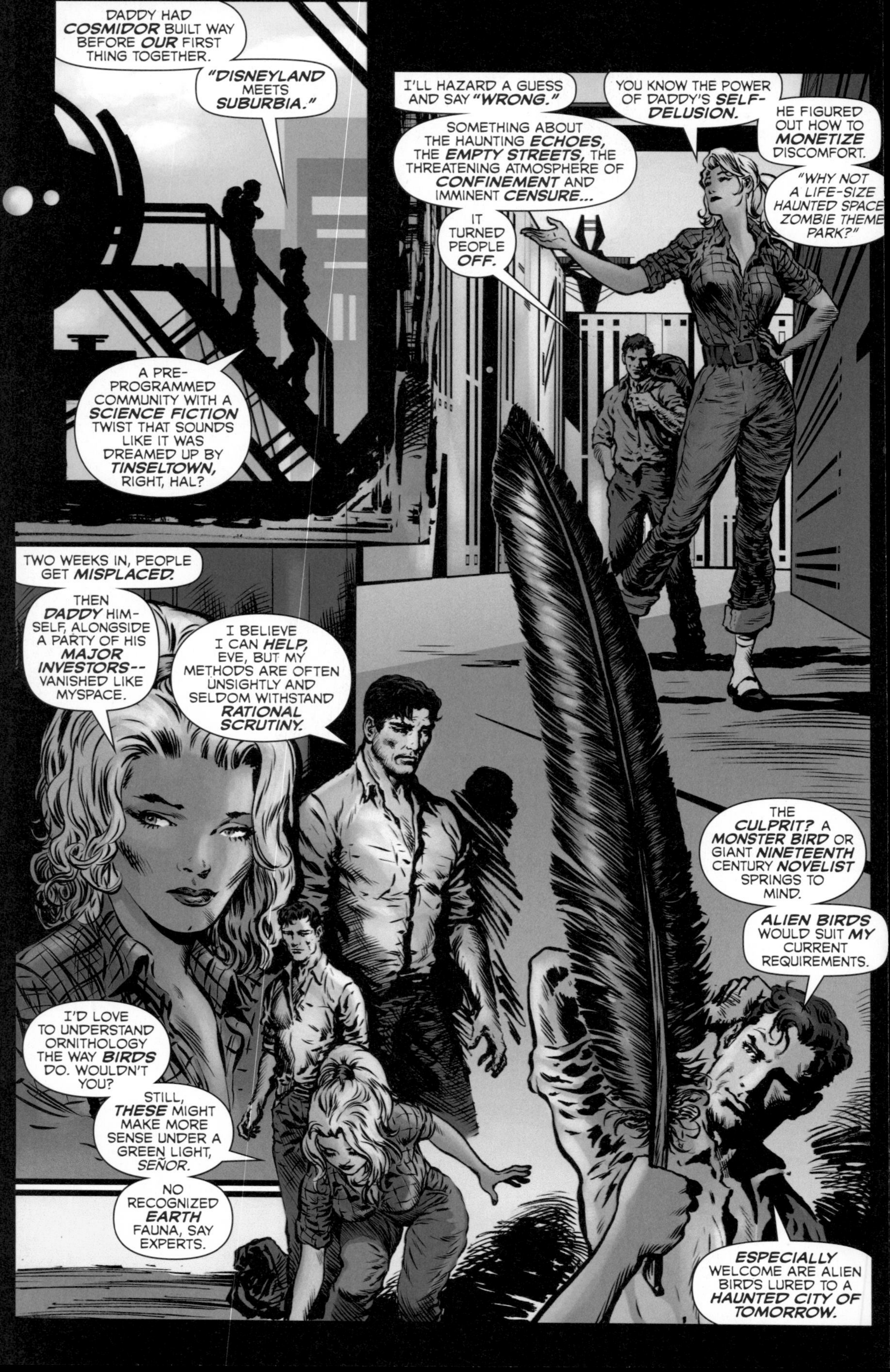
DADDY HAD COSMIDOR BUILT WAY BEFORE OUR FIRST THING TOGETHER.
"DISNEYLAND MEETS SUBURBIA."
A PRE-PROGRAMMED COMMUNITY WITH A SCIENCE FICTION TWIST THAT SOUNDS LIKE IT WAS DREAMED UP BY TINSELTOWN, RIGHT, HAL?
I'LL HAZARD A GUESS AND SAY "WRONG."
SOMETHING ABOUT THE HAUNTING ECHOES, THE EMPTY STREETS, THE THREATENING ATMOSPHERE OF CONFINEMENT AND IMMINENT CENSURE...
IT TURNED PEOPLE OFF.
YOU KNOW THE POWER OF DADDY'S SELF-DELUSION.
HE FIGURED OUT HOW TO MONETIZE DISCOMFORT.
"WHY NOT A LIFE-SIZE HAUNTED SPACE ZOMBIE THEME PARK?"
TWO WEEKS IN, PEOPLE GET MISPLACED.
THEN DADDY HIMSELF, ALONGSIDE A PARTY OF HIS MAJOR INVESTORS-- VANISHED LIKE MYSPACE.
I BELIEVE I CAN HELP, EVE, BUT MY METHODS ARE OFTEN UNSIGHTLY AND SELDOM WITHSTAND RATIONAL SCRUTINY.
THE CULPRIT? A MONSTER BIRD OR GIANT NINETEENTH CENTURY NOVELIST SPRINGS TO MIND.
ALIEN BIRDS WOULD SUIT MY CURRENT REQUIREMENTS.
I'D LOVE TO UNDERSTAND ORNITHOLOGY THE WAY BIRDS DO. WOULDN'T YOU?
STILL, THESE MIGHT MAKE MORE SENSE UNDER A GREEN LIGHT, SEÑOR.
NO RECOGNIZED EARTH FAUNA, SAY EXPERTS.
ESPECIALLY WELCOME ARE ALIEN BIRDS LURED TO A HAUNTED CITY OF TOMORROW.

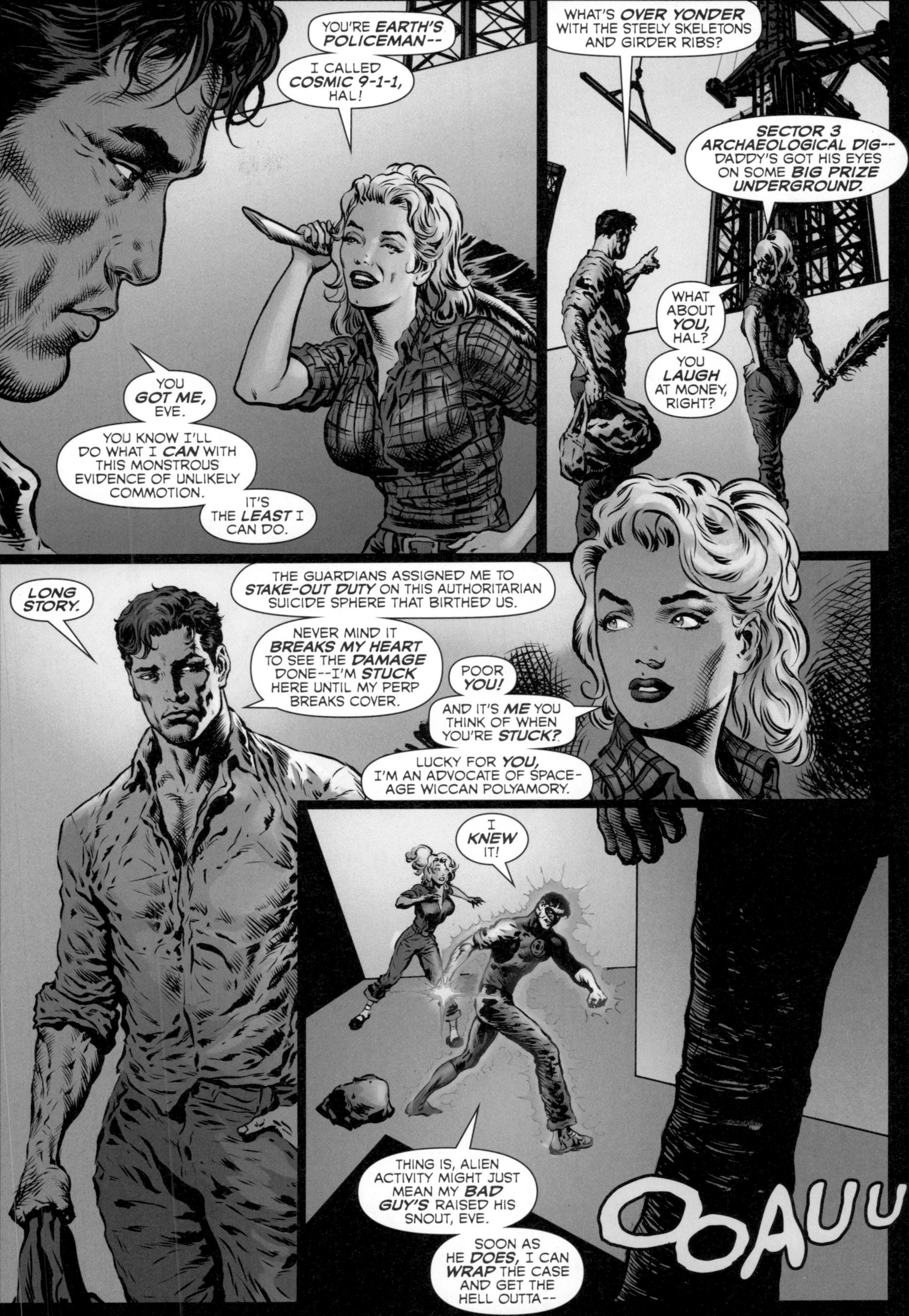

YOU'RE *EARTH'S POLICEMAN--*
I CALLED *COSMIC 9-1-1,* HAL!
YOU *GOT ME,* EVE.
YOU KNOW I'LL DO WHAT I *CAN* WITH THIS MONSTROUS EVIDENCE OF UNLIKELY COMMOTION.
IT'S THE *LEAST* I CAN DO.
WHAT'S *OVER YONDER* WITH THE STEELY SKELETONS AND GIRDER RIBS?
SECTOR 3 ARCHAEOLOGICAL DIG-- DADDY'S GOT HIS EYES ON SOME *BIG PRIZE UNDERGROUND.*
WHAT ABOUT *YOU,* HAL?
YOU *LAUGH* AT MONEY, RIGHT?
LONG STORY.
THE GUARDIANS ASSIGNED ME TO *STAKE-OUT DUTY* ON THIS AUTHORITARIAN SUICIDE SPHERE THAT BIRTHED US.
NEVER MIND IT *BREAKS MY HEART* TO SEE THE *DAMAGE* DONE--I'M *STUCK* HERE UNTIL MY PERP BREAKS COVER.
POOR *YOU!*
AND IT'S *ME* YOU THINK OF WHEN YOU'RE *STUCK?*
LUCKY FOR *YOU,* I'M AN ADVOCATE OF SPACE-AGE WICCAN POLYAMORY.
I *KNEW* IT!
THING IS, ALIEN ACTIVITY MIGHT JUST MEAN MY *BAD GUY'S* RAISED HIS SNOUT, EVE.
SOON AS HE *DOES,* I CAN *WRAP* THE CASE AND GET THE HELL OUTTA--
OOAUU

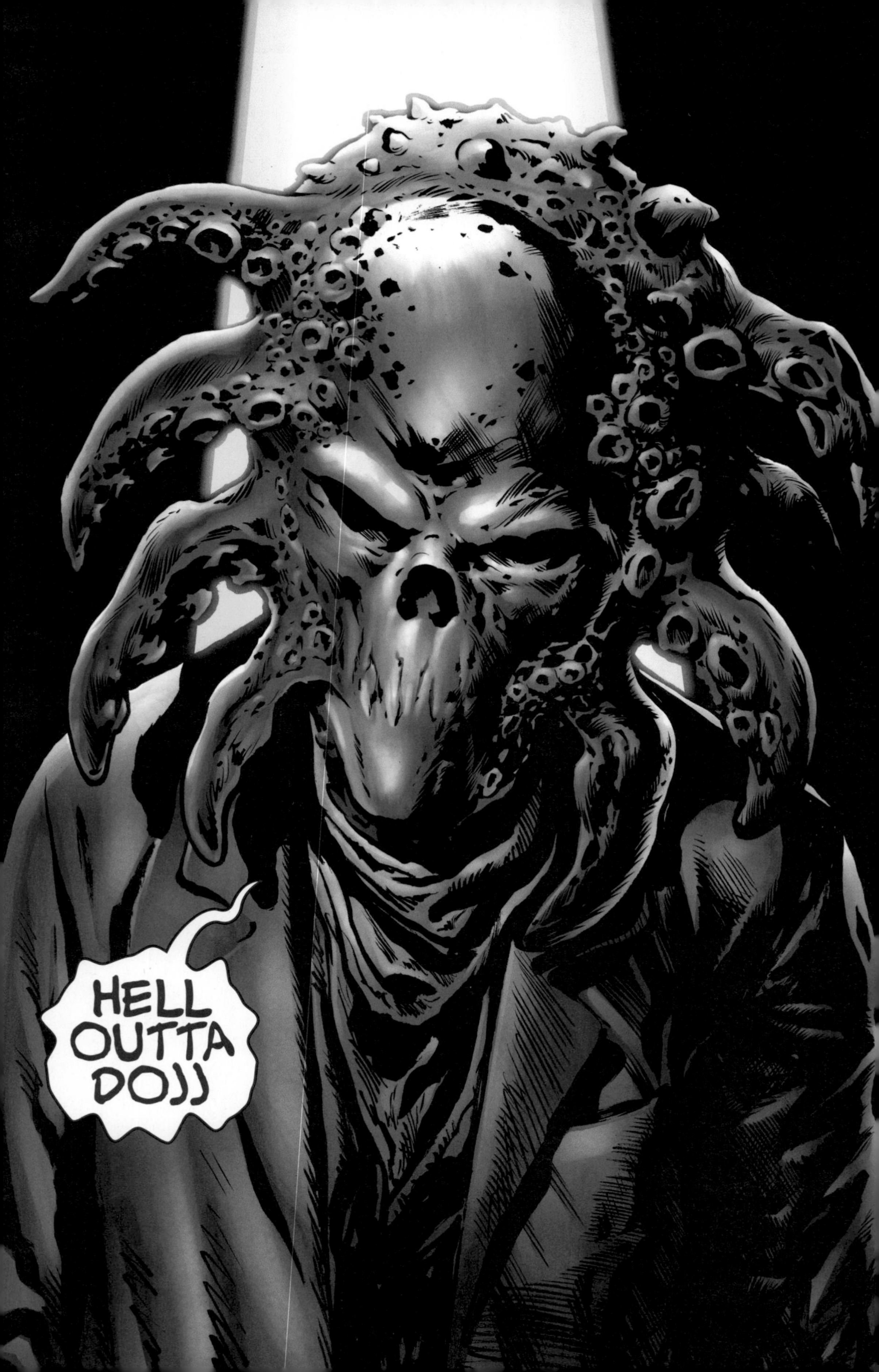
HELL OUTTA DOJJ

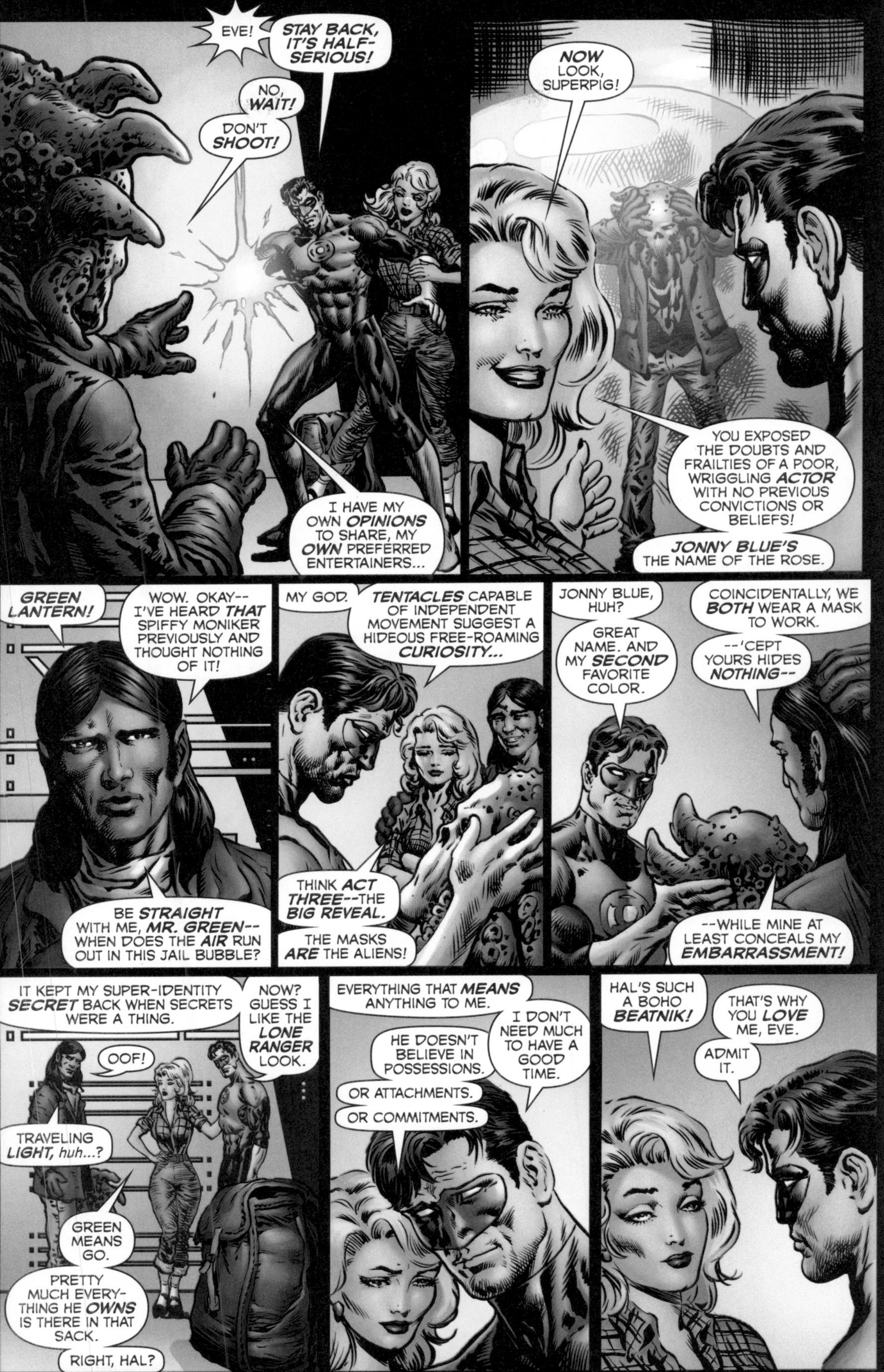
EVE!
STAY BACK, IT'S HALF-SERIOUS!
NO, WAIT!
DON'T SHOOT!
I HAVE MY OWN OPINIONS TO SHARE, MY OWN PREFERRED ENTERTAINERS...
NOW LOOK, SUPERPIG!
YOU EXPOSED THE DOUBTS AND FRAILTIES OF A POOR, WRIGGLING ACTOR WITH NO PREVIOUS CONVICTIONS OR BELIEFS!
JONNY BLUE'S THE NAME OF THE ROSE.
GREEN LANTERN!
WOW. OKAY-- I'VE HEARD THAT SPIFFY MONIKER PREVIOUSLY AND THOUGHT NOTHING OF IT!
BE STRAIGHT WITH ME, MR. GREEN-- WHEN DOES THE AIR RUN OUT IN THIS JAIL BUBBLE?
MY GOD.
TENTACLES CAPABLE OF INDEPENDENT MOVEMENT SUGGEST A HIDEOUS FREE-ROAMING CURIOSITY...
THINK ACT THREE--THE BIG REVEAL.
THE MASKS ARE THE ALIENS!
JONNY BLUE, HUH?
GREAT NAME. AND MY SECOND FAVORITE COLOR.
COINCIDENTALLY, WE BOTH WEAR A MASK TO WORK.
--'CEPT YOURS HIDES NOTHING--
--WHILE MINE AT LEAST CONCEALS MY EMBARRASSMENT!
IT KEPT MY SUPER-IDENTITY SECRET BACK WHEN SECRETS WERE A THING.
NOW? GUESS I LIKE THE LONE RANGER LOOK.
OOF!
TRAVELING LIGHT, huh...?
GREEN MEANS GO.
PRETTY MUCH EVERY-THING HE OWNS IS THERE IN THAT SACK.
RIGHT, HAL?
EVERYTHING THAT MEANS ANYTHING TO ME.
I DON'T NEED MUCH TO HAVE A GOOD TIME.
HE DOESN'T BELIEVE IN POSSESSIONS.
OR ATTACHMENTS.
OR COMMITMENTS.
HAL'S SUCH A BOHO BEATNIK!
THAT'S WHY YOU LOVE ME, EVE.
ADMIT IT.

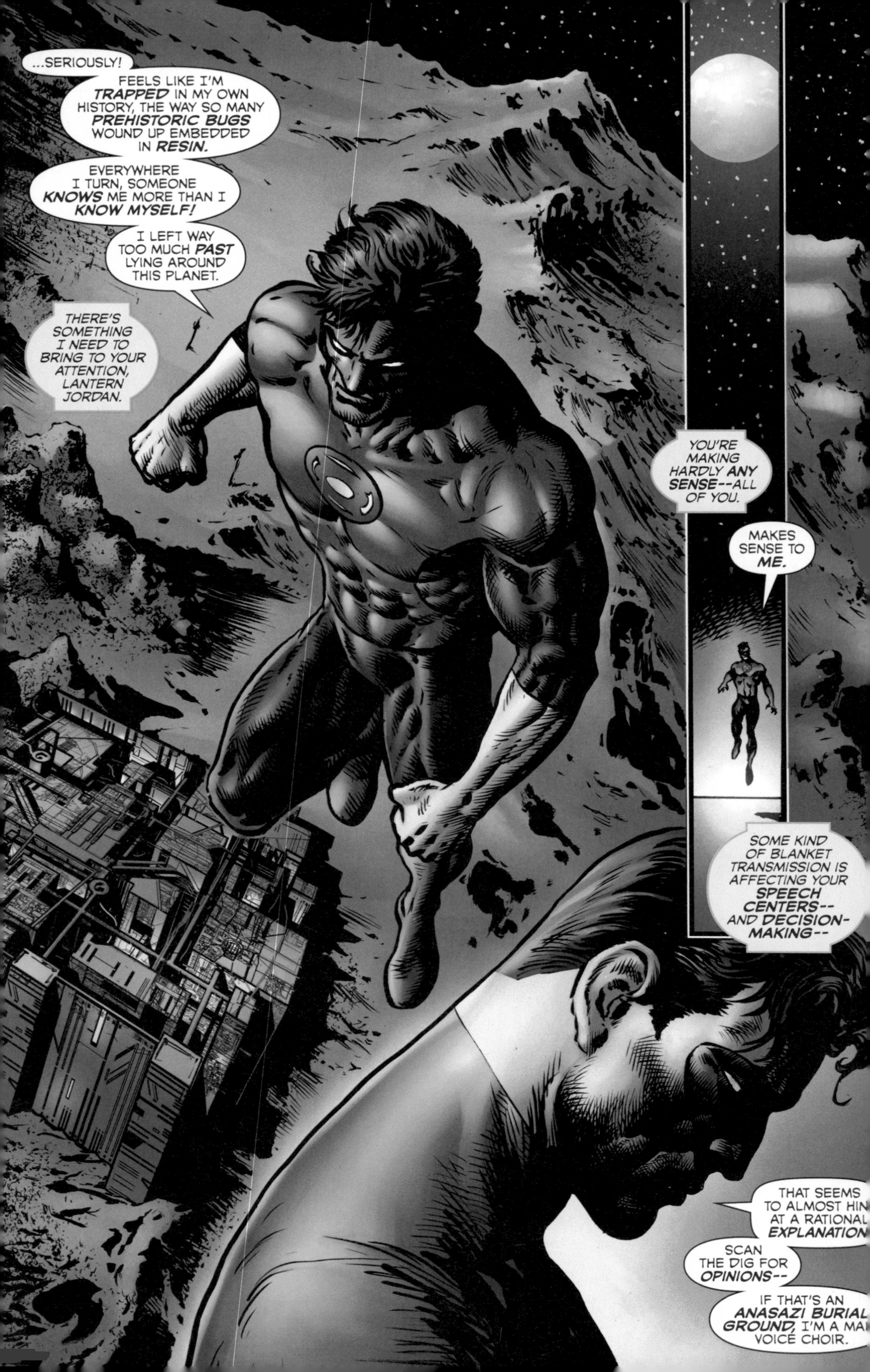
...SERIOUSLY!
FEELS LIKE I'M TRAPPED IN MY OWN HISTORY, THE WAY SO MANY PREHISTORIC BUGS WOUND UP EMBEDDED IN RESIN.
EVERYWHERE I TURN, SOMEONE KNOWS ME MORE THAN I KNOW MYSELF!
I LEFT WAY TOO MUCH PAST LYING AROUND THIS PLANET.
THERE'S SOMETHING I NEED TO BRING TO YOUR ATTENTION, LANTERN JORDAN.
YOU'RE MAKING HARDLY ANY SENSE--ALL OF YOU.
MAKES SENSE TO ME.
SOME KIND OF BLANKET TRANSMISSION IS AFFECTING YOUR SPEECH CENTERS-- AND DECISION-MAKING--
THAT SEEMS TO ALMOST HIN AT A RATIONAL EXPLANATIO
SCAN THE DIG FOR OPINIONS--
IF THAT'S AN ANASAZI BURIAL GROUND, I'M A MA VOICE CHOIR.

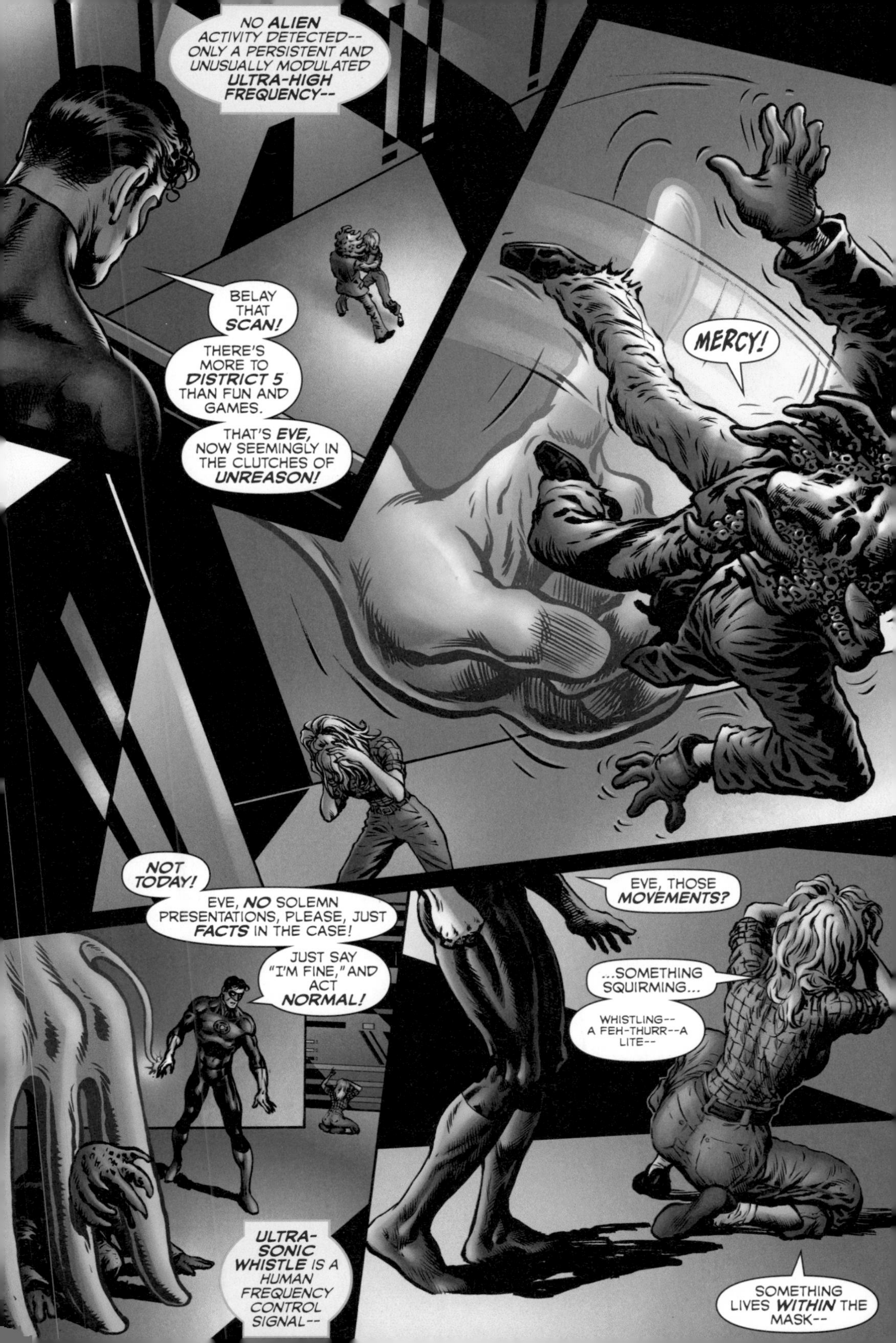
NO ALIEN ACTIVITY DETECTED-- ONLY A PERSISTENT AND UNUSUALLY MODULATED ULTRA-HIGH FREQUENCY--
BELAY THAT SCAN!
THERE'S MORE TO DISTRICT 5 THAN FUN AND GAMES.
THAT'S EVE, NOW SEEMINGLY IN THE CLUTCHES OF UNREASON!
MERCY!
NOT TODAY!
EVE, NO SOLEMN PRESENTATIONS, PLEASE, JUST FACTS IN THE CASE!
JUST SAY "I'M FINE," AND ACT NORMAL!
ULTRA-SONIC WHISTLE IS A HUMAN FREQUENCY CONTROL SIGNAL--
EVE, THOSE MOVEMENTS?
...SOMETHING SQUIRMING...
WHISTLING-- A FEH-THURR--A LITE--
SOMETHING LIVES WITHIN THE MASK--

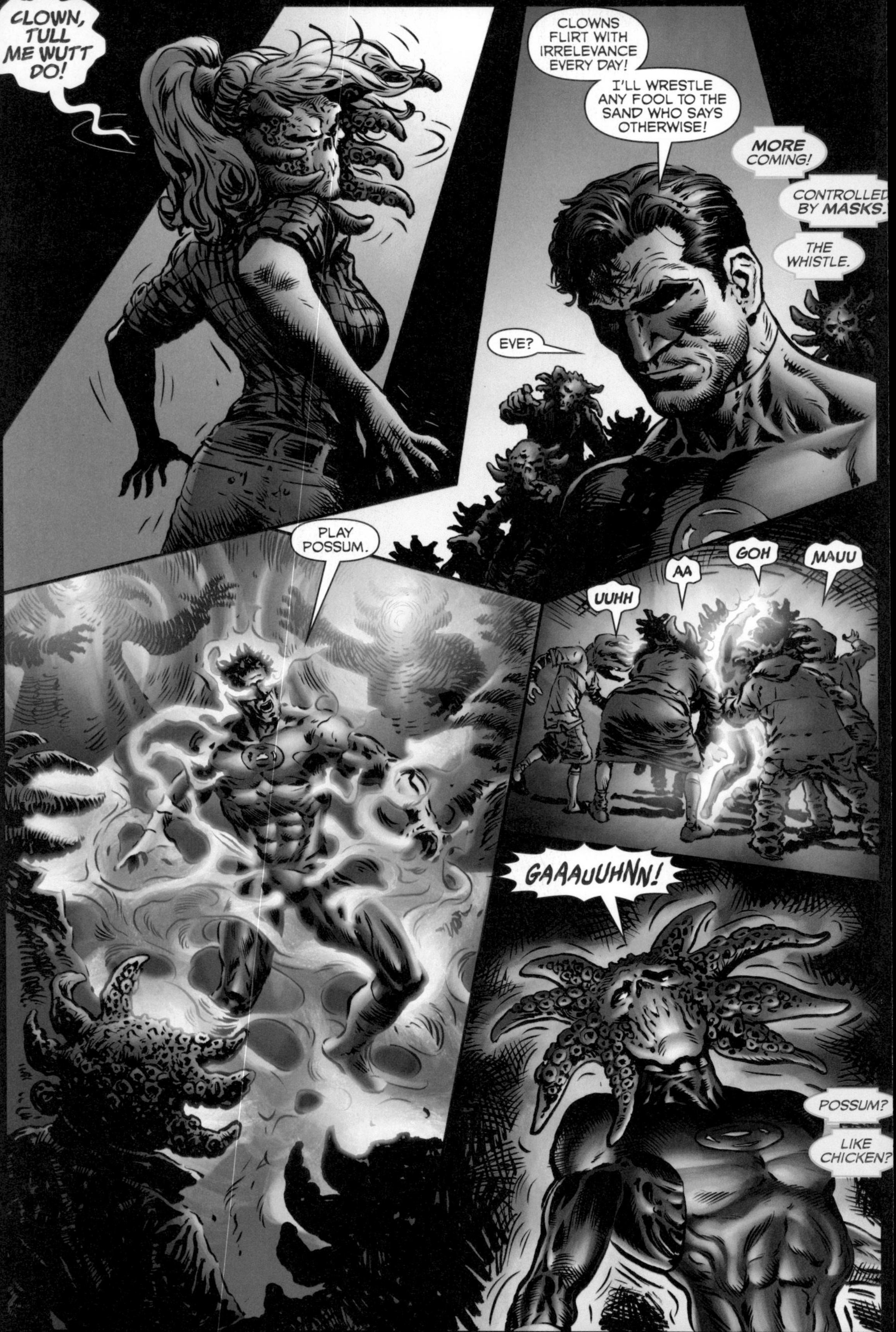
CLOWN, TULL ME WUTT DO!
CLOWNS FLIRT WITH IRRELEVANCE EVERY DAY!
I'LL WRESTLE ANY FOOL TO THE SAND WHO SAYS OTHERWISE!
MORE COMING!
CONTROLLED BY MASKS.
THE WHISTLE.
EVE?
PLAY POSSUM.
UUHH
AA
GOH
MAUU
GAAAUUHNN!
POSSUM?
LIKE CHICKEN?

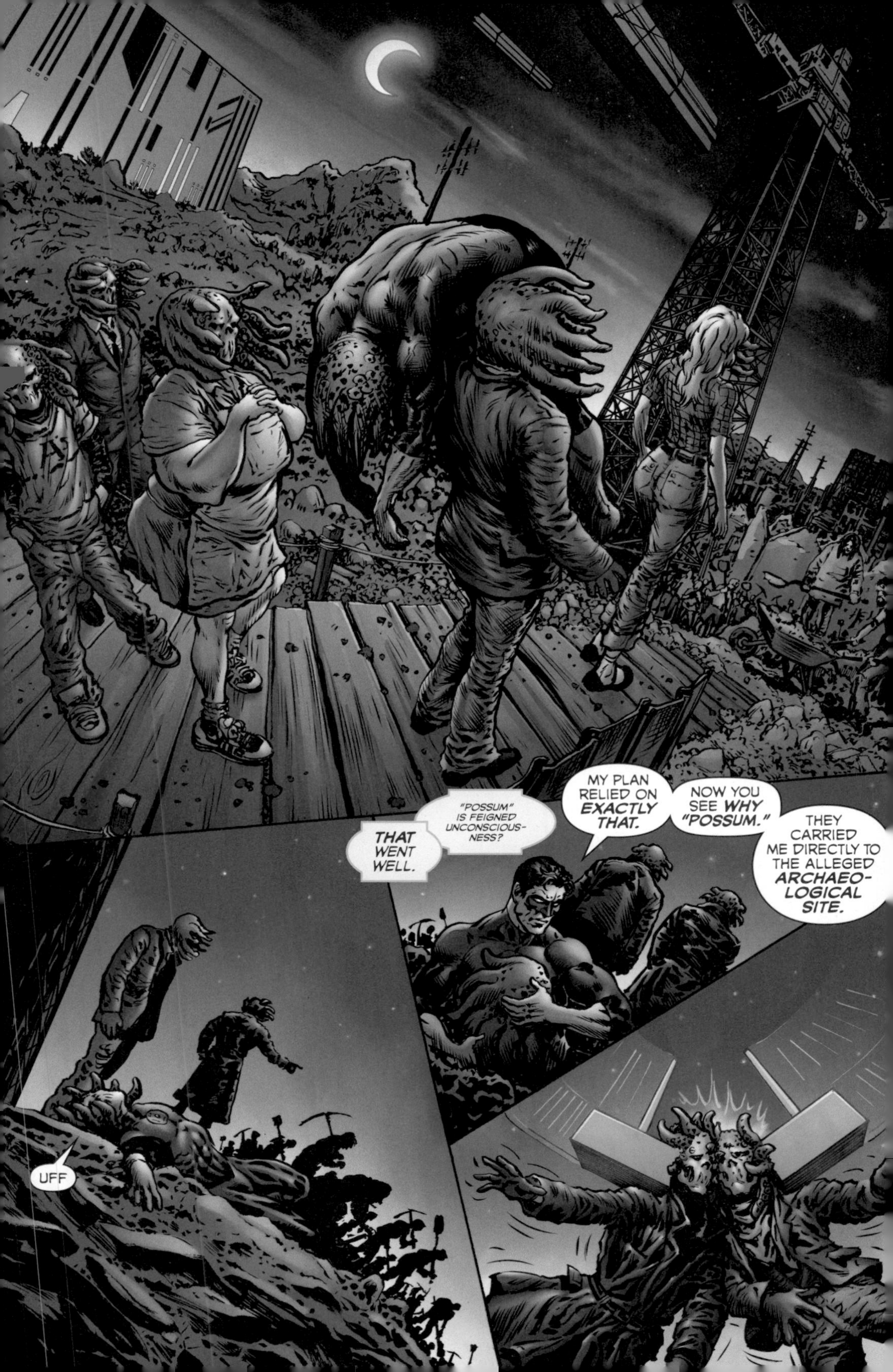

THAT WENT WELL.
"POSSUM" IS FEIGNED UNCONSCIOUS-NESS?
MY PLAN RELIED ON EXACTLY THAT.
NOW YOU SEE WHY "POSSUM."
THEY CARRIED ME DIRECTLY TO THE ALLEGED ARCHAEO-LOGICAL SITE.
UFF

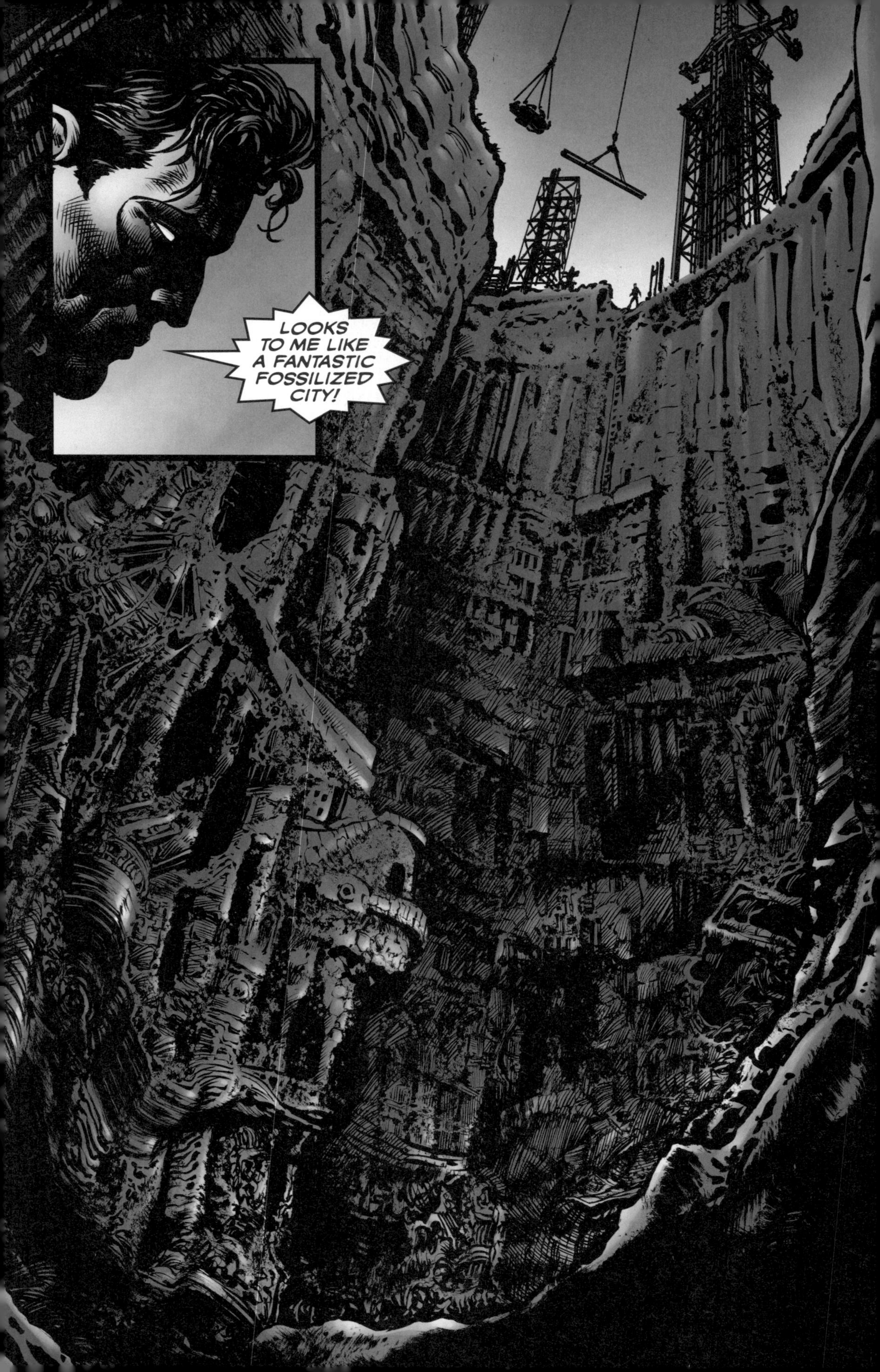
LOOKS TO ME LIKE A FANTASTIC FOSSILIZED CITY!

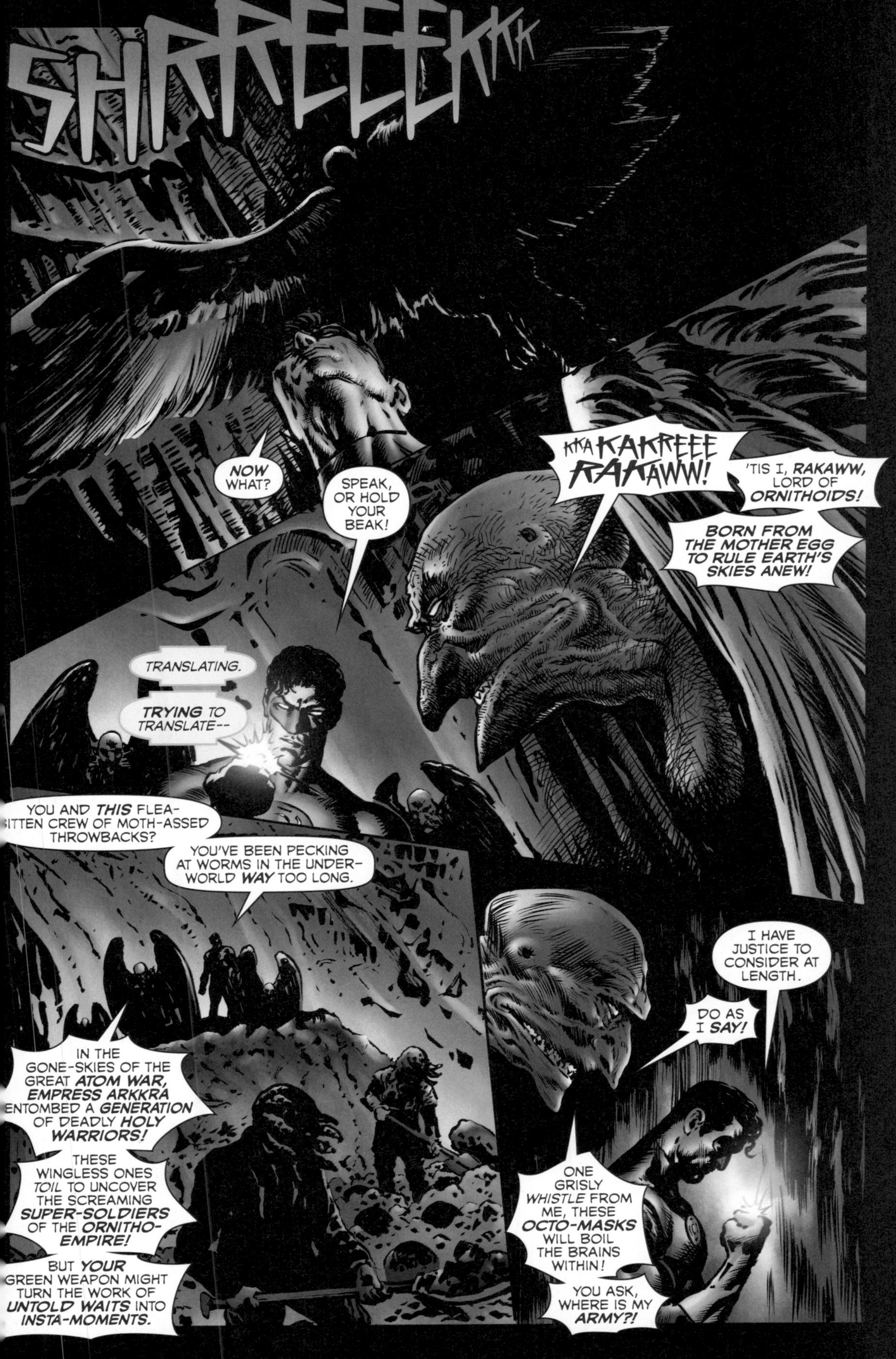
SHRREEEKKKK
NOW WHAT?
SPEAK, OR HOLD YOUR BEAK!
KKA KAKREEE RAKAWW!
'TIS I, RAKAWW, LORD OF ORNITHOIDS!
BORN FROM THE MOTHER EGG TO RULE EARTH'S SKIES ANEW!
TRANSLATING.
TRYING TO TRANSLATE--
YOU AND THIS FLEA-BITTEN CREW OF MOTH-ASSED THROWBACKS?
YOU'VE BEEN PECKING AT WORMS IN THE UNDER-WORLD WAY TOO LONG.
I HAVE JUSTICE TO CONSIDER AT LENGTH.
DO AS I SAY!
IN THE GONE-SKIES OF THE GREAT ATOM WAR, EMPRESS ARKKRA ENTOMBED A GENERATION OF DEADLY HOLY WARRIORS!
THESE WINGLESS ONES TOIL TO UNCOVER THE SCREAMING SUPER-SOLDIERS OF THE ORNITHO-EMPIRE!
BUT YOUR GREEN WEAPON MIGHT TURN THE WORK OF UNTOLD WAITS INTO INSTA-MOMENTS.
ONE GRISLY WHISTLE FROM ME, THESE OCTO-MASKS WILL BOIL THE BRAINS WITHIN!
YOU ASK, WHERE IS MY ARMY?!

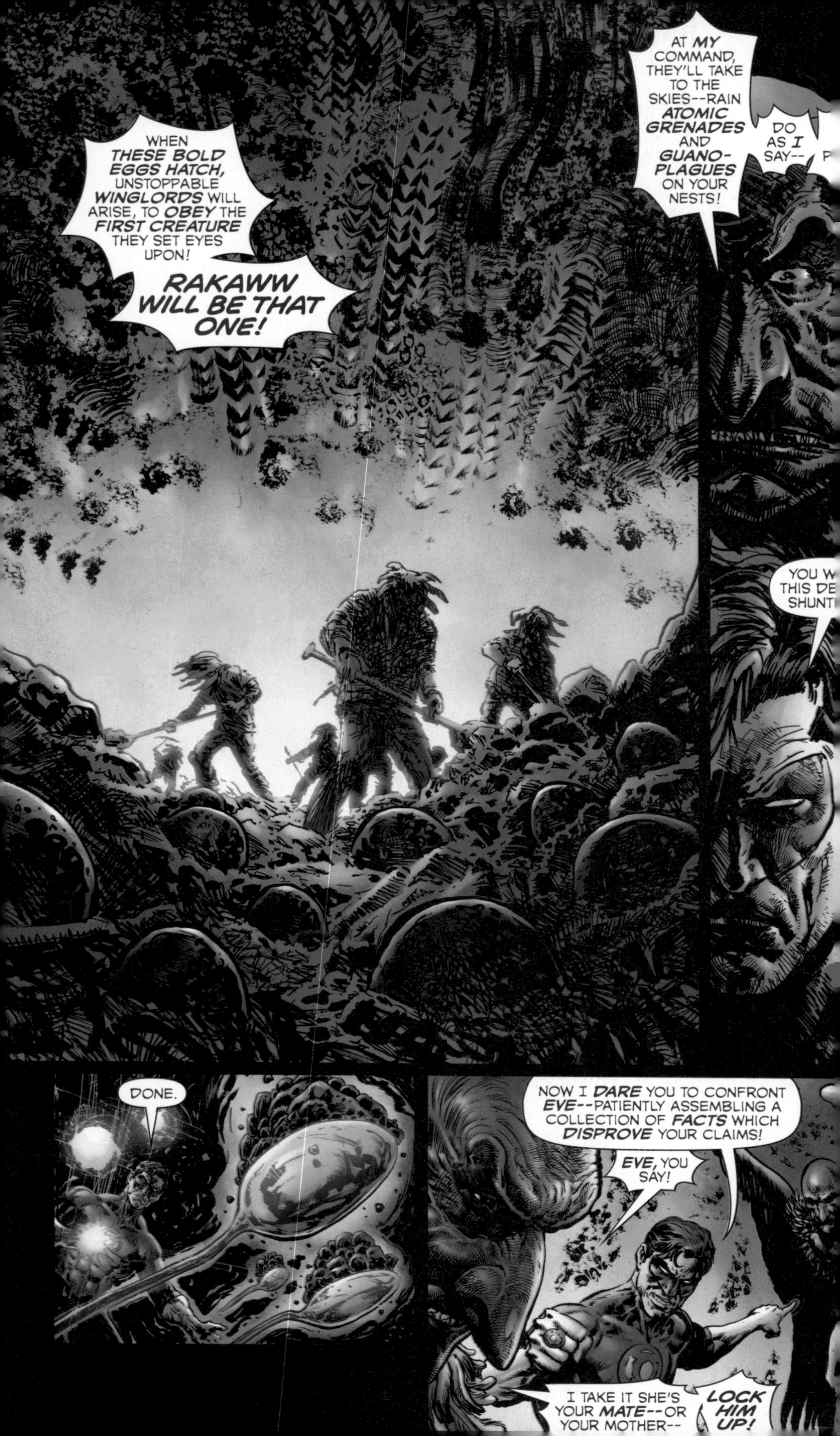
WHEN THESE BOLD EGGS HATCH, UNSTOPPABLE WINGLORDS WILL ARISE, TO OBEY THE FIRST CREATURE THEY SET EYES UPON!
RAKAWW WILL BE THAT ONE!
AT MY COMMAND, THEY'LL TAKE TO THE SKIES--RAIN ATOMIC GRENADES AND GUANO-PLAGUES ON YOUR NESTS!
DO AS I SAY--
DONE.
NOW I DARE YOU TO CONFRONT EVE--PATIENTLY ASSEMBLING A COLLECTION OF FACTS WHICH DISPROVE YOUR CLAIMS!
EVE, YOU SAY!
I TAKE IT SHE'S YOUR MATE--OR YOUR MOTHER--
LOCK HIM UP!

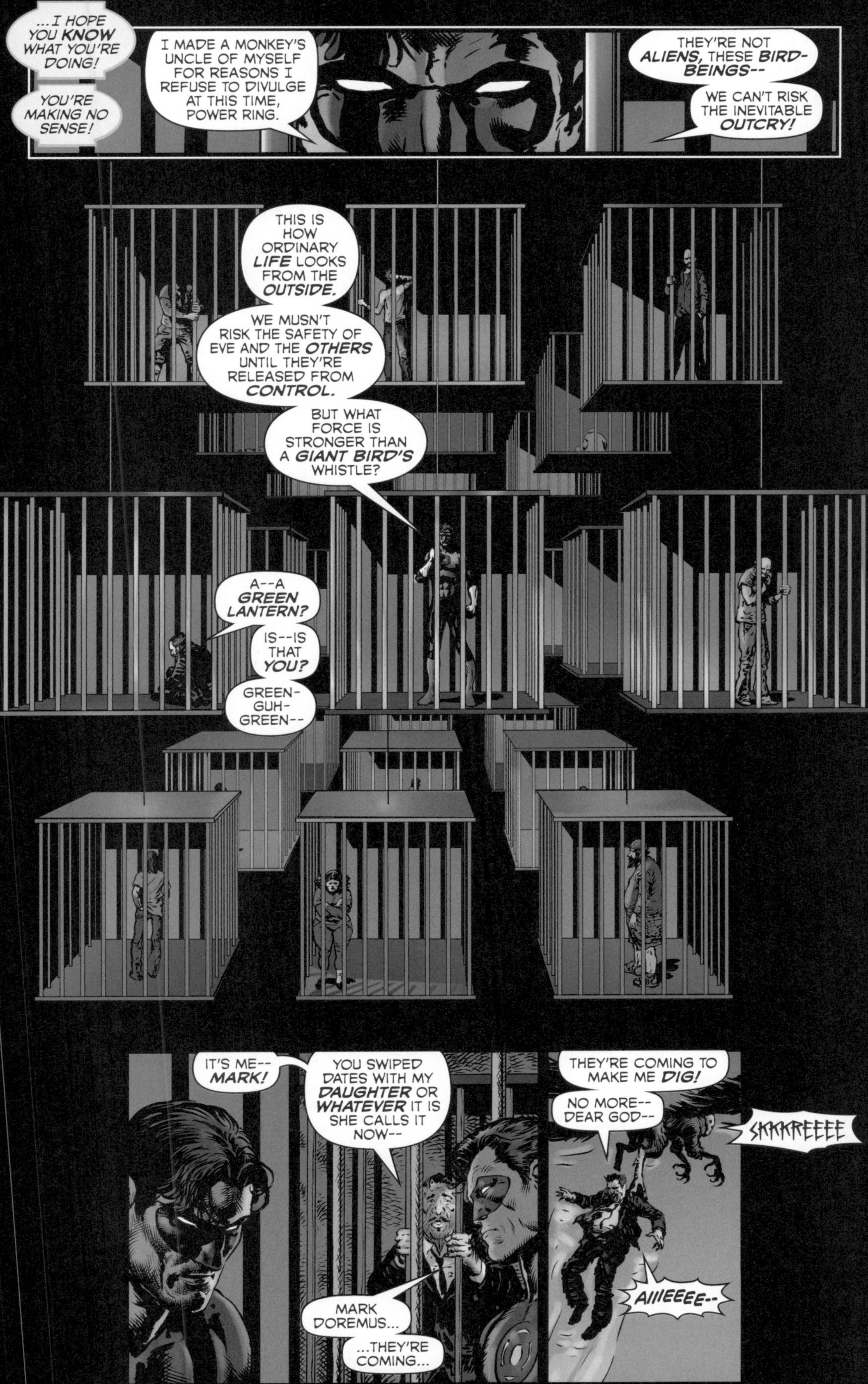
...I HOPE YOU KNOW WHAT YOU'RE DOING!
YOU'RE MAKING NO SENSE!
I MADE A MONKEY'S UNCLE OF MYSELF FOR REASONS I REFUSE TO DIVULGE AT THIS TIME, POWER RING.
THEY'RE NOT ALIENS, THESE BIRD-BEINGS--
WE CAN'T RISK THE INEVITABLE OUTCRY!
THIS IS HOW ORDINARY LIFE LOOKS FROM THE OUTSIDE.
WE MUSN'T RISK THE SAFETY OF EVE AND THE OTHERS UNTIL THEY'RE RELEASED FROM CONTROL.
BUT WHAT FORCE IS STRONGER THAN A GIANT BIRD'S WHISTLE?
A--A GREEN LANTERN?
IS--IS THAT YOU?
GREEN-GUH-GREEN--
IT'S ME--MARK!
YOU SWIPED DATES WITH MY DAUGHTER OR WHATEVER IT IS SHE CALLS IT NOW--
MARK DOREMUS...
...THEY'RE COMING...
THEY'RE COMING TO MAKE ME DIG!
NO MORE--DEAR GOD--
SKKKREEEE
AIIIEEEE--

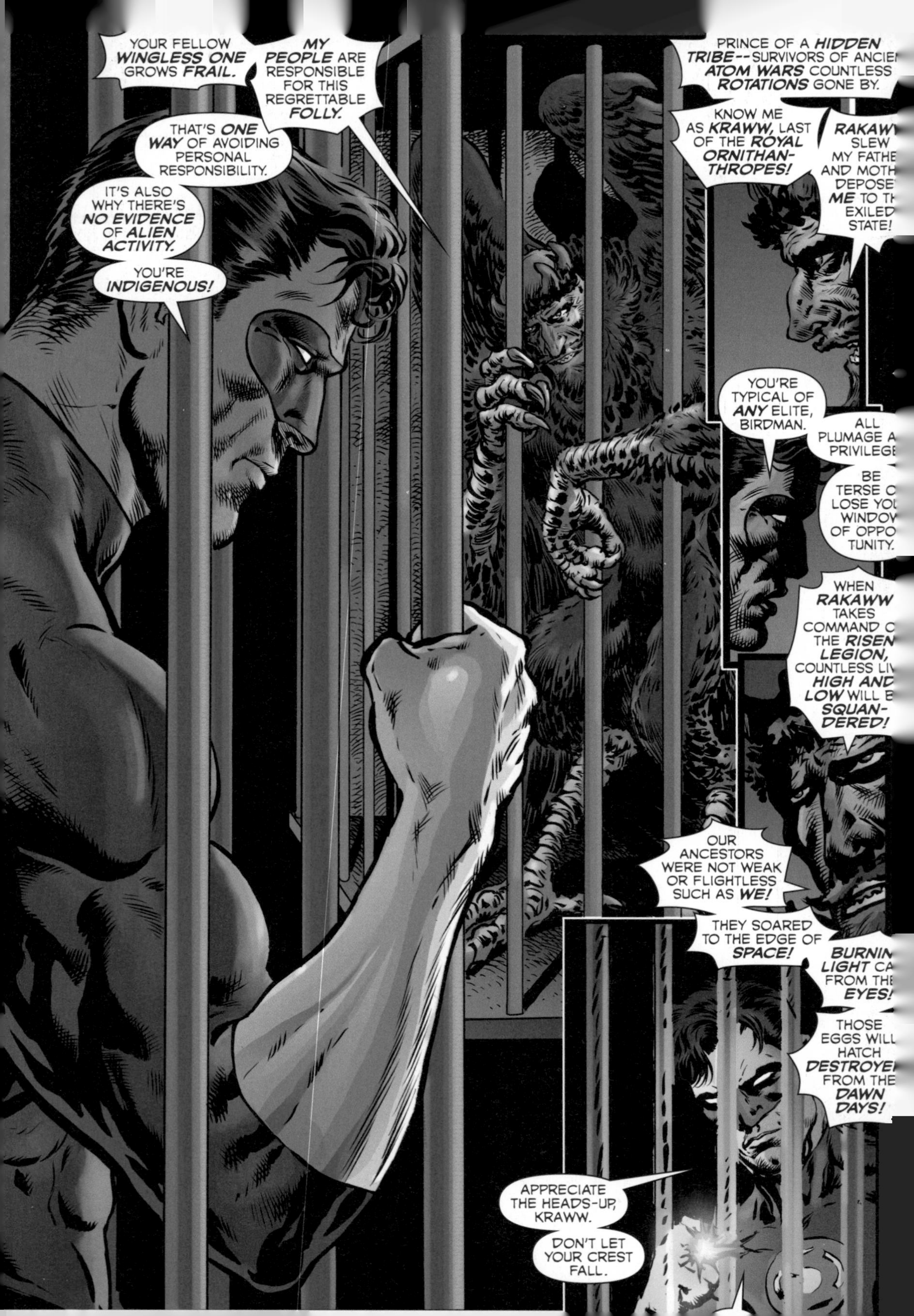
YOUR FELLOW WINGLESS ONE GROWS FRAIL.
MY PEOPLE ARE RESPONSIBLE FOR THIS REGRETTABLE FOLLY.
THAT'S ONE WAY OF AVOIDING PERSONAL RESPONSIBILITY.
IT'S ALSO WHY THERE'S NO EVIDENCE OF ALIEN ACTIVITY.
YOU'RE INDIGENOUS!
PRINCE OF A HIDDEN TRIBE--SURVIVORS OF ANCIE ATOM WARS COUNTLESS ROTATIONS GONE BY.
KNOW ME AS KRAWW, LAST OF THE ROYAL ORNITHAN-THROPES!
RAKAW SLEW MY FATHE AND MOTH DEPOSE ME TO TH EXILED STATE!
YOU'RE TYPICAL OF ANY ELITE, BIRDMAN.
ALL PLUMAGE A PRIVILEGE
BE TERSE O LOSE YO WINDOW OF OPPO TUNITY.
WHEN RAKAWW TAKES COMMAND O THE RISEN LEGION, COUNTLESS LIV HIGH AND LOW WILL B SQUAN-DERED!
OUR ANCESTORS WERE NOT WEAK OR FLIGHTLESS SUCH AS WE!
THEY SOARED TO THE EDGE OF SPACE!
BURNIN LIGHT CA FROM THE EYES!
THOSE EGGS WILL HATCH DESTROYE FROM THE DAWN DAYS!
APPRECIATE THE HEADS-UP, KRAWW.
DON'T LET YOUR CREST FALL.

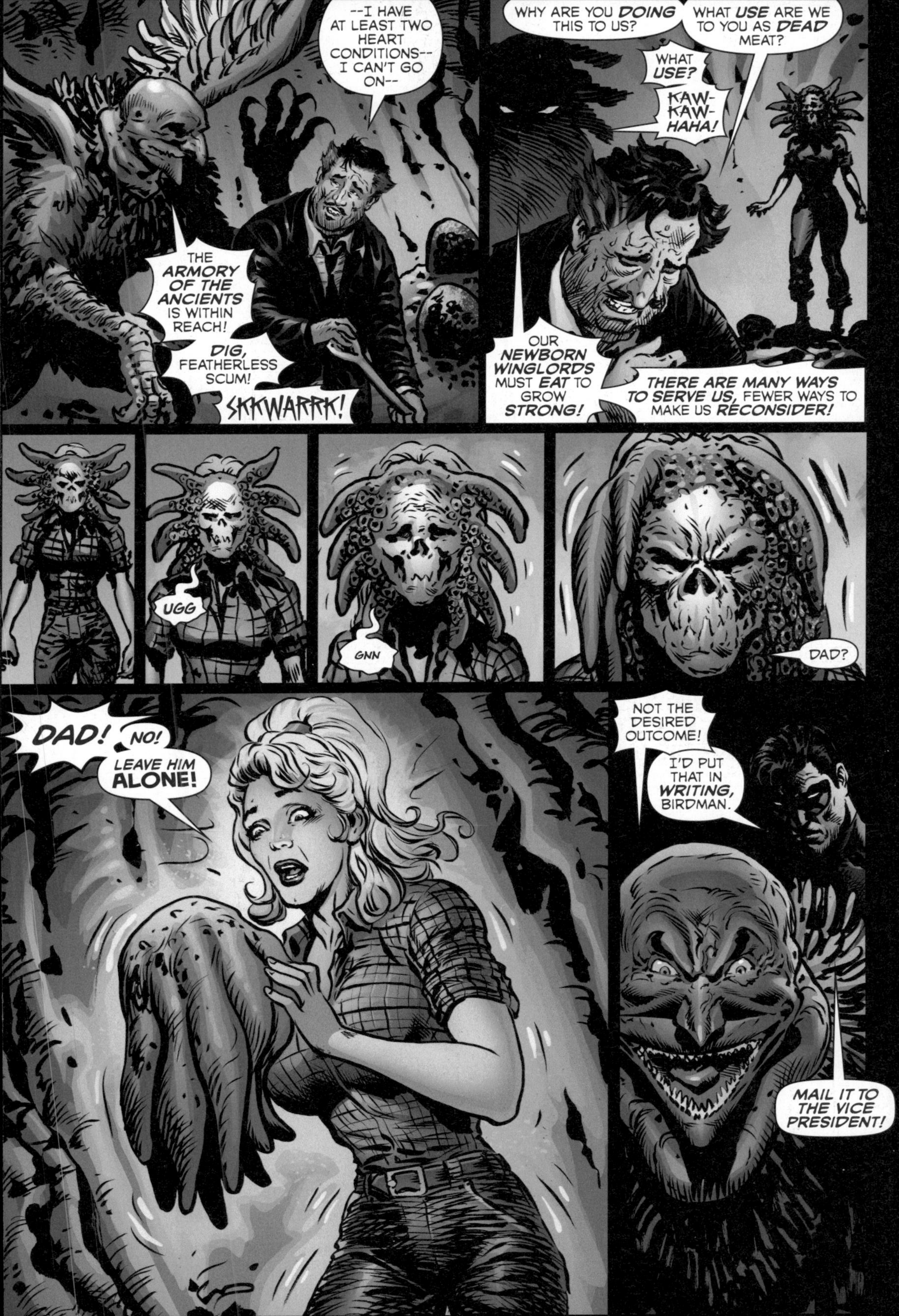
--I HAVE AT LEAST TWO HEART CONDITIONS-- I CAN'T GO ON--
THE ARMORY OF THE ANCIENTS IS WITHIN REACH!
DIG, FEATHERLESS SCUM!
SKKWARRRK!
WHY ARE YOU DOING THIS TO US?
WHAT USE ARE WE TO YOU AS DEAD MEAT?
WHAT USE?
KAW-KAW-HAHA!
OUR NEWBORN WINGLORDS MUST EAT TO GROW STRONG!
THERE ARE MANY WAYS TO SERVE US, FEWER WAYS TO MAKE US RECONSIDER!
UGG
GNN
DAD?
DAD!
NO! LEAVE HIM ALONE!
NOT THE DESIRED OUTCOME!
I'D PUT THAT IN WRITING, BIRDMAN.
MAIL IT TO THE VICE PRESIDENT!

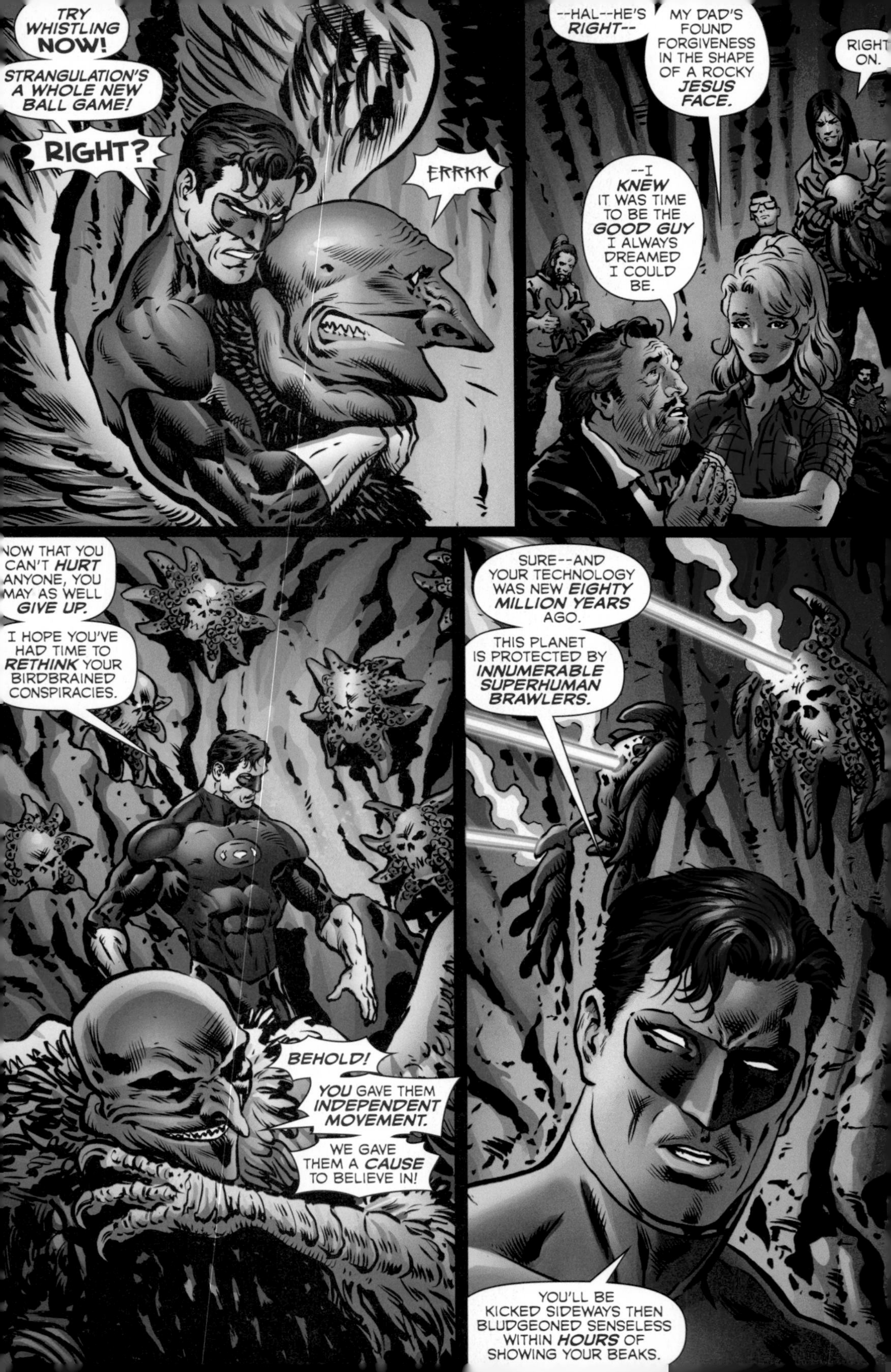
TRY WHISTLING NOW!
STRANGULATION'S A WHOLE NEW BALL GAME!
RIGHT?
ERRKK
--HAL--HE'S RIGHT--
MY DAD'S FOUND FORGIVENESS IN THE SHAPE OF A ROCKY JESUS FACE.
RIGHT ON.
--I KNEW IT WAS TIME TO BE THE GOOD GUY I ALWAYS DREAMED I COULD BE.
NOW THAT YOU CAN'T HURT ANYONE, YOU MAY AS WELL GIVE UP.
I HOPE YOU'VE HAD TIME TO RETHINK YOUR BIRDBRAINED CONSPIRACIES.
BEHOLD!
YOU GAVE THEM INDEPENDENT MOVEMENT.
WE GAVE THEM A CAUSE TO BELIEVE IN!
SURE--AND YOUR TECHNOLOGY WAS NEW EIGHTY MILLION YEARS AGO.
THIS PLANET IS PROTECTED BY INNUMERABLE SUPERHUMAN BRAWLERS.
YOU'LL BE KICKED SIDEWAYS THEN BLUDGEONED SENSELESS WITHIN HOURS OF SHOWING YOUR BEAKS.

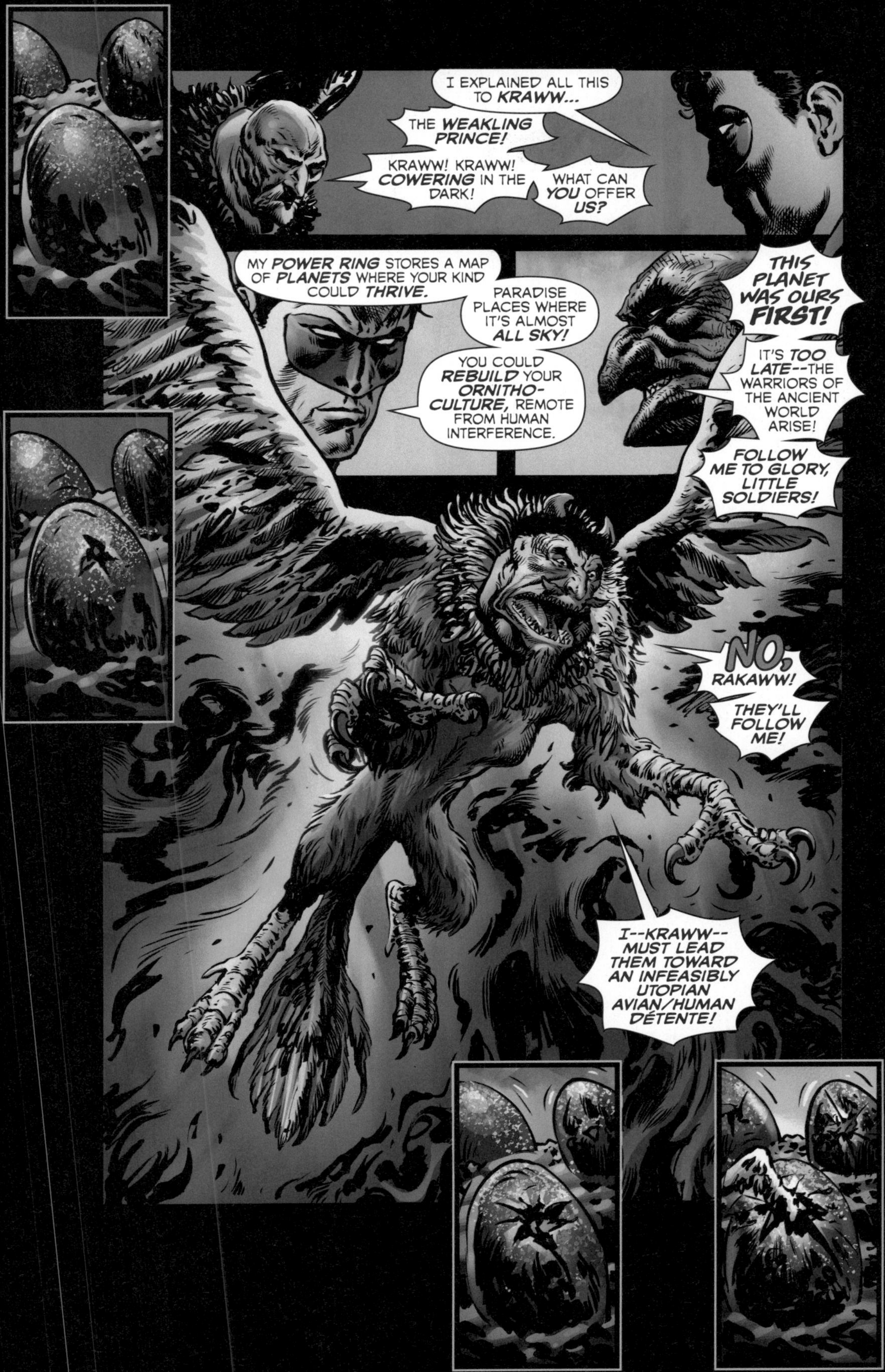

I EXPLAINED ALL THIS TO KRAWW...
THE WEAKLING PRINCE!
KRAWW! KRAWW! COWERING IN THE DARK!
WHAT CAN YOU OFFER US?
MY POWER RING STORES A MAP OF PLANETS WHERE YOUR KIND COULD THRIVE.
PARADISE PLACES WHERE IT'S ALMOST ALL SKY!
YOU COULD REBUILD YOUR ORNITHO-CULTURE, REMOTE FROM HUMAN INTERFERENCE.
THIS PLANET WAS OURS FIRST!
IT'S TOO LATE--THE WARRIORS OF THE ANCIENT WORLD ARISE!
FOLLOW ME TO GLORY, LITTLE SOLDIERS!
NO, RAKAWW!
THEY'LL FOLLOW ME!
I--KRAWW--MUST LEAD THEM TOWARD AN INFEASIBLY UTOPIAN AVIAN/HUMAN DÉTENTE!

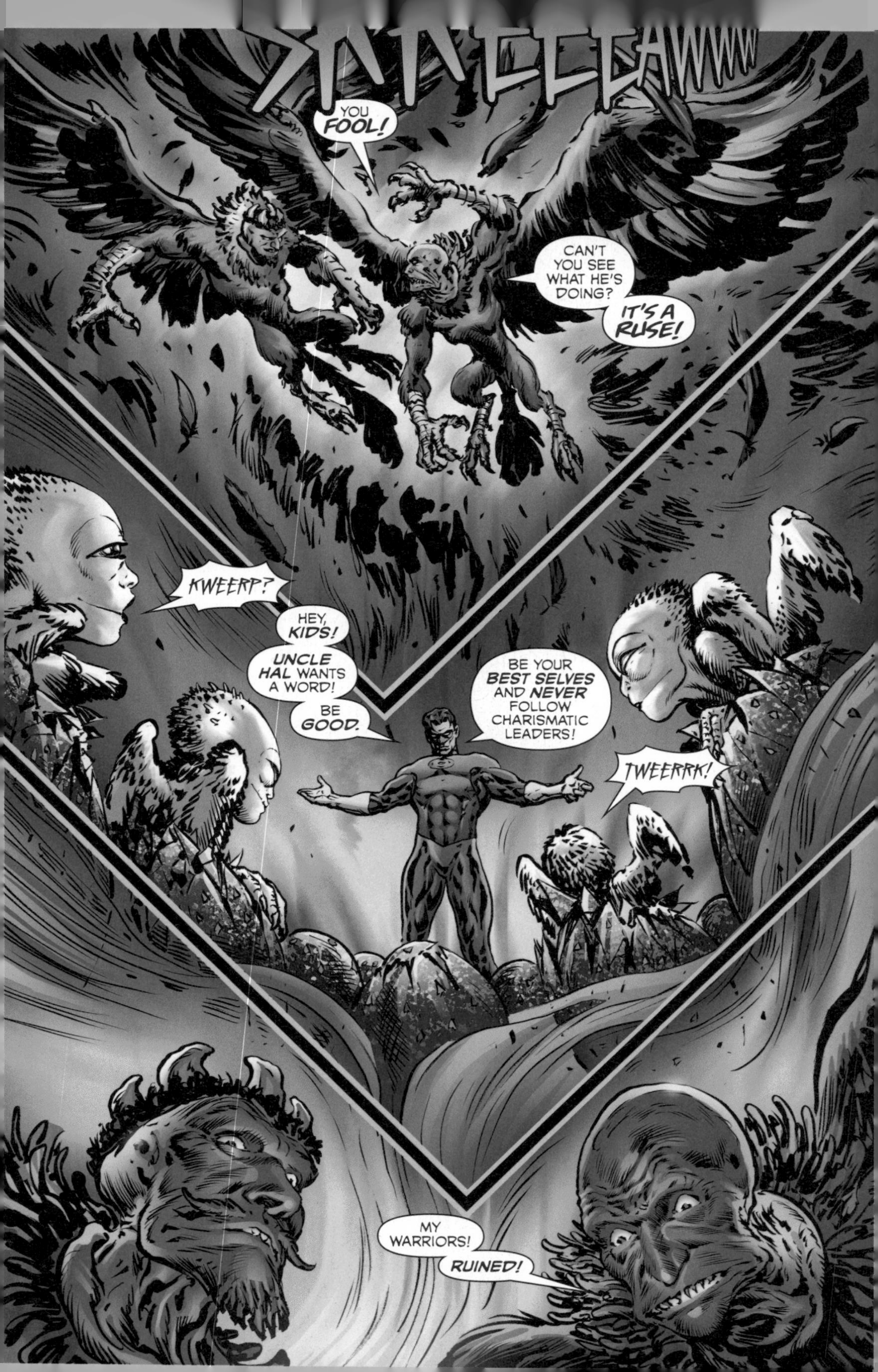
YOU FOOL!
CAN'T YOU SEE WHAT HE'S DOING?
IT'S A RUSE!
KWEERP?
HEY, KIDS!
UNCLE HAL WANTS A WORD!
BE GOOD.
BE YOUR BEST SELVES AND NEVER FOLLOW CHARISMATIC LEADERS!
TWEERRK!
MY WARRIORS!
RUINED!

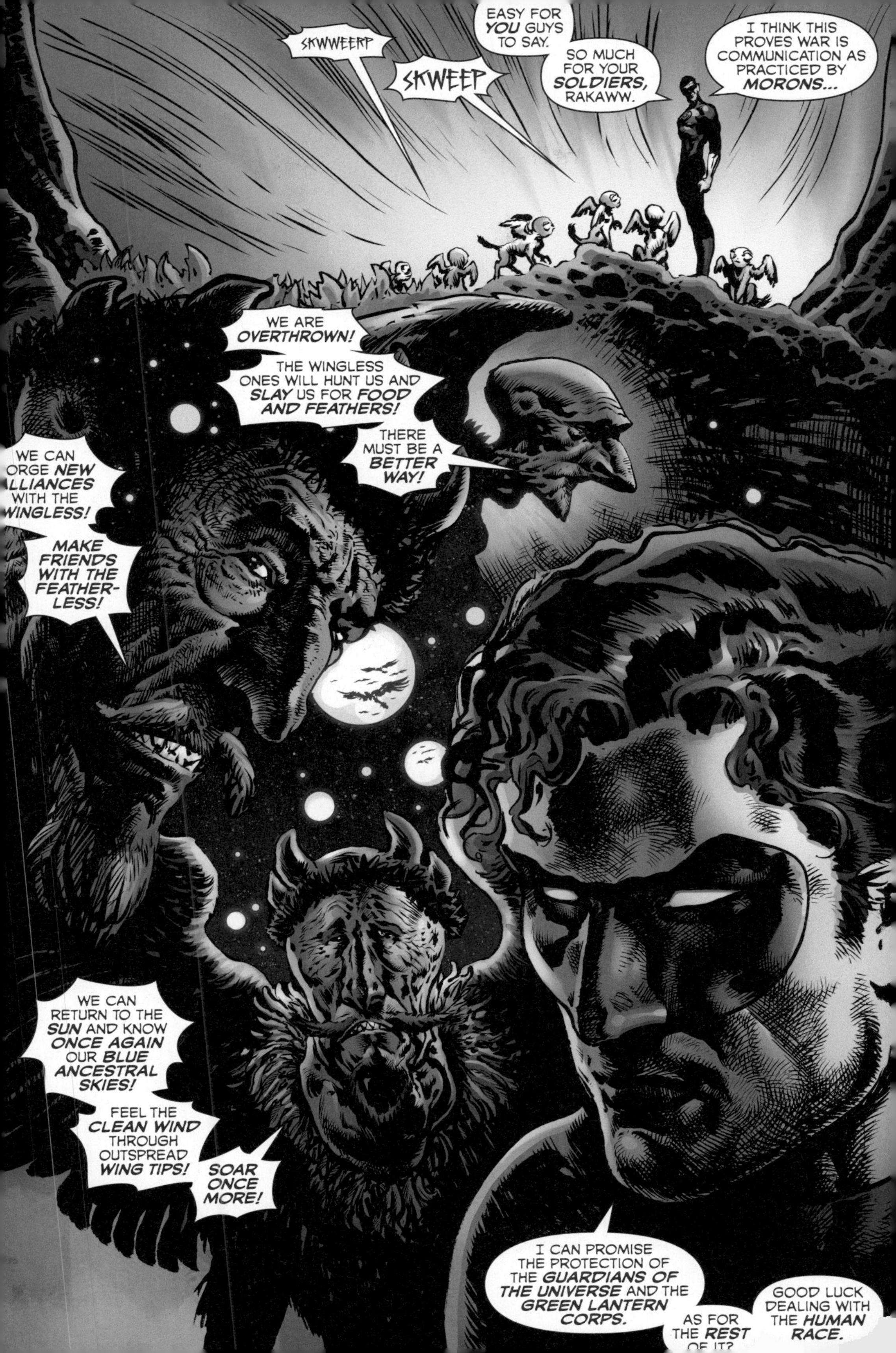
SKWWEERP
SKWEEP
EASY FOR YOU GUYS TO SAY.
SO MUCH FOR YOUR SOLDIERS, RAKAWW.
I THINK THIS PROVES WAR IS COMMUNICATION AS PRACTICED BY MORONS...
WE ARE OVERTHROWN!
THE WINGLESS ONES WILL HUNT US AND SLAY US FOR FOOD AND FEATHERS!
THERE MUST BE A BETTER WAY!
WE CAN ORGE NEW LLIANCES WITH THE WINGLESS!
MAKE FRIENDS WITH THE FEATHER-LESS!
WE CAN RETURN TO THE SUN AND KNOW ONCE AGAIN OUR BLUE ANCESTRAL SKIES!
FEEL THE CLEAN WIND THROUGH OUTSPREAD WING TIPS!
SOAR ONCE MORE!
I CAN PROMISE THE PROTECTION OF THE GUARDIANS OF THE UNIVERSE AND THE GREEN LANTERN CORPS.
AS FOR THE REST
GOOD LUCK DEALING WITH THE HUMAN RACE.

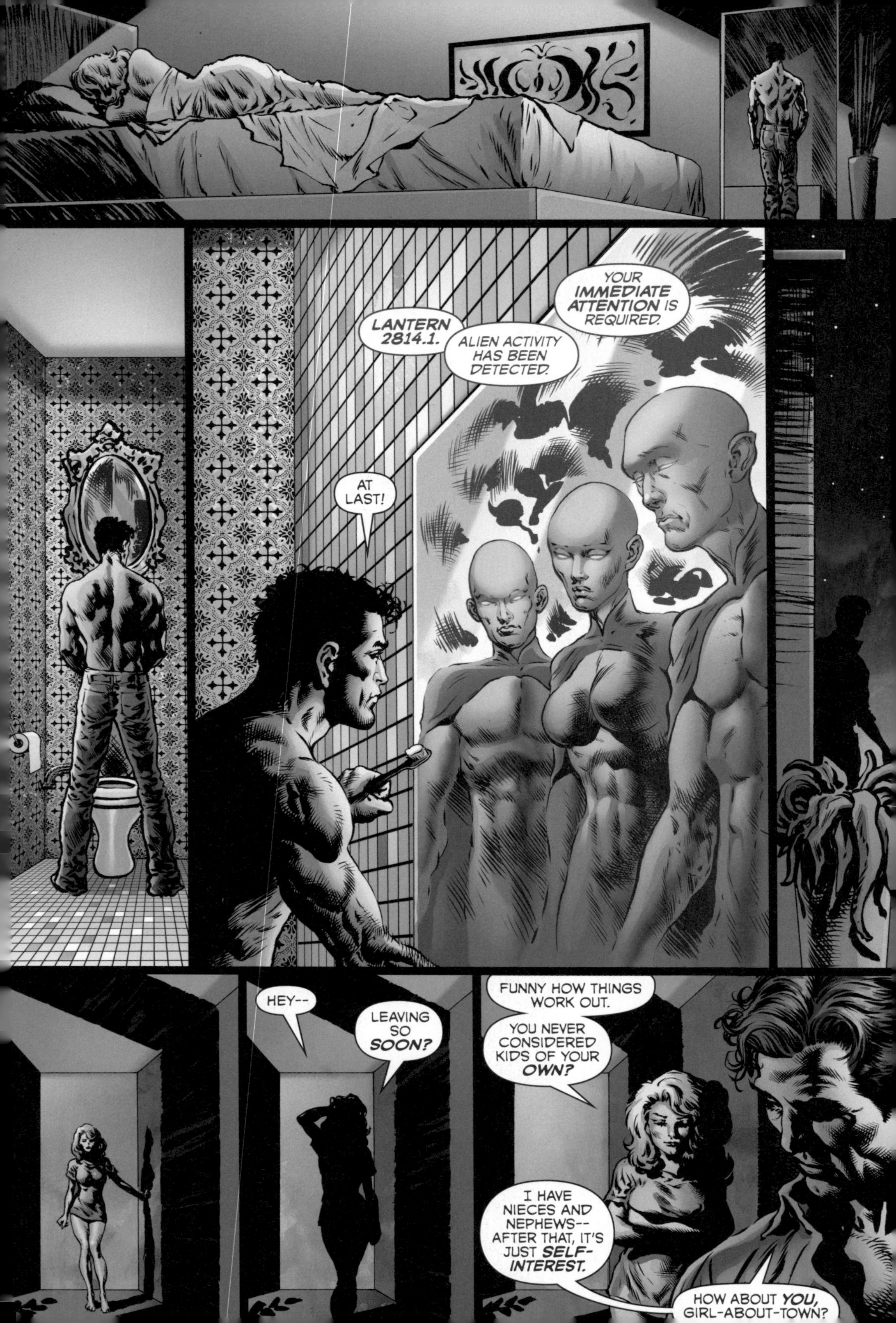
LANTERN 2814.1.
ALIEN ACTIVITY HAS BEEN DETECTED.
YOUR IMMEDIATE ATTENTION IS REQUIRED.
AT LAST!
HEY--
LEAVING SO SOON?
FUNNY HOW THINGS WORK OUT.
YOU NEVER CONSIDERED KIDS OF YOUR OWN?
I HAVE NIECES AND NEPHEWS-- AFTER THAT, IT'S JUST SELF-INTEREST.
HOW ABOUT YOU, GIRL-ABOUT-TOWN?

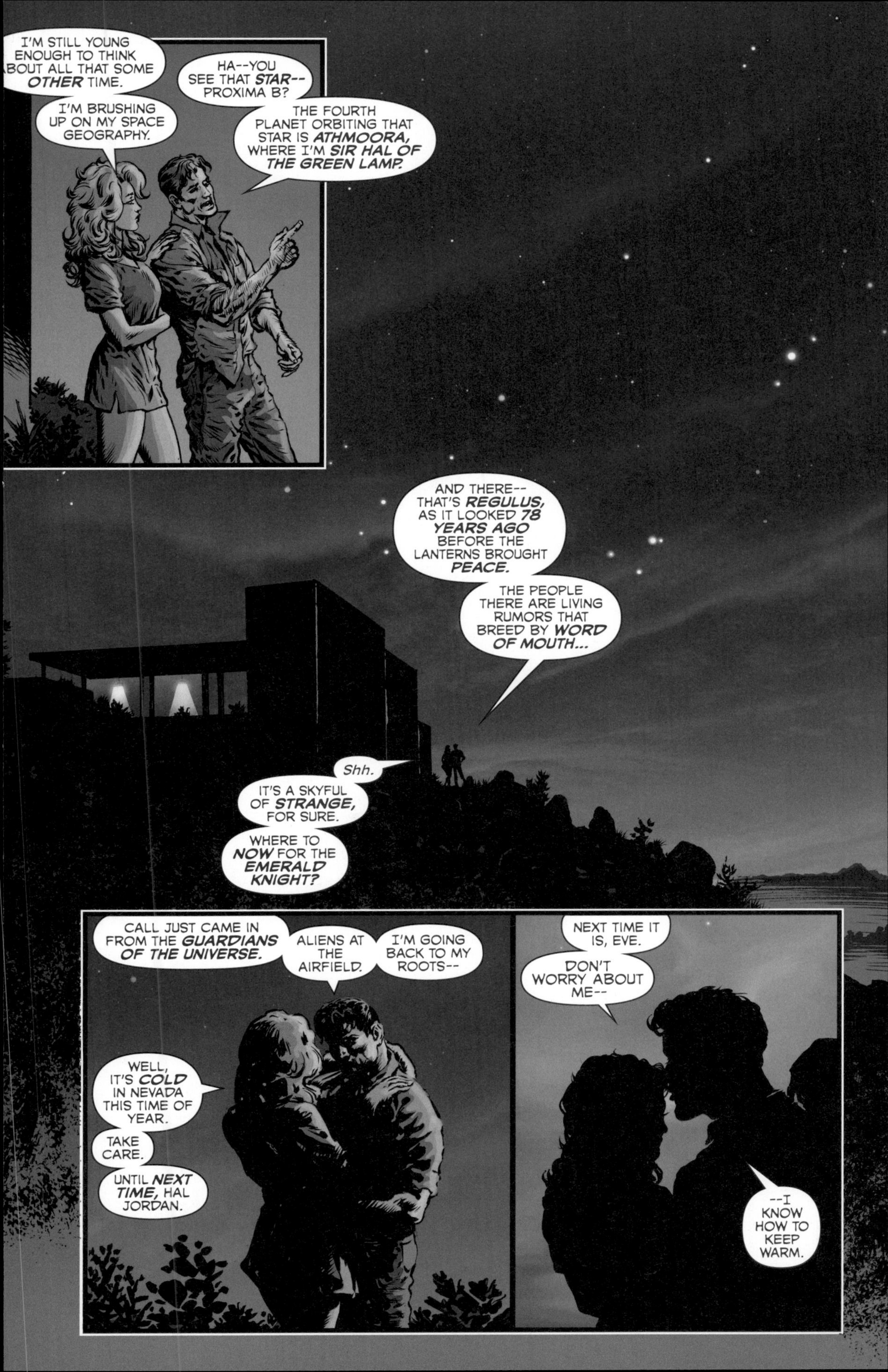
I'M STILL YOUNG ENOUGH TO THINK ABOUT ALL THAT SOME OTHER TIME.
I'M BRUSHING UP ON MY SPACE GEOGRAPHY.
HA--YOU SEE THAT STAR-- PROXIMA B?
THE FOURTH PLANET ORBITING THAT STAR IS ATHMOORA, WHERE I'M SIR HAL OF THE GREEN LAMP.
AND THERE-- THAT'S REGULUS, AS IT LOOKED 78 YEARS AGO BEFORE THE LANTERNS BROUGHT PEACE.
THE PEOPLE THERE ARE LIVING RUMORS THAT BREED BY WORD OF MOUTH...
Shh.
IT'S A SKYFUL OF STRANGE, FOR SURE.
WHERE TO NOW FOR THE EMERALD KNIGHT?
CALL JUST CAME IN FROM THE GUARDIANS OF THE UNIVERSE.
ALIENS AT THE AIRFIELD.
I'M GOING BACK TO MY ROOTS--
WELL, IT'S COLD IN NEVADA THIS TIME OF YEAR.
TAKE CARE.
UNTIL NEXT TIME, HAL JORDAN.
NEXT TIME IT IS, EVE.
DON'T WORRY ABOUT ME--
--I KNOW HOW TO KEEP WARM.

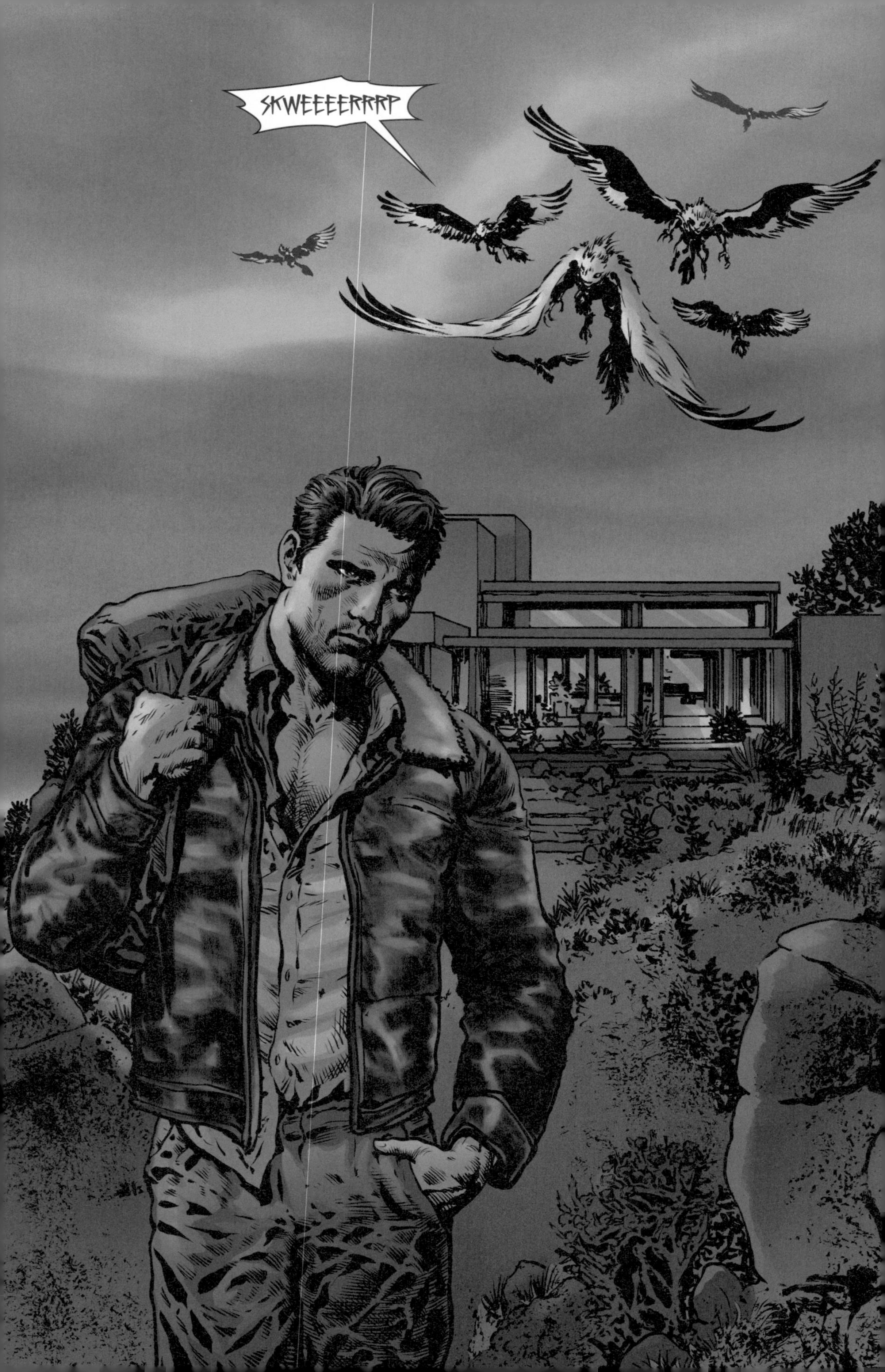
SKWEEEERRRP

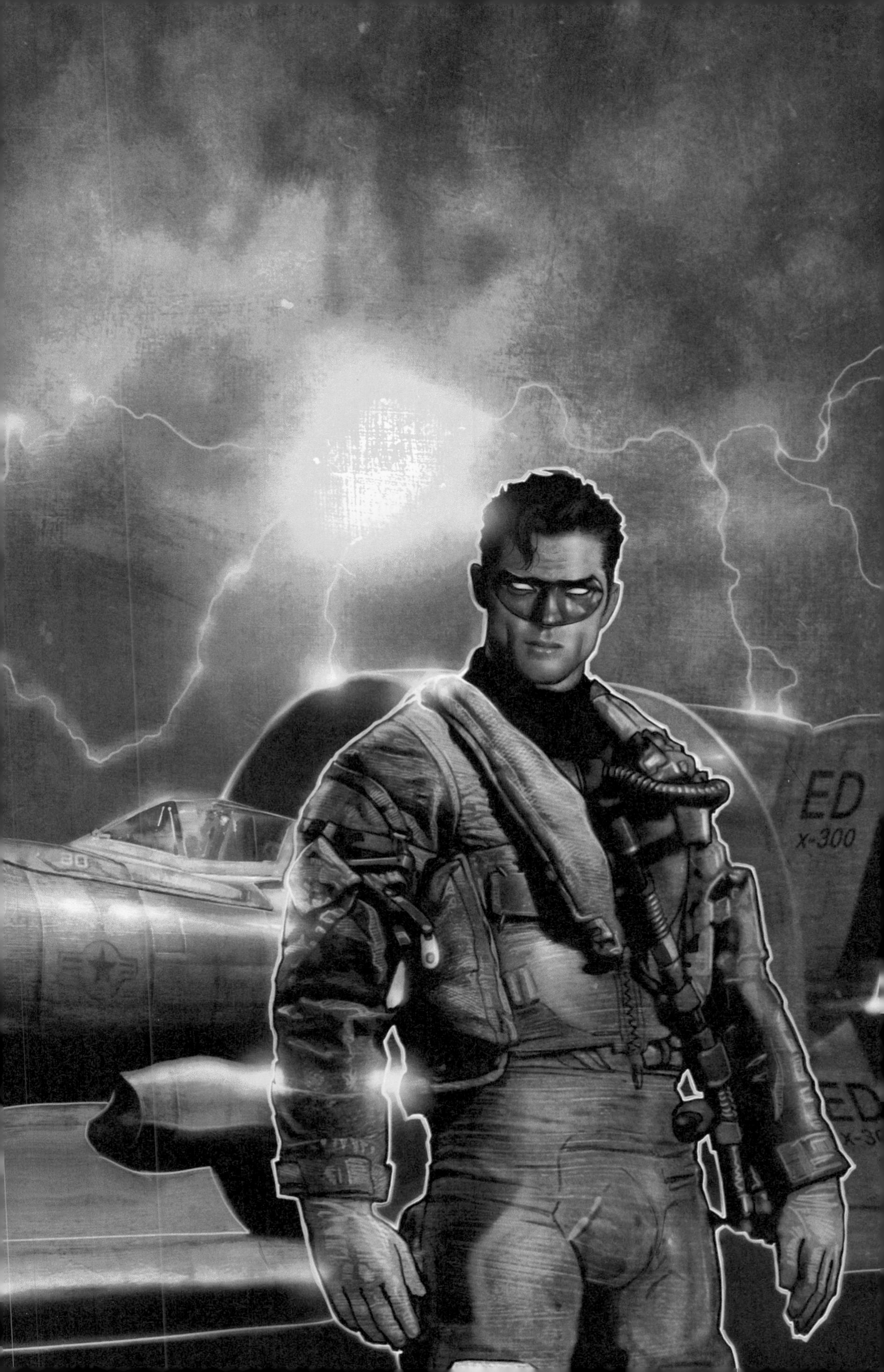
ED
X-300

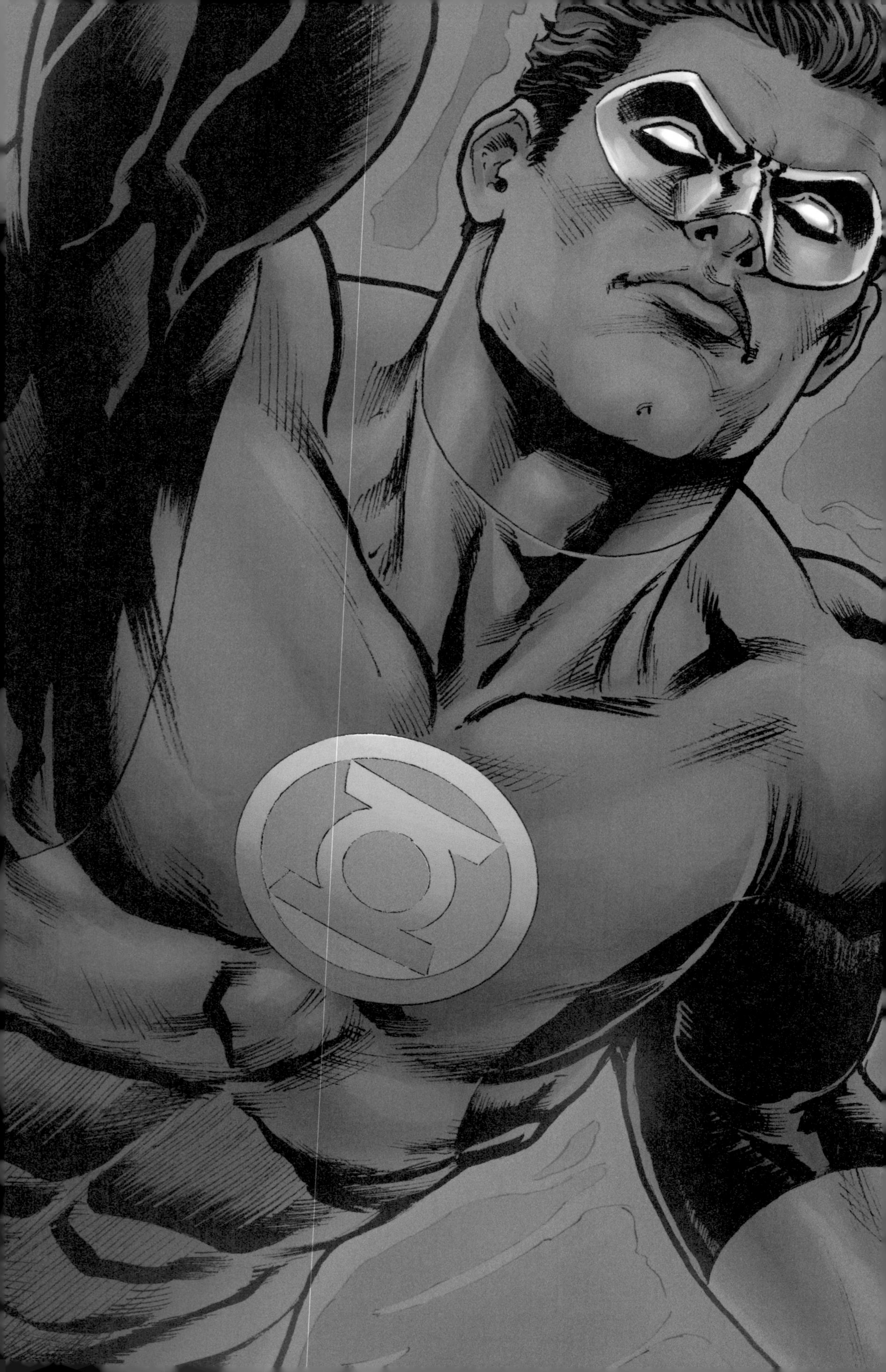

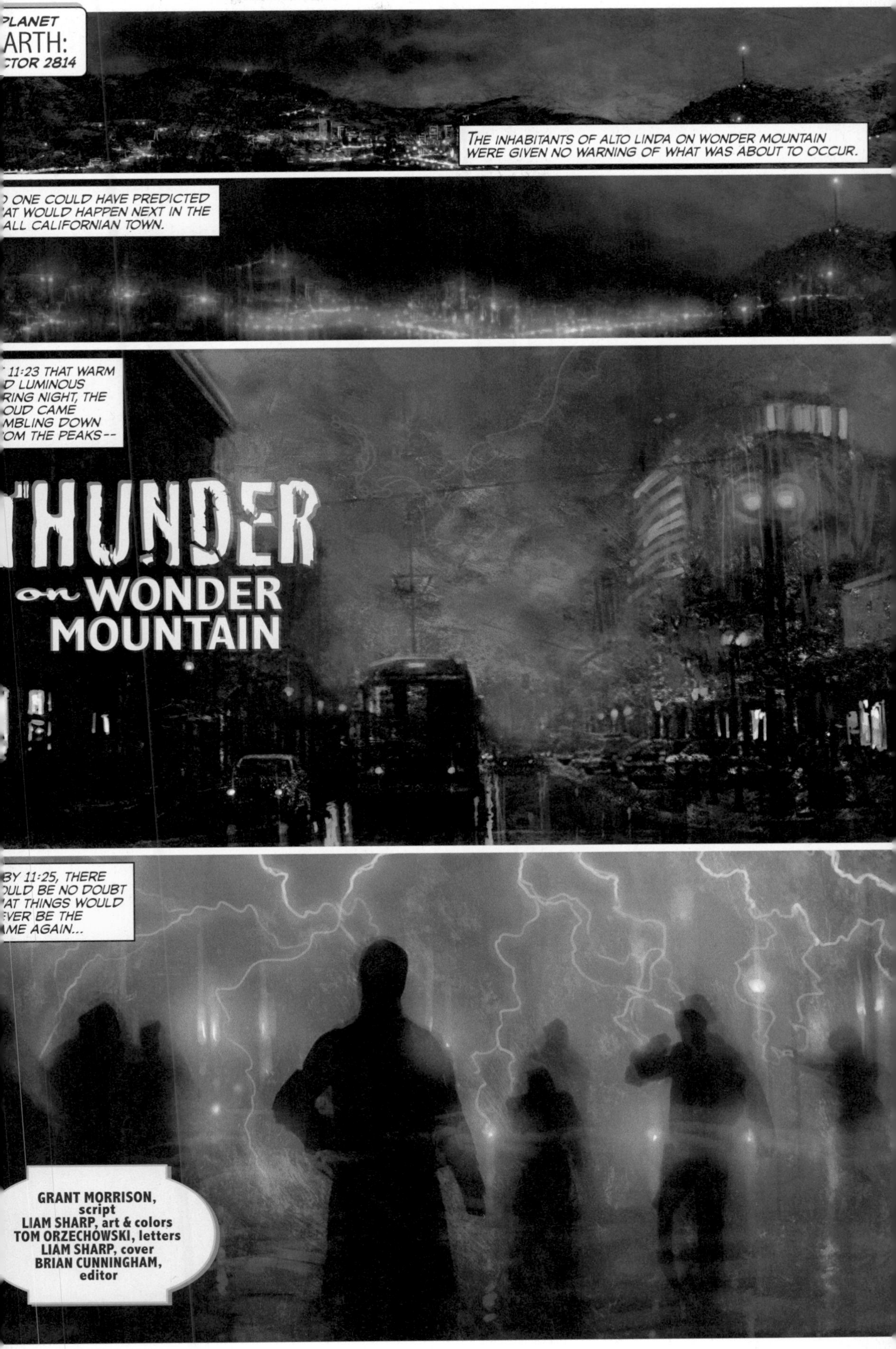
PLANET
ARTH:
CTOR 2814
THE INHABITANTS OF ALTO LINDA ON WONDER MOUNTAIN WERE GIVEN NO WARNING OF WHAT WAS ABOUT TO OCCUR.
O ONE COULD HAVE PREDICTED AT WOULD HAPPEN NEXT IN THE ALL CALIFORNIAN TOWN.
11:23 THAT WARM D LUMINOUS RING NIGHT, THE OUD CAME MBLING DOWN OM THE PEAKS--
THUNDER on WONDER MOUNTAIN
BY 11:25, THERE ULD BE NO DOUBT AT THINGS WOULD VER BE THE ME AGAIN...
GRANT MORRISON, script
LIAM SHARP, art & colors
TOM ORZECHOWSKI, letters
LIAM SHARP, cover
BRIAN CUNNINGHAM, editor

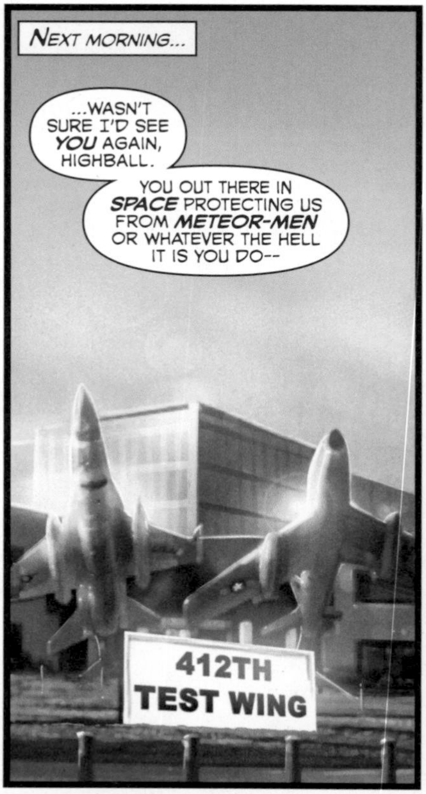
NEXT MORNING...
...WASN'T SURE I'D SEE YOU AGAIN, HIGHBALL.
YOU OUT THERE IN SPACE PROTECTING US FROM METEOR-MEN OR WHATEVER THE HELL IT IS YOU DO--
412TH TEST WING

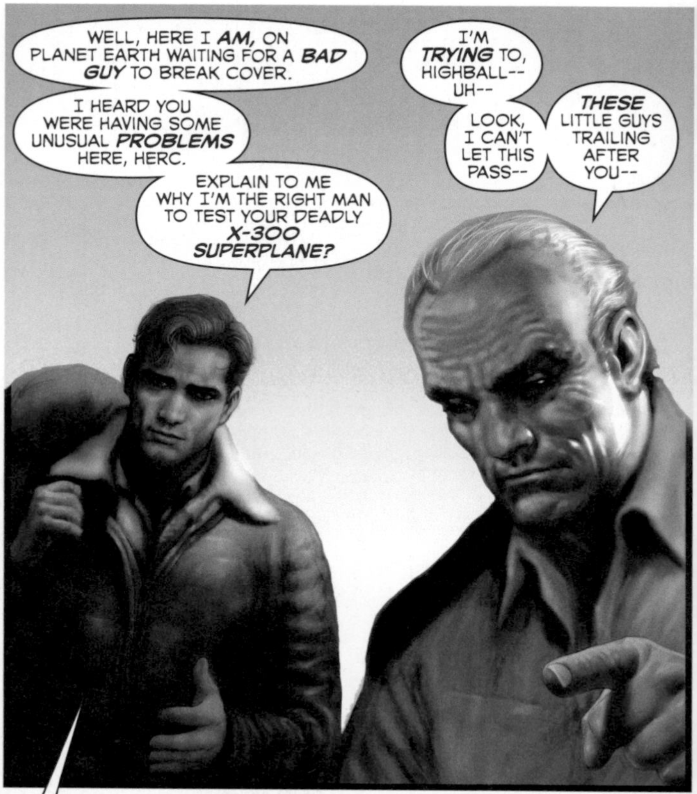
WELL, HERE I AM, ON PLANET EARTH WAITING FOR A BAD GUY TO BREAK COVER.
I HEARD YOU WERE HAVING SOME UNUSUAL PROBLEMS HERE, HERC.
EXPLAIN TO ME WHY I'M THE RIGHT MAN TO TEST YOUR DEADLY X-300 SUPERPLANE?
I'M TRYING TO, HIGHBALL-- UH--
LOOK, I CAN'T LET THIS PASS--
THESE LITTLE GUYS TRAILING AFTER YOU--

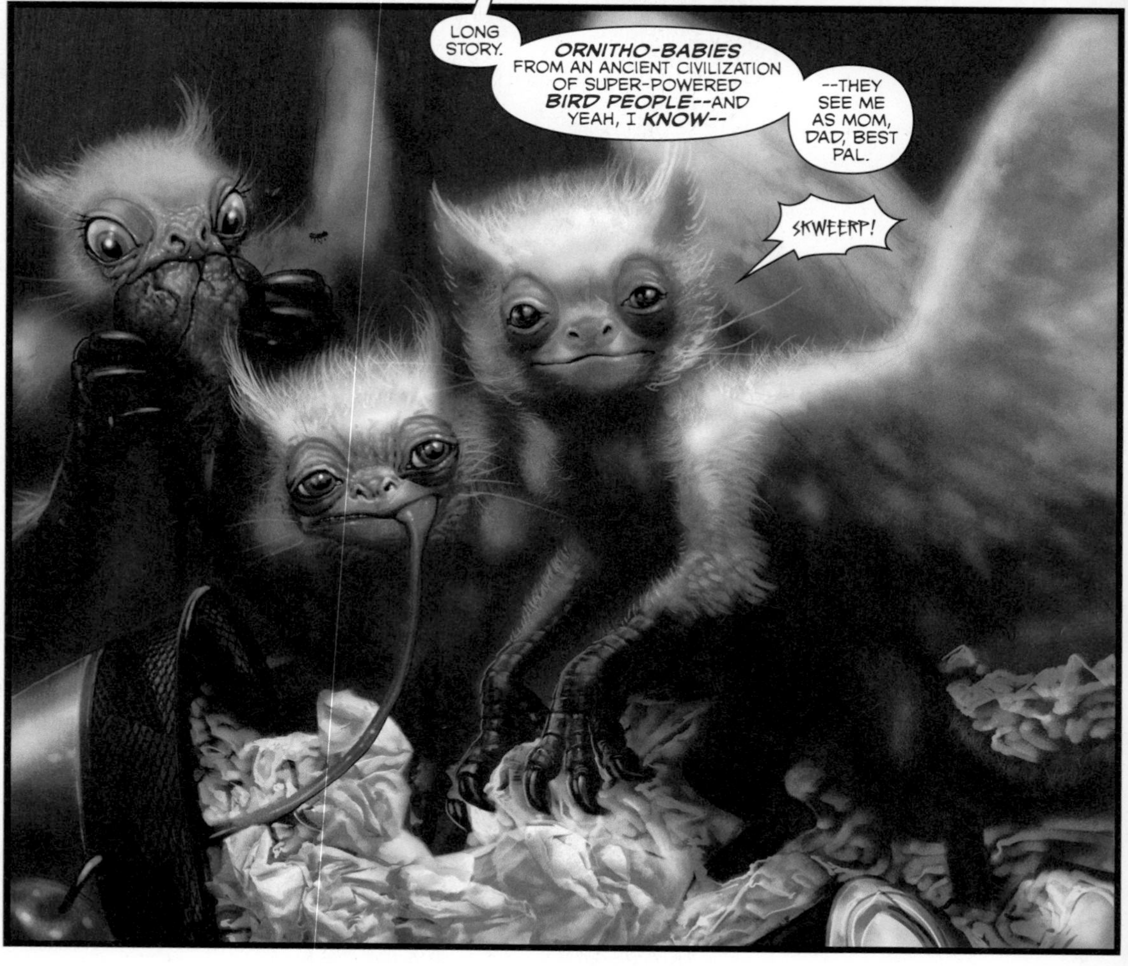
LONG STORY.
ORNITHO-BABIES FROM AN ANCIENT CIVILIZATION OF SUPER-POWERED BIRD PEOPLE--AND YEAH, I KNOW--
--THEY SEE ME AS MOM, DAD, BEST PAL.
SKWEERP!

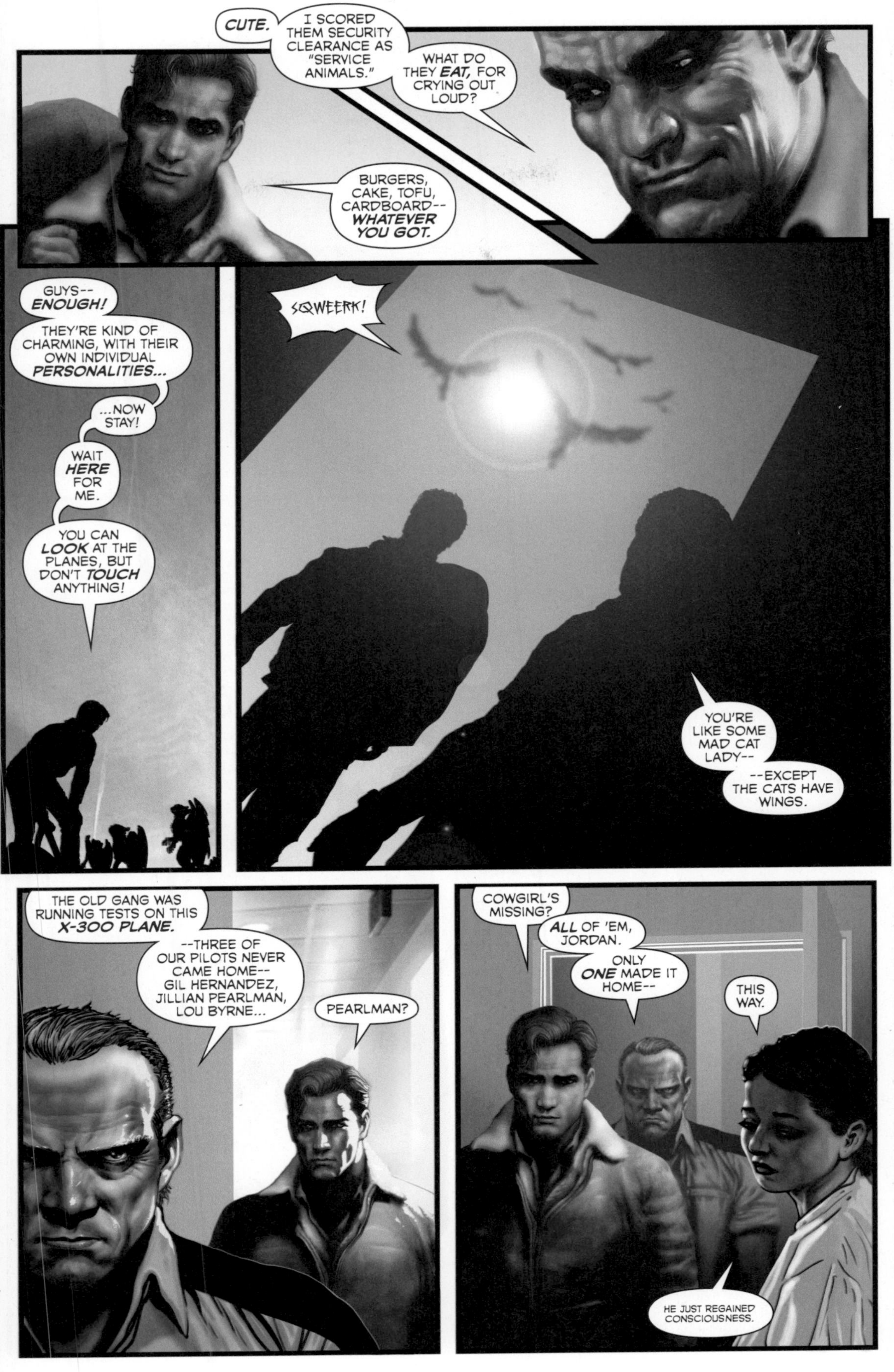

CUTE.
I SCORED THEM SECURITY CLEARANCE AS "SERVICE ANIMALS."
WHAT DO THEY EAT, FOR CRYING OUT LOUD?
BURGERS, CAKE, TOFU, CARDBOARD-- WHATEVER YOU GOT.
GUYS-- ENOUGH!
THEY'RE KIND OF CHARMING, WITH THEIR OWN INDIVIDUAL PERSONALITIES...
...NOW STAY!
WAIT HERE FOR ME.
YOU CAN LOOK AT THE PLANES, BUT DON'T TOUCH ANYTHING!
SQWEERK!
YOU'RE LIKE SOME MAD CAT LADY--
--EXCEPT THE CATS HAVE WINGS.
THE OLD GANG WAS RUNNING TESTS ON THIS X-300 PLANE.
--THREE OF OUR PILOTS NEVER CAME HOME-- GIL HERNANDEZ, JILLIAN PEARLMAN, LOU BYRNE...
PEARLMAN?
COWGIRL'S MISSING?
ALL OF 'EM, JORDAN.
ONLY ONE MADE IT HOME--
THIS WAY.
HE JUST REGAINED CONSCIOUSNESS.

MY GOD. ROCKET- SHANE.
MAN.

hsskk

highhball

whuh juss HIT me, bro?

WHAT HAPPENED TO YOU?

WHAT HAPPENED TO JILL?

ROCKET-MAN.

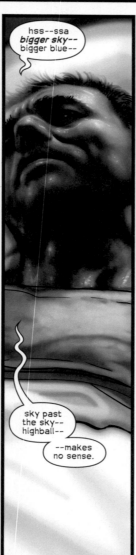

hss--ssa
bigger sky--
bigger blue--

sky past the sky--
highball--

--makes no sense.

Get 'em highball.

Cowgirl's there.

You go get 'em.

SHOW ME THE *X-300.*

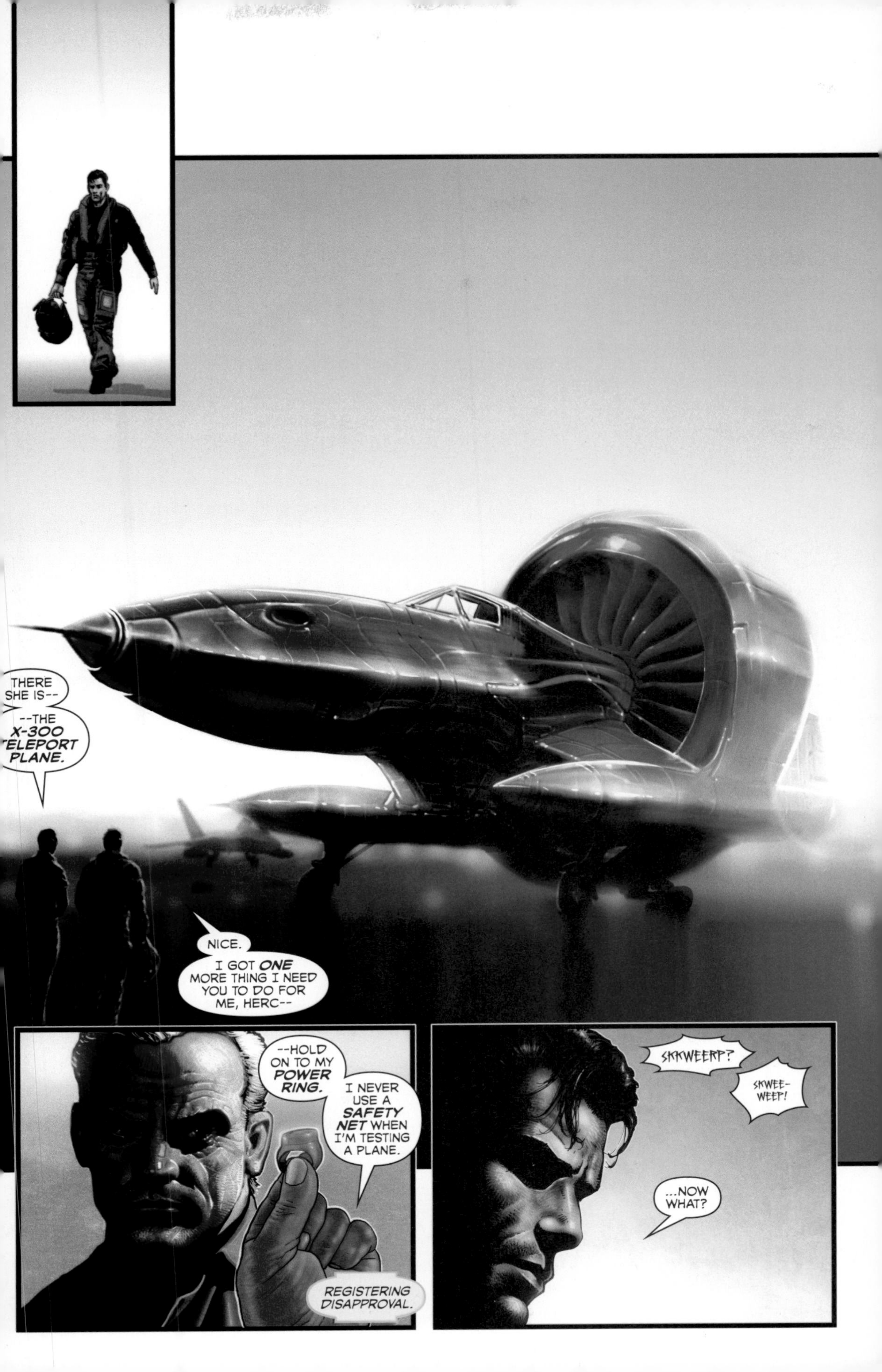
THERE SHE IS--
--THE X-300 TELEPORT PLANE.
NICE.
I GOT ONE MORE THING I NEED YOU TO DO FOR ME, HERC--
--HOLD ON TO MY POWER RING.
I NEVER USE A SAFETY NET WHEN I'M TESTING A PLANE.
REGISTERING DISAPPROVAL.
SKKWEERP?
SKWEE-WEEP!
...NOW WHAT?

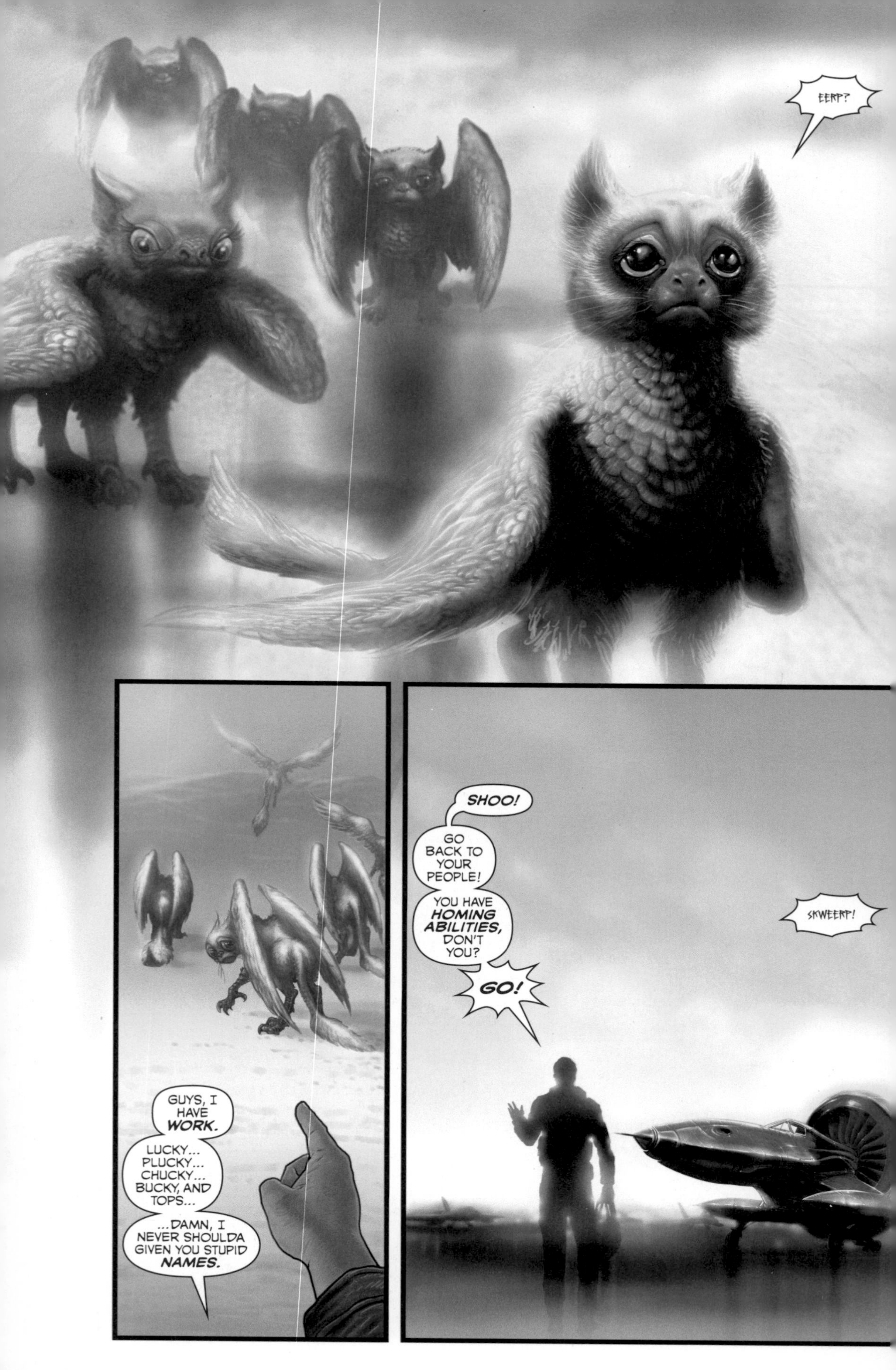
EERP?
GUYS, I HAVE WORK.
LUCKY... PLUCKY... CHUCKY... BUCKY, AND TOPS...
...DAMN, I NEVER SHOULDA GIVEN YOU STUPID NAMES.
SHOO!
GO BACK TO YOUR PEOPLE!
YOU HAVE HOMING ABILITIES, DON'T YOU?
GO!
SKWEERP!

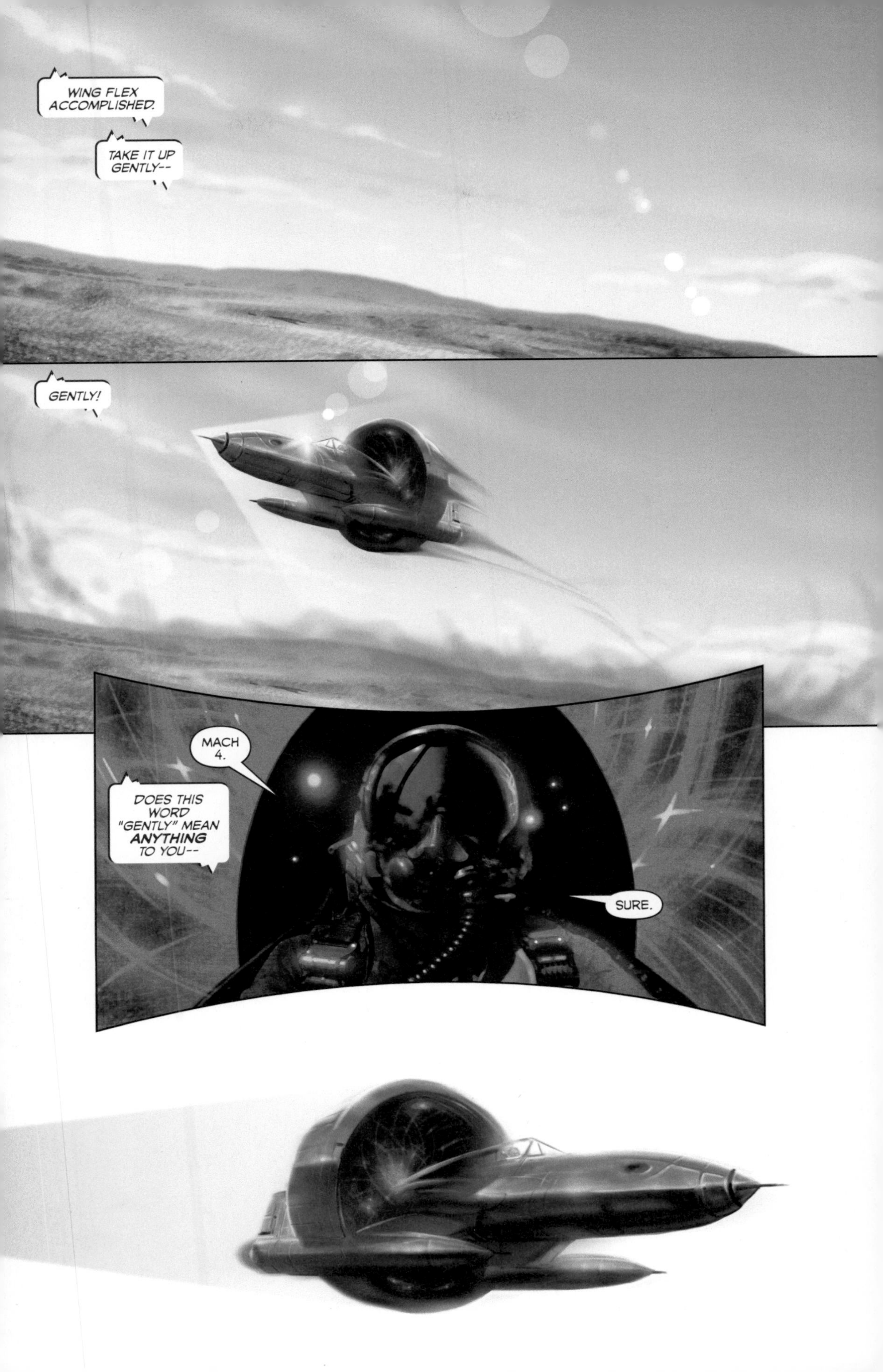

WING FLEX ACCOMPLISHED.
TAKE IT UP GENTLY--
GENTLY!
MACH 4.
DOES THIS WORD "GENTLY" MEAN ANYTHING TO YOU--
SURE.

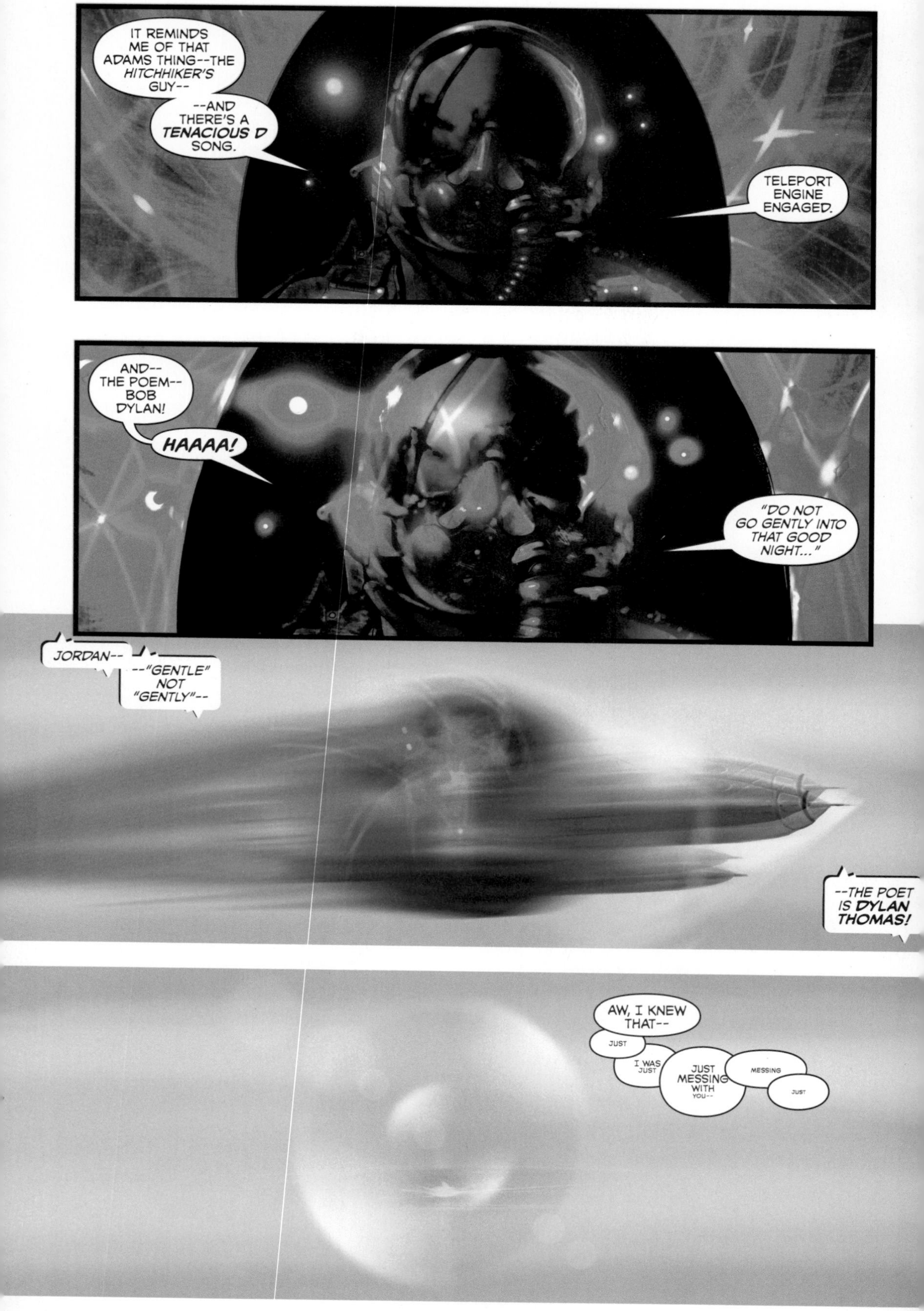
IT REMINDS ME OF THAT ADAMS THING--THE HITCHHIKER'S GUY--
--AND THERE'S A TENACIOUS D SONG.
TELEPORT ENGINE ENGAGED.
AND-- THE POEM-- BOB DYLAN!
HAAAA!
"DO NOT GO GENTLY INTO THAT GOOD NIGHT..."
JORDAN--
--"GENTLE" NOT "GENTLY"--
--THE POET IS DYLAN THOMAS!
AW, I KNEW THAT--
JUST
I WAS JUST
JUST MESSING WITH YOU--
MESSING
JUST

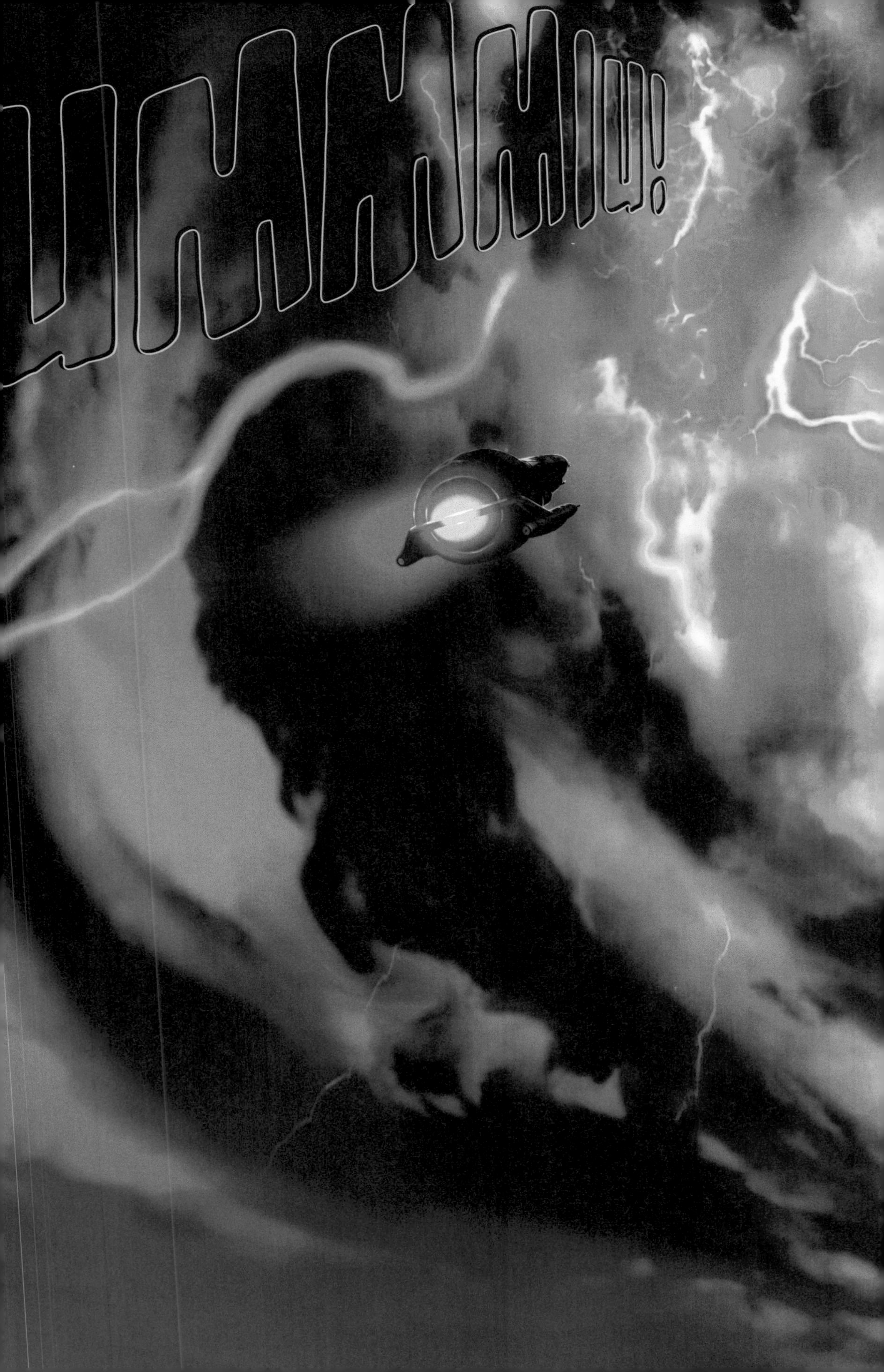

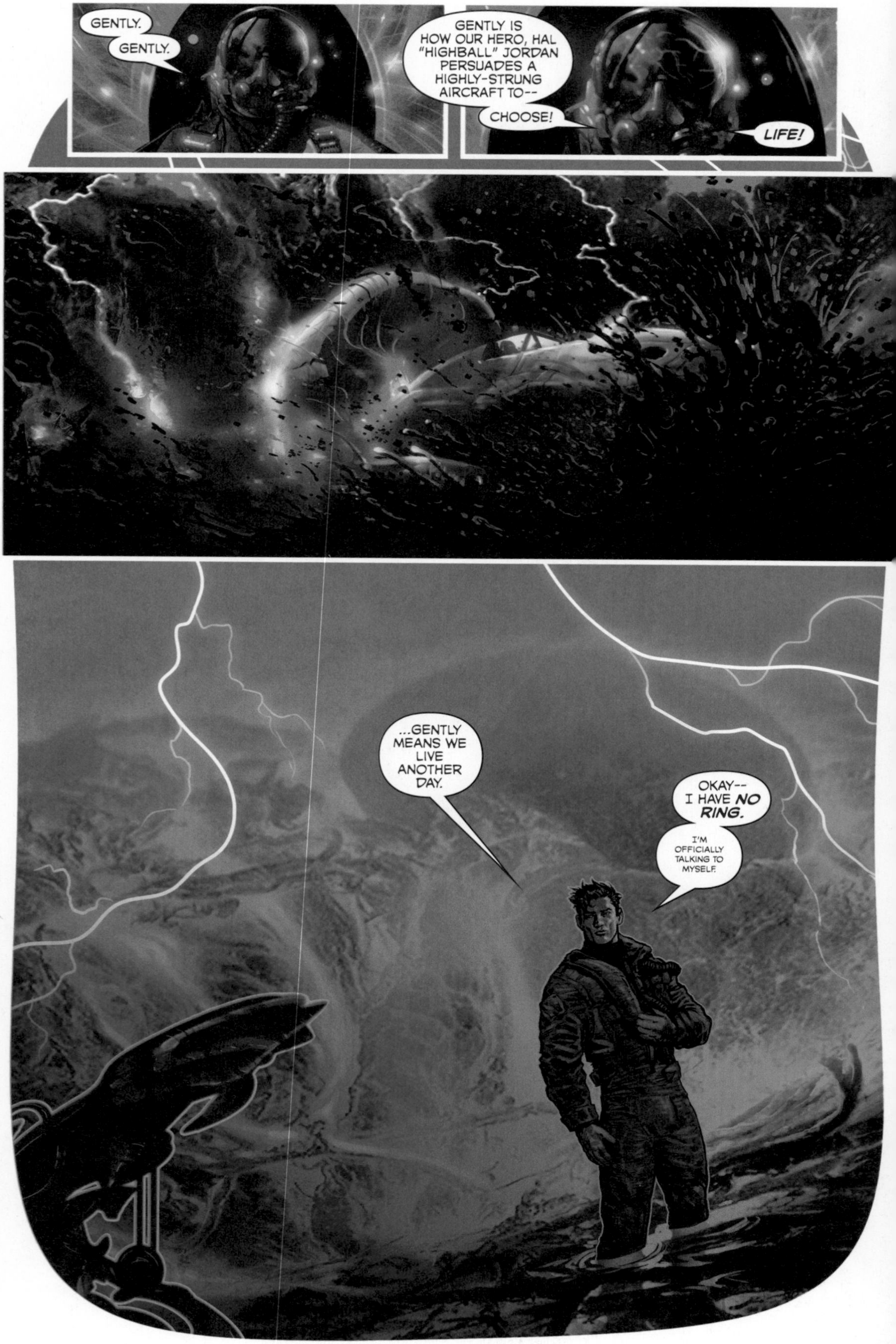
GENTLY.
GENTLY.
GENTLY IS HOW OUR HERO, HAL "HIGHBALL" JORDAN PERSUADES A HIGHLY-STRUNG AIRCRAFT TO--
CHOOSE!
LIFE!
...GENTLY MEANS WE LIVE ANOTHER DAY.
OKAY-- I HAVE NO RING.
I'M OFFICIALLY TALKING TO MYSELF.

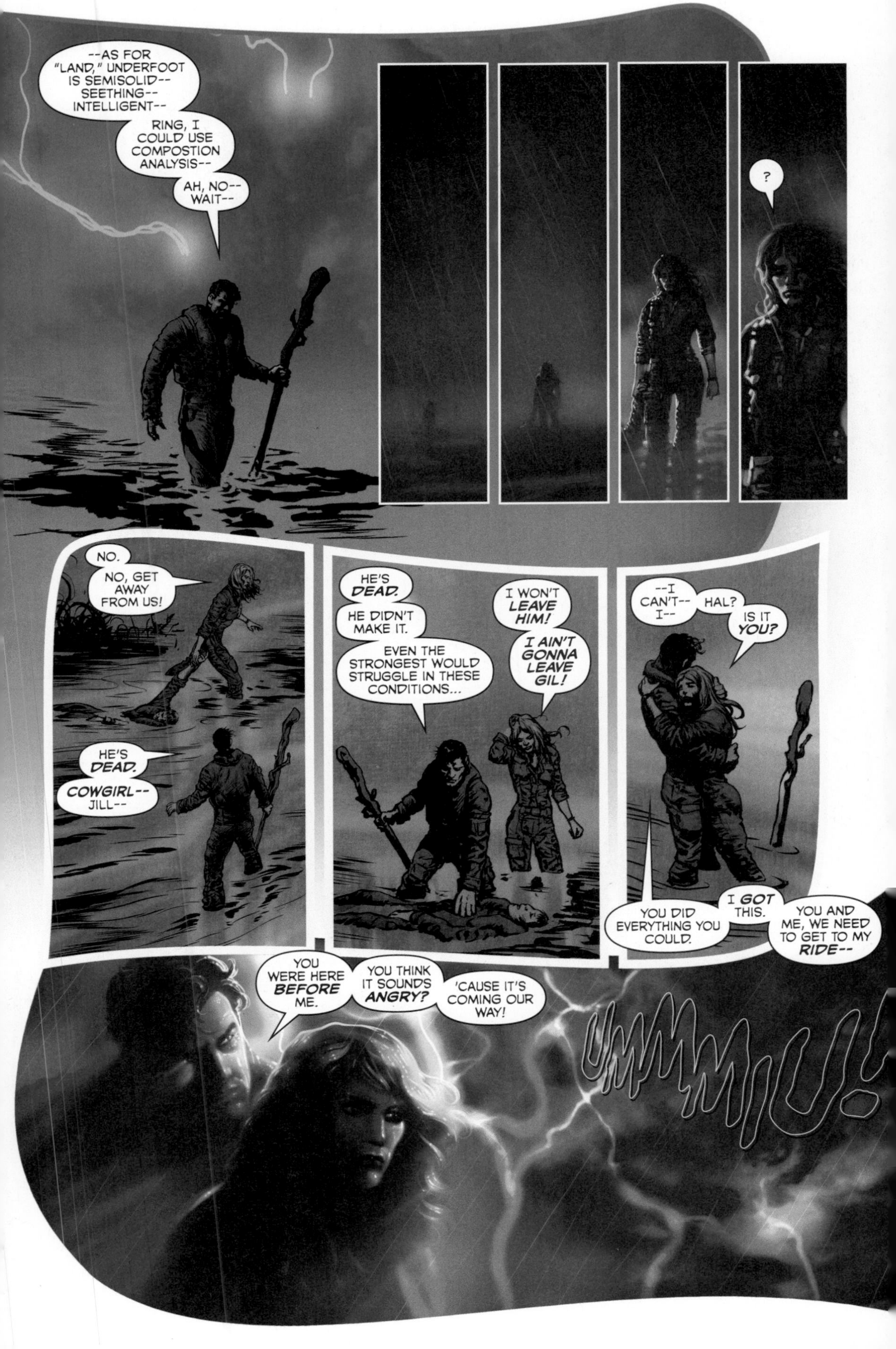
--AS FOR "LAND," UNDERFOOT IS SEMISOLID-- SEETHING-- INTELLIGENT--
RING, I COULD USE COMPOSTION ANALYSIS--
AH, NO-- WAIT--
?
NO.
NO, GET AWAY FROM US!
HE'S DEAD.
COWGIRL-- JILL--
HE'S DEAD.
HE DIDN'T MAKE IT.
EVEN THE STRONGEST WOULD STRUGGLE IN THESE CONDITIONS...
I WON'T LEAVE HIM!
I AIN'T GONNA LEAVE GIL!
--I CAN'T-- I--
HAL?
IS IT YOU?
YOU DID EVERYTHING YOU COULD.
I GOT THIS.
YOU AND ME, WE NEED TO GET TO MY RIDE--
YOU WERE HERE BEFORE ME.
YOU THINK IT SOUNDS ANGRY?
'CAUSE IT'S COMING OUR WAY!
UMMMMU!

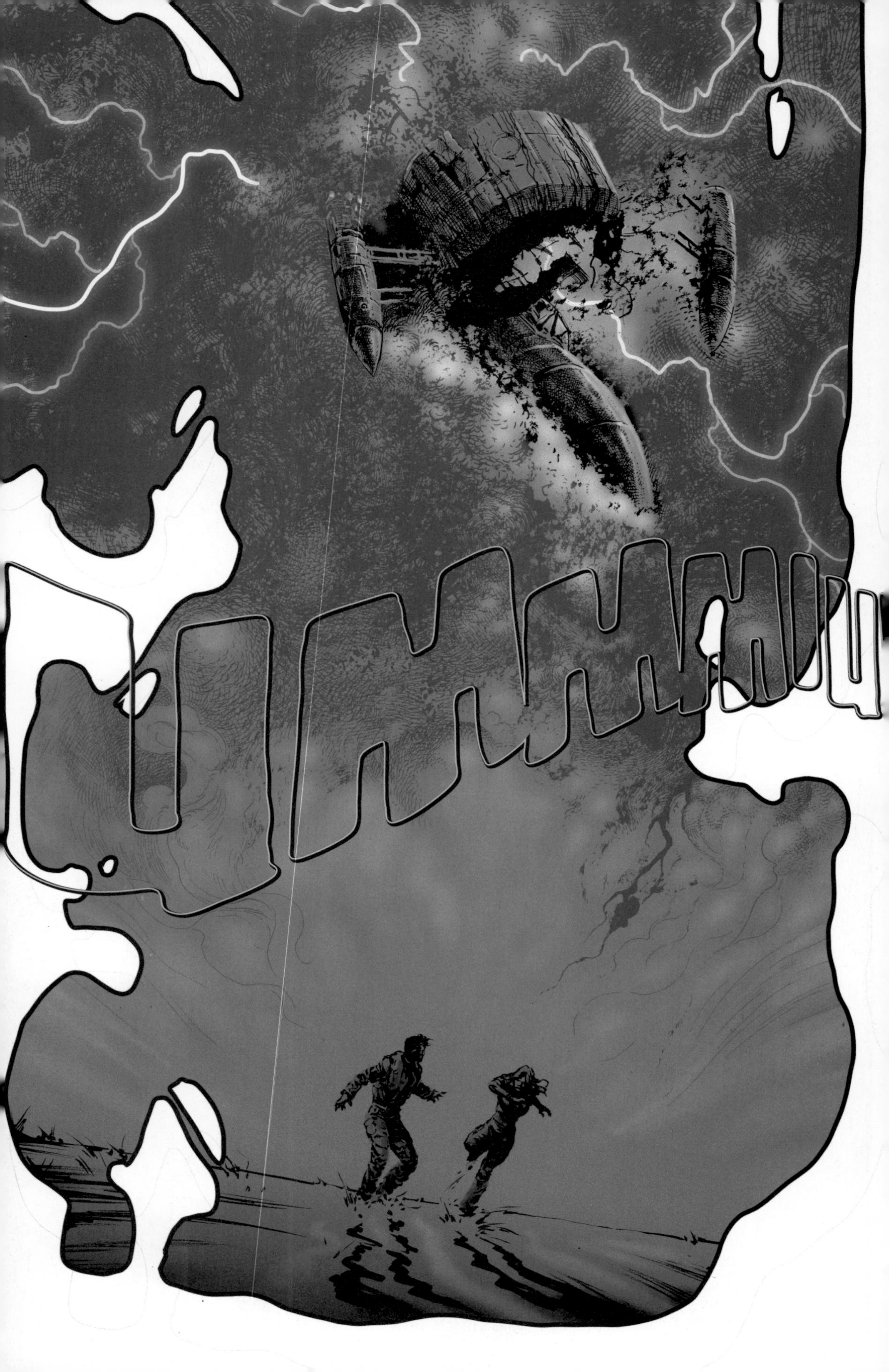

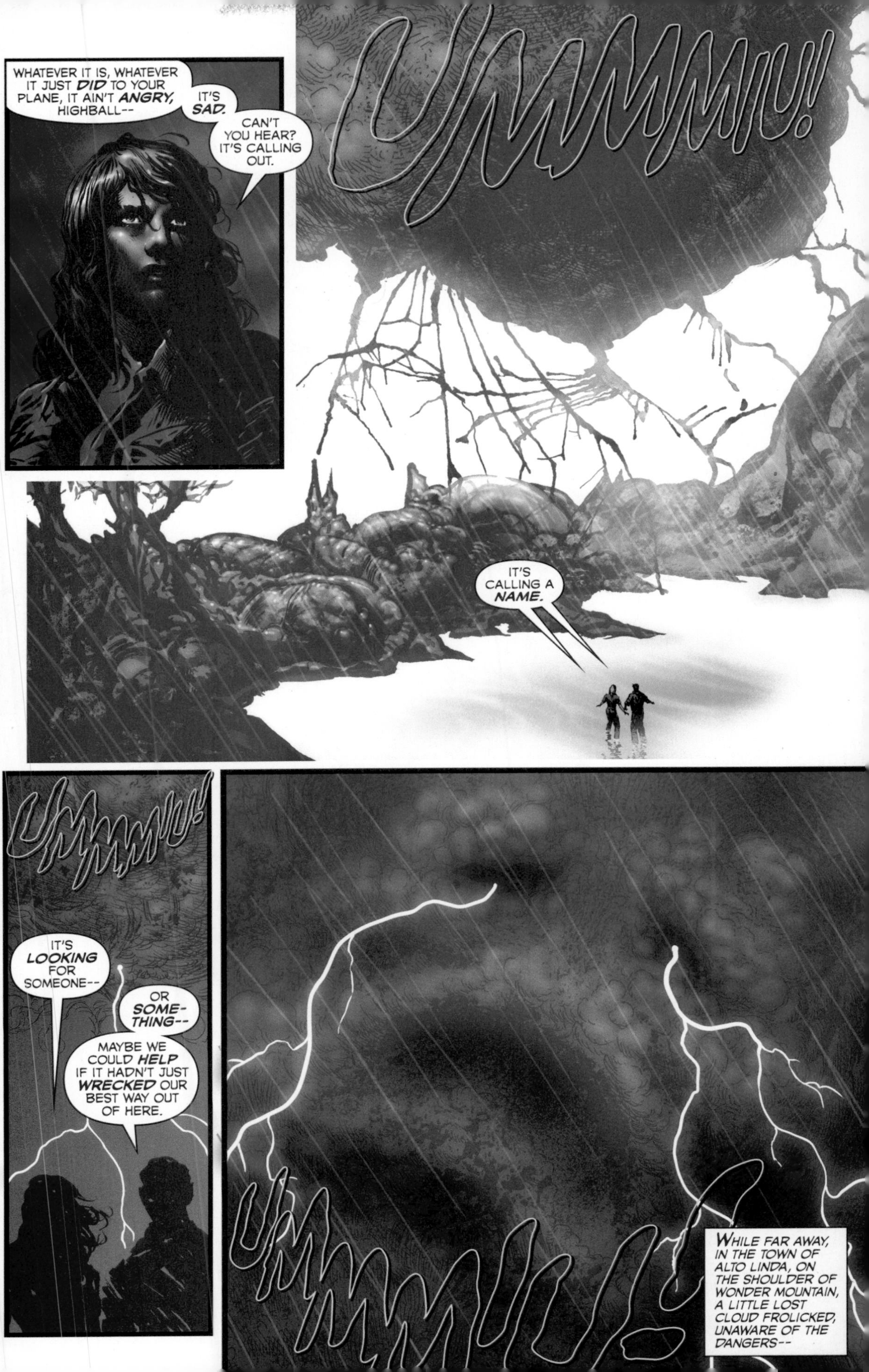
WHATEVER IT IS, WHATEVER IT JUST DID TO YOUR PLANE, IT AIN'T ANGRY, HIGHBALL--
IT'S SAD.
CAN'T YOU HEAR? IT'S CALLING OUT.
UMMMU!
IT'S CALLING A NAME.
UMMMU!
IT'S LOOKING FOR SOMEONE--
OR SOME-THING--
MAYBE WE COULD HELP IF IT HADN'T JUST WRECKED OUR BEST WAY OUT OF HERE.
UMMMU!
WHILE FAR AWAY, IN THE TOWN OF ALTO LINDA, ON THE SHOULDER OF WONDER MOUNTAIN, A LITTLE LOST CLOUD FROLICKED, UNAWARE OF THE DANGERS--

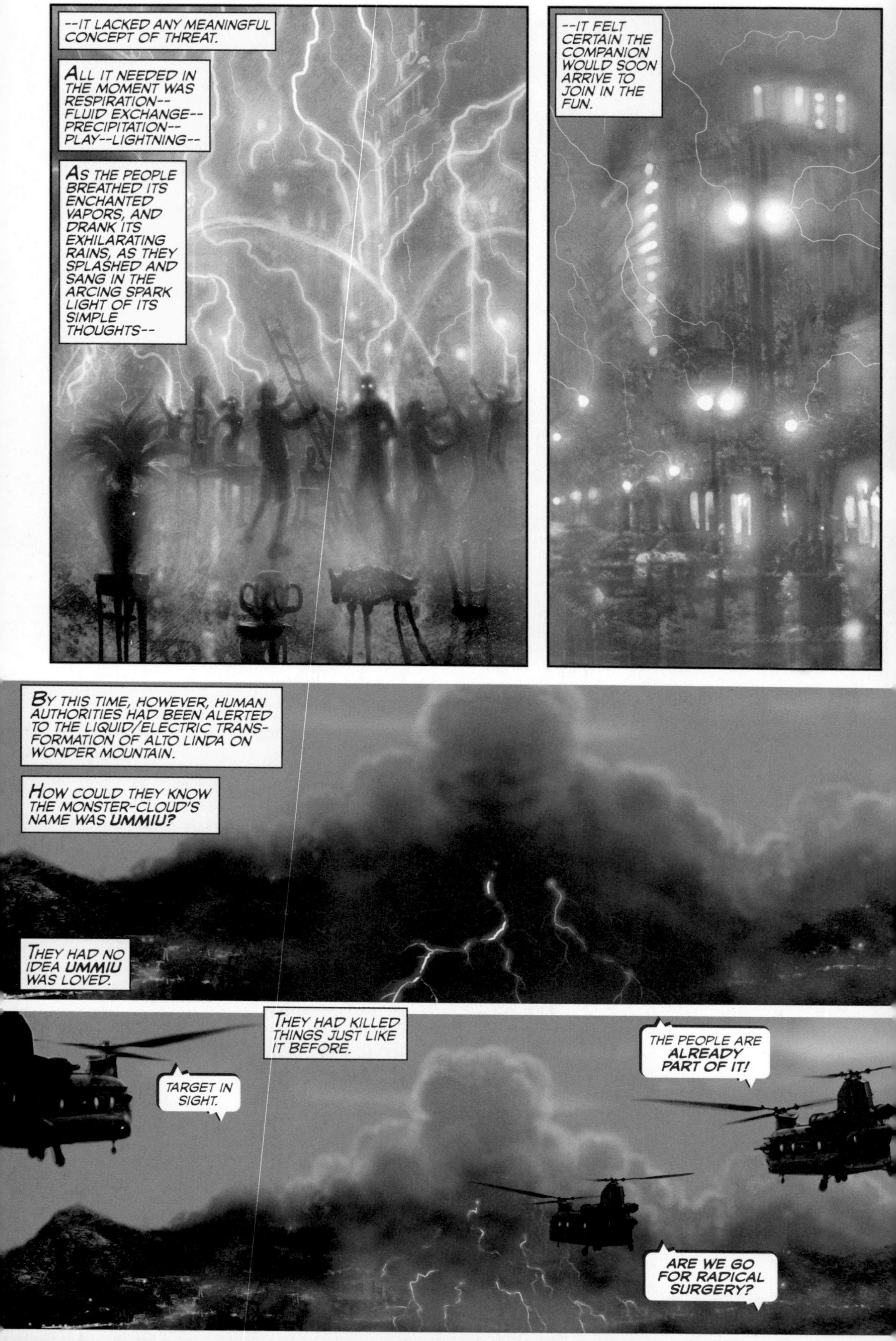
--IT LACKED ANY MEANINGFUL CONCEPT OF THREAT.
ALL IT NEEDED IN THE MOMENT WAS RESPIRATION-- FLUID EXCHANGE-- PRECIPITATION-- PLAY--LIGHTNING--
AS THE PEOPLE BREATHED ITS ENCHANTED VAPORS, AND DRANK ITS EXHILARATING RAINS, AS THEY SPLASHED AND SANG IN THE ARCING SPARK LIGHT OF ITS SIMPLE THOUGHTS--
--IT FELT CERTAIN THE COMPANION WOULD SOON ARRIVE TO JOIN IN THE FUN.
BY THIS TIME, HOWEVER, HUMAN AUTHORITIES HAD BEEN ALERTED TO THE LIQUID/ELECTRIC TRANSFORMATION OF ALTO LINDA ON WONDER MOUNTAIN.
HOW COULD THEY KNOW THE MONSTER-CLOUD'S NAME WAS UMMIU?
THEY HAD NO IDEA UMMIU WAS LOVED.
THEY HAD KILLED THINGS JUST LIKE IT BEFORE.
TARGET IN SIGHT.
THE PEOPLE ARE ALREADY PART OF IT!
ARE WE GO FOR RADICAL SURGERY?

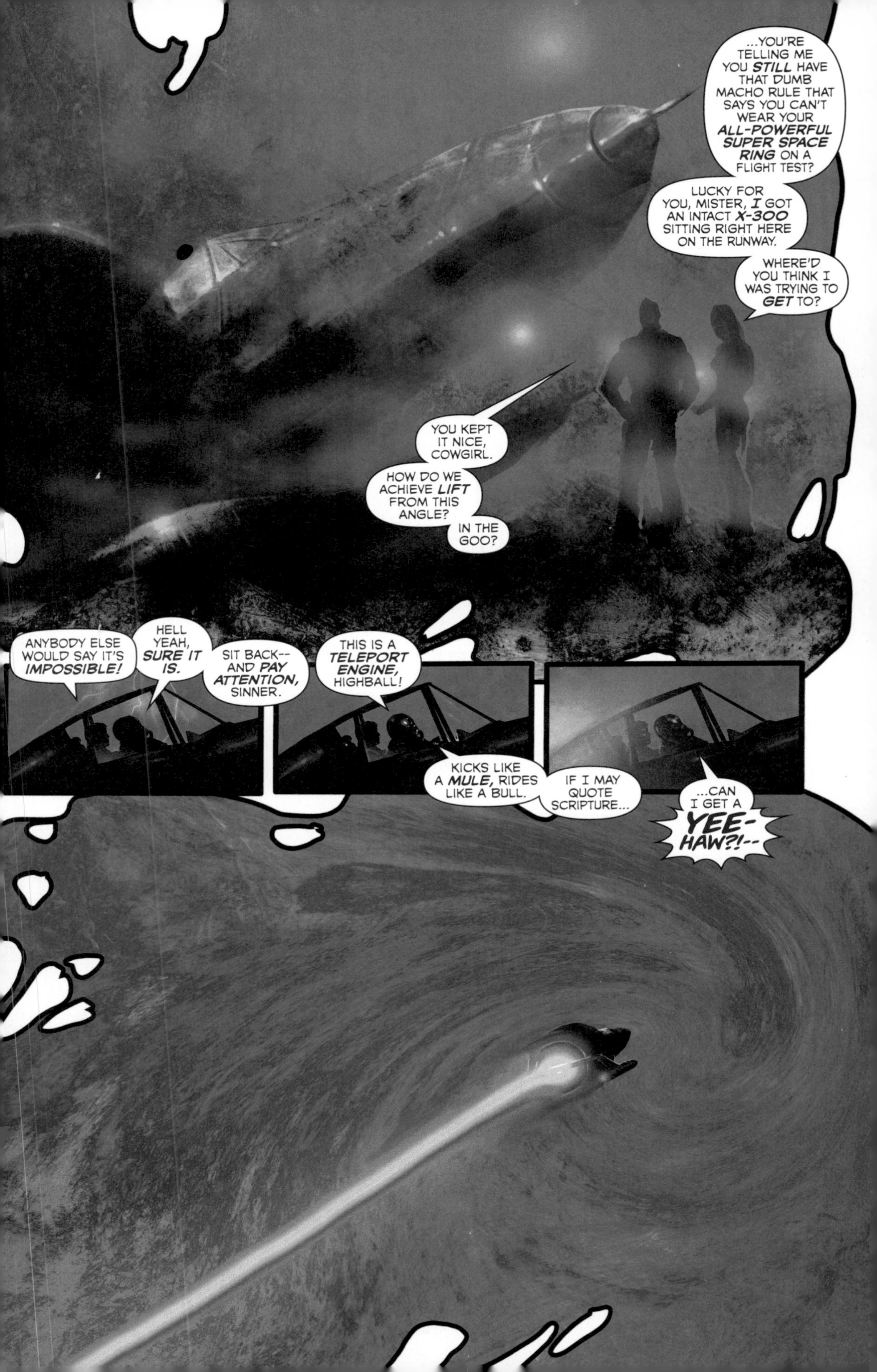
...YOU'RE TELLING ME YOU STILL HAVE THAT DUMB MACHO RULE THAT SAYS YOU CAN'T WEAR YOUR ALL-POWERFUL SUPER SPACE RING ON A FLIGHT TEST?
LUCKY FOR YOU, MISTER, I GOT AN INTACT X-300 SITTING RIGHT HERE ON THE RUNWAY.
WHERE'D YOU THINK I WAS TRYING TO GET TO?
YOU KEPT IT NICE, COWGIRL.
HOW DO WE ACHIEVE LIFT FROM THIS ANGLE?
IN THE GOO?
ANYBODY ELSE WOULD SAY IT'S IMPOSSIBLE!
HELL YEAH, SURE IT IS.
SIT BACK-- AND PAY ATTENTION, SINNER.
THIS IS A TELEPORT ENGINE, HIGHBALL!
KICKS LIKE A MULE, RIDES LIKE A BULL.
IF I MAY QUOTE SCRIPTURE...
...CAN I GET A YEE-HAW?!--

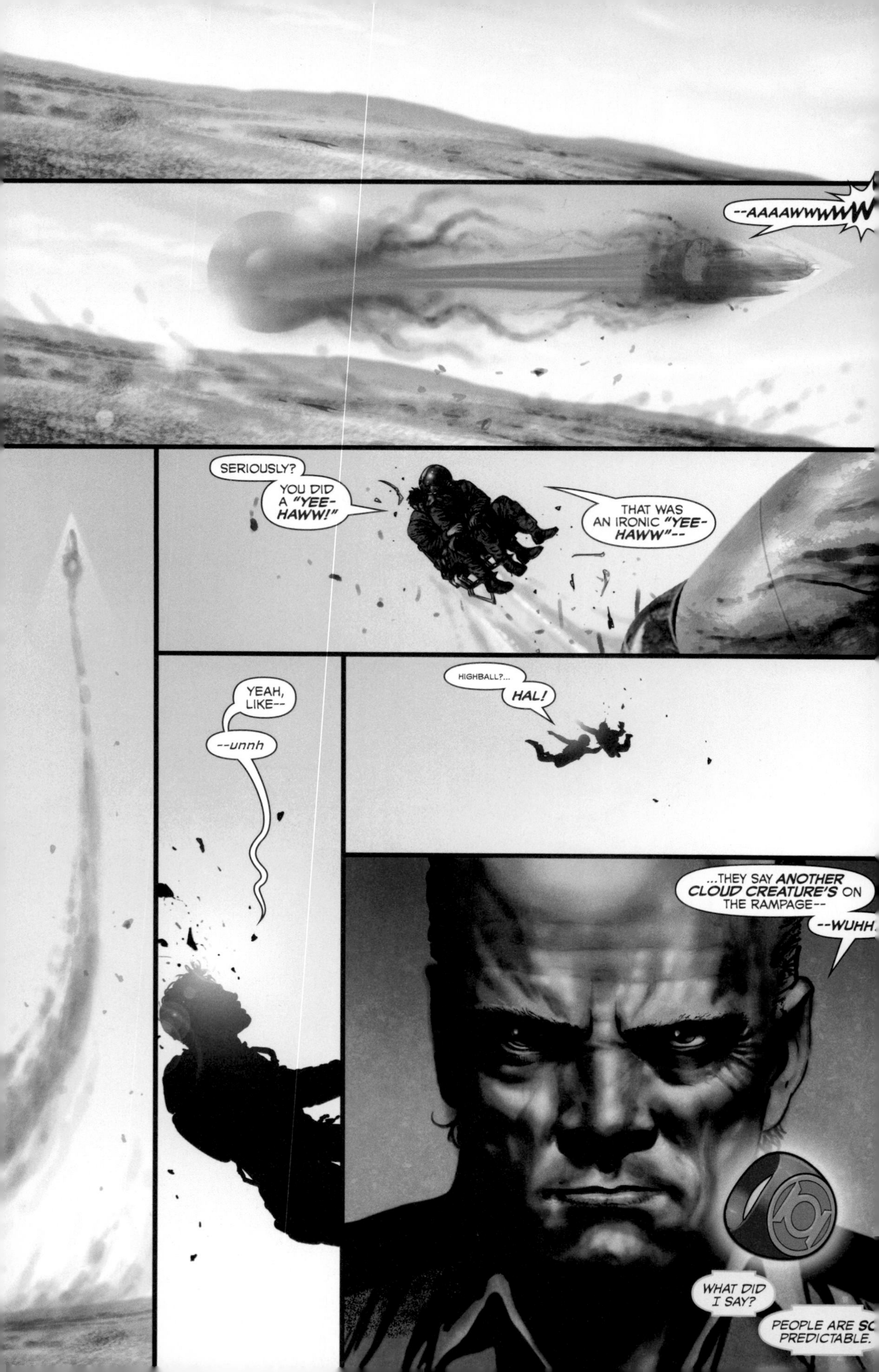

--AAAAWWWWWW
SERIOUSLY?
YOU DID A "YEE-HAWW!"
THAT WAS AN IRONIC "YEE-HAWW"--
YEAH, LIKE--
--unnh
HIGHBALL?...
HAL!
...THEY SAY ANOTHER CLOUD CREATURE'S ON THE RAMPAGE--
--WUHH.
WHAT DID I SAY?
PEOPLE ARE SO PREDICTABLE.

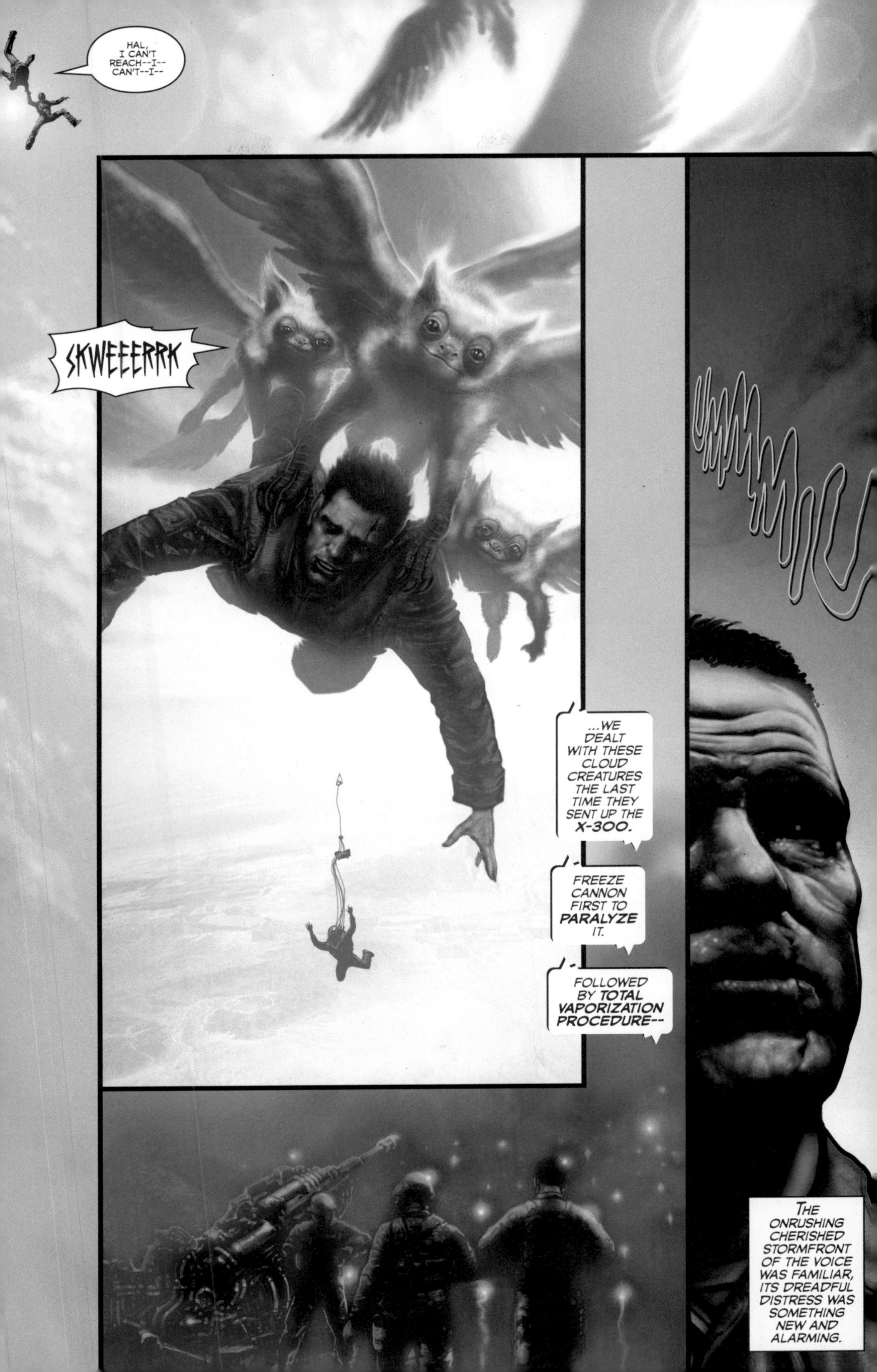
HAL, I CAN'T REACH--I--CAN'T--I--
SKWEEERRK
UMMMMMM
...WE DEALT WITH THESE CLOUD CREATURES THE LAST TIME THEY SENT UP THE X-300.
FREEZE CANNON FIRST TO PARALYZE IT.
FOLLOWED BY TOTAL VAPORIZATION PROCEDURE--
THE ONRUSHING CHERISHED STORMFRONT OF THE VOICE WAS FAMILIAR, ITS DREADFUL DISTRESS WAS SOMETHING NEW AND ALARMING.

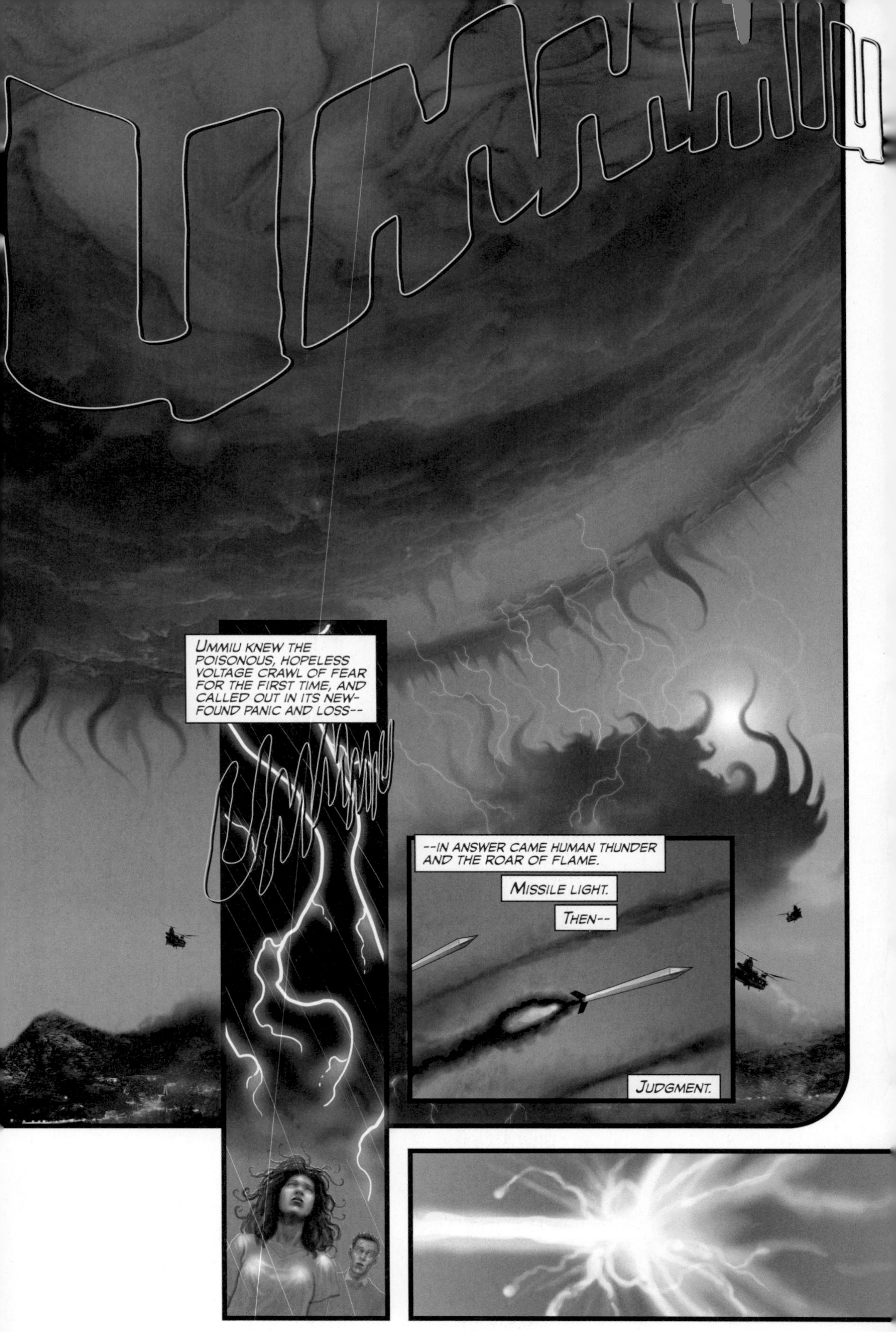

UMMIU KNEW THE POISONOUS, HOPELESS VOLTAGE CRAWL OF FEAR FOR THE FIRST TIME, AND CALLED OUT IN ITS NEW-FOUND PANIC AND LOSS--
--IN ANSWER CAME HUMAN THUNDER AND THE ROAR OF FLAME.
MISSILE LIGHT.
THEN--
JUDGMENT.

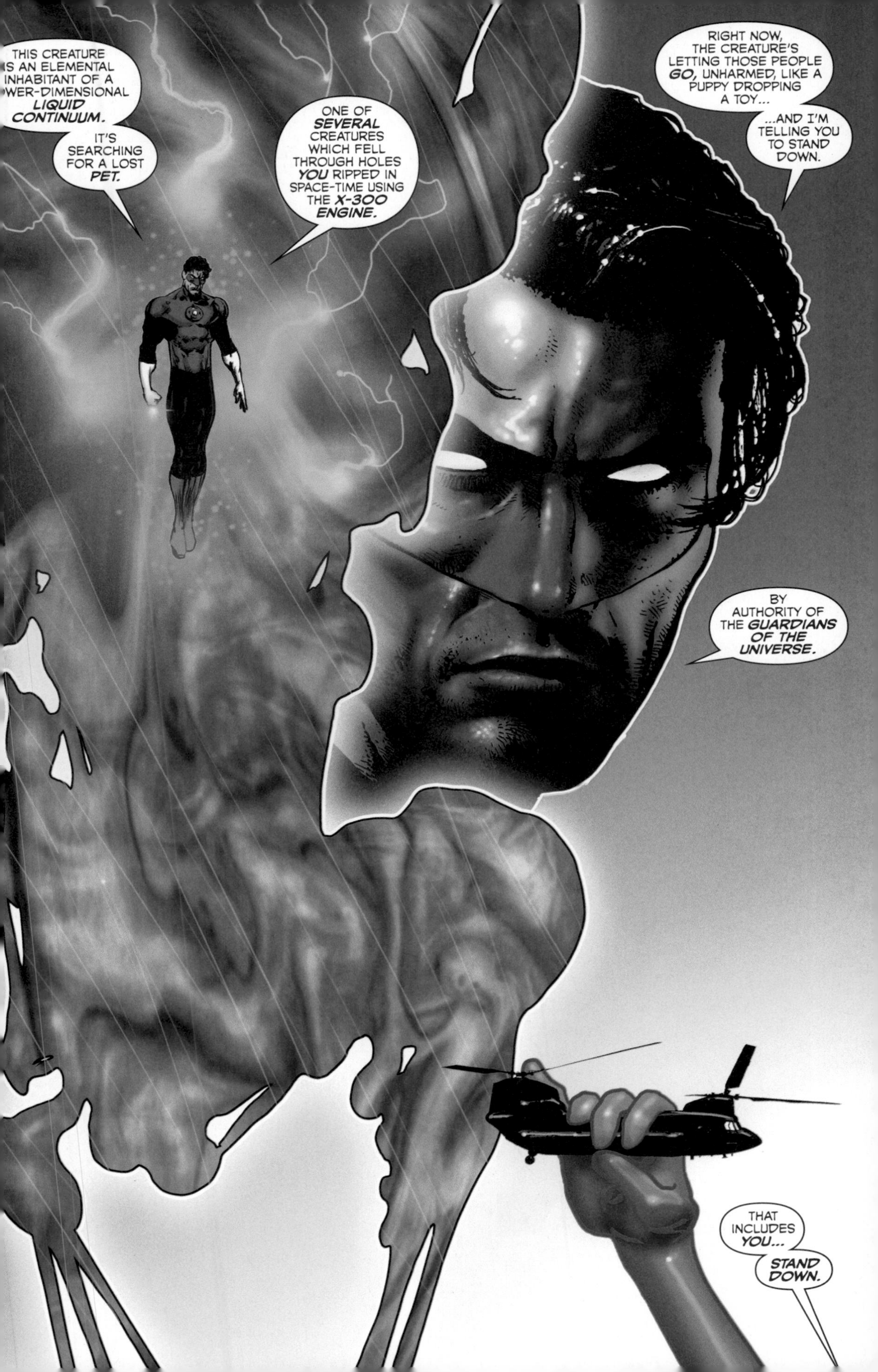

THIS CREATURE S AN ELEMENTAL INHABITANT OF A WER-DIMENSIONAL LIQUID CONTINUUM.
IT'S SEARCHING FOR A LOST PET.
ONE OF SEVERAL CREATURES WHICH FELL THROUGH HOLES YOU RIPPED IN SPACE-TIME USING THE X-300 ENGINE.
RIGHT NOW, THE CREATURE'S LETTING THOSE PEOPLE GO, UNHARMED, LIKE A PUPPY DROPPING A TOY...
...AND I'M TELLING YOU TO STAND DOWN.
BY AUTHORITY OF THE GUARDIANS OF THE UNIVERSE.
THAT INCLUDES YOU...
STAND DOWN.

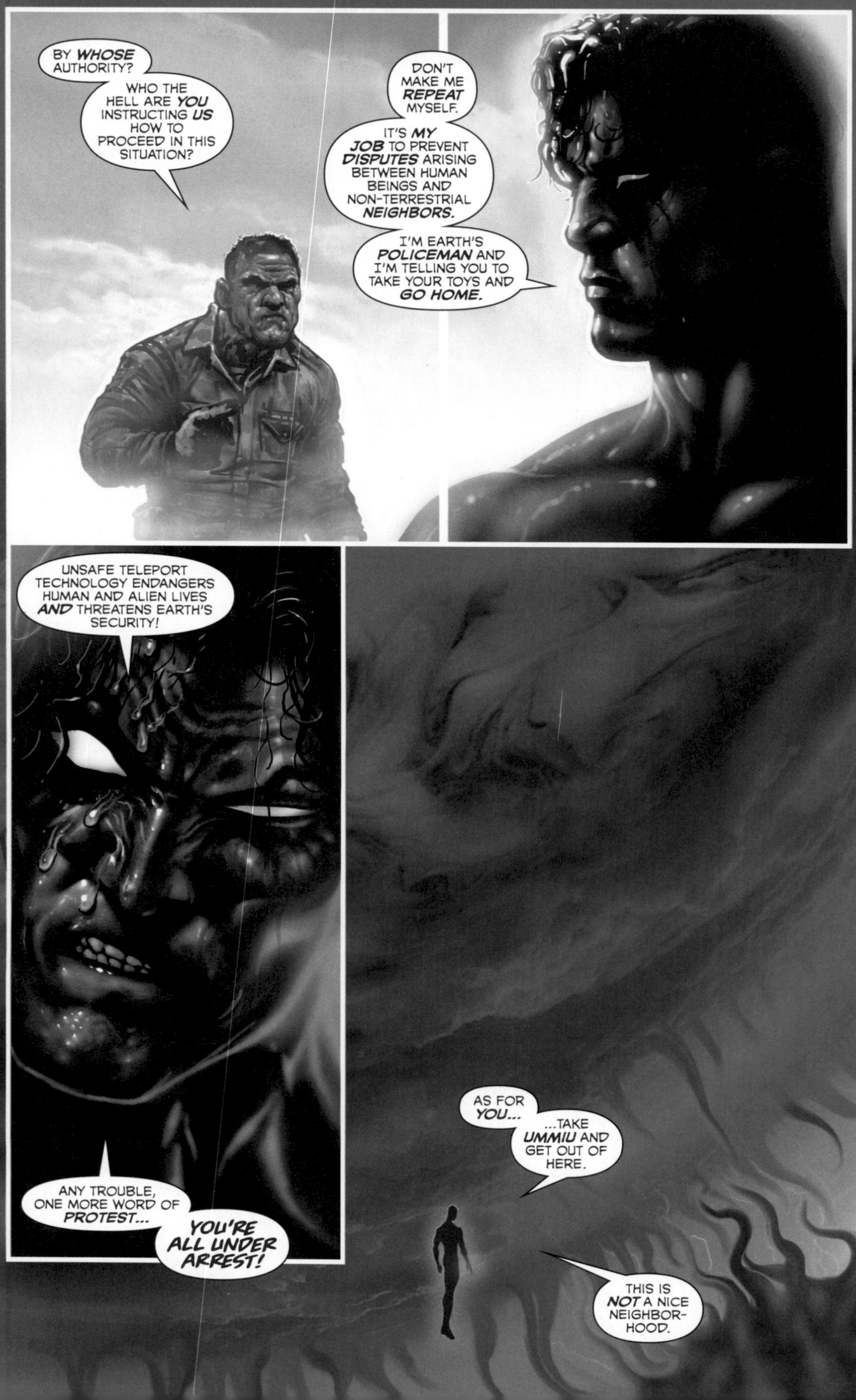

BY ***WHOSE*** AUTHORITY?
WHO THE HELL ARE ***YOU*** INSTRUCTING ***US*** HOW TO PROCEED IN THIS SITUATION?
DON'T MAKE ME ***REPEAT*** MYSELF.
IT'S ***MY JOB*** TO PREVENT ***DISPUTES*** ARISING BETWEEN HUMAN BEINGS AND NON-TERRESTRIAL ***NEIGHBORS.***
I'M EARTH'S ***POLICEMAN*** AND I'M TELLING YOU TO TAKE YOUR TOYS AND ***GO HOME.***
UNSAFE TELEPORT TECHNOLOGY ENDANGERS HUMAN AND ALIEN LIVES ***AND*** THREATENS EARTH'S SECURITY!
ANY TROUBLE, ONE MORE WORD OF ***PROTEST...***
YOU'RE ALL UNDER ARREST!
AS FOR ***YOU...***
...TAKE ***UMMIU*** AND GET OUT OF HERE.
THIS IS ***NOT*** A NICE NEIGHBOR-HOOD.

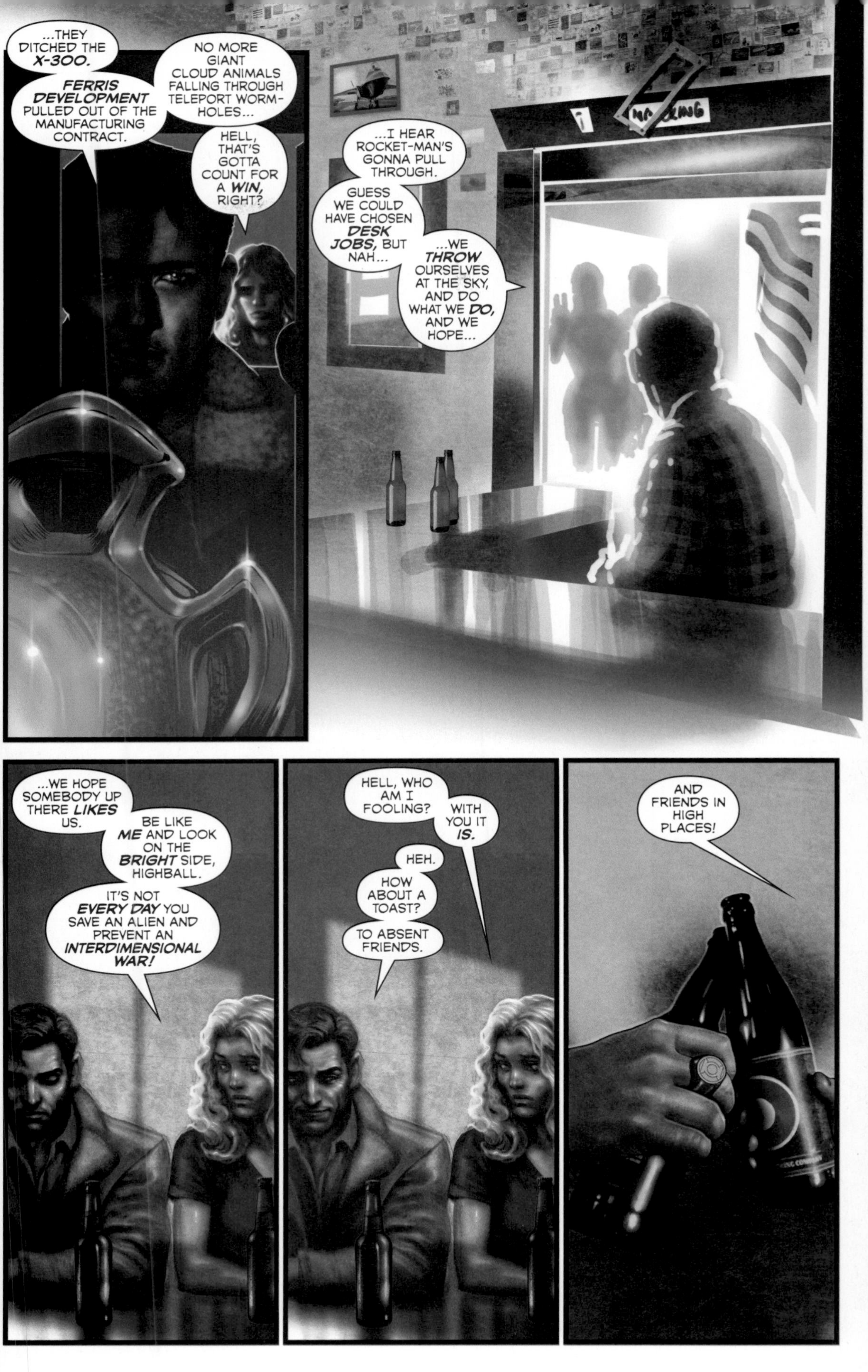
...THEY DITCHED THE X-300.
FERRIS DEVELOPMENT PULLED OUT OF THE MANUFACTURING CONTRACT.
NO MORE GIANT CLOUD ANIMALS FALLING THROUGH TELEPORT WORM-HOLES...
HELL, THAT'S GOTTA COUNT FOR A WIN, RIGHT?
...I HEAR ROCKET-MAN'S GONNA PULL THROUGH.
GUESS WE COULD HAVE CHOSEN DESK JOBS, BUT NAH...
...WE THROW OURSELVES AT THE SKY, AND DO WHAT WE DO, AND WE HOPE...
...WE HOPE SOMEBODY UP THERE LIKES US.
BE LIKE ME AND LOOK ON THE BRIGHT SIDE, HIGHBALL.
IT'S NOT EVERY DAY YOU SAVE AN ALIEN AND PREVENT AN INTERDIMENSIONAL WAR!
HELL, WHO AM I FOOLING?
WITH YOU IT IS.
HEH.
HOW ABOUT A TOAST?
TO ABSENT FRIENDS.
AND FRIENDS IN HIGH PLACES!

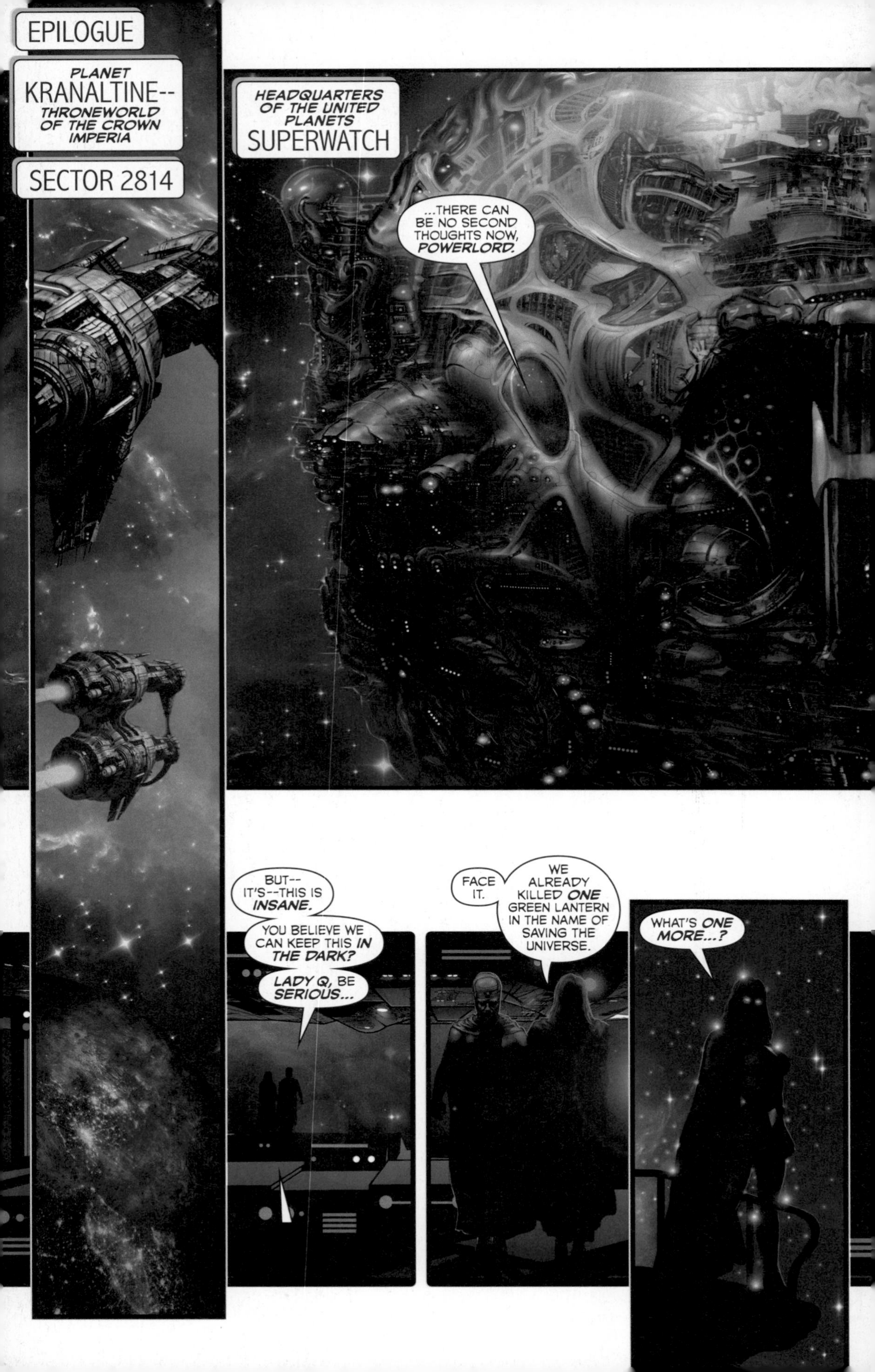
EPILOGUE
PLANET KRANALTINE-- THRONEWORLD OF THE CROWN IMPERIA
SECTOR 2814
HEADQUARTERS OF THE UNITED PLANETS SUPERWATCH
...THERE CAN BE NO SECOND THOUGHTS NOW, POWERLORD.
BUT-- IT'S--THIS IS INSANE.
YOU BELIEVE WE CAN KEEP THIS IN THE DARK?
LADY Q, BE SERIOUS...
FACE IT.
WE ALREADY KILLED ONE GREEN LANTERN IN THE NAME OF SAVING THE UNIVERSE.
WHAT'S ONE MORE...?

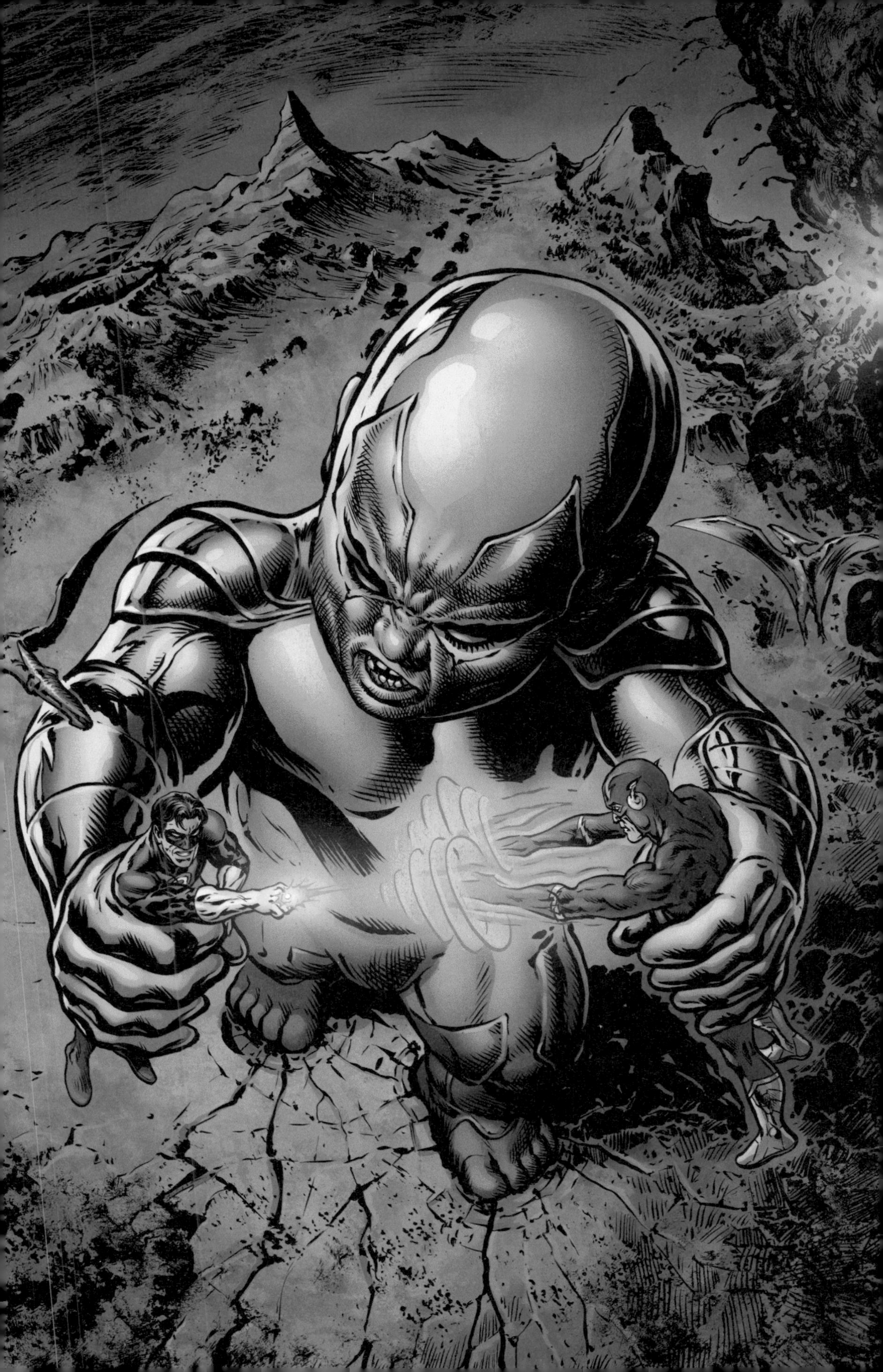

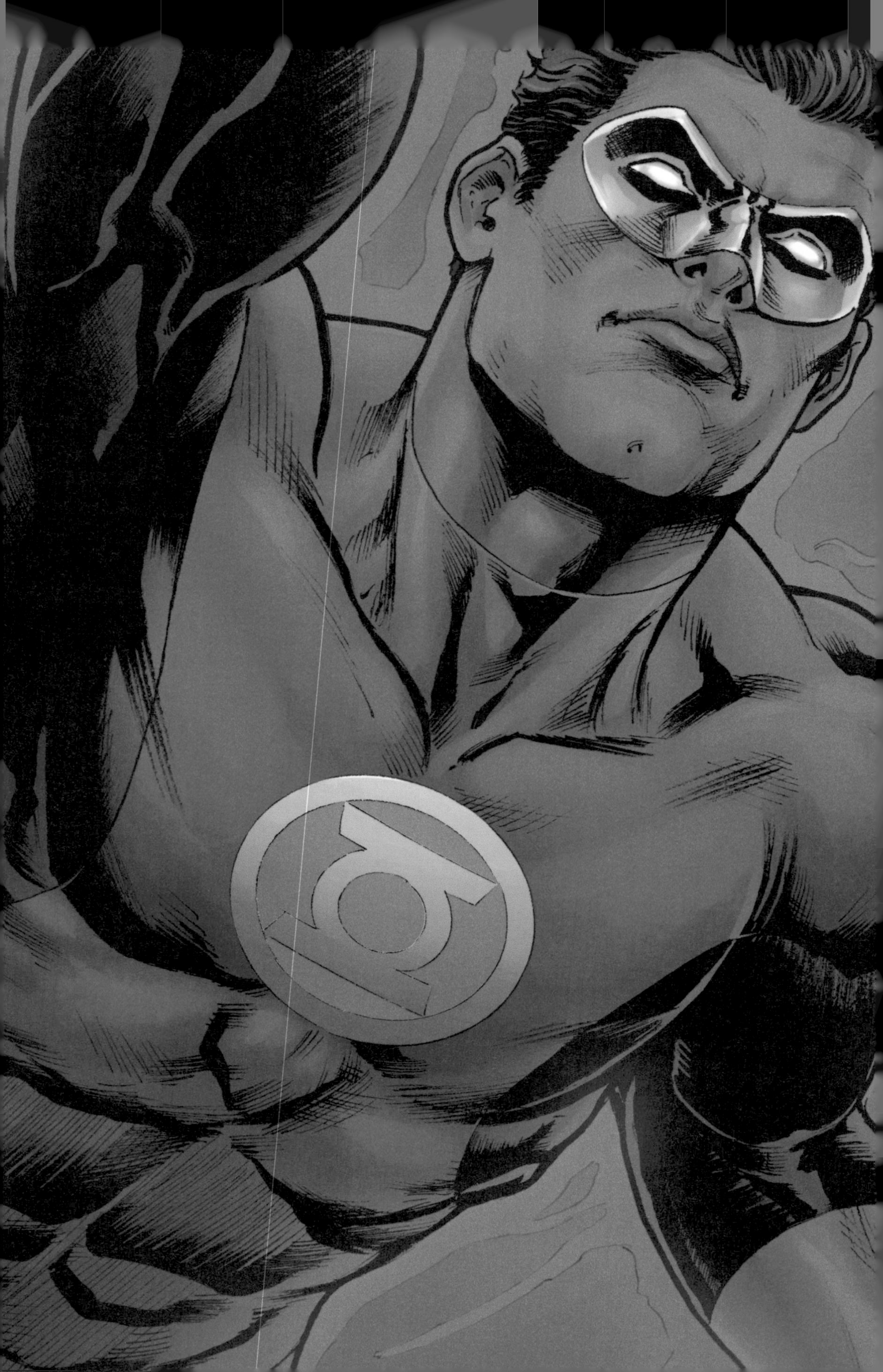

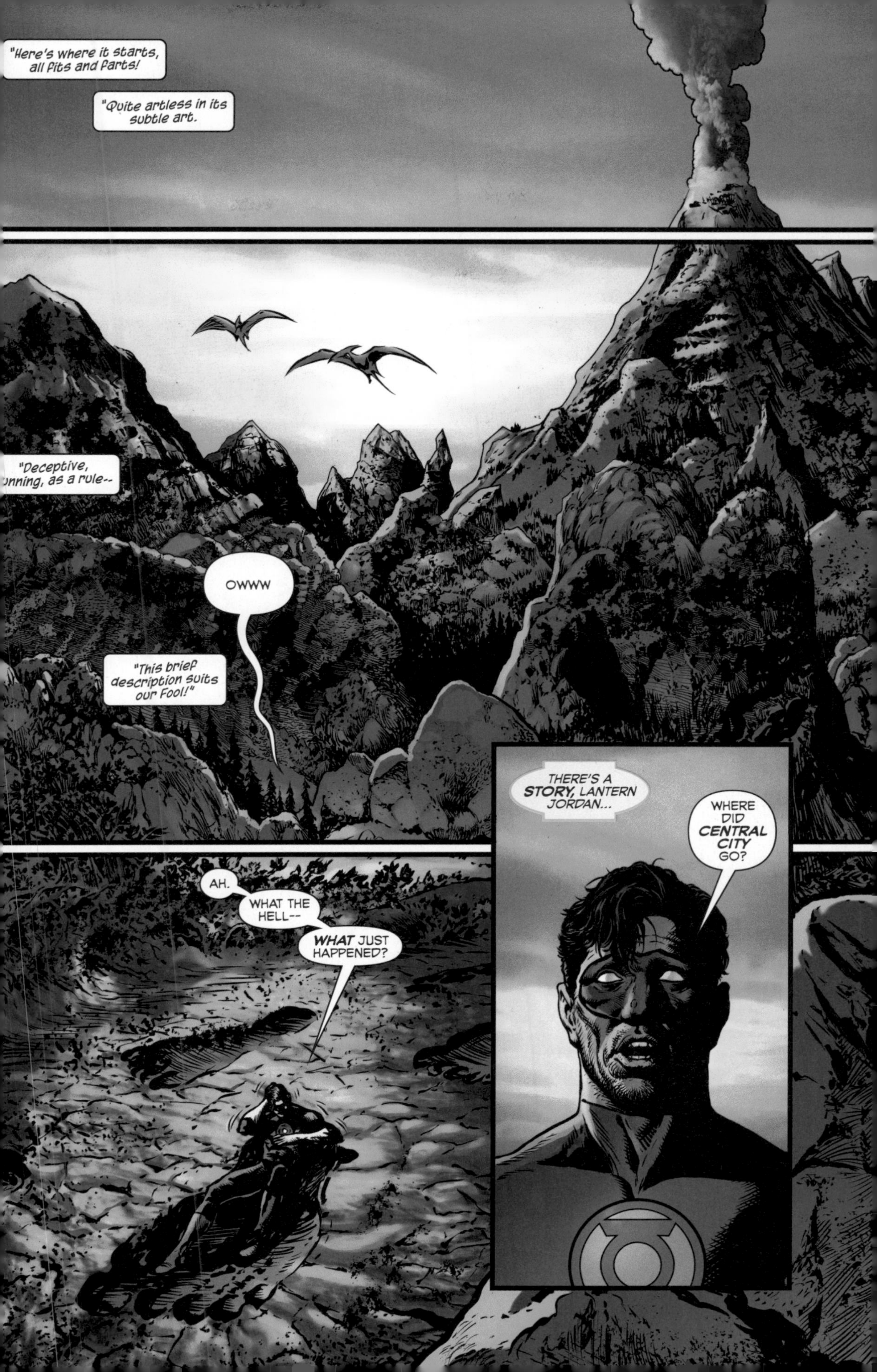
"Here's where it starts, all fits and farts!
"Quite artless in its subtle art.
"Deceptive, ...nning, as a rule--
OWWW
"This brief description suits our Fool!"
AH.
WHAT THE HELL--
WHAT JUST HAPPENED?
THERE'S A STORY, LANTERN JORDAN...
WHERE DID CENTRAL CITY GO?

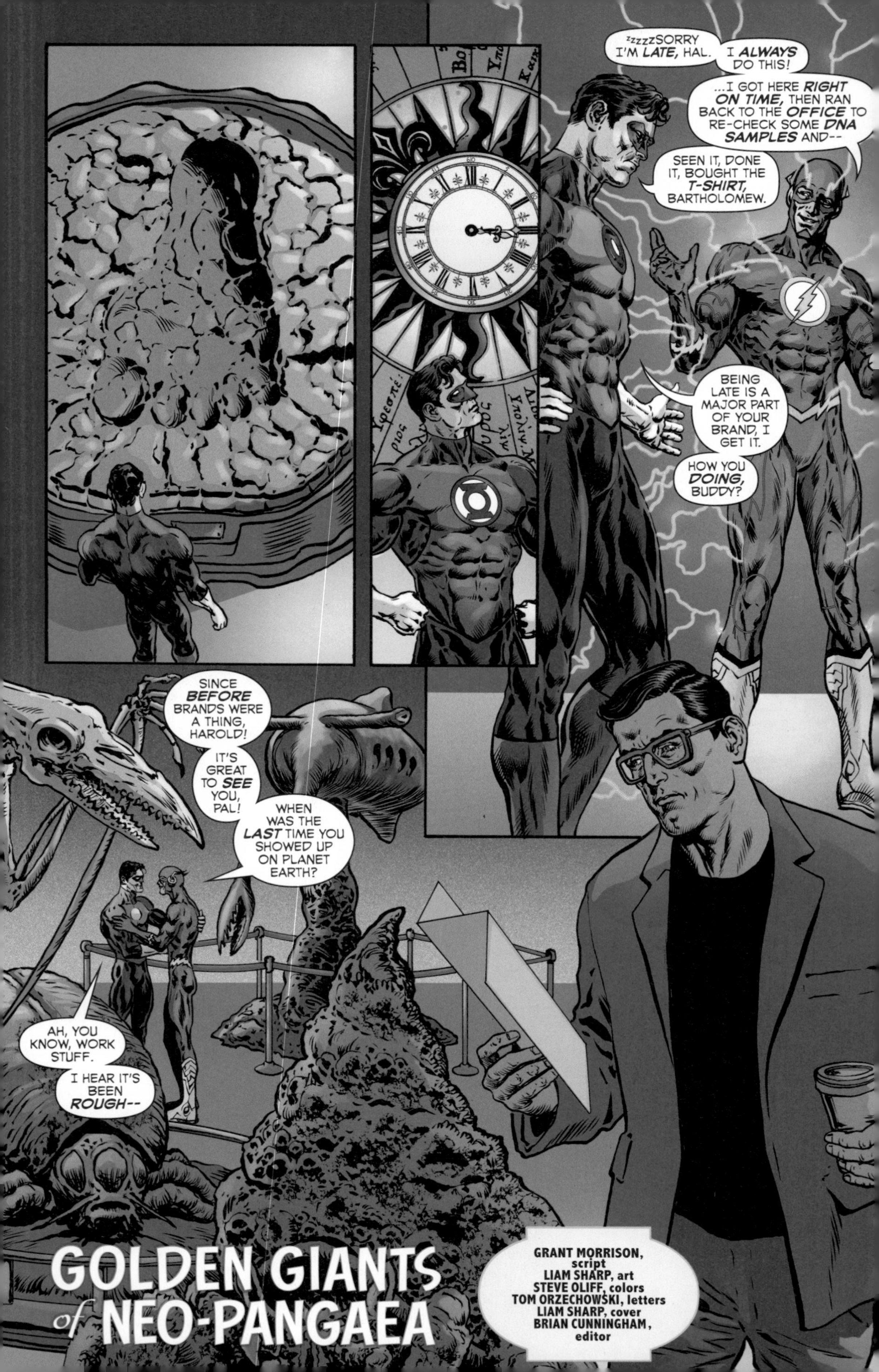
zzzzzSORRY I'M LATE, HAL.
I ALWAYS DO THIS!
...I GOT HERE RIGHT ON TIME, THEN RAN BACK TO THE OFFICE TO RE-CHECK SOME DNA SAMPLES AND--
SEEN IT, DONE IT, BOUGHT THE T-SHIRT, BARTHOLOMEW.
BEING LATE IS A MAJOR PART OF YOUR BRAND, I GET IT.
HOW YOU DOING, BUDDY?
SINCE BEFORE BRANDS WERE A THING, HAROLD!
IT'S GREAT TO SEE YOU, PAL!
WHEN WAS THE LAST TIME YOU SHOWED UP ON PLANET EARTH?
AH, YOU KNOW, WORK STUFF.
I HEAR IT'S BEEN ROUGH--
GOLDEN GIANTS of NEO-PANGAEA
GRANT MORRISON, script
LIAM SHARP, art
STEVE OLIFF, colors
TOM ORZECHOWSKI, letters
LIAM SHARP, cover
BRIAN CUNNINGHAM, editor

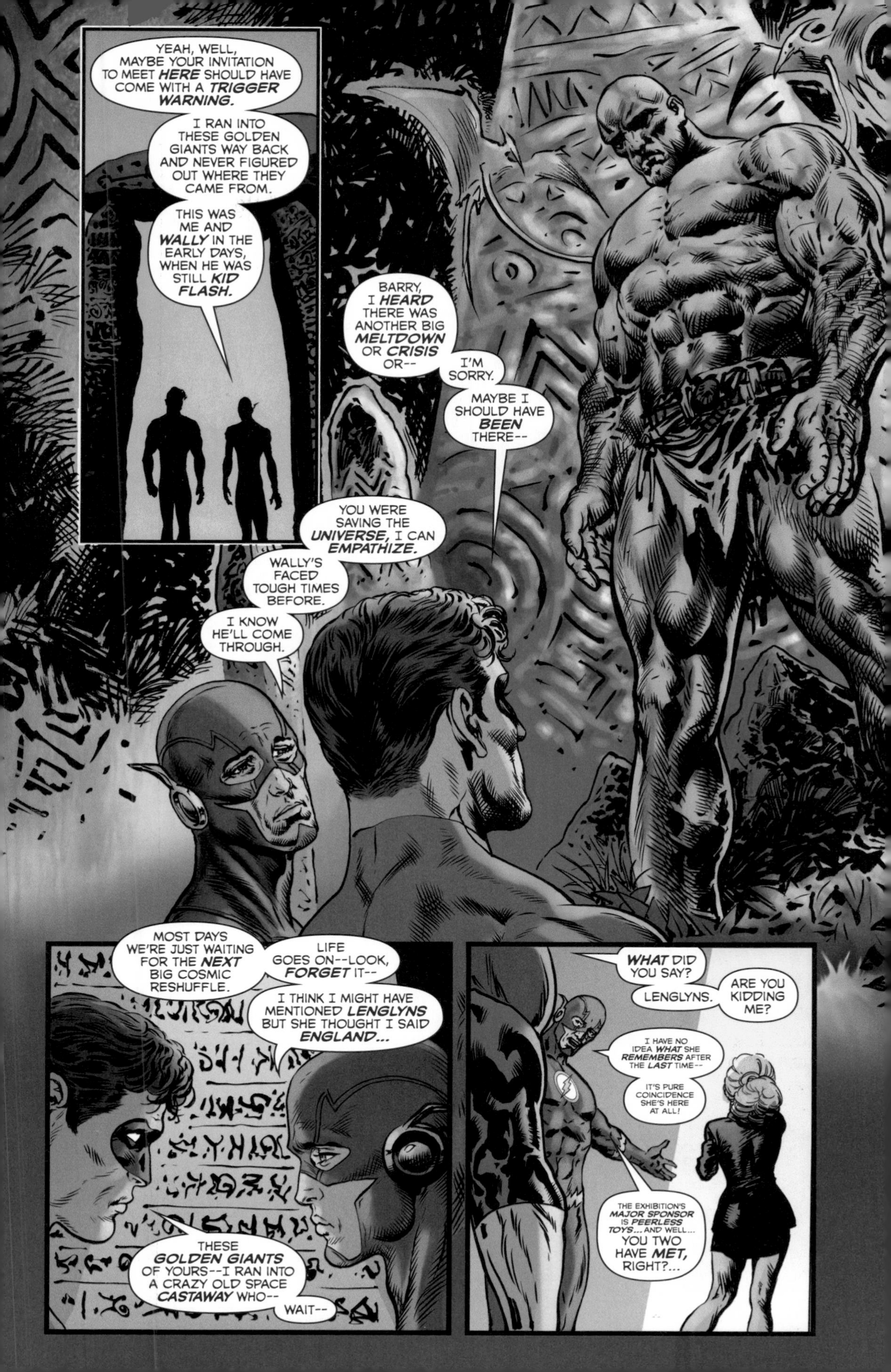
YEAH, WELL, MAYBE YOUR INVITATION TO MEET HERE SHOULD HAVE COME WITH A TRIGGER WARNING.
I RAN INTO THESE GOLDEN GIANTS WAY BACK AND NEVER FIGURED OUT WHERE THEY CAME FROM.
THIS WAS ME AND WALLY IN THE EARLY DAYS, WHEN HE WAS STILL KID FLASH.
BARRY, I HEARD THERE WAS ANOTHER BIG MELTDOWN OR CRISIS OR--
I'M SORRY.
MAYBE I SHOULD HAVE BEEN THERE--
YOU WERE SAVING THE UNIVERSE, I CAN EMPATHIZE.
WALLY'S FACED TOUGH TIMES BEFORE.
I KNOW HE'LL COME THROUGH.
MOST DAYS WE'RE JUST WAITING FOR THE NEXT BIG COSMIC RESHUFFLE.
LIFE GOES ON--LOOK, FORGET IT--
I THINK I MIGHT HAVE MENTIONED LENGLYNS BUT SHE THOUGHT I SAID ENGLAND...
THESE GOLDEN GIANTS OF YOURS--I RAN INTO A CRAZY OLD SPACE CASTAWAY WHO--
WAIT--
WHAT DID YOU SAY?
LENGLYNS.
ARE YOU KIDDING ME?
I HAVE NO IDEA WHAT SHE REMEMBERS AFTER THE LAST TIME--
IT'S PURE COINCIDENCE SHE'S HERE AT ALL!
THE EXHIBITION'S MAJOR SPONSOR IS PEERLESS TOYS... AND WELL... YOU TWO HAVE MET, RIGHT?...

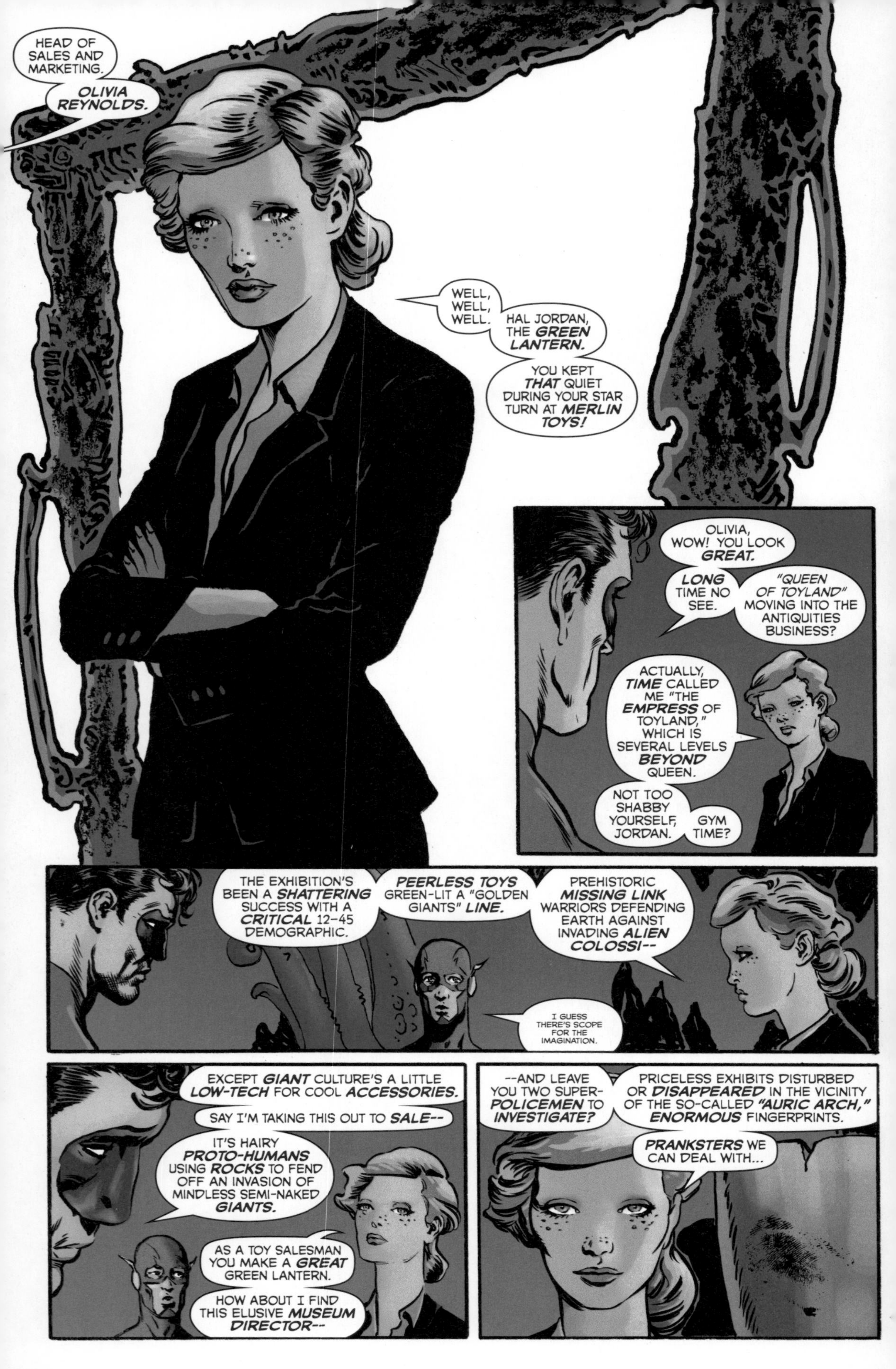
HEAD OF SALES AND MARKETING.
OLIVIA REYNOLDS.
WELL, WELL, WELL.
HAL JORDAN, THE GREEN LANTERN.
YOU KEPT THAT QUIET DURING YOUR STAR TURN AT MERLIN TOYS!
OLIVIA, WOW! YOU LOOK GREAT.
LONG TIME NO SEE.
"QUEEN OF TOYLAND" MOVING INTO THE ANTIQUITIES BUSINESS?
ACTUALLY, TIME CALLED ME "THE EMPRESS OF TOYLAND," WHICH IS SEVERAL LEVELS BEYOND QUEEN.
NOT TOO SHABBY YOURSELF, JORDAN.
GYM TIME?
THE EXHIBITION'S BEEN A SHATTERING SUCCESS WITH A CRITICAL 12-45 DEMOGRAPHIC.
PEERLESS TOYS GREEN-LIT A "GOLDEN GIANTS" LINE.
PREHISTORIC MISSING LINK WARRIORS DEFENDING EARTH AGAINST INVADING ALIEN COLOSSI--
I GUESS THERE'S SCOPE FOR THE IMAGINATION.
EXCEPT GIANT CULTURE'S A LITTLE LOW-TECH FOR COOL ACCESSORIES.
SAY I'M TAKING THIS OUT TO SALE--
IT'S HAIRY PROTO-HUMANS USING ROCKS TO FEND OFF AN INVASION OF MINDLESS SEMI-NAKED GIANTS.
AS A TOY SALESMAN YOU MAKE A GREAT GREEN LANTERN.
HOW ABOUT I FIND THIS ELUSIVE MUSEUM DIRECTOR--
--AND LEAVE YOU TWO SUPER-POLICEMEN TO INVESTIGATE?
PRICELESS EXHIBITS DISTURBED OR DISAPPEARED IN THE VICINITY OF THE SO-CALLED "AURIC ARCH," ENORMOUS FINGERPRINTS.
PRANKSTERS WE CAN DEAL WITH...

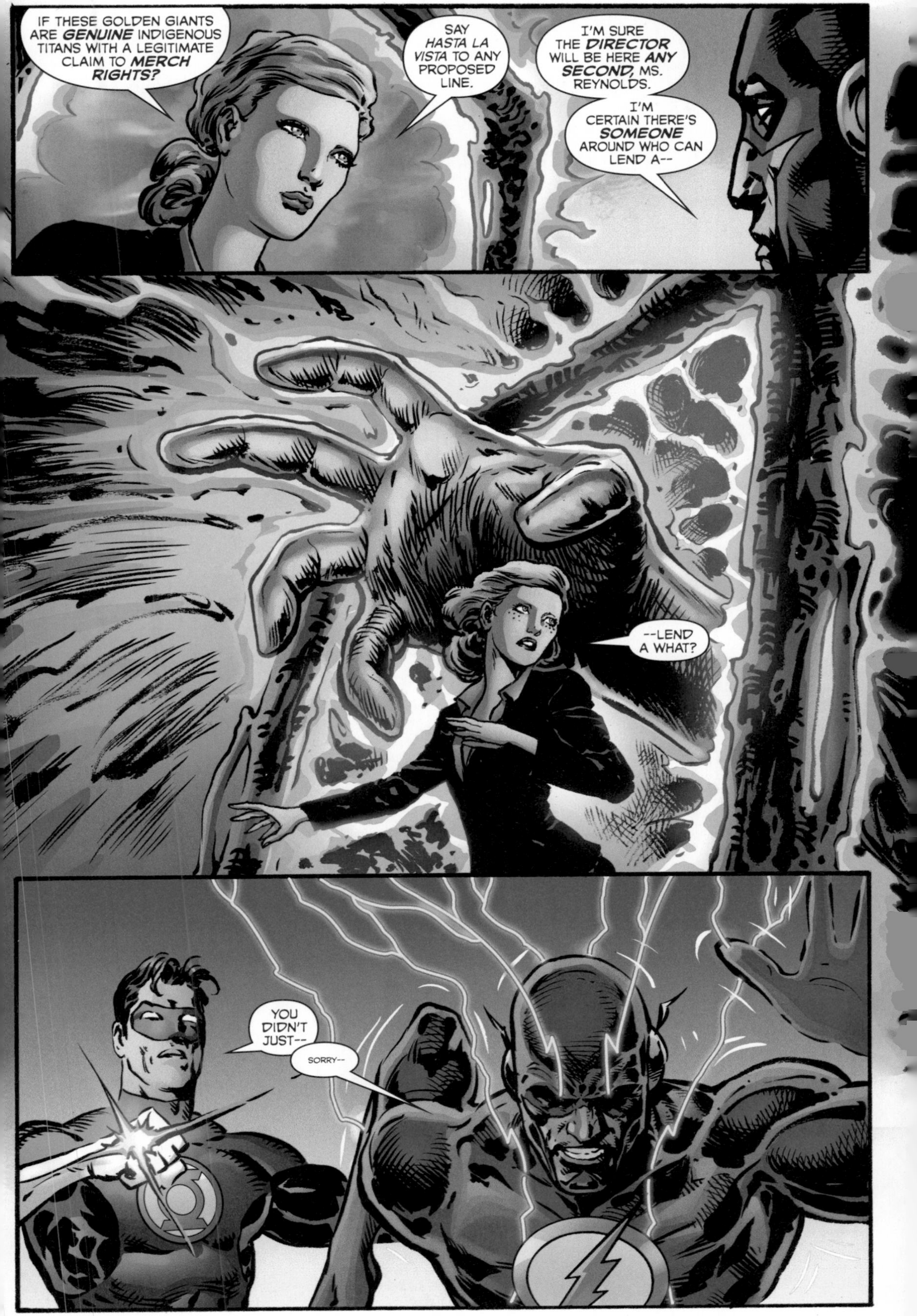
IF THESE GOLDEN GIANTS ARE GENUINE INDIGENOUS TITANS WITH A LEGITIMATE CLAIM TO MERCH RIGHTS?
SAY HASTA LA VISTA TO ANY PROPOSED LINE.
I'M SURE THE DIRECTOR WILL BE HERE ANY SECOND, MS. REYNOLDS.
I'M CERTAIN THERE'S SOMEONE AROUND WHO CAN LEND A--
--LEND A WHAT?
YOU DIDN'T JUST--
SORRY--

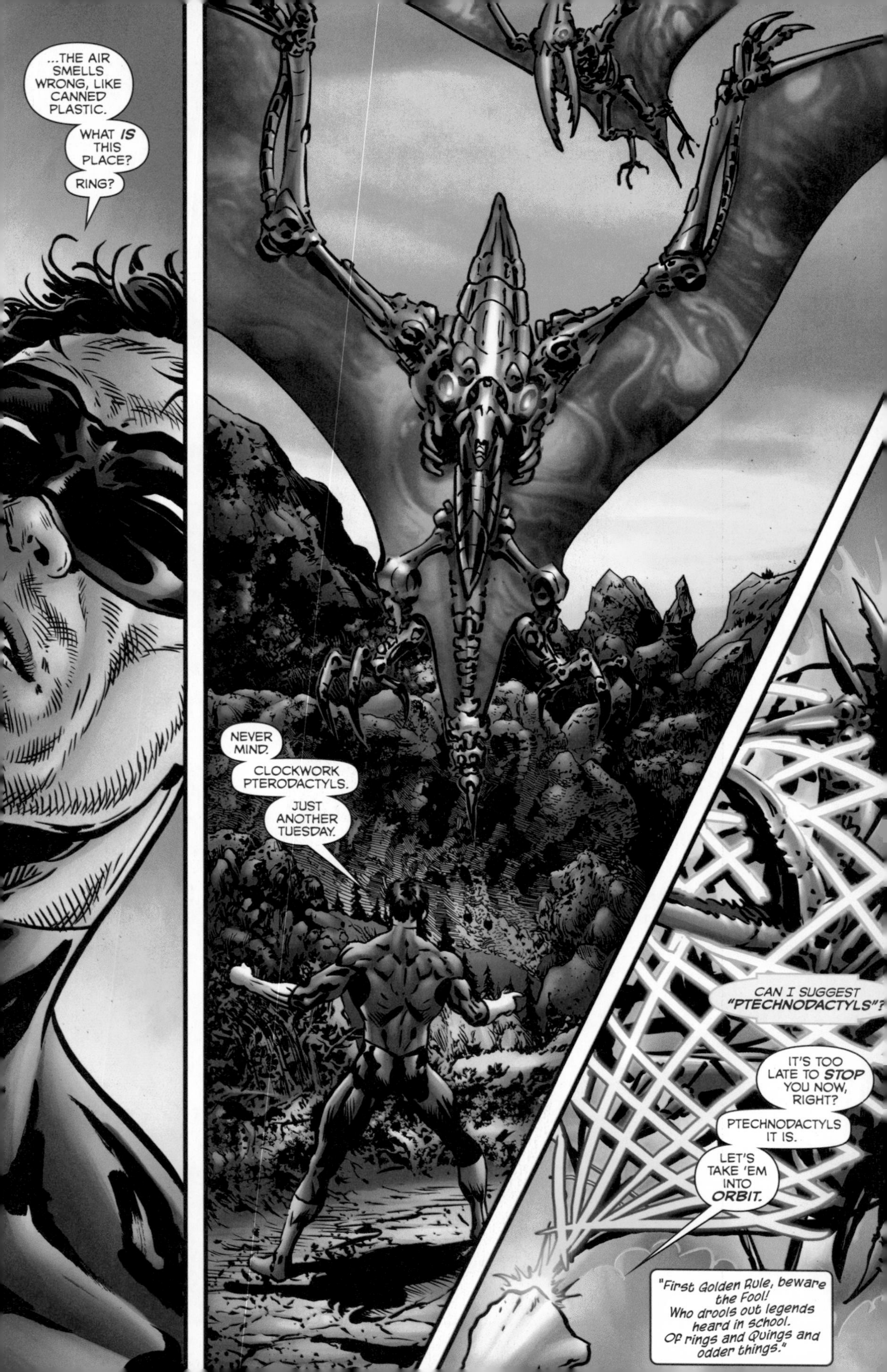
...THE AIR SMELLS WRONG, LIKE CANNED PLASTIC.
WHAT IS THIS PLACE?
RING?
NEVER MIND.
CLOCKWORK PTERODACTYLS.
JUST ANOTHER TUESDAY.
CAN I SUGGEST "PTECHNODACTYLS"?
IT'S TOO LATE TO STOP YOU NOW, RIGHT?
PTECHNODACTYLS IT IS.
LET'S TAKE 'EM INTO ORBIT.
"First Golden Rule, beware the Fool! Who drools out legends heard in school. Of rings and Quings and odder things."

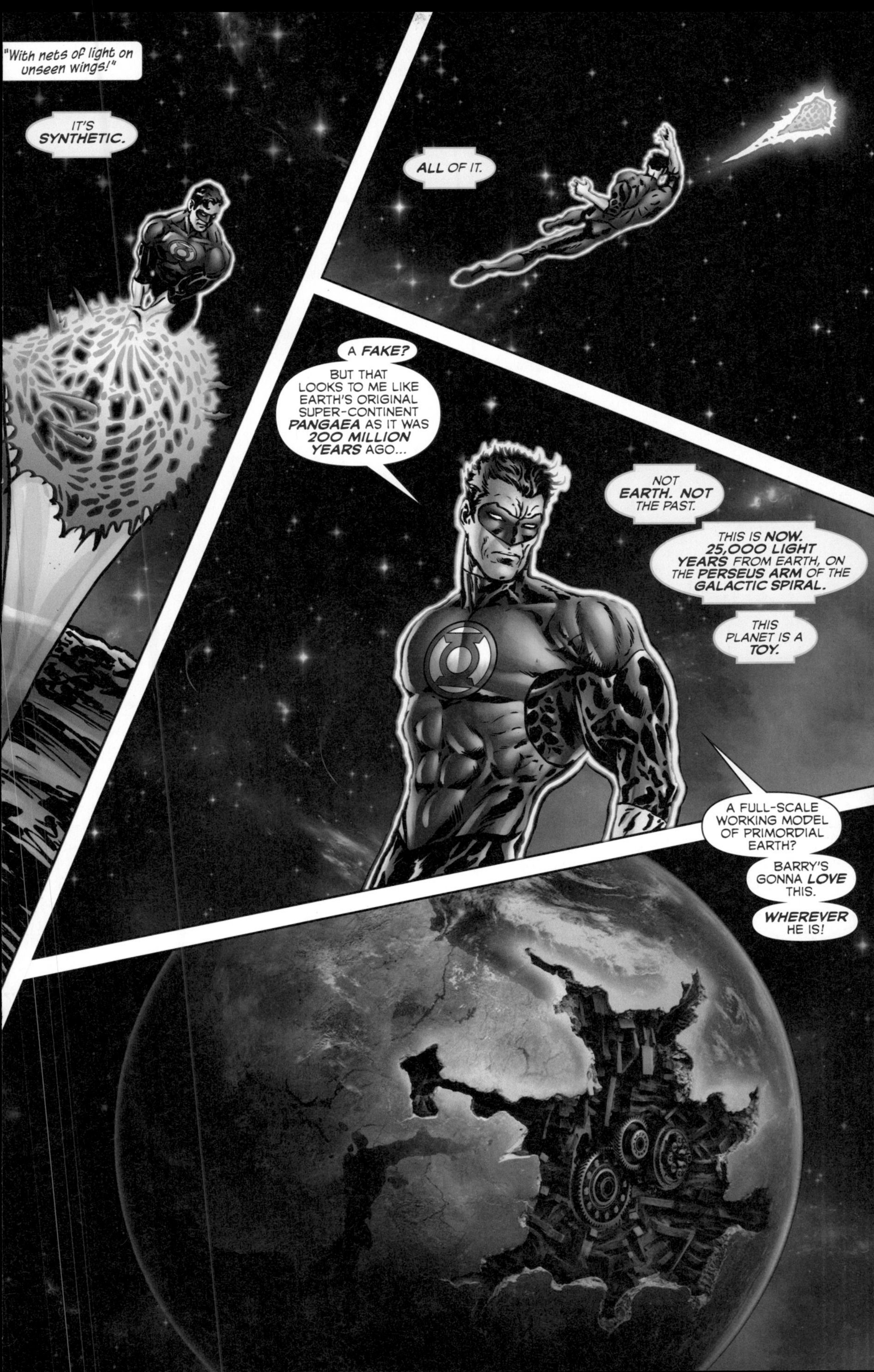
"With nets of light on unseen wings!"
IT'S SYNTHETIC.
ALL OF IT.
A FAKE?
BUT THAT LOOKS TO ME LIKE EARTH'S ORIGINAL SUPER-CONTINENT PANGAEA AS IT WAS 200 MILLION YEARS AGO...
NOT EARTH. NOT THE PAST.
THIS IS NOW. 25,000 LIGHT YEARS FROM EARTH, ON THE PERSEUS ARM OF THE GALACTIC SPIRAL.
THIS PLANET IS A TOY.
A FULL-SCALE WORKING MODEL OF PRIMORDIAL EARTH?
BARRY'S GONNA LOVE THIS.
WHEREVER HE IS!

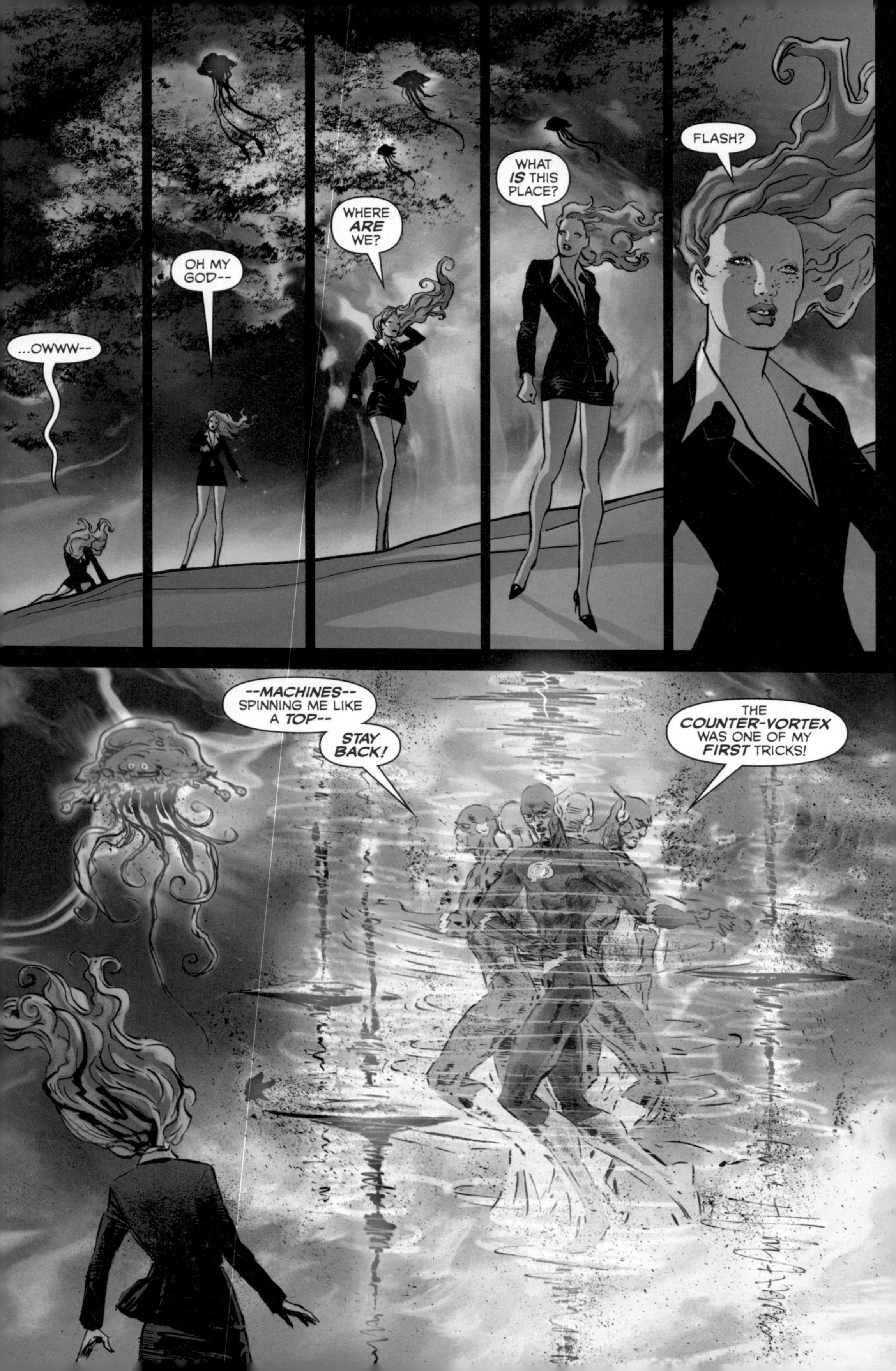
...OWWW--
OH MY GOD--
WHERE ARE WE?
WHAT IS THIS PLACE?
FLASH?
--MACHINES-- SPINNING ME LIKE A TOP--
STAY BACK!
THE COUNTER-VORTEX WAS ONE OF MY FIRST TRICKS!

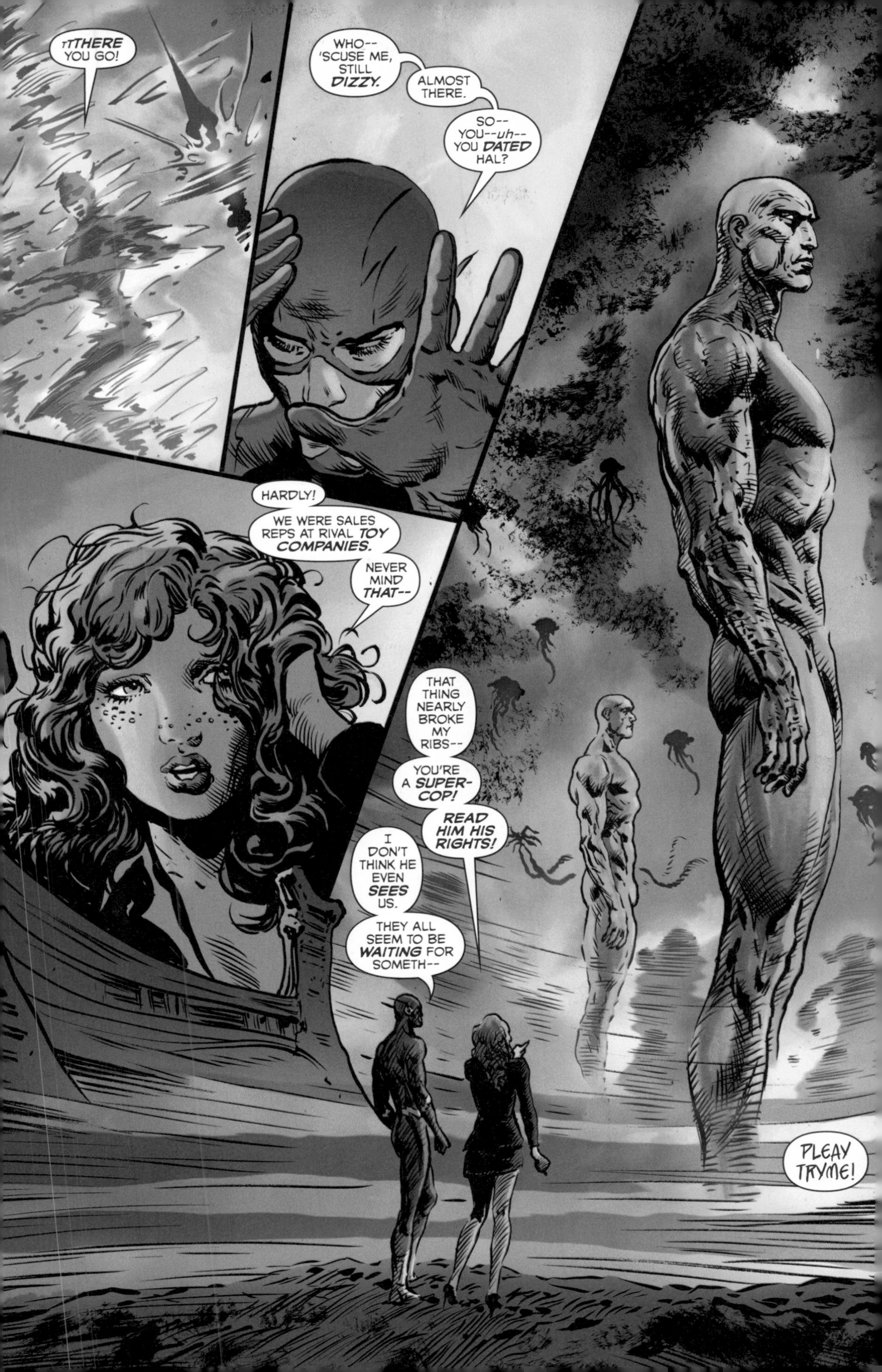
TTTHERE YOU GO!
WHO-- 'SCUSE ME, STILL DIZZY.
ALMOST THERE.
SO-- YOU--uh-- YOU DATED HAL?
HARDLY!
WE WERE SALES REPS AT RIVAL TOY COMPANIES.
NEVER MIND THAT--
THAT THING NEARLY BROKE MY RIBS--
YOU'RE A SUPER-COP!
READ HIM HIS RIGHTS!
I DON'T THINK HE EVEN SEES US.
THEY ALL SEEM TO BE WAITING FOR SOMETH--
PLEAY TRYME!

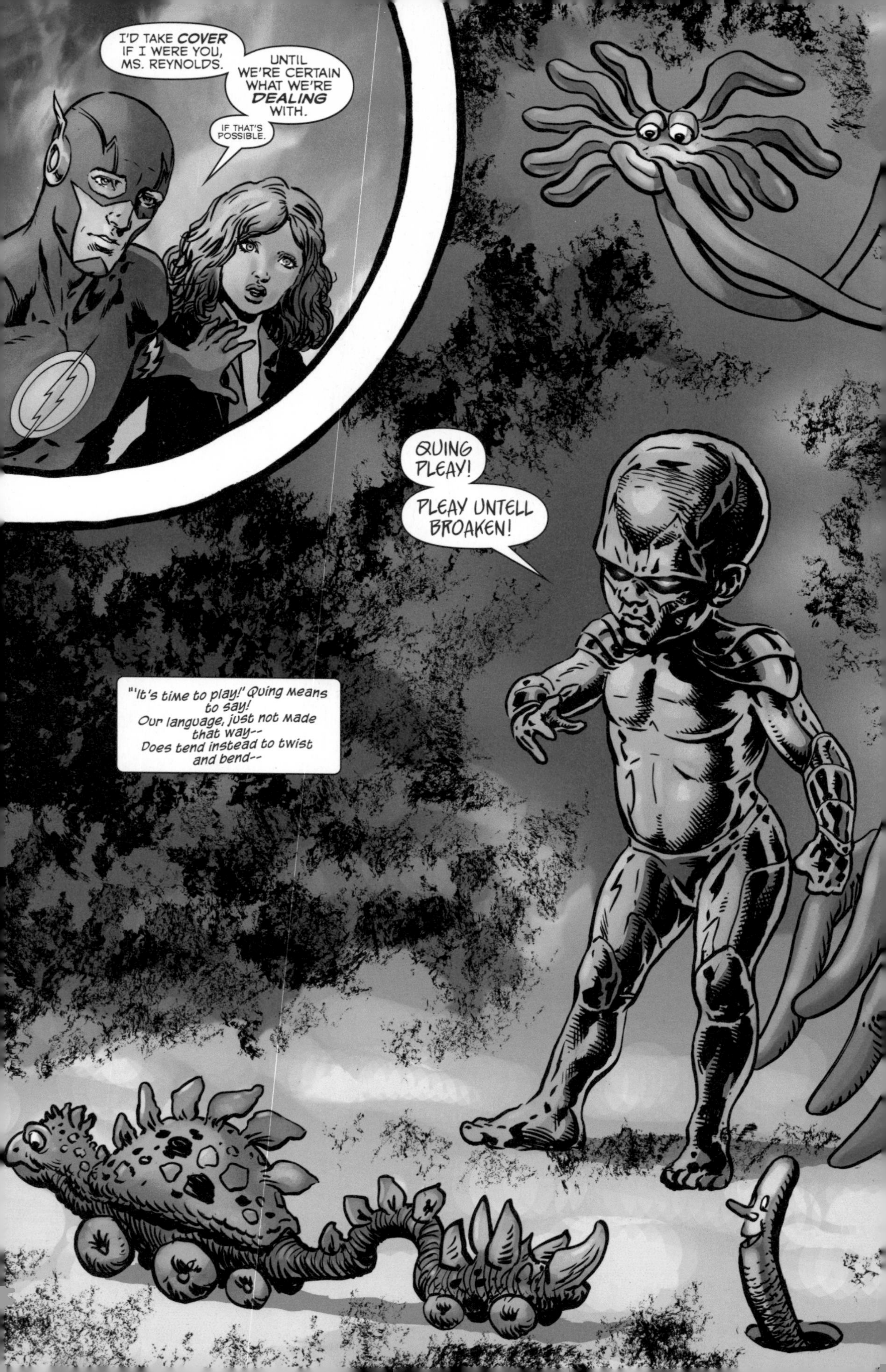
I'D TAKE COVER IF I WERE YOU, MS. REYNOLDS.
UNTIL WE'RE CERTAIN WHAT WE'RE DEALING WITH.
IF THAT'S POSSIBLE.
QUING PLEAY!
PLEAY UNTELL BROAKEN!
"It's time to play!" Quing Means to say! Our language, just not Made that way-- Does tend instead to twist and bend--

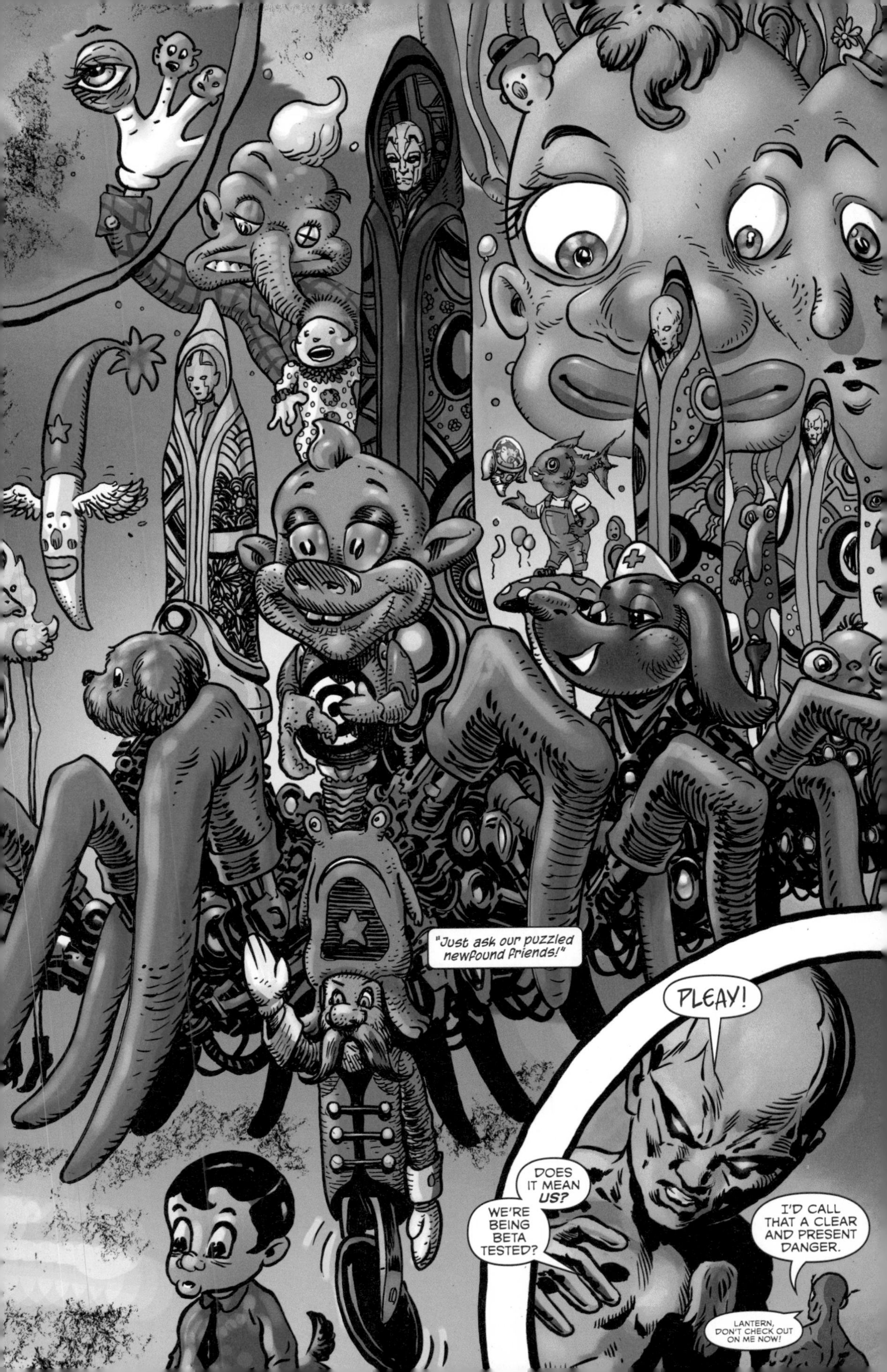
"Just ask our puzzled newfound friends!"
PLEAY!
DOES IT MEAN US?
WE'RE BEING BETA TESTED?
I'D CALL THAT A CLEAR AND PRESENT DANGER.
LANTERN, DON'T CHECK OUT ON ME NOW!

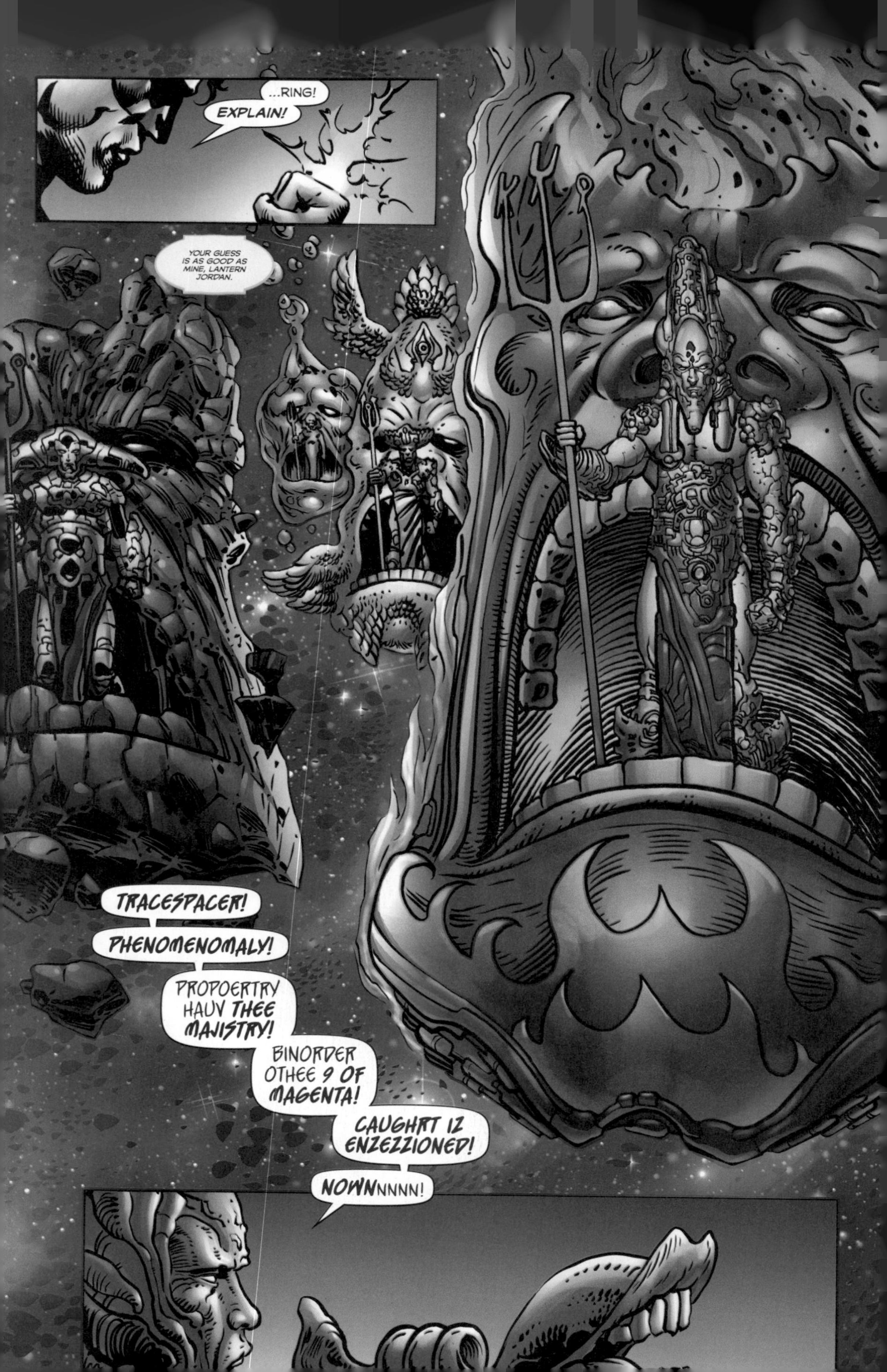
...RING!
EXPLAIN!
YOUR GUESS IS AS GOOD AS MINE, LANTERN JORDAN.
TRACESPACER!
PHENOMENOMALY!
PROPOERTRY HAUV THEE MAJISTRY!
BINORDER OTHEE 9 OF MAGENTA!
CAUGHRT IZ ENZEZZIONED!
NOWNNNNN!

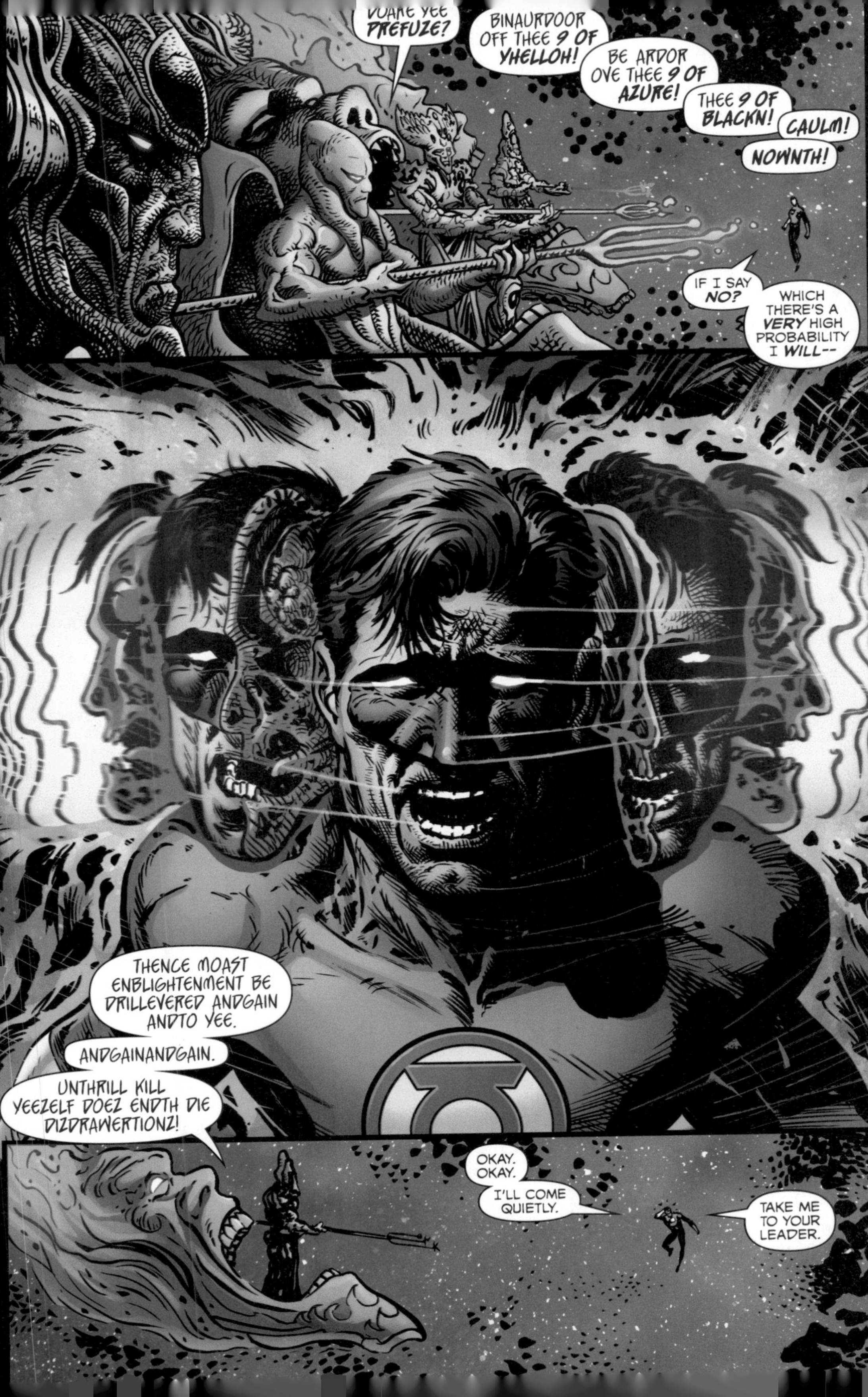
VOAKE YEE PREFUZE?
BINAURDOOR OFF THEE 9 OF YHELLOH!
BE ARDOR OVE THEE 9 OF AZURE!
THEE 9 OF BLACKN!
CAULM!
NOWNTH!
IF I SAY NO?
WHICH THERE'S A VERY HIGH PROBABILITY I WILL--
THENCE MOAST ENBLIGHTENMENT BE DRILLEVERED ANDGAIN ANDTO YEE.
ANDGAINANDGAIN.
UNTHRILL KILL YEEZELF DOEZ ENDTH DIE DIZDRAWERTIONZ!
OKAY. OKAY.
I'LL COME QUIETLY.
TAKE ME TO YOUR LEADER.

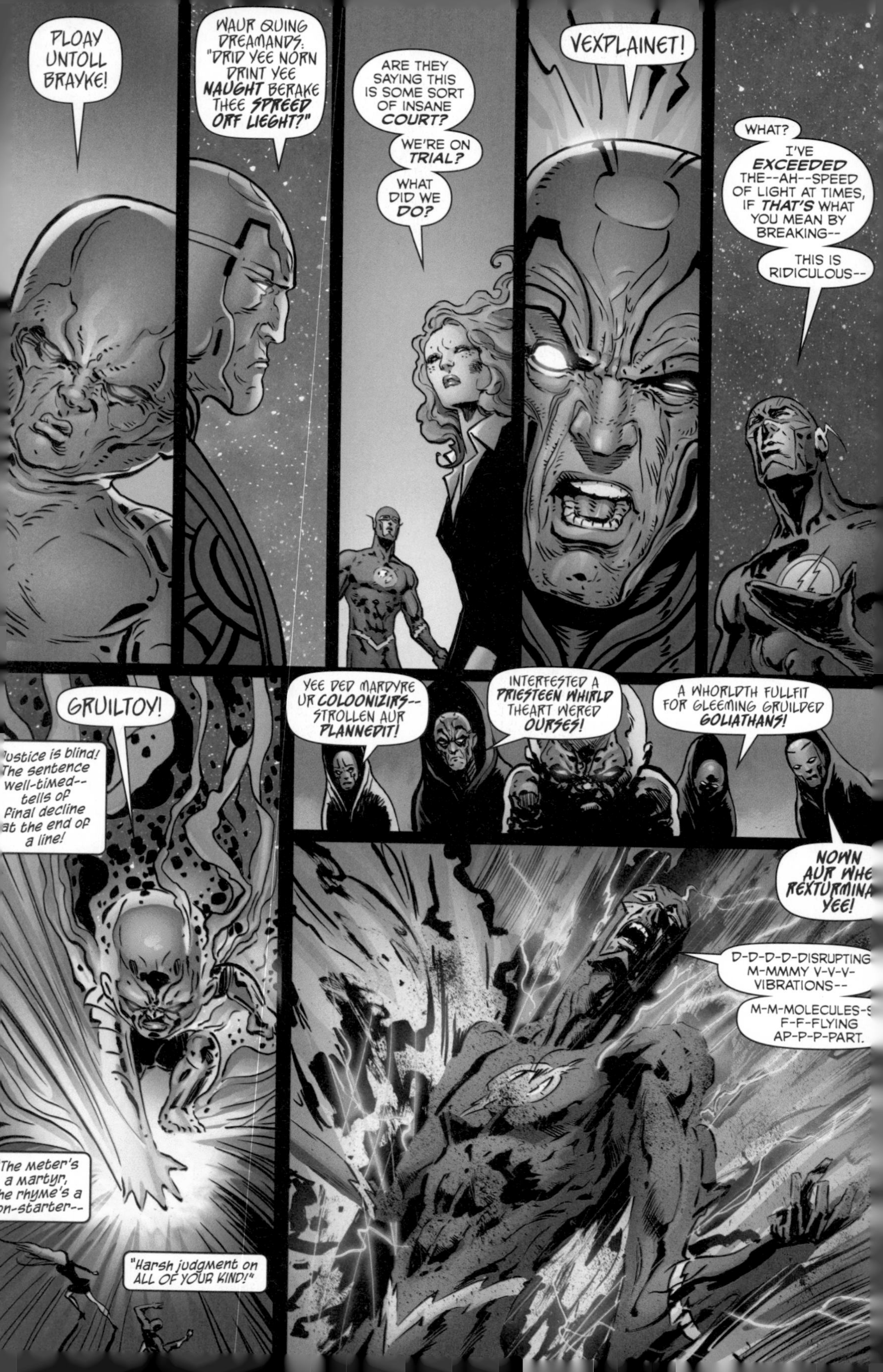

PLOAY UNTOLL BRAYKE!
WAUR QUING DREAMANDS: "DRID YEE NORN DRINT YEE NAUGHT BERAKE THEE SPREED ORF LIEGHT?"
ARE THEY SAYING THIS IS SOME SORT OF INSANE COURT?
WE'RE ON TRIAL?
WHAT DID WE DO?
VEXPLAINET!
WHAT?
I'VE EXCEEDED THE--AH--SPEED OF LIGHT AT TIMES, IF THAT'S WHAT YOU MEAN BY BREAKING--
THIS IS RIDICULOUS--
GRUILTOY!
Justice is blind! The sentence well-timed-- tells of final decline at the end of a line!
YEE DED MARDYRE UR COLOONIZIRS-- STROLLEN AUR PLANNEDIT!
INTERFESTED A PRIESTEEN WHIRLD THEART WERED OURSES!
A WHORLDTH FULLFIT FOR GLEEMING GRUILDED GOLIATHANS!
NOWN AUR WHE REXTURMINA YEE!
D-D-D-D-DISRUPTING M-MMMY V-V-V-VIBRATIONS--
M-M-MOLECULES-S F-F-FLYING AP-P-P-PART.
The meter's a martyr, he rhyme's a on-starter--
"Harsh judgment on ALL OF YOUR KIND!"

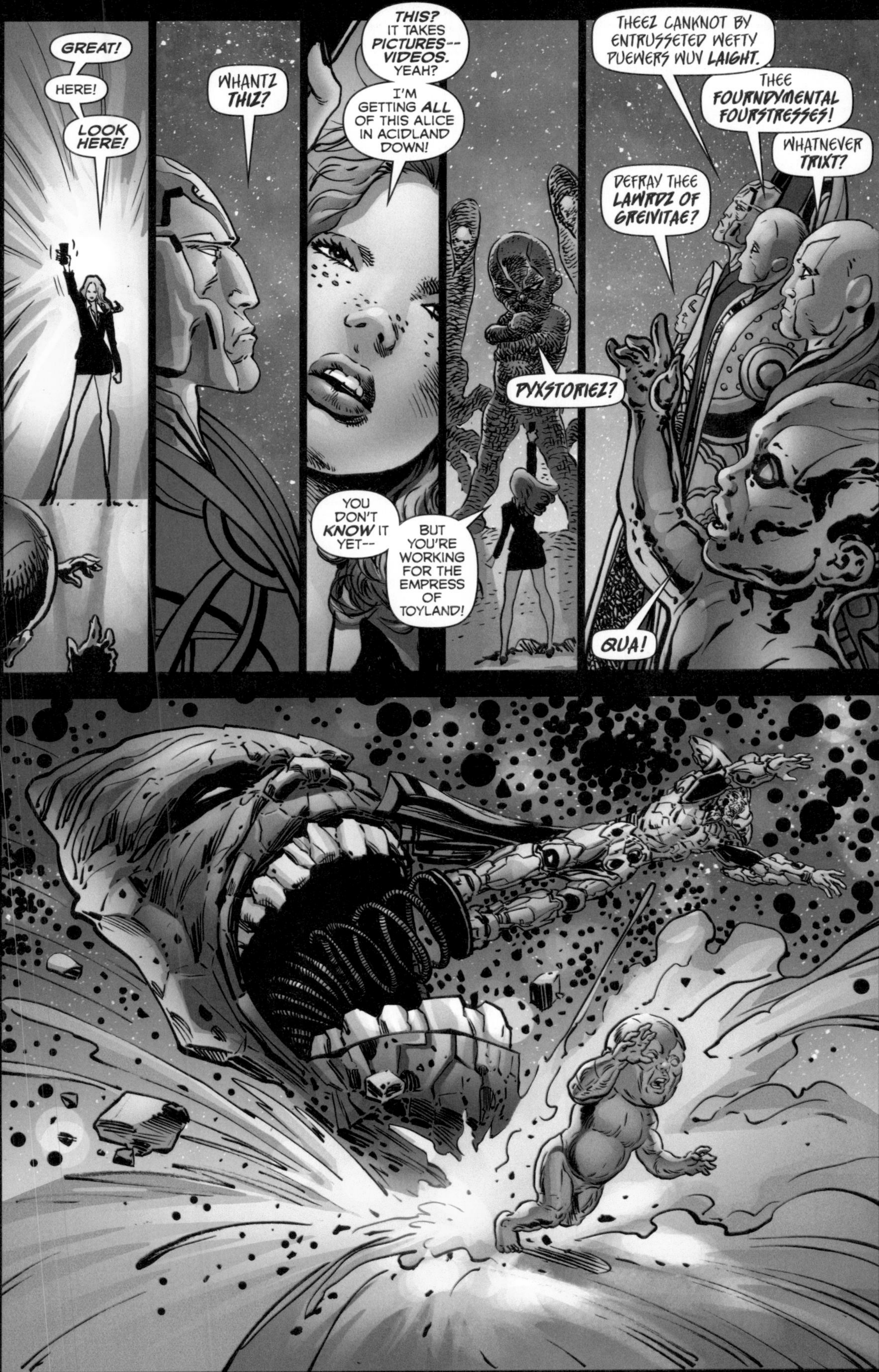
GREAT!
HERE!
LOOK HERE!
WHANTZ THIZ?
THIS? IT TAKES PICTURES-- VIDEOS. YEAH?
I'M GETTING ALL OF THIS ALICE IN ACIDLAND DOWN!
YOU DON'T KNOW IT YET--
BUT YOU'RE WORKING FOR THE EMPRESS OF TOYLAND!
PYXSTORIEZ?
THEEZ CANKNOT BY ENTRUSSETED WEFTY PUEWERS WUV LAIGHT.
THEE FOURNDYMENTAL FOURSTRESSES!
WHATNEVER TRIXT?
DEFRAY THEE LAWRDZ OF GREIVITAE?
QUA!

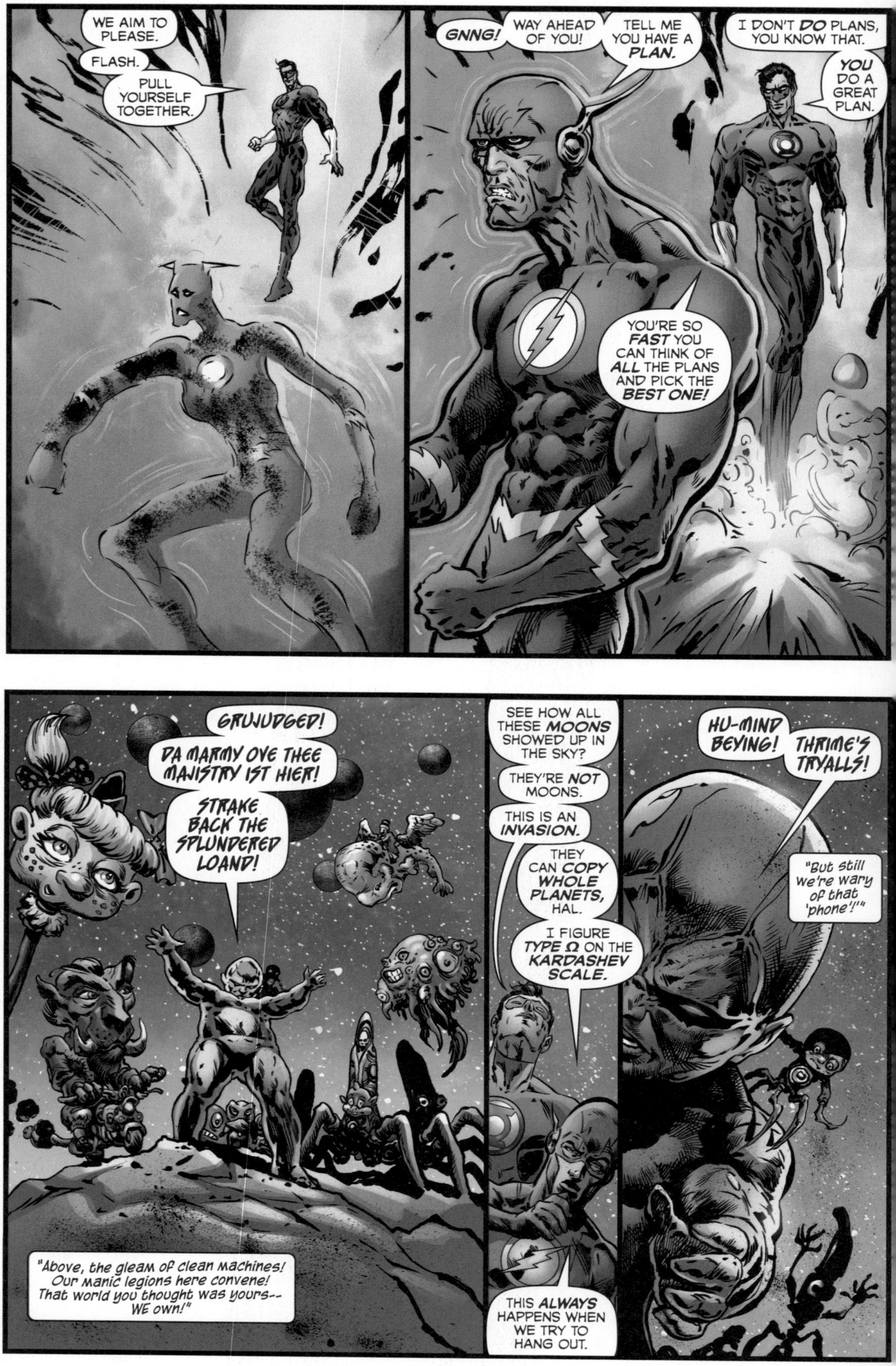
WE AIM TO PLEASE.
FLASH.
PULL YOURSELF TOGETHER.
GNNG!
WAY AHEAD OF YOU!
TELL ME YOU HAVE A PLAN.
I DON'T DO PLANS, YOU KNOW THAT.
YOU DO A GREAT PLAN.
YOU'RE SO FAST YOU CAN THINK OF ALL THE PLANS AND PICK THE BEST ONE!
GRUJUDGED!
DA MARMY OVE THEE MAJISTRY IST HIER!
STRAKE BACK THE SPLUNDERED LOAND!
"Above, the gleam of clean machines! Our manic legions here convene! That world you thought was yours-- WE own!"
SEE HOW ALL THESE MOONS SHOWED UP IN THE SKY?
THEY'RE NOT MOONS.
THIS IS AN INVASION.
THEY CAN COPY WHOLE PLANETS, HAL.
I FIGURE TYPE Ω ON THE KARDASHEV SCALE.
THIS ALWAYS HAPPENS WHEN WE TRY TO HANG OUT.
HU-MIND BEYING!
THRIME'S TRYALLS!
"But still we're wary of that 'phone'!"

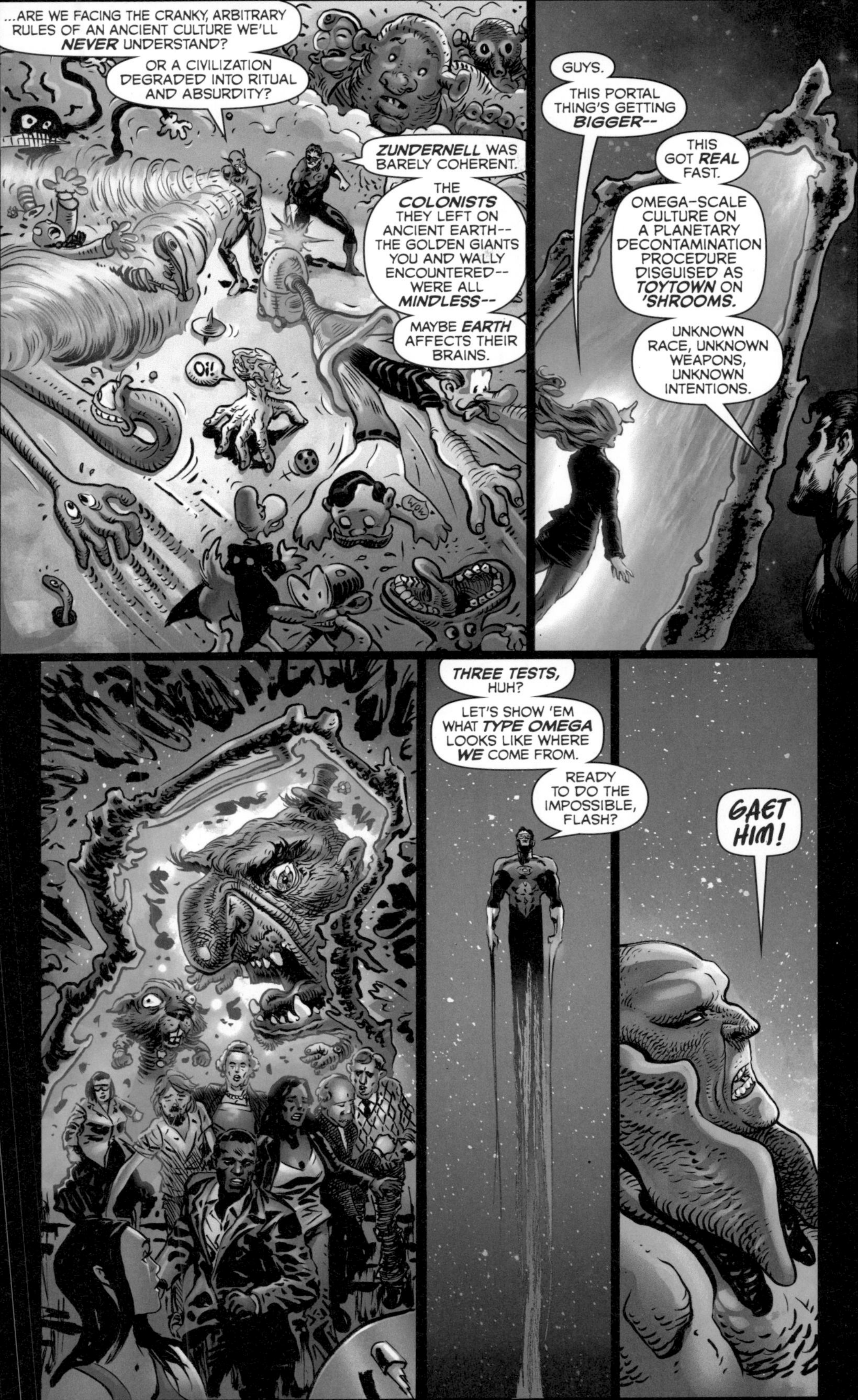

...ARE WE FACING THE CRANKY, ARBITRARY RULES OF AN ANCIENT CULTURE WE'LL NEVER UNDERSTAND?
OR A CIVILIZATION DEGRADED INTO RITUAL AND ABSURDITY?
ZUNDERNELL WAS BARELY COHERENT.
THE COLONISTS THEY LEFT ON ANCIENT EARTH-- THE GOLDEN GIANTS YOU AND WALLY ENCOUNTERED-- WERE ALL MINDLESS--
MAYBE EARTH AFFECTS THEIR BRAINS.
OI!
WOW
GUYS.
THIS PORTAL THING'S GETTING BIGGER--
THIS GOT REAL FAST.
OMEGA-SCALE CULTURE ON A PLANETARY DECONTAMINATION PROCEDURE DISGUISED AS TOYTOWN ON 'SHROOMS.
UNKNOWN RACE, UNKNOWN WEAPONS, UNKNOWN INTENTIONS.
THREE TESTS, HUH?
LET'S SHOW 'EM WHAT TYPE OMEGA LOOKS LIKE WHERE WE COME FROM.
READY TO DO THE IMPOSSIBLE, FLASH?
GAET HIM!

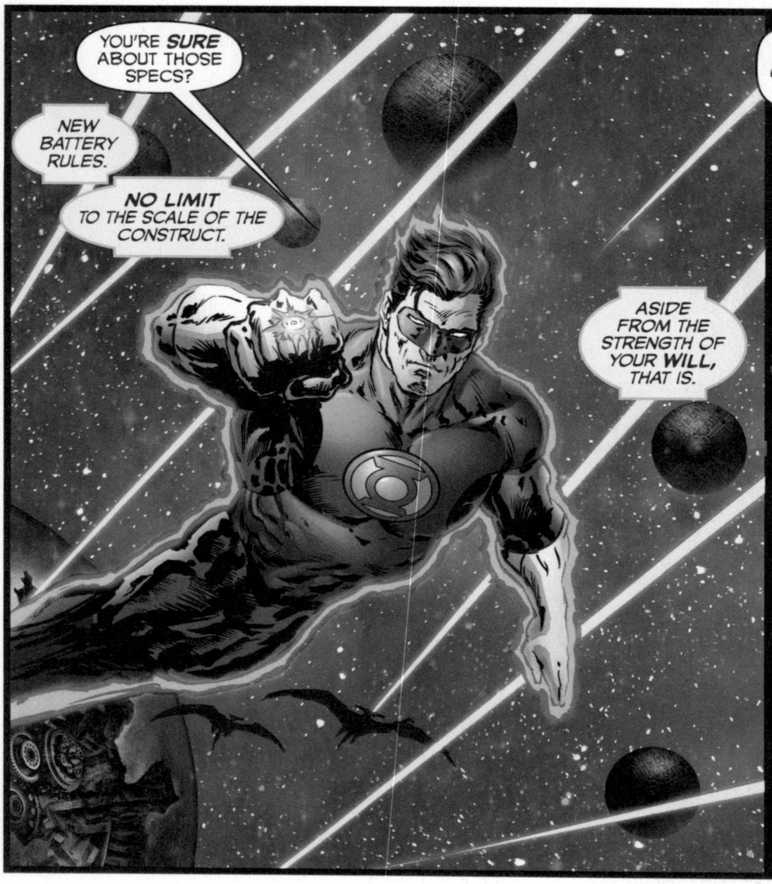
YOU'RE SURE ABOUT THOSE SPECS?
NEW BATTERY RULES.
NO LIMIT TO THE SCALE OF THE CONSTRUCT.
ASIDE FROM THE STRENGTH OF YOUR WILL, THAT IS.

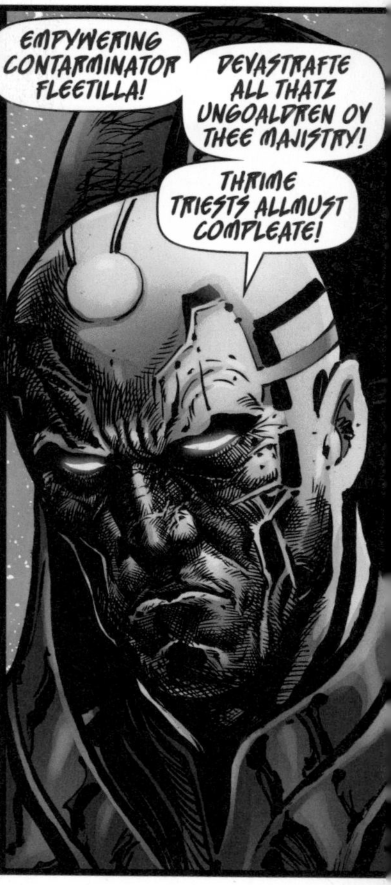
EMPYWERING CONTARMINATOR FLEETILLA!
DEVASTRAFTE ALL THATZ UNGOALDREN OV THEE MAJISTRY!
THRIME TRIESTS ALLMUST COMPLEATE!

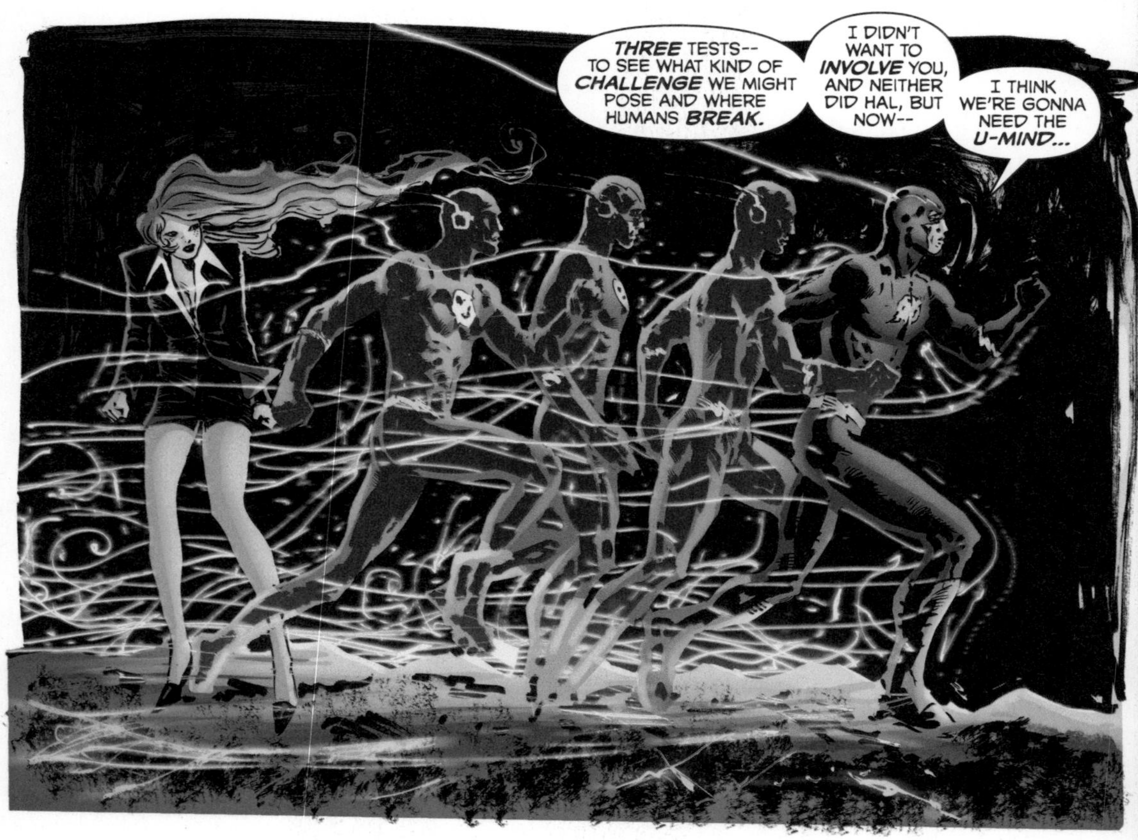
THREE TESTS-- TO SEE WHAT KIND OF CHALLENGE WE MIGHT POSE AND WHERE HUMANS BREAK.
I DIDN'T WANT TO INVOLVE YOU, AND NEITHER DID HAL, BUT NOW--
I THINK WE'RE GONNA NEED THE U-MIND...

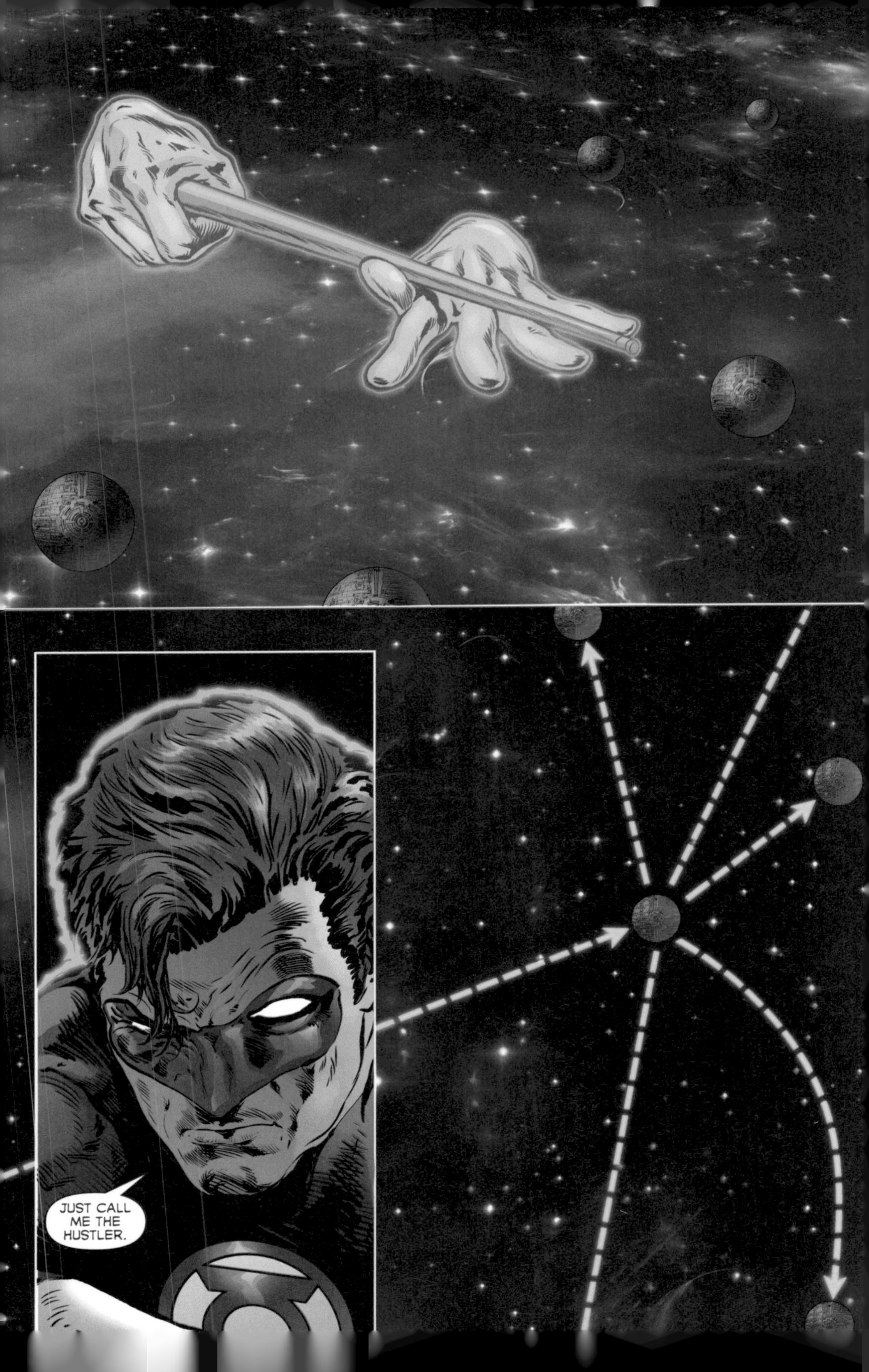
JUST CALL ME THE HUSTLER.

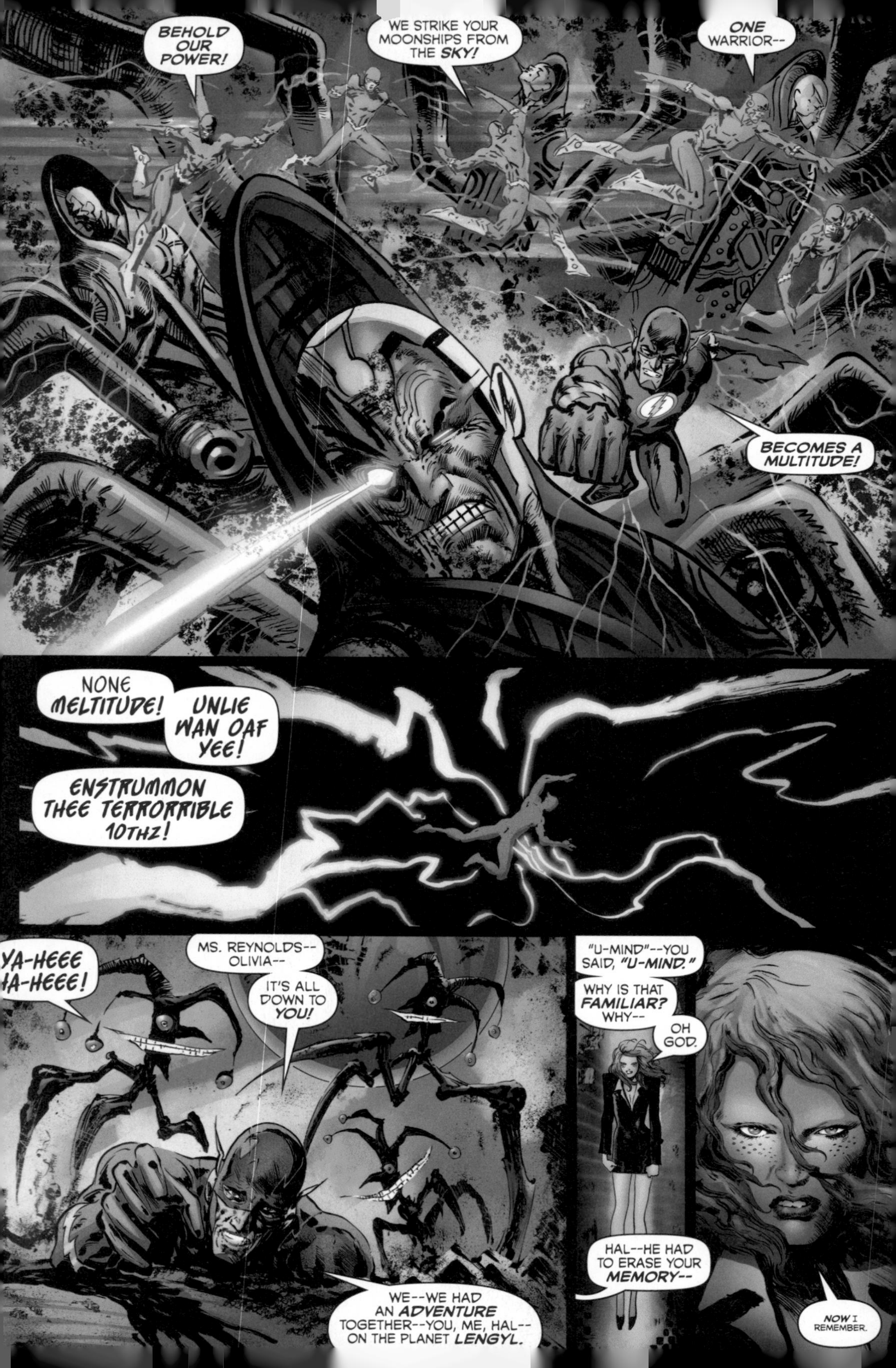

BEHOLD OUR POWER!
WE STRIKE YOUR MOONSHIPS FROM THE SKY!
ONE WARRIOR--
BECOMES A MULTITUDE!
NONE MELTITUDE!
UNLIE WAN OAF YEE!
ENSTRUMMON THEE TERRORRIBLE 10THZ!
YA-HEEE HA-HEEE!
MS. REYNOLDS-- OLIVIA--
IT'S ALL DOWN TO YOU!
WE--WE HAD AN ADVENTURE TOGETHER--YOU, ME, HAL-- ON THE PLANET LENGYL.
"U-MIND"--YOU SAID, "U-MIND."
WHY IS THAT FAMILIAR? WHY--
OH GOD.
HAL--HE HAD TO ERASE YOUR MEMORY--
NOW I REMEMBER.

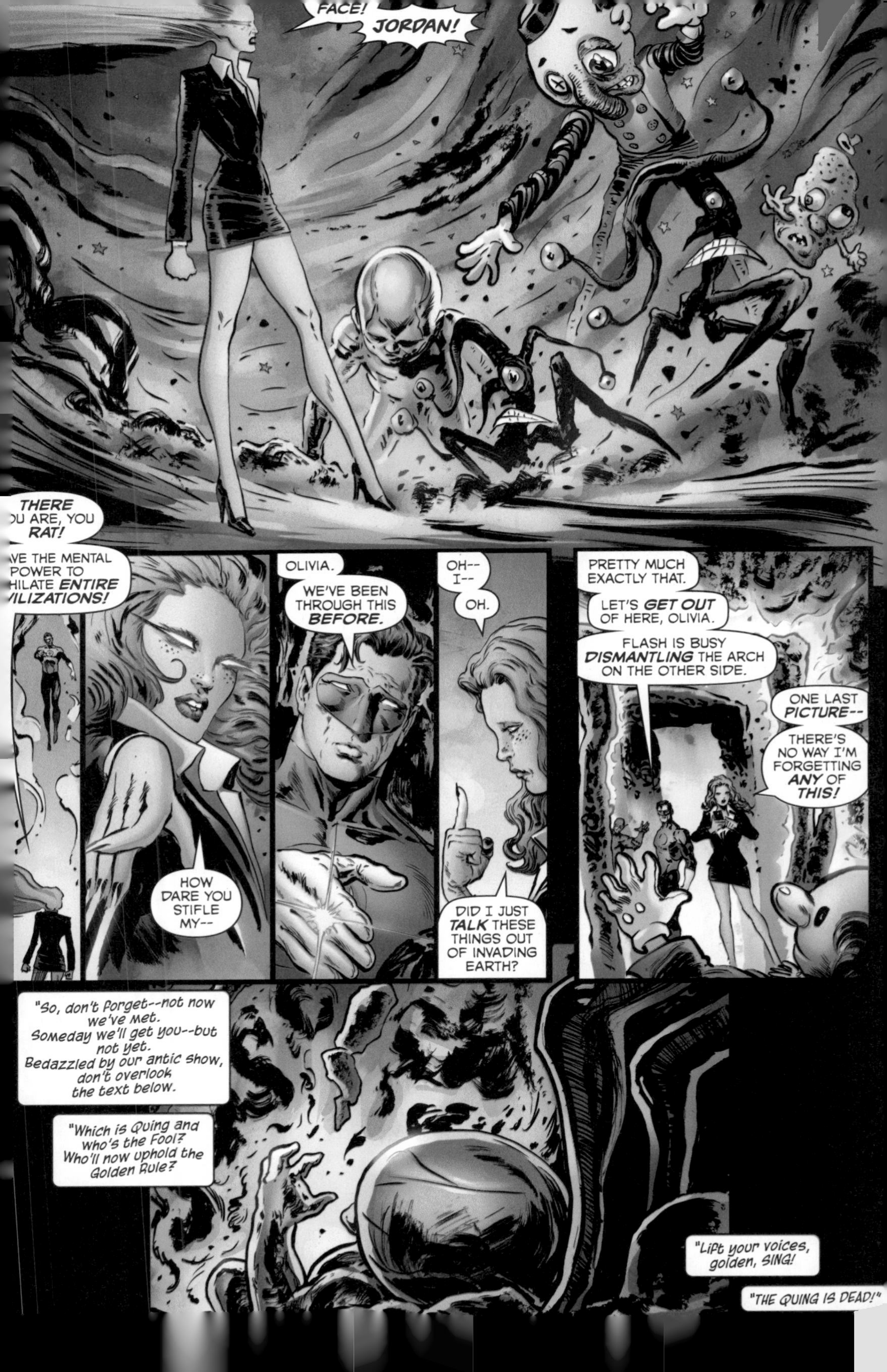

FACE!
JORDAN!
THERE
OU ARE, YOU
RAT!
AVE THE MENTAL
POWER TO
HILATE ENTIRE
VILIZATIONS!
HOW
DARE YOU
STIFLE
MY--
OLIVIA.
WE'VE BEEN
THROUGH THIS
BEFORE.
OH--
I--
OH.
DID I JUST
TALK THESE
THINGS OUT
OF INVADING
EARTH?
PRETTY MUCH
EXACTLY THAT.
LET'S GET OUT
OF HERE, OLIVIA.
FLASH IS BUSY
DISMANTLING THE ARCH
ON THE OTHER SIDE.
ONE LAST
PICTURE--
THERE'S
NO WAY I'M
FORGETTING
ANY OF
THIS!
"So, don't forget--not now we've met. Someday we'll get you--but not yet. Bedazzled by our antic show, don't overlook the text below.
"Which is Quing and who's the Fool? Who'll now uphold the Golden Rule?
"Lift your voices, golden, SING!
"THE QUING IS DEAD!"

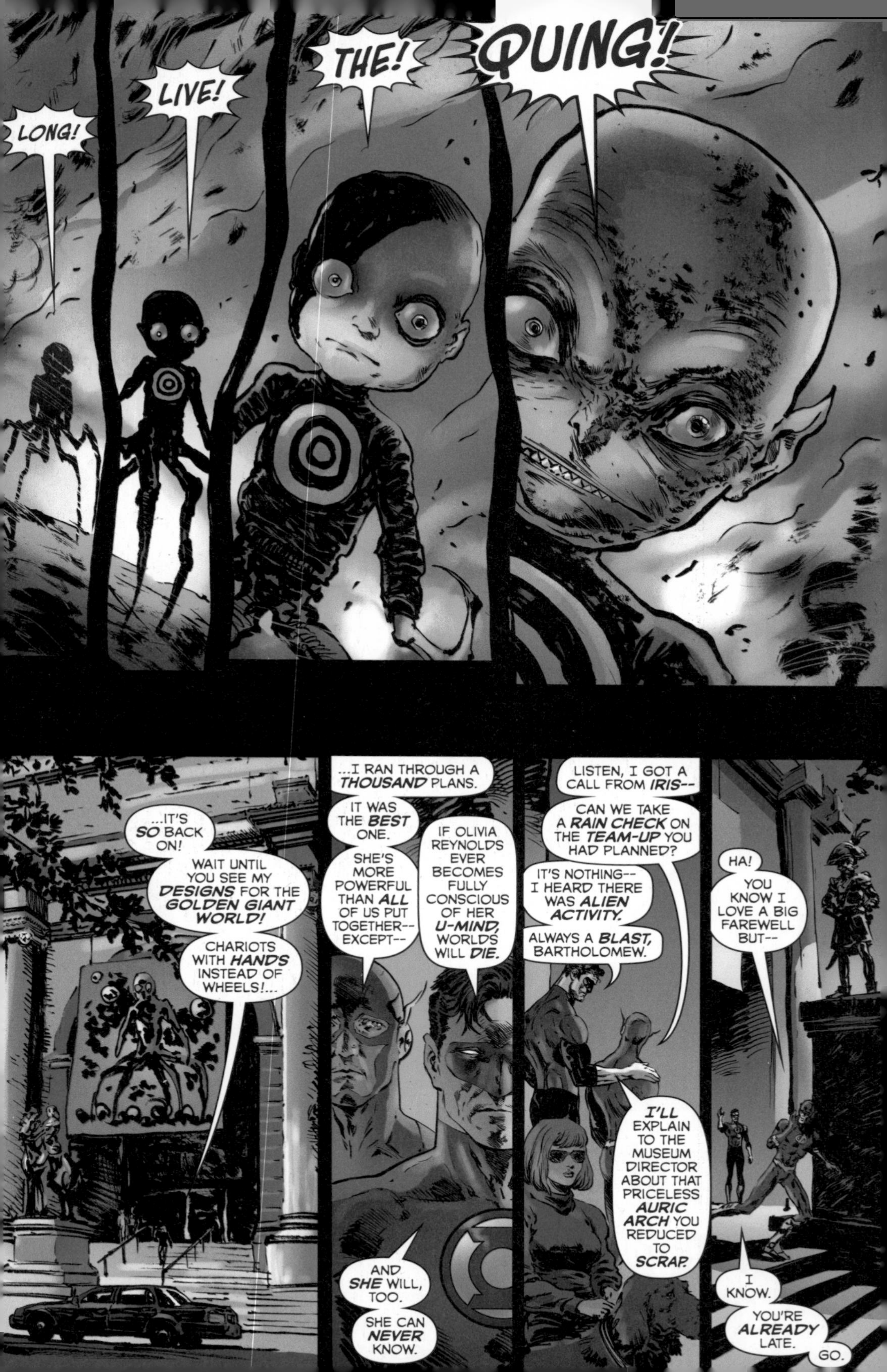
LONG!
LIVE!
THE!
QUING!
...IT'S SO BACK ON!
WAIT UNTIL YOU SEE MY DESIGNS FOR THE GOLDEN GIANT WORLD!
CHARIOTS WITH HANDS INSTEAD OF WHEELS!...
...I RAN THROUGH A THOUSAND PLANS.
IT WAS THE BEST ONE.
SHE'S MORE POWERFUL THAN ALL OF US PUT TOGETHER-- EXCEPT--
IF OLIVIA REYNOLDS EVER BECOMES FULLY CONSCIOUS OF HER U-MIND, WORLDS WILL DIE.
AND SHE WILL, TOO.
SHE CAN NEVER KNOW.
LISTEN, I GOT A CALL FROM IRIS--
CAN WE TAKE A RAIN CHECK ON THE TEAM-UP YOU HAD PLANNED?
IT'S NOTHING-- I HEARD THERE WAS ALIEN ACTIVITY.
ALWAYS A BLAST, BARTHOLOMEW.
I'LL EXPLAIN TO THE MUSEUM DIRECTOR ABOUT THAT PRICELESS AURIC ARCH YOU REDUCED TO SCRAP.
HA!
YOU KNOW I LOVE A BIG FAREWELL BUT--
I KNOW.
YOU'RE ALREADY LATE.
GO.

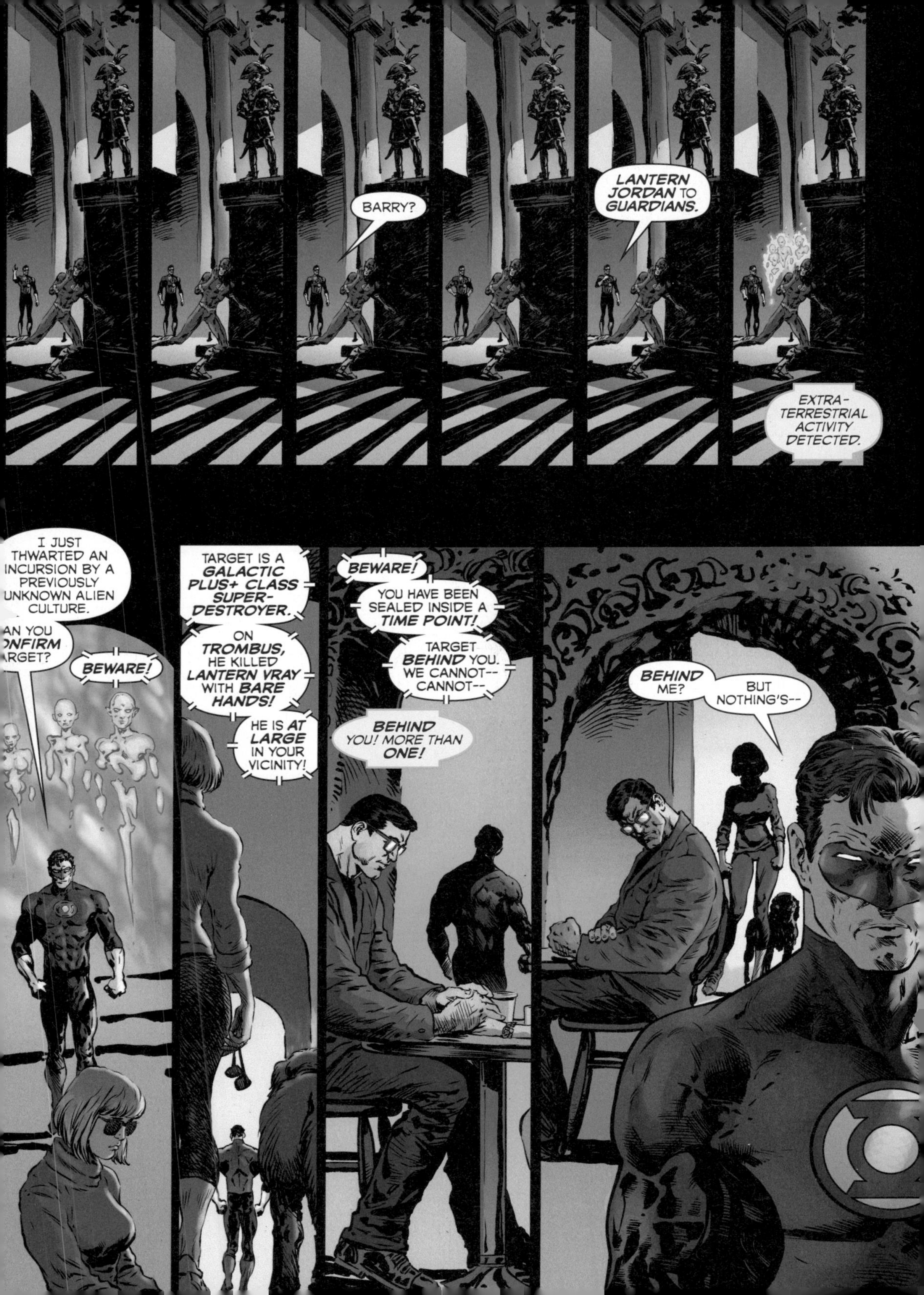
BARRY?
LANTERN JORDAN TO GUARDIANS.
EXTRA-TERRESTRIAL ACTIVITY DETECTED.
I JUST THWARTED AN INCURSION BY A PREVIOUSLY UNKNOWN ALIEN CULTURE.
AN YOU ONFIRM ARGET?
BEWARE!
TARGET IS A GALACTIC PLUS+ CLASS SUPER-DESTROYER.
ON TROMBUS, HE KILLED LANTERN VRAY WITH BARE HANDS!
HE IS AT LARGE IN YOUR VICINITY!
BEWARE!
YOU HAVE BEEN SEALED INSIDE A TIME POINT!
TARGET BEHIND YOU. WE CANNOT-- CANNOT--
BEHIND YOU! MORE THAN ONE!
BEHIND ME?
BUT NOTHING'S--

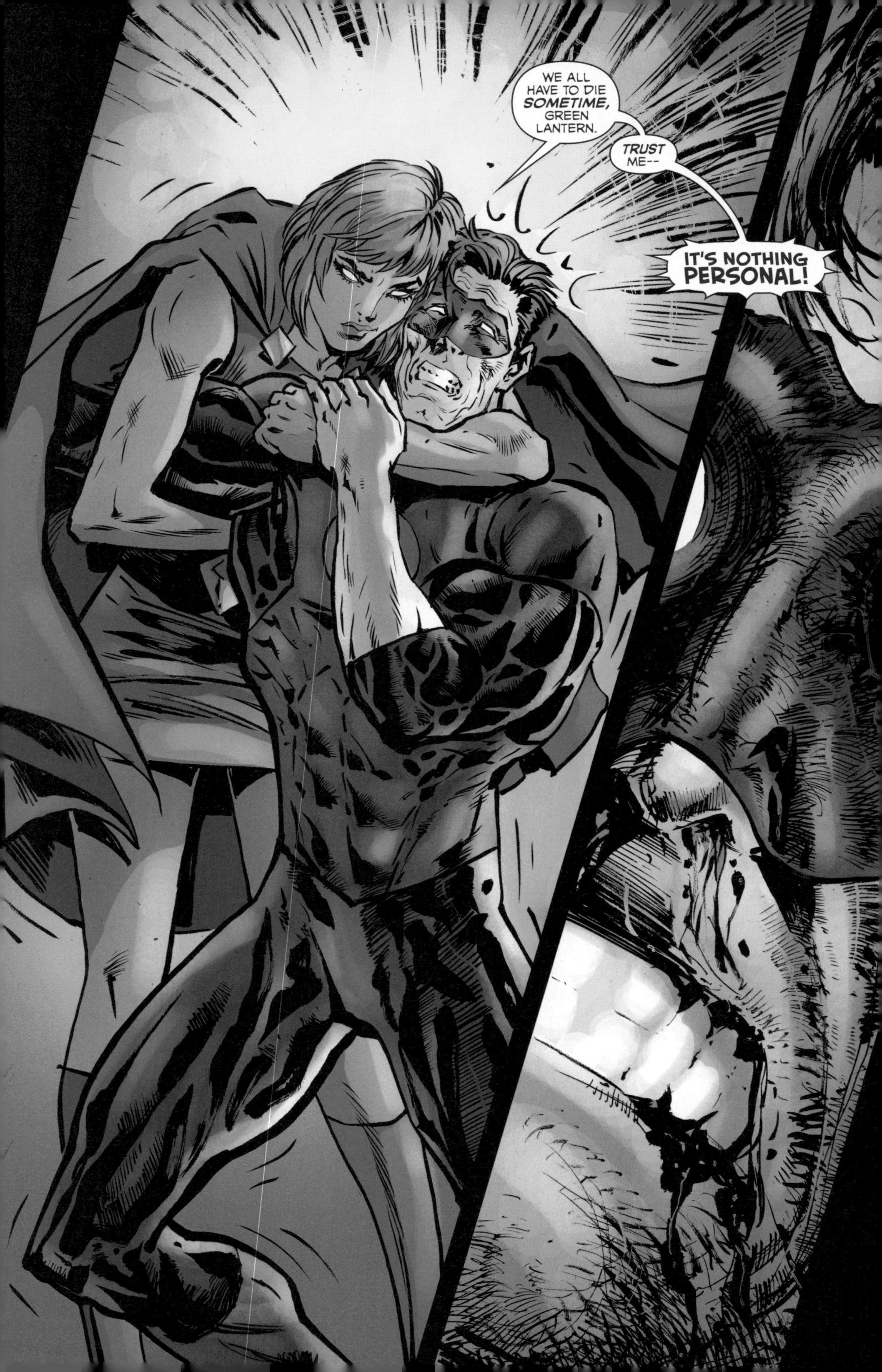
WE ALL HAVE TO DIE SOMETIME, GREEN LANTERN.
TRUST ME--
IT'S NOTHING PERSONAL!

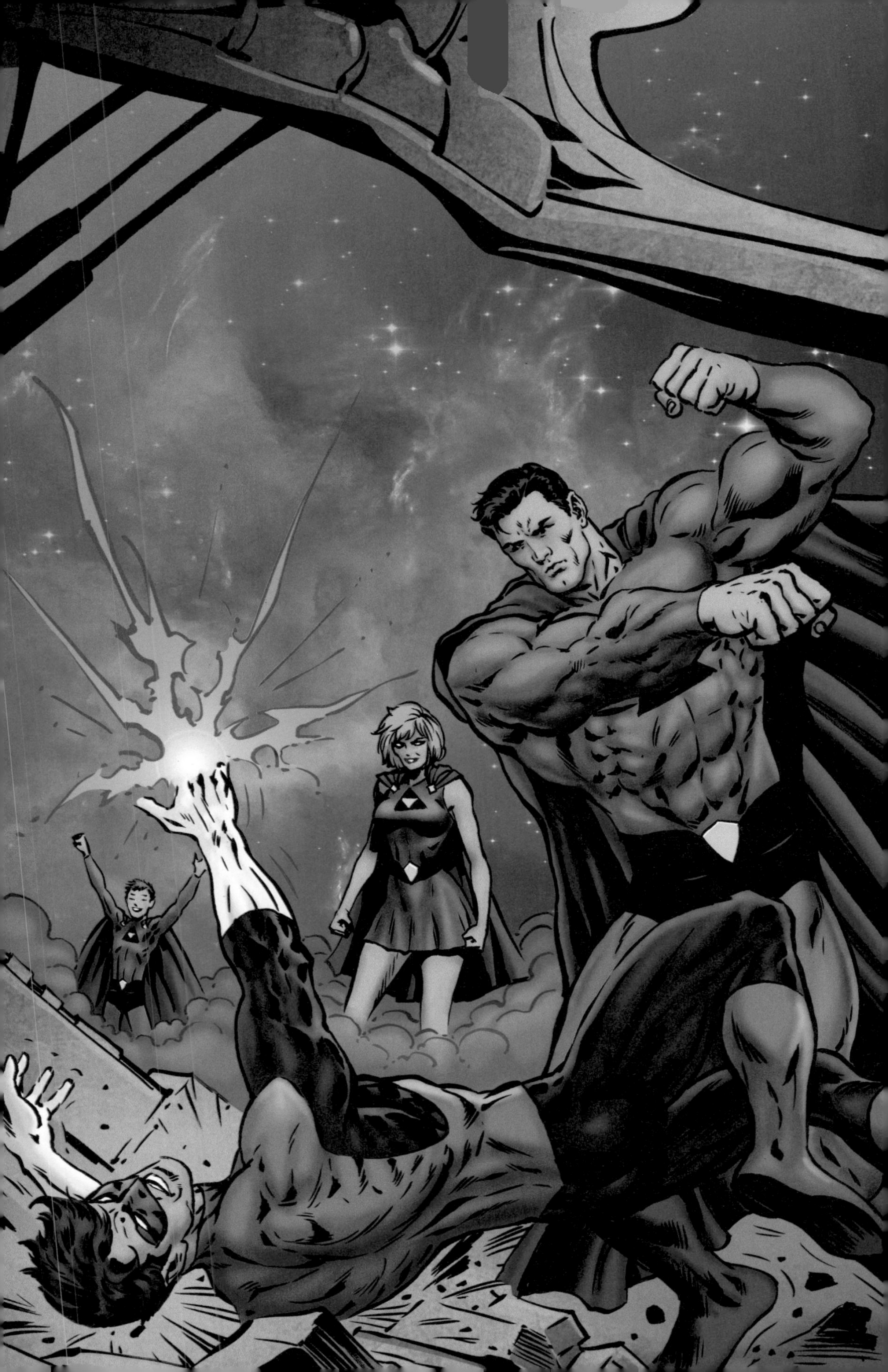

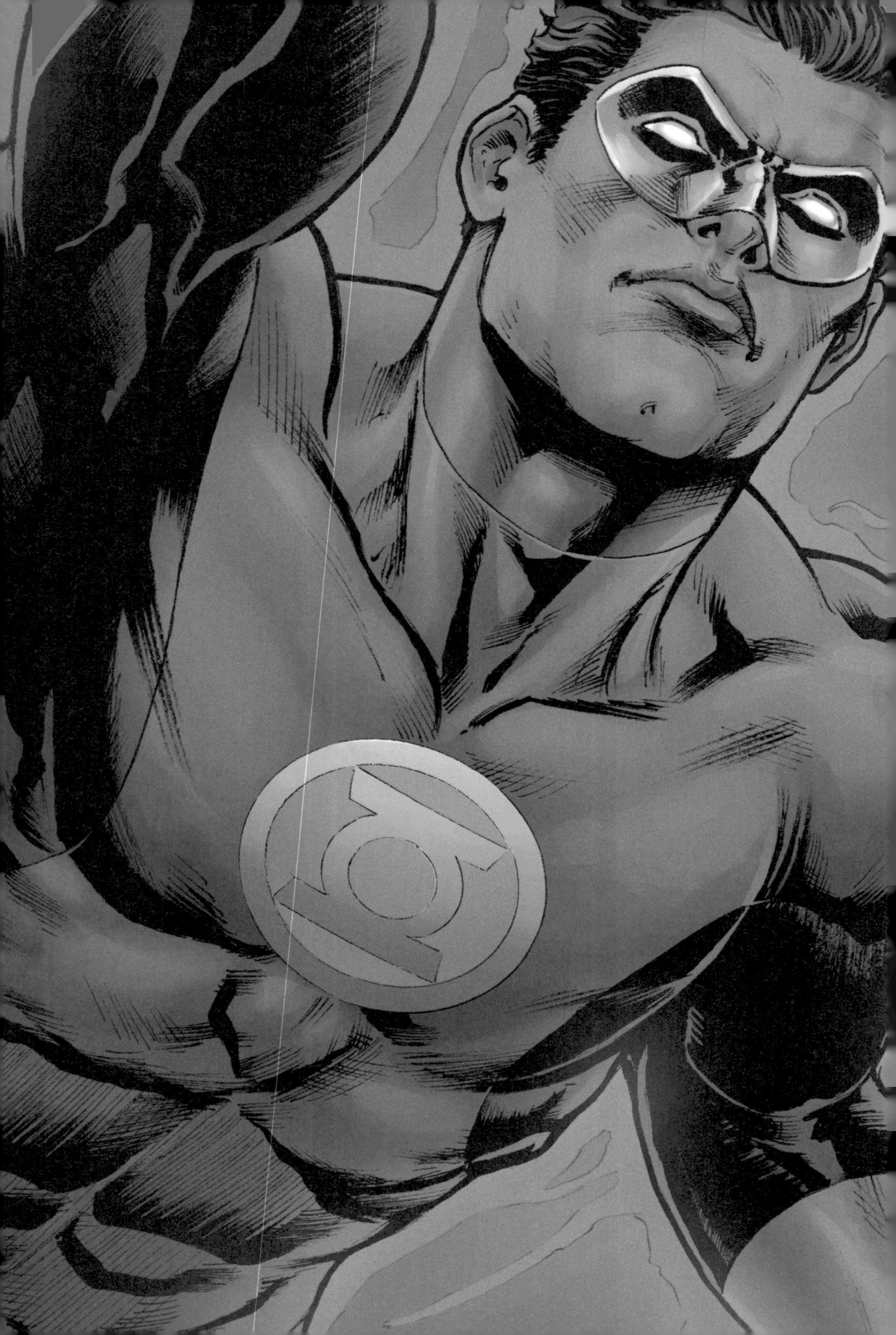

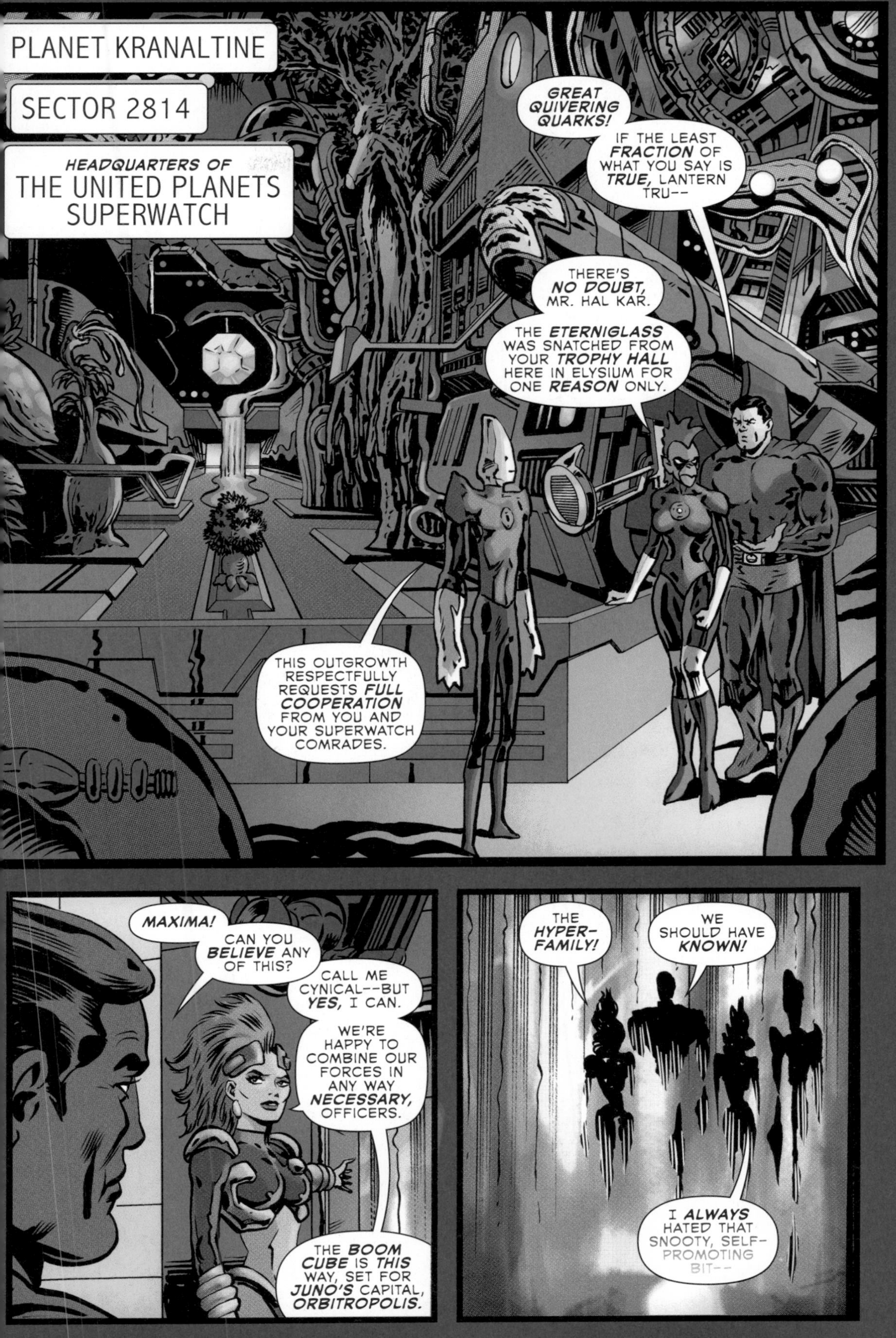

PLANET KRANALTINE
SECTOR 2814
HEADQUARTERS OF THE UNITED PLANETS SUPERWATCH
GREAT QUIVERING QUARKS!
IF THE LEAST FRACTION OF WHAT YOU SAY IS TRUE, LANTERN TRU--
THERE'S NO DOUBT, MR. HAL KAR.
THE ETERNIGLASS WAS SNATCHED FROM YOUR TROPHY HALL HERE IN ELYSIUM FOR ONE REASON ONLY.
THIS OUTGROWTH RESPECTFULLY REQUESTS FULL COOPERATION FROM YOU AND YOUR SUPERWATCH COMRADES.
MAXIMA!
CAN YOU BELIEVE ANY OF THIS?
CALL ME CYNICAL--BUT YES, I CAN.
WE'RE HAPPY TO COMBINE OUR FORCES IN ANY WAY NECESSARY, OFFICERS.
THE BOOM CUBE IS THIS WAY, SET FOR JUNO'S CAPITAL, ORBITROPOLIS.
THE HYPER-FAMILY!
WE SHOULD HAVE KNOWN!
I ALWAYS HATED THAT SNOOTY, SELF-PROMOTING BIT--

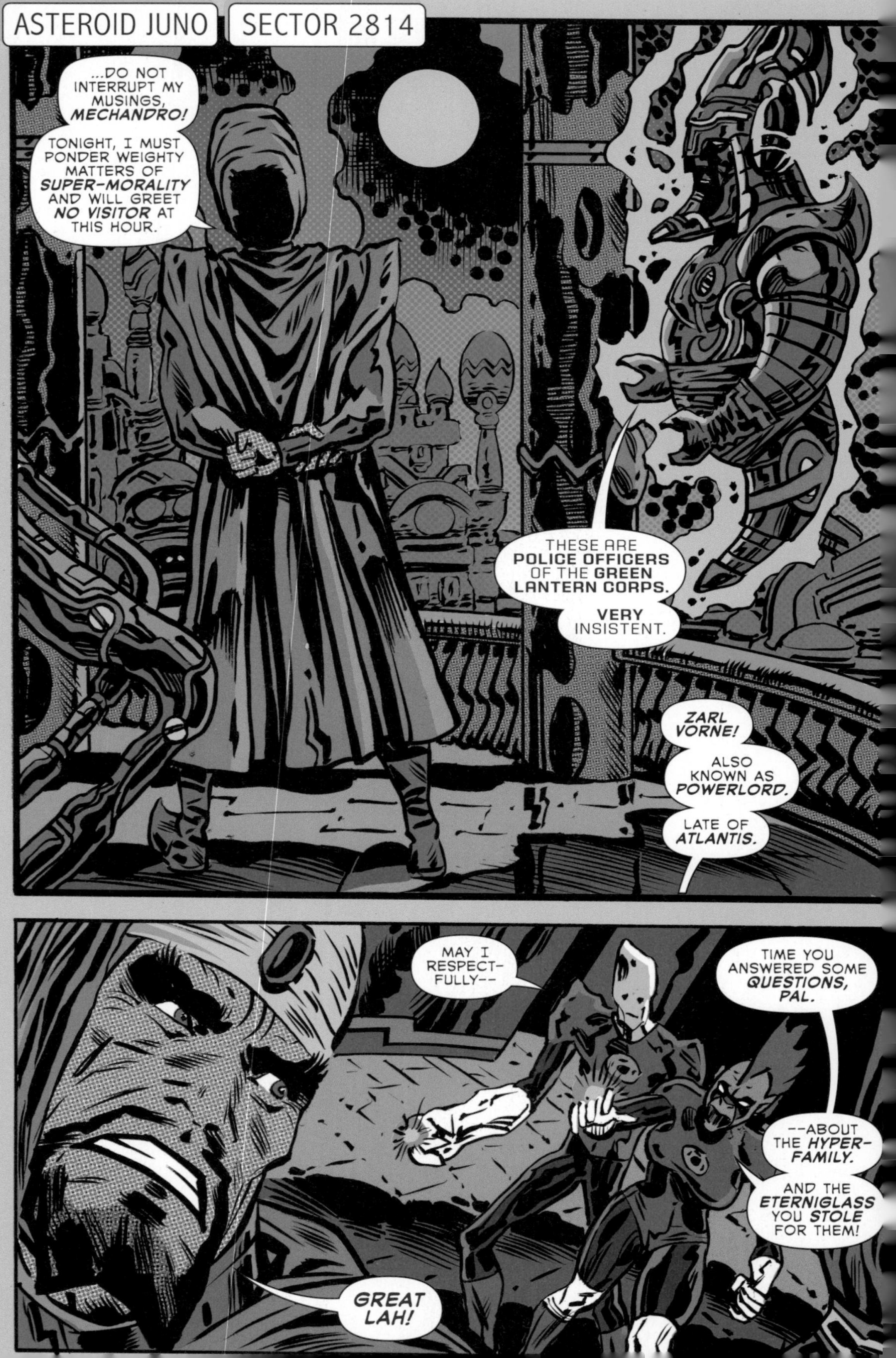
ASTEROID JUNO
SECTOR 2814
...DO NOT INTERRUPT MY MUSINGS, MECHANDRO!
TONIGHT, I MUST PONDER WEIGHTY MATTERS OF SUPER-MORALITY AND WILL GREET NO VISITOR AT THIS HOUR.
THESE ARE POLICE OFFICERS OF THE GREEN LANTERN CORPS.
VERY INSISTENT.
ZARL VORNE!
ALSO KNOWN AS POWERLORD.
LATE OF ATLANTIS.
MAY I RESPECT-FULLY--
TIME YOU ANSWERED SOME QUESTIONS, PAL.
--ABOUT THE HYPER-FAMILY.
AND THE ETERNIGLASS YOU STOLE FOR THEM!
GREAT LAH!

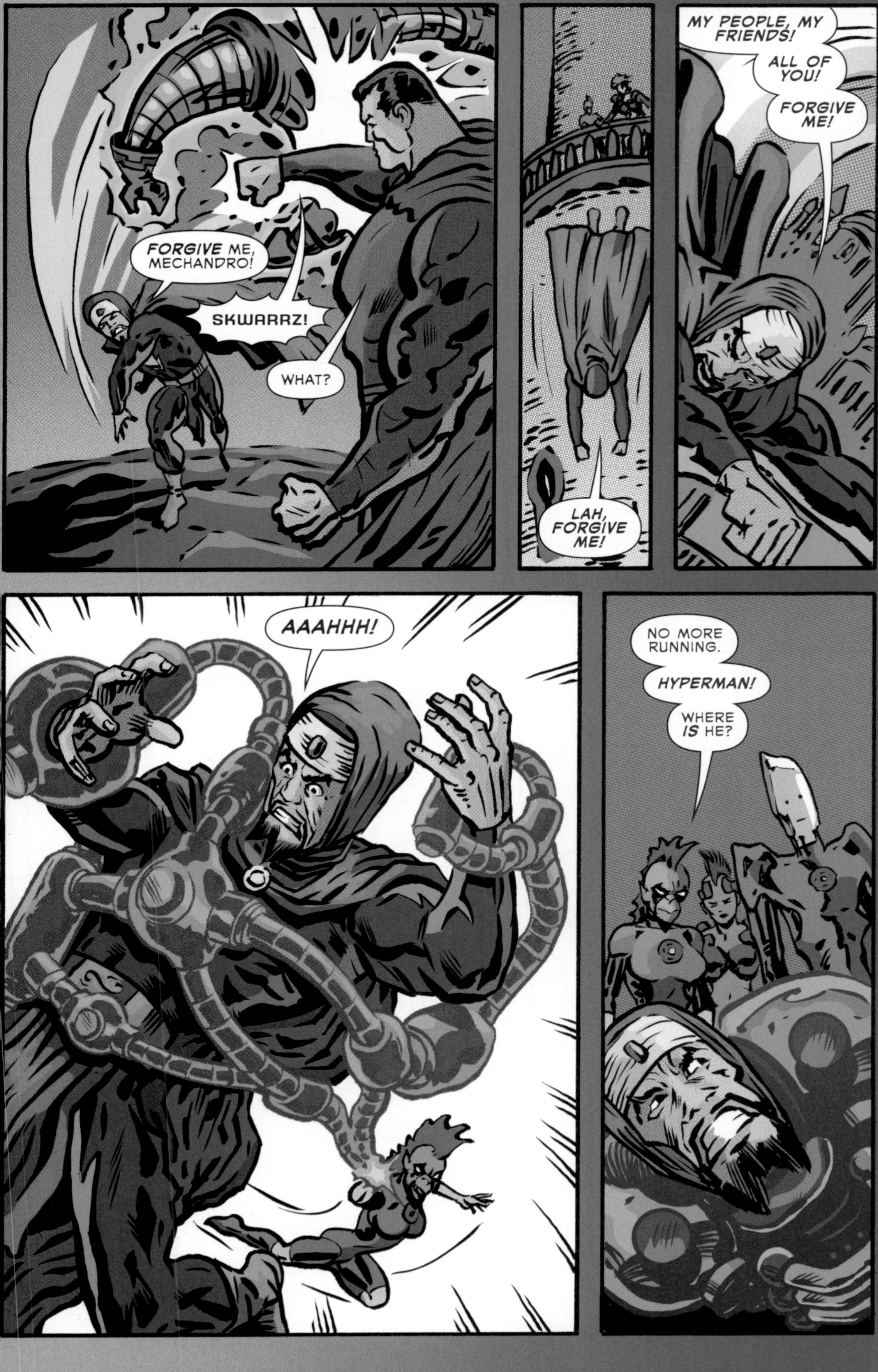
FORGIVE ME, MECHANDRO!
SKWARRZ!
WHAT?
LAH, FORGIVE ME!
MY PEOPLE, MY FRIENDS!
ALL OF YOU!
FORGIVE ME!
AAAHHH!
NO MORE RUNNING.
HYPERMAN!
WHERE IS HE?

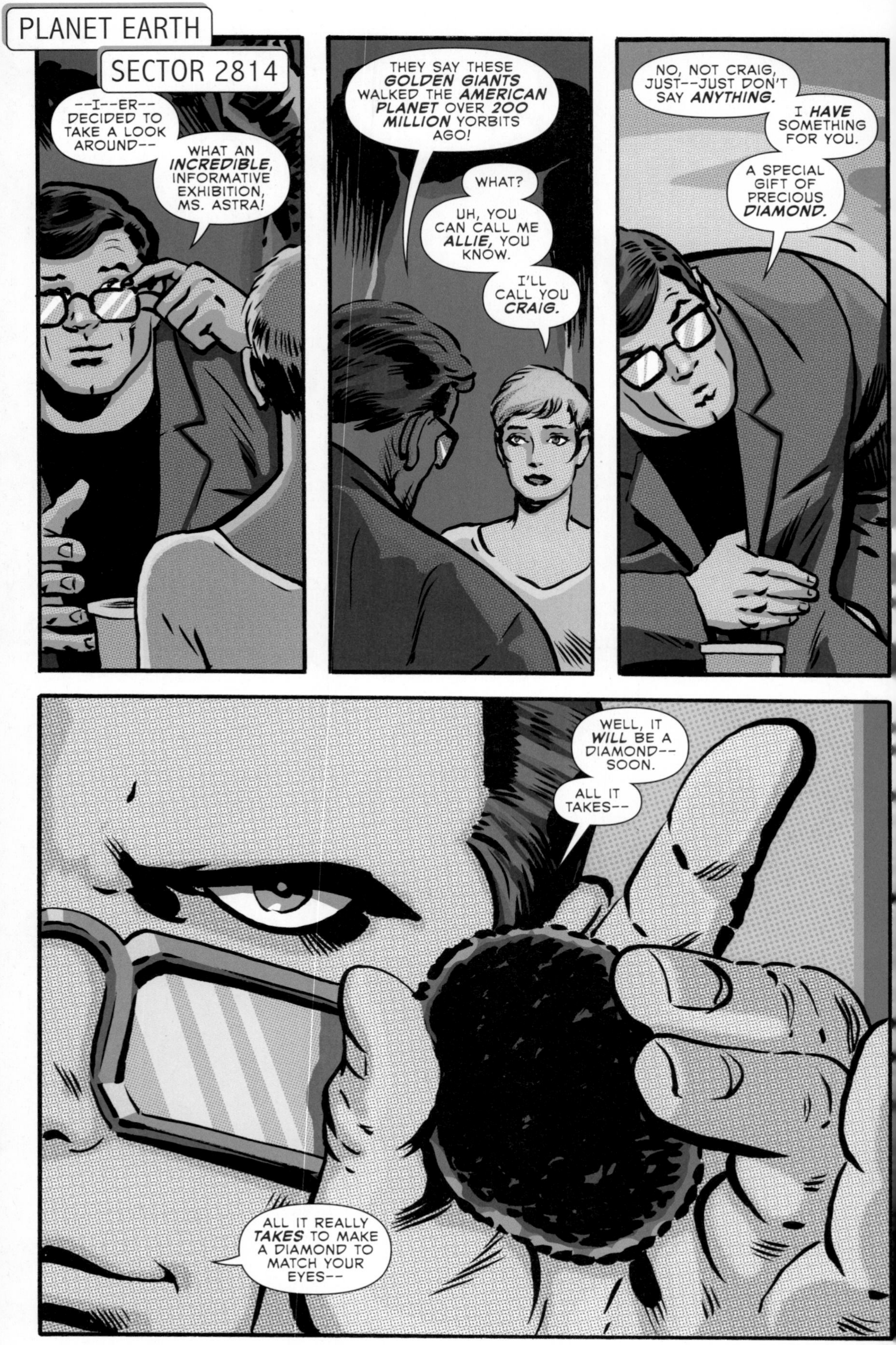

PLANET EARTH
SECTOR 2814
--I--ER--DECIDED TO TAKE A LOOK AROUND--
WHAT AN INCREDIBLE, INFORMATIVE EXHIBITION, MS. ASTRA!
THEY SAY THESE GOLDEN GIANTS WALKED THE AMERICAN PLANET OVER 200 MILLION YORBITS AGO!
WHAT?
UH, YOU CAN CALL ME ALLIE, YOU KNOW.
I'LL CALL YOU CRAIG.
NO, NOT CRAIG, JUST--JUST DON'T SAY ANYTHING.
I HAVE SOMETHING FOR YOU.
A SPECIAL GIFT OF PRECIOUS DIAMOND.
WELL, IT WILL BE A DIAMOND--SOON.
ALL IT TAKES--
ALL IT REALLY TAKES TO MAKE A DIAMOND TO MATCH YOUR EYES--

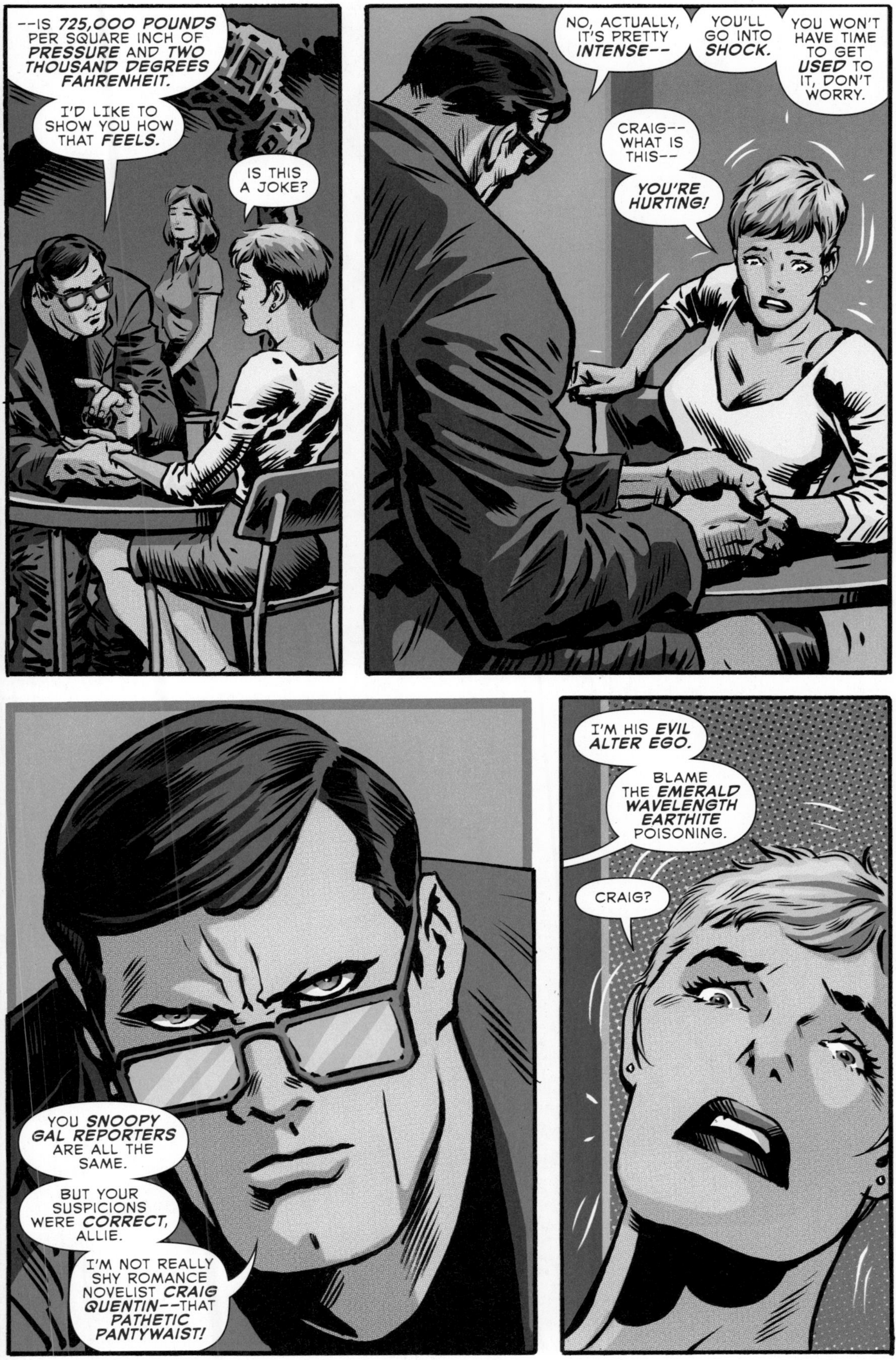
--IS 725,000 POUNDS PER SQUARE INCH OF PRESSURE AND TWO THOUSAND DEGREES FAHRENHEIT.
I'D LIKE TO SHOW YOU HOW THAT FEELS.
IS THIS A JOKE?
NO, ACTUALLY, IT'S PRETTY INTENSE--
YOU'LL GO INTO SHOCK.
YOU WON'T HAVE TIME TO GET USED TO IT, DON'T WORRY.
CRAIG-- WHAT IS THIS--
YOU'RE HURTING!
YOU SNOOPY GAL REPORTERS ARE ALL THE SAME.
BUT YOUR SUSPICIONS WERE CORRECT, ALLIE.
I'M NOT REALLY SHY ROMANCE NOVELIST CRAIG QUENTIN--THAT PATHETIC PANTYWAIST!
I'M HIS EVIL ALTER EGO.
BLAME THE EMERALD WAVELENGTH EARTHITE POISONING.
CRAIG?

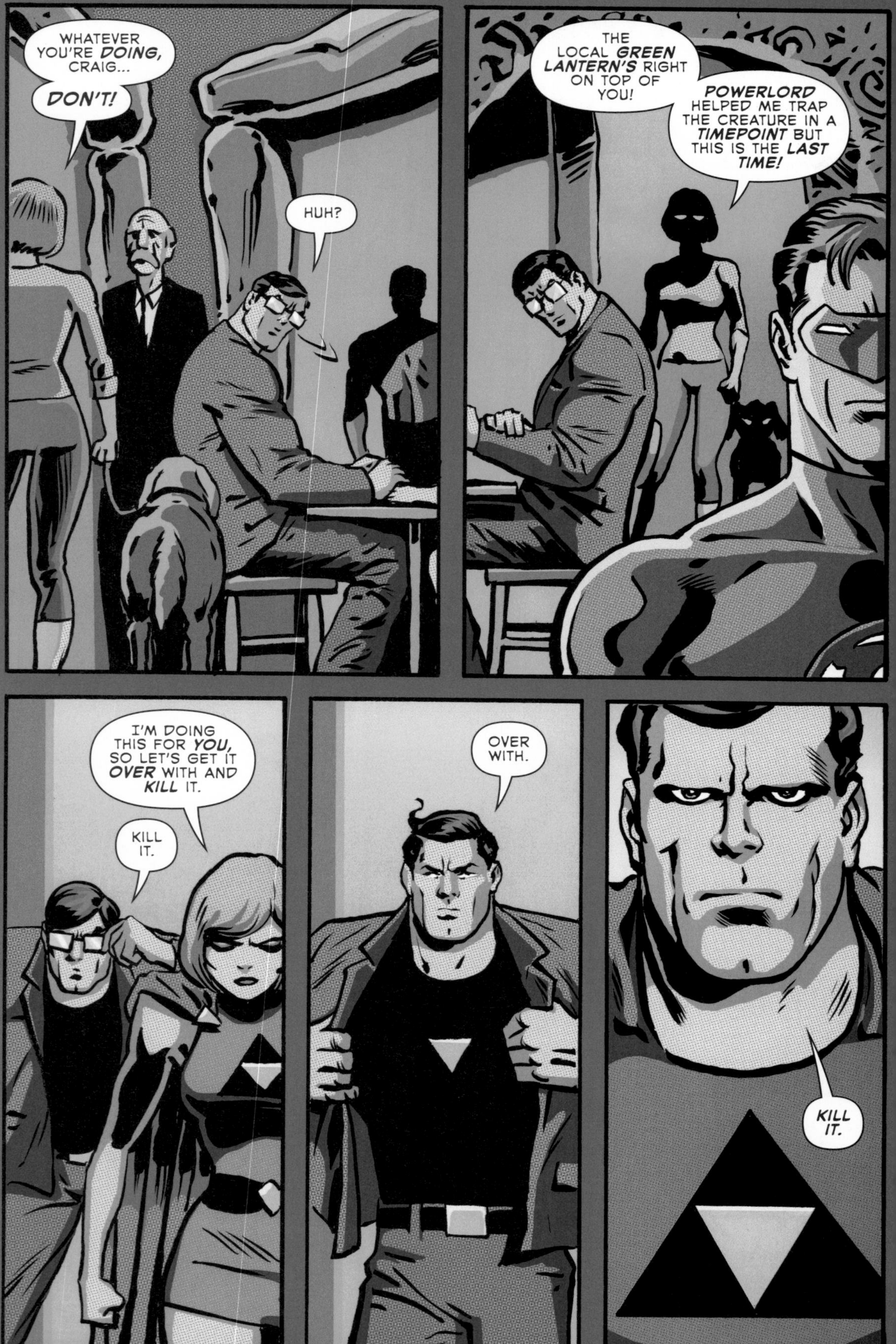
WHATEVER YOU'RE DOING, CRAIG...
DON'T!
HUH?
THE LOCAL GREEN LANTERN'S RIGHT ON TOP OF YOU!
POWERLORD HELPED ME TRAP THE CREATURE IN A TIMEPOINT BUT THIS IS THE LAST TIME!
I'M DOING THIS FOR YOU, SO LET'S GET IT OVER WITH AND KILL IT.
KILL IT.
OVER WITH.
KILL IT.

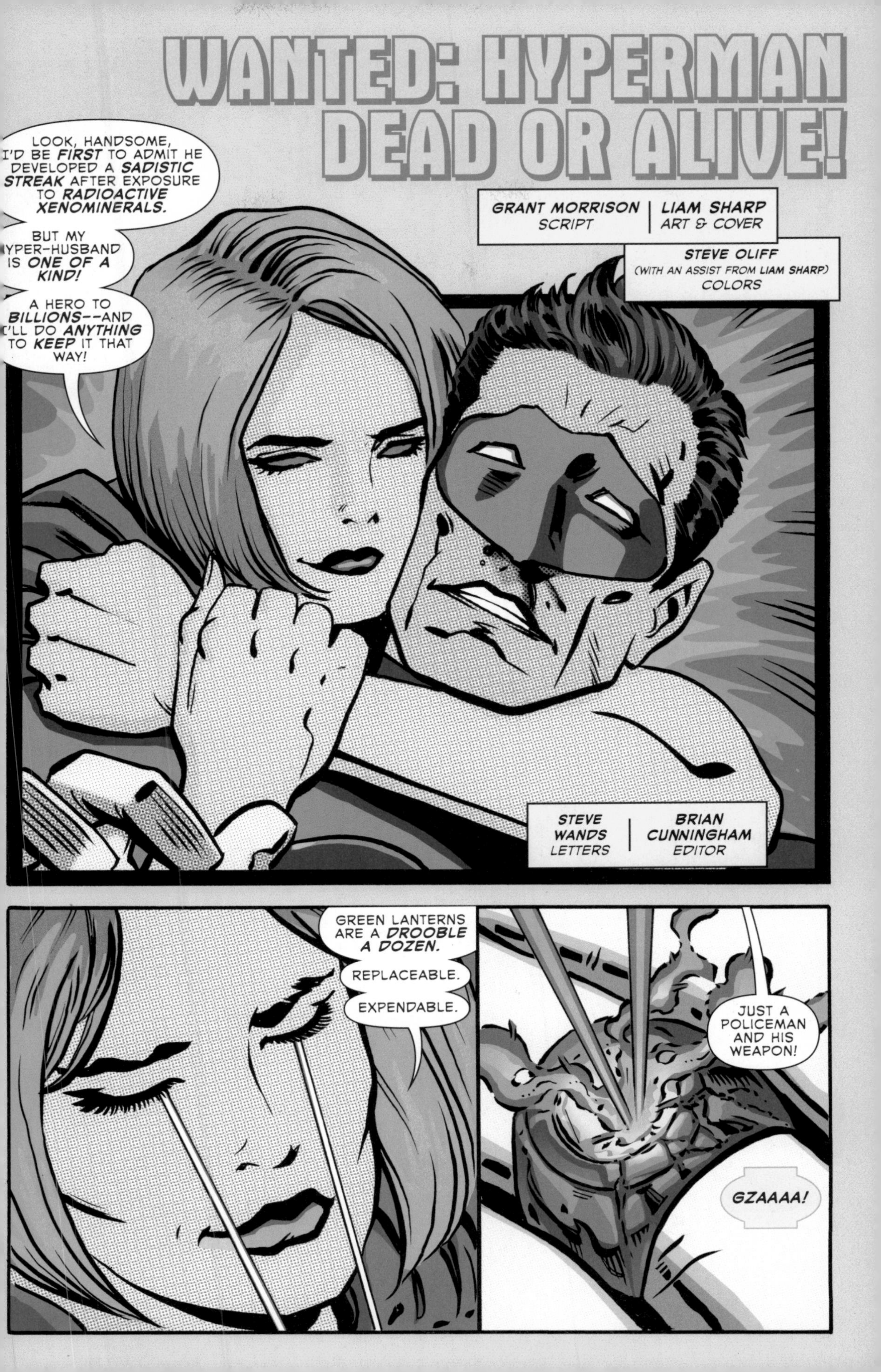
WANTED: HYPERMAN DEAD OR ALIVE!
LOOK, HANDSOME, I'D BE FIRST TO ADMIT HE DEVELOPED A SADISTIC STREAK AFTER EXPOSURE TO RADIOACTIVE XENOMINERALS.
BUT MY HYPER-HUSBAND IS ONE OF A KIND!
A HERO TO BILLIONS--AND I'LL DO ANYTHING TO KEEP IT THAT WAY!
GRANT MORRISON SCRIPT
LIAM SHARP ART & COVER
STEVE OLIFF (WITH AN ASSIST FROM LIAM SHARP) COLORS
STEVE WANDS LETTERS
BRIAN CUNNINGHAM EDITOR
GREEN LANTERNS ARE A DROOBLE A DOZEN.
REPLACEABLE.
EXPENDABLE.
JUST A POLICEMAN AND HIS WEAPON!
GZAAAA!

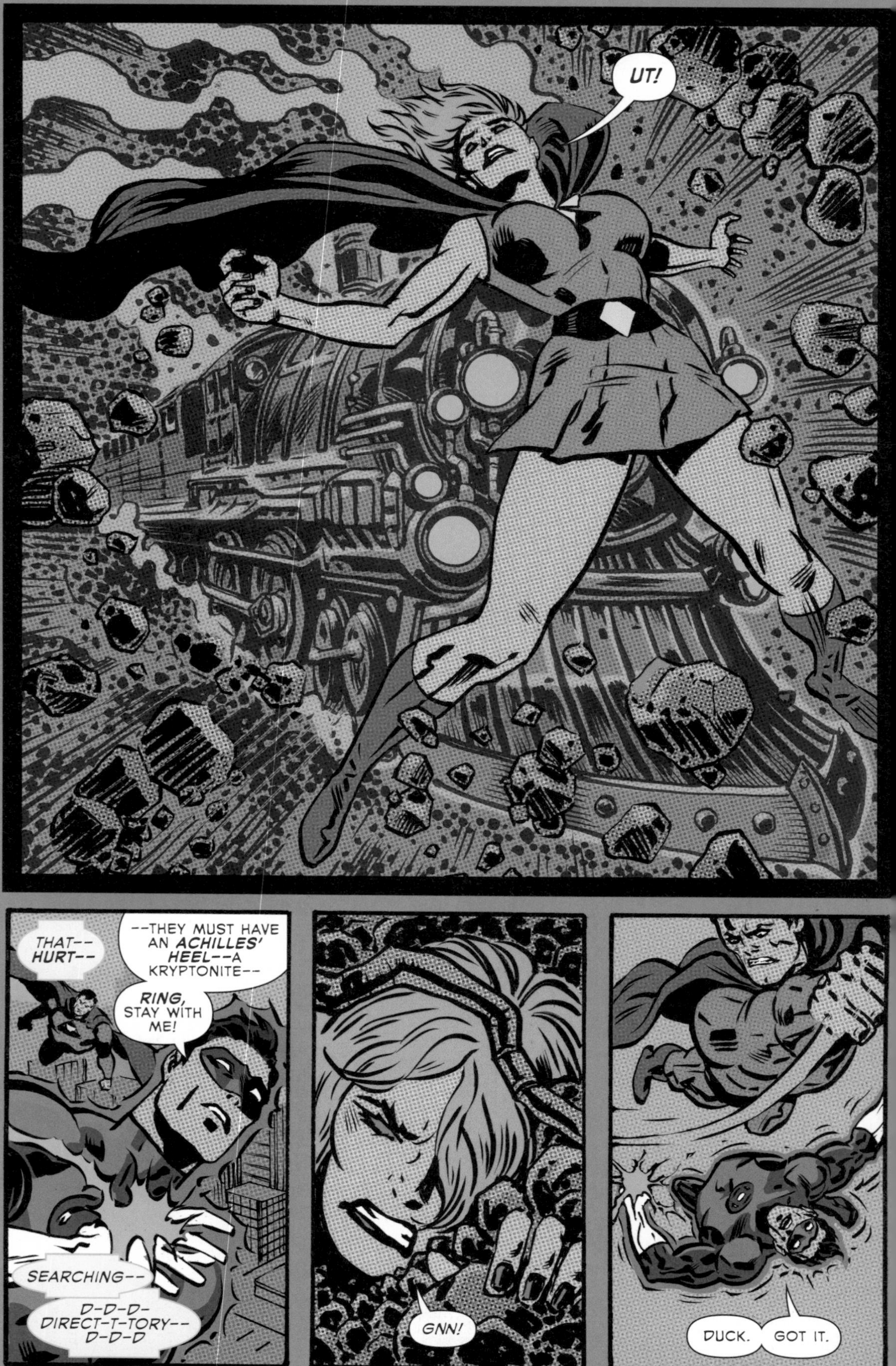
UT!
THAT-- HURT--
--THEY MUST HAVE AN ACHILLES' HEEL--A KRYPTONITE--
RING, STAY WITH ME!
SEARCHING--
D-D-D- DIRECT-T-TORY-- D-D-D
GNN!
DUCK.
GOT IT.

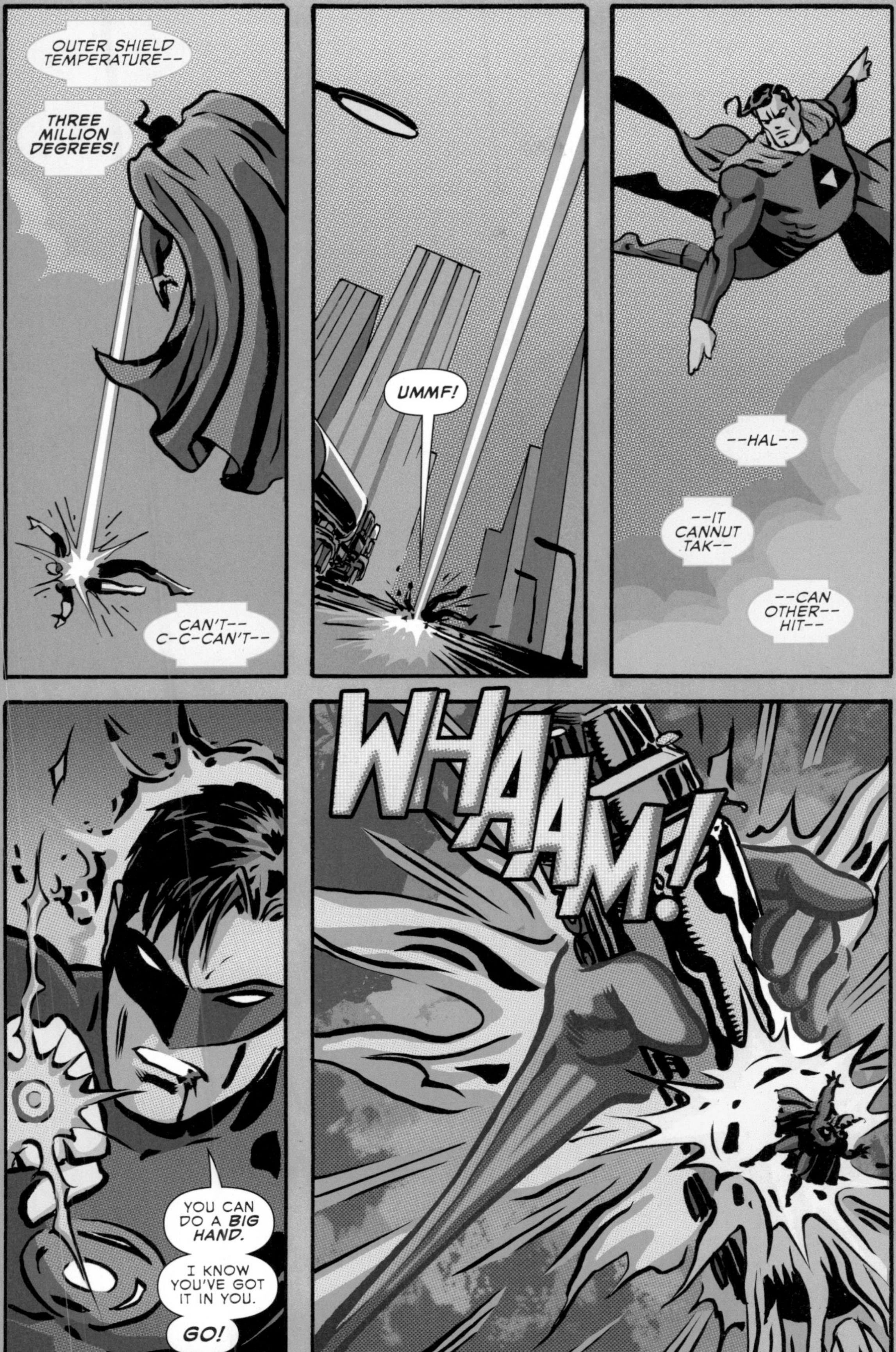
OUTER SHIELD TEMPERATURE--
THREE MILLION DEGREES!
CAN'T-- C-C-CAN'T--
UMMF!
--HAL--
--IT CANNUT TAK--
--CAN OTHER-- HIT--
YOU CAN DO A BIG HAND.
I KNOW YOU'VE GOT IT IN YOU.
GO!
WHAAAM!

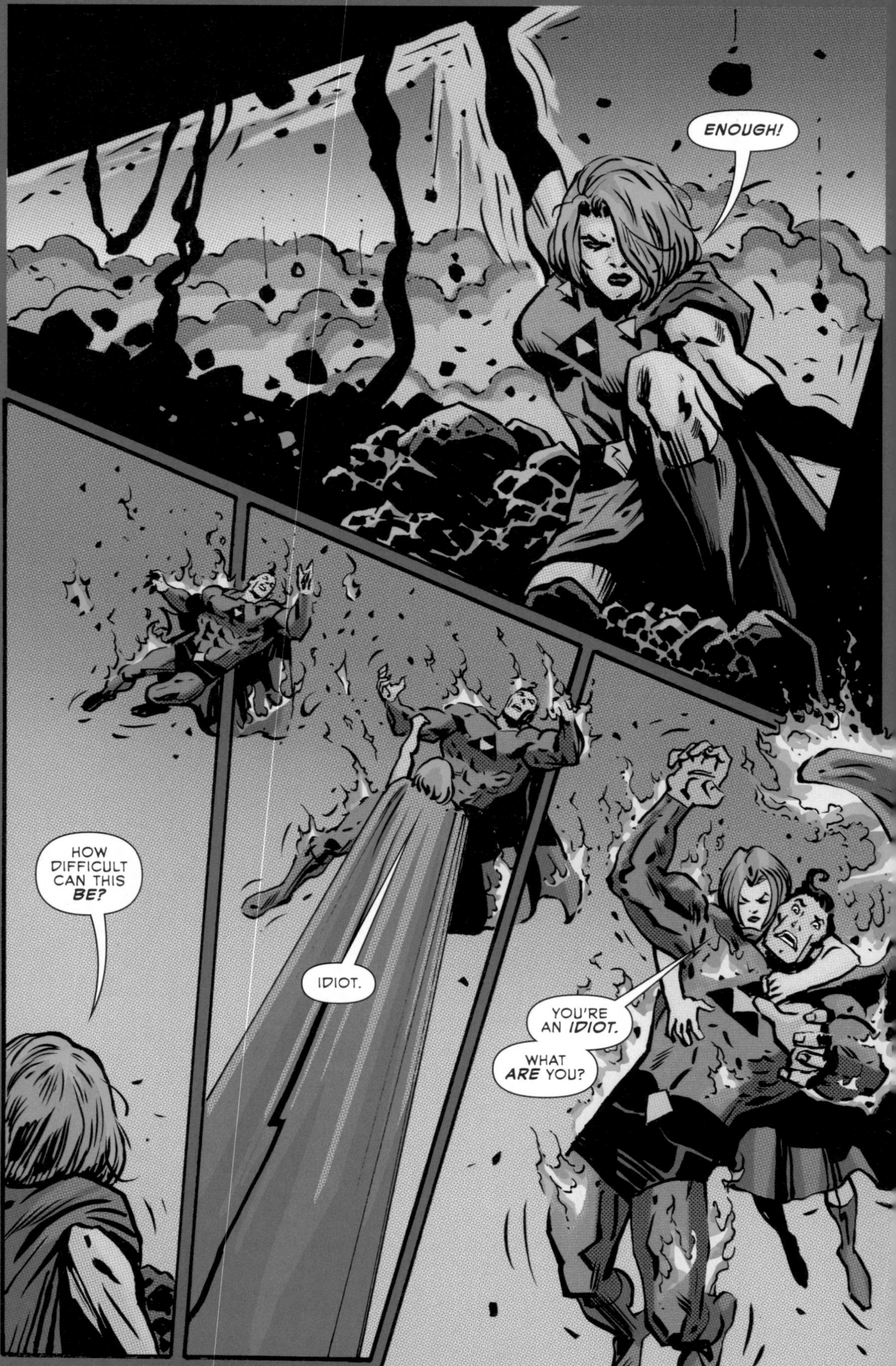
ENOUGH!
HOW DIFFICULT CAN THIS BE?
IDIOT.
YOU'RE AN IDIOT.
WHAT ARE YOU?

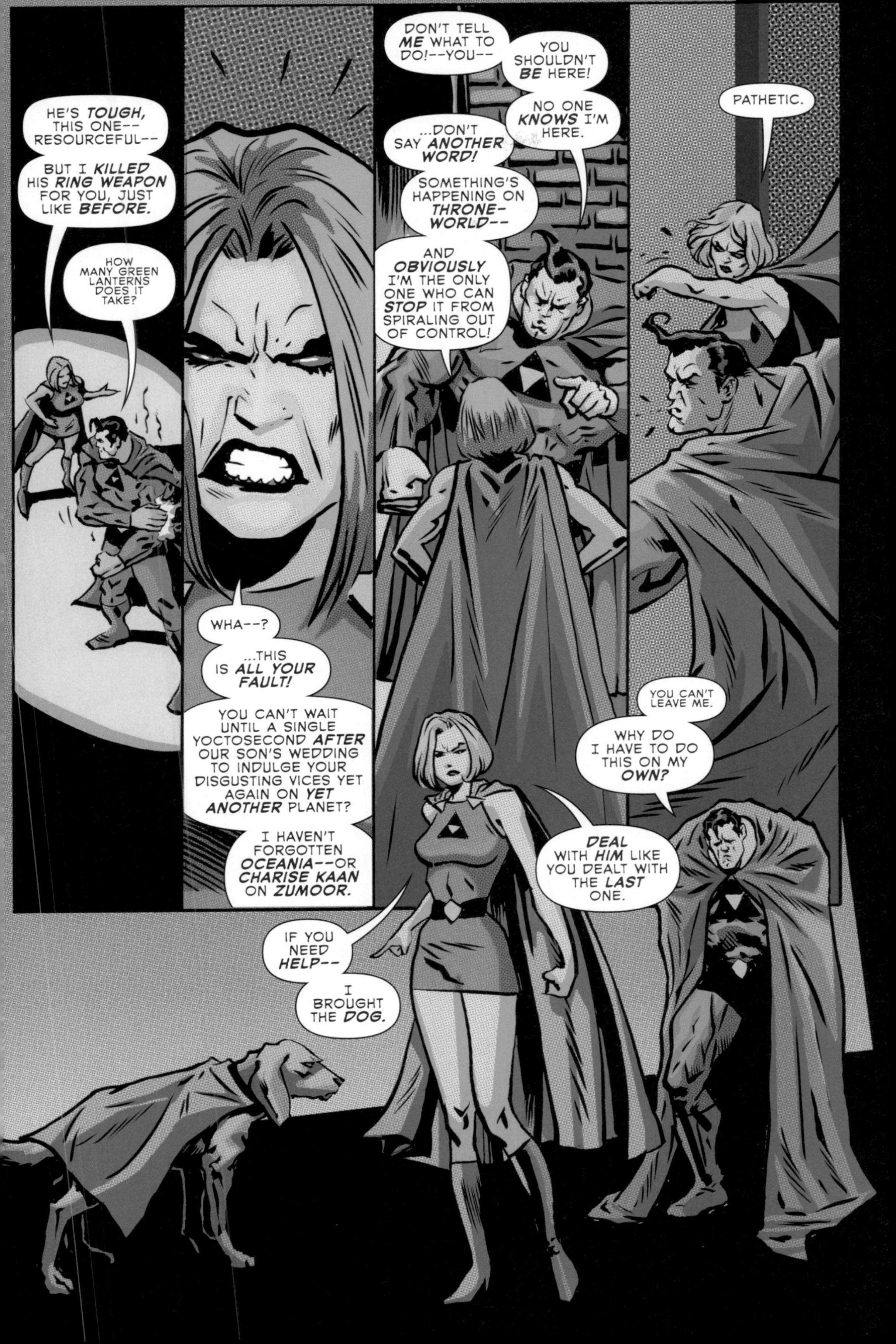
HE'S TOUGH, THIS ONE--RESOURCEFUL--
BUT I KILLED HIS RING WEAPON FOR YOU, JUST LIKE BEFORE.
HOW MANY GREEN LANTERNS DOES IT TAKE?
WHA--?
...THIS IS ALL YOUR FAULT!
YOU CAN'T WAIT UNTIL A SINGLE YOCTOSECOND AFTER OUR SON'S WEDDING TO INDULGE YOUR DISGUSTING VICES YET AGAIN ON YET ANOTHER PLANET?
I HAVEN'T FORGOTTEN OCEANIA--OR CHARISE KAAN ON ZUMOOR.
DON'T TELL ME WHAT TO DO!--YOU--
YOU SHOULDN'T BE HERE!
NO ONE KNOWS I'M HERE.
...DON'T SAY ANOTHER WORD!
SOMETHING'S HAPPENING ON THRONE-WORLD--
AND OBVIOUSLY I'M THE ONLY ONE WHO CAN STOP IT FROM SPIRALING OUT OF CONTROL!
PATHETIC.
YOU CAN'T LEAVE ME.
WHY DO I HAVE TO DO THIS ON MY OWN?
DEAL WITH HIM LIKE YOU DEALT WITH THE LAST ONE.
IF YOU NEED HELP--
I BROUGHT THE DOG.

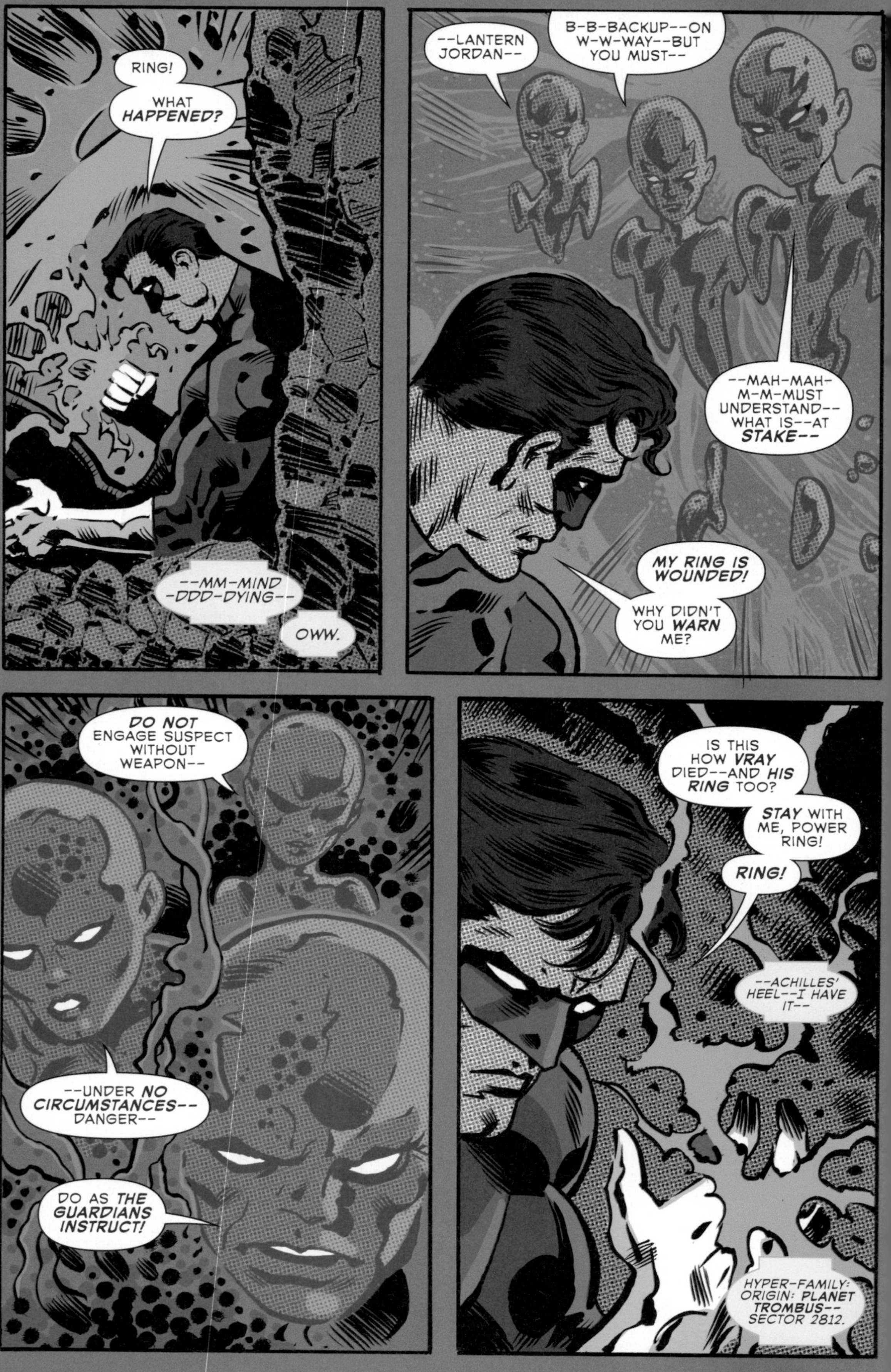
RING!
WHAT HAPPENED?
--MM-MIND -DDD-DYING--
OWW.
--LANTERN JORDAN--
B-B-BACKUP--ON W-W-WAY--BUT YOU MUST--
--MAH-MAH-M-M-MUST UNDERSTAND--WHAT IS--AT STAKE--
MY RING IS WOUNDED!
WHY DIDN'T YOU WARN ME?
DO NOT ENGAGE SUSPECT WITHOUT WEAPON--
--UNDER NO CIRCUMSTANCES--DANGER--
DO AS THE GUARDIANS INSTRUCT!
IS THIS HOW VRAY DIED--AND HIS RING TOO?
STAY WITH ME, POWER RING!
RING!
--ACHILLES' HEEL--I HAVE IT--
HYPER-FAMILY: ORIGIN: PLANET TROMBUS--SECTOR 2812.

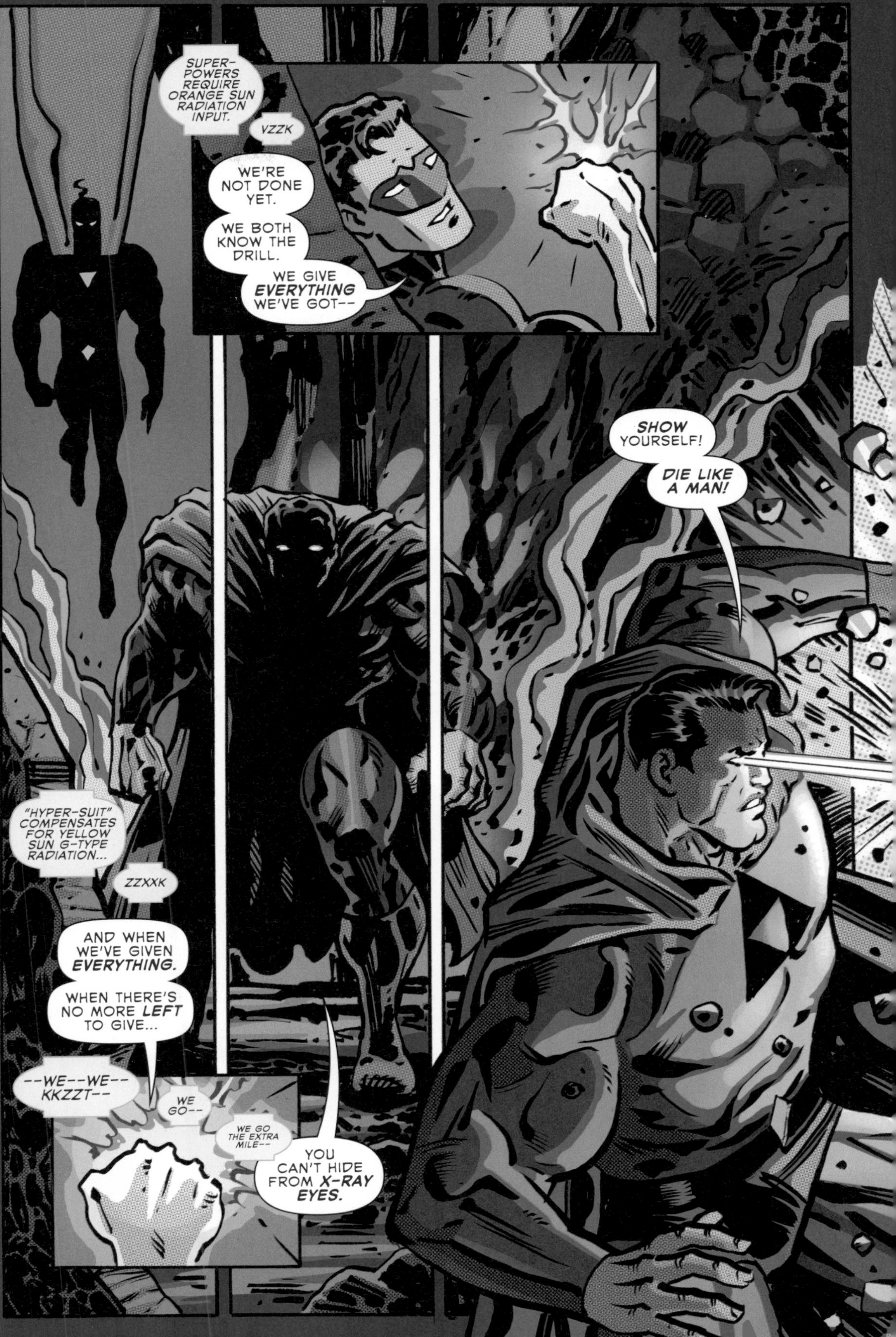
SUPER-POWERS REQUIRE ORANGE SUN RADIATION INPUT.
VZZK
WE'RE NOT DONE YET.
WE BOTH KNOW THE DRILL.
WE GIVE EVERYTHING WE'VE GOT--
SHOW YOURSELF!
DIE LIKE A MAN!
"HYPER-SUIT" COMPENSATES FOR YELLOW SUN G-TYPE RADIATION...
ZZXXK
AND WHEN WE'VE GIVEN EVERYTHING.
WHEN THERE'S NO MORE LEFT TO GIVE...
--WE--WE--KKZZT--
WE GO--
WE GO THE EXTRA MILE--
YOU CAN'T HIDE FROM X-RAY EYES.

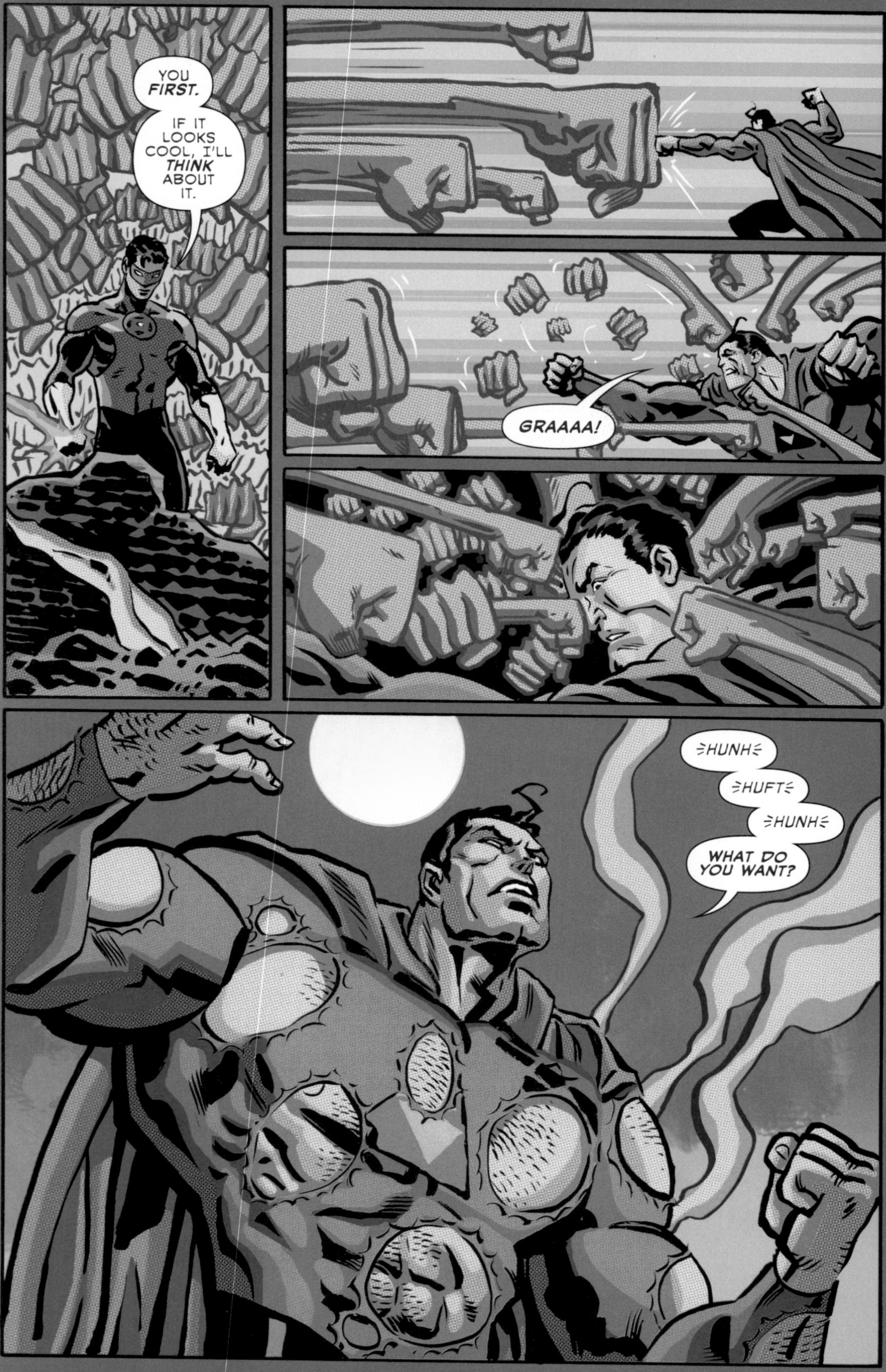
YOU FIRST.
IF IT LOOKS COOL, I'LL THINK ABOUT IT.
GRAAAA!
HUNH
HUFT
HUNH
WHAT DO YOU WANT?

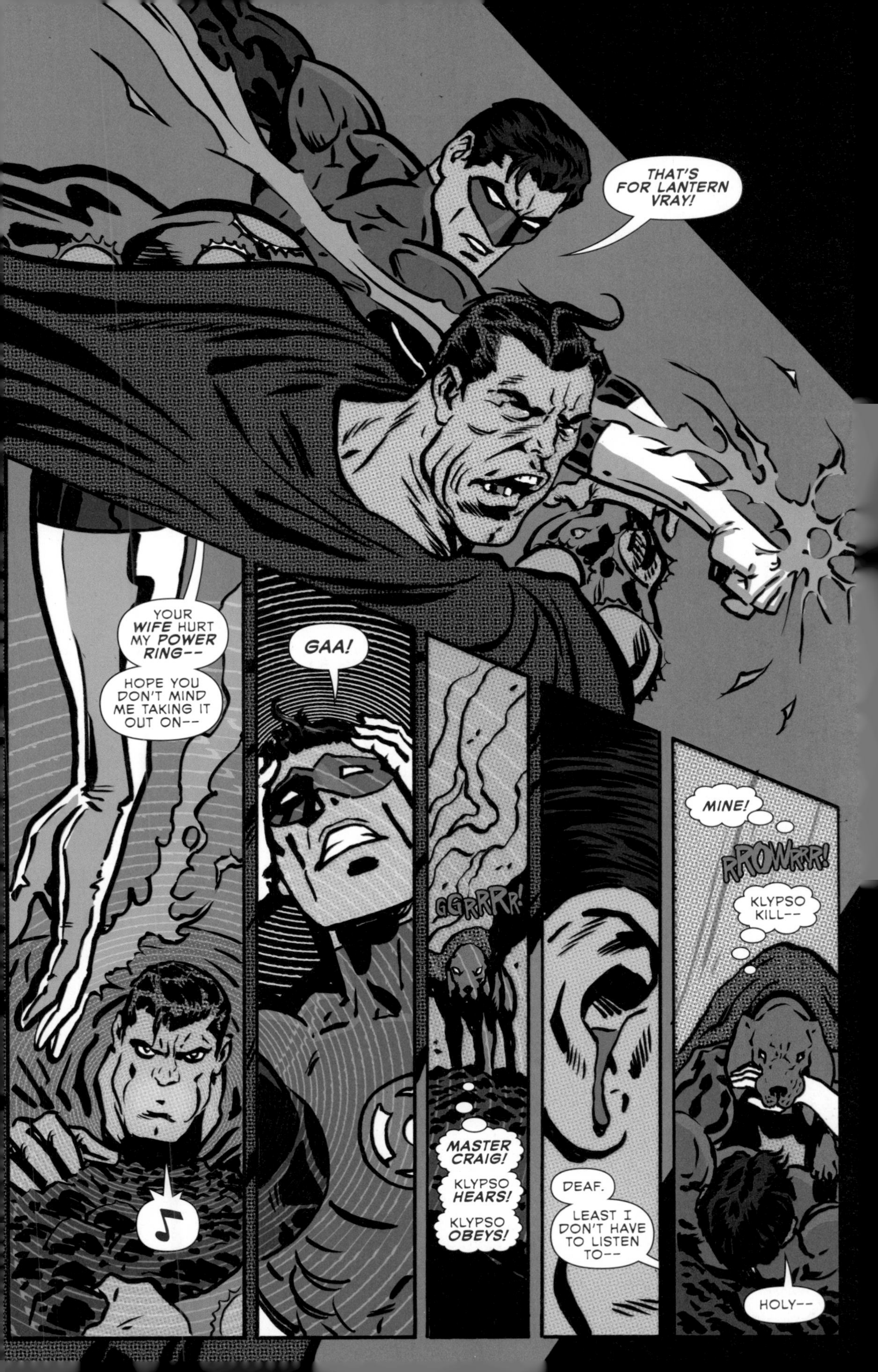
THAT'S FOR LANTERN VRAY!
YOUR WIFE HURT MY POWER RING--
HOPE YOU DON'T MIND ME TAKING IT OUT ON--
♪
GAA!
GGRRRR!
MASTER CRAIG!
KLYPSO HEARS!
KLYPSO OBEYS!
DEAF.
LEAST I DON'T HAVE TO LISTEN TO--
MINE!
RROWRRR!
KLYPSO KILL--
HOLY--

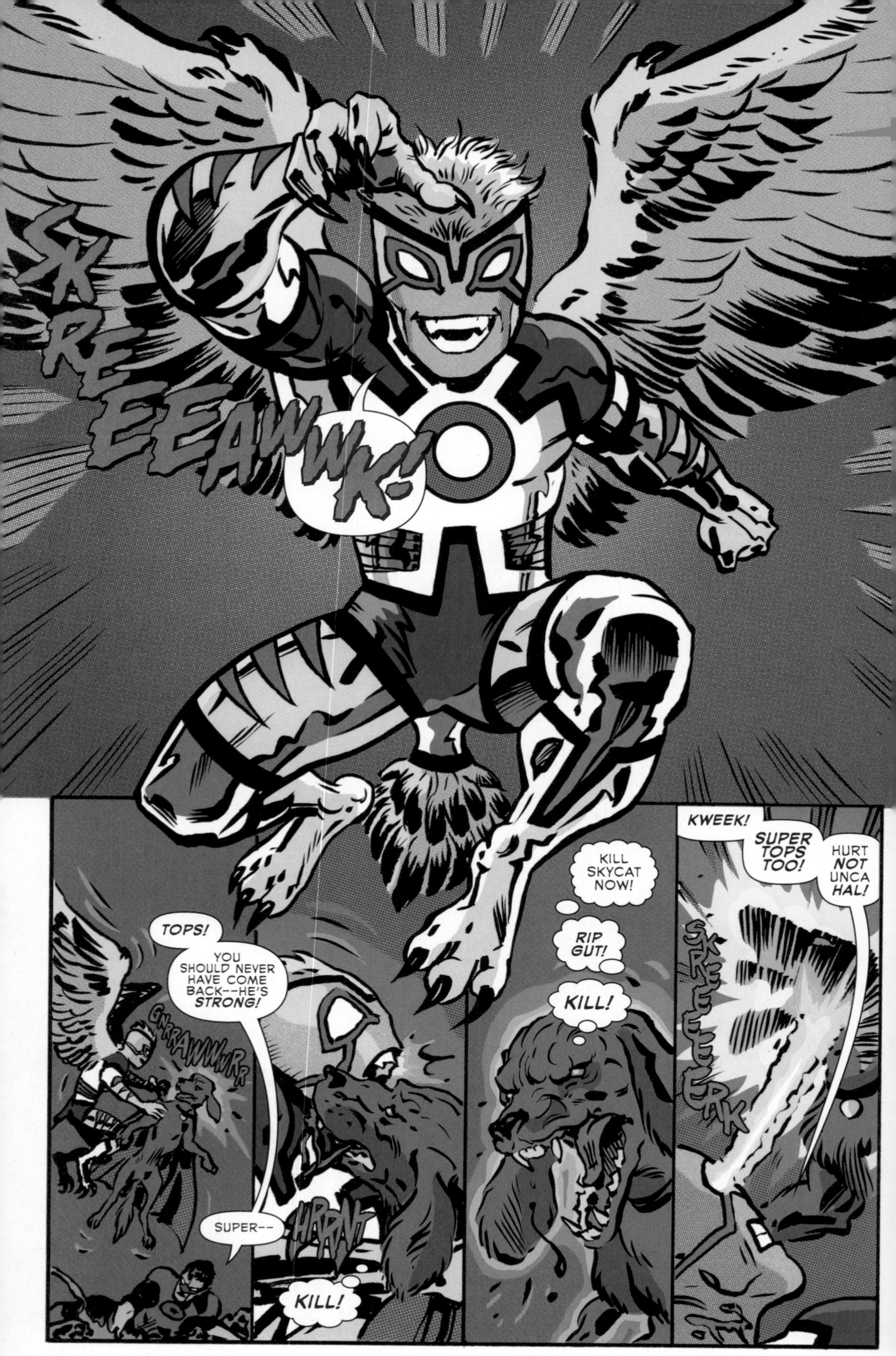
SKREEEAWWK!
TOPS!
YOU SHOULD NEVER HAVE COME BACK--HE'S *STRONG!*
GNRRAWWWRR
SUPER--
HRRNT
KILL!
KILL SKYCAT NOW!
RIP GUT!
KILL!
KWEEK!
SUPER TOPS TOO!
HURT *NOT* UNCA *HAL!*
SKREEEERK

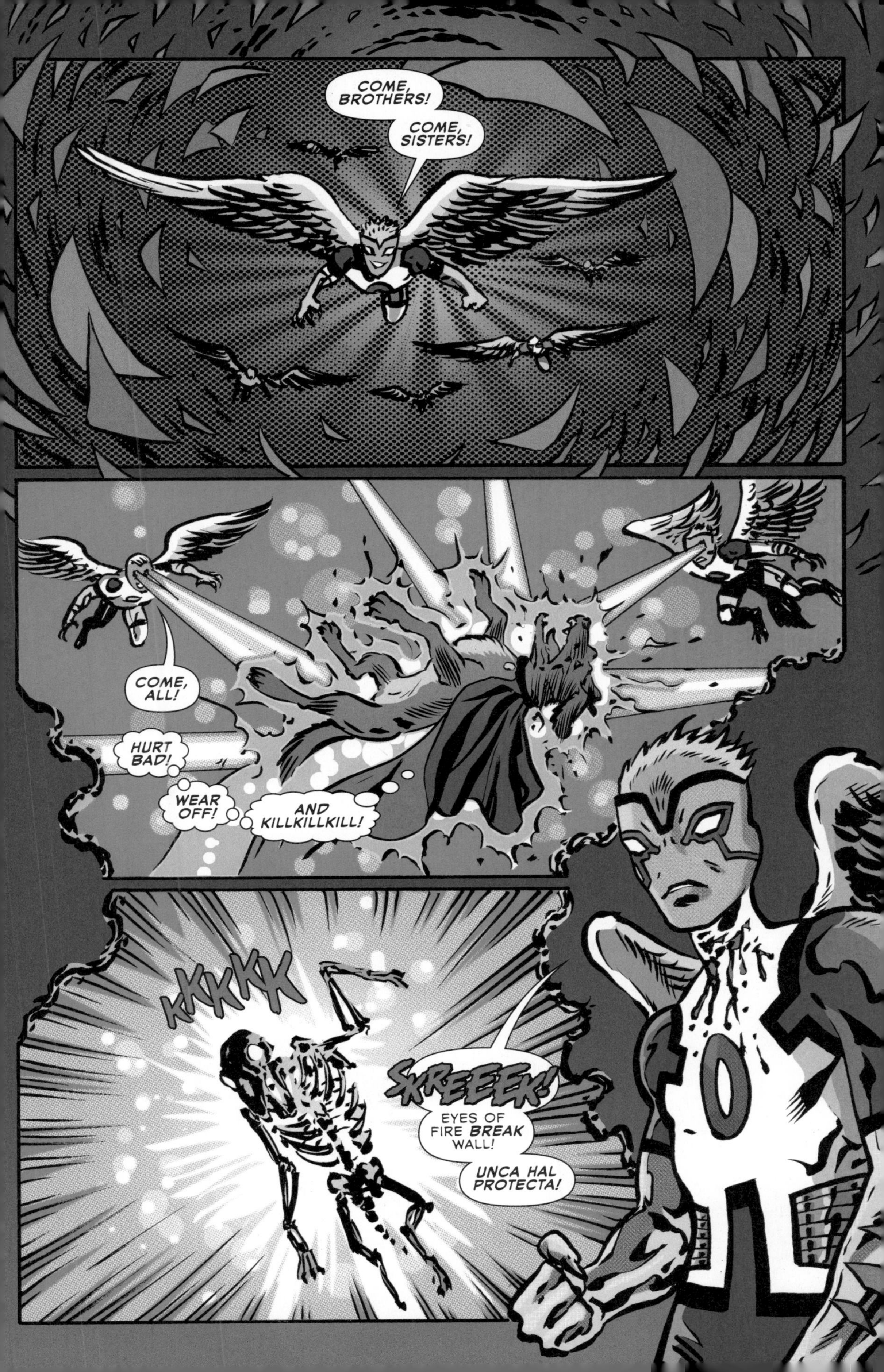
COME, BROTHERS!
COME, SISTERS!
COME, ALL!
HURT BAD!
WEAR OFF!
AND KILLKILLKILL!
KKKKK
SKREEEK!
EYES OF FIRE BREAK WALL!
UNCA HAL PROTECTA!

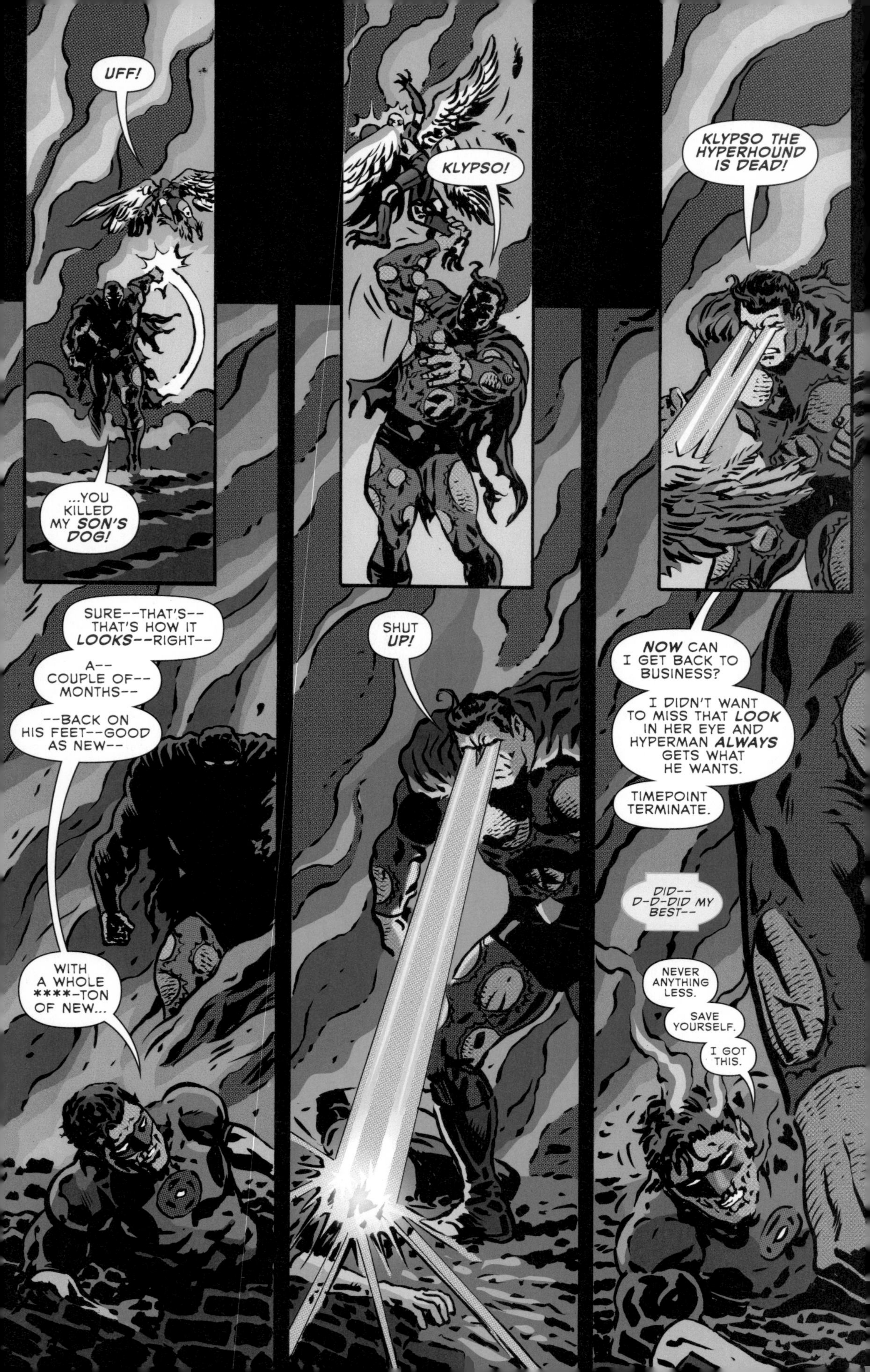
UFF!
...YOU KILLED MY SON'S DOG!
KLYPSO!
KLYPSO THE HYPERHOUND IS DEAD!
SURE--THAT'S--THAT'S HOW IT LOOKS--RIGHT--
A--COUPLE OF--MONTHS--
--BACK ON HIS FEET--GOOD AS NEW--
WITH A WHOLE ****-TON OF NEW...
SHUT UP!
NOW CAN I GET BACK TO BUSINESS?
I DIDN'T WANT TO MISS THAT LOOK IN HER EYE AND HYPERMAN ALWAYS GETS WHAT HE WANTS.
TIMEPOINT TERMINATE.
DID--D-D-DID MY BEST--
NEVER ANYTHING LESS.
SAVE YOURSELF.
I GOT THIS.

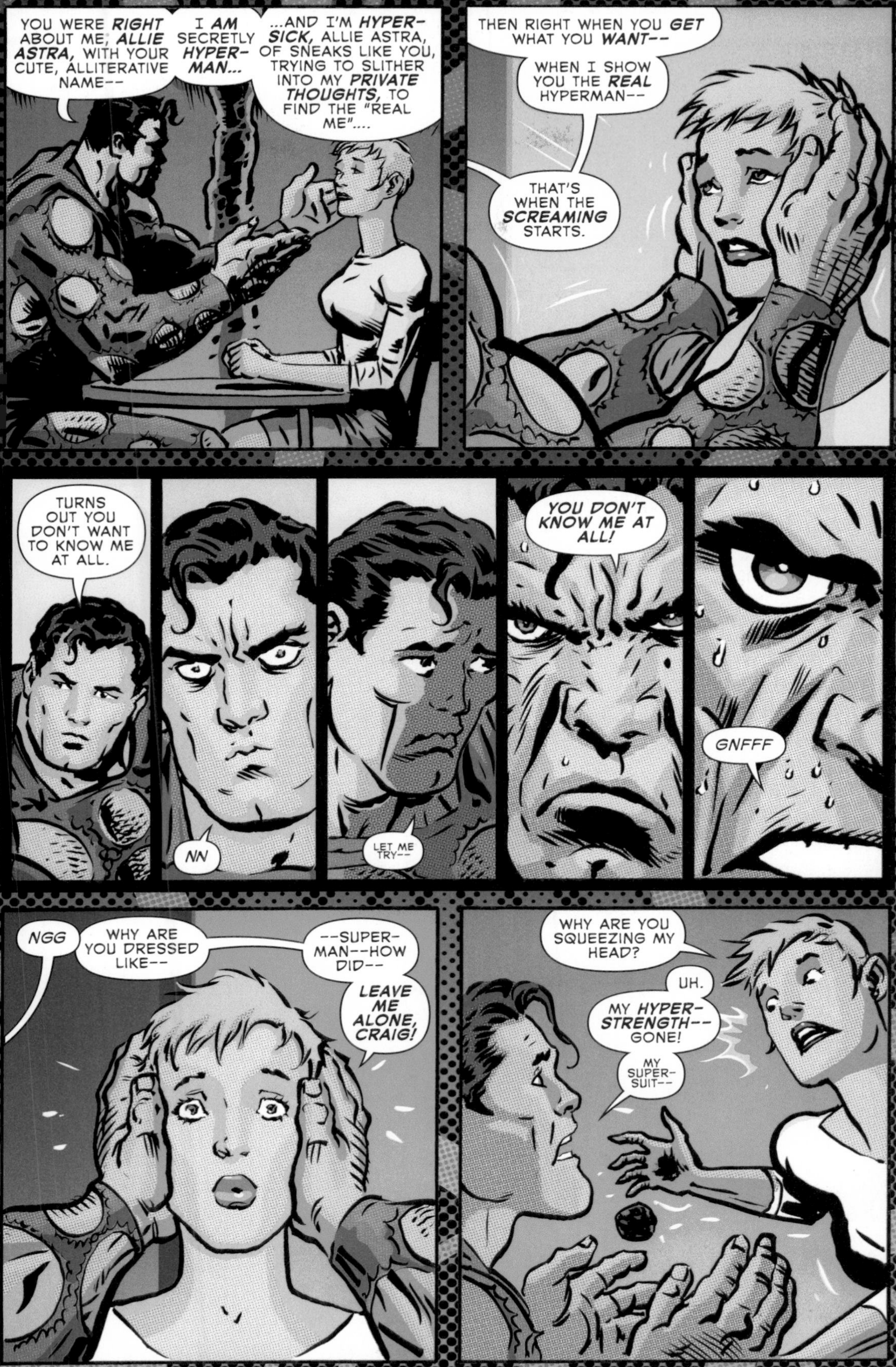
YOU WERE RIGHT ABOUT ME, ALLIE ASTRA, WITH YOUR CUTE, ALLITERATIVE NAME--
I AM SECRETLY HYPER-MAN...
...AND I'M HYPER-SICK, ALLIE ASTRA, OF SNEAKS LIKE YOU, TRYING TO SLITHER INTO MY PRIVATE THOUGHTS, TO FIND THE "REAL ME"....
THEN RIGHT WHEN YOU GET WHAT YOU WANT--
WHEN I SHOW YOU THE REAL HYPERMAN--
THAT'S WHEN THE SCREAMING STARTS.
TURNS OUT YOU DON'T WANT TO KNOW ME AT ALL.
NN
LET ME TRY--
YOU DON'T KNOW ME AT ALL!
GNFFF
NGG
WHY ARE YOU DRESSED LIKE--
--SUPER-MAN--HOW DID--
LEAVE ME ALONE, CRAIG!
WHY ARE YOU SQUEEZING MY HEAD?
UH.
MY HYPER-STRENGTH--GONE!
MY SUPER-SUIT--

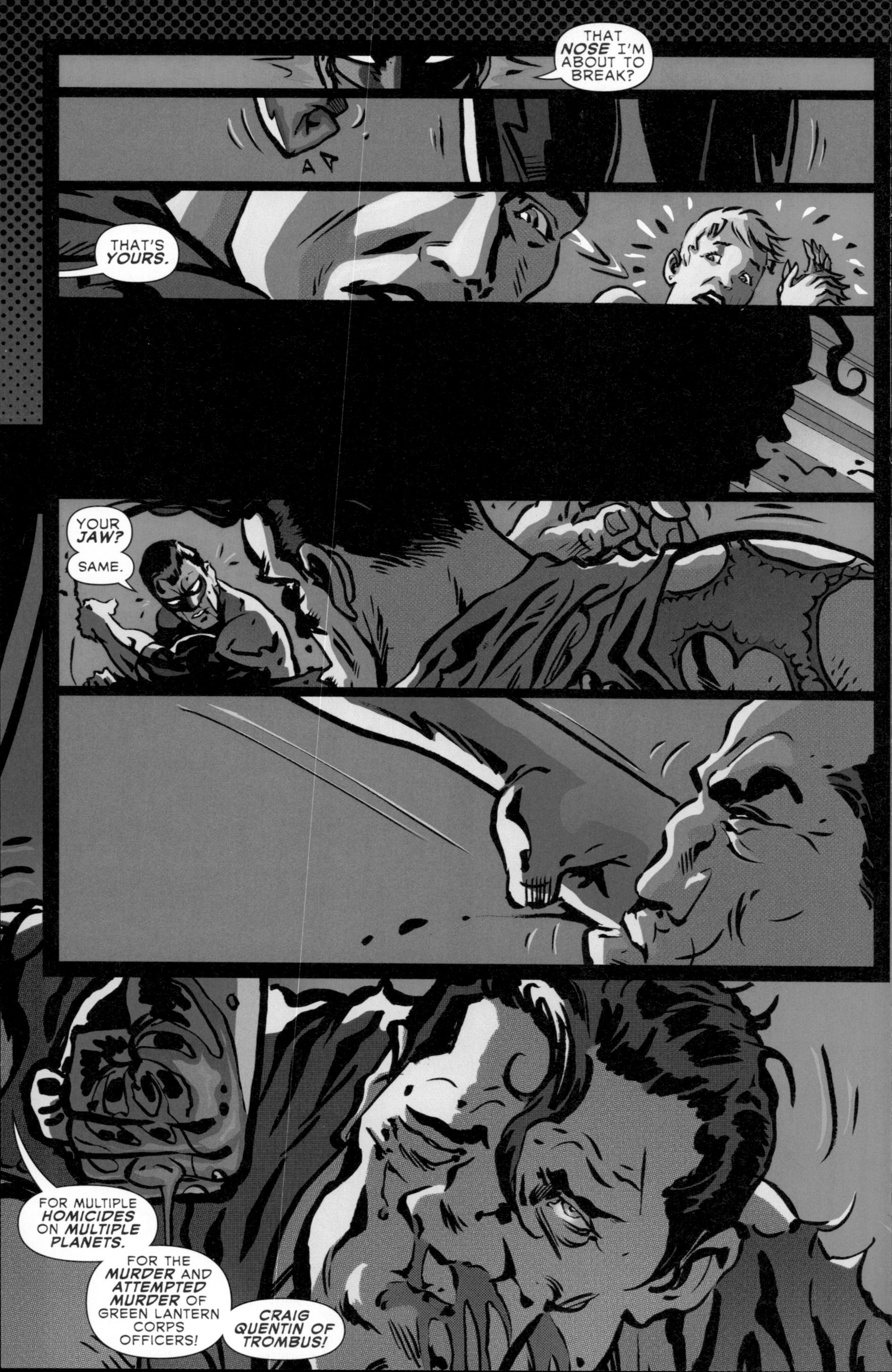
THAT NOSE I'M ABOUT TO BREAK?
THAT'S YOURS.
YOUR JAW?
SAME.
FOR MULTIPLE HOMICIDES ON MULTIPLE PLANETS.
FOR THE MURDER AND ATTEMPTED MURDER OF GREEN LANTERN CORPS OFFICERS!
CRAIG QUENTIN OF TROMBUS!

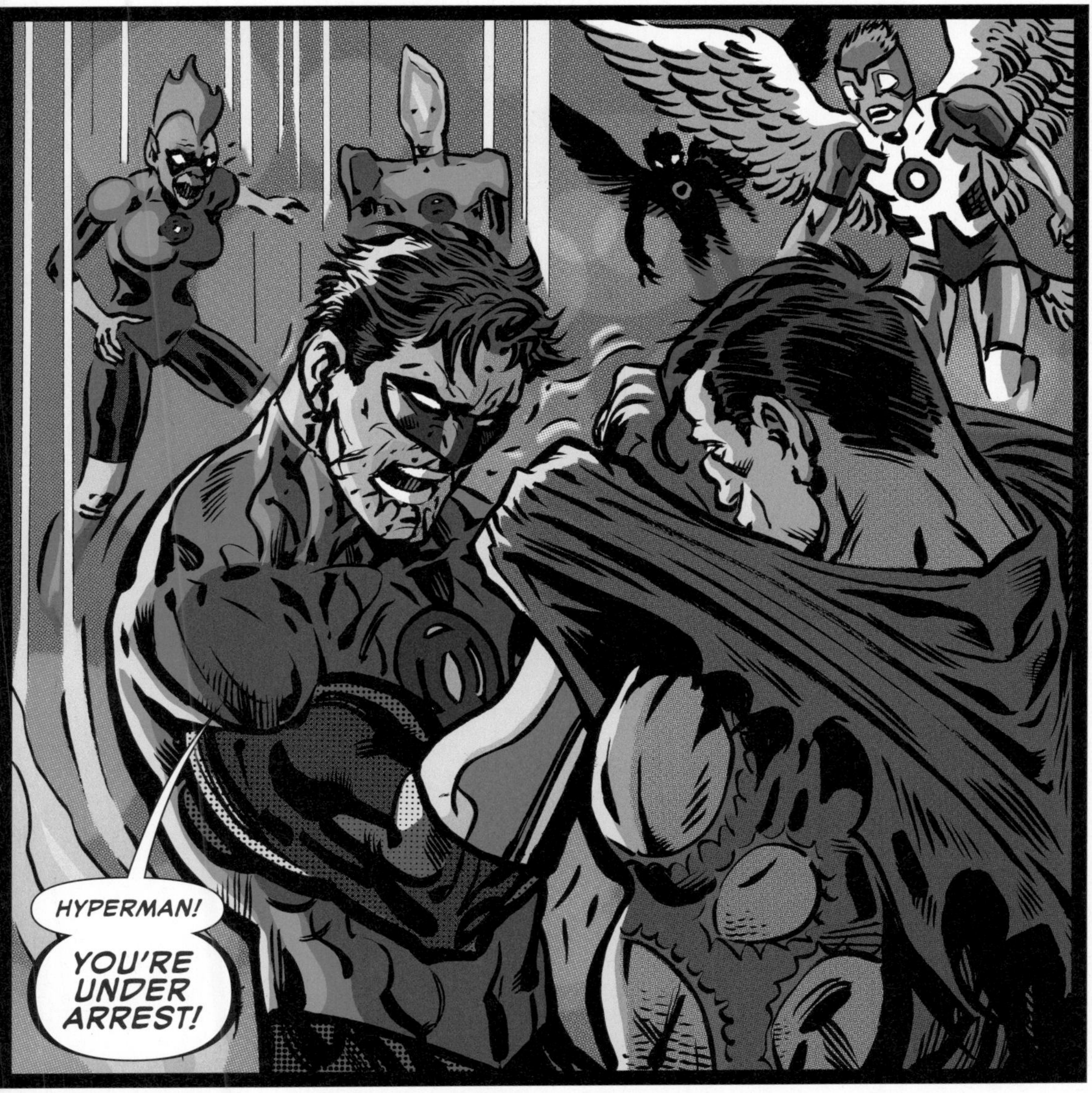
HYPERMAN!
YOU'RE UNDER ARREST!

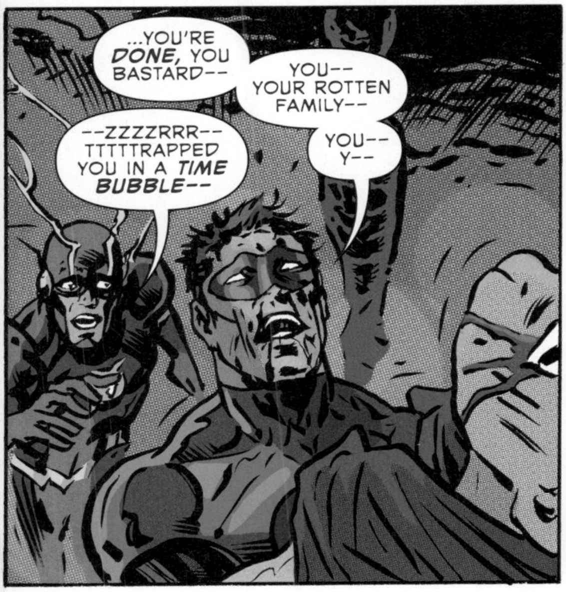
...YOU'RE DONE, YOU BASTARD--
YOU-- YOUR ROTTEN FAMILY--
--ZZZZRRR-- TTTTTRAPPED YOU IN A TIME BUBBLE--
YOU-- Y--

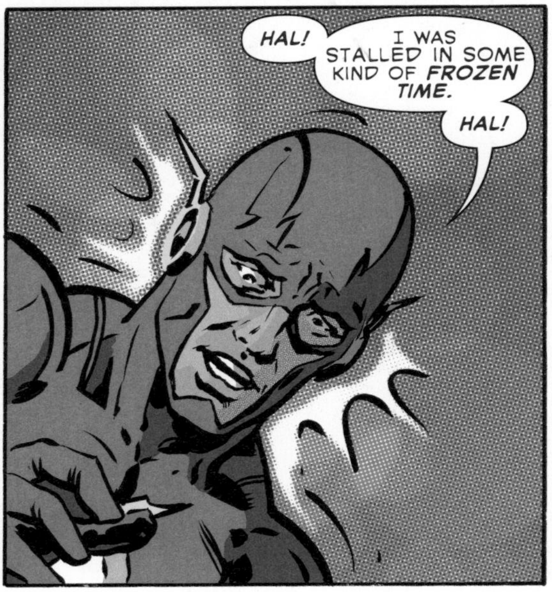
HAL!
I WAS STALLED IN SOME KIND OF FROZEN TIME.
HAL!

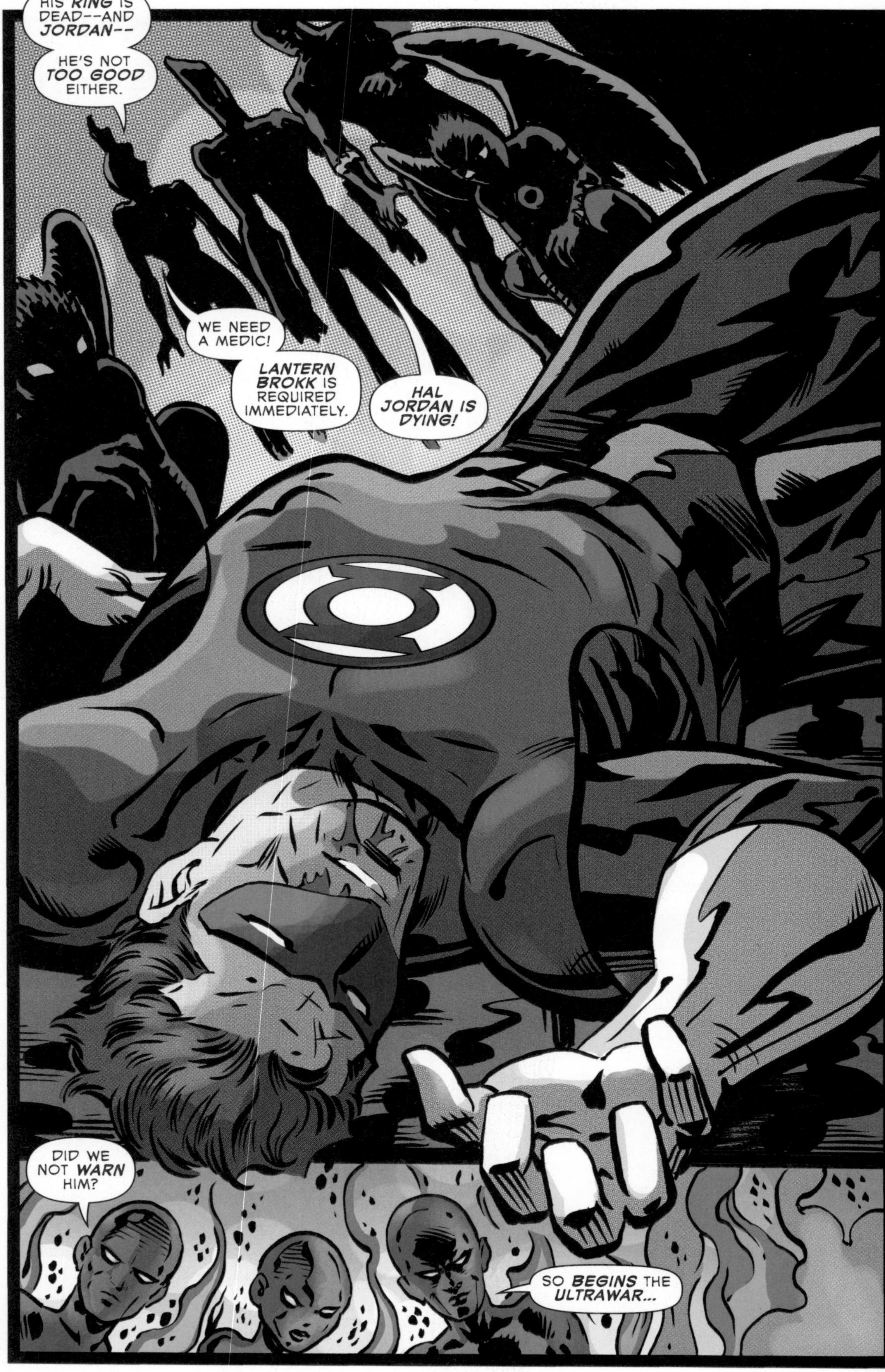
HIS RING IS DEAD--AND JORDAN--
HE'S NOT TOO GOOD EITHER.
WE NEED A MEDIC!
LANTERN BROKK IS REQUIRED IMMEDIATELY.
HAL JORDAN IS DYING!
DID WE NOT WARN HIM?
SO BEGINS THE ULTRAWAR...

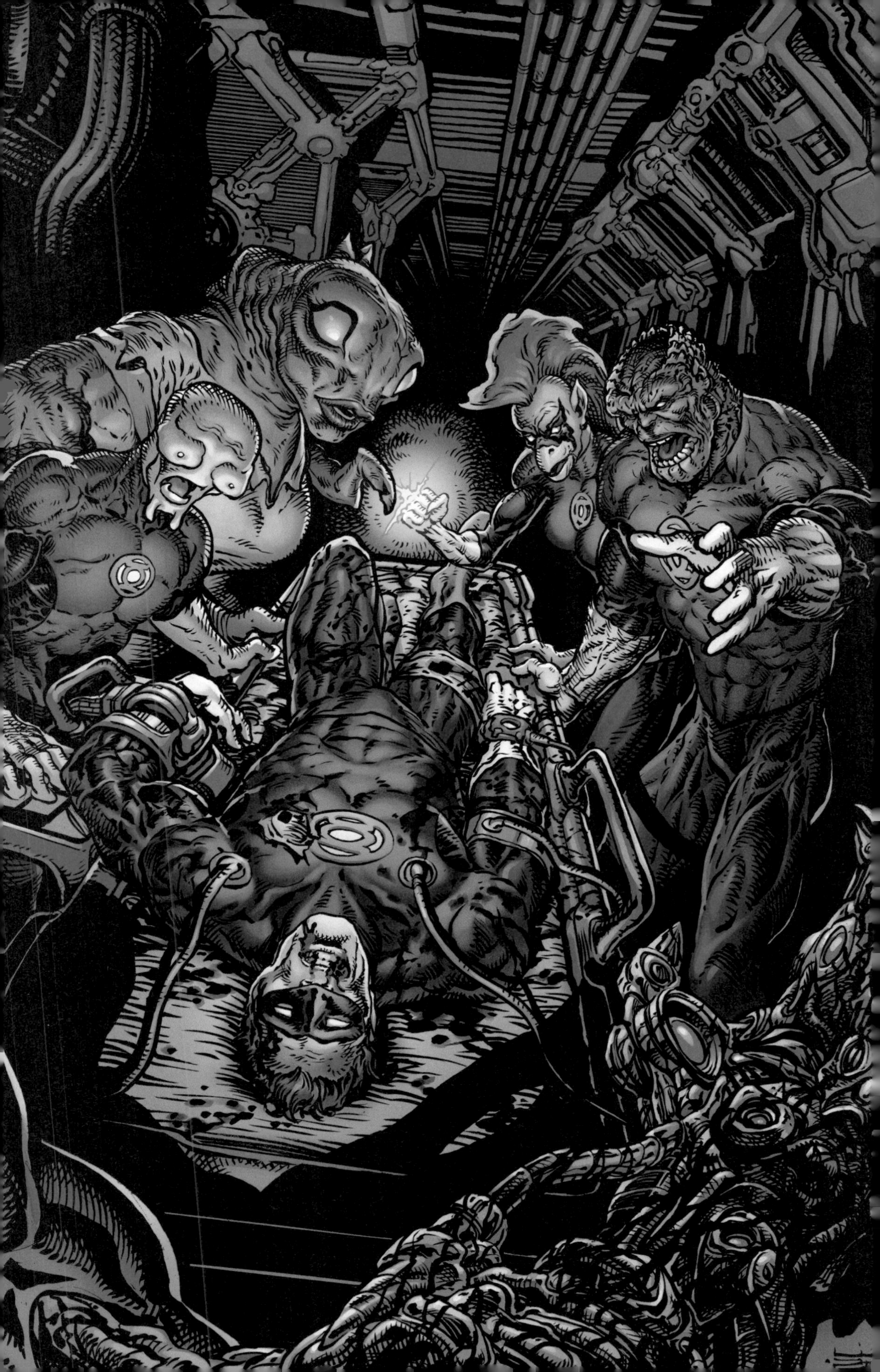

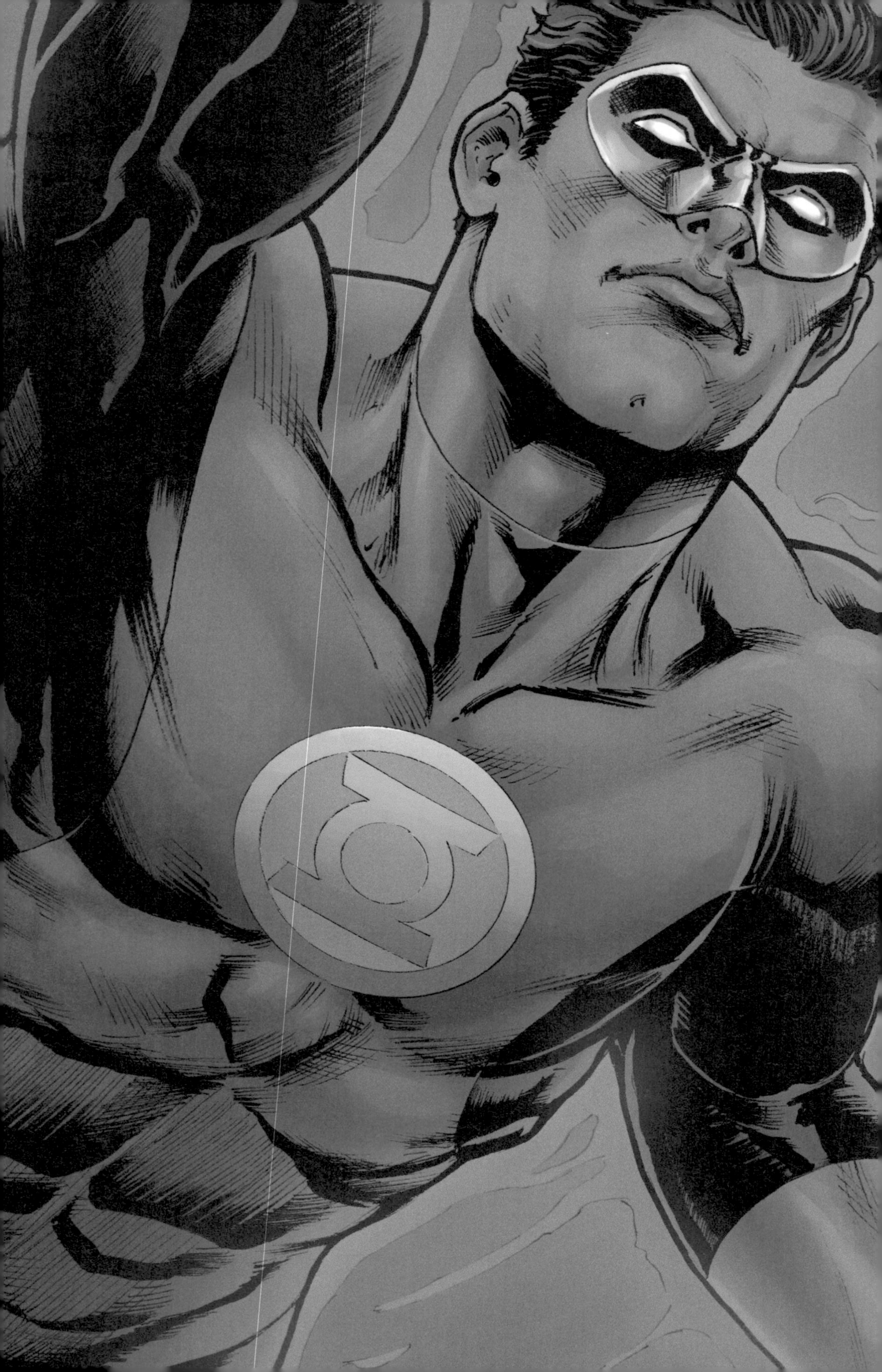

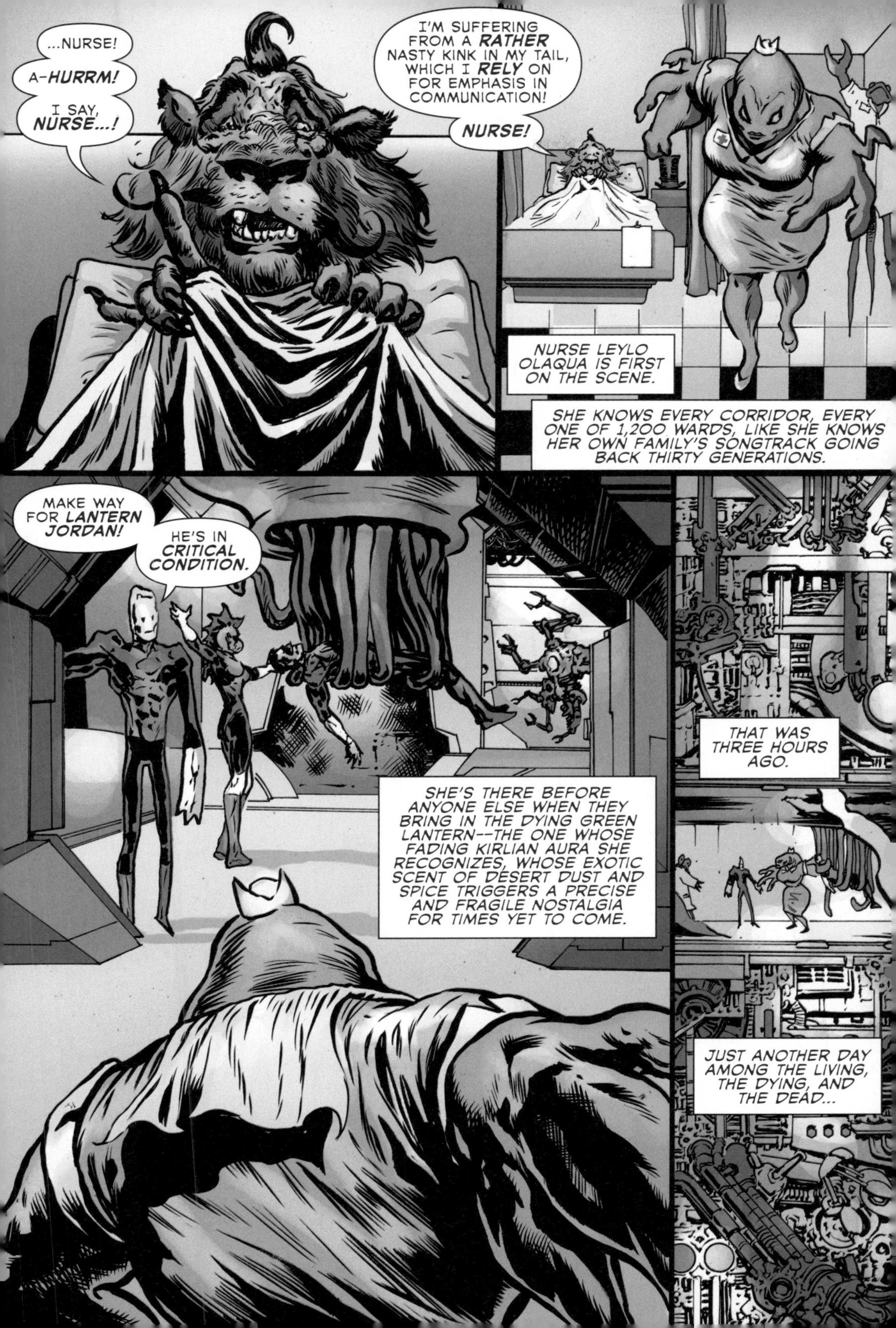

...NURSE!
A-HURRM!
I SAY, NURSE...!
I'M SUFFERING FROM A RATHER NASTY KINK IN MY TAIL, WHICH I RELY ON FOR EMPHASIS IN COMMUNICATION!
NURSE!
NURSE LEYLO OLAQUA IS FIRST ON THE SCENE.
SHE KNOWS EVERY CORRIDOR, EVERY ONE OF 1,200 WARDS, LIKE SHE KNOWS HER OWN FAMILY'S SONGTRACK GOING BACK THIRTY GENERATIONS.
MAKE WAY FOR LANTERN JORDAN!
HE'S IN CRITICAL CONDITION.
SHE'S THERE BEFORE ANYONE ELSE WHEN THEY BRING IN THE DYING GREEN LANTERN--THE ONE WHOSE FADING KIRLIAN AURA SHE RECOGNIZES, WHOSE EXOTIC SCENT OF DESERT DUST AND SPICE TRIGGERS A PRECISE AND FRAGILE NOSTALGIA FOR TIMES YET TO COME.
THAT WAS THREE HOURS AGO.
JUST ANOTHER DAY AMONG THE LIVING, THE DYING, AND THE DEAD...

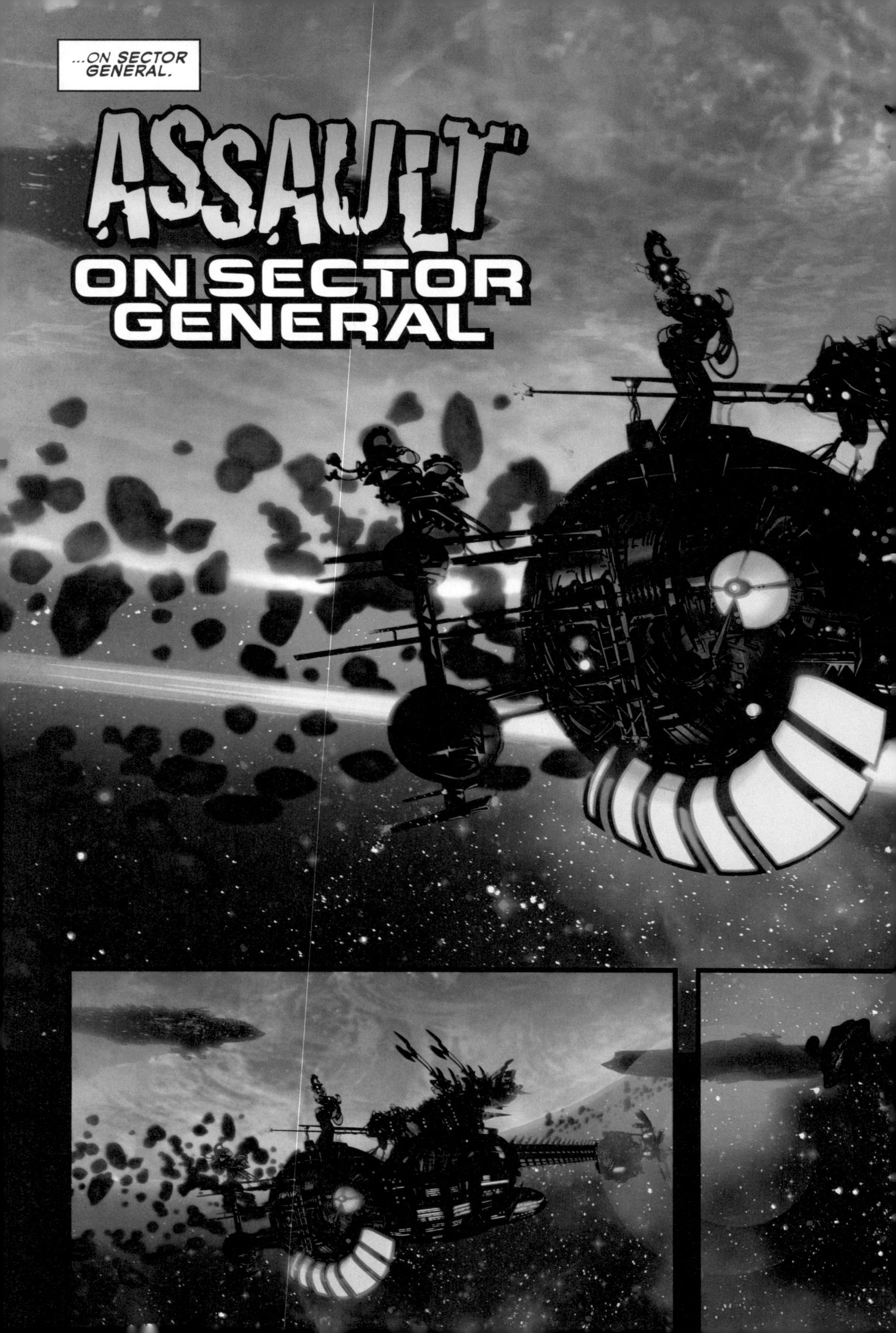
...ON SECTOR GENERAL.
ASSAULT ON SECTOR GENERAL

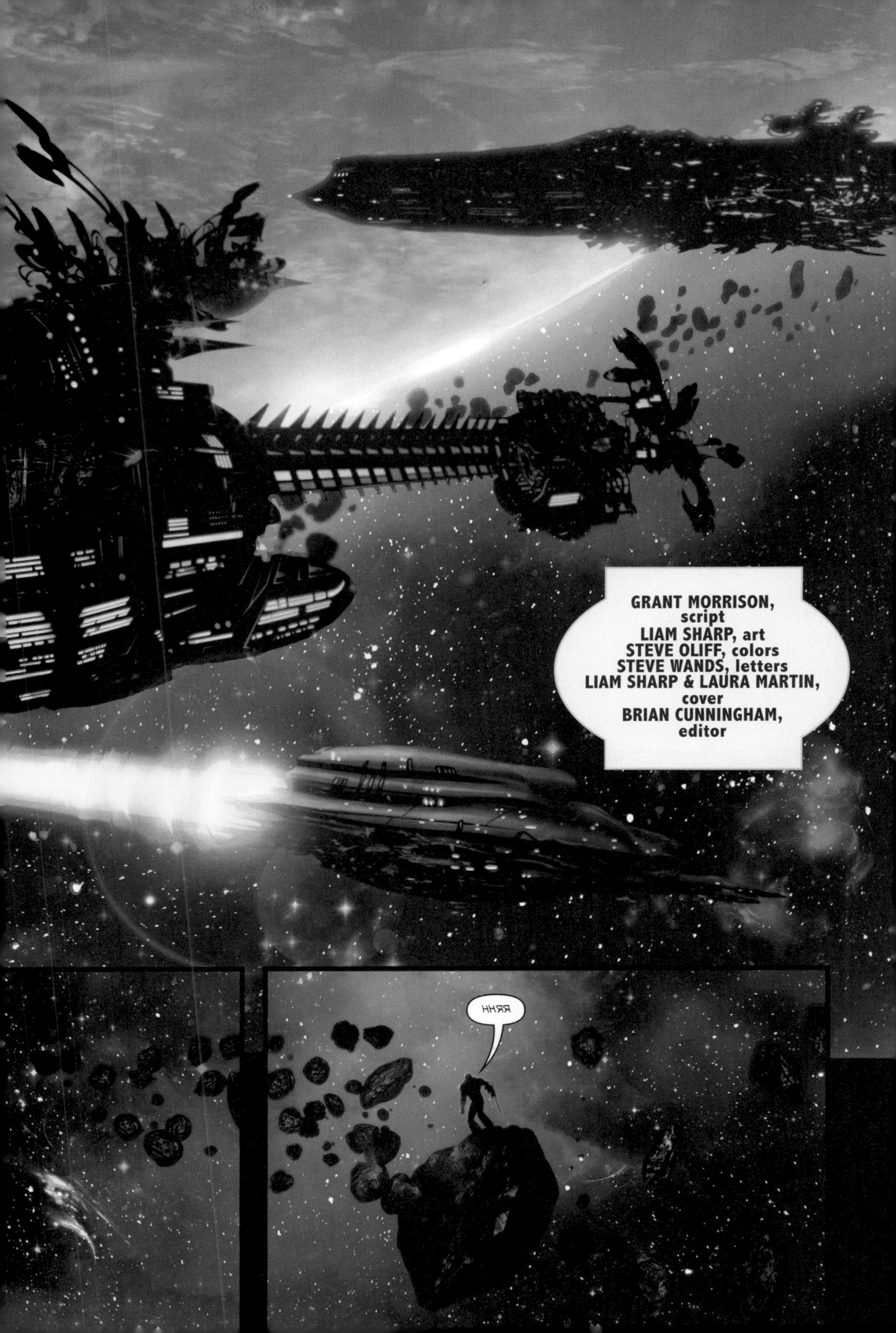
GRANT MORRISON, script
LIAM SHARP, art
STEVE OLIFF, colors
STEVE WANDS, letters
LIAM SHARP & LAURA MARTIN, cover
BRIAN CUNNINGHAM, editor
HHЯЯ

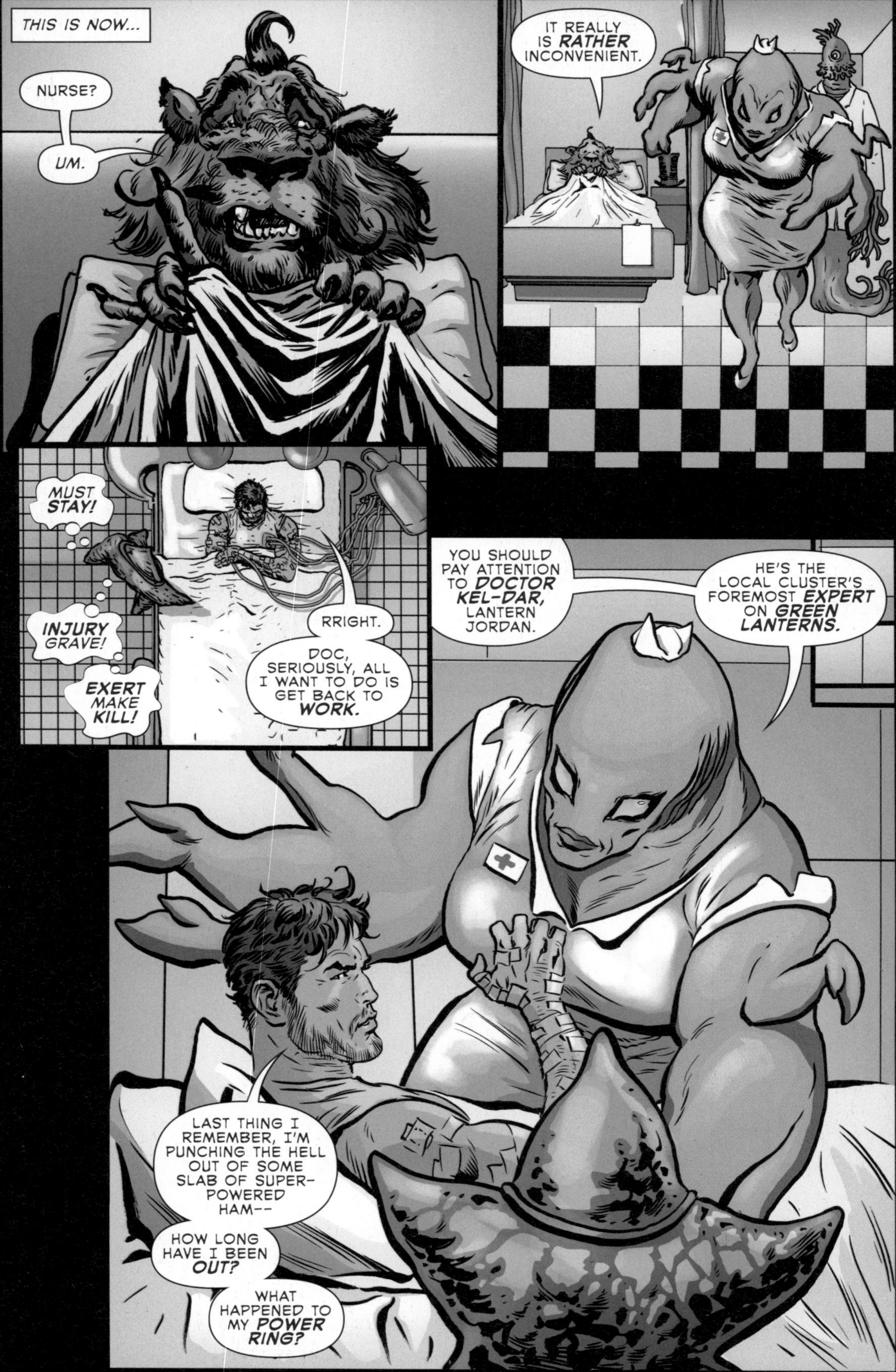
THIS IS NOW...
NURSE?
UM.
IT REALLY IS RATHER INCONVENIENT.
MUST STAY!
INJURY GRAVE!
EXERT MAKE KILL!
RRIGHT.
DOC, SERIOUSLY, ALL I WANT TO DO IS GET BACK TO WORK.
YOU SHOULD PAY ATTENTION TO DOCTOR KEL-DAR, LANTERN JORDAN.
HE'S THE LOCAL CLUSTER'S FOREMOST EXPERT ON GREEN LANTERNS.
LAST THING I REMEMBER, I'M PUNCHING THE HELL OUT OF SOME SLAB OF SUPER-POWERED HAM--
HOW LONG HAVE I BEEN OUT?
WHAT HAPPENED TO MY POWER RING?

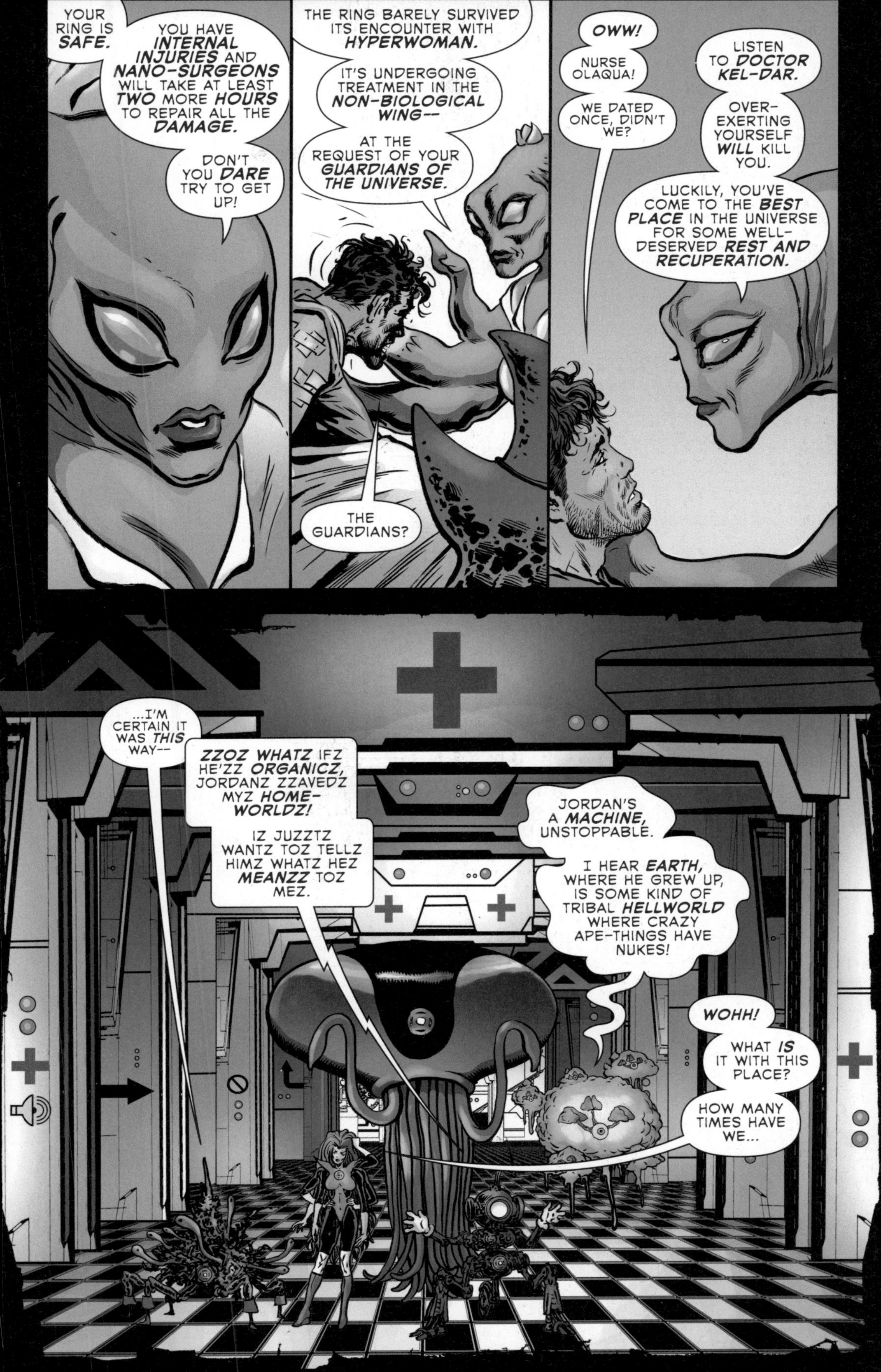
YOUR RING IS SAFE.
YOU HAVE INTERNAL INJURIES AND NANO-SURGEONS WILL TAKE AT LEAST TWO MORE HOURS TO REPAIR ALL THE DAMAGE.
DON'T YOU DARE TRY TO GET UP!
THE RING BARELY SURVIVED ITS ENCOUNTER WITH HYPERWOMAN.
IT'S UNDERGOING TREATMENT IN THE NON-BIOLOGICAL WING--
AT THE REQUEST OF YOUR GUARDIANS OF THE UNIVERSE.
THE GUARDIANS?
OWW!
NURSE OLAQUA!
WE DATED ONCE, DIDN'T WE?
LISTEN TO DOCTOR KEL-DAR.
OVER-EXERTING YOURSELF WILL KILL YOU.
LUCKILY, YOU'VE COME TO THE BEST PLACE IN THE UNIVERSE FOR SOME WELL-DESERVED REST AND RECUPERATION.
...I'M CERTAIN IT WAS THIS WAY--
ZZOZ WHATZ IFZ HE'ZZ ORGANICZ, JORDANZ ZZAVEDZ MYZ HOME-WORLDZ!
IZ JUZZTZ WANTZ TOZ TELLZ HIMZ WHATZ HEZ MEANZZ TOZ MEZ.
JORDAN'S A MACHINE, UNSTOPPABLE.
I HEAR EARTH, WHERE HE GREW UP, IS SOME KIND OF TRIBAL HELLWORLD WHERE CRAZY APE-THINGS HAVE NUKES!
WOHH!
WHAT IS IT WITH THIS PLACE?
HOW MANY TIMES HAVE WE...

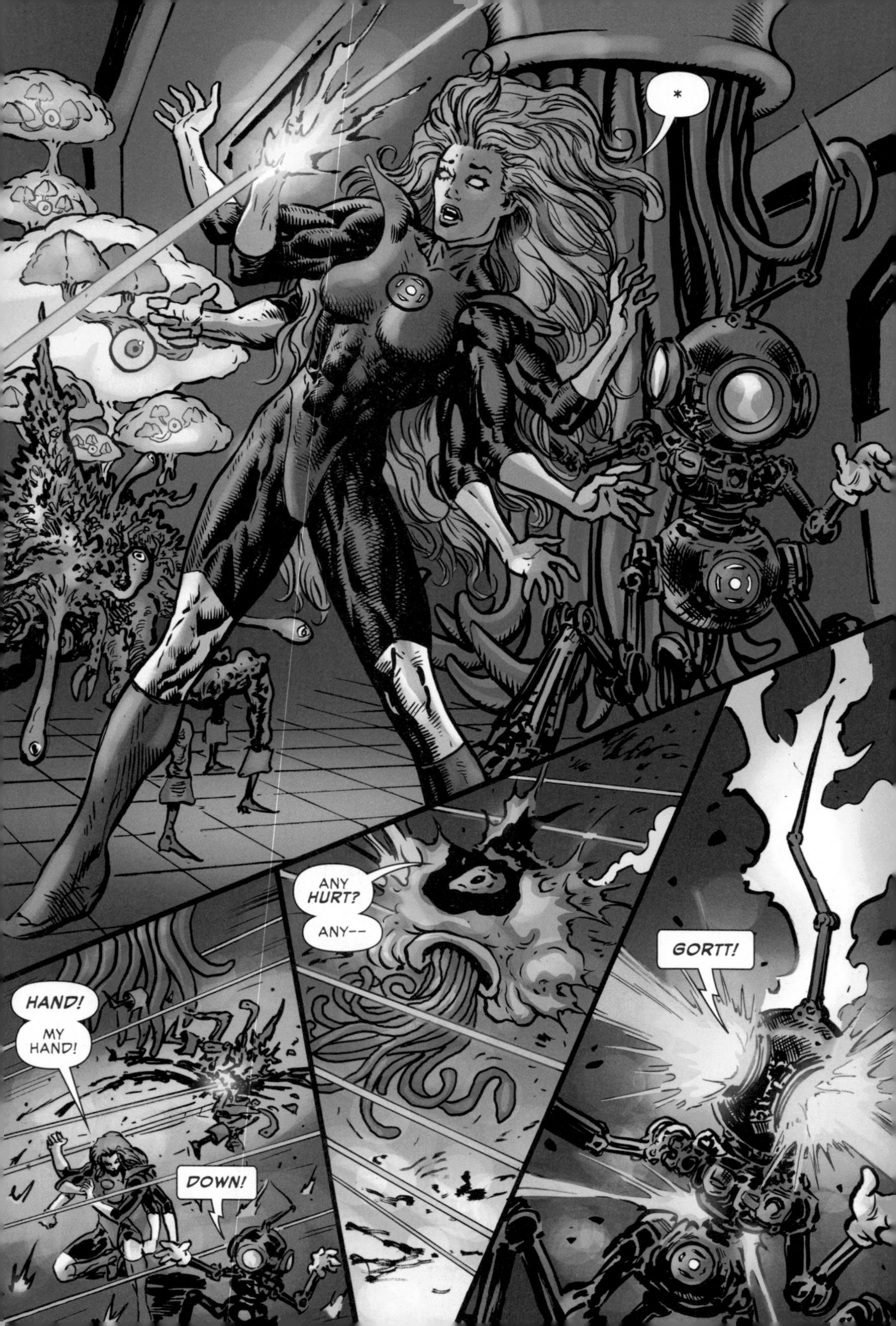
*
HAND!
MY HAND!
DOWN!
ANY HURT?
ANY--
GORTT!

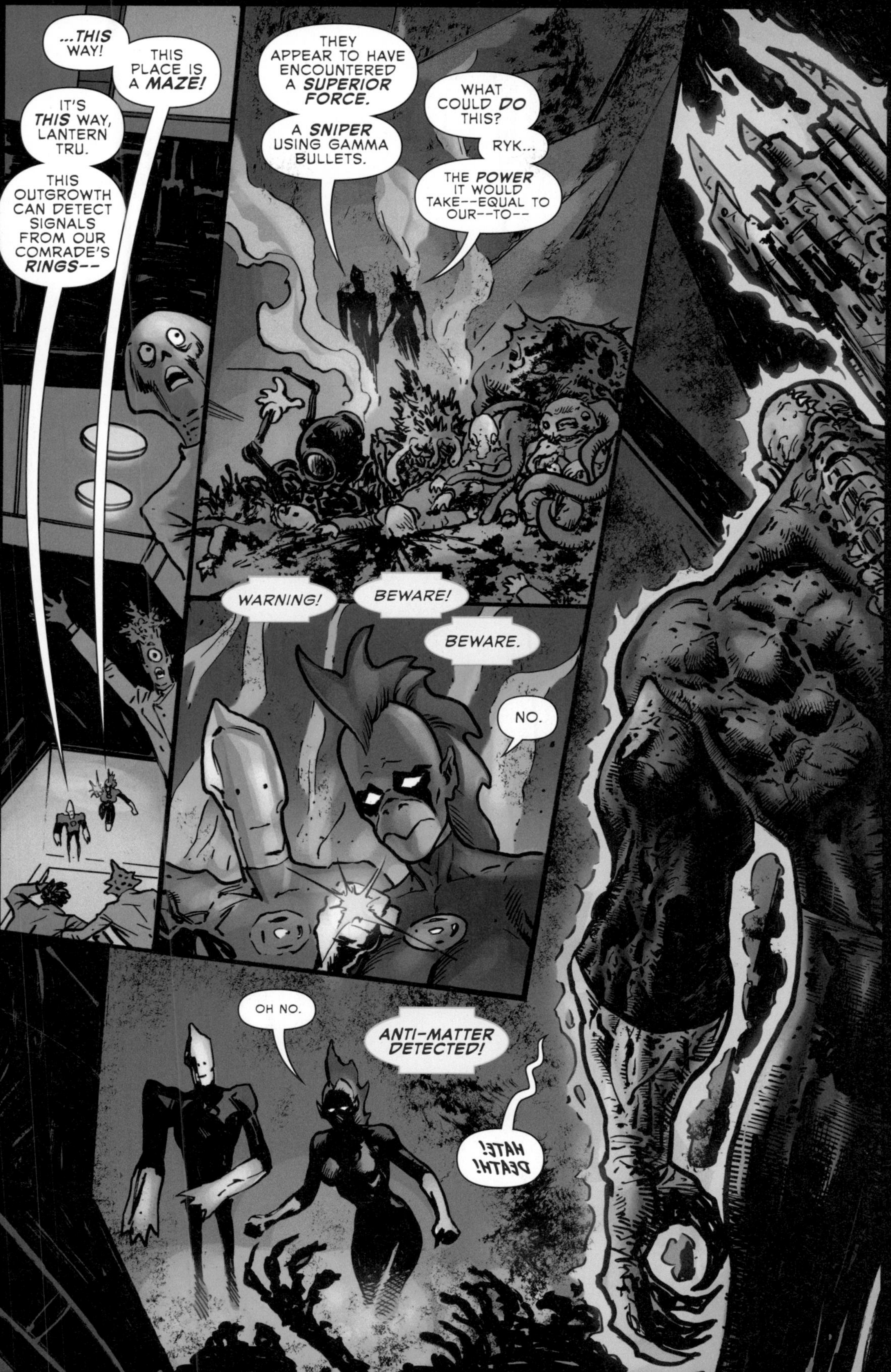

...THIS WAY!
THIS PLACE IS A MAZE!
IT'S THIS WAY, LANTERN TRU.
THIS OUTGROWTH CAN DETECT SIGNALS FROM OUR COMRADE'S RINGS--
THEY APPEAR TO HAVE ENCOUNTERED A SUPERIOR FORCE.
A SNIPER USING GAMMA BULLETS.
WHAT COULD DO THIS?
RYK...
THE POWER IT WOULD TAKE--EQUAL TO OUR--TO--
WARNING!
BEWARE!
BEWARE.
NO.
OH NO.
ANTI-MATTER DETECTED!
HATE! DEATH!

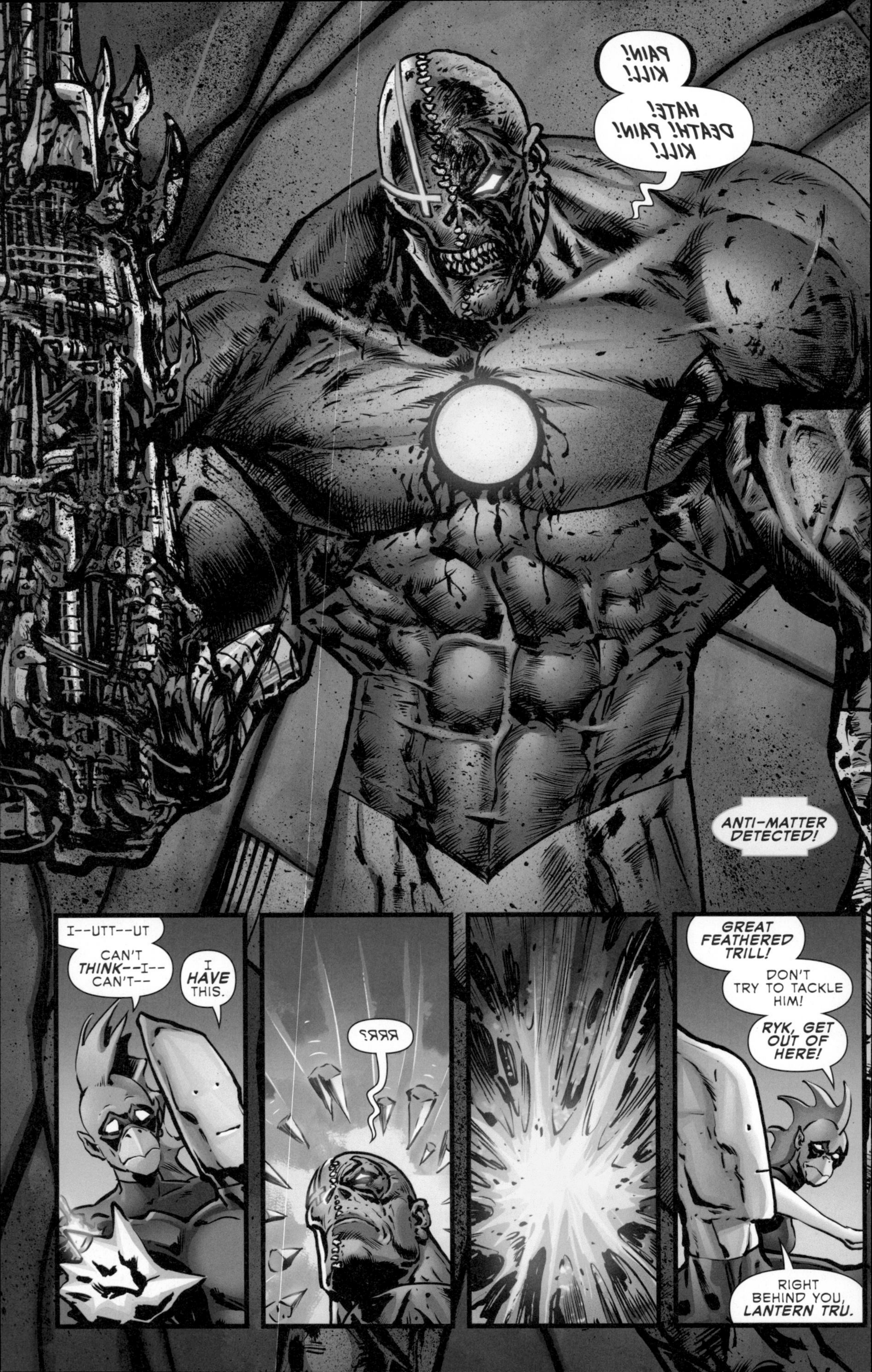
PAIN! KILL!
HATE! DEATH! PAIN! KILL!
ANTI-MATTER DETECTED!
I--UTT--UT
CAN'T THINK--I--CAN'T--
I HAVE THIS.
RRR?
GREAT FEATHERED TRILL!
DON'T TRY TO TACKLE HIM!
RYK, GET OUT OF HERE!
RIGHT BEHIND YOU, LANTERN TRU.

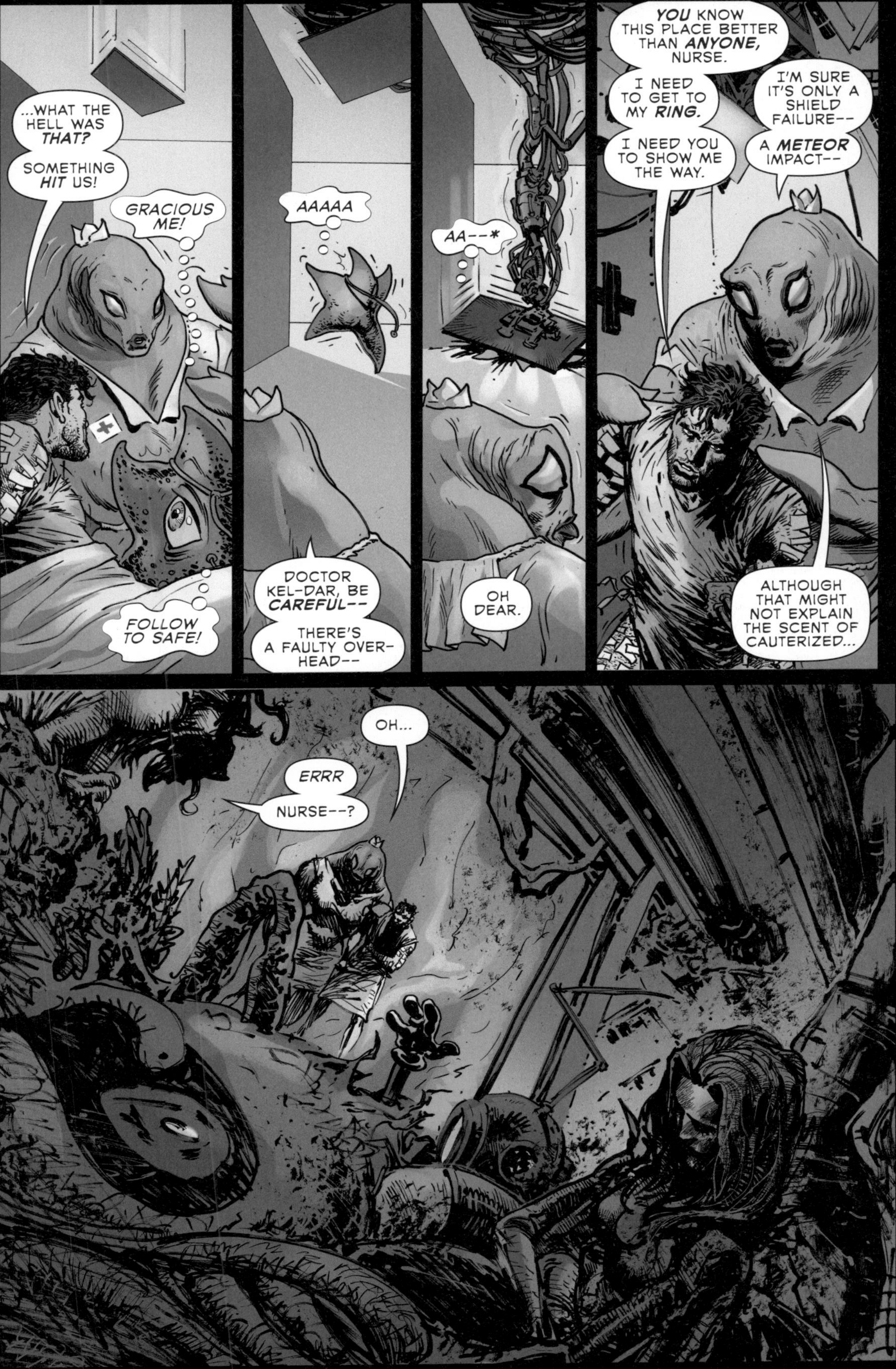
...WHAT THE HELL WAS THAT?
SOMETHING HIT US!
GRACIOUS ME!
FOLLOW TO SAFE!
AAAAA
DOCTOR KEL-DAR, BE CAREFUL--
THERE'S A FAULTY OVER-HEAD--
AA--*
OH DEAR.
YOU KNOW THIS PLACE BETTER THAN ANYONE, NURSE.
I NEED TO GET TO MY RING.
I NEED YOU TO SHOW ME THE WAY.
I'M SURE IT'S ONLY A SHIELD FAILURE--
A METEOR IMPACT--
ALTHOUGH THAT MIGHT NOT EXPLAIN THE SCENT OF CAUTERIZED...
OH...
ERRR
NURSE--?

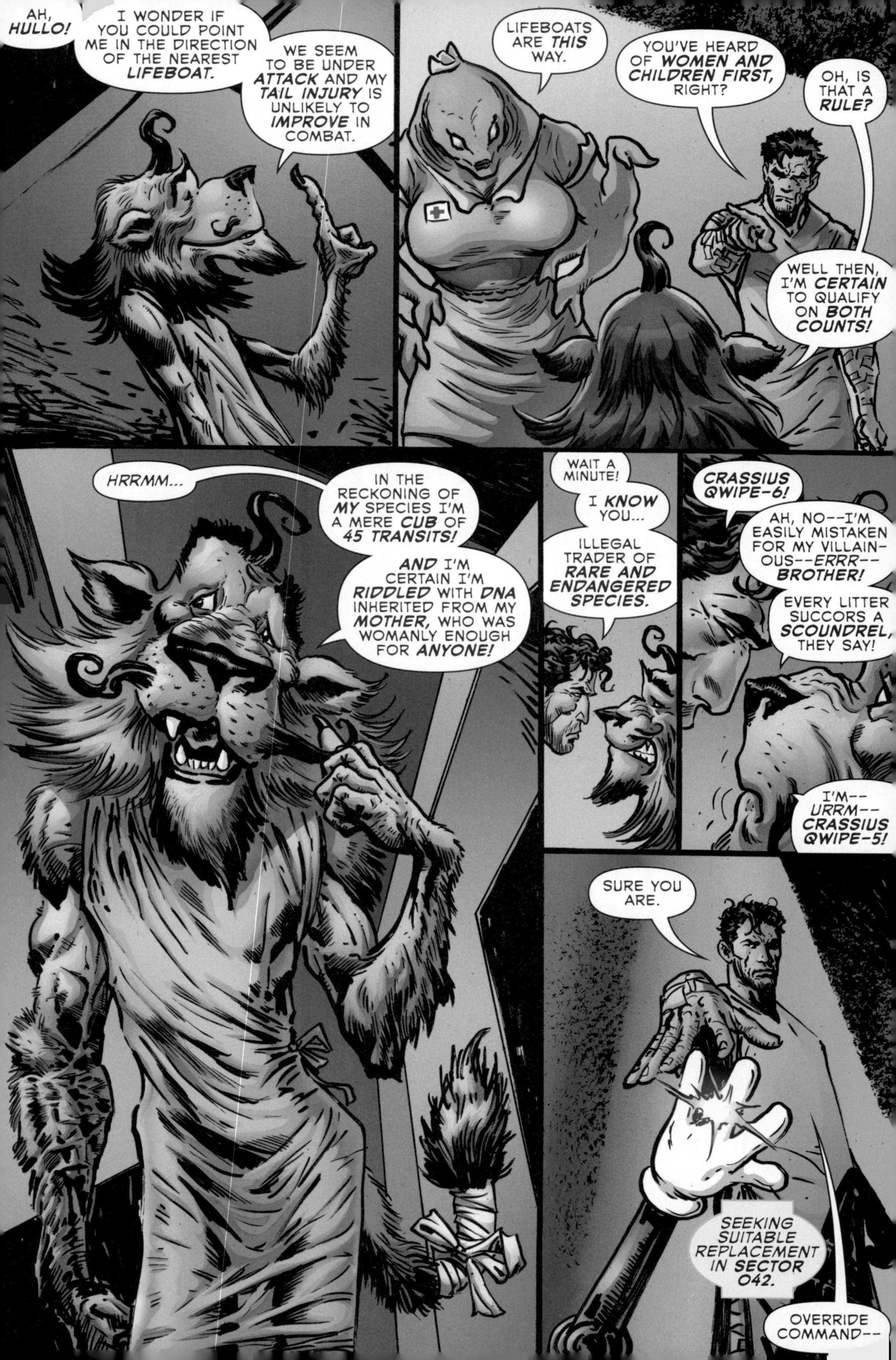

AH, HULLO!
I WONDER IF YOU COULD POINT ME IN THE DIRECTION OF THE NEAREST LIFEBOAT.
WE SEEM TO BE UNDER ATTACK AND MY TAIL INJURY IS UNLIKELY TO IMPROVE IN COMBAT.
LIFEBOATS ARE THIS WAY.
YOU'VE HEARD OF WOMEN AND CHILDREN FIRST, RIGHT?
OH, IS THAT A RULE?
WELL THEN, I'M CERTAIN TO QUALIFY ON BOTH COUNTS!
HRRMM...
IN THE RECKONING OF MY SPECIES I'M A MERE CUB OF 45 TRANSITS!
AND I'M CERTAIN I'M RIDDLED WITH DNA INHERITED FROM MY MOTHER, WHO WAS WOMANLY ENOUGH FOR ANYONE!
WAIT A MINUTE!
I KNOW YOU...
ILLEGAL TRADER OF RARE AND ENDANGERED SPECIES.
CRASSIUS QWIPE-6!
AH, NO--I'M EASILY MISTAKEN FOR MY VILLAIN-OUS--ERRR--BROTHER!
EVERY LITTER SUCCORS A SCOUNDREL, THEY SAY!
I'M--URRM--CRASSIUS QWIPE-5!
SURE YOU ARE.
SEEKING SUITABLE REPLACEMENT IN SECTOR 042.
OVERRIDE COMMAND--

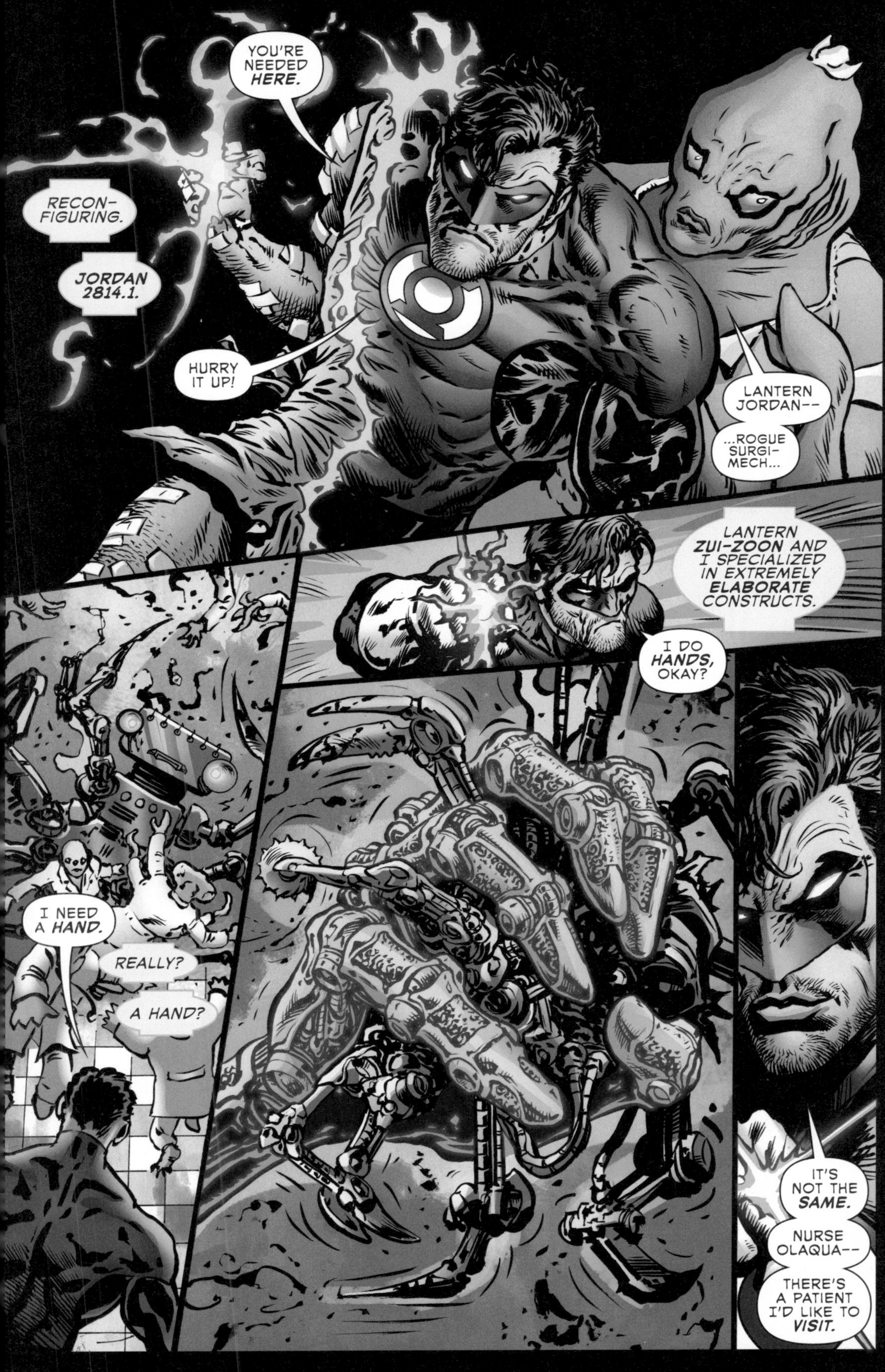
YOU'RE NEEDED HERE.
RECON-FIGURING.
JORDAN 2814.1.
HURRY IT UP!
LANTERN JORDAN--
...ROGUE SURGI-MECH...
LANTERN ZUI-ZOON AND I SPECIALIZED IN EXTREMELY ELABORATE CONSTRUCTS.
I DO HANDS, OKAY?
I NEED A HAND.
REALLY?
A HAND?
IT'S NOT THE SAME.
NURSE OLAQUA--
THERE'S A PATIENT I'D LIKE TO VISIT.

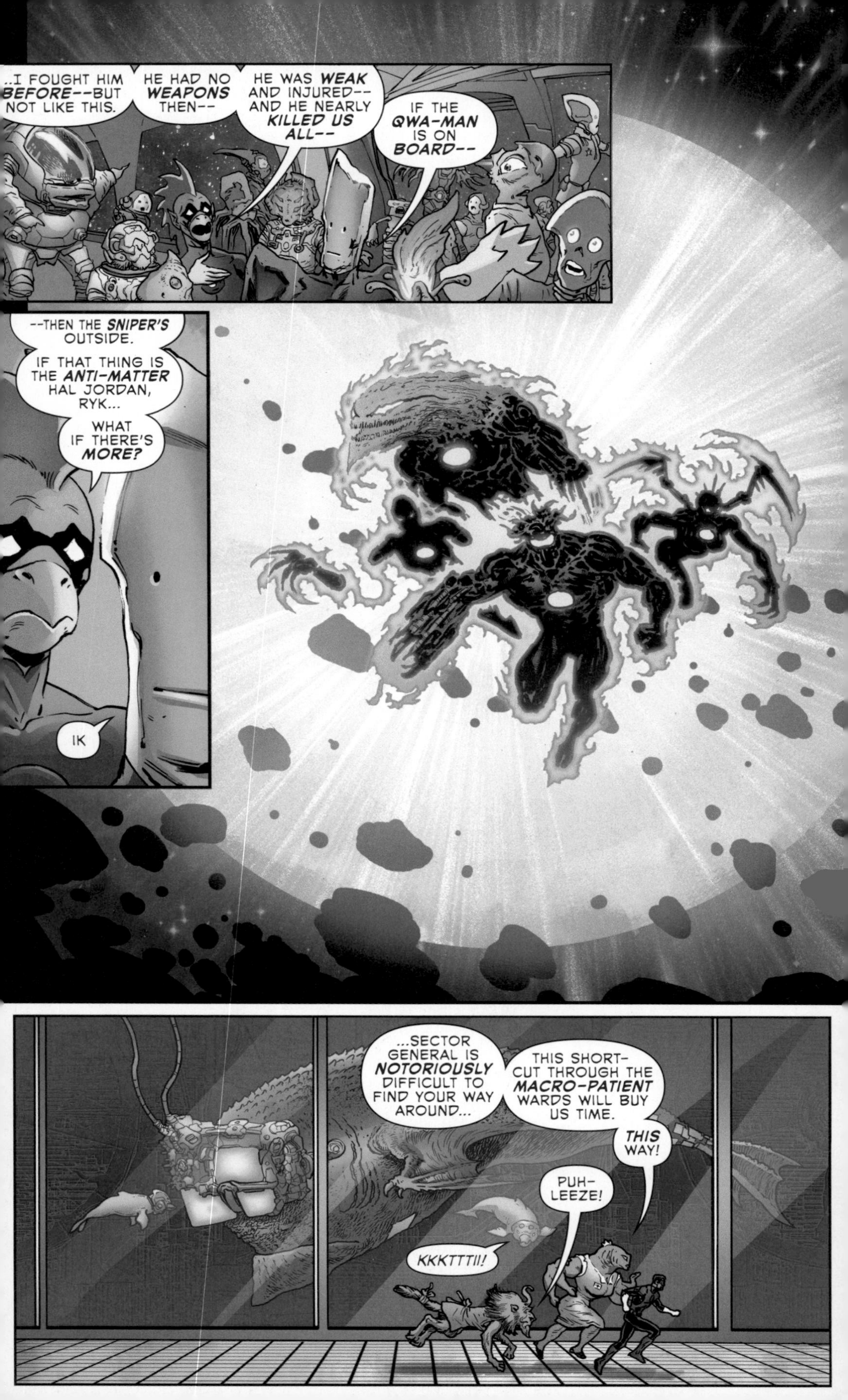
..I FOUGHT HIM BEFORE--BUT NOT LIKE THIS.
HE HAD NO WEAPONS THEN--
HE WAS WEAK AND INJURED-- AND HE NEARLY KILLED US ALL--
IF THE QWA-MAN IS ON BOARD--
--THEN THE SNIPER'S OUTSIDE.
IF THAT THING IS THE ANTI-MATTER HAL JORDAN, RYK...
WHAT IF THERE'S MORE?
IK
...SECTOR GENERAL IS NOTORIOUSLY DIFFICULT TO FIND YOUR WAY AROUND...
THIS SHORT-CUT THROUGH THE MACRO-PATIENT WARDS WILL BUY US TIME.
THIS WAY!
PUH-LEEZE!
KKKTTTI!!

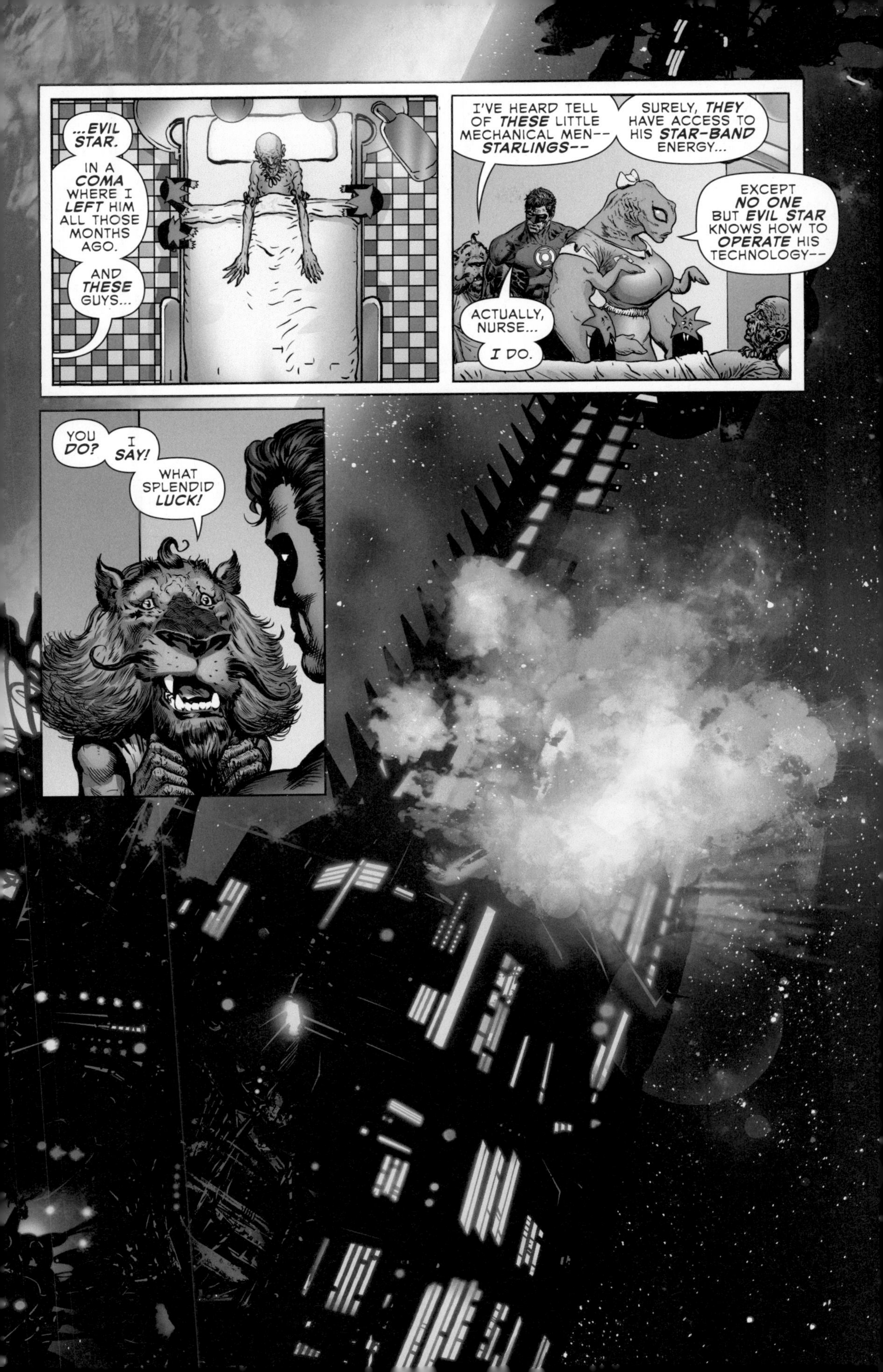
...EVIL STAR.
IN A COMA WHERE I LEFT HIM ALL THOSE MONTHS AGO.
AND THESE GUYS...
I'VE HEARD TELL OF THESE LITTLE MECHANICAL MEN-- STARLINGS--
SURELY, THEY HAVE ACCESS TO HIS STAR-BAND ENERGY...
EXCEPT NO ONE BUT EVIL STAR KNOWS HOW TO OPERATE HIS TECHNOLOGY--
ACTUALLY, NURSE...
I DO.
YOU DO?
I SAY!
WHAT SPLENDID LUCK!

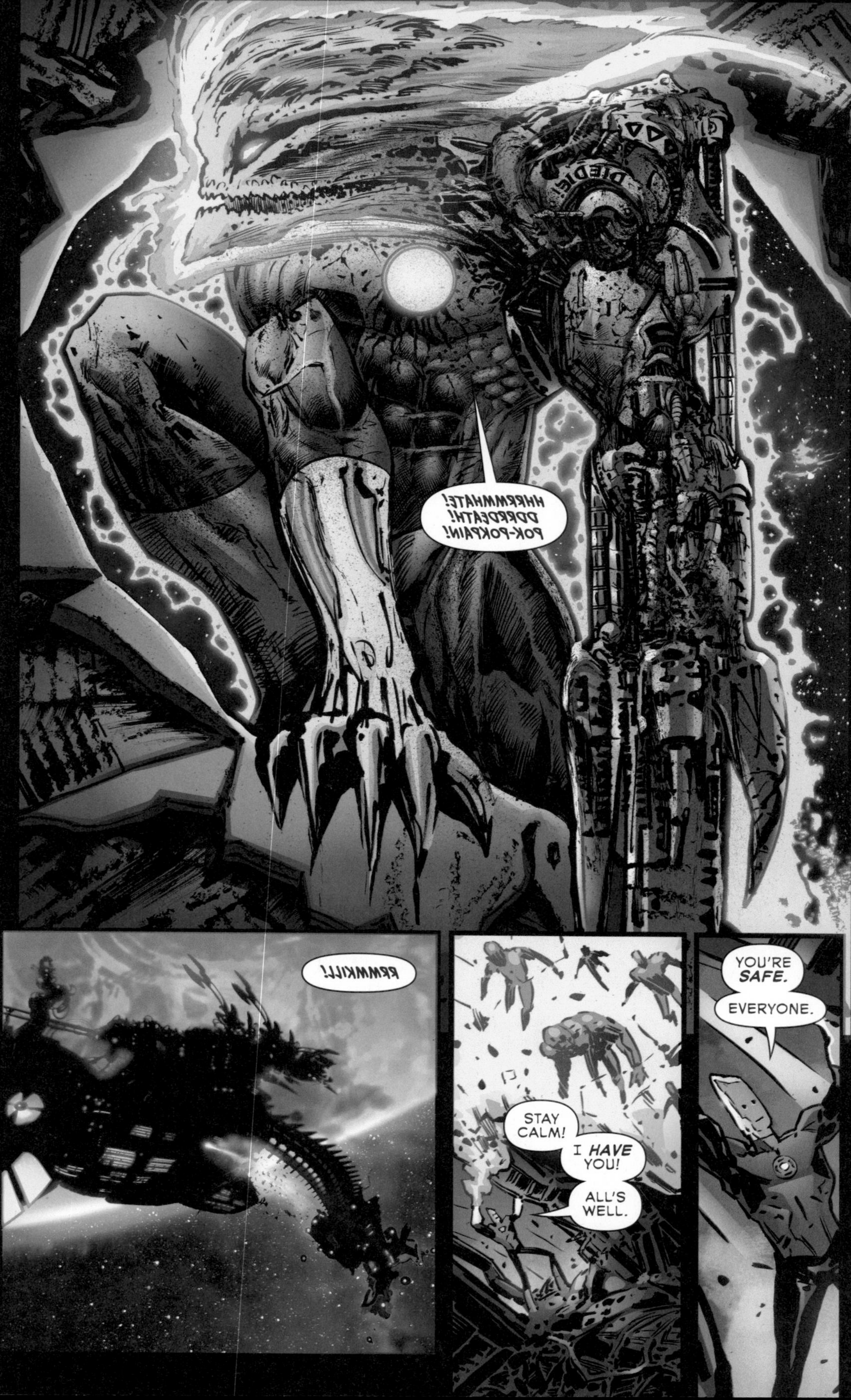
HHRRMMHATE! DORRDEATH! POK-POKPAIN!
RRMMKILL!!
STAY CALM!
I *HAVE* YOU!
ALL'S WELL.
YOU'RE *SAFE.*
EVERYONE.

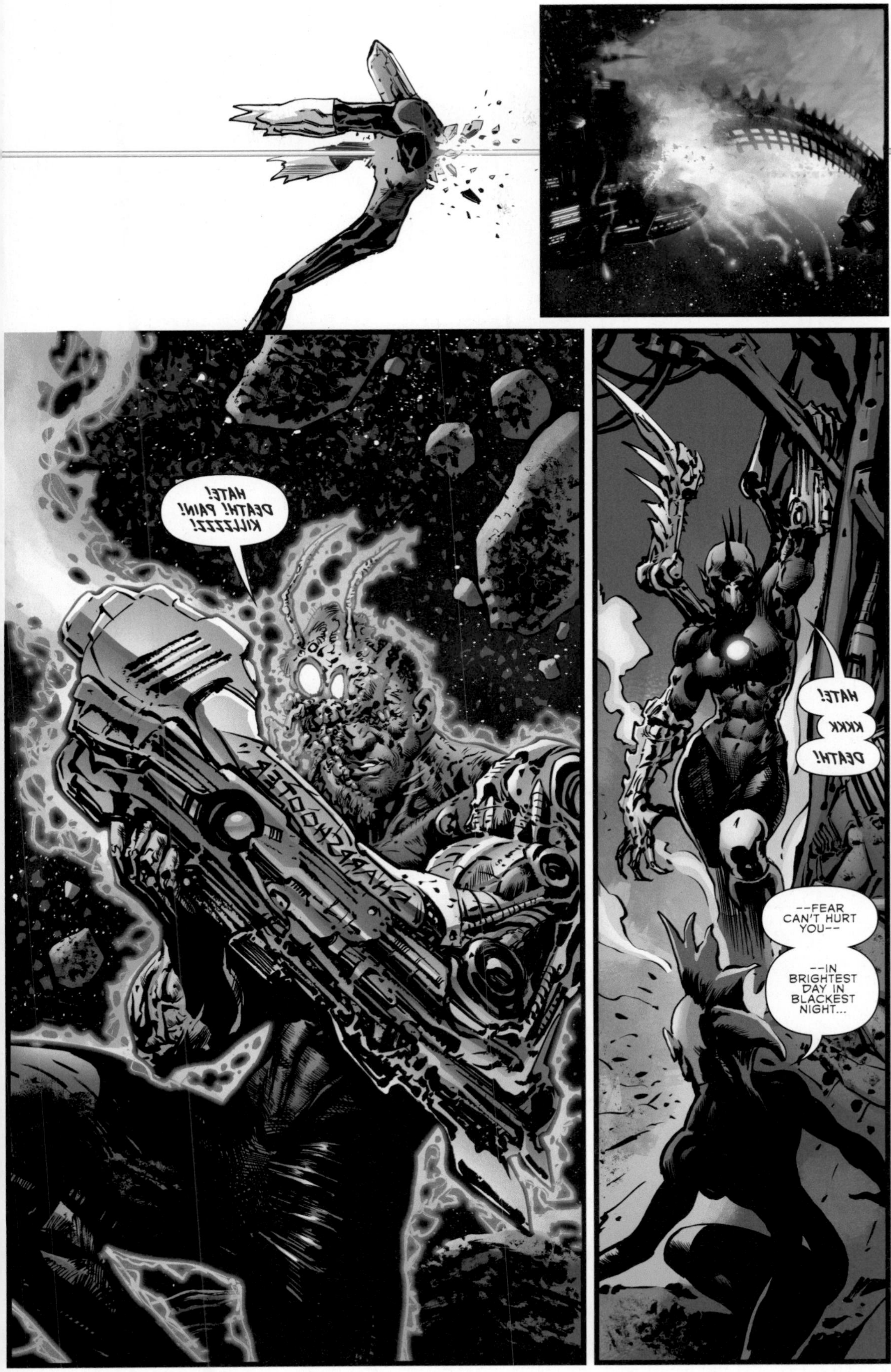
HATE! DEATH! PAIN! KILLZZZ!
HATE! KKKK DEATH!
--FEAR CAN'T HURT YOU--
--IN BRIGHTEST DAY IN BLACKEST NIGHT...

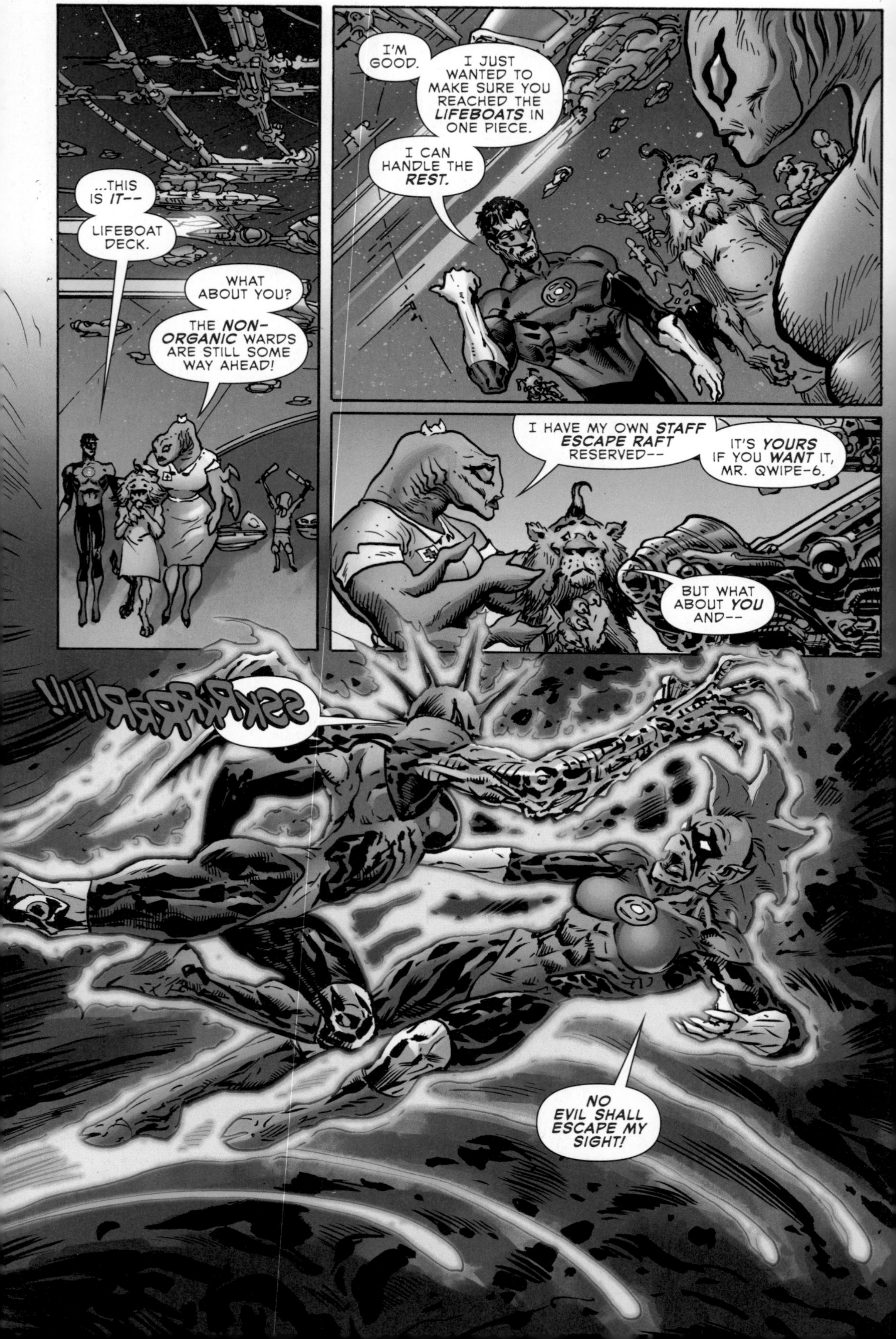
...THIS IS IT--
LIFEBOAT DECK.
WHAT ABOUT YOU?
THE NON-ORGANIC WARDS ARE STILL SOME WAY AHEAD!
I'M GOOD.
I JUST WANTED TO MAKE SURE YOU REACHED THE LIFEBOATS IN ONE PIECE.
I CAN HANDLE THE REST.
I HAVE MY OWN STAFF ESCAPE RAFT RESERVED--
IT'S YOURS IF YOU WANT IT, MR. QWIPE-6.
BUT WHAT ABOUT YOU AND--
SSKRRRRR!!!
NO EVIL SHALL ESCAPE MY SIGHT!

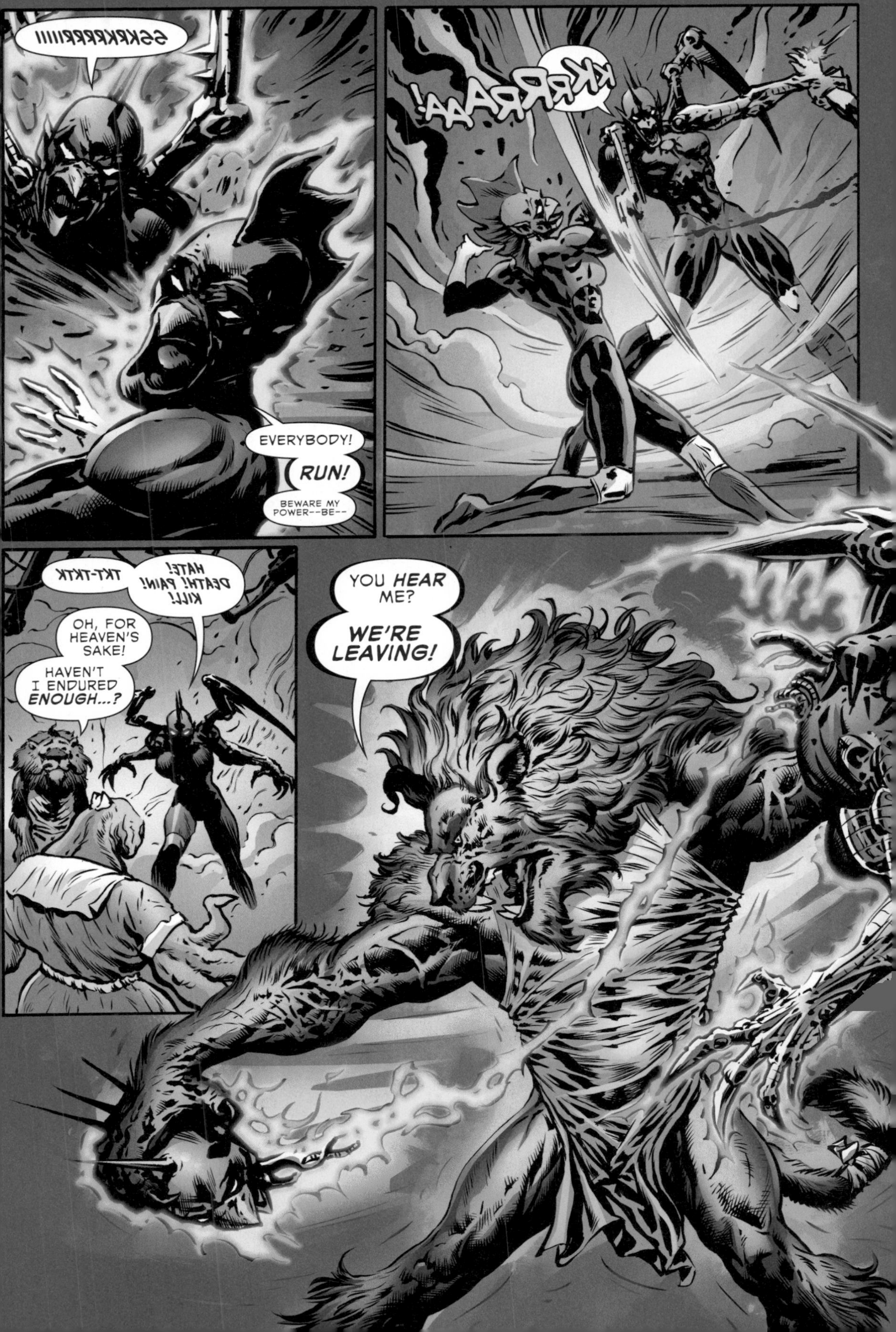
GSKRKRRRII!!!
EVERYBODY!
RUN!
BEWARE MY POWER--BE--
KKRRRAAA!
TKT-TKTK
HATE! DEATH! PAIN! KILL!
OH, FOR HEAVEN'S SAKE!
HAVEN'T I ENDURED ENOUGH...?
YOU HEAR ME?
WE'RE LEAVING!

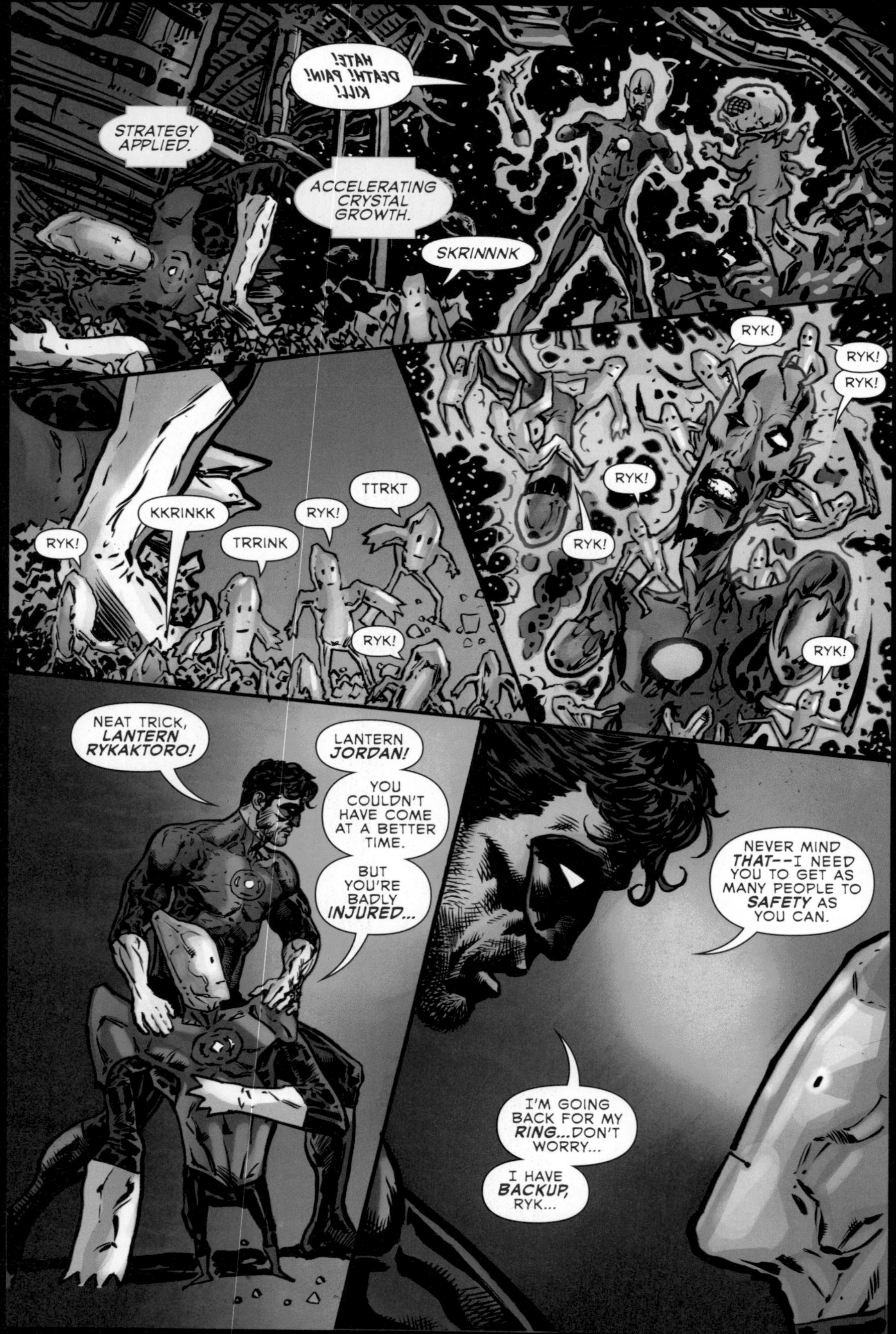
STRATEGY APPLIED.
HATE! DEATH! PAIN! KILL!
ACCELERATING CRYSTAL GROWTH.
SKRINNNK
RYK!
KKRINKK
TRRINK
RYK!
TTRKT
RYK!
RYK!
RYK!
RYK!
RYK!
RYK!
RYK!
NEAT TRICK, LANTERN RYKAKTORO!
LANTERN JORDAN!
YOU COULDN'T HAVE COME AT A BETTER TIME.
BUT YOU'RE BADLY INJURED...
NEVER MIND THAT--I NEED YOU TO GET AS MANY PEOPLE TO SAFETY AS YOU CAN.
I'M GOING BACK FOR MY RING...DON'T WORRY...
I HAVE BACKUP, RYK...

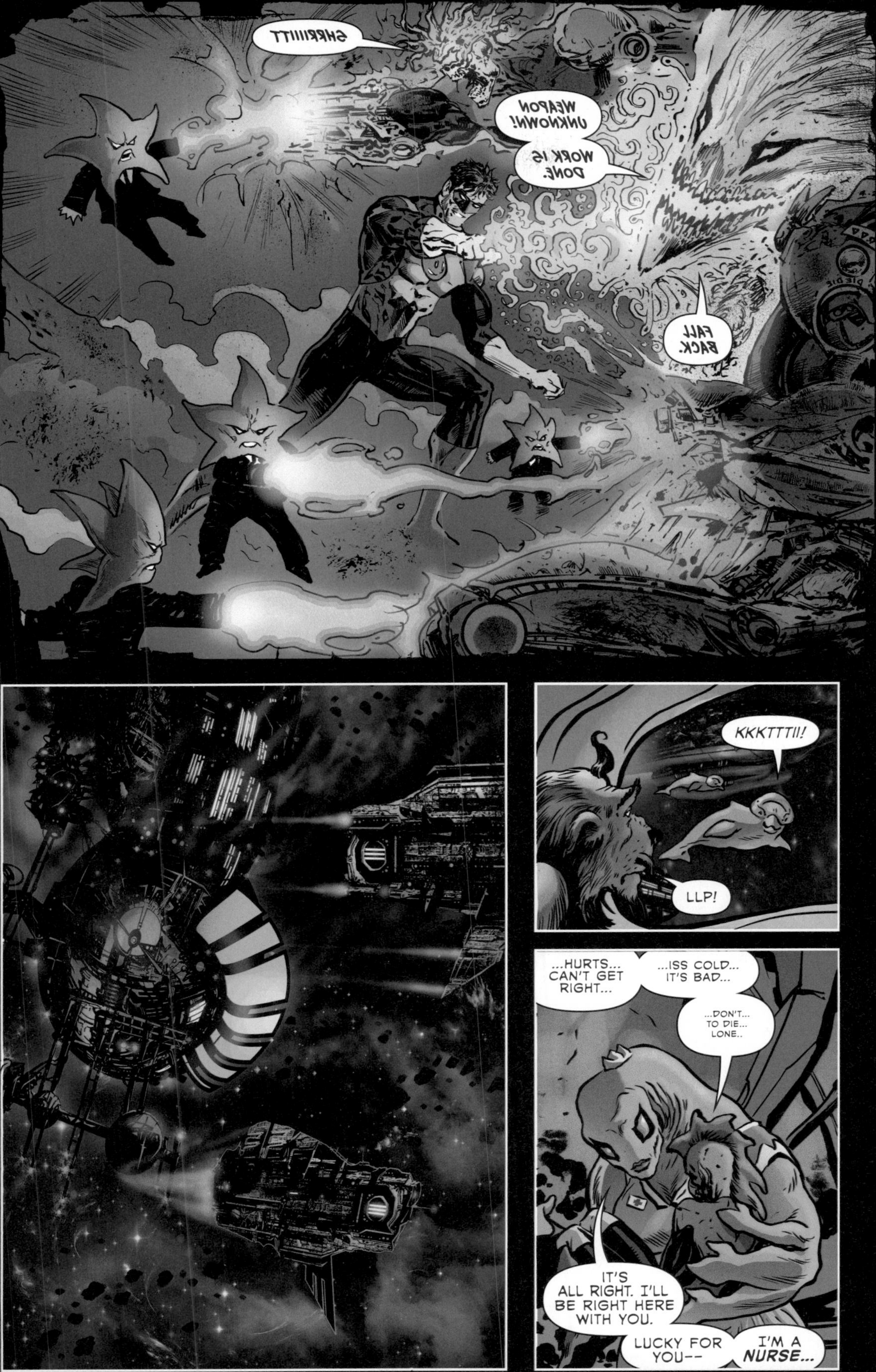
SHRIIIITT
WEAPON UNKNOWN!
WORK IS DONE.
FALL BACK.
KKKTTTII!
LLP!
...HURTS... CAN'T GET RIGHT...
...ISS COLD... IT'S BAD...
...DON'T... TO DIE... LONE..
IT'S ALL RIGHT. I'LL BE RIGHT HERE WITH YOU.
LUCKY FOR YOU--
I'M A *NURSE...*

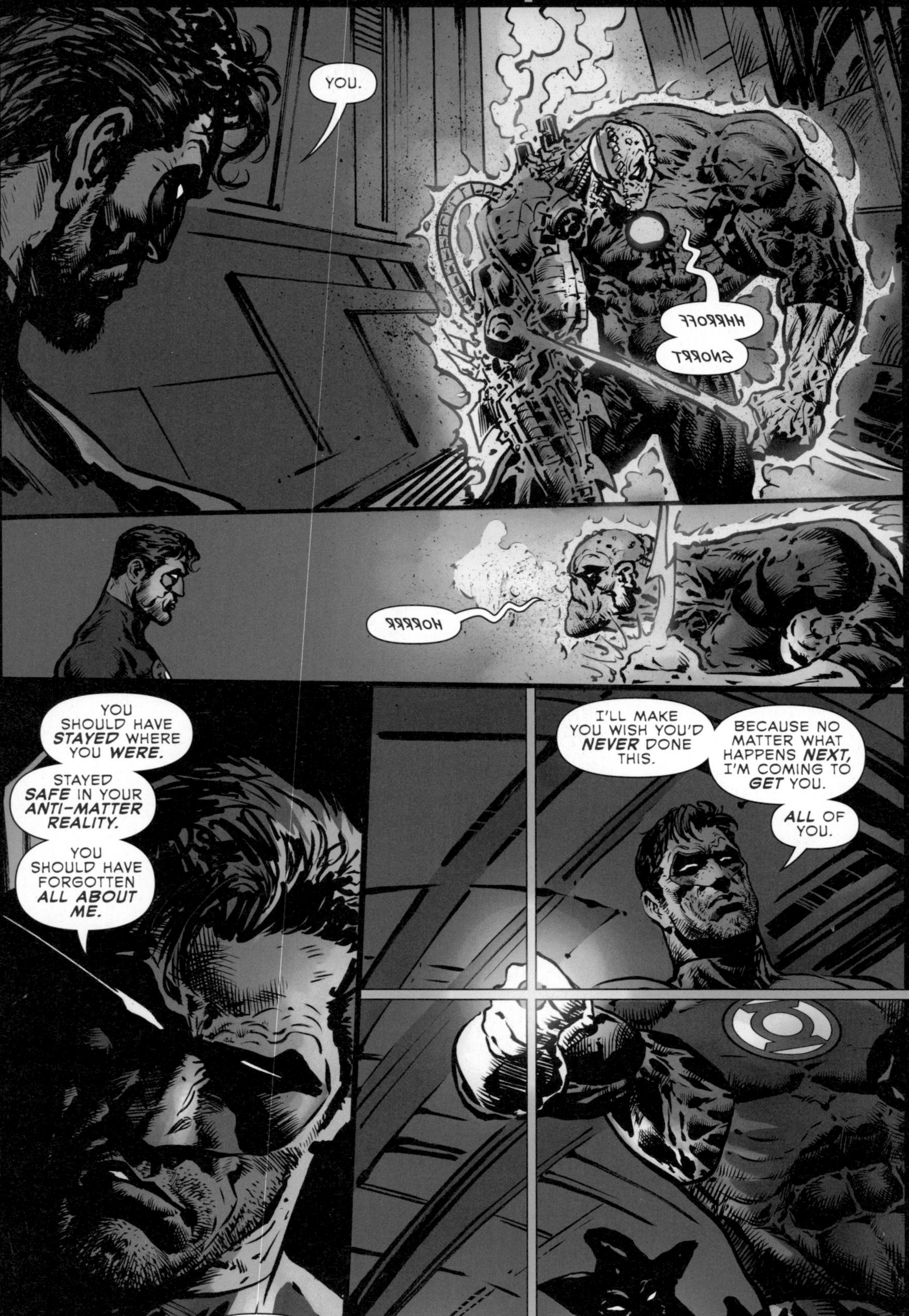
YOU.
HHRROFF
SNORRT
HORRRR
YOU SHOULD HAVE STAYED WHERE YOU WERE.
STAYED SAFE IN YOUR ANTI-MATTER REALITY.
YOU SHOULD HAVE FORGOTTEN ALL ABOUT ME.
HHNRRRR
I'LL MAKE YOU WISH YOU'D NEVER DONE THIS.
BECAUSE NO MATTER WHAT HAPPENS NEXT, I'M COMING TO GET YOU.
ALL OF YOU.

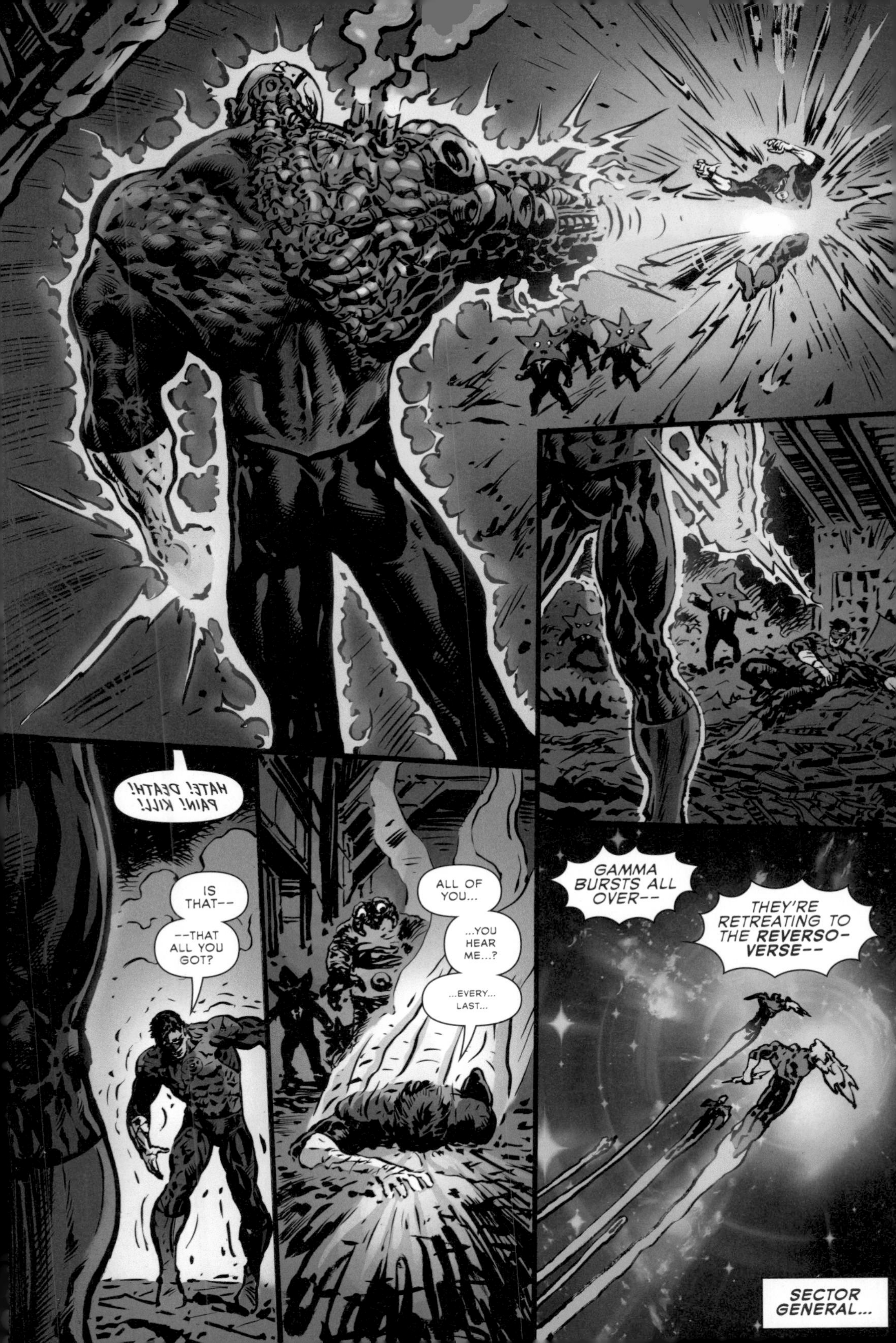
HATE! DEATH! PAIN! KILL!
IS THAT--
--THAT ALL YOU GOT?
ALL OF YOU...
...YOU HEAR ME...?
...EVERY... LAST...
GAMMA BURSTS ALL OVER--
THEY'RE RETREATING TO THE **REVERSO-VERSE**--
SECTOR GENERAL...

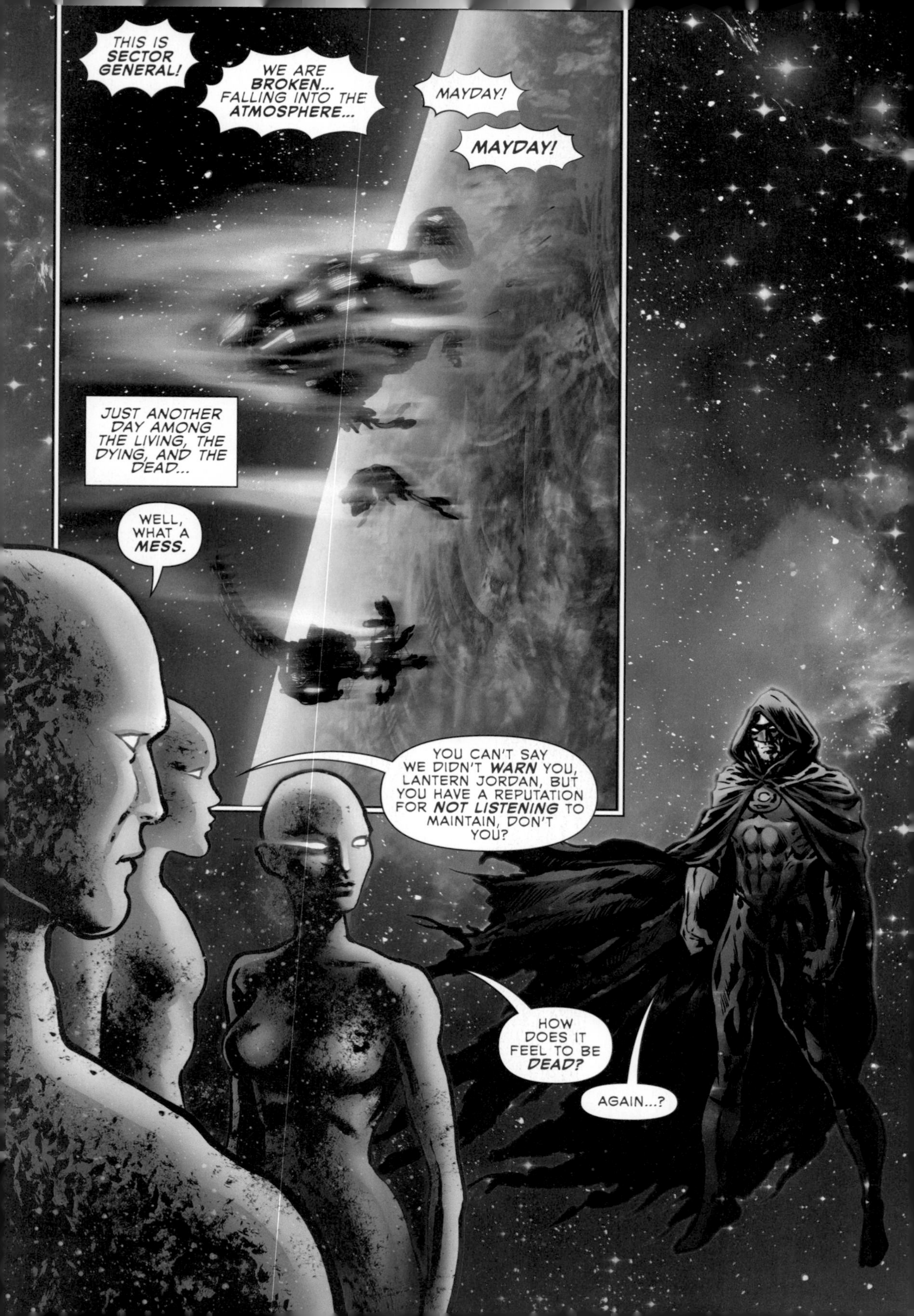
THIS IS SECTOR GENERAL!
WE ARE BROKEN... FALLING INTO THE ATMOSPHERE...
MAYDAY!
MAYDAY!
JUST ANOTHER DAY AMONG THE LIVING, THE DYING, AND THE DEAD...
WELL, WHAT A MESS.
YOU CAN'T SAY WE DIDN'T WARN YOU, LANTERN JORDAN, BUT YOU HAVE A REPUTATION FOR NOT LISTENING TO MAINTAIN, DON'T YOU?
HOW DOES IT FEEL TO BE DEAD?
AGAIN...?

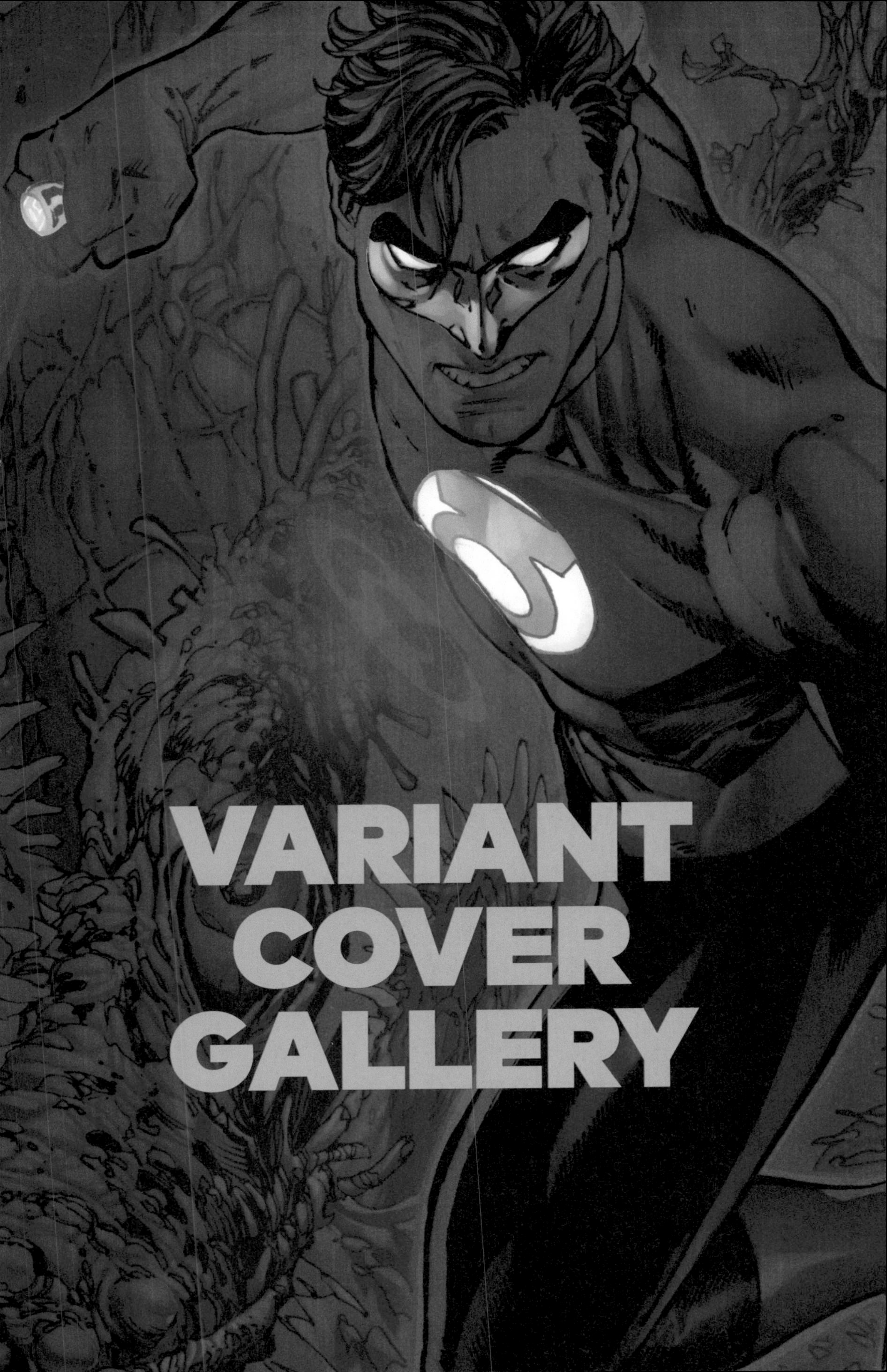

VARIANT COVER GALLERY

***GREEN LANTERN: BLACKSTARS* #1**
variant cover by **DARICK ROBERTSON** and **DIEGO RODRIGUEZ**

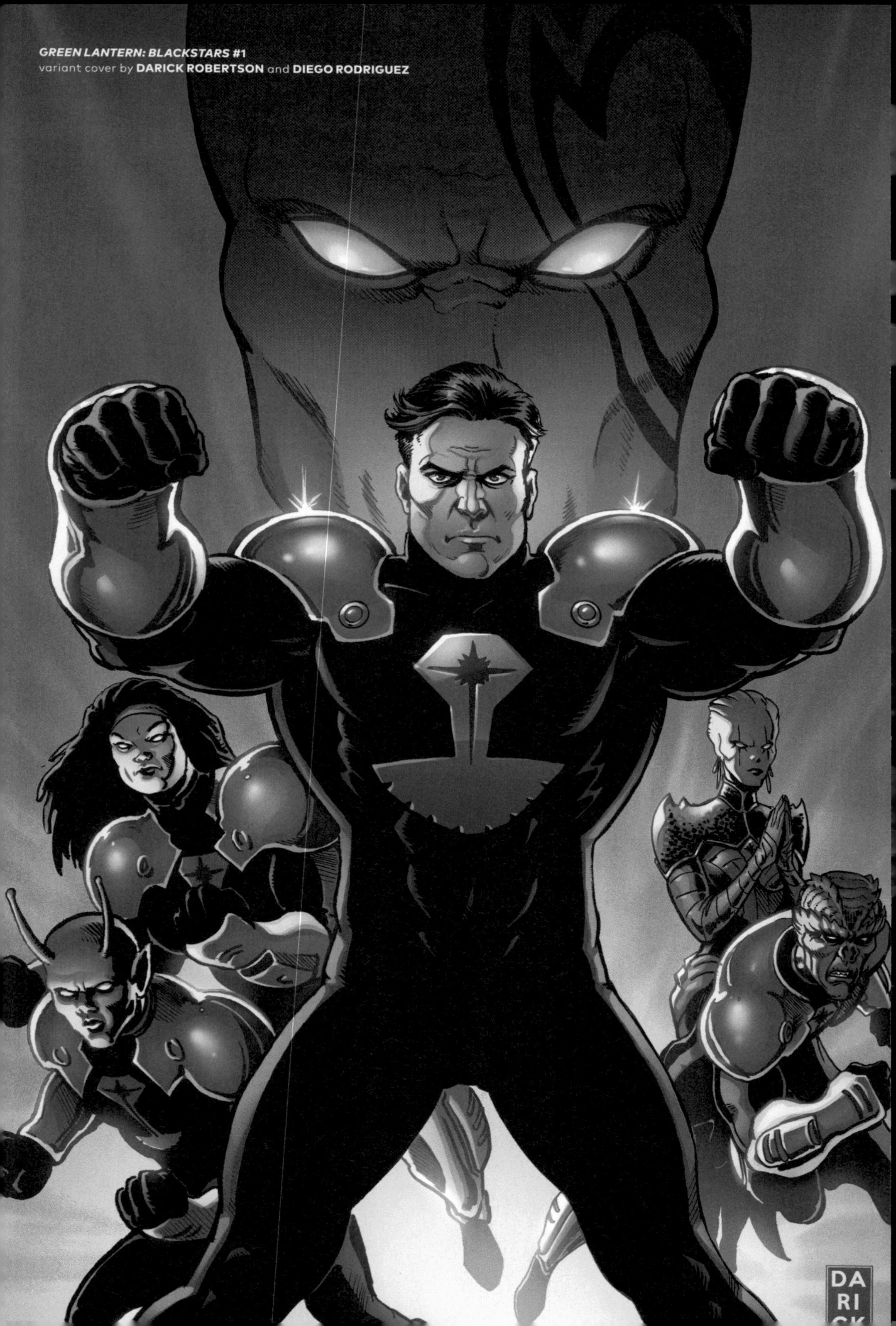

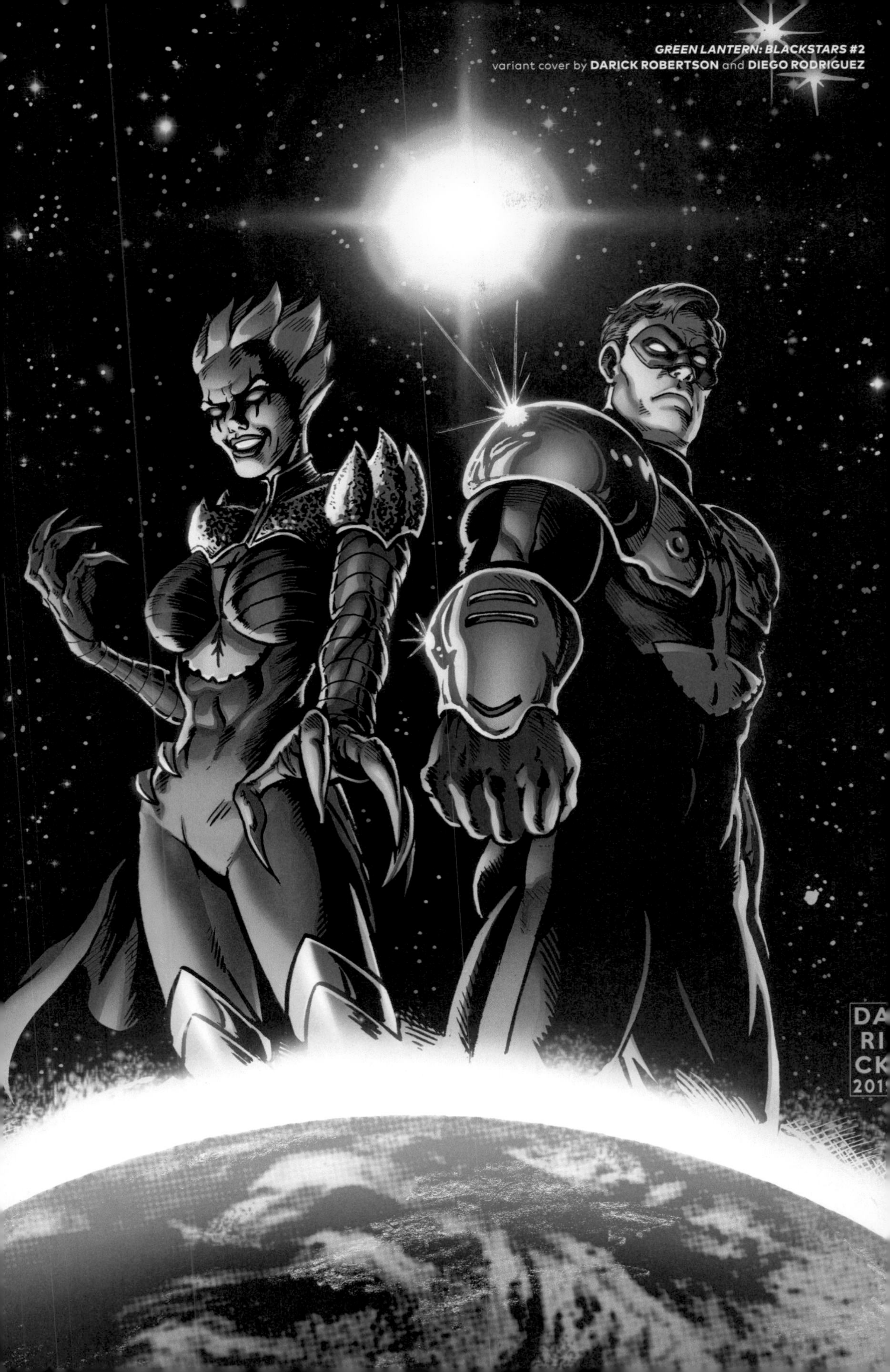

GREEN LANTERN: BLACKSTARS **#2**
variant cover by **DARICK ROBERTSON** and **DIEGO RODRIGUEZ**

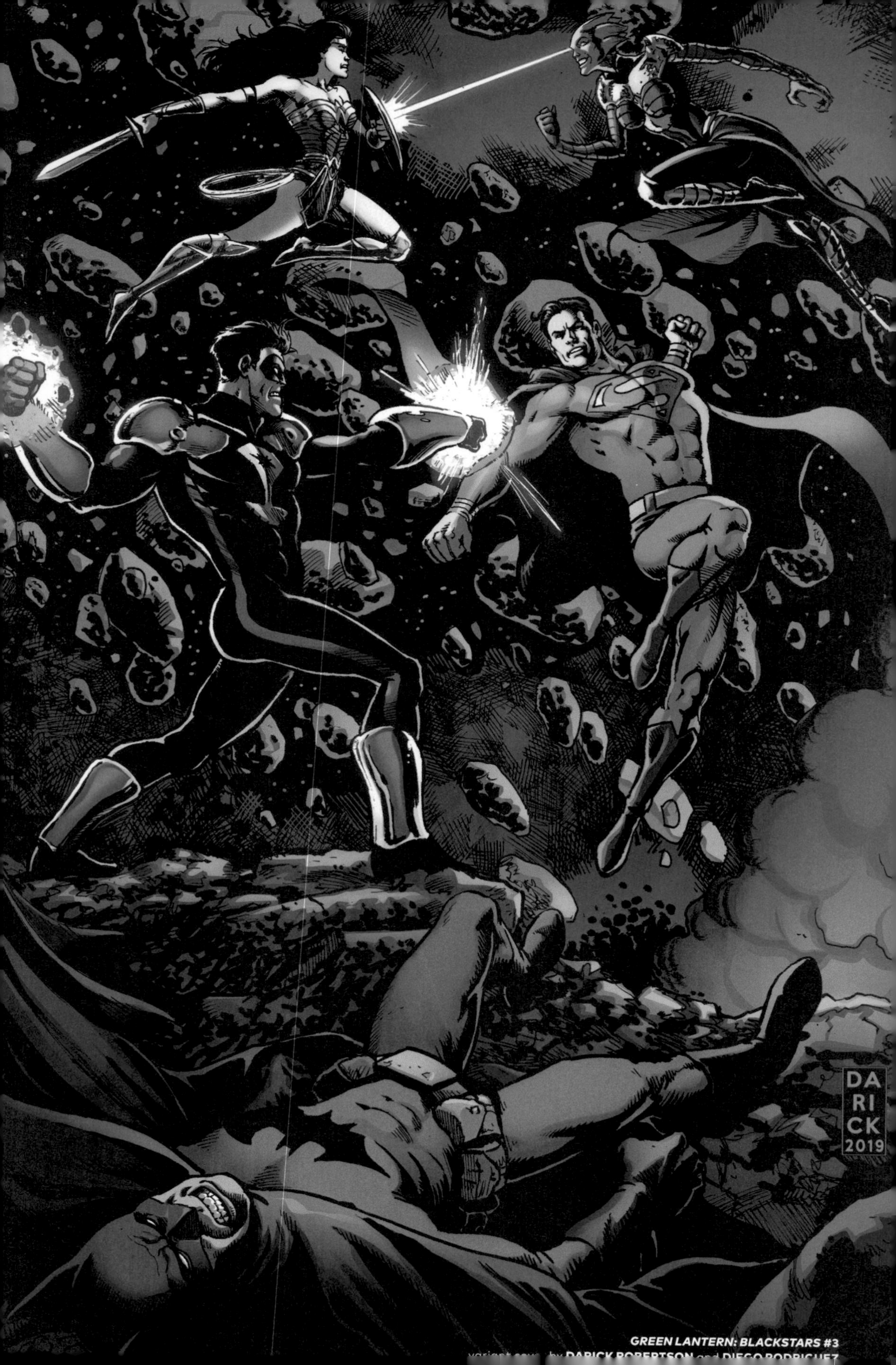
DA
RI
CK
2019

GREEN LANTERN: BLACKSTARS #3
variant cover by **DARICK ROBERTSON** and **DIEGO RODRIGUEZ**

variant cover by GERALD PAREL

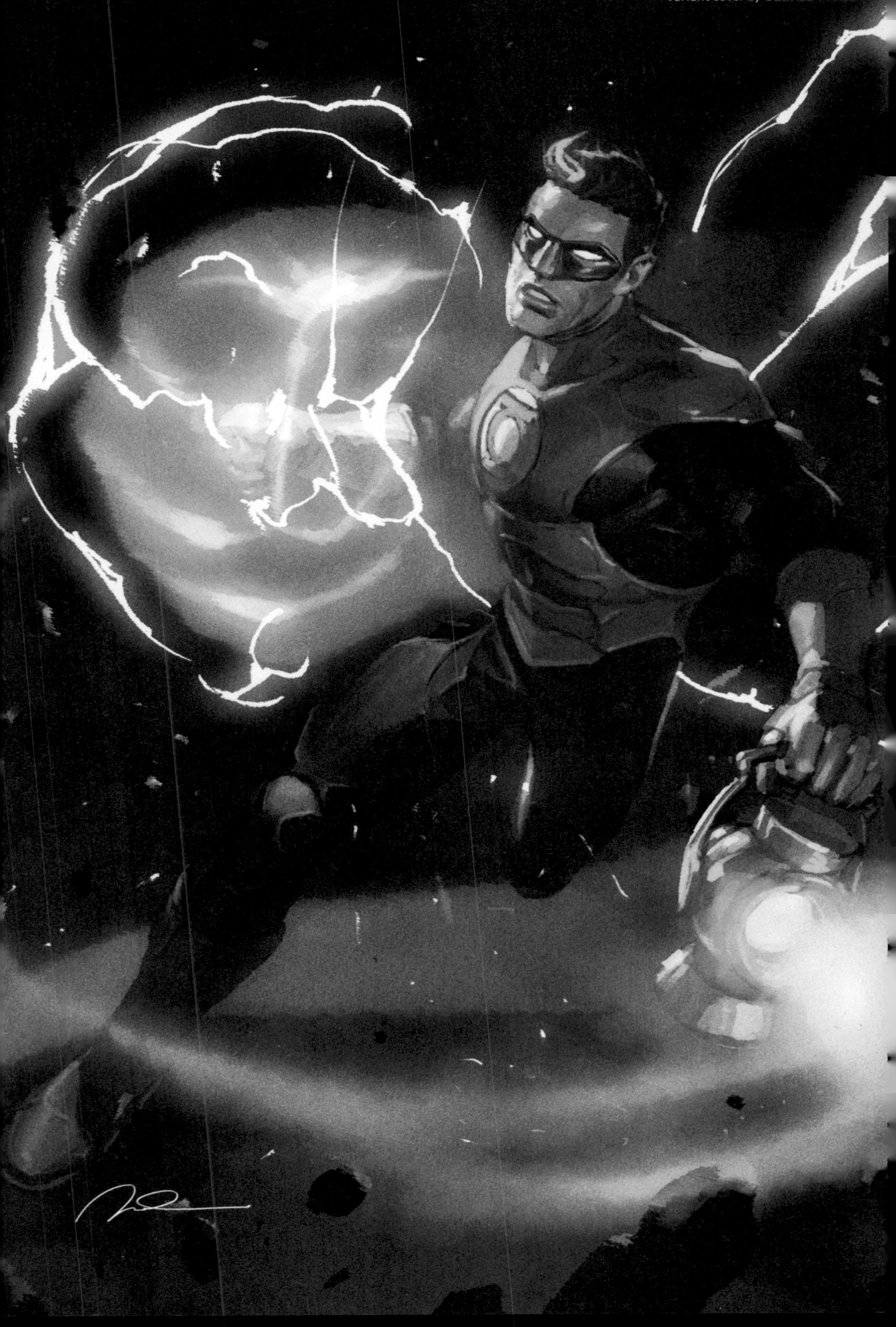

THE GREEN LANTERN SEASON TWO #2
variant cover by **NICOLA SCOTT** and **ANNETTE KWOK**

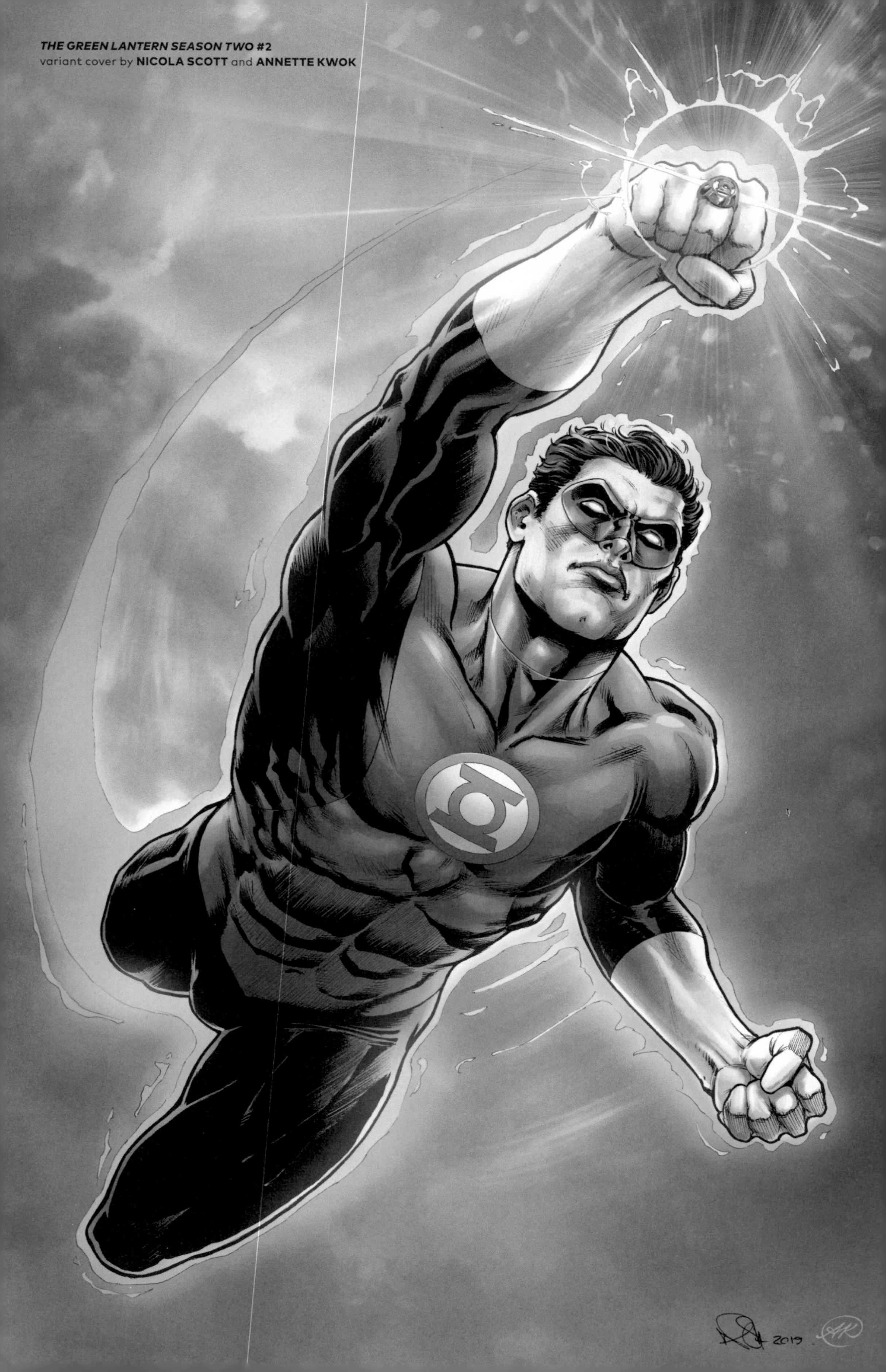

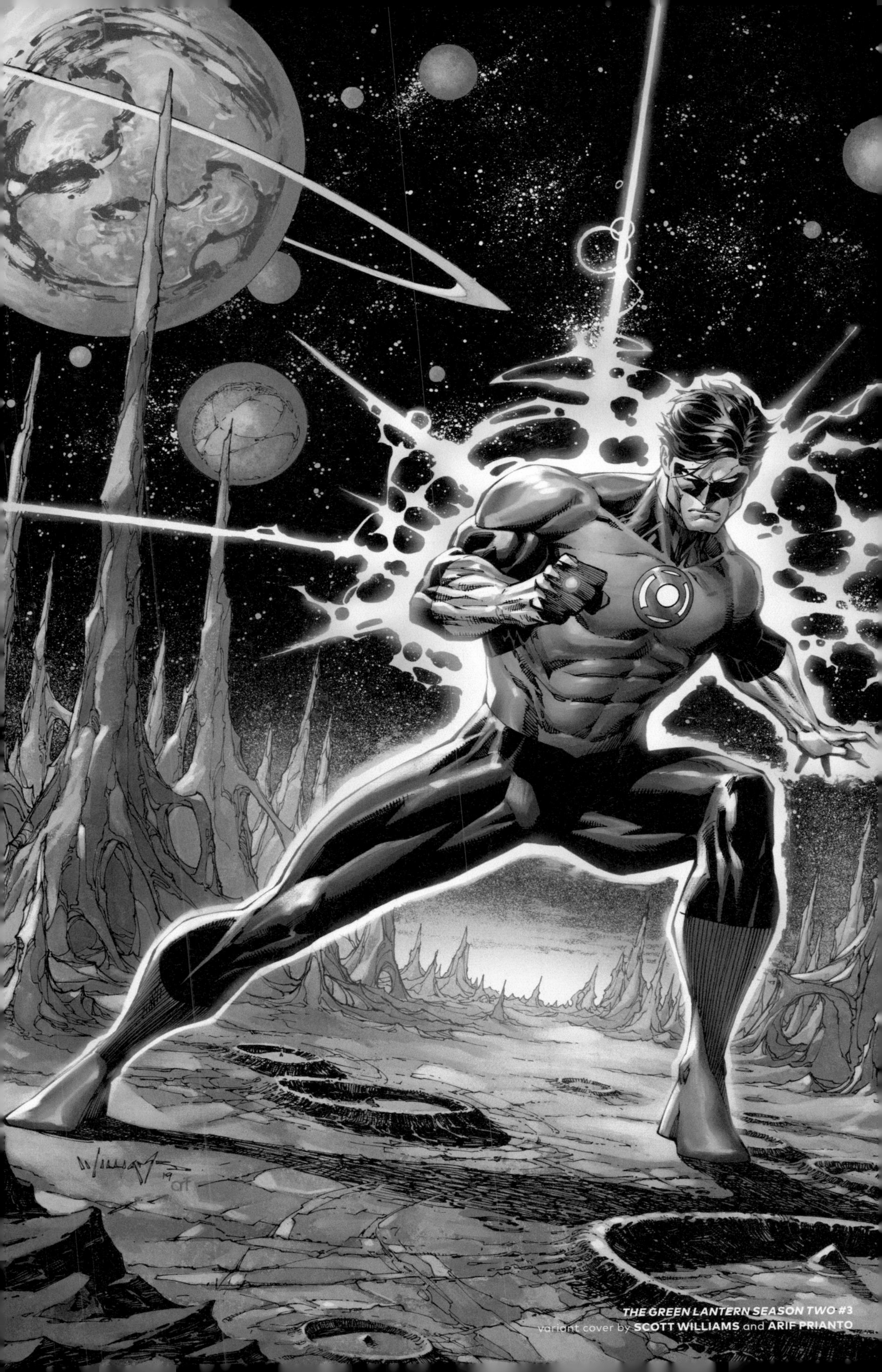

THE GREEN LANTERN SEASON TWO #3
variant cover by **SCOTT WILLIAMS** and **ARIF PRIANTO**

THE GREEN LANTERN SEASON TWO #4
variant cover by **MATTEO SCALERA**
and **MORENO DINISIO**

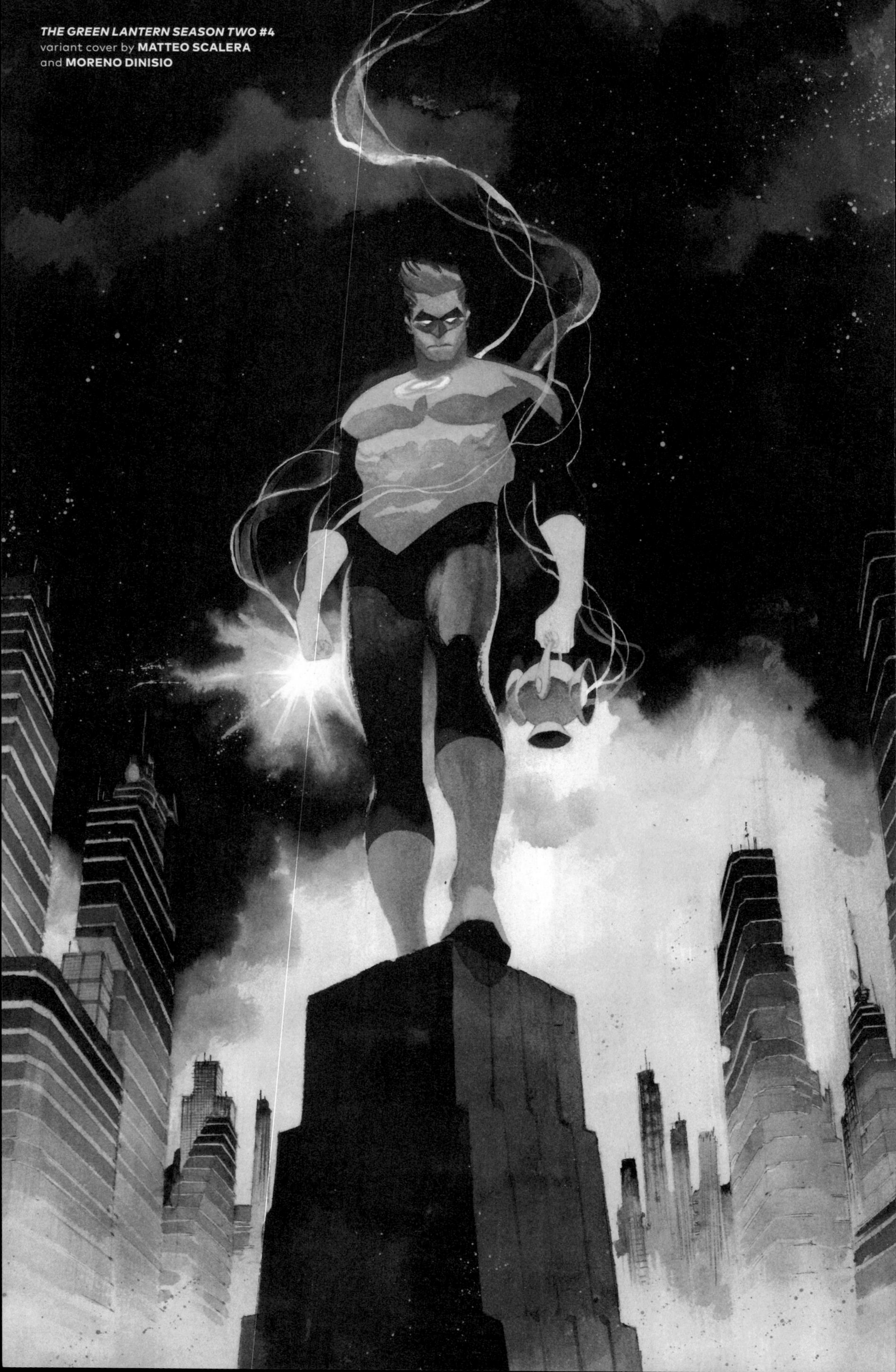

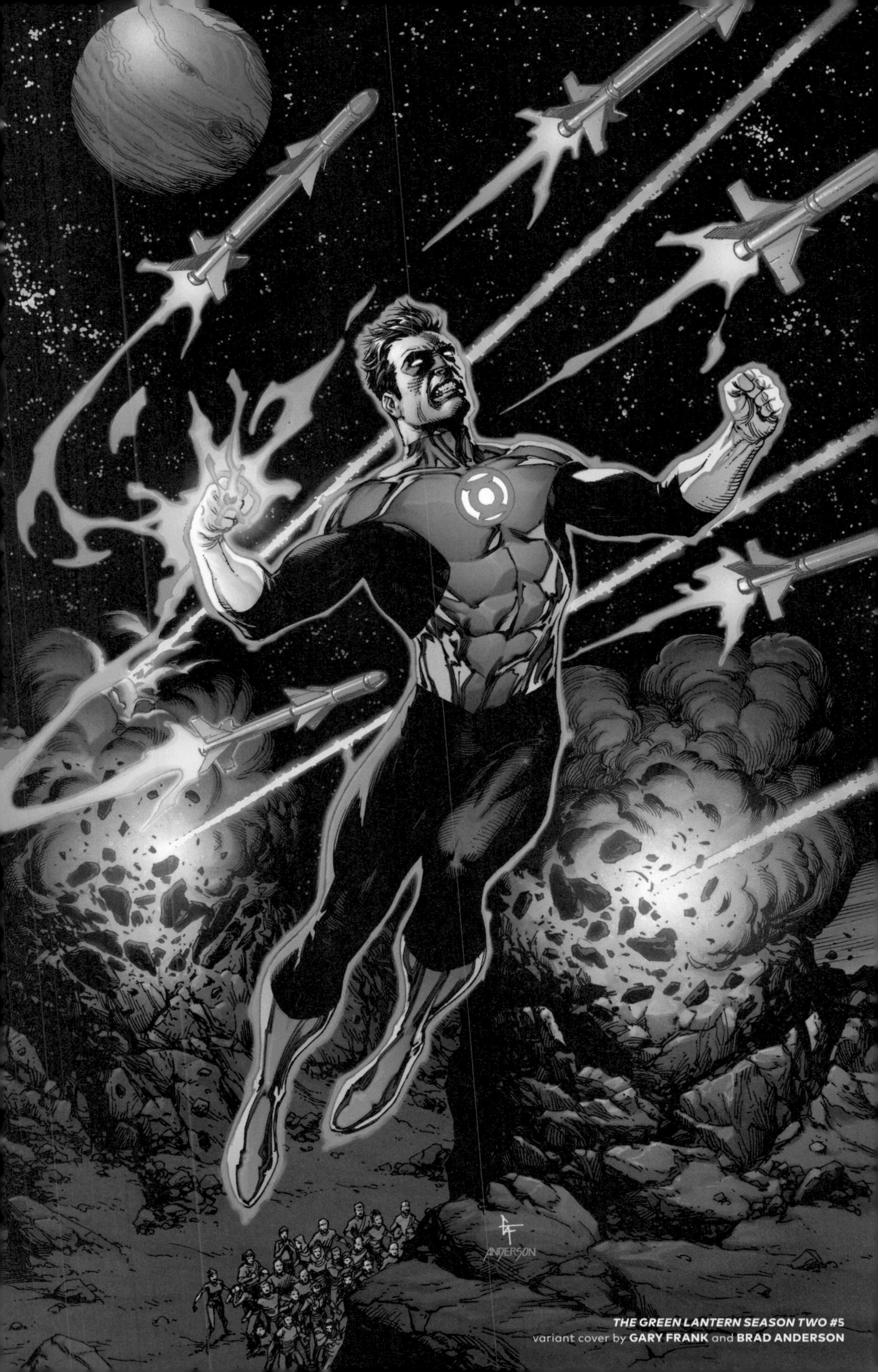
ANDERSON

THE GREEN LANTERN SEASON TWO #5
variant cover by **GARY FRANK** and **BRAD ANDERSON**

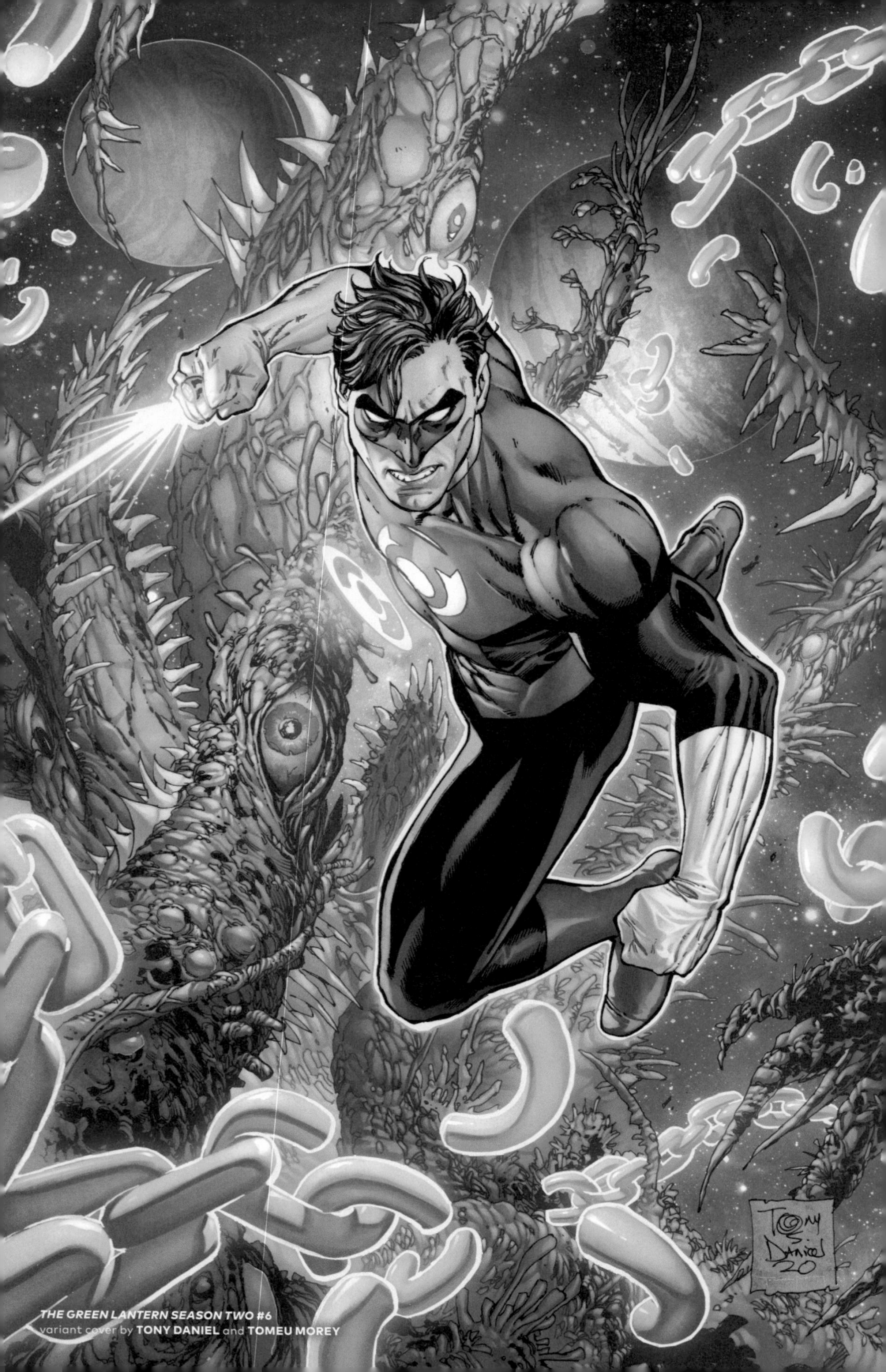
TONY DANIEL 20

***THE GREEN LANTERN SEASON TWO* #6**
variant cover by **TONY DANIEL** and **TOMEU MOREY**

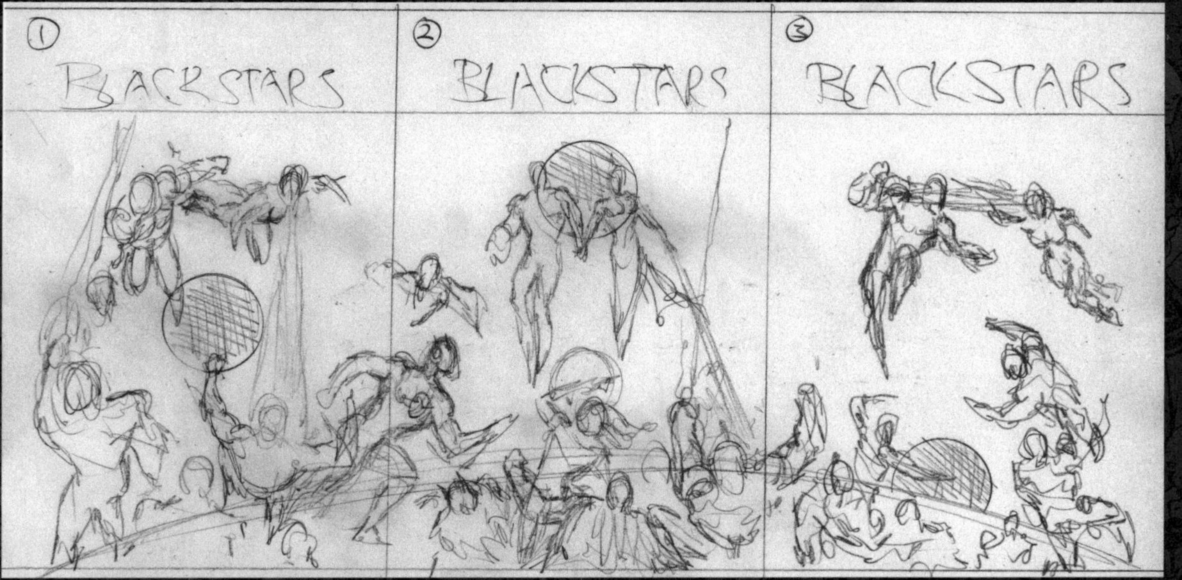
1
BLACKSTARS
2
BLACKSTARS
3
BLACKSTARS

***GREEN LANTERN: BLACKSTARS* #1-3** cover sketch and final inks

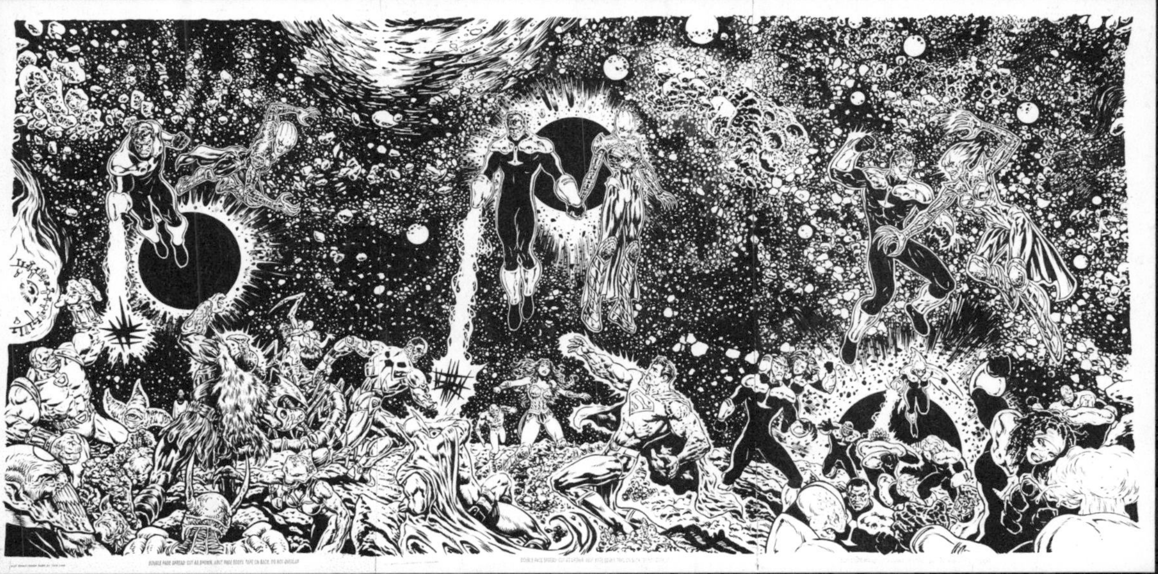

GREEN LANTERN: BLACKSTARS #1-3 final cover spread

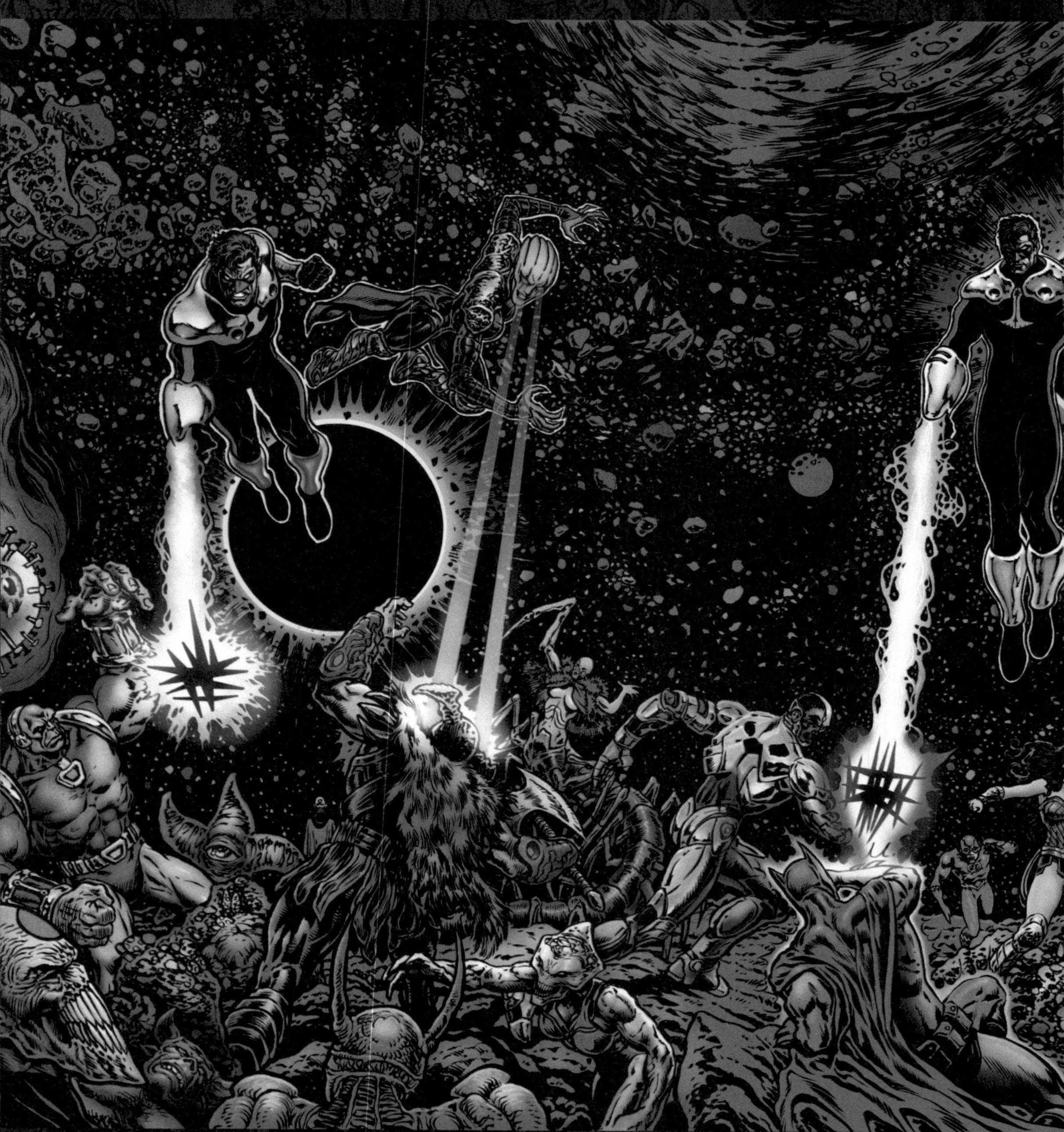

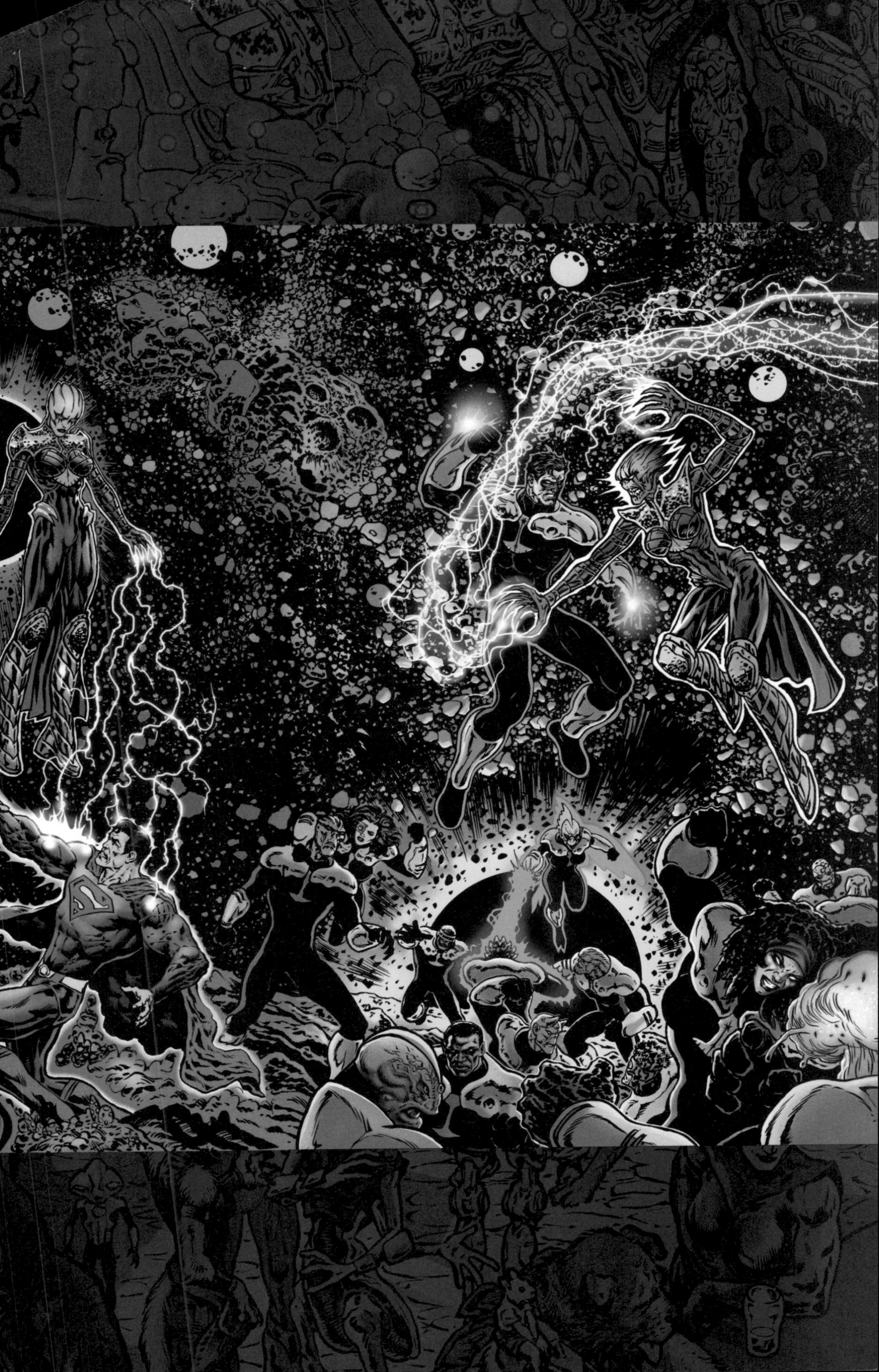

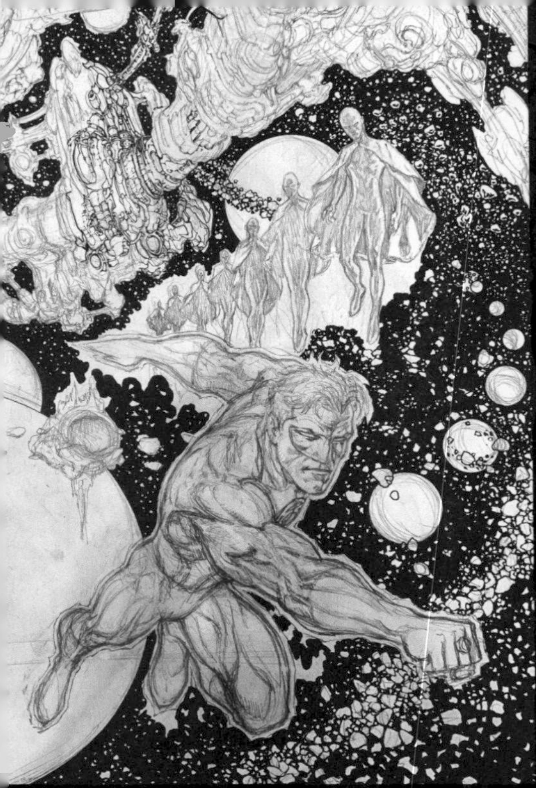

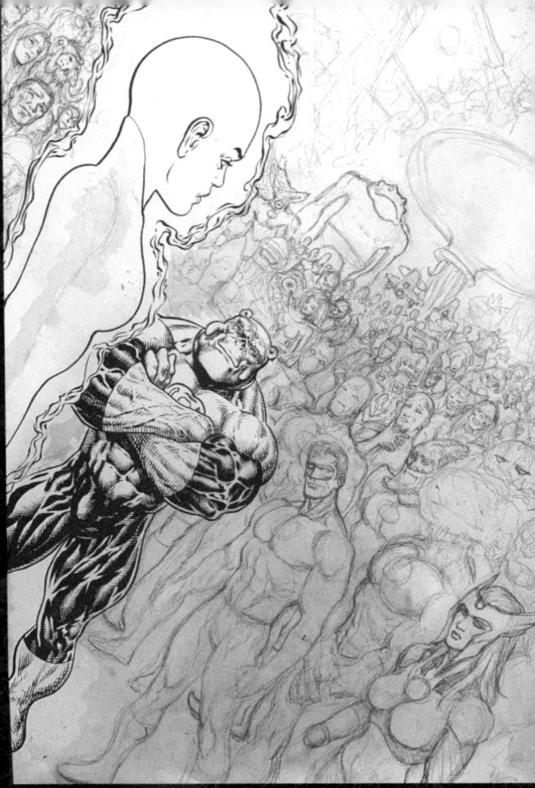

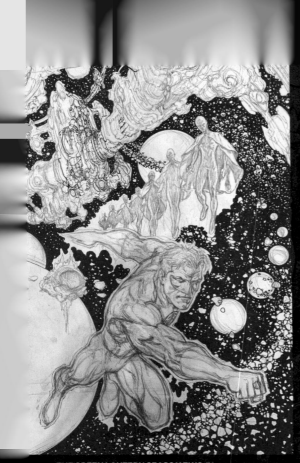

THE GREEN LANTERN SEASON TWO #1 cover proces

THE GREEN LANTERN SEASON TWO #1 pg. 28 process

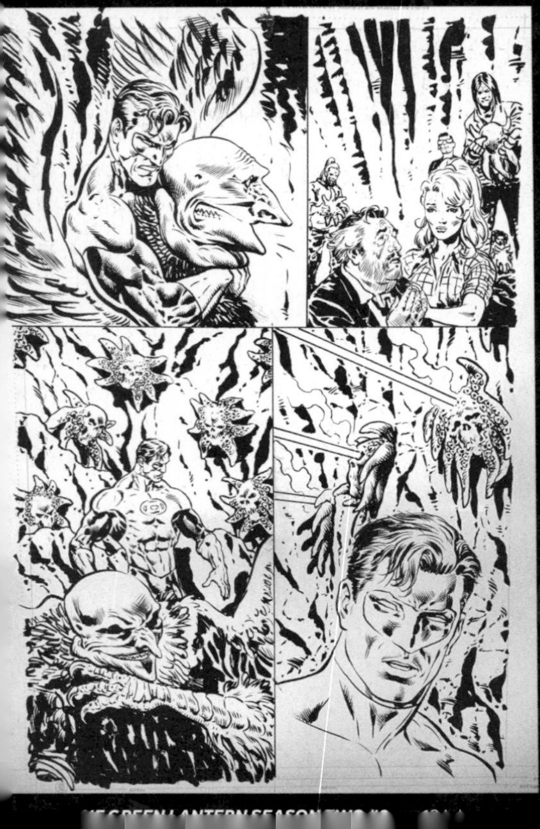

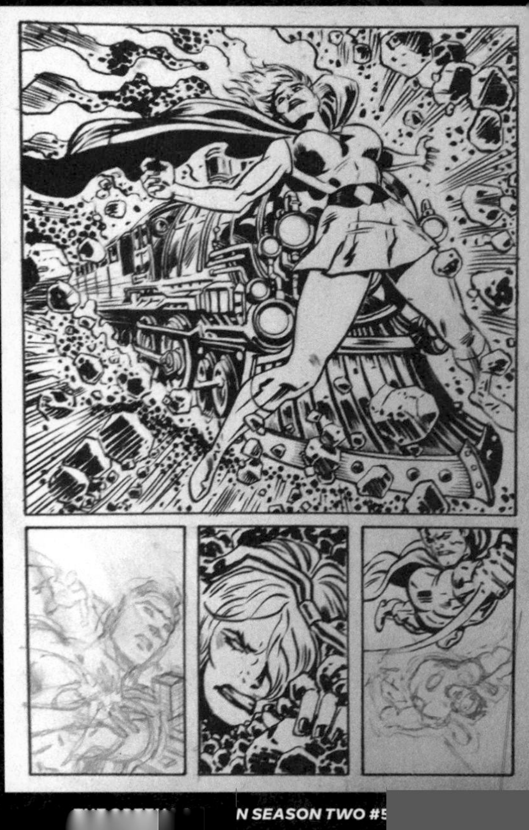

N SEASON TWO #5